Remove this page
leave the next blank in place

THE
Quest
FOR
TRUTH

Answering Life's Inescapable Questions

THE
Quest
FOR
TRUTH

Answering Life's
Inescapable Questions

F. Leroy Forlines

PUBLICATIONS • WORLDWIDE MINISTRIES

114 Bush Road • P.O. Box 17306
Nashville, Tennessee 37217 USA

www.randallhouse.com

Acknowledgements

Unless otherwise indicated, all Scripture quotations in this volume are from the authorized *King James Version* of the Bible.

Scripture quotations marked "NKJV" are taken from the New King James Version, Copyright © 1979, 1980, 1982 by Thomas Nelson, Inc. Used by permission. All rights reserved. Scripture quotations marked "NASB" are taken from the *New American Standard Bible,* Copyright © 1960, 1962, 1963, 1968, 1971, 1972, 1975, 1977 by The Lockman Foundation. Used by permission. Scripture quotations marked "NIV" are taken from the *Holy Bible,* New International Version®. Copyright © 1973, 1978, 1984 by International Bible Society. Used by permission of the Zondervan Publishing House. All rights reserved.

Quotations from *Predestination & Free Will* by David Basinger and Randall Basinger are used by permission of InterVarsity Press. Quotations from *The Justification of God* by John Piper (Copyright © 1983), *Christian Theology* by Millard J. Erickson (Copyright © 1985), *The Grace of God, the Bondage of the Will,* edited by Thomas R. Schreiner and Bruce A. Ware (Copyright © 1995) are used by permission of Baker Books. Quotations from *Systematic Theology* by Louis Berkhof are used by permission of Wm. B. Eerdmans Publishing Co. Quotations taken from *A Systematic Theology of the Christian Church* (or *A Systematic Theology of the Christian Religion,* Volume 1 or Volume 2) by James Oliver Buswell, Jr., (Copyright © 1963 by Zondervan Publishing House) are used by permission of Zondervan Publishing House. Quotations from *Protestant Thought and Natural Science* by John Dillenberger are used by permission of the author. Quotations from *A Case for Arminianism: The Grace of God and The Will of Man* by Clark Pinnock are used by permission of the author.

The Quest for Truth:
Answering Life's Inescapable Questions
by F. Leroy Forlines

Printed in the United States of America.

ISBN: Hardcover 0-89265-864-9
          Paper 0-89265-962-9

Dedication

This book is dedicated to my wife Fay with love and appreciation.

Table of Contents

Foreword

Only occasionally does one find a theology book that seriously discusses profound truths while at the same time connecting with everyday life. The study of theology is thought by many people to be a pedantic exercise, unrelated to real-world concerns. In this book, a major revision and expanded edition of his earlier work entitled *Biblical Systematics* (1975), F. Leroy Forlines offers his readers a penetrating treatment of the main topics of systematic theology that seeks to interact with lived experience. This combination is the result of what Professor Forlines terms his "total personality approach" to theology. He insists that theology must be wrested free from a methodology that would rely solely on intellectual concerns. Rather, it must be made applicable to the total personality–the intellect, the emotions, and the will.

Forlines' total personality approach is skillfully displayed in his book *Biblical Ethics* (1973). It may also be seen in his forthcoming manuscript that develops a theological approach to human personality. This forthcoming work is the outgrowth of more than twenty years in a dual role as not only a professor of theology but also a student dean and counselor. These experiences compelled him to develop an approach to theology that is designed to influence not merely one's thinking, but all of one's life. Thus, he deals with the *"inescapable questions of life"*–questions that arise from the heart as well as the mind, from the marketplace as well as the classroom. Given this approach, the book provides an ideal opportunity for inquisitive laypeople as well as college and seminary students to approach the field of theology from numerous vantage points. Therefore, the book will be found useful as a college textbook or for introductory seminary courses in systematic theology. Yet, at the same time, the work will be helpful to pastors and scholars who will benefit from Forlines' unique approach.

The first edition of this book, which appeared in 1975, was ahead of the game in anticipating some of the postmodern dissatisfaction with the "detached rational analysis" characteristic of Enlightenment thought. That edition, unlike his *Romans* commentary (1987), threw off some of the conventions of academic writing and assumed a more first-person, conversational style. Thus, Forlines does not hesitate to weave personal experiences and life-related illustrations into his theological exposition. His interaction with the reader feels more like a lively discussion than a staid, academic discourse.

One such experience was Professor Forlines' six-month teaching tour of institutes and seminaries in Russia and Ukraine. This trip helped to fuel his interest in the growing intellectual phenomenon of postmodernism. Emerging from this experience, Forlines increasingly realized the importance of relating Christian theology to the intellectual currents of our day. Many of these trends seem to be propelling our culture away from notions of objective truth. Hence, the theologian is faced with the daunting task of trying to communicate truth about God and from God within a culture that undermines belief in the possibility of divine revelation. This book is Forlines' attempt to explain traditional theological concepts in a way that is relevant to the contemporary intellectual landscape, which will help people to cope with current challenges to the Christian worldview. Readers who are familiar with postmodernism will be aided in their understanding of how to articulate Christian ideas in a postmodern setting. Conversely, readers who are unfamiliar with post-modernism will find themselves progressively better acquainted with it in this readable discussion.

This book includes a number of interpretations that make it unique. Perhaps the most note-worthy of these is Forlines' Classical Arminian approach to the doctrine of salvation. Forlines' Arminianism, like that of Jacobus (James) Arminius himself, differs from what most people think of as Arminianism. Forlines emphasizes human inability in salvation, as well as the priority and neces-sity of divine grace for salvation. He also subscribes to the Reformed view of the nature of atone-ment and justification (the view of both Calvin and Arminius). In this view, Christ's atonement satis-fies the just demands of a holy God and provides the believing sinner with Christ's own righteous-ness, which is imputed through faith. Likewise, Forlines' understanding of sanctification is Reformed. He eschews any notion of a second work of grace or entire sanctification. Yet he insists that sanctification, while distinct from justification, is the necessary outgrowth of it. Forlines' view of perseverance also differs from that of most traditional Arminianism. He sees salvation through-out as the work of God which is by grace alone, through faith alone, in Christ alone. Yet, because of the believer's freedom, the possibility of apostasy is real.

Forlines' Classical Arminianism, it should be noted, is radically different from what has unfor-tunately come to be known as "Freewill Theism"–a view that posits, among other things, God's lim-ited omniscience or foreknowledge. Forlines articulates a contemporary reworking of traditional Arminian thought, which holds that God has perfect foreknowledge of the future, free acts of His creatures.

The first edition of this work was recommended by *Christianity Today* as one of the signifi-cant books of 1975. The book was soon translated into Spanish, and in 1996 it was translated into Russian. Since then, ten thousand copies have circulated in Russia and Ukraine. Thus, *Systematics* has influenced the lives of countless numbers of students, pastors, laypeople, and scholars. Professor Forlines has instructed them and has demonstrated for them how to do theology in such a way that it influences the whole personality–mind, heart, and will–and enables one to glorify God more effectively in all of life. There is no doubt that this revised and greatly expanded edition will affect many, many more. Because of the fresh and thoughtful insights, because of its thoroughly readable style, and because it presents a model of how to do theology within the postmodern cul-ture of today, it is our sincere hope that this book will enjoy the wide readership that it so richly deserves.

Stephen M. Ashby and J. Matthew Pinson

Preface

It has been my privilege to teach systematic theology on the college level for forty years. My book *Biblical Systematics,* which I used as a text, was published in 1975. The 1975 edition was translated into Spanish. This translation has been used in ministering to Spanish-speaking people in the United States, Spain, Mexico, Uruguay, Panama, and Cuba.

A few years ago, Randall House Publications and I decided that I should revise the 1975 edition. At that time, Randall House scanned the book and put it on a computer disk. That has proved to be an invaluable asset in making the present revision possible.

In 1995, the Reverend Eugene Waddell and others representing the Free Will Baptist Foreign Missions Department went to Russia and Ukraine and met with Russian Baptist leaders. A decision was made to have *Systematics* translated into Russian. It was also decided that my wife Fay and I would go to Ukraine and Russia in 1996. I would lecture on Arminian theology.

I lectured on Arminian theology in Baptist Bible institutes and Baptist seminaries in Kiev, Odessa, and Moscow, and in churches in several other cities across Russia. Prior to going to the Former Soviet Union, I reorganized and enlarged the chapter on perseverance for translation into Russian. With still further revisions while I was in Russia, this became the chapter on perseverance. While in Russia, I also made limited revisions of the other chapters. This revised version was published by Bible for Everyone Publishing House in St. Petersburg (Leningrad), Russia.

In preparing the current book, I worked from the disks that were used for the Russian translation. The revisions and expansion are of such a nature that the current book is a new book. Chapters 2, 15, 16, 17, and 18 are altogether new chapters.

The Target Audience

The target audience of this book is upper-level college students, seminary students, pastors, and laymen who would like to think their way through the Christian worldview.

I have tried to write the book so that it can be understood by a broad audience. It has been my desire to deal meaningfully with substance, but at the same time to make it as easy as possible to be understood.

I was saved in 1944 just before I turned eighteen. Though I had been very regular in church and Sunday school for ten years, I discovered that I did not know how to be saved. The Reverend R. N. Hinnant was the revival speaker that year. He spoke with great clarity. He made it clear that the only way that anyone could be saved was by faith in Jesus Christ. He also made it clear that faith in Christ was the only condition of salvation. I gave my heart to Jesus Christ. The following Sunday afternoon I was baptized. That night I joined the Winterville Free Will Baptist Church in Winterville, North Carolina. About two years later, after going through a time during which the Holy Spirit made it unquestionably clear that He was calling me to preach His Word, I answered that call. In January of 1948, I learned about Free Will Baptist Bible College. I enrolled as a student in September 1948 to prepare for the ministry.

I had attended church for ten years before it was made clear to me how to be saved. This made a deep impression on me. As a result of that experience, I have always desired to make things as understandable as possible. I made a commitment that I would do my very best to communicate the Truth so that it could be understood. At the same time I have been motivated by the conviction that people need a meaningful grasp of the substance of truth. Layman need a grasp of the substance of their faith.

In order to live up to my commitment to make things as clear as possible, I prefer simple words to complex words. Yet I have made no attempt to shy away from important theological terms. It has been my aim to be sure that the meaning of these terms is made clear to the reader who may not already be familiar with them. I am particularly concerned that we make popular use of those theological terms that are also biblical terms such as justification, regeneration, sanctification, etc. If the terms are not familiar to people, they need to be used so much that they will become familiar.

In order to make the reading of this book easier to those who do not have a background in the subject, I have at times quoted what I have said previously in the book rather than referring the reader back to the earlier treatment. Occasionally, this may occur in the same chapter. Another reason for repeating what I have already said in previous chapters is that I know that many people will select a particular chapter to read. As much as is possible, I want what I am saying in these chapters to be understandable for the person who has not read the previous chapters. I do cross reference a good bit of what is said in the book when I think it will be helpful to the person in getting a better understanding of the chapter under study.

The reader may notice that I make liberal use of longer quotations. There are several reasons for this. My first reason is that I think the longer quotations will be helpful to those not familiar with theological works. Also, when I criticize what another person has said, I like to give enough of what he has said so that the reader can judge for himself whether I have properly understood the other person's thinking. Are my criticisms of what the person said justified? Or, if I quoted the person as supporting my position, does what the person said really support my position? There are also times that I am depending on the expertise of the other person in an area in which I am not well qualified. I am using the person as an authority to back up what I am saying. In such cases the longer quotation will enable the reader to decide whether the other person is saying what I think he is. I think it would be in order to quote the words of Jacques Barzun and Henry F. Graff on this point. They comment:

> Quoting other writers and citing the places where their words are to be found are by now such common practices that it is pardonable to look upon the habit as natural, not to say instinctive. It is of course nothing of the kind, but a very sophisticated act, peculiar to a civilization that uses printed books, believes in evidence, and makes a point of assigning credit or blame in a detailed, verifiable way.[1]

For those who do not have a background of reading theology, I would like to offer this bit of advice. If you do not understand everything you read, keep reading as long as you feel like you are gaining worthwhile knowledge from what you read. That will go for reading other books as well as for reading this book. I use that principle to guide me in my reading.

The Paradigm Shift From Modernism to Postmodernism

In the "Preface" to the first edition, I said, "Truth is unchanging, but the scene to which truth addresses itself, while having the common ingredient of sin and the need of redemption, undergoes change." I am even more convinced of the truth of that statement now than I was when I wrote it 25 years ago. I went on to say, "While presenting timeless truth, I have tried to be aware of and address the current scene. I have been more concerned about the current scene [the 1970's] as influenced by secularism than the current scene of conflict and controversy in the theological world, though the theological scene has not been totally neglected." I think that assessment is still true of this present work.

As I look back on it, I now know that the first edition was written when the secular culture was in the midst of a paradigm shift. In the current edition, I point out that from 1960-1990 secular culture in America, on the grassroots level, was undergoing a paradigm shift. I knew in the 1970's that some drastic changes were taking place in our culture. But I had no idea that in 1975 we were halfway through a major paradigm shift in the secular culture.

The 1975 edition was basically addressed to the modernist secular paradigm. However, attention was given to Francis Schaeffer's mention of the irrational upper story, which I recognize now was a part of the history of postmodernism. It has been said that Francis Schaeffer was a man ahead of his times. Though, in the index to his complete works, the word *postmodernism* does not occur, a reading of his works is essential for a person who would like to have a working knowledge of postmodernism.

A Total Personality Approach to Thought and Life

At the time I wrote the 1975 edition of *Systematics,* I was deeply concerned that my treatment of theology should speak to life's concerns. That concern has grown over the years. At no point in my experience as a student or a teacher have I ever had any serious questions about my commitment and confidence in the truth of orthodox, conservative Christianity. But I had some deep struggles in bringing Truth and life together. Things were not as simple for me in the application of Truth to life as it seemed that others were saying that it was for them. The strong emphasis on integrity that was instilled in me by my parents made me too honest to claim that things were glorious when they were not. But I knew that it was the design of Truth to set people free. I knew that it had to be true because Jesus said so in John 8:32. I do not have time here to relive the journey of my struggles in coming to the confidence that I now have in the reality that the Truth makes us free. I have learned to take my hurts to the Bible and the Bible to my hurts.

I should make mention of a very significant factor in my interest in the relationship between Truth and life. At the time I wrote the book, I was Dean of Students at Free Will Baptist Bible College. For several years before, I had been Dean of Men. I felt that it was my obligation to help those who came to me for help to find answers to their problems. I refused to believe that there were no answers. There must be answers that will help people live in a world filled with harsh reality. My own struggles and my work with others as they dealt with the harsh realities of life were a very significant factor in developing my approach to theology.

By the time I wrote the 1975 edition, I had developed a strong interest in the total personality approach to apologetics and the study of the Bible and theology. That interest is present and far more visible in this book than it was in the first edition. In retrospect I believe that this total personality approach was preparing me to confront and minister to the postmodern culture once I was able to recognize it for what it was.

The concept of the design of God in the creation of man and the design of God in redemption was already a significant part of my thinking in the understanding of human needs and how God addresses those needs. My conviction about the importance of recognizing divine design is stronger now and receives more emphasis in the present book.

One of the products of divine design is what I call the *inescapable questions of life*. Every human being as he or she develops into adulthood is faced with questions such as: Is there a God? If so, what is He like? How do I know what is right and what is wrong? Is there life after death? and other such questions. What is the meaning of life? How can I have a meaningful life? The *inescapable questions of life* were in evidence in the first edition. They are a driving concern in this book.

The concern for the *total personality* approach is seen in the following quotation from the 1975 edition regarding the criteria for testing a system of thought that claims to give an explanation of the whole of reality:

> So far as rational tests are concerned, a system that proposes to explain the whole of reality must prove to be satisfactory to our total personality as thinking, feeling, acting beings. Logic cannot divorce itself from life and become an accurate judge of a system. I believe the following tests are a step in the right direction to establishing criteria that will protect the interest of the total personality: (1) Is there internal consistency, i.e., is the structure logically related to the foundation? Do all the parts fit consistently together? (2) Is there internal sufficiency, i.e., are the causes adequate to produce the effects attributed to them? (3) Does it conform to that which is undeniably true? (4) Does it answer the inescapable questions of life? Regardless of how well a system passes the first three tests, if it cannot pass the fourth test, it is not an adequate system and must be rejected (*Biblical Systematics*, p. 9).

In the current book, that passage reads this way:

> A system that proposes to explain the whole of reality (or a worldview) must prove to be satisfactory to our *total personality* as thinking, feeling, acting beings. Logic cannot divorce itself from life and become an accurate judge of a system. I believe the fol-

lowing tests are a step in the right direction to establishing criteria that will protect the interest of the *total personality:* (1) Does it answer the *inescapable questions of life?* (2) Is there internal consistency, i.e., is the structure logically related to the foundation? Do all the parts fit consistently together? (3) Is there causal adequacy? i.e., are the causes adequate to produce the effects attributed to them? (4) Does it conform to that which is undeniably true?

If a worldview cannot answer the *inescapable questions of life,* it is not worthy of our consideration. (*Quest for Truth,* p. 18)

The only difference in the wording is the change from "Is there internal sufficiency?" to "Is there causal adequacy?" This does not represent a change in substance. I think that "causal adequacy" is a better way of saying what I wanted to say. The significant change from the 1975 edition is seen in making the first test, "Does it answer the *inescapable questions of life?*"

In 1975, modernism was being challenged, but it had not been dethroned. With the emphasis that was given to reason in modernism, it was fitting to start with: "Is there internal consistency, i.e., is the structure logically related to the foundation? Do all the parts fit consistently together?" That was the rational test of coherence.

I was not familiar with anyone who had come up with a test that would forthrightly demand that a true worldview must be effectively life related; I stated that as "Does it answer the *inescapable questions of life?*" I felt driven to requiring that test by two different factors: First, the drive for the quest for Truth was motivated by the demands of my own inner nature. I was convinced that just as these questions were of deep concern to me, they were to others. While I believe in the uniqueness of each person's experience, I also was convinced of the commonality of human experience

The second factor, and a very important one, was what I detected to be the driving force behind the hippie movement, the student unrest of the 1960s, and the rise and spread of the drug culture. As I perceived it, the real problem for these movements was that they had recognized that reason and science had not been able to minister to the deep inner needs of human nature. To use my terminology, "Naturalism had not been able to answer the *inescapable questions of life."* Science had performed wonders in the area of technology, but it had left people empty as it related to their deepest inner needs. Deep within every human heart is a deep need for purpose and meaning for life. I became strongly convinced that if a worldview does not answer the *inescapable questions of life,* it is not worthy of consideration.

In the preparation of this book, it became apparent that the test: Does it answer the *inescapable questions of life?* should be the first test. However, if it seems to pass that test it should be subjected to the other tests. We do not want to trust the care of our total being for time and eternity to that which is not true.

Feeling the pain that both modernism and postmodernism have inflicted on our culture, I believe that it is imperative that, as Christians, we must show to a hurting world that we feel their pain and let them know that we care. We must let them know that there is, to quote Francis Schaeffer, "true Truth." We must let them know that the biblical accounts of the creation, the fall, the covenants made with Abraham and Israel, the birth, the life, His sacrificial death for our sins, and the bodily resurrection of Jesus Christ are all factual historical realities. His promises are true. He will come again.

We must share with this hurting world that we believe the words of the Apostle Peter when he said, "For we have not followed cunningly devised fables, when we made known unto you the power and coming of our Lord Jesus Christ, but were eyewitnesses of his majesty" (2 Pet. 1:16).

As a part of this *total personality* approach to Truth, I have abandoned the concept that objectivity should be the guiding ideal in our quest for Truth. I believe very strongly in objective Truth, but I do not believe that the best approach to finding Truth is a dispassionate search for Truth. Rather, I believe that our search for Truth must be a passionate search under the control of integrity. We should think and feel our way through a study of theology.

I do not believe that anyone will see, at any point in this book, where this emphasis on the total personality approach to Truth has weakened my commitment to objective Truth, the objective authority of the Bible, and a significant place given to reason. My favorite verse of Scripture is, "And ye shall know the truth, and the truth shall make you free" (Jn. 8:32).

Differences Between the Current and 1975 Editions

As a technical point, I made a mistake in the 1975 edition when I said, "I do not believe that knowledge of God is innate" (p. 73). My problem was a misunderstanding of the meaning of "innate." What I meant was that I did not believe that day-old babies have thoughts about God. While I am still of that opinion, that is not what is meant by saying that knowledge of God is innate. To say that knowledge of God is innate is to say that it is a natural byproduct of the image of God in a human being for him or her to believe in God. There is an inborn nature in a human being that in natural development leads to belief in God.

So far as the content is concerned, I think the current edition will reflect a maturing and a clarifying of what was in the first edition. The concept of worldview thinking was prevalent in the 1975 edition, but the term *worldview* did not occur in the book. The term *worldview* was around long before 1975, but it had not gained the prominence in use by that time that it has in recent years. I did not use the terms *modernism* or *postmodernism* in the 1975 edition. What I said in the book would have been addressed mainly to the modernist paradigm. But I think the *total personality* approach was significant preparation for addressing the postmodern paradigm. I was already heading in the right direction.

In order to deal adequately with modernism and postmodernism, it was necessary to add a new chapter, Chapter 2: "The Acquisition of Upper Story Knowledge."

The subject of election was referred to, but was not developed in the 1975 edition. In this edition Chapters 15, 16, and 17 give a thorough development of the doctrine of election. Chapter 18, the concluding chapter, is entitled, "Communicating the Christian Message in a Postmodern Culture." Though this chapter is not what one would expect to find in a treatment of systematic theology, I felt that since the ground work had been laid for it in the book, the need for such a treatment made it incumbent upon me to do so.

Though this edition covers areas not dealt with in the first edition, it still fails to cover a minimum of what should be covered in an introduction to systematic theology. Tentative plans have been made, perhaps on a joint authorship basis, to deal with ecclesiology and eschatology.

Where This Book Fits in the Theological Spectrum

This is a conservative treatment of systematic theology. I am strongly committed to the inspiration and inerrancy of the Bible. I believe in the Trinitarian view of God. Without hesitation, I believe that Jesus was born of a virgin, and that Jesus, though one person, was fully God and fully man (two natures), that His suffering and death on the cross paid the full penalty for our sins, that the same body that was placed in the tomb was raised by God and was God's confirmation of the claims and the teaching of Jesus Christ. I believe in the bodily return of Christ. Though it is not dealt with in this book, I am premillennial in my eschatology. My thinking in this area is developed around the redemptive covenants. I believe in a conjunctive relationship between Old Testament Israel and the New Testament Church, as distinguished from a disjunctive one.

As has already been indicated by my mention above of teaching Arminian theology in Ukraine and Russia, this book is a treatment of Arminian theology. My treatment of Arminian theology is what I have chosen to call Classical Arminianism. This is in distinction from Wesleyan Arminianism. The term "classical" is used because I think this view is in essential agreement with James Arminius. I believe that there are some important distinctions between my view and Wesleyan Arminianism besides that Wesleyan Arminians believe in a second work of grace. Wesleyan Arminians, for the most part, believe in the governmental view of atonement or some modification of that view. Classical Arminianism, in agreement with Arminius, is strongly committed to the satisfaction view of atonement.

In theological seminaries in the last thirty years or so there has been a revival of Classical Five-Point Calvinism and Four-Point Calvinism. (A strong trend in this direction has taken place in Southern Baptist seminaries.) As theological students moved on into upper-level seminary studies and into doctoral studies, they were confronted with far more scholarly treatments of Calvinistic theology than they were of Arminian theology. They were also confronted with the weakened form of Arminianism that was being promoted by scholars such as Clark Pinnock. Seeing those alternatives, many chose Four- or Five-Point Calvinism.

I think the climate is right for a revival of Classical Arminianism. On the grassroots level there is a growing discontent with the trend toward Calvinism. This is particularly true as it relates to the question of election.

I believe that Classical Arminianism is particularly suited to deal with the challenge. It has a strong view on the effect of the fall of Adam on the race. In agreement with Arminius, Classical Arminianism takes the position that the guilt of Adam's sin is imputed to each member of the human race and that as a result of Adam's sin every human being is born with a depraved nature. It takes the position that infants are "saved" rather than "safe."

On atonement, Classical Arminianism is strongly committed to the penal satisfaction view. Justification is based on the imputation of the death and righteousness of Christ—that and that alone, nothing more and nothing less. The condition for receiving this justification is faith in Jesus Christ as Lord and Savior—that and that alone, nothing more and nothing less. We are saved by Christ alone on the condition of faith alone.

No person can come to Christ apart from the drawing power of the Holy Spirit. That drawing power is extended to all. The drawing power of the Holy Spirit enables a person to come to a point that he can make a positive decision. But the person can resist and say no. The moment a person believes, he or she is instantly regenerated by the Holy Spirit and becomes a new creature in Christ. Sanctification begins at regeneration and progresses in life.

A person remains saved as long as he or she continues to keep faith in Christ as Lord and Savior. If there should be a wilful and defiant return to unbelief that person will cease to be saved and will be beyond redemption. It is important to keep in mind that Christians do not live without sin. It is not sinning through weakness that causes a person to cease to be saved. Rather, it is a wilful return to unbelief.

I do not believe that we are to achieve unity between Calvinists and Arminians by choosing to be silent. It is an abridged view of Christianity that does not deal with subjects like election, the extent of atonement, whether grace can be resisted, and the perseverance of the saints. We must be able to have Christian fellowship with one another and at the same time have forthright exchanges about these issues.

An Invitation for Criticism

In the 1975 edition, I said:

> I have a high respect for the opinion of those who are devout scholars of the Bible, but I have not hesitated to be critical of their views when they appear to me to be in error.
> I expect my own ideas to be criticized by others (Preface).

I would affirm those same comments with respect to the current edition. One of the reasons for putting ideas into print is so they can be evaluated and critiqued by others. I want what I have said to be examined critically. I welcome responses.

A Word of Explanation About Use of Bible Translations

If it is not otherwise indicated, the KJV is used. I have a great deal of respect for the KJV, but I am not a "KJV-only" person. I have made frequent use of other translations.

In the 1975 edition I used the KJV as the basic text. As I have indicated earlier, the 1975 edition was scanned and put on a disk for me. I made use of the disk in preparing the manuscript to be used for the Russian translation. It was my intent to switch to using the NASB for that manuscript on the doctrine of perseverance. I thought it would be better for use in Russia. I was forced to abandon my plan.

There is more involved in changing from one Bible translation to another than meets the eye. It is not as simple as just going through and changing the wording of the verses. In discussing a passage, we use the wording of the verse in our comments about the verse. To change from the KJV to the NASB meant that I would have to examine the comments that I had made about the passage to be sure that the wording that was used in my comments was consistent with the wording in the NASB. For example, in Acts 3:19 the KJV says "that your sins may be blotted out." The NASB reads, "that your sins may be wiped away." If you use the KJV on Acts 3:19, in the comments you would speak about having your "sins blotted out." If you used the NASB, you would speak of having your "sins wiped away." The meaning is the same, but you would like to keep your wording consistent with the translation. I made changes when it seemed to be wise, but it saved considerable time to keep the KJV as the basic text.

No person is going to go very far in biblical and theological training without having at least a working knowledge of the language of the KJV. The great hymns of the past that inform our minds and bless our hearts are filled with "thees" and "thous." Anyone who wants to do theological research is not going to go very far before he finds great theological works and Bible commentaries that were either written in Elizabethan English or were translated from another language into Elizabethan English.

Also, some of the terms used in the KJV have become fixed in theology and will not disappear from usage anytime soon. For example, the term the "seed of Abraham." While it means descendant or offspring, a person will not get very far in a study of eschatology without becoming acquainted with the expression "seed of Abraham." We are holding on to the KJV terminology when we speak of the "imputation" of Adam's sin to the race or the "imputation" of the death and righteousness of Christ to the believer. We will not likely forfeit that terminology in theology.

Acknowledgments

This is the hardest part of the preface to write. There are so many that have in one way or another contributed to making this book a reality. I feel that it would be the height of ingratitude not to mention several who have made a significant contribution. But I am afraid that I will fail to mention some who have made a significant contribution.

I will start with my wife, Fay. She has read portions of the manuscript and has made valuable suggestions. She has held up the standard of excellence before me. Because of her, I have a much broader view of life than I would have otherwise had. She has stood by me in difficult times. It would be impossible for me to understand the many ways that she has contributed to making it possible for this edition of this book to come to pass.

I would be remiss if I did not mention my parents who gave me a Christian home and Christian background. Outstandingly strong was the character training in honesty, integrity, a sense of duty, loyalty, purity, fairness, thoughtfulness, and within the range of their limited means an emphasis on beauty and excellence.

I want to give thanks to the memory of the Reverend R. N. Hinnant, whom I have already mentioned, for making the plan of salvation clear to me. He laid it out so clearly before me that we are saved by faith alone. This has meant more to me than I will ever know. I have never wavered on that.

It would be impossible for me to explain how important the theological and biblical training that I received at Free Will Baptist Bible College has been to me. I owe much to Dr. J. P. Barrow, Dr. L. C. Johnson, Dr. LaVerne Miley, and Dr. Charles A. Thigpen for their example and their teaching of courses in Bible and theology.

The course that impacted the shaping of my theology more than any other course that I have ever taken was the course "Arminian Theology" which was taught by Dr. L. C. Johnson, the founding president of Free Will Baptist Bible College. It was in that course that the foundations were laid for what I am calling "Classical Arminianism." In that class theology became alive to me. The greatest single contribution of the course for me was that it helped me nail down forever my belief in the penal satisfaction view of atonement.

Another significant person in those days was Robert E. Picirilli. We had had some exchanges on theology as students. He was in the class "Arminian Theology." I joined the faculty at Free Will Baptist Bible College in 1953. He joined the faculty in 1954. We were working our way through issues. We had many strong exchanges that sharpened my mind and helped shape my thinking. You might say that we were sparring buddies. Dr. Picirilli later became academic dean. Both of us became too busy to hash things out like we once did. Those discussions were of great value to me.

I would also like to mention another one of my colleagues, Ralph C. Hampton. I have called his number many times over the years for information. It has always been helpful to talk things over with him.

In my seminary training, I had the privilege of being subjected to some of the greatest minds in the evangelical world from 1954-1970. I attended Winona Lake School of Theology, Northern Baptist Theological Seminary, and Chicago Graduate School of Theology (formerly Winona Lake School of Theology). I would like to mention a few of the professors who contributed much to my thinking. Dr. Arnold C. Schultz, Dr. H. Dermot McDonald, Dr. Edward J. Young, Dr. Kenneth Kantzer, Dr. Milford Henkel, and Dr. Carl F. H. Henry have all made their impact on my thinking.

During the time that I have been working on the book, I have consulted with many different people whose suggestions and reassurances have been helpful. Among these have been Dr. Darrell Holley, Dr. Garnett Reid, Dr. Stephen M. Ashby, and the Reverend J. Matthew Pinson, Dr. Fisher Humphries, and Dr. Jonathan Wilson.

Steve Ashby and the Matt Pinson have read and commented on the entire manuscript. They have served as consultants. Dr. Ashby is assistant professor of philosophy and religion at Ball State University, Muncie, Indiana. Brother Pinson is pastor of the Colquitt Free Will Baptist Church, Colquitt, Georgia. Matt is engaged in Ph.D. studies in church history at Florida State University in Tallahassee and part time instructor of history and religion at Bainbridge College, Bainbridge, Georgia. Both of these gentlemen are well acquainted with both theological education and university education. They are well grounded in theology and philosophy. They are abreast of the current scene in the culture. They have been an invaluable aid to me.

In the light of the paradigm shift from modernism to postmodernism, it has been particularly helpful to be able to consult with Steve and Matt as I went along. I called each of them often. Sometimes it was to toss around some ideas. Sometimes it was to be sure that I was on the right track, especially when it came to matters relating to the culture. Sometimes it was to check out the best wording to say what I wanted to say.

Ultimately, the responsibility of what is in the book is mine. I deeply appreciate the contribution that each of the above mentioned has made to helping this book become a reality.

Having brought this project to a close, I join with the hymn writer, George Keith, when he said, "How firm a foundation, ye saints of the Lord, is laid for your faith in His excellent Word!"

F. Leroy Forlines
Nashville, Tennessee

1

Introduction

I can remember as far back as the 1930s and the 1940s. Within my memory, the increase of people's knowledge of the physical universe has been astounding. This includes making knowledge available to the masses that once was known only by a few, and many discoveries of which most had never dreamed. It is common knowledge now that the nearest star other than the sun is said to be four and one-half light years away, with a light year being the distance light travels in a year at the rate of 186,000 miles per second. We are also told that some stars are millions of light years away. The last 60 years introduced the splitting of the atom, the harnessing of atomic energy, television as a form of mass media, space travel, heart transplants, laser surgery, computers, etc. Someone has said, "I was born in one age, and I will die in another." That applies to me.

At the same time that people's knowledge of the physical universe has increased, the certainty that many had with regard to Christian truth has been widely diminished. The culture of my youth was strongly influenced by Christian thought. Such is not the case today.

Pluralism and relativism set the mood for the day. The only thing that some people are sure about is that nothing is true and nothing is false. Beliefs are determined by preference and culture. There is tolerance for everything except for those who believe that ultimate Truth exists and is knowable.

The Inescapable Questions of Life

The prevailing mood of doubt and uncertainty in today's culture presents real problems for human beings. It is impossible for us to escape asking such questions as: Is there a God? If so, what is He like? How can I know Him? Who am I? Where am I? How can I tell right from wrong? Is there life after death? What should I and what can I do about guilt? How can I deal with my inner pain? These are what I call the *inescapable questions of life*. When an individual fails to find satisfying answers to these questions, he or she will fail to find meaning in life.

While it is true that some people have more of a passion for these questions than others, there is no one who has grown into adulthood without giving some attention to questions of this kind. In early 1996, my wife, Fay, and I spent four months in Ukraine and Russia. Nothing that I learned there raised any doubts in my mind about the universality of these observations. The influence of atheistic Russian communism had not by any means silenced these questions.[1]

The Tragic Picture of Our Times

The person who has learned of the vastness of the universe and the potential that lies within it, but has found himself with no sure and satisfactory answers to the *inescapable questions of life* is in deep trouble. He is capable of experiencing a feeling of lostness that few people could have experienced before this present time. He is overwhelmed by the vastness of the universe. He is over-whelmed by the secrets that have been unlocked that have made so many inventions and discover-ies possible. He is frustrated because scientists have been able to navigate the universe and send space ships to the moon and planets, but they have given him no means of answering these ques-tions he cannot avoid asking. He cannot find purpose and meaning in life. He does not know how to deal with guilt, loneliness, depression, and despair. Out of his despair he cries out, "Who am I?" "Where am I?" "What direction should I take?" With his ear turned toward naturalism, he hears no voice that bears Truth that will set him free. Empiricism has no satisfactory answers to these ques-tions. From the emptiness of unsatisfied thirst, many are turning to illegal drugs, alcohol, and promiscuous sex. These may bring temporary thrills, but in the long run they become a part of the problem. The odor of unbelief, uncertainty, fear, loneliness, boredom, depression, despair, and pes-simism permeate the atmosphere.

We live in the midst of confused, and frustrated people. Jesus said, "And you shall know the truth, and the truth shall make you free" (Jn. 8:32, NKJV). It is my conviction that these words of Jesus are of particular importance for people experiencing the problems prevalent in our society. There is no remedy apart from Truth. The culture which denies that Truth exists or is accessible *is in desperate need of Truth.*

The Purpose of This Study

This study is designed to present the basic truths of the Christian faith. It is written out of a heart of redemptive concern. I am concerned evangelistically for the person who is not a Christian that he may come to know Jesus Christ, whom to know is eternal life (Jn. 6:68). I am concerned for the person who is already saved, that he or she may grow in the likeness of Christ (Rom. 8:29), and that he may be able to appropriate the all-sufficient grace of God in the midst of the complexities of life (2 Cor. 12:9). This redemptive concern has a twofold motivation: (1) that people may be deliv-ered from both misery and distress that accompany the powers of darkness both in this life and the life to come, and further be translated into the kingdom of God's dear Son experiencing that joy, peace, and satisfaction that belong to Christ's kingdom both in this life and the life to come (Col. 1:13) and (2) that God may be given His rightful place of honor and glory in our hearts and minds as our Sovereign Lord and Redeemer (Phil. 2:9-11).

The Approach of This Study

LIFE-ORIENTED

For a long time there was a tendency in the world of scholarship to make a sharp distinction between the academic, which deals with the content of Truth, and the practical, which deals with the application of Truth. In studying the content of Truth, the ideal was to be objective. It was felt that to combine the study of the content of Truth with the application of Truth was to contaminate objectivity with subjectivity. To be objective was to seek to be detached from the subject under study.

A person was to study as if it made no difference what conclusions he reached. It was felt that objectivity was necessary in order to maintain intellectual honesty.

To challenge objectivity as a guiding ideal in the pursuit of Truth should not be considered a challenge to the notion that Truth itself is objective. Truth exists outside of the mind of the knower. At the same time Truth is for life. It is not just a cold, dry collection of abstract and impersonal ideas.

In my early years of teaching in the 1950s, I worked hard to maintain objectivity. I demanded that students write their papers in the third person. I insisted that in an exegetical paper that the students refrain from introducing anything into their papers besides bare exegesis of the text. I rebuked one student for placing a poem in his paper.

I have come to believe that there are some serious problems in trying to maintain objectivity as the guiding ideal in the search for Truth. Objectivity seeks to make a person a neutral investigator of Truth. Why is a person supposed to be more capable of discovering Truth if he is a neutral investigator rather than one who is deeply involved in what he is doing and who feels strongly about it? Who learns the most about art—a person who is neutral about art, or a person who loves art? Who learns more about baseball—one who studies with a feeling of detachment or one who is deeply involved? We are not to wring all the feeling out of Truth if we expect it to speak to life. Thinking and feeling must be found together.

It is an absolute must that we maintain honesty and integrity in our pursuit of Truth. To speak of a dishonest search for Truth is a contradiction of terms. However, to become married to objectivity as a means of trying to guarantee honesty means to divorce the mind from the rest of the personality. Truth is for the *total personality*. It may take a strong commitment to honesty to be honest when a person is deeply involved in a matter. Yet, this is what must take place. Honesty and deep involvement must be found in the same person in order to reach the highest degree of proficiency in discovering the Truth.

We are not spectators in our search for Truth. We are deeply concerned and involved. We study with a passion. It is particularly important that we study theological truth as interested and involved persons because theological truth is for life. It must not be a mere mental exercise. It must be experience oriented. As a person studies the breadth of material covered in a study of systematic theology, he or she should feel spoken to. He should experience a wide range of emotions. He may, depending on his or her relationship with Jesus Christ, experience feelings of fear, dread, rebuke, or relief, peace, satisfaction, calm and gratitude. He should develop an increased concern for other people. He should feel challenged and motivated. Life should take on meaning and purpose.

Many times authors have chosen to write in the third person as a means of maintaining a higher degree of objectivity.[2] This caused the author to write as a detached person. To a large extent, this removed his writings from life. There was a missing dimension that kept many outstanding works on theology from speaking to the heart. They were not designed to speak to the heart. That was left for devotional studies.

My aim here is not objectivity. I am writing as a deeply involved and deeply concerned person. I want the reader to feel that I care and that what I say is real to me. Therefore, I will write in the first person. I will endeavor to be honest. Since I am subject to human frailties, I may not always achieve this; nevertheless, this is my guiding ideal.

Combining the academic and the practical in this study does not presuppose that the full implications of the practical will be developed, as might be in a book more completely devoted to the practical. However, it will be life-oriented in its approach. Any presentation of Truth that does not speak to life has a missing element. We may not be able to show a life application from every sentence or paragraph, or even every page, but the process of discovering Truth should be a process of learning more about how to live in a complex world. I believe Truth is practical. Truth is for life.

SYSTEMATICALLY ORIENTED

When the term doctrine, as distinguished from systematic theology, is applied to a study of the Christian system of Truth, it refers to a topical study of basic Christian truths. As a rule, such a study is designed to set forth the biblical teachings on these subjects. Little or no attention is given to gaining a rational understanding of one's faith and to showing the interrelatedness of doctrines one to another. Also, only limited attention is given to differing views of interpretation.

Systematic theology covers essentially the same areas that a more or less complete work on doctrine covers. It attempts to help a person develop a rational understanding of his faith. In its attempt to be systematic, it seeks to lay a foundation and build a structure of thought on that foundation. Attention is given to how the structure grows logically out of the foundation and how the doctrines relate one to another to produce harmony in the system. As a rule, a systematic theology is more thorough than a doctrinal treatment. It gives more documentation for what is set forth and gives more attention to different views. My experience has been in teaching systematic theology rather than doctrine. This study will be systematic in its approach.

It will be helpful at this point if we distinguish between systematic theology and that branch of theology called biblical theology. Biblical theology is a study of biblical teachings as they are progressively revealed, or as they are set forth in a particular section of the Bible, a particular book, or the writings of a particular author. In speaking of biblical theology, we talk about Old Testament theology, New Testament theology, Theology of the Pentateuch, Pauline theology, etc.

Systematic theology is a topical study of the whole of Christian Truth, using any and all sources of Truth, with a view to seeing the parts as making up an integrated and harmonious whole, resulting in a Christian worldview. To speak of biblical theology as distinguished from systematic theology, is not intended to suggest that systematic theology is not biblically based. When systematic theology is properly done, it rests squarely on the authority of the Bible. When speaking of biblical theology as a branch of theology, it seeks to show how a particular doctrine is unfolded and developed in the Bible. It does not have the same interest that systematic theology does in harmonizing doctrines and developing a total worldview.

The Presuppositions

By presuppositions, I mean the basic beliefs that are essential for a particular type of study to be conducted. At this point, I am not raising the question of how or whether these presuppositions can be proved. That will be discussed when these presuppositions come up for elaboration in the study. I am saying that at all times these presuppositions will be treated as true and that they are necessary for the study as a whole. There is no neutral platform from which to start. We cannot start from "nowhere." We must start somewhere. Honesty requires us to make this admission.

• That God Exists As the Triune God and His Self-revelation Is Seen in:
1. Jesus Christ
2. The Bible
3. In nature and the experience of men

• That God's Revelation Is for Man and Can Be Known by Him

Man is created in God's image for a relationship with God. The Truth the Maker reveals is designed to meet the needs of the one He has made in the condition his experiences have put him. It is the very purpose of God's Truth to set us free (Jn. 8:32). Truth must always be studied with that in mind.

The *design* of our being created in the image of God, along with the divine aid that is provided for us, creates the possibility for us to understand the Truth. Apart from this confidence there would be no proper theology.

• That Truth Is an Integrated and Harmonious Whole

I will not propose to treat all Truth. However, I affirm that all Truth is an integrated and harmonious whole. For those who wish to see all Truth in this way, a study of theology is foundational. It puts all Truth in proper perspective. To deprive one's knowledge of theology is to deprive it of the perspective that is necessary to meet the needs of the *total personality*.

• That All of Life's Experiences Operate Within the Framework of Four Basic Relationships and Involve Four Basic Values

The *four basic relationships* are: (1) man's relationship with God, (2) man's relationship with other people, (3) man's relationship with himself, and (4) man's relationship with the created order. Man is *designed* for relationships. All of our experiences in one way or another involve one or more of these four basic relationships. This involves both our actions and our thoughts.

The *four basic values* are holiness, love, wisdom, and ideals. Man is a value oriented personal being. He is so constructed that he cannot erase the categories of right and wrong, good and bad, from his being. One or more of these values is involved in all of life's experiences including both actions and thoughts. The four basic values furnish the guiding principles for the proper functioning of the four basic relationships.

It is the function of theology to identify God, man, and the created order and to show the system of Truth that is derived from the *application* of the *four basic values* to the *four basic relationships*. This system of Truth becomes the foundation for the application of the four basic values to its four basic relationships in actual life.

The Aim

My aim in this study will be to present a system of doctrinal Truth that is: (1) Christ-centered, (2) Bible-based, and (3) life-oriented.

2

The Acquisition of Upper Story Knowledge

In my early years (1930s and 1940s), most people in the U.S. believed in God and thought the Bible was the Word of God. There was what Francis Schaeffer would call a "Christian consensus." The vast majority of people accepted the ideals of basic Christian morality. This was true even if they did not live by these ideals. Though it did not produce an ideal society, the existence of a Christian consensus did have a positive impact and served as a restraining influence on society. Today that consensus does not exist. How do we account for so much change?

There has been a major shift in worldview thinking on the grass roots level in my lifetime. A person's worldview is his explanation of the whole of reality. In Chapter 1, I referred to what I call the *inescapable questions of life.* These questions that voice themselves from within deal with questions about God, the origin of the universe, the origin of man, right and wrong, life after death, and the meaning and purpose of life. When a person attempts to answer these questions, he or she is developing a worldview.

When developing a worldview, one of the most basic questions that must be dealt with is: How do you know, and how do you know you know? This is the domain of epistemology. Epistemology deals with how you *acquire* knowledge and how you *test* knowledge. Our interest is in how you acquire and test knowledge as it relates to answering the *inescapable questions of life.*

We will first give attention to how a person acquires knowledge. When a person determines how he or she thinks knowledge is acquired, much has already been determined about the worldview he will develop. Our interest in this book is with what Francis Schaeffer called "upper story knowledge."

The Lower Story and the Upper Story

I have found Schaeffer's distinction between *lower story* and *upper story* knowledge very useful.[1] The *lower story* deals with particulars, mathematics, mechanics, the physical sciences, etc. It can be adequately studied by the mind as it reflects upon the data of observation and experience. The *upper story* deals with the moral and the religious concerns of life. Or, to put it another way, the *upper story* deals with the *inescapable questions of life.* In a rational worldview, the upper story deals with universals. Non-rational approaches to the *upper story* deny the existence of universal Truth.

Our concern in this book is with how you acquire *upper story* knowledge. The chart below will illustrate the *upper* and *lower* stories.

UPPER STORY
Answers to the *inescapable questions of life:* knowledge of God,
universals, moral knowledge, religious knowledge,
meaning and purpose for life, etc.

LOWER STORY
Particulars, mathematics, mechanics, the physical sciences, etc.

The Sources of Data

In learning, the mind gathers data and reflects upon that data. An important question to be decided by epistemology is: What are the sources of data? Everybody recognizes the validity of observation and experience as sources of data. The question is: What about divine revelation and innate knowledge?

The view that limits data to observation and experience is called *empiricism.* It rejects both divine revelation and innate ideas as valid sources for data. David A. Rausch defines empiricism as, "The philosophical theory that all ideas are derived from experience, asserting that both internal and external experience are the sole foundation of true knowledge and of science."[2]

As an approach to epistemology, empiricism works on the assumption that the only valid approaches to gaining knowledge are observation and experience. In its narrowest approach, empiricism assumes that the only valid knowledge is that which is gained by reflection upon sense data (that which is discovered through the five senses assisted by instruments of precision). This was the approach used by logical positivists.[3] One of their sayings was, "If it is not based on sense data, it is 'nonsense.'"

In its broader use, empiricism accepts data other than sense data. For example, the data gathered by opinion polls is considered data for empirical research.

The epistemology of those who accept the Christian worldview recognizes the validity of empirical research as a means of learning, but it also recognizes divine revelation as a source of data. Empiricism rejects divine revelation as a valid source of data. So while Christian thought would certainly recognize the validity of empirical research as a means of learning, it would reject empiricism.

There can be no real understanding of the American or Western scene without taking a look at the journey our culture has traveled to get to where we are. It will be observed that changes in culture, to a large extent, reflect changes in the way the *acquisition of knowledge* is approached.

Another approach that tried to put a worldview together without divine revelation was *rationalism.* Rationalism tried to develop a rational worldview based on reason using innate ideas without the input of data from divine revelation. Since empiricism has been the prevailing epistemology in modernism in America, my major attention will be given to it.

The History of Epistemology in Western Thought

On the grass roots level, the culture of my youth was informed by Christian thought and Christian morals and ideals. At the same time, there was a powerful force at work that was impacting the culture. That was the influence of secular thought. It had been a powerful force in the universities for some time. By 1960 it became evident that it was a major force on the grass roots level. In retrospect, we know that at the same time the influence of secular thought was becoming more evident on the grass roots level; a significant shift was taking place in secular thought. We now know that it was the beginning of a manifestation of a paradigm[4] shift from modernism to postmodernism.

To get an understanding of what *has* taken place and what is taking place in our culture, it will be helpful to look at how the acquisition of knowledge has been dealt with since the time of Copernicus. We gain very little insight into the thinkers of the past or those of today if we read their conclusions but do not know the sources of data that they accept and the sources of data that they reject. The *only* truth a person can discover is that which is allowed by his *epistemology*.

Yuri A. Gagarin, the first Russian cosmonaut who orbited the earth, came back and declared, "I did not see God up there." His epistemology excluded a priori his believing in God. If he could not see God he concluded that He was not there. An inadequate epistemology shut him off from a knowledge of God.

The Ascendancy of Empiricism

It will help if we will take a look at how empiricism came to occupy the throne in the mainstream of thought in Western universities. My presentation of the battle that led to the triumph of empiricism must be brief. For those who would like a thorough treatment, I would suggest that you read John Dillenberger's, *Protestant Thought and Natural Science,* which is cited below. While Dillenberger at the end of his treatment embraces neo-orthodoxy, I think he gives an accurate treatment of the conflict between the Copernican and Ptolemaic views of the universe.

Prior to the time of Copernicus (1473-1543), the Ptolemaic system was unchallenged in the church. The earth was viewed as an immobile planet at the center of the universe. The earth was cursed, but the rest of the universe was not thought to bear the marks of the curse. The rest of the universe served the earth. Dillenberger observes, "It was both philosophically and scientifically clear that the Christian drama was woven into the very texture of history and nature. A total coherent view had emerged in which everything had its place and its purpose. A picture so magnificent and so satisfying could not easily be abandoned."[5]

This geocentric understanding is referred to by Dillenberger as the Aristotelian-Ptolemaic view. It was viewed as having both the authority of theology and the authority of Aristotle behind it. The battle that ensued concerning the correctness of this view was to last about 140 years. By the time of Isaac Newton (1642-1727), the Copernican view had been declared the winner. It had come to be accepted by those outside and inside the church.

It is unfair to read the early rejection of the Copernican view by the church as a simple case of opposition by theologians. Dillenberger explains:

Much has been written about the manner in which theologians rejected Copernicus. But in any final assessment of the grounds for either acceptance or rejection of his views, it is of the utmost importance to pay close attention to dates. As early as 1525, Copernicus evidently had some fame, though his major work did not appear until 1543. The book, *De Revolutionibus Orbium Caelestiu,* was not widely accepted by astronomers in the decades immediately following its publication. This was the case in spite of the appearance of a new star in the Constellation Cassiopeia in 1572 and the tracing of the orbit of the comet of 1577. Both of these suggested that the traditional scientific conceptions were inadequate. However, genuine evidence for the basic Copernican position had to await the work of Kepler and Galileo in the early seventeenth century. Before that time, acceptance or non-acceptance could not be decided on what were later understood to be scientific grounds.[6]

Dillenberger goes on to say: "Professor Butterfield dates the breaking down of the Aristotelian-Ptolemaic system from the time of Galileo, but adds that there appeared no satisfactory alternative system until the time of Newton's *Principia* in 1687."[7]

Dillenberger further explains:

It is important to remember three periods whenever we consider the history of scientific advance. First is the period from Copernicus to Galileo. During this time there was no more compelling reason to accept than to reject the Copernican view. The balance was perhaps on the side of rejection. This can be said even if one discredits the strong bias of the Aristotelians in favour of the older position. The second period is that between Galileo and Newton. Here it is still possible to entertain alternative positions, though the weight of the evidence was certainly in the direction of the Copernican view. The third period is that of the Newtonian world-view. The genius of Newton had brought into being a unified conception of the universe. This position too had its problems; nevertheless, now the basic Copernican position was scientifically irrefutable.[8]

THE AUTONOMY OF SCIENCE

By the time of Galileo (1564-1643), science was beginning to be viewed as autonomous. With his telescope, Galileo gained observational support for the Copernican view. Robert G. Clouse explains, "In 1610, with the aid of his newly invented telescope, he discovered four moons that revolved around Jupiter. By analogy he reasoned that the planets revolve around the sun. This led him to support the Copernican explanation of the solar system."[9]

Certain essential steps were necessary in the development from Copernicus through Galileo to Newton which produced the decoupling effect of the burgeoning scientific method from any ultimate reference to the divine. As Dillenberger points out:

For Galileo the process could be described apart from God, but the credit or byline belonged to him. The seriousness of Galileo's religious concerns were clear enough. But insofar as the description could proceed without a reference to the divine, the stage was set for removing God from any vital relation to the order of nature.[10]

Concerning Newton's contribution Dillenberger explains:

It is generally agreed that the various components of the Newtonian picture were known prior to Newton. But it was Newton's genius to have a vision of, and experimentally verify, a single unified picture of what we may call scientific reality. Through the so-called universal law of gravitation, Newton was able to bring order out of confusion and with comparative simplicity at that. . . . It was now apparent that the new science of terrestrial mechanics, to which the experiments of Galileo contributed so much, was applicable to the celestial spheres. The last hope of an appreciable difference between the terrestrial spheres had disappeared.[11]

Dillenberger wishes to remind us that Newton had very strong theological interests and sought to protect those interests. However, "Whatever his intentions were, his influence was on the side of those who held a mechanical view of the world."[12]

By the time of Newton's contribution, in the thinking of many, science had become autonomous. Even though the major contributors to the Copernican victory had no intention of weakening theology, in the minds of many reason aided by experience and observation (empiricism) had triumphed over theology. God was no longer necessary. If God were still in the picture at all, the Bible would have to submit to science rather than having science to submit to the Bible. Empiricism was on the throne. A turning point had come in Western thought.

THE CONTRIBUTION OF DARWIN

While, for many, the direction had already been set to put together a view of life without God, those who were prone in this direction got another boost when Darwin, in 1859, published *Origin of Species.*

Dillenberger explains:

One difference between Newton and Darwin made it more difficult for the latter to gain acceptance. While Newton's theological views were not widely acceptable, he professed that the world had a Christian foundation. . . . On the other hand Darwin's views appeared to challenge a Christian understanding of the world. Moreover, it was known that Darwin was an agnostic.[13]

He further explains:

In the period between Copernicus and Newton, theologians had witnessed a change in men's thinking whereby God's relation to the cosmos has become more and more limited. For many, it was no longer necessary to think of God at all. Now man himself was no longer unique; he was essentially animal. He was the product of forces working without design or purpose, a being who essentially belonged to the nature from which he had emerged. Insofar as Darwinism was the end product of a long development in which not only the meaningful conceptions of the world and God, but also of man, had been called into question, it was inevitable that the battle should be bitter.[14]

Major Divisions in Western Thought

That which follows may be somewhat of an oversimplification. Nevertheless, I think it will help in grasping what has been happening in Western thought from Newton until the present.

OUTSIDE THE CHURCH

By the time of Isaac Newton, for many, the Bible could no longer be accepted as a divine revelation. The triumph of the Copernican view meant to them that the Bible was wrong on this most important view, i.e., the geocentric view of the universe. As a result of the influence of the Enlightenment, reason had been exalted as the final arbiter of Truth. For many the Bible failed the test of higher criticism. For such people, the Bible could no longer be viewed as an infallible authority. The remaining question was: Where do we go from here? Let us take a look at how thinking, as it relates to the *upper story,* was affected by the enthronement of empiricism and the dethroning of the Bible as a divine revelation communicating objective Truth.

Deism

With the loss of belief in the authority of the Bible as a divine revelation, many no longer believed in the Christian message of redemption through Jesus Christ. At the same time they were not ready to abandon God. They became deists. Jesus Christ and the Bible might be sources for moral Truth, but reason was the authority over what was true and what was false in the Bible.

H. M. McDonald is correct when he describes deism as "natural religion" which may be understood simply by a correct use of reason. On the other hand, what is decidedly not needed is revelational knowledge or that which comes from the teaching of the church.

He lists the basic doctrines of deism as follows:

(1) the belief in a supreme being;
(2) the obligation to worship;
(3) the obligation of ethical conduct;
(4) the need for repentance from sins; and
(5) divine rewards and punishments in this life and the next.[15]

Among well-known people who were deists were Voltaire, Thomas Jefferson, and Benjamin Franklin. Once one is familiar with the basic tenets of deism, it is not hard to see that these thought forms influenced the major documents of America's foundation.

While deists did not accept the need of redemption and the gospel, they did accept the concept of divine creation. Reality was rational. They believed in a moral order. They were advocates of natural law. They were imbued with the optimism of the Enlightenment.

They were at odds with orthodox Christianity on divine revelation, the fall of man, the deity of Christ, and the truth of the gospel. They were not at odds with Christianity on the essence of basic morality and that a rational explanation of the whole of reality was possible.

Deism is no longer a strong force in Western thought. Those who would have been appealed to by its approach have apparently sought refuge in modernism or some form of liberal Christianity.

Modernism

Modernists go further than deists. They hold to a naturalistic interpretation for the whole of reality. They believe that the only rational knowledge is empirical knowledge. They are empiricists. They hold to a secular worldview.

While some modernists would affirm atheism and some others would claim to be agnostics, most would probably affirm a belief in God. However, to them God is merely an appendage to their worldview. Their God serves no purpose in the development of their worldview. The result of such thinking is epistemological atheism. The worldview that is produced by epistemological atheism is atheistic. To move away from an atheistic worldview requires more than an acknowledgment of belief in God. It requires that this belief in God must also contribute to the development of the person's worldview.

Modernism shared the optimism of the Enlightenment. Its adherents believed that human reason alone, apart from divine revelation, could answer all of people's questions and solve all of people's problems. Nature had the answer. Nature was rational and moral. Modernism was optimistic and utopian. It was idealistic.

Modernism was at serious odds with Christianity. It completely wrote off divine revelation as a source of data. It stripped Jesus Christ of His deity. It had no room for the miracles of the Bible. It was married to the law of uniformity. All that ever had happened could be explained on the basis of natural causes and effects. All that will happen in the future will be produced by natural causes. Our only hope is in nature, but it is an optimistic hope. This view is commonly called *secular humanism*.

Postmodernism

Postmodernism is currently forcing itself on our attention. If you are not acquainted with it by name, as you read this explanation there will be a ring of familiarity about it. It is very obvious that there has been a major paradigm shift. We know that something new has made its appearance, but how do we describe it? When did it begin?

We are not to think that modernism has left the scene. But it is no longer ruling as king in secular thought. Modernism will likely be relegated to a place among history's failures because its epistemology made it *incapable of delivering on its promises.*

Postmodernism did not appear from nowhere. It arose from the failure of modernism. Modernism believed that Truth existed and that it could be found by reason. Modernism was optimistic. In times of highest hope it was utopian. Those who switched to postmodernism did so because they had supped at the table of modernism and went away starved.

The experiment of modernism had about 200 years to deliver. It failed to produce a unified view of the *lower* and *upper stories.* It failed to produce Truth. It was haunted by doubt and uncertainty.

The prevalence of drug and alcohol addiction, the crime rate, the suicide rate, the number of teenage pregnancies, the number of abortions, the prevalence of a feeling of emptiness and lostness, etc. all tell us that we are far from a utopia. We are currently doing well economically. But we are not sure about the future. We are amazed at technological advancement. But modernism did not find the answers to the *inescapable questions of life.* Modernism has left those who have looked to it for hope with a feeling of lostness, emptiness, and inward pain.

Modernism believed that Truth existed, but it could not find it. Postmodernism neither believes in nor desires to find ultimate Truth. Joseph Natoli and Linda Hutcheon explain this in the "Introduction" of *A Postmodern Reader* by saying, "an inevitable part of the general condition of postmodernity: [is] an acknowledgment of the impossibility (and indeed the undesirability) of reaching any absolute and final 'Truth.' "[16] The earmarks of postmodernism are doubt, uncertainty, ambivalence, contingency, relativism, pluralism, and tolerance.

Modernism believed that a rational worldview was possible, but they were always short of producing it. They are well described by Paul's words, "Ever learning, and never able to come to the knowledge of the truth" (2 Tim. 3:7).

Natoli and Hutcheon are incisive when they state:

> If one of the messages of the postmodern is that cultural values are always local and particular, and not universal and eternal, then we will also have to think about whether—for example—the French figuration of the postmodern should necessarily be the same as the Canadian, or the white American need resemble the African-American model. Jean-François Lytard's defining of the postmodern as marking the death of the grand "metanarratives" that used to make sense of our world for us comes out of a different intellectual and historical frame of reference than does Jurgen Habermas's counterargument that the modernist project of Enlightenment rationality requires completion first.[17]

The rejection of a metanarrative by postmodernism means that they reject the idea of a worldview that explains the whole of reality. There are worldviews, but there is not one worldview that is true and that judges other worldviews as being false. There is a rejection of the correspondence theory of Truth.

The question still remains: When did postmodernism start? There was not an exact point in time when postmodernism started. It emerged over a period of time. The affinity of postmodern thought with the thinking of Friedrich Nietzsche (1844-1900) is recognized. When World War I failed to be the war that would end all wars, the optimism of modernism began to wane. By the time of the end of World War II, many who were at the forefront of secular thought began to see that modernism as a worldview was a failure. It was about 1960 when the denial of *upper story* truth began to permeate the masses. It began to be seen through the rise of the hippie movement. They were dissatisfied with life. They assumed that nobody had been able to find meaning and purpose for life. They rebelled against the Establishment. The Establishment meant the government, the church, tradition, etc. They sought to tear down without knowing what to build in its place. They were searching for answers. Some experimented with mind-expanding drugs in hopes of finding answers while they were on drug trips. The failure of their search to find meaning and purpose for life only increased their despair. The influence of relativism began to permeate the culture.

What we now commonly refer to as "postmodernism" was for a while viewed as a divergent form of modernism. At least, that is the way it seemed to most Christian thinkers who were viewing it from the outside. It was all a part of what we called "secular humanism."

Probably no other writer and speaker prepared Christians as much to understand postmodernism, once it was completely unmasked, as Francis Schaeffer (1912-1984). Yet, the word *postmodernism* does not appear in his writings. He dealt clearly and forcefully with the concepts that we now understand to be postmodernism. When reading material that is addressing the thoughts and trends that we have been dealing with in this chapter, it is very important to check the date of publication. That will help us trace the progress of the development of the movement. The ideas, and even the term *postmodernism,* will be found earlier, but extensive use of the term began in the late 1980s.

The actual dethronement of modernism and the enthronement of postmodernism has taken place within the last few years. Thomas Oden is very precise about when this occurred. He explains:

> By postmodern, we mean the course of actual history following the death of modernity. By modernity we mean the period, the ideology, and the malaise of the time from 1789 to 1989, from the Bastille to the Berlin Wall.[18]

He further explains:

> The easiest way to identify the *time span* or epoch of modernity is as this precise 200-year period between 1789 and 1989, between the French Revolution and the collapse of Communism.
>
> While admitting that no dating of any historical period is ever unchallengeable, this one seems to cry out for special recognition. It was announced with such a spectacu-

lar beginning point (the opening up and storming of the wall of the Bastille prison in Paris with all its egalitarian fervor). It closed with a precise moment of collapse (the literal fall of a highly symbolic visible concrete wall in Berlin that the entire world watched tumble). The end of modernity can be timed precisely to the exact hour, even instant, of the fall of that wall in Germany.[19]

While not everyone would agree with Oden's precise dating of the transition of the modern to postmodern periods, it is generally recognized that by 1990 modernism had been dethroned and that postmodernism was on the throne.

In a sense we can say that in postmodernism everything is "true" and everything is "false." Postmodernism accepts everything and rejects everything. Postmodernism is not hindered by the law of non-contradiction.[20] Everything is true in the sense of "true for you" or "true for me." Nothing is true in the sense of true by a standard of absolute Truth. In that sense everything is false.

One of the things about modernism that was particularly offensive to postmodernists was the idea that those of us in the West would try to convince the rest of the world that anything that we have is superior to what they have. Postmodernism would say that it is just different. The desirability of competition in any form is abolished. The Christian concept of world evangelism is particularly offensive to the postmodernist. According to postmodernism no culture is superior to another in the way it seeks to gain knowledge and understanding. There are no valid and invalid ways of gaining knowledge. Nothing remains certain in postmodernism. Even science is in danger. Stanley J. Grenz tells us:

> Postmoderns are inclined to prize difference over uniformity and to respect the local and particular more than the universal. For this reason, postmodern thinkers do not regret the loss of science as a unifying enterprise. Postmodernism may spell the end of the "world," of "metanarratives," and of "science," but it marks the beginning of a revolution of knowledge.[21]

It must be remembered that empirical science did not originate in a vacuum. Scientific study requires the uniformity of nature. For a scientific study to proceed there must be the assumption that when you reproduce the same set of causes you have the same effect every time. It was the Christian view of an *ordered universe* that made the emergence of what we call *Modern Science* possible. A lower story which made science possible was dependent upon a Creator who gives order to nature. The problem with modernism was that there was nothing to give "nature" its nature. Modernism presupposed that nature was rational and moral, but it had no foundation to support this presupposition. Postmodernism rejects the presupposition that nature is rational and moral. It does not presuppose the law of uniformity. It undercuts the basis for science. Nature as it has been historically viewed is dead. How long can we enjoy the benefits of scientific research in a postmodern world? Can civilization continue to coexist with postmodernism? The barbarians are not only coming, they are already dwelling in the land.

WITHIN THE CHURCH

Many who accepted the victory of the Copernican view, and who also agreed that higher criticism had discredited the Bible as a source of authoritative truth, were not willing to completely accept either deism or modernism. They were not ready to abandon Christianity.

Liberalism

Theological liberalism believes that the knowledge gained through higher criticism and science has demolished the belief that the Bible can be viewed as a divine revelation conveying objective truth. However, liberals are not content to do away with Christianity. Friedrich Schleiermacher (1768-1834) sought to give Christianity empirical respectability by considering the data of religious experience to be valid empirical data. He is called the "father of liberalism."

Liberalism believed in the basic goodness of man. It was optimistic. Jesus Christ was a great moral teacher and example, but He was not deity. It had no room for the miracles of the Bible. It was a strong influence until around the time of World War II. The optimistic dream of liberal theology was not coming to pass. The devastation of two World Wars made it hard to maintain the optimism of theological liberalism.

Neo-orthodoxy

The neo-orthodox (Karl Barth 1886-1968 and Emil Brunner 1889-1966) agreed that the objective authority of the Bible had been destroyed, but they rejected the approach of the older form of liberalism. They rejected the liberal view of the goodness of man. They had no room for optimism based on human achievement. Man was deeply sinful. A great gulf separated man from God. Reason said that God was so Wholly Other (totally different) from man that God could not reveal Himself to man. For the one who has had an encounter with God, faith says that God has revealed Himself. Reason says that there could not be an incarnation of God in human flesh. Faith says that God became incarnate in Jesus Christ. Faith in such a case is irrational. The *upper story* is irrational.

Contemporary theology continues as some modification of neo-orthodox or liberal thought. Again we see that Paul's words "Always learning and never able to come to the knowledge of the truth" (2 Tim. 3:7) are appropriately applied.

Orthodox Biblical Christianity

There has been a consensus on the acceptance of the Copernican view both inside and outside the church. However, there is not a consensus within the church on the rejection of the Bible as an authoritative divine revelation.

Orthodox Christians accept the Copernican view of the universe, but see it as being in harmony with the Bible. If we use Francis Schaeffer's view of the *upper* and *lower stories,* orthodox Christians believe in a unified view of *upper* and *lower stories*. They accept divine revelation as an objective authority. They believe that man is created in the image of God and that some ideas are innate. For example, the law of God is written in our hearts. Orthodox Christians accept data from divine revelation (the Bible), innate ideas, as well as observation and experience. Advocates of this approach are referred to as *conservatives, evangelicals,* and *fundamentalists.* This view can simply be referred to as biblical Christianity. Biblical Christianity takes the Bible to be a divine revelation and develops its theology from the Bible. My treatment here will be brief since this view is the view that will be set forth throughout the book.

Testing Upper Story Knowledge for Validity

The concern of this chapter is with the acquisition of *upper story* knowledge. Another concern of epistemology is: How do we test the validity of what is presented as *upper story* knowledge? Or, how do we test the Truth claims of a worldview? At this point, I will just set forth the tests. They will receive further elaboration in later chapters.

A system that proposes to explain the whole of reality (or a worldview) must prove to be satisfactory to our *total personality* as thinking, feeling, acting beings. Logic cannot divorce itself from life and become an accurate judge of a system. I believe the following tests are a step in the right direction to establishing criteria that will protect the interest of the *total personality*: (1) Does it answer the *inescapable questions of life?* (2) Is there internal consistency, i.e., is the structure logically related to the foundation? Do all the parts fit consistently together? (3) Is there causal adequacy? i.e., are the causes adequate to produce the effects attributed to them? (4) Does it conform to that which is undeniably true?

If a worldview cannot answer the *inescapable questions of life,* it is not worthy of our consideration. It would be an unbearable universe if human beings were so constituted that they could not escape asking certain questions, and yet there were no answers that could be found. I am not saying that all imaginable questions must have answers, but I am saying that questions that are written indelibly into the constitution of man must be answered.

The Challenge Before the Church

One of the advantages of having lived a long time is that you can see things from a greater perspective. The longer you have lived the greater is your context of time. The challenge before the church is always: How can we reach people for Christ? How can we show the implications of the Christian message for life and thought?

The challenge for Christians today is much harder than it was in the 1930s and the 1940s. That challenge has been made progressively more difficult until the present time. The ascendancy of postmodernism to the throne in secular thought has drastically changed the nature and the difficulty of our challenge. With the coming of postmodernism, there has been a major paradigm shift in the way people approach knowledge. That paradigm shift has given the church a different and a drastically more difficult challenge.

Personal Reflections

I have spent a lot of time in reflection on the difference between the way things were in my youth and the way things are now. There would be no value in my taking the space in this book to think through why things were different then than now if it was simply to take a nostalgic look at the good old days. I am reminded of Carl Hurley's story of two ladies who were talking about the past. One of the ladies said, "Things are not like they used to be." The other lady said, "They never were." There is a lot of truth in what the lady said. When we get older, we try to glamorize the past. If my review of the journey our culture has taken in the last 60 years does not help us to better understand the present and how to deal with it, it will serve no useful purpose in this book.

MORALS AND IDEALS [22]

When it comes to morality and ideals, the *culture* that I was brought up in did a better job of training people than the *church* does now. There was a strong emphasis on right and wrong, honesty, integrity, purity, modesty, responsibility, duty, diligence, faithfulness, loyalty, self-control, respect for age, respect for authority, concern for others, thoughtfulness, kindness, courtesy, politeness, manners, dignity, beauty, and excellence. I do not want to leave the impression that everyone was a shining example of all of these virtues. Some were not. But these virtues were extolled, and that made a difference in people.

There were differences of opinion on the finer points of the application in moral areas, but there was no conflict on the basic morality of the Ten Commandments. When it came to ideals, there was some variation on details, but there was no conflict over the substance involved in these virtues.

There were some who lived in serious violation of these ideals, but they did not idealize such behavior. Violation of the basic morality of the Ten Commandments was considered to be sin. When it came to violation of basic morality, it was attributed to "the flesh" or depravity. When it came to politeness, manners, dignity, beauty, and excellence, failure in this regard was attributed to not caring. It was said that such a person did not have good breeding. It was a reflection on his or her parents.

The emphasis on right and wrong helped people develop a sense of responsibility, duty, and a commitment to diligence. The emphasis on the virtues: thoughtfulness, kindness, and courtesy motivated concern for your fellow man. The emphasis on the virtues: politeness, manners, dignity, beauty, and excellence lifted people's sights. It gave people something to which to aspire. People looked forward to dressing up. Sloppiness was not in. While not everyone was equally committed to these virtues, many people were and many could testify of how these virtues helped them find satisfaction and move ahead in life.

EVANGELISM

In the 1930s and 1940s, almost everybody in my environment thought Christianity was true. They planned to get saved before they died. The main responsibilities of Christians in evangelism were: (1) to remind sinners of the dangers of putting off salvation and (2) to clarify the gospel for them.

Every evangelist had illustrations of those who died while they were putting off salvation. They told of those who tragically lost their lives while they were young. They also reminded people that with age there tended to be a hardening of the heart. They had illustrations of those who hardened their hearts even in the face of death. The plea of the preacher was, "Behold, now is the day of salvation" (2 Cor. 6:2).

These warnings helped sinners to listen more attentively. The preacher would explain that good works, baptism, church membership, and other things that people might depend upon would not save a person. Then, he would explain that the only way of salvation was to receive Jesus Christ by faith as Lord and Savior. The Holy Spirit moved mightily in many of those services. Many responded and were saved.

I do not have to tell you that what I have just said does not describe our day. Some drastic changes have occurred.

THE PROBLEM OF THEOLOGICAL LIBERALISM

Prior to 1930 the hottest battles between fundamentalism and theological liberalism had been fought. The liberals had won so far as votes were concerned. In mainline denominations, liberals were in control of the seminaries and foreign mission programs; many pulpits were occupied by liberals. It was a real problem for a young ministerial student to find a conservative seminary to attend. Many lost their faith while in seminary.

It is much easier now to find a good conservative seminary to attend than it was 30 years ago. The situation has improved some over what it was 50 or 60 years ago.

AN EXPLANATION OF THE CULTURE OF MY YOUTH

For several years I have pondered the question: What accounted for the strong influence of Christian thought in my early years? I am particularly concerned with what was taking place on the grass roots level. We are tempted to say that the difference is to be explained by the difference between the churches then and now. Certainly, a great deal of credit belongs to the churches of those days. But I do not believe that the influence of the churches in those days is the total answer.

To find an answer for the difference in the culture then and now, we must look at the forces that were shaping the culture then and now. To understand the success or failure of churches in evangelistic efforts and on impacting the values of the culture at a given time, we must take a look at the *opposition* the churches faced during the time under consideration.

Many cultural changes can be explained on the basis of sociological principles. But I think the deep changes that have taken place in our society, such as the rejection of the existence of ultimate Truth and the rise of moral and cultural relativism, must look to changes in worldview thinking for an explanation. If we are going to understand the culture of the 1930s and the 1940s, we must take a look at how that culture was impacted by worldview thinking.

What, besides Christian thought, impacted the culture then? Modernism was a strong influence. The modernism of that day promoted the opposite of what postmodernism is promoting today. It was rational, moral, and optimistic so far as its major thrust was concerned. I remember that sometime in the mid or late 1940s I read in the newspaper that some university professor somewhere was advocating "free love" (the term then used to approve sex outside marriage). The professor was viewed as being eccentric.

Modernism did pose a threat to Christian beliefs, but it was not a threat to high ideals. It promoted excellence. The modernism of the time would not have supported an outright attack on the basic morality of the Ten Commandments. What could be said about the modernism of the time could also be said about the theological liberalism of the time. There was no significant voice that was undercutting moral ideals. The problem existing then was that the power of depravity caused people to violate their conscience as well as their best judgment.

When moral ideals are kept intact, it is much easier for the Christian message to be heard on the grass roots level. Modernism and liberalism were a problem, but they did not pose the same threat in the area of morals and ideals that postmodernism does.

What I have said about the 1930s and the 1940s applies, to a lesser degree, to the 1950s. Changes were in the making that would prepare the way for the turbulent time of the 1960s.

The 1960s

The optimism of modernism was no longer convincing. In an experiment of more than 150 years, autonomous reason (reason not informed by divine revelation) had failed to deliver on its promise to find a solution to human need. This failure gave rise to the hippie movement. The Hippies rebelled against the Establishment. The Establishment was the institutions of society. The church was a part of this Establishment. It, too, was written off as having failed to find answers to life's questions and problems. However, their main concern was with modernism. Christianity was viewed as a relic of the past. It was assumed that Christianity died as a viable option with the rise of modernism. So far as the hippie movement was concerned, there was no reason to reexamine Christianity as a possible answer for people's problems. This no doubt occurred in a few instances. But such an examination was never a subject of concern for the hippie movement.

Rioting and burning took place on many university campuses. There was a distrust of everybody over 30. They did not know what direction to go in, but they were convinced that the answers were not to be found in the past. In a desperate attempt to find answers to the problems of life, many sought to find answers through mind-expanding drugs. They found none. This led to more despair.

The optimistic hope that man by reason would be his own Savior could no longer be maintained. In retrospect, we know that modernism was entering its death sickness. Postmodernism with its denial of truth, doubt, uncertainty, ambivalence, moral and cultural relativism, pluralism, etc. was emerging.

The turbulence of the 1960s died down in the 1970s, but the move toward a full blown postmodernism continued. For a while it looked as though we were simply witnessing a change within modernism. It was all called "secular humanism." Now that it is clearer what has happened, we no longer call it secular humanism. The term humanism suggests that there is hope. It suggests an aspiration for the better things of life. That is not what we are seeing. Hope is gone. There is nothing better to which to aspire. One thing is as good as another. It is all a matter of preference and taste.

Preference and taste are culturally conditioned. Postmodernism is what we call it now. Postmodernism is on the throne.

The 1990s

It is evident that a major paradigm shift has occurred. It has changed our society. The high ideals of modernism are gone. The high ideals of Christianity have lost their appeal. The concept of Truth is rejected. We are in desperate need of a revival of morals.

David Wells tells us:

> Western culture once valued the higher achievements of human nature—reasoned discourse, the good use of language, fair and impartial law, the importance of our collective memory, tradition, the core of moral axioms to which collective assent was given, those aesthetic achievements in the arts that represented the high-water marks of the human spirit. These are now all in retreat. Reasoned discourse has largely disappeared; in a nation of plummeting literacy, language has been reduced to the lowest common denominator, to the vulgar catch phrases of the youth culture; the core of values has disintegrated; the arts are degraded; the law is politicized.[23]

Christianity is Truth based. Jesus said, "And you shall know the truth, and the truth shall make you free" (Jn. 8:32, NKJV). Postmodernism denies the existence of ultimate Truth. Christianity is rational. It believes in the law of non-contradiction. Postmodernism is irrational. It is not bothered by the law of non-contradiction. Christianity believes in absolute moral Truth. Postmodernism believes in moral relativism.

I am not suggesting that everybody has given up on all that is good and noble. It is not necessary for a person to buy the whole package of postmodernism to be influenced by it. There is a *post-modern mood,* and that mood is conditioning our culture. People's feelings about Truth and about right and wrong have been desensitized. People do not have the feeling about sin that is required to support the doctrines of judgment, Hell, and the necessity of atonement as set forth by Christian theology.

Concluding Observations

I hope it has become evident in this chapter that what people believe about the acquisition of *upper story* knowledge is extremely important. If we only admit the data of observation and experience, we rule out a Christian worldview. It is not a matter of intelligence. It is a matter of what data is admissible. No person can build a Christian worldview when the only data that is admitted is the data of observation and experience. No person who accepts the data of divine revelation could accept modernism or postmodernism.

It should be obvious that 200 years of experiments tell us that empiricism cannot solve the problem of human need. It was the failure of that experiment that gave rise to postmodernism. Postmodernism is not a solution. It is the announcement of a failed experiment.

In the tracing of the history of culture in my own lifetime, it should be obvious that people are in desperate need of answers to the *inescapable questions of life*. It should be obvious that worldview thinking affects behavior for good or bad.

The failure of the experiment of modernism and the lack of any hope from postmodernism should present us as Christians with an opportunity. We need to let people know that though the experiment of modernism failed that does not mean that all hope is lost. We need to let people know that modernism could do nothing but fail because it left out the important data of divine revelation.

Paul tells us in Romans 3:11, *"There is none who understands"* (NKJV). The Greek for "understand" is *suniemi*. Concerning this word, Randolf O. Yeager explains:

> To understand in this sense is "to put it all together." Such a thinker seeks and finds maximum concrescence. Truth is consistent, coherent and correspondent to reality. There are no parts of the truth that oppose one another. Each part coheres with all other parts and all parts correspond to the real world."[24]

To put what Paul said in modern terms is to say that without God it is impossible to put together a true and adequate worldview. A worldview without God, the Bible, and Jesus Christ is inadequate. It cannot meet the needs of a person in this life or the life to come.

By leaving God, Jesus Christ, and divine revelation out of the picture, modernism put itself at cross purposes with the image of God. It led to pessimism and despair. It created an empty and troubled society.

That is where modernism has left people. Postmodernism recognizes the problem, but offers no solution. It has concluded that *there is no solution*. We are *determined* by our culture and our language community. *We are not free*.

We need to be able to explain this emptiness that people are experiencing. We need to speak to that emptiness. We need to show people that there is hope. Jesus said, " I am come that they might have life, and that they might have it more abundantly" (Jn. 10:10). Paul said, "Godliness is profitable unto all things, having promise of the life that now is, and of that which is to come" (1 Tim. 4:8).

The impact of postmodernism on culture presents a far greater problem for the advancement of Christian concerns than was the case with modernism. Modernism left moral ideals essentially intact. The pluralism and relativism of postmodernism undermine morals and desensitize the way people feel about the morals they do accept.

If we expect to make a significant impact on people in today's culture, we must make people aware of where we are and how we got here. We must learn to confront people with Truth who have been conditioned by relativism. We must learn to do this in such a way that it gives hope. We must help those who have been deluded into thinking that there is no meaning and purpose for life. The only message that gives people's lives meaning and purpose is the gospel. That is what we have been commissioned by Jesus Christ to do.

3

God's Self-revelation

If we use the division between the *lower story* and the *upper story* as set forth in the previous chapter, everybody would recognize that human beings have *upper story* experiences. Undeniably, people have moral and religious experiences. It is also undeniable that these experiences are very significant in the development of a healthy or unhealthy personality. The question is: Is there truth that guides these experiences, making some ideas true or false and some actions right or wrong? It is at this point that agreement ends.

I used to think that everybody believed that Truth existed. I knew there were differences of opinion on what the Truth was. I also knew there was not agreement on how you might find Truth. I knew some people were agnostic about finding Truth. I believe my understanding did describe the vast majority of people until recent years, including those in the academic world. With the paradigm shift from modernism to postmodernism, that has now changed.

In describing the scene on university campuses in 1987, Allan Bloom says:

> There is one thing a professor can be absolutely certain of: almost every student enter-ing the university believes, or says he believes, that truth is relative. If this belief is put to the test, one can count on the students' reaction: they will be uncomprehending. That anyone should regard the proposition as not self-evident astonishes them, as though he were calling into question $2 + 2 = 4$. These are things you don't think about.[1]

Bloom goes on to say, "There is no enemy other than the man who is not open to everything."[2]

As I understand Bloom, he is telling us that there was a time when universities insisted on aca-demic liberty for their teachers. They did this because they believed that Truth did exist. They did not want to hinder the teacher's search for Truth. Now, they stand for *openness* because they believe there is no such thing as Truth. He says, "Thus what is advertised as a great opening is a great clos-ing."[3] The mind that *denies* the existence of Truth is *closed* to the Truth.

Some people have thought of God as a killjoy. Such people think that belief in God inflicts guilt on people and interferes with the joy of living. These people think that if we could get God out of the picture, people could get on with the joy of living.

Once God is removed, there is no authority to inflict guilt. Each person, it is thought, is free to make his or her own morals. The dream is that a society conditioned by such thought will be free to enjoy unhindered pleasure. One of the main areas to be redirected by this dream is the area of sex. It is thought that deliverance from divine restrictions on sex would open the way for a happy life. The only concern is for safe sex that will protect against unwanted pregnancy and disease. In such a society living together without marriage gets the same approval as marriage. Homosexuality is viewed as having the same moral standing as heterosexuality.

Our society has moved a long way in the direction that I have described. We have seen a wide scale casting away of moral standards and high ideals. The question is: Has it brought the happiness that had been expected? I do not think many would claim that it has. The widespread addiction to drugs and alcohol should tell us that the casting away of moral ideals has not succeeded in bringing happiness. Depression, pessimism, and despair are widespread. This is true in spite of the economic prosperity that we have experienced as a country. We live in a troubled society. The attempt to deny real guilt has not solved people's problems.

With many, it is the allurements of hedonism that makes the denial of Truth and the casting off of moral authority appealing. However, that is not what has brought on the paradigm shift from modernism to postmodernism. This shift was not made because people thought the key to happiness was to be found in moral autonomy. The leaders in the paradigm shift chose the plunge into postmodernism because they thought all attempts to find truth for *upper story* experiences had failed and would continue to fail. They believe that the search for Truth is over. There are no answers to the *inescapable questions of life.*

I respect postmodernists for realizing that empiricism, by reflecting on the data of observation and experience, cannot find *upper story* truth. I respect the postmodernists for realizing that modernism is bankrupt. I respect those who reject oversimplified answers for the problems that plagues us as human beings. However, I believe there are answers. I believe there is hope. I do not have a dream-world view of life. I do not subscribe to oversimplified answers. We live in a world filled with harsh reality. There is no guarantee that a person can escape partaking of some of this harsh reality. But it is possible to find answers that will give purpose and meaning to life. There is help for the journey.

A Lesson From Copernicus

Copernicus was faced with a problem for which he could find no answers. When he could not find answers, He went to the past and found help. Edward Rosen explains:

> At an early stage in his career Copernicus became aware of serious defects in the Ptolemaic astronomical system that he had learned as a student. Hoping to get rid of these grave errors, he began to review the older literature of the subject and found that a minority opinion had been long neglected. This opinion placed the sun rather than the earth at the center of the universe, and it was this heliocentric concept that Copernicus chose for the basics of his system.[4]

A feeling of need and a willingness to make an inquiry into the past put Copernicus on the road that would revolutionize our understanding of the universe. His search was rewarded and we are the beneficiaries.

An Assessment of the Current Crisis

I believe any honest assessment of the current situation will tell us that the culture is in serious trouble. We are in a crisis. I would suggest that we look at the casualties of postmodernism.

THE DEATH OF TRUTH

Postmodernism spells the death of Truth. Dennis McCallum comments, "Postmodernism, as it applies to our everyday lives, is the death of truth as we know it."[5]

In support of this assessment let me refer to the quotation from Joseph Natoli and Linda Hutcheon that I used in the previous chapter. They shed light on this assessment in the "Introduction" of *A Postmodern Reader* by saying, "an inevitable part of the general condition of postmodernity: [is] an acknowledgment of the impossibility (and indeed the undesirability) of reaching any absolute and final 'Truth.'"[6]

Can we afford to follow an approach that denies the existence of Truth—indeed, even rejects the idea that we should desire to find Truth?

THE DEATH OF REASON

With its emphasis on relativism and pluralism, postmodernism is irrational so far as the *upper story* is concerned. It is not bothered by the law of non-contradiction. Reason is dead when the law of non-contradiction is ignored.

Can we afford to follow an approach that has killed reason?

THE DEATH OF NATURE

Both Christianity and modernism recognized that there is an order to nature. Nature has a "nature." This "nature" was thought to be orderly and capable of being studied by the mind. Those who made a scientific study of nature spoke of the laws of nature. The "nature" of nature was viewed by both Christianity and modernism as being rational and moral. When this "nature" is denied, nature as it has been historically believed has disappeared. It is dead. There is no order to nature. There are no laws of nature. There is no foundation for science. Nature is not inherently moral.

Can we afford to follow an approach that robs nature of any consistent essence?

THE DEATH OF HOPE FOR A METANARRATIVE (OR WORLDVIEW)

Jim Leffel and Dennis McCallum tell us, "Metanarratives are the overarching explanations of reality based on central organizing 'truths.'"[7] A *metanarrative* would be the same as what I call a *worldview* if it is considered to be a true explanation of the whole of reality. Postmodernism has no room for a metanarrative nor a true worldview. (I prefer the term "worldview.")

Can we afford to follow an approach that writes off any hope of a true worldview?

THE DEATH OF A MORAL CONSENSUS

As I pointed out in the previous chapter, in the 1930s and 1940s there was a moral consensus at the grass roots level of society. While on the finer points of application there would not have been an agreement between conservative Christianity, modernism, and theological liberalism, they were not at war with one another on the basic morality of the Ten Commandments. This moral consensus made a difference. It did not produce a perfect society, but it did produce a healthier society than we have now. Moral relativism and pluralism are wreaking havoc on the people in our society. They offer no solution to people's problems. They are a part of the problem. They are making it much harder to reach people with the Christian message.

Chuck Colson reminds us:

There has never been a case in history in which a society has been able to survive for long without a strong moral code. And there has never been a time when a moral code has not been informed by religious truth. Recovering our moral code—our religious truth—is the only way our society can survive. The heaping ash of Auschwitz, the killing fields of Southeast Asia, and the frozen wastes of the gulag remind us that the city of man is not enough; we must also seek the city of God.[8]

David Wells is addressing the spread of moral relativism when he says:

Beneath all other major cultures were religious assumptions, whether these came from Hinduism, Islam, or Christianity itself. There are no such religious assumptions beneath our culture, however, and this is the first time any major civilization has attempted to build itself this way.[9]

Wells further observes:

In the nineteenth century in particular, there were numerous attempts to establish a system of morals that did not need to assume the existence of God and His revelation. These experiences were all conducted by a small avant-garde made up of philosophers, novelists, and artists. What has changed is that now the whole society has become avant-garde. It is the whole society that is now engaged in this massive experiment to do what no other major civilization has done—to rebuild itself deliberately and self-consciously without religious foundations. And the bottom line of this endeavor is that truth in any absolute sense is gone. Truth, like life, is fractured. Like experience, it is disjointed. Like our perceptions of ourselves, it is uncertain. It takes on different appearances as we move between the small units of meaning that make up our social experience. Like our manners, it must be adapted to each context and it must remain flexible. It is simply a type of etiquette. It has no authority, no sense of rightness, because it can no longer find any anchorage in anything absolute. If it persuades, it does so because our experience has given it its persuasive power—but tomorrow our experience might be different.[10]

Can we afford to continue this path of devastation?

THE DEATH OF A CONSENSUS ON HIGH IDEALS

My earliest memories take me back to the days of the Great Depression. Even as a pre-school aged child I heard the adults talking enough about it that I knew that the country was experiencing a severe depression. But in spite of the severity of the depression, my parents always made certain the family had what we called in those days a "Sunday outfit." My parents could very easily have said, "We are not able to buy you any Sunday clothes." But they were driven by a determination that we were not going to be denied all experience of beauty and excellence. They were at least going to furnish us a symbolic acquaintance with high ideals. I believe the provision of a Sunday outfit on the part of my parents lifted my sights and helped me choose a higher road in life. Everybody agreed there was a *higher* and a *lower* road a person could travel. There was no confusion about what was *higher* and what was *lower.* Now, there is a resistance to the very idea that there is a distinction between a *higher* and a *lower* road.

There were some people in those days who did not give as much personal emphasis on dress and other ways of demonstrating a concern for ideals as my parents did. But no one extolled sloppiness and lack of concern. There was a consensus in holding up the goal of high ideals. If a person had previously been culturally deprived, it was expected that if he went to college he would experience refinement.

I do not have to tell you that what I have just said does not describe the 1990s. Instead of promoting high ideals, educational institutions bear a lot of the blame for the barbarism that pervades our culture.

Should we continue the way we are going? Is this what you want for yourself, your children, and your grandchildren?

A Summary Look at the Developments
That Brought Us to Where We Are

As I pointed out in the previous chapter, around the time of Isaac Newton (1642-1727), there was a turning point in Western thought. With the triumph of the Copernican view, many thought God was no longer necessary. Empiricism was on the throne in secular thought. With many, all hope that the Bible was a divinely revealed authority had vanished. The only valid approach to knowledge was for the mind to reflect upon the data gained by observation and experience. Theism was abandoned and naturalism was pursued. This challenge was one that empiricism welcomed. It faced the challenge with great optimism.

There were those who accepted the Copernican view, welcomed the discoveries of science, and continued to have confidence in the Bible as a divine revelation. This view has survived and is continued by those Christian groups who wear the name conservatives, fundamentalists, or evangelicals. But our present concern is with those who chose to limit data for rational reflection to observation and experience. This did not necessarily mean that all who accepted the secular view rejected the existence of God. The point to keep in mind is that God was left out of their worldview thinking. Such people may acknowledge a belief in God, but this belief in God does not contribute to their worldview. This is what I call "epistemological atheism."

This devotion to empiricism has been found among those we refer to as modernists. As we observed in the last chapter, modernism was on the throne for about 200 years. The relationship between postmodernism and empiricism is a strange one. In a sense empiricism is the parent of postmodernism. In another sense postmodernism is the rejection of empiricism. Postmodernism would have never existed had it not been for empiricism and modernism. Empiricism demands epistemological atheism. The logical end of epistemological atheism is the denial of Truth. It fathers relativism, pluralism, nihilism, pessimism, and despair. What we call postmodernism was inherent in empiricism from the outset. It took two centuries for this to work itself out and permeate the grass roots of society.

A Challenge to Follow the Example of Copernicus

I would like to challenge those who have been influenced by postmodernism to follow the example of Copernicus. Copernicus found that there had been those in the past who had advocated a heliocentric view of the universe. But those who followed the geocentric (or Ptolemaic) view had prevailed. Copernicus looked back and picked up a discarded view and it changed history. Suppose Copernicus had been unwilling to learn from the past. Suppose he had been unwilling to change his mind.

Look back to the time in the history of Western thought when the mainstream of university thought chose to discard Christian Theism and chose instead naturalism. There was a rejection of divine revelation as a source of data. A choice was made to restrict the data for rational reflection to observation and experience. The failure of modernism should make a person give serious thought to a reconsideration of Christian Theism that was rejected by so much of Western thought. The human heart and mind cries out for more than the hopelessness and despair of postmodernism.

Copernicus checked out a discarded view. I challenge you to check out the view that was rejected by mainstream university thought. Join with us as we examine and expound the Christian worldview. Allow yourself to think it through. Allow your *total personality* to enter into this study.

Can you in all seriousness believe that all that exists is indifferent or maybe even hostile to human need? Are we lost on the sea of life with no compass and no North Star to guide us? Is there no basis for hope for something better?

I think we can safely say that empiricism has taken those who trust it to the only place it could. It has dumped them off at a place where: There is no place for Truth. Reason, so far as *upper story* experiences are concerned, is dead. Nature, as possessing order and capable of rational study, is dead. The hope of a rational worldview is dead. The hope of moral consensus is dead. The hope of any return to an aspiration for high ideals is dead. Is there nothing that we can do other than to develop steel nerves and grit our teeth while we wait for annihilation?

Is the major reason for the failure of modernism and the tragedy of postmodernism rooted in a wrong choice made by some Western thinkers 200 years ago? As I see it there are only two choices: Christianity or despair. I am convinced that Christianity is true. I urge those who are in the grip of the hopelessness of postmodernism to go back to the fork in the road. Look where empiricism has led. Take an honest look at the view that accepts both observation and experience and divine revelation as valid sources of data for rational reflection. If there is a God, the only hope of knowing Him would be for Him to reveal Himself to us.

Michael Bauman puts forth the challenge in very strong words when he said:

> If you believe in the sixties, or if you believe in the nineties, you believe a lie. As I did, you need an undeception. In order to get it, you need to go back well beyond the sixties, back to the wisdom that is older than time. You need to go back to God and to the wisdom that spoke this universe into existence. You need to go back to the God who made you and redeemed you. Real answers are found nowhere else.[11]

Bauman's testimony is:

> I had to learn in this last half of the twentieth century what was already old news even in the days of Jeremiah, the ancient prophet, who wrote, "Stand at the cross-roads, and look, and ask for the ancient paths, where the good way lies; and walk in it, and find rest for your souls" (Jer. 6:16).[12]

God's Self-revelation the Only Answer

It should not be thought strange that empiricism cannot find *upper story* truth. I used to hear the well-known Christian philosopher, Gordon Clark, say, "Empiricism leads to skepticism." When I first heard him say that I did not understand what he was saying. Now I know he was saying that those who restrict rational knowledge to that which is known by experience and observation cannot find God. They cannot find *upper story* truth.

Empirical research and reasoning cannot answer the questions we have about God. God must reveal Himself if He is to be known. I see two basic reasons why our knowledge of God must come through His revealing Himself: (1) God is not perceivable to the five senses, nor to any instruments of precision that we have at our disposal. (2) Since God is personal, He cannot be known unless He reveals Himself.

As human beings, we cannot know what is in the mind of another person unless he or she reveals it to us. At the same time, because we are thinking, feeling, acting beings, one person can reveal to another what is on his mind. Since God is personal, He can speak. That is exactly what we as Christians believe has taken place. We are not lost on the sea of life. God has revealed Himself to us and He has given answers to the *inescapable questions of life.*

The vast majority of the world religions assume that God is impersonal. Only Christianity, Judaism, and Islam claim to have a written divine revelation from a personal God. Consider for a moment, if God be viewed as impersonal: He (It) is an object that cannot be perceived through the senses. If He (It) be impersonal, He (It) cannot speak. Therefore, He (It) cannot be known. In such a case, a person can only speculate about a god which he is not sure is there.

Paul said, "The world by wisdom knew not God" (1 Cor. 1:21). Paul probably has reference to the point that the finest strivings of the human mind (illustrated by the Greek philosophers Socrates, Plato, and Aristotle) have failed to find or know God. The same verdict would be pronounced upon the strivings of philosophers since that time. Pantheism, deism, agnosticism, and atheism all show the futility of man's attempts to locate the Ultimate. The very idea that God must be found implies the idea of an impersonal god.

If God be personal but He has not spoken to the human race, the words of Elijah to the prophets of Baal would be in order, "Cry aloud: for he is a god; either he is talking [to someone other than the human race], or he is pursuing, or he is in a journey, or peradventure he sleepeth, and must be awaked" (1 Kg. 18:27).

However, if God is personal, He can speak. As Christians, it is our conviction that He has spoken. The Christian God is not one to be found by us, but one who has spoken to us. God has revealed Himself to us. Concerning this revelation, Bernard Ramm says: "Revelation is the autobiography of God, i.e., it is the story which God narrates about himself. It is that knowledge about God which is from God."[13]

General Revelation

In studying the subject of divine revelation, a distinction is made between general revelation and special revelation. General revelation refers to the revelation of God in the created order and the basic nature of man. In special revelation, God communicates, in a direct way, knowledge of Himself and His plan to a particular person or group.

Sometimes general revelation is referred to as natural revelation. A distinction is made between natural and supernatural revelation. The term "general" is better than "natural" since natural revelation, when distinguished from supernatural revelation, gives a possible inference that natural revelation is not supernatural. All revelation of God is supernatural. Louis Berkhof observes: "The distinction between natural and supernatural revelation was found to be rather ambiguous, since all revelation is supernatural in origin and, as a revelation of God, also in content."[14]

Since the content of special revelation is so much greater than the content of general revelation, it is easy to overlook the importance of general revelation. It is a mistake to conclude that since we have special revelation we should only give a passing reference to general revelation.

GENERAL REVELATION IN ROMANS 1

The most important chapter in the Bible on general revelation is Romans 1. There have been a variety of viewpoints on the subject of general revelation. Karl Barth took the position that there was no knowledge of God apart from the revelation of God in Jesus Christ. Therefore, the revelation of God in nature could be known only by those who have the revelation of God in the gospel.[15] Among conservative theologians, general revelation is accepted, but with a variety of opinions about its role.

THE MEANING OF *GNOSTOS* IN ROMANS 1:19

In trying to settle the question of the nature of general revelation, we need to examine Romans 1:19. The Greek word *gnostos* in the KJV and the NIV is taken to mean "may be known." In the NASB, it is taken to mean "known." There is no debate over the meaning of *gnostos* in the other places that it is used in the New Testament (Lk. 2:44, 23:49; Jn. 18:15, 16; Acts 1:19; 2:14; 4:10, 16; 9:42; 13:38; 15:18; 19:17; 28:22, 28). In all of these places it refers to "knowing," not "the possibility of knowing."

Those who are knowledgeable in Greek tell us that in classical Greek *gnostos* has the meaning "knowable." Commentators are divided over whether the meaning in Romans 1:19 is "that which may be known" or "that which is known."[16]

The question that needs to be decided is: Is Paul, in Romans 1, telling us that general revelation is of such a nature that it is *possible* for people to have a knowledge of God, or is he telling us that people *actually* have a knowledge of God through general revelation. I believe Paul is telling us that people have a knowledge of God.

The Meaning of the Image of God in Man

The meaning of being made in the image of God will be developed much more in the chapter on "The Nature of Man." At this point let me say that in Christian thought a human being is made in the image of God (Gen. 1:26). This means that human beings are rationally (Col. 3:10) and morally (Eph. 4:24) constituted. Human beings are not blank tablets. We are *designed* beings. I believe this is what Paul is telling us, that knowledge of God and knowledge of basic morality are written into our very being.

We have not been hurled into space to drift aimlessly. We have been preprogrammed by God with a knowledge of God and what He is like. An understanding of basic morality is written in our hearts. It is a violation of our very nature to silence the revelation of God and the moral revelation that is written within. When we sin against God, we sin against ourselves.

As we pursue this study of what Paul is telling us about general revelation, our inner being will bear witness that a knowledge of God and a knowledge of basic morality has been indelibly written into our innermost being. Truth speaks to us. It will help us understand what is happening within. In a sense, we can say that Truth is self-authenticating.

Nothing is more rational than believing in God. However, we are not talking about cold, dispassionate logic. We are looking for answers to questions that we cannot avoid asking. We are looking for meaningful answers for deeply felt needs. We are in desperate need of answers. Solomon addressed the internal nature of human beings when he said, "He [God] set eternity in their heart" (Ec. 3:11, NASB). Concerning these words, Franz Delitzsch explains concerning man, "It lies in his nature not to be contented with the temporal, but to break through the limits which it draws around him, to escape from the bondage and the disquietude within which he is held, and amid the ceaseless changes of time to console himself by directing his thoughts to eternity."[17]

General Revelation and Moral Knowledge

ROMANS 2:14, 15

We are dealing with two concerns: (1) Knowledge of God, and (2) Moral knowledge. It will be easier if we first establish that Paul is telling us that moral knowledge is written in our hearts. This is exactly what he tells us in Romans 2:15. In speaking of those who had never seen the Bible he said:

> For when the Gentiles, who do not have the Law do instinctively [KJV, by nature] the things of the Law, these, not having the Law, are a law to themselves: in that they show the work of the Law written in their hearts (Rom. 2:14, 15, NASB).

Paul is telling us that no one can plead ignorance of God's law because it is written in the heart of every human being. The law that is written in our hearts is the same law that is written in the moral law of the Ten Commandments. Sin, both within us and in the culture around us, has confused many issues, but when we address people with the basic morality of the Ten Commandments, we never inform a moral blank. Regeneration, the enlightenment of the Holy Spirit, and the instruction of Scripture will clarify things and sharpen a person's moral perceptions, but these experiences will never be the beginning of moral knowledge. When people put themselves in conflict with these moral concepts that God has programmed into their innermost being, they do so to their own hurt.

ROMANS 1:32

I started this discussion about moral knowledge with Romans 2:15 because of the undeniable clarity with which it addressed the subject. Now I want to return to Romans chapter one and show from it that Paul is asserting that people *do* have knowledge of God and morals. He is not talking about the *mere possibility* of knowledge of God and morals.

In speaking about those who had never received special revelation, Paul explained: "Who knowing the judgment of God, that they which commit such things are worthy of death" (Rom. 1:32). Paul clearly said that these people *do* know the judgment of God. They *do* know they are worthy of death.

I know the idea that people already have a knowledge of the basic morality revealed in the Ten Commandments raises a lot of questions. Many would challenge this claim. They would call attention to the fact that many people have ideas about morals that are in conflict with the morality of the Ten Commandments.

ROMANS 1:18

In order to deal with this concern, we need to look at Romans 1:18. According to this verse, God's wrath is universally extended against: (1) ungodliness, (2) unrighteousness, and (3) the suppression of the Truth. Our present concern is with the suppression of the Truth. The KJV translates "who hold the truth in unrighteousness." The vast majority of biblical scholarship understands *katecho* in this verse as meaning to suppress "the truth." It is so translated in most translations.[18] The context favors the meaning "suppress the truth."

The concept of suppressing the Truth is essential to understanding what Paul is saying in Romans 1. How could it be claimed that all people, whether they admit it or not, do know that those who violate basic morality know "the judgment of God, that they which commit such things are worthy of death" as stated in Romans 1:32? The answer is that *suppressed knowledge is nevertheless knowledge.* We can have some success with suppressing knowledge from the conscious mind into the subconscious mind. But we cannot drive it out of the mind. No matter how hard a person tries to deny the truthfulness of the moral teachings of the Ten Commandments, he or she can never eradicate the concern for the basic morality of the Ten Commandments that is written in our innermost being. Human beings are not moral blanks.

I am not saying that from general revelation a person has a well developed doctrine of judgment and Hell. I am saying that when a person is addressed by special revelation on these subjects a blank in his or her mind is not being addressed. Rather, a level of moral awareness and concern that is already there is being addressed, clarified, and developed.

General Revelation and Knowledge of God

Just as many people suppress moral knowledge, some suppress the knowledge of God that has been preprogrammed into their minds. As I pointed out above, in Romans 1:19 Paul is not simply telling us that it is possible to know God. He is telling us that God *is known* in general revelation. He is telling us that knowledge of God is innate. When a person makes a claim to be an atheist, he is suppressing the knowledge of God that is in the subconscious mind. He or she is held responsible for the knowledge he is suppressing.

ROMANS 1:20

This knowledge of God, whether suppressed or not, led Paul to say that God's wrath is against ungodliness and unrighteousness (Rom. 1:18). In verse 20 he tells us that based on the knowledge gained in general revelation alone any defense made for people's ungodliness (failure to reverence God) and unrighteousness (failure to live up to God's moral law) is disallowed. Paul's case is built on the principle that general revelation destroys any possibility of a person successfully pleading ignorance for his or her sin as a defense before God.

Romans 1 is not dealing with whether a person can prove the existence of God. Paul is telling us that every human being has a knowledge of God.[19] I will deal with the question of proofs for God's existence in chapter 7, "Testing Worldviews" (page 93).

The Content of General Revelation

In Romans 1:20, concerning the content of general revelation, Paul points out that it is a knowledge of His "eternal power and Godhead." The first point Paul makes is that through general revelation people know God is eternal and that He is powerful. The second point he makes is conveyed in the Greek word *theiotēs*. The KJV translates *theiotēs* as "Godhead." Both the NASB and the NIV translate *theiotēs* as "divine nature." It seems that most would favor the translation "divine nature." Through general revelation, people grasp what God is like. We could say that through general revelation people know that God is eternal, powerful, sovereign, holy, just, caring, and fair. Even people who deny the existence of God have an image of the kind of being they claim does not exist. Human beings do not start off blank when it comes to the existence and nature of God.

David tells us, "The heavens declare the glory of God; And the firmament shows his handiwork" (Ps. 19:1, NKJV). Paul and Barnabas in speaking to the people at Lystra said the following about general revelation, "Nevertheless he left not himself without a witness, in that he did good, and gave us rain from heaven, and fruitful seasons, filling our hearts with food and gladness" (Acts 14:17). According to these verses, through general revelation a person can know about the glory of God and His goodness.

In Acts 17:28, Paul reminded the pagans at Mars Hill that "certain of your own poets have said, For we are also his [God's] offspring." Through general revelation people can know that God created us.

Some of the knowledge of general revelation is innate or "preprogrammed." Other aspects of the knowledge gained by general revelation are based on observation and experience. It is empirically learned. Both the data of innate knowledge and the data of observation and experience are fed to the mind for reflection.

The knowledge gained by general revelation is not redemptive. However, it does help prepare a person for the reception of the message of redemption. One of the big problems with postmodernism is that it not only robs people of special revelation, it also attempts to silence general revelation and cut people off from its message. To the extent that it succeeds, postmodernism is not just a threat to Christianity, but also a threat to civilization. Civilization needs the benefit of general revelation.

Special Revelation

THE NECESSITY OF SPECIAL REVELATION

It is sometimes thought that it was only after the fall of Adam and Eve that special revelation became necessary. Such is not the case. Special revelation is made necessary because God is personal. There was nothing about unfallen man that could enable him to read the mind of God concerning His plan. For example, the only way for Adam and Eve to know they would die if they ate of the fruit of the tree of the knowledge of good and evil was for God to tell them. This is special revelation.

Kenneth Kantzer stated the case well when he said: "Special revelation was no afterthought introduced to circumvent the fall of man, but was a part of the original divine economy. Only as a result of the curse and expulsion from the garden did such immediate converse between men and God become 'special' (Gen. 3:24)."[20]

The message of judgment can be read from general revelation, but the message of redemption cannot. Paul tells us in 1 Corinthians 2:9, "But as it is written, Eye hath not seen, nor ear heard, neither have entered into the heart of man, the things which God hath prepared for them that love him." In current language, Paul is saying that empirical research and reasoning has not discovered redemptive knowledge. It cannot. Regardless of how intelligent the researcher may be and how sophisticated the tools of research may be, he or she cannot discover the gospel of redemption by reflecting on the data of observation and experience. Knowledge of God's plan of redemption must be received by special revelation.

Just as emphatically as Paul denies that we can read redemptive revelation from general revelation, He positively asserts that God has given us a redemptive message. He says, "But God hath revealed them unto us by his Spirit" (1 Cor. 2:10).

THE MESSAGE OF SPECIAL REVELATION

After the fall, God's special revelation, of necessity, included a message of judgment. A holy God must judge sin.

It was necessary that special revelation involve a message of *judgment*. But it was not necessary that this message of special revelation involve a message of *redemption*. Judgment of sin is a necessary act of a holy God. The offer of redemption is *a free act of a loving God.*

Though it was not out of necessity, thanks be to God, special revelation to a fallen race has as its basic theme the message of redemption. It is centered in Jesus Christ. The initiative on God's part in providing redemption is rooted solely in His free and unparalleled love (Rom. 5:7, 8). With the first sin of Adam and Eve, God could have revealed Himself in judgment and closed the books on the human race so far as any positive relationship is concerned. If something within you balks at this statement, keep in mind that God has never spoken to fallen angels with a message of redemption. God's holiness demands that sin be punished, but there is *nothing* in God's nature that demands He offer redemption. It is the *free act of His love.*

THE PROBLEM OF THE COMMUNICATION AND RECEPTION OF GOD'S SPECIAL REVELATION

As we have seen in Romans 1:18-32, fallen man does read from general revelation that, as a result of God's judgment, he is worthy of death (verse 32), but he tries to deny this by suppressing this knowledge.

Man changed from a willing recipient of God's revelation to one who suppresses God's revelation. God's revelation is no longer addressed to one who is holy, but to one who has sinned.

The communication and reception of redemptive revelation is fraught with difficulty. The fact that man is made in the image of God remains true, but the image has suffered damage. Men have resisted the revelation of God's righteousness (Jn. 3:19). They have not welcomed with outstretched arms the Redeemer and His message (Jn. 1:11). The damage caused by the fall created a problem in man's grasp of revelation, but it did not destroy the possibility of a grasp. Carl F. H. Henry explains: "The divine image in man did not, in the fall, suffer to such an extent that man's *ratio* is now unable on the basis of general and special revelation to receive conceptual knowledge of the supernatural spiritual world."[21]

THE RELATIONSHIP BETWEEN GENERAL AND SPECIAL REVELATION

The message of judgment in special revelation does not address itself to a person who is totally void of such knowledge. The moral knowledge of general revelation forms the basis of a point of contact for the message of judgment in special revelation. Special revelation seeks to clarify this knowledge of sin and judgment as a means of opening the way for the reception of the redemptive revelation. Special revelation is needed to overcome the proneness of depravity to distort and suppress that which is clearly revealed in general revelation.

General revelation sets the stage for special revelation. The stage is set for a person to receive a clearer message of sin and judgment. A feeling of need is present, that when clarified by special revelation is understood to be the need of redemption. A longing is present that can be clarified as a longing for redemption. I am reminded of the words of Augustine when he said, "Thou madest us for thyself, and our heart is restless, until it repose in Thee."[22]

It is extremely doubtful that a person who had never had any thoughts about sin or God, right or wrong, confused or unconfused, could expect to take seriously a redemptive message. To the mind that is longing for an understanding that will make sense out of the whole of reality, special revelation in the Bible will speak. Special revelation is a necessary complement to general revelation. To that person who realizes something is missing, it is special revelation and its message of redemption which speaks.

While standing firm upon our insistence that general revelation does not and cannot speak the message of redemption, we must keep in mind the words of G. C. Berkouwer when he says, "We must insist that 'general' revelation does not and cannot mean an attack upon the special revelation in Jesus Christ."[23]

As B. B. Warfield observes: "It is important that the two species or stages of revelation should not be set in opposition to one another, or the closeness of their mutual relations or the constancy of the interaction be obscured. They constitute a unitary whole, and each is incomplete without the other."[24]

The Over-All Form of Revelation

God did not choose to give us His revelation in the form of a systematic theology. Romans gives a logical treatment of doctrine, but it would not be considered a systematic theology. On first thought, it might appear that we would have been better off if God had chosen to give us a systematic presentation of doctrines. This would likely have eliminated most of the controversy between Calvinism and Arminianism. Any number of theological controversies either would have never occurred, or they would have had only small areas of difficulty.

While a systematic theology might have had some advantages in clarifying some ideas, the way in which God has given His revelation does a much better job of addressing life. God's revelation is presented, for the most part, as a record of God's speaking, acting, and dealing with people, basically with Israel and the church, and their experiences with God. We see truth demonstrated in terms of relationships. We see God's faithfulness to His promises. We see judgment fall upon sin. We see the sorrows and agony brought by sin. We see the joy brought by righteous living and submission to God. We see people living in the midst of a real world and hear them say: "We are troubled on every side, yet not distressed; we are perplexed, but not in despair; Persecuted, but not forsaken; cast down, but not destroyed" (2 Cor. 4:8, 9). God's special revelation, as it comes to us, is woven into the fabric of life. It is for life in the real world.

That God did not choose to give His revelation in the form of a systematic treatment of doctrines does not cast reflection upon such an undertaking on our part. Such an attitude would fail to appreciate the type of reasoning demonstrated in the Book of Romans. However, when it comes to addressing life and preparing to live, we gain far more from seeing the Truth as it is demonstrated in God's experiences with people and in people's experiences with God.

The Effects of the Rejection of Divine Revelation

THE EFFECTS OF THE REJECTION OF SPECIAL REVELATION

When we think about the rejection of divine revelation, we are usually thinking about the rejection of special revelation as it has come to us in the Bible. It is obvious that to reject the Bible as a divine revelation is to shut a person off from the gospel of redemption through Jesus Christ. The truth of the gospel depends upon the truth of the divine revelation of God in the Bible. Any form of Christianity (so called) that is not based on the truth-claims of the Bible is not the Christianity set forth in Scripture.

A total rejection of special divine revelation, on the part of the human race, would mean the death of Christianity. My mention of the total rejection of special divine revelation by all human beings is not to suggest that it could happen. I mention it, only in a theoretical sense, to show the essential relationship between the special divine revelation given in Scripture and the preservation and promotion of the gospel of redemption through Jesus Christ. I know it will not happen because Jesus said, "I will build my church; and the gates of hell shall not prevail against it" (Mt. 16:18).[25]

While there is no danger that Christianity will cease to exist, when special divine revelation is not respected by the general population the work of the church becomes much harder. It is harder to reach people for Christ. It is also harder to show the implications of biblical Christianity for the Christian life.

The rejection of special divine revelation involves more than closing the door to the gospel of redemption. In speaking of the plight of those who leave the Bible and Jesus Christ out of the picture, Paul said in Romans 3:11, "There is none who understands" (NKJV). As we noted in the previous chapter, to put what Paul is saying in today's language is to say that without God, the Bible, and Jesus it is impossible to put together a true and adequate worldview.

Modernism failed in its ambition of developing a worldview that would make the hope that it promised a reality. Postmodernism pronounces doom on all attempts to produce a metanarrative (or worldview). So far as attempts to put together a worldview without God, the Bible, and Jesus Christ are concerned, *postmodernists have arrived at the same conclusion as Paul.*

THE EFFECTS OF THE REJECTION OF GENERAL REVELATION

General revelation, as we have seen, helps prepare the way for the gospel that is given by special revelation. Rejection of general revelation will have a devastating negative influence on evangelism. But the negative influence goes beyond its effect on evangelism. It has a devastating influence on our hope of a meaningful sojourn in this life.

Modernism did not recognize general revelation, but its negative influence in this regard was not so devastating as that of postmodernism. Though it denied general revelation, it did not silence the voice of general revelation. This was true because modernism thought that somehow rationality and morality were woven into the fabric of reality. It had no foundation for it, but it did not deny the reality of our moral constitution. Thus the voice of the moral constitution in general revelation was not totally silenced.

Postmodernism rejects the presupposition that nature is rational and moral. Nature, as it has been historically viewed, is dead. There is no "nature" to nature. There is no innate moral knowledge. There is no natural law.

This rejection of the reality that nature is morally constituted is devastating our culture. Paul B. Henry says, "Virtually all societies have established ethical prescriptions against murder and incest on the basis of what might be called a natural law or instinct."[26]

It is only when those made in the image of God *suppress* the knowledge that God has designed within them that they *openly approve* sex outside marriage, homosexuality, abortion, assisted suicide, etc. Even when people acknowledged Christian ideals as what they ought to live by, the power of depravity dragged many down into the depths of sin. But something worse has come upon us.

Human beings are in desperate need of a rational worldview. When the rational nature of reality is denied, that closes any hope of a rational worldview. Postmodernism closes the door of hope for a rational worldview (or metanarrative).

THE CONTRIBUTION TO KNOWLEDGE OF THOSE WHO REJECT DIVINE REVELATION

Since we live in the same world as those who reject the Christian worldview, we are faced with a real problem. Can we learn anything from a person who rejects and may even be hostile to the Christian worldview?

It is hard to understand the exact nature of the effect of the fall on the rational nature of man. No one can deny that human ingenuity has accomplished much when it comes to scientific and technological achievements. Success has not been as great in the area of human behavior and meeting personality needs.

It seems that when the human mind accepts and is committed to the right premises it can do good reasoning. The problem is that sin blinds people and puts them in opposition to that which is most fundamental to sound reasoning. When this blindness and opposition puts a person at odds with the recognition of God and the Bible as a divine revelation, Truth in terms of comprehensive and systematic thinking is not possible. That is why Paul said in Romans 3:11, *"There is none who understands"* (NKJV). Without God, the Bible, and Jesus Christ, it is impossible to put together a true and adequate worldview.

Though a person cannot have an adequate worldview without God, this is not the same as saying that such a person cannot make any worthwhile contribution to the world of knowledge. A great deal of scientific research that we benefit from is done by people who do not give God the proper place in their thinking.

We do not have to work on the assumption that those who leave God out of the picture can never say anything that is true. The image of God is not totally silent and fruitless even in people who reject God. There can even be some worthwhile insight into some upper story experiences.

Such people can develop fragments of knowledge or even segments of knowledge that are worthwhile for mankind and Christians as they live in this world. However, when put in the broader context of life and thought, such knowledge is flawed. The more a person tries to deal with personality and the problems of life, the more *inadequate* and the more *flawed* such a view will be when God, the Bible, and Jesus Christ are left out or ignored.

Concluding Comments

Postmodernists are correct in recognizing that modernism failed to produce a true and adequate worldview. Postmodernists are also correct in their conclusions that it is impossible through reflecting on the data of observation and experience to produce a metanarrative. However, they are not correct in writing off all hope of a metanarrative. Hope returns when we recognize that a personal God exists and that He has revealed Himself in the Bible and Jesus Christ. The Apostle Paul speaks of godliness as "having promise [hope] of the life that now is, and of that which is to come" (1 Tim. 4:8).

Our next step in expounding the Christian worldview will be a study of the inspiration and authority of the Bible.

4

Inspiration and Authority

A study of revelation is not complete unless it involves a study of the inspiration and authority of the Bible. Special revelation has come to us in the Bible. We are intensely interested in this Book. We want to know what it claims for itself. We want to know if it answers for us the *inescapable questions of life*. We want to know if we can depend upon it. If we believe that we already know the answers to these questions, we want a rational comprehension of our faith. We want to add assurance to assurance. We are rational beings. We cannot escape this fact. At the same time, we cannot separate our reason from the rest of our personality. We want something that speaks to our total personality and helps us face the total responsibilities of life in the midst of the complexities of life.

With great interest, we study this book which makes the claim of divine revelation. Modernism has failed to deliver on its promises. Postmodernism offers no hope. Our whole being cries out for hope. But we cannot afford to commit ourselves to a false hope. In a later chapter, we will take a serious look at why we believe the Bible to be a divine revelation. In this chapter, we will examine the claims that the Bible makes for itself.

The Origin of Scripture

THE DIVINE AUTHORSHIP

Second Timothy 3:16 speaks of the divine origin of Scripture. The Greek word which is translated in the KJV as "given by inspiration of God" is *theopneustos*. This word means God-breathed. It is so translated in the NIV. The Scriptures are a product of the breath of God. They are of divine origin. In commenting on this passage, Warfield observes:

> No term could have been chosen . . . which would have more emphatically asserted the Divine production of Scripture than that which is here employed. The 'breath of God' is in Scripture just the symbol of His almighty power, the bearer of His creative word. 'By the word of Jehovah,' we read in the significant parallel Ps. xxxiii.6, 'were the heavens made; and all the host of them by the breath of his mouth.' And it is particularly where the operations of God are energetic that this term . . . is employed to designate them—God's breath is the irresistible outflow of His power. When Paul declares, then, that 'every scripture,' 'is God-breathed,' he asserts with as much energy as he could employ that Scripture is the product of a Divine operation.[1]

The word *theopneustos* occurs nowhere else in Scripture. However, it is clear that Paul used this strong term to ascribe to Scripture what it had already ascribed to itself. Expressions such as, "Thus saith the LORD," "The LORD saith," and "The word of the LORD came to . . ." or the equivalent are found more than 3,800 times in the Old Testament. Jesus referred to the Old Testament as being invested with that type of authority that no one but God could give (Mt. 4:4, 7, 10; 5:17, 18; Lk. 24:44, 45; Jn. 5:39; 10:34, 35; and many others). Second Peter 1:21 gives evidence that the message of the prophets was God's Word.

It is clear that when Paul said in 2 Timothy 3:16, "All scripture is God-breathed," he meant to include the whole Old Testament. The problem is: Did he also embrace the New Testament? I believe he did.

In 2 Peter 3:2, Peter puts the writings of the apostles on the level with that of the prophets when he admonishes his readers: "That ye may be mindful of the words which were spoken before by the holy prophets, and of the commandment of us the apostles of the Lord and Savior." In 2 Peter 3:16 after referring to Paul's epistles, Peter refers to "other scriptures." To speak of "other" Scriptures means that Peter was considering Paul's writings as Scripture.

Paul, apparently, referred to Luke's writings as Scripture when he said in 1 Timothy 5:18, "For the scripture saith, Thou shalt not muzzle the ox that treadeth out the corn. And, the labourer is worthy of his reward." The first part of the verse is taken from Deuteronomy 25:4. The last part is taken from Luke 10:7. If Paul intends for "the scripture saith" to refer to the entire verse, he is considering Luke's Gospel to be Scripture.

Paul considered his own writings to be of divine origin when he said: "If any man think himself to be a prophet, or spiritual, let him acknowledge that the things that I write unto you are the commandments of the Lord" (1 Cor. 14:37).

The evidence given above supports the inclusion of the part of the New Testament that had been written up to the time of Paul's reference to "all scripture" in 2 Timothy 3:16. What about that part of the Bible that was written after 2 Timothy 3:16? I believe a case can be built for including that too as part of inspired Scripture.

If we ask a contractor what kind of brick he is using in a building, and he names a particular kind of brick we expect that he is not only telling us the kind he has been using, but also the kind he plans to use in the remainder of the building. When Paul said, "All scripture is God-breathed," he was telling us a characteristic of all writings that were appropriately called Scripture as he was using the term. The term would be equally applied to any later writing if it could be appropriately called Scripture. As Warfield explains:

> What must be understood in estimating the testimony of the New Testament writers to the inspiration of Scripture is that 'Scripture' stood in their minds as the title of a unitary body of books, throughout the gift of God through His Spirit to His people, but that this body of writings was at the same time understood to be a growing aggregate, so that what is said of it applies to the new books which were being added to it as the Spirit gave them, as fully as to the old books which had come down to them from their hoary past. . . . Whatever can lay claim by just right to the appellations of "Scripture," as employed in its eminent sense by those writers, can by the same just right lay claim to the 'inspiration' which they ascribe to this "Scripture."[2]

THE HUMAN AUTHORSHIP

Several factors indicate a human authorship of the Bible. The most obvious is that in many books the writer identifies himself (Is. 1:1; Jer. 1:1; Am. 1:1; Rom. 1:1; 1 Cor. 1:1; 2 Cor. 1:1; Gal. 1:1-3; and others). Also, others refer to the writings of a particular author as being his writings (Rom. 9:27, 29; 2 Pet. 3:15, 16; and others).

That the Bible was written by human beings is too obvious to be debated. The question is: Were they amanuenses (secretaries) or were they in a real sense authors? Did the writers merely receive dictation or did their personalities as thinking, feeling, acting beings enter into their writings?

The evidence that the writers were more than secretaries is abundant.. If Romans had been dictated by God, it is not likely that God would have dictated it to Paul, and Paul in turn would have dictated it to Tertius (Rom. 16:22). One would have expected it to have been given directly to Tertius.

Throughout the Bible one can detect the traces of the personalities of the writers. Their own style and vocabularies show in their writings. The personality of the writer does not manifest itself as strongly in some writings as in others. Books such as Kings and Chronicles, which depended to a great extent upon written records, would not reflect as much of the human author as the Book of Romans where Paul's thinking entered strongly into the book. However, the same is true in these types of writings even when divine authorship is not involved. The total personality of the author is naturally less involved in some types of writings than others.

I am not claiming that there is not any dictation presented in Scripture at any time. The Ten Commandments would have been copied into the Book of Exodus from stones upon which God had written (Ex. 32:15-19; 34:1-4). In principle, this would be the same as dictation. At times, the prophets seemed to have been bearers of messages that would not have differed drastically from dictation (Jer. 34:1-7). Whatever else may be said concerning the possible use of dictation, it was not the usual method used by God in the employment of human authors to give us the Bible.

THE NATURE OF THE DIVINE INFLUENCE UPON THE HUMAN AUTHORS

The nature of the divine influence upon the human authors is not fully explained to us. That there was such a relationship and that it guaranteed that what they said was the Word of God is made clear by Peter when he said: "For the prophecy came not in old time by the will of man: but holy men of God spake as they were moved by the Holy Ghost" (2 Pet. 1:21). The word which is translated "moved" is the Greek word *pherō*. It means to bear, carry, or bring. Concerning this word, Warfield explains:

> The term here used is a very specific one. It is not to be confounded with guiding, or directing, or controlling, or even leading in the full sense of that word. It goes beyond all such terms, in assigning the effect produced specifically to the active agent. What is 'borne' is taken up by the 'bearer,' and conveyed by the bearer's goal, not its own. The men who spoke from God are here declared, therefore, to have been taken up by the Holy Spirit and brought by His power to the goal of His choosing.[3]

There have been several attempts to explain the nature of the divine influence which is referred to by the term *inspiration*. Some have used the term *illumination* to describe this influence. It is said that the natural perceptions of the writer were elevated and intensified by the Holy Spirit. Illumination is experienced by all believers. The difference between Bible writers and other believers would be only a matter of degree.

To describe inspiration as illumination fails to do justice to 2 Timothy 3:16 and 2 Peter 1:21. Illumination is not an adequate explanation of how the Bible writers were borne along by the Holy Spirit to produce a product that can rightly be ascribed to God. It is obvious that illumination would not produce a product that could rightly be called *God-breathed.*

Another word that has been used to describe this divine influence is the word *dynamic*. Usually this view is explained more in terms of the type product produced than in the nature of the influence, though the word itself speaks of the influence. It is used to refer to a much stronger influence than illumination. There is a particular interest that the writers be authors, not just penmen. The result produced is an infallible guide in matters of faith and practice, but not inerrant in matters not pertaining to faith and practice. As a rule, those who hold this view would speak of "concept inspiration" rather than "verbal inspiration." A discussion of the weaknesses of this view will be given later when we look at the extent of the divine influence in inspiration and the authority of Scripture. At this time let us pass by raising the question: Does this view do justice to 2 Timothy 3:16 and 2 Peter 1:21?

Plenary verbal is the name given to the view, according to which, the Holy Spirit used the writers to produce an infallible and inerrant Bible. However, these words do not describe the nature of the divine influence. Rather, they speak of the nature of the product. There is *no* commonly used and accepted term that describes this influence.

In the quotation from Warfield above, he pointed out that the divine influence, as spoken of in 2 Peter 1:21, "is not to be confounded with guiding, or directing, or controlling, or even leading in the full sense of that word." We have no word which will adequately describe it. This probably accounts for the reason more attention has been given to the extent of inspiration and biblical authority than the nature of the divine influence.

The difficulty of describing the divine influence on the human authors of the Bible arises because we are dealing with *a relationship between persons*. The Holy Spirit is a *person*. The writers were *persons*. Mechanical relationships are more easily described and measured. Language tends to give us the choice between viewing a relationship as either active or passive. Where personal relationships and personal responses are involved, they do not submit to the simple analysis of active or passive.

We are not to think of the human authors as being passive only. In 2 Peter 1:21, we see both the active and the passive voice used with respect to the authors. They "spoke" (active) as they were "borne" (passive) by the Holy Spirit. The Holy Spirit acted upon one who was actively involved.

Though we cannot fully describe the relationship between the human authors and the divine author, we can make certain definite conclusions:

1. The divine authorship is of such a nature that the Scriptures are God-breathed. They are of divine origin.
2. The relationship of the divine authorship to the human author guaranteed that what the authors wrote was the Word of God.
3. The human authors were authors in the true sense of the word. Their personalities were actively involved in preparations to write and in their writing.

The Extent of the Divine Influence in Scripture

Our approach throughout this chapter is to find out: (1) What the Bible specifically says about itself. (2) What can be inferred and what can be logically deduced about the Bible from its own statements. It is of vital interest what a book that claims to be a divine revelation says about itself. We would expect a book that is a divine revelation to make such a claim. We are concerned about anything it says about its basic nature. We do not accept every book that proposes to be a divine revelation. But to reject all of them leaves us on the sea of life without a compass and without a North Star. We cannot chart the ocean of reality. To find a book that we truly believe to be a divine revelation gives us answers to the *inescapable questions of life*. We come to know who we are, where we are, and where we are going. It takes away our lostness. It gives us purpose and meaning in life. We cry out for this from the depth of our being. We dare not separate our rational mind from the rest of our personality and let it cause us to reject the revelation God gives. I reserve for a later chapter a discussion of why we believe the Bible. It will be treated along with why we believe in God. At present, let us return to our examination of what the Bible says about itself.

Regarding the extent of the divine influence, we have two areas of concern: (1) Does it extend to *all portions* of Scripture? (2) Does it extend to the *words* of Scripture?

PLENARY IN SCOPE

It has been pointed out above that both Old and New Testaments are God-breathed (2 Tim. 3:16). There is a difference of opinion concerning whether the Greek should be rendered "all" or "every." All would refer to the entire body of Scripture as a whole. Every would embrace the whole, but would give stress to the parts that make up the whole. Concerning the significance of which is used, all or every, Warfield observes:

> In both cases these Sacred Scriptures are declared to owe their value to their Divine origin; and in both cases their Divine origin is energetically asserted of the entire fabric.[4]

The term *plenary* is used to embrace the idea that the Bible is inspired *both in the whole and in every part*. Warfield describes plenary inspiration as:

the doctrine that the Bible is not in part but fully, in all its elements alike,—things discoverable by reason as well as mysteries, matters of history and science as well as of faith and practice, words as well as thoughts.[5]

VERBAL AS TO DETAIL

The word "verbal" is frequently added to plenary to make it clear that the inspiration extended to the words used. The claim of verbal inspiration is clearly made in 1 Corinthians 2:13. Paul denied that redemptive truth can be discovered by human investigation in 2:9. In 2:10, he affirms that God has revealed redemptive truth by the Holy Spirit. In 2:13 concerning the truth received by revelation, he says, "Which things also we speak, not in the words which man's wisdom teacheth, but which the Holy Ghost teacheth."

The very fact that the Scriptures are spoken of as God-breathed (2 Tim. 3:16) means that the inspiration extended to the words used. It is the *product* that is said to be God-breathed. If the product itself is appropriately spoken of as God-breathed, it was necessary for God to bear a relationship to every part for it to be so described. Also, for the writers to be so borne along by the Holy Spirit that they spoke the message of God (2 Pet. 1:21) we must necessarily infer that the inspiration extended to the words.

The words of Jesus, "For verily I say unto you, Till heaven and earth pass, one jot or one tittle shall in no wise pass from the law, till all be fulfilled" (Mt. 5:18), cannot be understood apart from verbal inspiration. The same can be said for Jesus' statement in John 10:35: "The scripture cannot be broken."

THE RELATIONSHIP BETWEEN CONCEPTS AND WORDS

Some have spoken of *thought* or *concept inspiration* rather than *verbal inspiration.* It is held that God gave the writers the thoughts and they expressed these thoughts in their own words. In reality, this view is a view of revelation without inspiration. Revelation has to do with the giving of truth on the part of God. Inspiration is the divine work of God in which the writers were borne along in the process of communicating that truth which they received by revelation.

If we truly speak of *thought inspiration,* it *cannot* be separated from *verbal inspiration.* To speak of Thought Inspiration is to mean that God so moved upon the Bible writers that they communicated God's thoughts. The Bible has come to us in the words of human language. If God inspired the writers to write in such a way that it guaranteed the communication of God's thoughts, it would of necessity mean that inspiration guaranteed the use of words that would convey these thoughts. If this is not the case, there is no inspiration, or it did not extend to the thoughts.

We cannot divorce the process of inspiration from words. Though we cannot divorce inspiration from words, it is not necessary to conclude that in no instance could any other word have been used by the writer. What we must insist upon is that in every case appropriate words were chosen that would convey God's thoughts. In cases where only one word would convey God's thought, we can rest assured that that particular word was used. This allows room for the particular writer to enter into his writing, but at the same time guarantees the communication of God's message. A comparison of different speeches by Jesus in the gospels seems to support this conclusion. We have the same message, but some variation in words.

While it was of utmost importance that *appropriate* words be used, we must keep in mind that the ultimate focus of God centered on the message. *Appropriate* words are important because they serve as a necessary means in the communication of God's message to us. Words are the *means.* The *message (concepts* or *thoughts)* is the *end.* Another way of saying this is: The *message* is the *substance.* The *words* are the *form* used to convey this substance.[6]

It is often said that *thoughts* cannot exist without *words.* I think this statement is in error. Thoughts exist independent of words. Let me illustrate.

A person can take a course that is taught in French. The knowledge that is learned is stored as *thoughts* or *concepts. Thoughts* and *concepts* are *substance.* The words used in languages are *form.*

In communicating those *thoughts* or *concepts* that he or she learned in a course where the *form* used was French words, he can communicate what he has learned in the *form* of English words or the words of any other language that he or she may be fluent in without going through a word for word translation. If this be true, *thoughts* must be independent of *words.*

Another illustration is our frequent use of "in other words." On occasions like that we are expressing the same thoughts in different words. In order for this to happen, thoughts must be independent of words.

While thoughts and words are independent of one another, there is an essential relationship between thoughts and words in learning and communication. Words give birth to thoughts. Therefore, words are essential in the learning process and the communication process. The communication that we can have from one person to another without words is very limited. But there is a freedom that we can have in the choice of words in communicating ideas from one person to another.

These observations should shed light on the statement, "Words are the *means.* The message (concepts or thoughts) is the *end."* This is a very important observation for the following reasons:

1. The Bible can be translated into other languages. If words, in which no other word could have been acceptable in any case, had been the main aim of God in giving us the Bible, the translation of the Bible would have been ruled out. Priority is given to the texts in the original language because in these we have the Word of God (substance) in words (form) inspired of God. However, in so far as the message is properly translated from the Hebrew and Greek texts we have God's Word in our own language. We have the message (substance) of God, but not in the words (form) in which it was originally given.

2. We need not be hesitant in calling a good translation the inspired Word of God. We do not claim verbal inspiration for translations because translators are not inspired in their work. This statement is true regardless of how accurate the translation may be. We do have God's message, and it is an inspired message.

3. We do not just read or memorize the Bible. Since the message is the end and words are the means, it follows that the Bible can and must be interpreted. Scripture memorization is

good, but we must go beyond quoting the Bible. We must interpret its message and apply it to life.

4. It helps us as we face the subject of textual criticism. The labor of textual critics is important in assuring us, as much as possible, that we have the same words that were used in the original texts. However, when we realize that concepts are the main concern of God in giving us the Bible, we will see that in the unsettled points there is no real reason for alarm. Very seldom is the concept significantly altered in the variant readings no matter which is chosen. No biblical doctrine is at stake because of variant readings.

THE QUESTION OF PLENARY VERBAL INSPIRATION AND DICTATION

Those who criticize plenary verbal inspiration have constantly accused its advocates of believing that the Bible was given from God by dictation. Plenary verbal speaks of the product, not of how it was produced. It would be possible for a person to believe in a plenary verbally inspired Bible and believe that it did come by dictation. However, works in which this is done are extremely few. It is very unlikely that most of those who accuse the advocates of verbal inspiration of believing in dictation could name even one who is a dictationist and could then support the charge.

No false charge is more inexcusable than the blanket accusation that claims all advocates of the plenary verbal view believe in dictation. I attended a Bible college for four years. I have spent more than four years in seminary. I attended several summers at a seminary which for many years gathered some of the leading conservative scholars from America and from other countries. I have heard many people preach, both educated and uneducated. In all of my experience I have never heard one person advocate the dictation theory. The only case in print, in recent years, to advocate the dictation theory was John R. Rice in his book, *Our God-breathed Book—The Bible* (Murfreesboro, Tennessee: Sword of the Lord, 1969). To the best of my knowledge this book did not attract many to subscribe to the dictation view.

R. Laird Harris comments:

> No creed of any consequence in the Christian Church has taught the dictation theory, though, as we shall see, the creeds are full of assertions that there are no contradictions in Scripture, that all of it is to be believed, that God is the author of the whole, etc. And there are few if any theological authors of importance who have held to the dictation theory, even though the usual view through the history of the Christian Church has been that the Scriptures are true to the smallest detail.[7]

H. D. McDonald, in his book, *Theories of Revelation, An Historical Study 1860-1960* says, "Prior to the year 1860, the idea of an infallibly inerrant Scripture was the prevalent view."[8] Concerning the period that began with 1860, McDonald explains:

> The whole period following the general repudiation of inerrancy and the introduction of higher criticism has been marked by an attack on the 'mechanical' theory of inspi-

ration. It is just, however, to point out that this was a view of inspiration credited to the traditionalists generally rather than actually taught by them.[9]

Later in the same chapter, McDonald explains that there were three important volumes in the period 1860-1960 that might so state the traditionalists' point of view in such a way that some might understand them to be advocating the mechanical view. These are: (1) C. Wordsworth, *The Inspiration of the Bible,* 1861, page 5; (2) L. Gaussen, *Theopneustia: The Plenary Inspiration of the Holy Scriptures* (translated by David Scott in 1863), page 24 (cf. p. 281); and (3) J. W. Burgon, *Inspiration and Interpretation,* reprinted in 1905, page 86. (The latter refers to a sermon preached by J. W. Burgon at Oxford in 1860.) McDonald explains that upon examination these men are not properly understood as supporting a mechanical view to the exclusion of human authorship.[10]

It should be quite obvious that there is absolutely no justification for the general charge that accuses the advocates of verbal inspiration of believing in the dictation view of inspiration. Such charges either represent poor scholarship on the part of people because they have not examined the writings of those who believe in verbal inspiration, or they represent dishonesty on the part of those making the claim. If they want to say that verbal inspiration logically requires dictation, they would have a right to make the statement though it would be an error in judgment. However, to make a *blanket statement* that those who believe in verbal inspiration believe in dictation is nothing short of academic irresponsibility or dishonesty.

The Interpretation of Scripture

Before dealing with the subject of biblical authority, I would like to give brief attention to biblical interpretation. This will help provide a proper context in which to discuss biblical authority.

Any serious discussion of the authority of Scripture, whether for or against, must assume that Truth exists. It must either assume that Truth exists and that the Bible is an authority on Truth, or it must assume that there is an authority of Truth that is above the Bible. If there is no Truth, the whole subject of biblical authority is meaningless.

Modernism believed that Truth existed, but reason was the final arbiter of Truth. In modernism, reason rejected biblical authority. The Bible as a book had no authority. Reason treated the Bible just like it did any other book. It sat in judgment to decide what was true and what was not true in the Bible. In postmodernism Truth does not exist. The whole subject of the authority of Scripture, or the question of the inerrancy of the Bible is meaningless.

In the Christian worldview, things are different. Truth exists. The question of whether something is true or false is meaningful. This brings up the subject of interpretation.

Much has been said in recent years that would raise serious doubts about any hope of communication from one person to another. The focus in postmodernism has changed from the intent of the author to the interpretation given by the reader. Authorial intent is irrelevant. The meaning given by the reader is culturally conditioned. Language is considered to be inadequate to convey the meaning of the author to the reader. Objective Truth and meaning are dismissed. Subjective meaning differs from one person to another and from one culture to another. What is important is for each person to decide what is "true for me." If it works for you it is "true for you." If it does not work for you, it is not true for you.

In a culture that is conditioned by the Postmodern Mood, word meanings, parts of speech, and syntax have lost their importance. A feeling of gloom has settled over the whole enterprise of trying to understand what another person means.

Christian thought is not willing to join in with this spirit of gloom. Christians believe in a personal God who has created man in His own image (Gen. 1:26). God is rational and the author of rationality. God has created man so that he can understand the divine revelation given in the Bible. It is not simply a matter of the adequacy of language to convey meaning. It is a matter of what human beings created in the rational image of God can do with language. The Bible leaves no doubt that language is capable of conveying meaning to human beings. Peter told his readers:

> Grace and peace be multiplied to you in the knowledge of God and of Jesus our Lord; seeing that His divine power has granted to us everything pertaining to life and godliness, *through the true knowledge of Him* who called us by His own glory and excellence (2 Pet. 1:2, 3, NASB). [Italics mine]

It is possible to understand the Bible. For those who believe that it is possible for meaning to be conveyed from one person to another through the use of human language, it is encouraging to know that the One who is King of Kings, Lord of Lords, and the Creator of the universe and human beings has spoken to us a message of hope.

The Bible has come to us in human language. It uses language in the same sense that it was used in ordinary speech and writing. That means that the Bible is to be interpreted by the normal laws of language. In the Bible, a noun is a noun. An adjective is an adjective. A verb is a verb. An adverb is an adverb, etc.

The approach to biblical hermeneutics that studies the Bible in the light of the ordinary laws of language is called grammatico-historical interpretation. Terry explains, "The grammatico-historical sense of a writer is such an interpretation of his language as is required by the laws of grammar and the facts of history."[11]

This type of interpretation is referred to most frequently as literal interpretation. Terry says, "Sometimes we speak of the literal sense, by which we mean the most simple, direct, and ordinary meaning of phrases and sentences."[12]

While I accept what is referred to as literal interpretation, I go along with E. R. Cravens in preferring to use the word normal instead of literal. He comments:

> Normal is used instead of literal (the term generally employed in this connection) as more expressive of the correct idea. No terms could have been chosen more unfit to designate the two great schools of prophetical exegetes than literal and spiritual. These

terms are not antithetical, nor are they in any proper sense significant of the peculiarities of the respective systems they are employed to characterize. They are positively misleading and confusing. Literal is opposed not to spiritual but figurative: spiritual is in antithesis on the one hand to material, on the other to carnal (in a bad sense). The Literalist (so called) is not one who denied that figurative language, that symbols, are used in prophecy, nor does he deny that great spiritual truths are set forth therein: his position is, simply, that the prophecies are to be normally interpreted (i.e., according to the received laws of language) as any other utterances are interpreted—that which is manifestly literal is regarded as literal, that which is manifestly figurative is so regarded.[13]

The diagram below will show the problem that arises from speaking of literal interpretation.

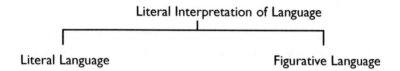

Though such a conclusion is not intended, it looks as if figurative language is to be interpreted literally. Literal interpretation seems to be far more appropriate for literal language than for figurative language.

The diagram below will show the advisability of speaking of normal interpretation.

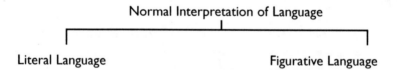

In normal interpretation, we treat literal language as literal and figurative as figurative. We do this in life, and we should do this in our Bible study.

Normal interpretation or as it is more commonly called, literal interpretation, is the same approach as the grammatico-historical method of interpretation. *Normal* stresses that the same basic principles involved in biblical interpretation are involved in other uses of language. Grammatico-historical interpretation is descriptive of what normal interpretation is. It interprets in keeping with the laws of grammar and the historical context.

In studying the Bible, we must keep in mind that the Bible is addressed to the *total personality,* not just to the mind. The Bible must be studied in the arena of life. You bring the Bible to life and you bring life to the Bible. You bring the Bible to your pains and you bring your pains to the

Bible. When the Bible is properly understood, it makes us free (Jn. 8:32). It gives meaning and purpose to life. We have something to live for, and we have something to die for.

The Authority of Scripture

The big question to be decided is: Is the Bible authoritative on all matters about which it speaks, or is the Bible limited in its authority? Very strong support exists today for the viewpoint that the Bible is inerrant on all matters about which it speaks. Others have taken the position that the Bible is authoritative on all matters of faith and practice, but not on matters such as history, geography, and science. Still others, who claim to be evangelical, are willing to admit that there are errors in the Bible in the area of faith and practice. They prefer to speak of the Bible as having sufficient authority in matters of faith and practice.

Does the Bible teach its own inerrancy? Some, who may not deny inerrancy, say it does not. Everett F. Harrison says:

> Unquestionably the Bible teaches its own inspiration. It is a Book of God. It does not require us to hold to inerrancy, though this is a natural corollary of full inspiration. The phenomena which present difficulties are not to be dismissed or underrated. They have driven many sincere believers in the trustworthiness of the Bible as a spiritual guide to hold a modified position on the non-revelation material. Every man must be persuaded in his own mind.[14]

Many disagree with Harrison. They believe the Bible does teach its inerrancy. I take my stand with those who believe the Bible does require us to believe in its inerrancy.

Roger Nicole says:

> From beginning to end, the New Testament authors ascribe unqualified authority to Old Testament Scripture. Whenever advanced, a quotation is viewed as normative. Nowhere do we find a tendency to question, argue, or repudiate the truth of any Scripture utterance.[15]

As we read the Bible we are met with a compelling impression that its contents are without error. The Bible gives not the slightest hint that error is affirmed anywhere in its pages. Jesus and the writers of the New Testament used the Old Testament in such a way we feel compelled to believe that they understood it to be without error.

We do not draw our conclusions from a general impression alone. Jesus' statement: "Till heaven and earth pass, one jot or one tittle shall in no wise pass from the law, till all be fulfilled" (Mt. 5:18) requires us to believe that He thought the Old Testament was true in its smallest detail.

Jesus' statement, "The Scripture cannot be broken" (Jn. 10:35) is synonymous with the statement, "The Scripture cannot be in error."

In the light of Matthew 5:17, 18 and John 10:35, it seems strange that anyone should say that the Bible does not require us to believe in its inerrancy. No one can deny that it claims to be true. Jesus said in John 17:17, "Thy word is truth." That is a positive statement. The negative that is necessarily implied from it is, "Thy word is without error."

The Bible teaches two inescapable conclusions which require us to believe in a third. The first is that God cannot lie (Num. 23:19, Tit. 1:2, along with all the biblical teaching on God's holiness and righteousness). The second is that the Bible is God's Word (2 Tim. 3:16, as well as the numerous references where the Bible writers claim to be speaking the message of God). These can be stated as follows:

Major Premise: God cannot lie.
Minor Premise: The Bible is God's Word.
Therefore, The Bible cannot lie.

To say that the Bible cannot lie is to say that it cannot be in error.

The Origin of the Concern Over Biblical Inerrancy[16]

Though I believe the Bible teaches its own inerrancy, I do not believe the origin of people's concern over biblical inerrancy begins with the teaching of the Bible. Most people who believe in biblical inerrancy could not, on the spot, show that the Bible teaches its own inerrancy.

The root of concern for biblical inerrancy comes out of the *design* of our being. I adhere to the *total personality* approach to learning and the *total personality* approach to apologetics. The personality is concerned with thinking (the activity of the mind), feeling (the activity of the heart, which refers to the seat of our emotions), and acting (the activity of the will). While we can distinguish the activity of the mind, heart, and will, we cannot separate the activity. The activity of each is deeply involved in the other. The mind, heart, and will are a functional unity. It is also important to keep in mind that the personality exists on both the conscious and subconscious levels. On the subconscious level each person has programmed a vast storehouse of ideas and attitudes. There is a rational process which draws from the data stored in the subconscious mind. What a person believes is based on more than what he consciously elaborates as his reasons. The *inescapable questions of life* are written deep within the subconscious mind of every person. A person may give the wrong answers to these questions, but he cannot keep from having them arise at times from his subconscious mind into his conscious mind.

Along with these questions that are implanted in our subconscious mind are certain a priori conclusions (*a priori* means before there is an investigation of the facts of the case). One of these conclusions is: If there is a God, He is a perfect being. He is holy, just, and fair. Our whole being abhors the idea of a god who is less than perfect, holy, just, and fair. It is this a priori view of what God is like if He exists that causes some people to doubt or even reject the existence of God. They do not know how to harmonize what is happening to them or what they see around them with the holiness, justice, and fairness of God. As a result, their belief in God runs into trouble. Sometimes instead of doubting God's existence, the person may blame God for being unfair. Even this grows out of an a priori belief that God is sovereign.

The very idea of God apart from a belief in His existence already has built into it the belief that if God exists He is perfect, holy, just, fair, and sovereign. Here is where my total personality approach to learning and apologetics comes in. The only way that a person can possibly imagine, except as a temporary emotional response to disappointment, that God is less than perfect, holy, just, and fair is to divorce the mind from the rest of his personality. Such a person may claim to believe that God could be less than perfect, holy, just, fair, and sovereign, but I doubt he takes the view seriously. At least no one has ever developed such a view and developed a following of any consequence.

I have said what I have up to this point to build a case for another a priori belief. That a priori belief is that if there is a book that can rightly be called God's Word, it is without error, or stated positively, whatever this book affirms, is true. I believe it to be a self-evident truth that any book that would be the Word of God would surely be inerrant. I know that there are those who say that they do not believe in biblical inerrancy, but I am reasonably certain that such people have at least been faced with the question of inerrancy from their own inner being. For a person to entertain the idea of a less than inerrant Word of God, in my opinion, does violence to his personality as a functional unity. I think it would be interesting to know how many people who reject inerrancy did accept it at one time. You do not have to teach people to believe in the inerrancy of whatever they call the Word of God. If they reject it, they have to be led away from it. Our *whole being* is repulsed by the idea of a book that is the Word of God being *less than inerrant*.

We do not go to a book that we consider to be the Word of God with no opinion about its inerrancy; we go to it expecting it to be inerrant. This does not mean we blindly believe that a book that claims to be the Word of God is without error. It does mean that serious problems are created for us in believing it to be the Word of God if we are convinced that it has errors. I am well aware of those who say they believe the Bible is the Word of God *and* that it contains errors, but I doubt that they would have believed at the outset if they had been convinced of error in the Bible.

Some might argue that this approach places too much emphasis on subjective experience in giving significance to an a priori belief that any book that can rightfully be called the Word of God is without error. They may say that it would open the floodgate for all kinds of beliefs based on a person's subjective experience. It is very important that we distinguish between those ideas that we are inescapably forced to face because of our inner nature, and those ideas that do not fit into this category.

A good illustration of what I am referring to is a proposed answer to Anselm's ontological argument for the existence of God. Anselm used the idea that God is a perfect being in order to argue for the existence of God since the idea of perfection would include existence. Gounilo responded, I have the idea of a perfect island, but that does not mean that such an island exists. While I am not sure of the exact significance that we should give to Anselm's ontological argument, the objection referred to above does not overthrow the argument. We have an a priori idea that if God exists, He must be perfect. We cannot escape being confronted with such an idea whether we believe in God or not. However, we do not have an a priori idea of a perfect island. We can escape being confronted with such an idea. Most people have never thought of a perfect island.

The ideas that I am suggesting that we must pay respect to are those ideas that we cannot escape confronting. *If* the *inescapable questions* referred to earlier have no positive answers, and if the a priori beliefs that I have referred to are to be cast aside, we live in an *irrational universe* and man is *hopeless*. *If* these *inescapable questions* do have answers in Christianity, and *if* these a priori beliefs are confirmed in Christianity we have a *rational universe*. There is a rational consistency between God and man. God has designed these questions and these ideas into our being as a means of helping us come to a knowledge of Truth. These ideas are innate in man. Just as growth and development and interaction with other people will activate a person toward talking and developing rational thought, so growth, and development, and interaction with other people activate these *inescapable questions* and ideas.

I am not saying that our belief in the inerrancy of that which we believe to be the Word of God is accepted solely on this a priori belief. We rationally consider the idea, but a part of the data in our rational consideration is this a priori belief.

I want to make it clear that I am not saying that we have an a priori conviction that the Bible is the Word of God. I am saying that *if we believe it to be the Word of God, we have an a priori belief that it is inerrant.* Why we believe the Bible to be the Word of God will be dealt with in Chapter 7.

Problems Raised for Those Who Believe in Inerrancy

With regard to the phenomena or facts of Scripture, everyone who has examined them, at least admits that it is difficult to harmonize all of the seeming contradictions of Scripture. A partial list of these problem passages are as follows. If the Bible is inerrant why did Paul require a second thought to remember how many he baptized at Corinth? (1 Cor. 1:14-16). Some problems with numbers can be found by comparing 2 Samuel 8:4 with 1 Chronicles 18:4 and 2 Samuel 10: 18 with 1 Chronicles 19:18. In Matthew 10:9, 10, Jesus said, "Provide . . . nor yet staves." While in Mark 6:8, He permitted the taking of a staff. In reporting the same account, Matthew mentions two men (Mt. 8:28), while Mark (Mk. 5:2) and Luke (Lk. 8:27) mention only one man. In Matthew 26:34, 74-75 and Luke 22:34, 60, 61, it is said that Peter would deny Christ thrice before the cock crew. In Mark 14:30, 72, it said that he would deny Christ thrice before the cock crew twice.

The above, while not complete, will illustrate the internal difficulties involved for one who believes in biblical inerrancy. My first observation about these difficulties is that some of the greatest minds in church history have been well acquainted with these problems, but have held firmly to the doctrine of inerrancy. Among these have been Charles Hodge, Benjamin Warfield, and Carl F. H. Henry in our own times. These problems are not new in the church. I do not think these problems are the crucial issue for those who currently reject inerrancy. I will deal with what I consider the problem to be at a later point.

Some observations need to be made at this point on how we deal with the kind of problems mentioned above. The first thing that we need to do is to decide what we mean by inerrancy.

The critics of inerrancy contend that it is almost impossible to decide what people mean by inerrancy, and that the way some defenders define inerrancy is almost a rejection of the doctrine. I see no real difficulty in deciding the meaning of inerrancy.

When we say the Bible is inerrant we simply mean that what it affirms to be true *is true*. The Bible affirms *nothing* to be *true* that is *false*. It declares *nothing* to be *false* that is *true*.

How do we discover what the Bible affirms to be true? We learn what the Bible affirms to be true by the approach to interpretation given above. We should not consider anything to be an error unless it would be considered an error in the ordinary use of language. Truth and absolute precision are not synonymous. In answer to a question concerning how many people were present on an occasion, all of the following answers could be true: 297, 300, 325 or some other figure in this general range. Only one of these could be precise. As a precise answer, 297 could be true. As an answer spoken of in round numbers, 300 could be true even if spoken by one who knew the answer was 297 if he did not claim it to be exact. The number 325 could be true as an estimate. Truthfulness is equated with precision only when precision is claimed. A summary of a speech, if properly prepared, is true. Yet, a degree of precision may of necessity be lost in condensing the speech.

Two partial reports may appear to be in contradiction. Yet, a complete report may show each partial report to be true and reconcilable with the other.

An illustration from my own experience shows how a partial report of something appears to be irreconcilable, but is clearly reconcilable when the whole story is told. I use this frequently with young people to have a little fun with them. I tell them I never was in the eleventh grade in high school, but that I graduated from the twelfth grade. I quickly explain that the possible solutions that most people would offer do not fit the case. I did not skip a grade. I did not take extra courses. I did not go to summer school.

Once these possible explanations to sustain the truth of the two statements are removed, it appears that one of the statements must be false. Since I am present at the time I raise the problem, I can explain to their satisfaction how both statements are true. They would be true whether I furnished the additional clarifying facts or not. Those who were convinced of my integrity and were convinced that I was not joking would believe both statements were true whether I ever furnished the rest of the information or not. Those who would refuse to believe without the clarifying information would be doubting my integrity or consider that I was too ignorant to know that what I was saying was not true.

The facts that make both statements true are as follows. The year that I was in the tenth grade the state decided to change from an eleven year system to a twelve year system for public schools. This was not done by simply adding an additional year of studies to what was already existing. Rather, the change started with the upcoming eighth grade. Those who the following year were to be in the eighth grade were the first ones to have the twelve year program.

The next year, the report cards for those who would have been in the ninth grade read tenth grade, for those who would have been in the tenth grade read eleventh grade, and for those who would have been in the eleventh grade the report cards read twelfth grade. So, according to my report card I graduated from the twelfth grade without having been in the eleventh grade.

It is very obvious that Scripture is full of partial accounts and abridged speeches. It should not be surprising that there would be some apparent contradictions that could not be easily reconciled without a complete account. If Scripture does not give us a complete account it is unlikely that a complete account will be found. If we believe the Bible to be the Word of God, and thus inerrant, we recognize the problem, but we have confidence that what appears to be a contradiction is apparent, but not real.

I am for neither denying nor dodging the difficulties that may be involved in apparent contradictions. However, I believe the problem is greatly reduced when we recognize that truth and absolute precision are not synonymous. In our experience truth is synonymous with precision only when precision is affirmed. The same is true in the Bible. Truth can be given in absolute statements, relative statements, and general statements. This is the way it is in life. It is also the way it is in the Bible. We do not have any great difficulty deciding which is which in life. We should have no great difficulty in the Bible. In life we use specific numbers; we use round numbers, and we use estimates. We have no great difficulties knowing which is which. We should have no great difficulty knowing which is which in the Bible.

Many of the difficulties with apparent contradictions are easily solved. Others may present some difficulty. Personally, I do not think we need to find a solution for every apparent contradiction. Critics make more mileage out of what appears to be strained attempts to explain some problems than they would if we plainly said that we did not feel the need to find answers for all problems. When a representative number of problems have been dealt with, that is enough. This has been done time and time again. Our faith in inerrancy does not depend upon our ability to have the answer to every problem.

The doctrine of inerrancy applies to the original manuscripts. We believe in the reliability of the Greek and Hebrew texts. We do not claim that copyists have made no mistakes over the years. Textual critics assure us that we have a basically reliable text. When we make the distinction between *words* and *ideas*, even when we are not sure about the exact *word*, the truthfulness of the *idea* may not be at stake. Copyists' mistakes, whether in matters of faith and practice or the phenomena of Scripture, are not to be equated with errors in the *ideas* of Scripture. I am not denying that a copyist's mistake could include a technical error, but it does not of necessity. Most of the seeming contradictions in the Bible, as we have it, can be explained without resorting to the conclusion that they were copyists' errors. Most are not errors at all.

It is only natural that a person would be concerned about what is referred to as errors in the Bible. As a rule, when a person examines these he finds answers to most without much difficulty. Soon he becomes so sure that answers can be found for others if all the information were available that he abandons his search and spends his energies on other things.

THE PROBLEM OF THE HUMAN AUTHORSHIP OF SCRIPTURE

Almost all the advocates of biblical inerrancy, who believing in the divine authorship of Scripture, also believe the human writers were genuinely involved in their writings and are to be called human authors. Some opponents of inerrancy insist that the genuineness of human author-ship introduces a fallible element into Scripture since human beings are fallible.

Those who advocate some form of limited inerrancy should say the Bible *contains* the Word of God, rather than it *is* the Word of God. However, this is *not* the case with those who claim to believe in limited inerrancy. They claim that the Bible *is* the Word of God, not that it *contains* the Word of God.[17] Some even say that they subscribe to "verbal inspiration." This means that the so-called errors in the Bible are the Word of God as well as the truth that is in it. Our *whole being* cries out against the idea that that which can rightly be called the Word of God includes *error.*

Anytime *human authorship* is used to argue for error, that error *cannot* be restricted to any particular aspect of Scripture. If the genuineness of human authorship required that there be error in matters such as history, geography, and science, it would undoubtedly introduce errors into mat-ters of faith and practice as well. Also, areas that are crucially relevant to faith and practice cannot be exempted from error as long as room for error is based on the genuineness of human author-ship. The genuineness of human authorship would have rendered the human author just as liable to communicate error in matters of faith and practice as it did the phenomena of Scripture. If any-thing, the author would have been more prone to introduce error in matters of faith and practice. Since the product is called the "Word of God," we must conclude that the inspiration of the Holy Spirit so influenced the writers of the Bible that they did *not* introduce error into their writing. We must not allow our concern for the genuineness of human authorship to undercut the genuineness of *divine* authorship. The genuineness of divine authorship of the Bible rules out the possibility of error being conveyed in the original manuscripts.

Some contend that since God has used fallible men whose fallibility has shown through in the history of the church, there is no logical reason that He could not have given us a Bible in which the human author's fallibility introduced error into his writings. There is a distinct difference in using the fallible efforts of men in the work of the church and allowing the fallibility of the human authors of the Bible to introduce error into the Bible. The works of preachers, theologians, and other Christians are not called the "Word of God." The Bible is the Word of God. We can accept the idea that even the best of Christians may be in error, but our entire being will not tolerate the idea that God's Word can be in error. I insist that the Bible is the Word of God and is, therefore, to state it positively, true in all that it affirms, and to state it negatively, is without error.

THE PROBLEM OF THE MISSING AUTOGRAPHS

The claim of biblical inerrancy is applied to the original manuscripts of the Bible writers, which are called the autographs. It is usually conceded that there might be at least some slight or insignif-icant error that may be in today's Hebrew Old Testament texts and Greek New Testament texts. It is argued by the critics of inerrancy that there is little, if any difference, in having errors in the origi-nal and having errors in the present Hebrew and Greek texts.

I contend that there is a vast difference. I have a deep a priori conviction that in the giving of what is called the Word of God, it must be without error. I do not have an a priori conviction that it would be impossible for a person copying the Bible to make an error.

I believe the problem of errors in today's texts has been greatly exaggerated. When we are talking about truth and error, we are talking about ideas. Textual problems do not have any serious bearing on the ideas, especially as it relates to making the ideas into an error. Hardly anybody is seriously concerned about the reliability of present Hebrew and Greek texts.

THE NECESSITY OF INERRANCY

The opponents of inerrancy argue that belief in inerrancy is not essential to the preservation of other evangelical doctrines. In fact, they seem to think that the doctrine of inerrancy is a hindrance to maintaining these doctrines. They point out that when inerrancy proponents insist that departing from the doctrine of inerrancy leads to other doctrinal errors, it causes many, who are unable to believe in inerrancy to give up other evangelical doctrines as well. Some who reject inerrancy say that their own belief in other evangelical doctrines is proof that the departure from inerrancy does not set in motion a rejection of other doctrines. This is the argument of Stephen T. Davis.[18]

I think Harold Lindsell has made a good case for the position that when inerrancy goes, in the course of time, the other evangelical doctrines also will be set aside. This may not happen in the lifetime of the individual, but history bears out that it will happen over time in denominations, schools, and other organizations.[19] In my reading, I have found no one trying to answer Lindsell's proof that historically departure from inerrancy led to further doctrinal departures. Davis tried to prove that there was no logical reason that giving up inerrancy would lead to the loss of other doctrines, but he did not deal at all with the historical evidence. We must learn from history in order not to repeat its mistakes.

THE REAL SOURCE OF DIFFICULTY

None of the reasons I have referred to in this chapter actually account for the drift away from inerrancy. These problems are not recent discoveries. Devout men have considered them in the history of the church without feeling it necessary to give up the doctrine of inerrancy. Until recent years, the real problem as I see it has been the theory of evolution and the desire to be considered respectable in the modernists' academic community. Since the time of Darwin, the main problem for those who have departed from the doctrine of inerrancy has been that they have felt the case for evolution was convincing. They could not harmonize evolution with biblical inerrancy so they gave up their doctrine of inerrancy. Some tried to harmonize evolution and Scripture, but the trend among these people has been toward a weaker view of Scripture. Once they have had trouble on a significant point such as the doctrine of creation, the matters such as I have mentioned before seemed to give added support for their weakening view of Scripture. Very few people seem to have departed from inerrancy simply because they could not harmonize all of the apparent contradictions of Scripture. It has in most cases been some other problem.

Evolution was particularly important to modernism for two basic reasons: (1) It bolstered their confidence that they could explain the whole of reality without God. Newtonian physics had convinced the modernists that they did not need God to explain *the physical universe*. The scientific respectability given by Darwin to evolution further strengthened their confidence. They could explain *man* without God. (2) The principle of change and progress embedded in the evolutionary hypothesis was also appealing to modernists. When this philosophy was applied to other areas of thought and life, it went hand in glove with the optimism of modernism. By social engineering they could hasten the progress toward an ideal society.

It does not appear that the proponents of postmodernism will share the same interest in evolution that modernism had. They may be glad for any damage done to Christian thought by evolution, but they will not likely use arguments for evolution against Christianity. That is because of their rejection of the categories of true and false in any absolute sense of the word. Postmodernism is not that fond of reason.

A Further Concern

The particular views that I have discussed which deny biblical inerrancy would view the Bible as having at least some kind of authority in matters of faith and practice. However, that relationship in some instances becomes so vague that it is hard to decide exactly what it is. This vagueness opens the door for a person claiming to believe such a view, and at the same time have a neo-orthodox view of revelation or some other form of contemporary theology. This is especially true when such words as sufficiency and adequacy are used.

The neo-orthodox view is based on the assumption that God is so Wholly Other (totally different) from man that there can be no communication from God to man. Reason says that God cannot reveal Himself to man. In spite of this, God breaks through and reveals Himself. The faith that believes God has revealed Himself to man is either contrary to reason or irrational. In spite of this, the person who experiences this encounter with God takes the leap of faith and believes that God has revealed Himself. God reveals Himself in Jesus Christ and as He speaks to man through the Bible.

The Bible is not a revelation about God. The Bible is a witness of the fact that God has revealed Himself and that He will reveal Himself. The view that the Bible is a witness to revelation makes it important in the revelation encounter with God, but there is no inspired message from God in the Bible. The Bible is a record of revelation, but not revelation. The Bible as written is not the Word of God. In some sense it becomes the Word of God or is an instrument of revelation when God speaks through it, but even then its words or message do not become the Word of God.

In neo-orthodoxy, there is no content revelation. Revelation is a revelation of God Himself, not a revelation about God. The Bible would be a reflection of the Bible writers about their encounter with God, not the communication of a message from God. Thus, it is called a witness to revelation. Theology would not result from an interpretation of a revealed message from God, but is a reflection about a person's encounter with God.

It is quite obvious that this view of the Bible is quite different from that of Jesus and the writers of the New Testament when they prefaced many of their statements from the Old Testament with "it is written." This certainly tells us that they did view the Old Testament as a content revelation from

God. A good example of this fact is Jesus' answer to Satan during His temptation, "It is written, Man shall not live by bread alone, but by every word that proceedeth out of the mouth of God" (Mt. 4:4).

Contemporary theology, with its many forms, is a modification of neo-orthodox theology. There is a serious epistemological conflict between biblical Christianity and contemporary theology. Biblical Christianity believes that God has given us a content revelation in the Bible. This revelation is true. There should be no fascination, on the part of evangelical Christians, with theological systems that reject the idea that God has given us a true, content revelation in the Bible.

While neo-orthodoxy predates postmodernism, it can be seen that it was wrestling with the same problems that postmodernism is now wrestling with. It should be clear that those of us who believe that objective Truth does exist will take a different approach than that of neo-orthodoxy, contemporary theology, or postmodernism. The doctrine of biblical inerrancy is meaningless to people who do not believe objective Truth exists. It is very meaningful to those of us who believe in a worldview that recognizes objective, universal, and timeless Truth.

Concluding Challenge

The Truth of the Bible is objective, timeless, universal, and unchanging. It has come to us in human language. It stands distinct from, is uncontaminated by, but is woven into the fabric of the lives and the cultures of the people of the Old and New Testaments. It stands ready to be woven into the lives and the cultures of people today. It judges and transforms culture. It must never be contaminated by culture.

The challenges that the Truth of the Bible faces from one culture to another change. However, the Truth of the Bible does not. There is a significant difference in the challenge that modernism presents to the Truth of the Bible from the challenge that postmodernism presents.

Modernism accepted the fact of universal Truth. Bible believers did not have to debate that fact with the modernists. The battle was over the truth of some of the particulars in the Bible. Believers had to deal with these problems. Their own internal make-up required satisfaction. If they were going to make a difference with unbelievers, they had to show an awareness of the problems and to deal with them with integrity. The interesting fact is that the list of challenges to the accuracy of the Bible that comes from historians, archaeologists, and scientists is the shortest that it has been at any time since the rise of modernism.

I want to make one point absolutely clear. *We do not believe that the Bible is the Word of God because it is inerrant.* Rather, *we believe the Bible is inerrant because we believe that it is the Word of God.* We expect the Bible to be inerrant because we believe it is the Word of God. There is *no established empirical fact* that *contradicts* the Bible. The lack of information on some matters may mean that we may not have a ready answer that will solve all problems. But there is no convincing case that says that the evidence clearly establishes a contradiction.

Postmodernism presents a different set of challenges. It challenges the very existence of Truth. That is a challenge that must be met with an appeal to the *total personality*. That is the challenge this whole book is addressing.

We must be very alert to the times in which we live. We must be alert that times can change. That has certainly happened in my lifetime. From 1930–1960, the paradigms in America were set by modernism and Christianity. They were competing over what Truth was, but not over whether Truth existed. From 1960–1990 was a period of transition. The paradigm of modernism was being dislodged. By 1990, the paradigm shift was completed modernism was dethroned, and postmodernism had usurped the throne. Jesus said, "I will build my church; and the gates of hell shall not prevail against it" (Mt. 16:8). Otherwise, we would probably say that Christianity is in a life or death struggle with postmodernism. But the One who is KING of KINGS and LORD of LORDS, and who knows the end from the beginning, has declared that His church will prevail.

While it is important to understand the times that we are living in when dealing with the question of the Truth of the Bible, it is more important to keep in mind *who we are serving and to whom we are ministering.* Jesus said in praying to the Father, "Thy word is truth" (Jn. 17:17). Our calling is to minister to those who are made in the image of God (Gen. 1:26). That image includes the fact that human beings are in the rational image of God (Col. 3:10). It is the Truth that sets people free (Jn. 8:32). While we need to understand the times we are living in to be able to administer God's Truth effectively, *God has not left it up to us* to negotiate His Truth away because of the prevailing mood of the culture.

We do not simply stand for the Truth in opposition to our culture. We must stand for the Truth *because of the need of our culture.* Our culture is hurting because it has rejected God's Truth. Human beings are made for Truth. We are in desperate need of Truth. The emptiness and confusion that exist because of the rejection of Truth present us with an opportunity. We dare not let our fellow human beings down.

5

Nature and Attributes of God

When that *inescapable question,* "Is there a God?" is answered in the affirmative, a question just as inescapable presents itself. What kind of being is God? The answer to this question is of greatest importance. The very fact that He is God means that He is the Sovereign Ruler and the Lord and Judge of my life. My relationship to Him is the most important of all my relationships. His nature and attributes form the foundation of the only valid value system. It is the value system by which I will be judged. It is the value system by which I must live if I am to have harmony within. My system of thought must acknowledge Him and must reflect a commitment to divine values.

In this chapter, I plan to discuss God as God, i.e., things that are equally true of each member of the Trinity. It is a mistake to understand the discussion of the nature and attributes of God to be a discussion of God the Father as distinguished from God the Son and God the Holy Spirit. What is true with regard to the nature and attributes of God is equally true of all members of the Trinity.

The Basic Nature of God

By the basic nature of God, I mean what God is within Himself apart from any consideration of His relationship with His creation. These facts about God are important when considering His relationship with His creation, but we can also think of them apart from His relationship to His creation.

GOD IS SPIRIT

God is a spirit-being (Jn. 4:24) as distinguished from a material being. It is proper to think of God as having essence or substance, but the substance is immaterial rather than material. Our minds are so accustomed to thinking of material substance that it is hard for us to think of a substance that is immaterial. Yet, we must think of immaterial substance if we are to think of the spirit-essence of God, or if we are to think of our own human spirit or the spirit-essence of angels.

There are two logical consequences of the truth that God is spirit: (1) He is incorporeal. (2) He is invisible.

By incorporeal, it is meant that God does not possess a physical body. It is of the very nature of spirit that spirit does not have flesh and bones (Lk. 24:39). It is true that the Bible speaks of God as having hands, feet, eyes, ears, etc. (Is. 59:2; Gen. 3:8; 1 Pet. 3:12; and others). These are to be understood as metaphorical expressions that serve as aids in communication. When Isaiah said, "Behold, the LORD's hand is not shortened, that it cannot save" (59:1), we do not think of the Lord as having a long arm with which He saves. What these anthropomorphic terms (terms describing God with human characteristics) do is to speak of God figuratively in terms of the organ with which we perform functions similar to those functions being ascribed to God. In view of the frequent use that we make of figurative language, it should not seem strange that such language would be used of God.

In accord with the concept that God is incorporeal, He is invisible. John said, "No man hath seen God at any time" (Jn. 1:18). Some problems are created by Genesis 32:30; Exodus 24:10; 33:18-23; Judges 13:22; and other passages where God is said to assume a visible form, but in the light of John's statement, we must conclude that these events involved something less than viewing the very essence of God.

GOD IS PERSONAL

In speaking of God as God, I prefer to say He is personal rather than say He is a person. "He is a person" would be appropriate to speak of one person. Since there are three persons in the Godhead, it is better to speak of God as personal. By personal we mean that He is a being who thinks, feels, and acts. That the God of the Bible thinks, feels, and acts is too obvious to require Scriptural documentation.

That God is personal means He is the living God. He is separated from idols who can neither see, hear, speak, nor act (Dt. 4:28; Ps. 115:5, 8; and others).

That God is personal separates Him from the impersonal god of philosophy. He is not an impersonal object to be found by our searching. He is a personal God who cares and has declared Himself.

That God is personal is not an observation to be made and passed over quickly. It deserves much thought in order to see and appreciate its far reaching implications. If God were impersonal, our relationship with Him (or better, It) would either be an unintelligible mystical relationship, or simply a relationship to laws. With God as personal, the ultimate relationship is personal. As personal beings we need personal relationships. We need to know that the highest of all beings cares for us. A personal relationship can be a warm relationship.

The doctrine of revelation is a logical outgrowth of and depends upon the fact that God is personal. A personal God who speaks gives us that which is beyond the reach of empiricism. He speaks Truth (Jn. 17:17). This Truth sets us free (Jn. 8:32). Belief in a personal God opens the way for answers to the *inescapable questions of life*. It gives meaning and purpose to life. The Truth spoken by God rescues us. We are not tossed about on the uncertain sea of postmodernism.

Miracles are no problem to a personal God who created and rules the universe. He is not locked in by the laws of nature. He does not have to suspend the laws of nature to work a miracle. He simply acts directly. His activity may counteract the laws of nature, but He does not have to suspend them. If a small child is riding with us and we have to stop suddenly, we reach out our hand to hold him to keep him from falling. If we had not reached out our hand and held him, the laws of nature in operation would have caused him to fall. As persons, we reach out the hand and introduce another law of nature that counteracts the law of nature that would have caused the child to fall. We did not suspend the law of nature. If we, as persons, can counteract one law of nature by another law of nature, cannot the personal Ruler of the universe interpose His own activity without suspending the laws of nature? Is He not free to do so?

The question of when to work miracles is a matter solely within God's control. The logical possibility of miracles is clearly present when we have a personal God. In our study of the Bible, we dare not be guided by a worldview that on an a priori basis rules out the possibility of miracles. Modernism used this kind of thinking in trying to deny or explain away the miraculous in the Bible.

GOD IS INDEPENDENT

God is not dependent upon anything outside Himself for His existence. He is the grounds of His own existence. We speak of the self-existence of God. God is not the cause of His existence because that which did not begin cannot be caused. God is an uncaused Being.

As Fred H. Klooster explains:

> The independence of God includes more than the idea of God's aseity or self-existence. His independence characterizes not only His existence, but His whole being and His attributes, His decrees and His works of creation, providence, and redemption.[1]

There is no force or person outside of God poses any threat to God or forces Him to take a particular path of action. God's actions are in accord with His own nature and His own plan.

God's independence does not mean He has not entered into personal relationships with the persons whom He has created, nor that He does not use them in His work. It does mean that the idea of these relationships and the use of those He has created to do His work was His own, not one imposed on Him. His independence does not mean He is not opposed, but it does mean that He is not in danger of being defeated by His foes. He can and does deal with them according to His own plans and purposes. When He chooses, He will call a halt to His opposition. His independence does not mean He will not respond to us, but it does mean the response is in keeping with His own nature, promises, and plans. We do not force God to respond to us.

GOD IS INFINITE IN RELATION TO SPACE

God's infinity in relation to space is usually spoken of by the term immensity. Immensity refers to the infinity of God's essence in relation to space (1 Kg. 8:27; Acts 17:24). The immensity of God forms the basis of His omnipresence which will be discussed later.

GOD IS INFINITE IN RELATION TO TIME

God is eternal. He had no beginning and He will have no end (Dt. 33:27; Job 36:26; Ps. 41:13; 90:2; Is. 43:13; 57:15; Rom. 1:20; and others).

To some extent we can comprehend eternity future. We can imagine a being not having an end. We cannot comprehend the eternity past of God. We cannot comprehend the idea of a Being without a beginning. Yet, we cannot comprehend God as having a beginning. It is non-imaginable that nothing could have produced God. Stephen Charnock's words are appropriate here:

> Though we cannot comprehend eternity, yet we may comprehend that there is an eternity; as though we cannot comprehend the essence of God, what he is, yet we may comprehend that he is; we may understand the notion of his existence, though we cannot understand the infiniteness of his nature.[2]

The most common way theologians describe God's eternity is to refer to it as timelessness. It is said that God has no past and no future. Everything with God is one eternal now. Time is said to be a creation of God and will be terminated by Him. Time is characterized by past, present, and future and has succession of events. Eternity has only the present, thus no succession of events.

Concerning God's relationship to time, Strong, who supports the eternal now view, comments:

> Yet, we are far from saying that time, now that it exists, has no objective reality to God. To him, past, present, and future are 'one eternal now,' not in the sense that there is no distinction between them, but only in the sense that he sees past and future as vividly as he sees the present. With creation time began, and since the successions of history are veritable successions, he who sees according to truth must recognize them.[3]

This explanation by Strong of God's relation to time would find general support among theologians holding to the eternal now view. It is my contention that to say the "past, present, and future are 'one eternal now,' . . . only in the sense that he sees the past and future as vividly as he sees the present," contradicts the eternal now view. It confuses omniscience with eternal now. To see with the vividness equal to the present that which God recognizes to be past and future is not the same as saying they are all *now* to Him.

A person has to make a choice between believing in eternal now and believing that God can observe human experiences as past, present, and future with equal vividness. If to God, eternity is one "now," all human experiences are one "now" to Him. It is not the same as saying God sees the past and future as vividly as He sees the present. To Him, what to us is past and future must be viewed as occurring now in the eternal now view. This would be a consistent presentation of the eternal now view. It is *only* when it is *consistently presented* that it can rightly be spoken of as *eternal now*.

When the eternal now view is consistently presented, it cannot stand. The present moment for me is the only moment that has objective reality. Yesterday had objective reality. Tomorrow will have objective reality. If my yesterday and my tomorrow are objectively real to God, He would have a different standard of objective reality as it relates to me for Himself than He has given to me for myself. This is inconceivable.

Some have argued that just as God fills all space, He fills all eternity, or just as His infinity fills one, it fills the other. Such a conclusion is not necessary. There is a vast amount of difference in the space filled by an elephant and a flea, but now is the same to both.

The essence of God fills space. Eternity cannot be filled in the same way. God is eternal in that He has no beginning and no end. The plain language of Scripture tells us that God has duration; a past, a present, and a future (Ps. 90:2; 102:12; Rom. 3:21; Heb. 13:8; and others). The question of the vividness with which God sees the past and future will be discussed under omniscience.

Some have sought support for the eternal now view from 2 Peter 3:8: "But, beloved, be not ignorant of this one thing, that one day is with the Lord as a thousand years, and a thousand years as one day." It is not meant that God sees no objective difference between a day and a thousand years. The meaning of the verse is explained in Psalm 90:4: "For a thousand years in thy sight are but as yesterday when it is past, and as a watch in the night."

It is obvious from Psalm 90:4 that it is the subjective experience of time that is under discussion. Objectively, time is the same for a child and an older person. Subjectively, it seems that time passes much more quickly with age. To us a thousand years seems like a long time. To God it does not.

Revelation 10:6 has been used to support the termination of time. The angel said "There should be time no longer." This is to be understood to mean that there will be no further delay. There is nothing in the passage to indicate that it has reference to an ending of time as such.

Part of the whole problem seems to be the problem of thinking of time as having a beginning and an end. Time usually is viewed as the succession of events. On the basis of this definition, it is thought that time began with creation.

Buswell's definition of time helps at this point. He says, "Time therefore should be defined as the mere abstract possibility of relationship in durational sequence."[4] Time is the possibility of now and then.

Viewed from this angle, time is the possibility of succession of events. The possibility exists whether the events are present or not. Looking at it from this viewpoint, there is no reason for not believing time to be eternal.

Following the same principle, "Space is the mere abstract possibility of dimensional relationships."[5] Space would be the possibility of "here and there." Space would be eternal. Space would not have to be created. The possibility of having distance between objects was eternal. Only objects needed to be created. Then, you would have distance between objects. When objects moved from one place to another you would have succession of events.

Buswell, as one who rejects the eternal now view, says:

> If the past is not past for God as well as man, then we are yet in our sins; Christ has not come and never will come, for He is Deity and therefore timeless. But He is said to have come in the fullness of time (*chronos*) and "in due time (*kairos*)." If the past is not past for God, we are yet under the wrath and curse of a righteous Judge.[6]

The view of time and eternity that has been set forth has no difficulty recognizing God as the God of history. It has no difficulty seeing the redemptive acts of God in history. It sees God as the King of Kings and Lord of Lords and the Supreme Judge of the universe, but He is not the Wholly Other whose revelation is an irrational breakthrough as neo-orthodox theologians say.

I am well aware that the majority of conservative theologians believe in some form of the eternal now view.[7] I do not accuse them of having neo-orthodox tendencies because the eternal now view is much older than neo-orthodoxy. However, I do raise these questions: For those who hold the eternal now view, are there not some logical difficulties avoiding the view of revelation set forth by neo-orthodoxy in connection with eternity and time? In coping with these difficulties, does not one in effect explain away the eternal now view?

GOD IS IMMUTABLE

By the immutability of God is meant that He is unchangeable in His essence and attributes. This unchangeableness of God is clearly taught in Scripture (Num. 23:19; 1 Sam. 15:29; Ps. 33:11; 119: 89-91; Mal. 3:6; Heb. 6:17; Jas. 1:17; and others).

Some problems are created by verses that speak of God as repenting (Gen. 6:6; Ex. 32:14; 2 Sam. 24:16; Jon. 3:10). Some verses like these are to be explained by the difficulty of describing God and His acts in human language. The experience of human beings that most nearly approximate the divine experience referred to may be repentance. Yet, some aspects of the human experience may not be applicable to the divine experience. This would be the case in Genesis 6:6 where "it repented the LORD that he had made man." Second Samuel 24:16 would also be explained this way.

In other places, repentance represents a change of attitude on the part of God in response to a change of attitude on the part of people. This is in full harmony with His unchangeableness. He is unchangeably committed to change His attitude toward those who change their attitude toward Him. He is also unchangeably committed to answer prayer under certain conditions. Such a change of attitude, instead of representing a change in His essence and attributes, actually demonstrates His unchangeableness in His essence and attributes. Exodus 32:14 and Jonah 3:10 would be explained this way.

Henry C. Thiessen's comment is helpful at this point:

> God's immutability is not like that of a stone that does not respond to changes about it, but like that of a column of mercury which rises and falls according as the temperature changes. His immutability consists in His always doing the right and in adapting the treatment of His creatures to the variations in their character and conduct.[8]

The Natural Attributes of God

In distinguishing attributes from the basic nature of God, I am viewing the attributes of God as the divine characteristics that in our conception of them, involve His relationship to His creation. I am not suggesting that He did not have these characteristics before He created. I am saying that in our understanding of them we tend to always think of His relationship to His creation. Any division in which we choose to discuss God will have its shortcomings. No approach has all the advantages.

GOD IS OMNIPRESENT

Frequently, there is no distinction made between omnipresence and immensity. When a distinction is made, immensity refers to the infinity of God's essence. Omnipresence speaks of God as being present everywhere for a relationship to His creation. It is the immensity of God that forms the basis for His omnipresence.

Wherever we go, God is there (Ps. 139:7-12; Jer. 23:23; Acts 17:24-28; and others). We cannot run from His presence to flee His judgment. We will never find ourselves at a place where He is not when we need Him. He is the ever present One.

GOD IS OMNISCIENT

When we speak of God as omniscient, we mean that His knowledge is infinite. There is nothing that has existed, does exist, or will exist outside His knowledge. As Thiessen explains:

> He knows Himself and all other things, whether they be actual or merely possible, whether they be past, present, or future, and that He knows them perfectly and from all eternity. He knows things immediately, simultaneously, exhaustively and truly.[9]

Our knowledge is known on two levels. We have a very limited amount of knowledge that is in our conscious mind. The majority of what we know exists in our subconscious mind. Some of it is available for instant recall for our conscious mind. Some of it is not recalled so readily. There is no subconsciousness with God. As Thiessen says, "He knows things immediately."

The Scriptural support of God's omniscience is abundant. The following are some selected passages: 1 Kings 8:39; 1 Chronicles 28:9; Job 34:21, 22; 42:2; Psalm 44:21; 147:4, 5; Isaiah 29:15; 40:27, 28; 46:10; Acts 15:18; Hebrews 4:13.

Now, let us pick up the discussion of the vividness with which God knows the past and future that was postponed from our discussion of God's eternity. God sees the past and future as vividly as He sees the present. This is a logical necessity if God is to be omniscient. However, only the present is objectively real to God. The past was objectively real. The future will be objectively real.

When we say that God sees the past and future with a vividness equal to His knowledge of the present, we are thinking about knowledge in two ways: (1) knowledge of facts, and (2) knowledge as subjective reality.

In considering God's knowledge of facts, there is nothing about the past that God knew then that He does not know now. There is nothing about the present that God knows now that He did not know in the past. He will not know more about the future when it becomes present than He knows now and has always known.

When we speak of knowing vividly, we are not only thinking of knowing facts, but also of knowing subjectively. The subjective experience of God's knowing the past is the same that it was when it was present. His subjective experience of the present is the same that it was when it was future. His subjective knowledge of the future is the same now that it will be when the future becomes present.

An illustration of subjective reality, where the objective reality is not present, is what happens when we relive an event of the past. The objective reality of the event is gone, but we still view it with subjective reality. The same could be said about anticipation of a future event.

God's factual knowledge of past, present, and future is exhaustive. The subjective reality of past, present, and future knows no difference. Yet, only the present is objectively real to God. We can say, then, that God views the past, present, and future with equal vividness. This is not the same as speaking of all things as being one eternal now with God. To me it is far easier to comprehend. It accords with all Scriptural evidence. It is more acceptable.

GOD IS OMNIPOTENT

By God's omnipotence, we mean that God can perform any act consistent with His nature. He is never limited in an activity by lack of power (Gen. 17:1; 18:14; Job 42:2; Mt. 19:26; Acts 26:8; Rev. 19:6; and others).

By omnipotence, we do not mean that God can do the ridiculous and the absurd. There are some things that God cannot do. He cannot lie (Tit. 1:2). He cannot make a square circle.

Frequently, in theological discussions, we hear the statement made, "I don't want to limit God." Certainly, we want to be careful, but we do not have to refuse to say under any circumstances, "God cannot do thus and so." Omnipotence does not preclude the possibility that there are some things God cannot do. It does preclude the possibility that He is ever limited by lack of power. The very nature of His being precludes the possibility that He could do some things.

The Moral Attributes of God

GOD IS HOLY

When we think of God as holy, we think of Him as being absolutely free from sin in thought, word, and deed. There is not the slightest taint of sin in Him. He is absolutely pure. As John says, "God is light, and in him is no darkness at all" (1 Jn. 1:5). He cannot in any way condone sin. As Habakkuk says, "Thou art of purer eyes than to behold evil, and canst not look on iniquity " (Hab. 1:13).

One of the main themes of the Old Testament is a declaration and demonstration of God's holiness (Ex. 15:11; Lev. 19:2; 1 Sam. 2:2; 6:20; Job 34:10; Ps. 47:8; 89:35; 119:9; Is. 6:3; 57:15; and others). This theme continues in the New Testament (Jn. 17:11; Jas. 1:13; 1 Pet. 1:15, 16; 1 Jn. 1:5; Rev. 4:8; 15:4; and others).

God as a holy God will not tolerate sin. It is because of God's holiness that "the wrath of God is revealed from heaven against all ungodliness and unrighteousness of men, who hold the truth in unrighteousness" (Rom. 1:18). The first revelation of God's holiness is a revelation of judgment. He said to Adam and Eve, "But of the tree of the knowledge of good and evil, thou shalt not eat of it: for in the day that thou eatest thereof thou shalt surely die" (Gen. 2:17). God's judgment against sin reveals His determination to remain holy.

The acts of judgment in biblical history bear testimony of God's hatred toward sin and His determination to remain holy. The flood, Sodom and Gomorrah, and the many other acts of judgment in the Scriptures leave us no doubt where God stands on the sin issue.

The eternal punishment of the wicked reveals the intolerant attitude of God toward sin. The Bible speaks of the punishment of the wicked with such expressions as, "outer darkness" (Mt. 8:12; 22:13; and 25:30), "furnace of fire" (Mt. 13:42, 50), "everlasting fire" (Mt. 18:8; 25:41), "everlasting punishment" (Mt. 25:46), "fire unquenchable" (Mk. 9:43-48), "everlasting destruction from the presence of the Lord, and from the glory of his power" (2 Th. 1:9), and "the lake which burneth with fire and brimstone: which is the second death" (Rev. 21:8).

The cross of Jesus Christ also reveals God's determination to remain holy. The cross of Christ is an eternal testimony that God will not forgive sin unless it is first punished. If we see in God a pattern of purity and righteousness but fail to see His hatred of sin, we have failed to understand the biblical view of holiness.[10]

God's holy will is an expression of God's holy nature. As Thiessen says: "In God we have purity of being before purity of willing. God does not will the good because it is good, nor is the good good because God wills it; else there would be a good above God or the good would be arbitrary and changeable. Instead, God's will is the expression of his nature, which is holy."[11]

We are not to imagine that God can by an arbitrary act of will declare a thing to be holy and it be holy. In Islamic thought, the will of Allah is supreme and arbitrary. In Christian thought God's will is always a true expression of His nature. It is incompatible with God's nature to declare one person obligated to the morality of the Ten Commandments and to declare a reverse morality for another. Under such an arrangement, God could reign by whim and fancy. We would not know what to expect next.

Since God's will is an expression of His holy nature, morality is rational. We can discover principles from our study of Scripture and apply them to things not mentioned in the Bible.

Holiness is the basic or fundamental attribute of God. As Thiessen explains: "Because of the fundamental character of this attribute, the holiness of God rather than the love, the power, or the will of God should be given first place. Holiness is the regulative principle of all three of them; for the throne is established on the basis of His holiness" (Ps. 47:8; 89:14; 97:2).[12]

This is one of the most important observations to be made in a doctrinal study. When love is made the basic attribute of God, it leads to the idea of universal salvation—an idea that finds no support whatever in Scripture. It also leads to compromise in moral issues. Love that is not subject to holiness is too ready to modify and compromise. It is only when holiness, not love, is seen to be the basic attribute of God that the biblical doctrines of Hell and atonement can be maintained. It is holiness, not love, that sends sinners to Hell. It is holiness, not love, that demanded that sin be punished before God would forgive sin.

Righteousness and justice flow from God's holiness. When we speak of God as righteous, we mean that He is right in all that He does. Righteousness is an overall term that refers to all of God's dealings as being right.

Justice is an aspect of righteousness. God is righteous in His judicial proceedings in handing out punishments and rewards. Remunerative justice is the justice of God that guarantees that obedience will receive its appropriate reward. Retributive justice is the justice of God that guarantees that disobedience will receive its appropriate punishment. Justice is the guardian of God's holiness.

GOD IS LOVING

That God is a God of love is made abundantly clear in Scripture (Dt. 4:37; 7:7, 8; Ps. 42:8; 63:3; 89:33; 103:13; Jer. 31:3; Hos. 11:1; Jn. 3:16; Rom. 5:8; 1 Jn. 3:1; 4:8-10; and others). By God's love is meant His affectionate concern. It is expressed in the Scriptures through the words "love," "lovingkindness," "compassion," and "mercy." This love is expressed in God's concern for both man's temporal and eternal welfare.

The loving concern of God is evidenced in the Old Testament, particularly in the Psalms, but the revelation of God's love reaches a high point with Jesus. Jesus had compassion in action. He was moved with compassion when He saw the sick, the bereaved, and the hungry. One of the most heartmoving scenes in the Scriptures is described for us when Matthew relates the lament of Jesus over Jerusalem: "O Jerusalem, Jerusalem, thou that killest the prophets, and stonest them which are sent unto thee, how often would I have gathered thy children together, even as a hen gathereth her chickens under her wings, and ye would not!" (Mt. 23:37).

As moving as the show of compassion was in the life of Christ, the high point in the revelation of God's love did not come in the life of Christ. The highest point in God's love came at the cross. As Paul tells us, "But God commendeth his love toward us, in that, while we were yet sinners, Christ died for us" (Rom. 5:8).

The death that Jesus died for sinners was not just an ordinary death. It was a death in which He paid the penalty for man's sin. He suffered the full wrath of God for man's sin. For the sinless Son of God to pay the full penalty for our sins in order that we who had sinned might be saved was the highest possible manifestation of God's love. God's love for us is real. It is love in action. It is love at a cost.[13]

The love of God manifests the deep feeling of concern that God has for us. Some have denied that there is any feeling in God. I am in agreement with Thiessen's comment when he says:

> Philosophers frequently deny feeling to God, saying that feeling implies passivity and susceptibility of impression from without, and that such a possibility is incompatible with the idea of the immutability of God. But immutability does not mean immobility. True love necessarily involves feeling, and if there be no feeling in God, then there is no love of God.[14]

God feels His love toward us. He feels His wrath toward sin. Explanations of God which deny that He is personal and deny that He has feeling make us think He is not approachable. It is hard for us to believe that He could or would care for us. I believe that such explanations of God grow out of the idea that reason divorced from the rest of our personality has a special gift for finding the

Truth. I think the reverse is true. We do not set our reason aside, but it functions as a part of our *total personality.*

When God's love is manifested toward those in misery and distress, we call it mercy. When God's love is manifested toward the ill-deserving, we call it grace because the emphasis is on the fact that it is unmerited. God's love toward sinners is mercy in that they are in misery and distress. It is grace in that they are ill-deserving.

To be technical, grace, *as saving grace,* is not an attribute of God. Saving grace is a *provision of God* made possible through atonement. God could not save sinners simply by exercising an attribute of grace. This would be incompatible with His holiness. He can exercise grace only in accord with the provision of atonement and the application of that atonement on the condition of faith.

It is also of interest to note that grace gets its characteristic not only from love, but from holiness. That grace is *offered* is owed to the *love* of God. That it is *free* is owed to the *holiness* of God. The same holiness which demanded that the full penalty of sin be paid before man could be forgiven also demanded that no more could be collected. Holiness will not tolerate an underpayment nor an overcharge. To charge more than what Christ paid through atonement for our forgiveness would have been an overcharge. Holiness would not tolerate this. Therefore, the characteristic of grace that describes it as an unmerited gift owes its origin to holiness.

The love of God as it is manifested to the good and bad alike is called benevolence. It was this kind of love that Jesus had in mind when He said, "For he maketh his sun to rise on the evil and on the good, and sendeth rain on the just and on the unjust" (Mt. 5:45).

GOD IS WISE

The Bible says a lot about the wisdom of God (Pr. 3:19; Dan. 2:20, 21; Lk. 2:40, 52; 11:49; Rom. 11:33; 1 Cor. 1:24; Eph. 3:10; and others). I am aware that it is not customary to list wisdom as a moral attribute of God. As a rule, it gets brief mention in connection with omniscience.

While it is not out of place to consider wisdom in connection with omniscience, I believe it belongs more logically under the moral attributes of God. It is only then that it will be given its proper significance. Consider the value that God places upon wisdom in the following references: Job 28:12-28; Proverbs 3:13-18; 4:5-9; 8:11-21; 16:16, 20-24. A study of God should call attention to the importance of God's wisdom and the corresponding responsibility in us to exercise wisdom. Yet, it is almost passed over in most studies of the attributes of God.

I believe wisdom should be considered under the moral attributes of God because it is impossible to consider wisdom apart from its moral tone. Strong says, "Omniscience, as qualified by holy will, is in Scripture denominated 'wisdom.' In virtue of his wisdom God chooses the highest ends and uses the fittest means to accomplish them."[15]

The following observations from Charnock show that wisdom is moral through and through. He explains:

But in particular, wisdom consists,

1. In acting for a *right* end. The chiefest part of prudence is in fixing a *right* end, and in choosing *fit* means, and directing them to that scope. . . .

2. Wisdom consists in observing all circumstances for action. He is counted a wise man that lays hold of the *fittest* opportunity to bring his designs about. . . .

3. Wisdom consists, in willing and acting according to the *right* reason, according to a *right* judgment of things.[16] [Italics mine]

Anthony A. Hoekema explains: "Wisdom means the application of knowledge to the reaching of a goal. God's wisdom implies that God uses the best possible means to reach the goals He has set for Himself."[17]

God's wisdom works in full harmony with His holiness and love. It sees to it that the best possible interests are carried out. Yet, the moral tone of wisdom is not simply that it acts in accord with holiness and love. The ability to achieve ends under complex circumstances is itself a virtue or a value. The exercise of wisdom is a moral obligation.

Wisdom is one of the most admirable characteristics of God. By His wisdom God is able to direct the affairs of the universe so that His plan will be carried out. This takes into account the freedom of man and the existence of evil. The sovereignty of God is maintained without constant reliance on the brute force of His omnipotence. By God's wisdom He created man a *personal being* and allows him the freedom inherent in being a person without forfeiting His sovereignty. It was the wisdom of God that arranged a plan whereby the *holiness* of God could be *satisfied* and the *love* of God could provide *redemption* for fallen man.

When we begin to see the wisdom of God in proper perspective, we heartily join with Paul when he said, "O the depth of the riches both of the wisdom and knowledge of God! how unsearchable are his judgments, and his ways past finding out!" (Rom. 11:33).

HOLINESS, LOVE, AND WISDOM ARE INTERRELATED

There is a sense in which holiness, love, and wisdom each embrace the other. To subtract love or wisdom from holiness would corrupt holiness. To subtract holiness or wisdom from love would corrupt love. To subtract holiness or love from wisdom would corrupt wisdom. Yet, they are distinct. We do not think of compassion as growing out of holiness. We do not think of wrath as growing out of love. We think of wisdom as arranging the plan of redemption. We think of love as providing it.

The Overall Characteristics of God

Some of what I will discuss as overall characteristics of God are usually considered attributes of God. I choose to treat them here because they seem to characterize God as a whole rather than describe a particular characteristic of God.

GOD IS A TRUE GOD AND THE GOD OF TRUTH

God is not a lie as idols are (Rom. 1:25). He is real. He exists. He speaks and He acts. Everything He says is true (Tit. 1:2). All that is true depends upon Him. Nothing that is true can be fully and ultimately explained without a reference to God.

Any discussion of a "true God and the God of truth" is meaningless and irrelevant to post-modernism. Modernism did not deny the existence or importance of Truth, but it thought that everything could be explained without God. Over a 200 year period, modernism tried in vain to develop a consistent and meaningful worldview. It tried in vain to make progress toward a utopian society. It now stands as one of the failures of history.

I believe that deep within the heart and mind of every human being there is a deep desire and longing for Truth. The *inescapable questions of life* cry out for answers that are true. The God of Truth has given us answers in the Bible.

In June 1996, as we were returning home from the Former Soviet Union, my wife and I spent three weeks with missionaries in Japan. On one occasion, missionary Dale Bishop invited me to meet with him for a Bible study with a man and his wife. His wife is a Christian, but he was not. He was retired from a position with the Japanese educational system. At the time, he was helping start homes for the handicapped and the elderly. Dale told him about our trip to Russia. He asked me several questions about Russia including questions about the the economic condition and the presidential election that was to take place at the end of June. He also asked about Christianity in Russia. Soon the discussion shifted to Japan. His questions made it very natural for us to talk about the inadequacy of approaches to a world- or life-view without God. He pointed out that before 1945 Japan lived in a *mystical era*. Since 1945, they have been in a *realistic era*. In this period, he explained, Japan has placed great value on scientific and economic achievement. They have been very successful in this regard. But in spite of economic success, he lamented that there is an emptiness now. People know there is more to life than technology and economics. It seems as if where there is the greatest economic and scientific success that there is the greatest emptiness. The human heart cries out for Truth.[18]

GOD IS GOOD

Goodness is frequently used to head the category of God's moral attributes. Others have tended to restrict it more to a category under which to consider love and related attributes.

I would agree that goodness embraces both the qualities of holiness and love, but it goes beyond that. It embraces all the qualities of an ideal person. Holiness and love are specific terms that carry great force. Goodness is a general term. It does not seem to do justice to holiness and love to consider them as sub-points under a general term such as goodness. I would prefer to consider it as an overall characteristic of God embracing all the characteristics of an ideal person.

GOD IS GLORIOUS

When we think of the glory of God, we think of His splendor. We stand before Him in amazement and wonder. We are awed by His presence. We praise Him. We honor Him. We worship Him.

THE QUEST FOR TRUTH

GOD IS MAJESTIC

When we think of the majesty of God, we think of His royal dignity. He is King of kings. He is kingly in the fullest possible sense of the word.

GOD IS PERFECT

Perfect means complete. Every quality of an ideal person is present in God. None of these qualities exist in short measure in Him.

Observations on the Awesomeness of God

The word "awesome" as it is used in the popular culture has made a change in the last few decades that has departed from its historical meaning in the English language. The current meaning in the youth culture is only remotely related to its use in the Bible.

The Oxford Dictionary of New Words: A Popular Guide to Words in the News helps us see how the word "awesome" has become weakened in its use. On its meaning, it explains:

> In North American slang (especially among young people): marvelous, great, stunningly good. *Awesome* originally meant 'full of awe,' but by the end of the seventeenth century could also be used in the sense 'inspiring awe, dreadful.' The apparent reversal of meaning that has now taken place started through a weakening of the word's meaning during the middle decades of the twentieth century to 'staggering, remarkable'; this was then further weakened and turned into an enthusiastic term of approval in the eighties.
>
> Within the youth culture, terms of approval come into fashion and go out rapidly. After becoming frequent in its weakened sense of 'mind-boggling' during the sixties and seventies, awesome was taken up in the eighties as one of the most fashionable words in general approval among young Americans. In particular it was associated with the speech of preppies and the New York smart set, and often seemed to be part of a fixed phrase preceded by totally. Surprisingly, it has remained popular among young people into the nineties, and has spread outside the U.S. to Canada and Australia. It has been used in British English in this sense too, but really only in caricature of U.S. speech.[19]

In order to see how far the word *awesome* has strayed from its biblical roots, let us look at the meaning of the word *awe* in the Bible. Paul G. Chappell explains the biblical meaning of the word *awe* as:

> A profound reverence and respect for God which is tempered with fear. This acute reverence is characterized by solemn wonder mingled with dread in view of the great and terrible presence of the Supreme Being. The Hebrew word *yir'a* and the Greek word

phobos are used most commonly to refer to this holy fear or "fear of God." Awe is the most characteristic meaning of the term "fear" in the Bible and is based upon recognition and awareness of the holiness and supreme majesty of God.[20]

With regard to the proper response to the awesomeness of God, Ralph Enlow comments:

> When confronted with God's awesome presence the inevitable human response is to quiver and cower. In fact, the Bible never records a direct personal encounter with God in which the individual was not visibly shaken by God's awesomeness. When God appeared to Moses in the burning bush, Moses hid his face and trembled before God (Exod. 3:6). When Isaiah saw the Lord in his glory and majesty, he cried, "Woe is me, I am ruined!" (6:5). When the risen Christ appeared to Saul the persecutor on the Damascus road, Saul prostrated himself in fear and trembling (Acts 9:3).[21]

It is true that God is "remarkable," "mind-boggling," or "extraordinary." But, as we have seen, these words do not get at the heart of what is meant by either the biblical or the historical use of the word "awesome" as it was used in the English language. It is important that we make young people aware of the difference between the popular use of awesome and the biblical use of the word awesome. There may be some legitimate use of "awesome" as it is used by the young people with reference to God. However, it seems to me that this use should be temporary and should be set aside as he or she grows into maturity. It may be appropriate for a young person to say that God is "neat," or God is "cool," but I hardly think such terminology would be appropriate when falling from the lips of a mature Christian.

Perhaps the best solution for the problem will be for us to make frequent and proper use of words like awesome and holy . We need to confront people with that view of God that Moses, Isaiah, and Paul had when they were encountered by God as told in Exodus 3:6; Isaiah 6:5; and Acts 9:3. There is a place for people to experience fear of God. When the sinner is faced with the true awesomeness of God, he or she will become interested in the love, mercy, and grace of God as it is manifested to us in Jesus Christ. When the Christian is confronted with the true awesomeness of God, he or she will be ready for true worship and true service.

Concluding Observations

What we believe about the nature and attributes of God is of utmost importance. It pervades every area of life and thought. Any thought and any action that is not consistent with the nature and attributes of God will not stand the test.

The four basic values of holiness, love, wisdom, and ideals, as human values, find their foundation in God. Holiness, love, and wisdom find their foundation in the moral attributes of God. Ideals find their foundation in the overall characteristics of goodness and perfection. God has woven these values into the fabric of Truth and life. If we ignore them, we do it to our own hurt. If our life and thought are guided by them, they form the foundation for true thought and a happy life.

6

The Trinity

What we know about God, we know through revelation. We know something of the nature of God through general revelation. Since God is a personal being, plus the fact that He does not come within the view of the five senses, we are dependent upon special revelation if we are to know some things about Him. Our knowledge that God is a Trinity fits into this category. As Warfield observes: "In point of fact, the doctrine of the Trinity is purely a revealed doctrine. That is to say, it embodies a truth which has never been discovered, and is indiscoverable, by natural reason."[1]

Our belief in the Trinity is not the product of our reason. On the other hand, our reason knows of nothing about the Trinity that is in contradiction to reason. There is no contradiction between "one" and "three" applying to God unless we mean one and three in the same sense. Reason does not have to originate what it believes. Neither does it have to see how what it believes could have originated, on its own. Some truths are received by revelation before reason believes. Reason does not need to fully comprehend what it believes. In fact, in the vast realm of reality, reason expects to encounter difficulty in comprehending some things. It is incomprehensible that our finite minds could completely comprehend every truth. Reason needs to see that what is believed does not violate the law of non-contradiction, and that it forms a part of a vital system of knowledge. Each truth must be seen as a part of an explanation that gives meaning to the whole of reality.

The question of the compatibility of Trinitarian thought with the law of non-contradiction is meaningful only for those who recognize the validity of truth and reason. In Western thought we are talking about biblical Christianity and modernism. I would like to encourage those whose roots are in modernism to give serious thought to biblical Christianity.

When postmodernism rejects Truth, the law of non-contradiction (which is the fundamental law of rational thought), the moral "nature" of nature, and the aspiration for high ideals, it offends that which is dear to both modernism and biblical Christianity. While it is understandable that postmodernists would view the 200-year modernist experiment as a failure, it offends our whole being as humans to write off the existence of Truth, to embrace irrationality, to reject the categories of right and wrong, and to erase the distinctions between lower and higher in ideals. We do not have to write off all hope.

For those who are under the influence of the Postmodern Mood, the whole idea of the doctrine of the Trinity is a matter of personal preference. The question of the law of non-contradiction is irrelevant. I applaud the postmodernists for seeing through the failure of modernism. However, I would like to reissue my challenge to them to follow the example of Copernicus and reexamine the trail that led to the failure of modernism. Check out biblical Christianity.

Let us now turn our attention to the biblical basis for the doctrine of the Trinity.

There Is Only One God

One of the burdens of the Old Testament was to firmly establish in the minds of God's people that there is only one God (Dt. 6:4, 5; 1 Kg. 8:60; Is. 45:5, 6; 14:18; 46:9). This conviction is also clearly adhered to in the New Testament (Mk. 12:29;1 Cor. 8:4-6; and Jas. 2:19).

By the very nature of things, there could be but one who could in the fullest sense of the word be God. We ascribe infinity to God. There can be only one infinite being. The idea of two infinite beings is a logical contradiction. If we try to conceive of two unlimited beings, we run into the problem that if one cannot control the other he is not infinite in power. If he can control the other, the one he controls is not infinite in power. In trying to conceive of two infinite beings, we either conclude that neither is infinite, or we conclude that only one is infinite. We cannot attribute infinity to both. Both Scripture and logic support the conclusion that there is only one God.

The truth of only one God rules out the possibility of *tritheism* which teaches there are three gods, each having a distinct and separate essence. Tritheism has had very few adherents in the history of the church. It mainly serves as an error with which we contrast the proper understanding of the Trinity. Tritheism would maintain that the unity of the Godhead is in purpose and endeavor. We do not question that there is unity of purpose and endeavor between the three persons in the Godhead. However, this is not what we mean when we talk about one God.

When we say that there is one God, we mean that there is only one Being. There is only one *essence.* There is only one spirit-essence that is shared fully by all three persons.

Father, Son, and Holy Spirit Are Each Deity

THE FATHER IS DEITY

Since there is no debate over the deity of the Father, I will mention only a few references in support and will not proceed to develop the argument (2 Cor. 1:3; Eph. 1:3; 5:20; Col. 1:3; and others).

THE SON IS DEITY

One of the most seriously contested truths in the history of the church is the deity of Christ. Yet, it is clearly and unquestionably taught in Scripture both by direct statement and by necessary inference.

He is called God (Jn. 1:1; 20:28; Tit. 2:13; Heb. 1:8; and others). The Jehovah's Witnesses, who deny the deity of Christ, have insisted that John 1:1 cannot be used in support of the deity of Christ. In the statement "the Word was God," there is no article in the Greek before the word "God." They insist that it should be translated "The Word was a god."

To insist on the translation "a god" will not stand for the following reasons: (1) It would contradict the clear teachings of Scripture in other places which clearly indicate that Jesus is God in the fullest sense of the word. (2) It shows a lack of understanding of the use of the article and the absence of the article in Greek. As Dana and Mantey explain: "The articular construction emphasizes identity; the anarthrous [without the article] construction emphasizes character." On the basis of this distinction they explain that the Greek construction without the article "in the Word was God" "emphasizes Christ's participation in the essence of the divine nature."[2] The emphasis is on the divine nature of the Word. This understanding is true to the Greek and consistent with the whole of Scripture. It should also be pointed out that the presence of the article with "Word" and the absence of the article with God make it clear that "The Word" is the subject of the sentence. (3) There are many clear-cut references to deity where the article is not used. There are so many that it is hard to conceive the idea that anyone would conclude that the absence of the article in John 1:1 would indicate that Jesus was less than God in the full sense of the word. Some references from John in which the reference is clearly to deity, which have no article in the Greek before God, should be adequate rebuttal to such claims (Jn. 1:6, 12, 18; 3:2—first occurrence of the word "God" in the verse; and 16:30).

Some may want to question the use of Titus 2:13 as a claim that Jesus is called God. They may want to say that "the great God and our Saviour Jesus Christ" refers to two persons rather than one. Dana and Mantey quote Granville Sharp, who explains:

> When the copulative *kai* connects two nouns of the same case, if the article *ho* or any of its cases precedes the first of the said nouns or participles, and is not repeated before the second noun or participle, the latter always relates to the same person that is expressed or described by the first noun or participle; i.e., it denotes a farther description of the first-named person.[3]

Dana and Mantey proceed to point out that the same Greek construction referred to by Granville Sharp is found in 2 Peter 2:20 where it indicates that Jesus is both Lord and Savior. They also point to 2 Peter 1:1 where it means that Jesus is our God and Savior and to Titus 2:13 where it is asserted that Jesus is our great God and Savior.[4]

In furthering our proof of the deity of Christ, we observe that He is called the Son of God (Mt. 14:33; 16:16; 17:5; Mk. 1:1; 5:7; 14:61, 62; 15:39; Lk. 9:35; 10:22; Jn. 1:34; 3:16; 9:35-37; 20:31; and others).

It is clear that the Jews understood Jesus to be claiming to be deity when He claimed to be the Son of God. We read: "Therefore the Jews sought the more to kill him, because he not only had broken the sabbath, but said also that God was his Father, making himself equal with God" (Jn. 5:18). It is also clear from their charge and Jesus' answer in John 10:33-36 that they equated the claim of being the Son of God with being God. Jesus did not deny the charge. Rather, He defended His right to make the claim (Jn. 10:34-38).

Warfield observes:

> It may be very natural to see in the designation "Son" an intimation of subordination and derivation of Being, . . . But it is quite certain that this was not the denotation . . . in the Semitic consciousness, which underlies the phraseology of Scripture; and it may be thought doubtful whether it was included even in their remote suggestions. What underlies the conception of sonship in Scriptural speech is just "likeness"; whatever

the father is that the son is also. The emphatic application of the term "Son" to one of the Trinitarian Persons, accordingly, asserts rather His equality with the Father than His subordination to the Father.[5]

A third proof of Jesus' deity is His power to forgive sins. In Mark 2:1-11, Jesus said to the paralytic, "Son, thy sins be forgiven thee" (verse 5). The scribes objected saying, "Why doth this man thus speak blasphemies? Who can forgive sins but God only? " (verse 7) .

Jesus did not deny their charge that no one but God could forgive sins. Rather, He said:

> Whether is it easier to say to the sick of the palsy, Thy sins be forgiven thee; or to say, Arise, and take up thy bed, and walk? But that ye may know that the Son of man hath power on earth to forgive sins, (he saith to the sick of the palsy,) I say unto thee, Arise, and take up thy bed, and go thy way into thine house (verses 9-11).

Another proof of Jesus' deity is that He was and is the object of worship (Mt. 2:2; 9:18; 14:33; 15:25; 20:20; 28:9; Mk. 5:6; Lk. 24:52; Jn. 5:23; Rev. 5:8-14; and others). The Scriptures make it clear that only God is to be worshiped. Yet, Jesus was worshiped. He never denounced anyone for worshiping Him. He accepted it.

In the temptation, Jesus made it clear that God and God alone was the object of worship. He said to Satan, "For it is written, Thou shalt worship the Lord thy God, and him only shalt thou serve" (Mt. 4:10).

When Cornelius met Peter he fell down at his feet to worship him. "But Peter took him up, saying; Stand up; I myself also am a man" (Acts 10:26).

After the healing of a crippled man in Lystra, the people thought Paul and Barnabas were gods and were going to offer sacrifices to them. At the thought of receiving worship, Paul and Barnabas rent their clothes and assured the people that they were fellow human beings and were not to be worshiped (Acts 14:8-18).

In the Book of Revelation, on two occasions John was going to worship an angel that was speaking to him. The angel assured John that he was a fellow servant and was not to be worshiped (Rev. 19:9, 10; 22:8, 9).

In Acts 12, we read of the fate of Herod who was ready to be acclaimed a god after delivering an oration. "And immediately the angel of the Lord smote him, because he gave not God the glory: and he was eaten of worms, and gave up the ghost" (Acts 12:23).

In the light of the above observations, there can be no doubt that the fact that Jesus is a proper object of worship is an unquestionable proof of His deity. He made no refusal like Peter, Paul and Barnabas, and the angel John was about to worship. He met with no fate such as Herod. Truly, He is God!

A fifth proof of His deity is His eternal existence (Mic. 5:2; Jn. 1:1-3; and Col. 1:17). Only God exists from eternity. Yet, Jesus has existed from eternity. Therefore, He is God.

Other proofs could be added, but the case already built is more than adequate. There can be no justification for denying the deity of Christ, or understanding the term to have any less or any different significance when applied to the Son than when applied to the Father.

THE HOLY SPIRIT IS DEITY

The main issue concerning the divine nature of the members of the Trinity has always centered in Jesus. There does not seem to have been any wide scale attempt to advocate a binitarian view of the Godhead consisting of the Father and Son, but failing to grant deity to the Holy Spirit. Therefore, I will give only limited attention to supporting the deity of the Holy Spirit.

When we see the Holy Spirit in Scripture, we always receive the impression that He is a member of the Godhead. The reference to the Holy Spirit in Matthew 28:19 and 2 Corinthians 13:14 view the Holy Spirit as being equal with the Father and the Son.

The strongest support for the deity of the Holy Spirit comes from references in which He is called God. In Acts 5:3 Peter asked Ananias, "Why hath Satan filled thine heart to lie to the Holy Ghost?" In Acts 5:4, Peter said to Ananias, "Thou hast not lied unto men, but unto God." In 1 Corinthians 3:16 Paul says, "Know ye not that ye are the temple of God, and that the Spirit of God dwelleth in you?" The Spirit of God dwells in the temple of God. It is clear that the Spirit of God is viewed as God. In 1 Corinthians 12:4-11, Paul elaborates on the various ways the Holy Spirit works in us through bestowing gifts upon us. In verse 6 with reference to this work of the Holy Spirit, Paul explains: "And there are diversities of operations, but it is the same God which worketh all in all." The Holy Spirit is clearly referred to here as God.

The Father, Son, and Holy Spirit Are Each Distinct Persons

MODALISM FAILS TO SEE THREE PERSONS IN THE GODHEAD

The support presented above for the belief in one God and for the belief in the deity of the Father, the Son, and the Holy Spirit has been acceptable to some who have fallen short of a Trinitarian view of the Godhead. The view known as modalism was introduced into the third century by Sabellius. Sabellius believed in a Trinity of *revelation,* not an *ontological* Trinity. (An ontological Trinity is a Trinity of being. God is a Trinity in the very nature of His being.)

There have been varying shades of modalism, but there are basically two types: (1) The names of God are names for particular periods in the history of revelation: The Father in creation and the giving of the Law, the Son in redemption, and the Holy Spirit in regeneration and sanctification. Some might say He was Father in the Old Testament, Son in the Gospels, and the Holy Spirit in Acts and continuing in the church. (2) The names are understood as titles relating to the different functions such as one person may be a father, husband, and businessman. This is similar to the first, but differs in that God can be viewed as all three at the same time.

SUGGESTED PROOFS OF MODALISM

Before setting forth the positive teaching of Scripture that will support Trinitarianism and show the fallacy of modalism, let us first take a look at two suggested proofs of modalism.

John 10:30

In John 10:30, Jesus said, "I and my Father are one." It is felt by some that they have found irrefutable proof that Jesus taught that the Father and the Son were one person.

A very interesting parallel is found in 1 Corinthians 3:8, "Now he that planteth and he that watereth are one." The Greek for "are one" is *hen eisin* in 1 Corinthians 3:8. The Greek for "are one" in John 10:30 is *hen esmen.* The construction is identical except that in 1 Corinthians 3:8 *eisin* is third person plural to correspond with the subject, "he that planteth and he that watereth." In John 10:30 *esmen* is first person plural to correspond with the subject, "I and my Father."

In 1 Corinthians 3:8, "he that planteth and he that watereth" definitely refer to two persons; namely, Paul and Apollos. If 1 Corinthians refers to two persons as "one," there is no reason whatever that the Father and Son cannot be two persons who are said to be one. The very fact that Jesus said, "My Father" makes it far more suitable to think of them as being two persons instead of one person.

In what sense were Paul and Apollos one? They were one in that there was no division among them. They were in agreement. The church was becoming divided over Paul and Apollos; yet, Paul and Apollos were in agreement. They were one.

Jesus and the Father are one in that they are in total agreement, but the oneness goes much deeper than that. That could be true in Tritheism. They are one in that they have the same essence.

Matthew 28:19

The singular use of the word "name" in Matthew 28:19 has frequently been urged as proof that "the Father, Son, and Holy Spirit" are all one person in this verse. The name of this person is said to be Jesus.

A case cannot be built for the conclusion that the singular use of the word "name" requires that the Father, Son, and Holy Spirit all have one name. In 1 Samuel 14:49, the first occurrence of the word "name" is in the plural in the English translation, but in the Hebrew it is singular, yet it is followed by two names. The same thing happens in 1 Samuel 17:13. The singular is used of the word "name" and it is followed by three names. It is not impossible that something similar to this could have happened in Matthew 28:19.

Though the above explanation shows that one cannot build a conclusive case from the singular use of "name" for saying that there must be one name applied to the Father, Son, and Holy Spirit, I think there is a more probable explanation for the verse. The use of the word "name" in Scripture, as can be seen by the use of a concordance, is not limited to the designation by which a person is called. "Name" refers to the person, his character, his reputation, his power, his authority, etc. When Proverbs 22:1 says, "A good name is rather to be chosen than great riches" it is clear that it is not referring to a good first name, nor a good last name, but a good reputation based on good character. When Peter said in Acts 3:16, "And his name through faith in his name hath made this man strong," he meant the power and authority of Jesus Christ.

In keeping with the biblical use of the word "name," which also finds parallels in our own use of the word, it seems best not to understand "name" in Matthew 28:19 as a designation, whether thinking of one or three, by which a person (or persons) is called. Rather, the name refers to the character, power, and authority of the Father, Son, and Holy Spirit.

PROBLEMS WITH MODALISM
The Father, Son, and Holy Spirit Have Objective Relationships One to Another

The Father says, "This is my beloved Son" (Mt. 3:17). The Father sent the Son (Jn. 3:34; 14:24). The Father loves the Son (Jn. 3:35). The Father sent the Holy Spirit (Jn. 14:16, 26).

The Son prayed to the Father (Jn. 17). The Son went to the Father (Jn. 16:16). The Son sent the Holy Spirit (Jn. 16:7).

The Holy Spirit testifies of the Son (Jn. 15:26). The Holy Spirit glorifies the Son (Jn. 16:14).

The interrelationships within the members of the Godhead rule out that form of modalism that sees the names Father, Son, and Holy Spirit as titles relating to the different functions of God. It is true that one person may be father, husband, and businessman, but he does not in these roles experience interpersonal relationships. All of us have more than one role in life, but a writing of our autobiography or biography would not lead people to think of one of us as being two or more sane, intelligent persons. We cannot escape the reality that in the New Testament we see God as three distinct persons.

The Father, Son, and Holy Spirit Are Concurrent

All three were present at the baptism of Jesus (Mt. 3:16, 17; Mk. 1:10, 11; Lk. 3:21, 22). The reference to the Father, Son, and Holy Spirit in Matthew 28:19 and 2 Corinthians 13:14 also indicate that the Father, Son, and the Holy Spirit are concurrent.

The concurrence of the Father, Son, and Holy Spirit rule out the modalism which says that the names of God are names for particular periods in the history of revelation.

An error is commonly made by Trinitarians when they speak of the Father being revealed in the Old Testament, the Son in the Gospels, and the Holy Spirit in Acts and the epistles. In the Old Testament, God was revealed as God without reference to which person was being revealed. In the New Testament, we have the revelation of the Trinity. It is true that Jesus is the center of the gospels, but it is also the time of the revelation of the Father and Holy Spirit as distinct members of the Godhead. It is true that we receive a greater understanding of the Holy Spirit beginning with Acts, but the Son continues to be the central person so far as the focus of redemptive revelation is concerned.

We know less about the doctrine of the Father, so far as His distinct role is concerned, than we do about the roles of the Son and Holy Spirit. In a few books, the section dealing with nature and attributes of God is called the doctrine of the Father. This is an error. What is said about the nature and attributes of God is equally true of the Father, Son, and Holy Spirit. Some books may make a few specific statements about the Father, but this does not justify calling the section the doctrine of the Father.

I am not aware of any well-developed doctrine of God the Father. Perhaps, this is not as unfortunate as it seems in view of the roles of the Son and Holy Spirit in redemption and our need of knowledge of these roles. Part of the reason for the lack of a well-developed doctrine of God the Father is that His role is not always as easily distinguished as that of the Son and Holy Spirit. Perhaps, for that reason, we are about as well off to have our discussion of the Father interwoven with our discussion of the Son and Holy Spirit.

The Trinity Is Intimated in the Old Testament

Without the aid of the New Testament revelation, no one would read a Trinitarian concept out of the Old Testament. However, once the Trinity is revealed we can with the aid of that revelation see that some statements of the Old Testament are better understood in the light of the Trinitarian revelation. As Warfield explains:

> The Old Testament may be likened to a chamber richly furnished but dimly lighted; the introduction of light brings into it nothing which was not in it before; but it brings out into clearer view much of what is in it but was only dimly or even not at all perceived before. The mystery of the Trinity is not revealed in the Old Testament; but the mystery of the Trinity underlies the Old Testament revelation, and here and there almost comes into view.[6]

CLEAR INTIMATIONS OF THE TRINITY

In speaking, God uses the plural pronoun "us" (Gen. 1:26; 3:22; 11:7). Once the revelation of the Trinity has been made known, it seems clear that we should understand the "us" in these references as referring to the persons in the Trinity.

Having seen the revelation of the Son in the New Testament, we would naturally interpret the Father and Son in Psalm 2:7 which reads: "I will declare the decree: the LORD hath said unto me, Thou art my Son; this day have I begotten thee." Having seen the Holy Spirit as a distinct person in the New Testament, we would interpret references such as Genesis 1:2; 6:3; and Psalm 51:11 as making references to the Holy Spirit.

In Hosea 1:7, it seems that we see two divine persons rather than one. "But I will have mercy upon the house of Judah, and will save them by the LORD their God." "I" and "the LORD their God" seem to be, in the light of the Trinitarian revelation, a reference to two persons in the Trinity.

SOME SUGGESTED INTIMATIONS OF THE TRINITY IN THE OLD TESTAMENT SEEM TO BE INVALID

One of the most commonly suggested intimations of the Trinity in the Old Testament is the use of the plural name for God, *Elohim*. Though it is plural it is used with a singular verb in Genesis

1:1, 26, and 48:15. The use of a plural, I think, is properly understood by G. F. Oehler. After rejecting various interpretations of the plural, among them being that it implies the Trinity, he explains:

> It is much better to explain *Elohim* as the *quantitative plural,* which is used to denote unlimited greatness in *shamayim* [heavens] and *mayim* [waters]. The plural signifies infinite fulness of the might and power which lies in the divine Being, and thus passes over into the *intensive plural,* as Delitzsch has named it.[7]

Another illustration of the intensive plural is found in Isaiah 53:9. The word "death" is plural in the Hebrew. The plural was used to show that this was not just an ordinary death.

There is justification for using the intensive plural to show the greatness of God. To seek to show the plurality of persons by using the plural for the name God would run the risk of Tritheism.

What is referred to as the Trisagia (an expression where the word "holy" is repeated three times with reference to God) in Isaiah 6:3 is thought by some to be an intimation of the Trinity. I fail to see in the repetition of the word holy three times any reference to three persons. It seems far more likely that it is intended to magnify the holiness of God.

Some see in the threefold blessing of the Aaronic benediction in Numbers 6:24-26 a blessing from each member of the Trinity. Again, I see no connection. The only connection is in three blessings and there are three persons in the Trinity. It seems to take more connection than that to read an inference of the Trinity from the passage.

How Do We Explain the Trinity?

Frequently, though a person has a clear faith in the Trinity, he will tend to drift toward tritheism or modalism in his attempt to explain the Trinity. For this reason, we must consider a person's training and ability to express himself before we judge him a heretic on the basis of the way he explains the Trinity. The explanation that explains the oneness of God as unity of purpose and endeavor does not distinguish itself properly from tritheism. There is unity of purpose and endeavor between the persons in the Godhead, but that is not what is meant by the statment that God is one God. When we say that there is only one God, we mean that there is only one divine essence. Each person shares the entire divine essence.·

We have to be careful when we explain the Trinity by saying that there are three personal manifestations. That could mean three persons who manifest themselves, or it could mean one person who manifests himself three ways as in modalism. It is better to use the word "persons" rather than personal manifestations to avoid confusion.

The word *person* is better than the word *personality*. Though it is possible to use person and personality in the same way, there is a tendency to think of personality more in terms of personality traits. If we say that there are three personalities in the Godhead, we run the risk of someone taking us to mean that the Father, Son, and Holy Spirit have different personality traits. This is not the case. The use of the word person helps avoid this misunderstanding.

The main thing to keep in mind is that there are three persons in one essence. As additional clarifying statements, we can say each person shares the entire essence. The personal distinctions are eternal. The persons are equal. Each person can say "I." With reference to others, He can address them as "Thou," or He can refer to each of the others as "He."

Illustrations of the Trinity are risky. They either illustrate tritheism or modalism. The one egg made up of yolk, white, and shell illustrates tritheism because the yolk, white, and shell each have a different essence. The illustration of the three members of a family making up one family illustrates tritheism because each member has a different essence. The illustration of water, steam, and ice illustrates modalism because, though they have the same substance or essence, they are not concurrent. No illustration properly illustrates both the oneness and threeness of God. I am not suggesting that illustrations should never be used. I am suggesting that we understand the problems involved with illustrations. The ultimate aim should be to get people to understand apart from illustrations.

By the Trinity is meant that the Father, Son, and Holy Spirit are three co-eternal and co-equal persons, who experience interpersonal relationships, existing in one divine essence with each person sharing the entire essence.

How Are We to Understand the Names Father, Son, and Holy Spirit?

Do the names have an ontological significance? Another way of putting it is: Is there something in the very nature of the Trinity that causes the Father by His nature to be called Father, the Son by His nature to be called Son, and the Holy Spirit by His nature to be called Holy Spirit? Or are the names Father, Son, and Holy Spirit related to their functions in the economy of redemption?

Since there should be less difficulty in making the decision, let us begin with the name Holy Spirit. Is there something about the very nature of the Holy Spirit that causes Him to be called Holy Spirit rather than one of the others, or is it because of His function? If the word "Spirit" is in His name because He has a spirit-essence, the same is equally true of the other members of the Trinity. If the word "Holy" is in His name because He is holy, the same is equally true of the other members of the Trinity. Is He not called the Holy Spirit because of His special ministry to convict us of sin, draw people to Christ, regenerate those who believe, and continue the work of sanctification in believers? In short, He is to work in us to make us holy people.

If we can accept the view of functional significance with reference to the name Holy Spirit, it should not be so painful to do the same with reference to the Father and Son. The problem here comes from the doctrine of the eternal generation of the Son from the Father.

Origen introduced the doctrine of the eternal generation of the Son in the third century. It has been generally accepted by orthodox theologians. There are some, however, who disagree. After carefully examining what is thought to be Scriptural support for the doctrine of the eternal generation of the Son, Buswell comments:

We have above examined all the instances in which "begotten" or "born" or related words are applied to Christ, and we can say with confidence that the Bible has nothing whatsoever to say about "begetting" as an eternal relationship between the Father and the Son. The suggestion that we completely drop the doctrine of eternal generation of the Son is somewhat revolutionary. We might be misunderstood. . . . Yet I do believe that the "eternal generation" doctrine should be dropped.[8]

The eternal generation of the Son from the Father refers to an eternal emanation of the Son from the Father. It is not an emanation or generation of the essence because He has the same essence as the Father. It is a generation of the person. This is not supposed to mean that the Father was before the Son because the generation was eternal. Those who hold to this view consider the generation of the Son by the Father to be the basis of the names Father and Son. The names Father and Son are thus considered to have an ontological significance.

After referring to John 3:16; 5:26; 10:38; 14:11; 17:21; and Hebrews 1:3 as verses used to support the eternal generation of the Son, Loraine Boettner remarks:

The present writer feels constrained to say, however, that in his opinion the verses quoted do not teach the doctrine in question. He feels that the primary purpose of these verses is to teach that Christ is intimately associated with the Father, that He is equal with the Father in power and glory, that He is, in fact, full Deity, rather than to teach that His Person is generated by or originates in an eternal process which is going on in the Godhead. Even though the attempt is made to safeguard the essential equality of the Son by saying that the process by which He is generated is eternal and necessary, he does not feel that the attempt is successful.[9]

To me the expression "eternal generation" is self-contradictory. Generation implies a process that has a beginning. Eternal denies the idea of beginning. To try to modify generation by eternal attempts to deny the idea of beginning. The whole idea of an eternal generation is incomprehensible. It is not incomprehensible simply because it is beyond comprehension, but because it speaks of a process that implies beginning as though it has no beginning.

We do not refuse to believe an idea because it is incomprehensible, but when it is incomprehensible because it appears self-contradictory, it would require unquestionable support in the biblical revelation before we should be expected to believe it. The verses cited above along with Psalm 2:7 fail to make such an impression on me. For those who would like a thorough examination of the main verses used to support eternal generation, I would recommend Buswell's treatment cited above, pages 106-111.

At this point attention needs also to be given to the eternal procession from the Father and Son of the Holy Spirit. It is basically the same as the eternal generation of the Son except the Son is generated from the Father while the Holy Spirit proceeds from the Father and the Son.

John 15:26 is the verse used to support the eternal procession of the Holy Spirit. The words "proceedeth from the Father" are adequately understood as being sent by the Father as He was sent on the day of Pentecost. I would present the same case against the eternal procession of the Holy Spirit that I did against the eternal generation of the Son. It is doubtful that anyone believes in the eternal procession of the Holy Spirit who does not believe in the eternal generation of the Son. Both Buswell and Boettner reject the doctrine of the eternal procession of the Holy Spirit.

I have already pointed out that I think the name Holy Spirit is a functional name rather than an ontological name. The name Holy Spirit is fully consistent with the ontological nature of the Holy Spirit, but the same could also be said about the Father and Son.

If the doctrine of the eternal generation of the Son from the Father fails, there are no grounds for granting an ontological significance to the name Father and Son as members of the Trinity. There is nothing distinctive in the ontological nature of the members of the Trinity that would make the names more appropriate for one than the other.

The names Father and Son seem to have been chosen for the members of the Trinity designated Father and Son because their functional relationship in redemption, particularly as it relates to the incarnation, somewhat parallels a father and son relationship. There is certainly no ontological subordination of one member of the Trinity to another, but there is some voluntary functional subordination in some developments in the economy of redemption. There is a voluntary subordination of the Son to the Father (Jn. 6:38, 39; Lk. 22:41, 42; and others). That the Holy Spirit is sent by the Father and Son (Jn. 14:16, 26; 15:26) implies some functional subordination.

Warfield observes:

> It may be natural to assume that a subordination in modes of operation rests on a subordination in modes of subsistence; that the reason why it is the Father that sends the Son and the Son sends the Spirit is that the Son is subordinate to the Father, and the Spirit to the Son. But we are bound to bear in mind that these relations of subordination in modes of operation may just as well be due to a convention, and agreement, between the Persons of the Trinity—a "covenant" as it is technically called—by virtue of which a distinct function in the work of redemption is voluntarily assumed by each.[10]

As long as we realize that the subordination refers to a voluntary arrangement, and not an ontological subordination, there is no inequality implied.

One more question remains: Are the names Father, Son, and Holy Spirit eternal names of the persons? I would say yes, not based on ontological significance, but on the concept that the redemptive plan is an eternal plan. In eternal anticipation of the functions ascribed to each member of the Trinity they have been eternally Father, Son, and Holy Spirit.

7

Testing Worldviews

In seeking to establish the truth of Christianity, some begin by trying to prove the existence of God. They do this by using *effect* to *cause* arguments such as the cosmological arguments and the teleological arguments. They seek to prove that the Bible is the Word of God through arguments based on the indestructibility of the Bible, the unity and nobility of thought of the Bible, the influence for good that the Bible has had, and fulfilled prophecy.

Others seek to prove that Jesus was raised bodily from the grave. It is their conviction that if the truth of the bodily resurrection of Christ is established that it establishes the truth of the claims of Christ. God's existence would be necessarily accepted and the truth of Scripture would necessarily follow.[1]

I prefer to take the approach of testing worldviews for validity. Since our interest is mainly with the Christian worldview, the modernist worldview, and the postmodern anti-worldview, we will test these views for truthfulness and adequacy.[2] This study will not be exhaustive. It will get to the heart of the matter. It will give a perspective on how we would go about testing these worldviews (or anti-worldviews).

One of the concerns that we have when we test worldviews is the relationship between *faith* and *reason*. By faith as we are using it now, we are referring to faith in God and the Bible, or to speak more broadly, religious faith, or knowledge of what is in the *upper story*. The *lower story* deals with the physical world. The *upper story* deals with moral and religious experiences. The *inescapable questions of life* reflect our concern for *upper story* knowledge.

Part of our problem when we talk about religious knowledge is that we are talking about faith-knowledge. In faith-knowledge, we believe something to be true that does not fall within the purview of the five senses.

Even in our daily experiences we have faith-knowledge. We believe something to be true that does not, at the time of our believing it, fall within this view of the five senses. It may, however, in principle be capable of being observed, but we believe it before it is observed.

Faith-knowledge is illustrated by what took place when some men took me 'coon (raccoon) hunting once. The dogs barked which indicated that they had treed something. I was a novice at 'coon hunting, but my partners were old hands at it. They assured me that there was a 'coon up the tree. I did not see it, neither did they because the leaves were too thick on the tree. One of the men did see what looked like a reflection from the eye of an animal when he shined his flashlight up the tree. They assured me that there was a 'coon up the tree on the following grounds: (1) The dogs would not continue to bark if they were not sure that something was up the tree. (2) The tree was larger than 'possums (opossums) usually climbed, but not too large for a 'coon. (3) If there was need for proof, the reflection of light was a sure indication that an animal was up the tree. Based on the integrity of the hunters, their experience in 'coon hunting, and their confidence in the dogs, I, too, believed that there was a 'coon up the tree. That was faith-knowledge because I did not see a 'coon.

While my knowledge of a 'coon up the tree was faith-knowledge, it was not without an involvement of reason. The reasons did not furnish absolute empirical proof that there was a 'coon up the tree, but the reasons did make believing completely compatible with reason.

I realize that my faith-knowledge in God differs from my faith-knowledge of the 'coon in the tree. These men had seen 'coons up trees. No person has seen God. Yet, I think the mere fact that I was believing something I did not see, hear, touch, taste, or smell means that there are at least some comparisons. The main comparisons with which I am concerned are: (1) We do make use of faith-knowledge. (2) Reason is involved in faith-knowledge.

The Relationship Between Reason and Faith

There are various opinions regarding the relationship between reason and faith. They range anywhere from complete confidence in reason to support faith to a total rejection of any possible involvement in faith.

COMPLETE CONFIDENCE IN REASON TO SUPPORT FAITH

Some are boldly confident that the arguments for the existence of God offer proof that God exists. It is thought to be impossible to refute these proofs.

REASON NOT INVOLVED IN FAITH

This view restricts the working area of reason to the *lower story*. Reason only works with data that are gathered by observation and experience. Reason does not apply to the *upper story*. The *upper story* is irrational.

According to the approach under consideration, the law of non-contradiction does not apply to *upper story* knowledge. Faith, with reference to the *upper story,* is neither produced by reason, nor is it subject to examination by reason. Contemporary theologians who deny that God has given us information about Himself, man, and His plan for human beings tend to take this position. Neo-orthodox theologians, Karl Barth and Emil Brunner were the first to popularize the idea of a denial of a place of reason in faith.

A DISTRUST IN REASON

This view does not accept the idea that what is in the *upper story* is irrational, but it does distrust the reasoning power of man, especially as it is affected by the fall of man into sin. The advocates of this view do not hesitate to use reason when it seems to be of value, but they retreat into distrust for reason when difficulty arises. They call attention to verses like 1 Corinthians 1:21 where Paul said: "For after that in the wisdom of God the world by wisdom knew not God, it pleased God by the foolishness of preaching to save them that believe." They also call attention to 1 Corinthians 2:14 which reads: "But the natural man receiveth not the things of the Spirit of God: for they are foolishness unto him: neither can he know them, because they are spiritually discerned." This approach is more of a popular approach than one held by scholars.

REASON INVOLVED IN FAITH

This view differs from the first view in that it does not propose to give absolute proof for faith-knowledge. It differs from the second view in that it has a place for reason in upper story knowledge. The difference between this view and the third view varies from person to person depending on the degree of distrust the person has of reason. Since the third view does not make a complete rejection of reason in faith-knowledge, there will be some likeness. The use the third view makes of reason will be far more in accord with the fourth view than the first view. At times those who distrust reason make it sound as if reason has no place at all in faith. In fact, they make it sound as if reason is an enemy of faith. At other times they use reason.

I believe the fourth view is the correct view. Human beings are deeply rational. According to Colossians 3:10, the image of God in man includes the fact that we are rational. It is impossible for a human being to completely suppress his rationality. We cannot avoid using reason and having rational concerns.

I do not think it is the place of reason to seek to find some neutral platform and seek to prove the existence of God and to prove that the Bible is the product of divine revelation. It is beyond doubt that a person cannot by rational reflection on the data of observation and experience find a way to be right with God. This is apparently what is meant by 1 Corinthians 1:21 and 2:9.

While Christian thought is anchored in both general revelation and special revelation, the message of redemption comes only by special revelation. The basics of the Christian worldview come to us as a given for our consideration. When reason is used with sincerity, diligence, and integrity, it is necessary and valuable in determining the truth or falsity of a worldview. While we may have to believe without having all of our questions answered and without having all of our problems solved, we dare not accept a worldview that our reason tells us fails the test of rational consistency.

The Way to Test Worldviews for Validity

I believe that there are four criteria that a worldview must pass if it is to be accepted as true and worthy of our serious consideration. These are: (1) Does it answer the *inescapable questions of life?* (2) Is there internal consistency, i.e., is the structure logically related to the foundation? Do all the parts fit consistently together? (3) Is there causal adequacy, i.e., are the causes adequate to produce the effects attributed to them? (4) Does it conform to that which is undeniably true?

The first test is: Does it give answers to the hard questions of life that will equip me to live in the real world? Or, does it help me to find answers that will help me cope with life?

The second and third tests would involve what philosophers call coherence. They deal with whether a worldview is logically consistent. If it is rationally consistent, it will not violate the law of non-contradiction. All of the parts will fit together to make up a systematic, integrated, and harmonious whole. While the third test is implied in the second test, I believe it is better to treat it separately. The significance of causal adequacy in apologetics means that it deserves separate treatment.[3]

The fourth test raises the question of whether the worldview contradicts that which we know to be unquestionably true based on our observation and experience. Does it pass the empirical test? This test involves what philosophers call the test of correspondence.

Testing the Modernist Worldview for Validity

Even though modernism is no longer on the throne in secular thought, it is still around. Many, even in academic circles, are still operating on the modernist paradigm. Therefore, it must still be dealt with. Also, it must be dealt with because it did profess to be a worldview (or at least was striving to develop a worldview).

Let's look at the third criterion. Is there causal adequacy? Are the causes capable of producing the effects ascribed to them?

Thorough going modernism ascribes no activity to a divine being. It is based on naturalism. Naturalism works on the assumption that the only kind of causes that are at work in the whole of reality are natural causes. That is true of both the past and the future.

Modernism is forced to believe that matter is eternal. Some may speak of energy rather than matter, but that is only a matter of terminology. From the viewpoint of naturalism either matter is eternal, or "nothing" created matter out of nothing. The latter is unthinkable. There can be no proof that matter is eternal, but in modernism it is a logical necessity.

The next problem is that either life must have been eternal, or it must have originated from lifeless matter. It is quite a burden to be borne by the intellect, but the usual belief of modernism is that life originated from lifeless matter. This is considered to be an easier burden on the mind than believing that life has been eternal.

Modernism is in effect giving many of the attributes and activities usually ascribed to deity to matter. Matter is eternal. Matter is the Creator. Does matter seem to be capable of all this? Modernism fails the test of causal adequacy.

Another weak point of modernism is that it gives no adequate explanation for the presence of the *inescapable questions of life* and for the concerns which are represented by these questions. Why the question, "Is there a God?" if there is no God? Modernism in its 200 year reign failed to give sure answers to questions such as: Is there life after death? If so, how can I prepare for it? Why am I so concerned about right and wrong? How can I know what is right and wrong? Why are human beings so prone to be religious? Why is it that we cannot just turn these questions off? Modernism gave no satisfactory answers to these questions nor to why we have these questions.

The image of God in man longs for all of our knowledge to be rationally consistent. This includes both *lower story* knowledge and *upper story* knowledge. Modernism sought to develop a rationally consistent and unified view of the whole of reality, but never succeeded.

No one can deny that human beings have *moral* and *religious* experiences. But empiricism cannot discover Truth to guide these experiences. Empirical research can take surveys and find what percentage of people, at a given time, believe that sex outside marriage is wrong, but it cannot tell us whether sex outside marriage is wrong. There is the problem of moving from the realm of IS to the realm of OUGHT. Empiricism *cannot* make this transition. This inability means that empiricism can never produce an adequate worldview.

Though empiricism tried valiantly to produce a true worldview and find answers for human need, it was an utter failure. When this failure was recognized, the modernist ship of secular humanism was abandoned. Postmodernism became the main mode of thought that shapes the direction of the culture.

Testing the Postmodernist "Anti-worldview" for Validity

It is hard to test a view that makes no Truth claims. Only one of the four tests for testing worldviews is relevant at all. Does it answer the *inescapable questions of life?* These questions come from our innermost being. They are a cry for help. The human heart is hoping for answers that will help in coping with lostness, emptiness, loneliness, boredom, and wretchedness. Rather than answering these questions, postmodernism rejects all Truth claims as "false" and accepts all Truth claims as "true." I am quite certain that deep within every human being there is something that revolts against such thinking (or should we say non-thinking?).

When postmodernists announced the sinking of the ship of secular humanism, they did not announce the arrival of a more seaworthy vessel. Instead of boarding a ship that, at least claimed to sail under the banner of Truth, they deny the existence of Truth. The stormy seas of life must be faced without Truth. There is no ship of Truth. There is no Captain who can navigate the sea of life. The only ships that sail the ocean of life are fictitious ships. Different societies construct their own narratives. These narratives are fictions that enable people who believe them to face the problems and struggles of life. With all of this talk about living by fictitious constructions of narratives, it is time for someone to boldly proclaim, "The emperor has no clothes."[4]

Since narratives are not to be judged as true or false, the postmodernists proclaim tolerance. Though they call for tolerance, they do not always practice tolerance. Gene Edward Veith reminds us:

> Those who celebrate the achievements of Western civilization are accused of a narrow-minded "Euro-centrism"; this view is challenged by "Afro-centrism," which exalts Africa as the pinnacle of civilization. Male-dominant thought is replaced by feminist models. "Patriarchal religions" such as Judaism and Christianity are challenged and replaced with matriarchal religions; the influence of the Bible is countered by the influence of "goddess-worship." Homosexuality must no longer be considered a psychological problem; rather, homophobia is.[5]

While preaching tolerance, postmodernists are prompting division and strife. I will never forget the words of a gentleman who was seated next to me on an airplane some years ago. He said,

"A slave's idea of freedom is to own slaves." It seems to me that for many postmodernists freedom from oppression means to bring someone else under oppression.

At the same time that they preach freedom to construct your own meaning for life, they proclaim determinism. Knowledge is socially constructed. The individual "I" is lost in the collective "We" of society. The individual is just a cog in the social machine. The cog is moved along by the machine. The image of God in man is not happy with this.

I commend postmodernists for recognizing that empiricism cannot produce an adequate worldview. This puts them on the side of the Apostle Paul.[6] However, their own approach is proving to be not only ineffective, but disastrous. Is there any other possible result that can come from: the death of Truth, the death of reason, the death of a moral consensus, the death of nature, and the death of a concern for and a consensus on high ideals? If the reign of postmodernism would remain unchecked, it would eventually be not only the death of the soul, but also the death of science (no order to nature) and the death of civilization (no moral consensus and no consensus on ideals).

For those who find themselves struggling on the sea of life, the "Old Ship of Zion" (the ship of salvation piloted by Jesus Christ) is sailing these same troubled waters. It is seaworthy. The passengers are singing:

> Jesus, Savior, pilot me,
> Over life's tempestuous sea;
> Unknown waves before me roll,
> Hiding rocks and treach'rous shoal;
> Chart and compass come from Thee—
> Jesus, Savior, pilot me!
>
> As a mother stills her child,
> Thou canst hush the ocean wild;
> Boist'rous waves obey Thy will
> When Thou say'st to them, "Be still!"
> Wondrous Sov'reign of the sea,
> Jesus, Savior, pilot me!
>
> When at last I near the shore,
> And the fearful breakers roar
> 'Twixt me and the peaceful rest,
> Then, while leaning on Thy breast,
> May I hear Thee say to me,
> "Fear not—I will pilot thee!"[7]

The Old Ship of Zion is well stocked with rescue equipment. The Captain is saying:

Throw out the Life-Line to danger fraught men,
Sinking in anguish where you've never been:
Winds of temptation and billows of woe
Will soon hurl them out where the dark waters flow.

Soon will the season of rescue be o'er,
Soon will they drift to eternity's shore;
Haste then, my brother—no time for delay,
But throw out the Life-line and save them today.

Throw out the Life-Line!
Throw out the Life-Line!
Someone is drifting away;
Throw out the Life-Line!
Throw out the Life-Line!
Someone is sinking today.[8]

If you are tired of struggling with guilt and the problems of life, if you long for purpose and meaning, if your being cries out for a rational view of life, heed the words of Jesus, when He said, "Come unto me all ye who labour and are heavy laden, and I will give you rest" (Mt. 11:28).

Testing the Christian Worldview for Validity

I will give brief attention later to the question of proofs for the existence of God. At the present, let me simply say that even if a well trained person could prove the existence of God, then prove that the Bible is the Word of God, and then prove that Jesus is God-incarnate, and then prove that all other worldviews are false that is not the way the vast majority of people come to faith. At the same time, I want to say that no person in coming to faith sets reason aside. Christian faith is rational.

We do not stand outside the Christian worldview and prove the main points of the Christian Worldview and then assemble the Christian worldview. The Christian worldview already exists. It predates us. We do not stand outside the Christian worldview and examine it. There is no place to stand outside the Christian worldview. Whatever the true worldview is, we are a part of it. We are deeply involved in it. We look at the worldview from within and apply the test. The basics of the Christian worldview come to us as given ideas. They are given to us for our examination. We test these ideas for reasonableness and adequacy.

Both modernism and postmodernism fail the test as it relates to the *inescapable questions of life*. At this point our belief in the Christian worldview comes in strong. To the question, "Is there a God?" the answer is yes. To the question, "How can we know Him?" the answer is through general revelation, the Bible, and Jesus Christ. To the question, "Is there life after death?" the answer is yes. To the question, "How can we prepare for life after death?" the answer is through faith in our Lord and Savior Jesus Christ. To the question, "How can we know what is right and what is wrong?" the answer is through our moral constitution and the moral revelation of God in the Bible.

These answers bring peace and satisfaction to the deepest longings of our innermost being. We expect any system of Truth that attempts to explain the whole of reality to do this. This makes us citizens of a rational universe. We are not abandoned. *Inescapable questions* have answers. These questions are not there to tantalize and confuse. They are there to prepare us to expect and receive the true answers. Just as thirst prepares one for water and hunger prepares one for food, these questions and the longings they represent prepare us for a knowledge of God and an experience with God.

I am aware that what I am saying does not prove there is a God. It does show that belief in God is reasonable. We are not dealing simply with *cause* and *effect* at this point. We are not saying that God is the cause and the *inescapable questions* are the *effect*. That is true, but these observations involve more than that.

In a rational worldview we have not only adequate *cause* and *effect* relationships, but also "togetherness," "cohesiveness," and "interrelatedness." Truth is a functioning system. Ideas fit together. In a rationally consistent worldview, the ideas have an interlocking relationship to each other. To believe in God answers the questions of our innermost being and fills the longings of our deepest being in such a way that these ideas and experiences fit together to form a part of a functioning system of Truth. Since there is togetherness, cohesiveness, and interrelatedness, we have—in another word—coherence.

While these observations do not prove that God exists, if we live in a rationally consistent universe we can certainly reject as false any worldview that does not adequately deal with the *inescapable questions of life*. We can reject any worldview that does not have this togetherness, cohesiveness, and interrelatedness. We certainly have a right to believe a worldview if it passes the test of all the criteria for testing a worldview. In fact, we will likely feel compelled to believe such a worldview.

An adequate worldview must meet the need of our *total personality,* i.e., our mind, heart, and will. It is for this reason that I started with the criterion of answering the *inescapable questions of life.* Truth must meet these needs. If a worldview does not speak to these needs, *it is not worthy of consideration.* We dare not accept a worldview or an anti-worldview that does not adequately deal with these needs. However, we must keep in mind that our rational mind is a part of our total personality. The image of God within us cries out for a rationally consistent worldview. Therefore, there are some other tests to which a system must be subjected other than whether it speaks to our inner being. I think it was appropriate to begin with this test since Truth is for life (Jn. 8:32) and only that which speaks to life is worthy of being considered.

Let us now apply the criterion: Is there causal adequacy? Here again the Christian worldview with its belief in a personal God passes the test. God, as described in Christian doctrine, is fully capable of creating the universe and its inhabitants. It makes sense to think of the universe and its inhabitants as being an *effect* and God as being the *cause.* Here again we see togetherness, cohesiveness, and interrelatedness. It all fits together as a part of a system of Truth.

It makes far more sense to look at God as an eternal Being who created matter out of nothing than it does to think of matter as being eternal and thus the Creator of the universe, life, and personality. There may be some difficulty in grasping the idea that God has existed from eternity past, but there is no difficulty in believing it. If we believe in God, we cannot conceive of God as being other than without beginning. It goes with the idea of God to believe in His eternity past. It does not go with our understanding of matter to believe it to have had no beginning. It fits the idea of God to believe that He has created matter, the universe, life, and personality. It does not fit the idea of matter to attribute to it the work of Creator of the universe, life, and personality. This is why we hear so little about it from those who propose to believe it. It is intellectually embarrassing to make matter the Creator.

Human beings are inescapably concerned with moral issues. How do we account for the inescapable presence of moral concern in human beings? A holy God who is man's Creator and the moral Lawgiver and Judge of the universe is an adequate answer. It makes sense to believe that God created man with a moral constitution from which man cannot totally escape. We never totally escape the categories of right and wrong. The moral imperative is too strong to be self-imposed. It is too strong to be culturally imposed. Secularism has no adequate explanation for the presence of this deep moral concern in human beings. It makes sense to believe that our moral concern is related to a moral relationship and a moral accountability to the holy Creator, Lawgiver, and Judge of the universe.

The *cause* and *effect* relationship between God and man as it relates to this indelible moral concern is very important. It is rationally sound, but its impact is also based on its ability to meet an experiential need within us. We have no need in our total existence that is more real to us than our moral need. There should be an adequate explanation of why this need is so great within us. The Christian worldview with its belief in God is an adequate explanation. We need a moral authority from which we can receive moral laws, moral guidelines, and moral principles. The Christian system with its belief in the Bible meets this need. Is there an answer to moral guilt? The Christian system gives us the answer through Jesus Christ. It also helps us distinguish false guilt from true guilt as we study its moral teachings.

Here again we see togetherness, cohesiveness, and interrelatedness. Our rational minds are satisfied. The needs of our innermost being are met. We dare not settle for less.

The Christian worldview presents the existence of God along with His relationship to man as being the *cause* of the existence in man of that inescapable presence of an idea of God. Here again we have a *cause* and *effect* relationship that is not only rationally sound, but also meets the needs of our innermost being. It speaks to the needs of life. It not only explains adequately the existence of the idea of God, but also why man is so deeply religious. Both the modernist worldview and the postmodernist anti-worldview are woefully lacking at this point.

It is an undeniable fact that some people say that they do not believe in God, and many others do not worship the true God. Any view of the whole of reality must have an adequate answer for this. The Christian worldview is fully aware of this problem. We are not caught off guard by this fact. The answer is found in sin and Satan. Sin has placed man in an awful predicament. Man is so deeply moral in his constitution that he cannot escape the categories of right and wrong. Yet, sin makes him want to cast off moral restraint. He wants to do that which he cannot do with total success. Man, because of sin, wants to cast off authority. It is to be expected that some will try to do so by denying the existence of God, while others will seek a god more to their own liking. Our observations of those who have tried these alternatives show us that they have not found satisfaction.

The Christian worldview has an adequate explanation of why most people believe in God and some do not. A place for the undeniable fact that some do not believe in God is found in the Christian worldview. Again, we see togetherness, cohesiveness, and interrelatedness.

Our examination of the Christian worldview with its belief in God has shown that it passes the test of the criteria: (1) It answers the *inescapable questions of life.* (2) It is internally consistent. (3) There is causal adequacy. (4) It conforms to that which is undeniably true. Belief in God passes all the tests of reasonableness. When we let our total personality be a part of our believing, we will be compelled to believe in God. There is no other alternative to believing in God that meets the deepest needs of our personality. To reject belief in God is a course that cannot be followed without great loss. To reject belief in God means to be lost on the sea of life.

To believe in God through Jesus Christ opens the door to a rationally and experientially satisfying life. It opens the way for unified knowledge of the lower and upper stories. It makes it so we can be an intelligent, functioning citizen of the lower story and the upper story.

To believe in God or not to believe in God is not a choice between faith-knowledge and sight-knowledge (or sense-knowledge). Naturalism is faith-knowledge. Nobody has observed that matter is eternal. Nobody has observed that matter is the Creator of the universe, life, and personality. To believe in God or not to believe in God are both faith-knowledge. We have two choices: (1) To have faith-knowledge in a worldview that forms the basis for unified knowledge of the whole of reality, that satisfies our mind, and that meets the deepest needs of our personality; or (2) To have faith-knowledge in a worldview that gives rationally unsatisfactory answers to the basic questions of origins leaves one lost on the sea of life concerning the deepest needs of human personality. As for me, I will continue in the faith-knowledge that meets the needs of my total personality.

It should also be pointed out that Christianity offers the foundation for the continuation of science. Science, as we know it, had its birth within the Christian community of thinkers. Christian thought believes that the physical universe is characterized by design and order. There is a consistency of *cause* and *effect* relationships that can be studied by the human mind. The problem with modernism is that it believed in an ordered universe, but had no basis for its belief. Christianity believes in an ordered universe and grounds it in a personal, rational God who created the physical universe with a rational consistency, and created human beings with a rational mind that could study the physical universe through reflecting on the data of observation and experience—thus the birth of science.

Christianity also forms the basis for the preservation of civilization. Morality finds its foundation in a holy God. High ideals find their foundation in a God who is the epitome of the high and the lofty. We are challenged to aspire to the high and the lofty (Phil. 4:8).

Observations on Why We Believe in God

OUR CONSTITUTION AND OUR BELIEF IN GOD

I believe we are made to believe in God. It is natural for us to believe in God, but it requires the proper environment or circumstances for us to believe in God.

It is natural for a grain of corn to sprout and produce a stalk of corn. However, it will do so only in the right environment. It must be in the soil, having the proper content of moisture, and the temperature must be right. If a grain of corn is placed on top of a table, it will never sprout because the right environment does not exist. This is the case regardless of its natural tendency to sprout. When the grain of corn is placed in the ground, it becomes activated by the soil, moisture, and temperature, and thus a sprout comes forth which will grow into a stalk.

If a member of the race from birth were to grow up in total isolation from other human beings, it is doubtful he would believe in God. In one sense, he would be less than human. He would, so to speak, have all the parts that go to make up a human being. The problem is he would not be in the environment that would activate him into being what a functioning human being is.

A human being cannot be described purely in individualistic terms. He is a member of a group. He is a relationship-creature. The grain of corn depends upon its relationships with soil, moisture, and temperature for it to develop in its fullest and truest nature. To become one's truest and fullest self, a human being is dependent upon other members of the race, the created order, and God. The mention of God comes from other human beings. The normal procedure is for a human being—through interaction with other people, reflection upon the created order, and interaction with God—to be activated into believing in God. A social context is required for a human being to be all that he or she is designed to be. A full development of knowledge requires a social context.

I am not suggesting that people who are brought up in an inadequate context would not believe in God. It would be impossible for a person to be brought up from birth in total isolation from other people. If such could happen, he or she would not be fully activated into all that it means to be a human being.

Every human being is in an environment that will activate the idea of God within him. It is the activation of something that is already there. You will never talk to a person about God and tell him or her something totally foreign to all that he has ever thought. Every person who calls himself an atheist has thought about God. Atheism is not the total absence of the idea of God. Rather, it is an attempt to reject the idea of God that is already there.

It is true that some people do not profess to believe in God. It is my opinion that such people do so to their own hurt. It introduces malfunction into their experience. Atheism puts a person at cross purposes with the image of God that is within. It produces troubled people.

THE PLACE OF REASON IN BELIEVING IN GOD

Even if it is possible for some people to prove that God exists, that is not the reason most people believe in God. Most people who believe in God would not claim to have proof that He exists. Many of the elaborate proofs that philosophers and theologians come up with are too hard to understand for most people to grasp them. For that reason, these proofs could not be the reason most people believe in God.

The vast majority of Christians are unable to do a good job of constructing proofs for God's existence. However, that is not the same as saying that reason is not involved in their belief in God. I am convinced that a certain knowledge of God, along with some basic ideas about the kind of being God is are innate within every human being. Questions will arise that will cause each person to give rational consideration of the existence of God. I believe that we test the idea of God's existence for its reasonableness, rather than establishing arguments for God's existence. Even those who do not involve themselves in formal study of their belief in God have a rational faith. Human beings cannot escape giving rational thought to what they believe.

We are so constructed that we cannot possibly set reason aside. Even those who propose to set reason aside give reasons for it. If John says to us, "I saw Joe at the airport," we subconsciously test the statement to see if it is reasonable to accept it as true. If John knows Joe; if John is an honest person; if we know of no reason to doubt that Joe was at the airport; and if we know of no bad motives John could have for saying he saw Joe at the airport if he were not; we accept his statement as true. If John does not know Joe well; if John's veracity is in question; if we had good reason to believe Joe was somewhere else; or if we know of a motive John would have for lying about whether Joe was at the airport; we will question John's statement or reject it altogether. If the answer is not immediately obvious, we will analyze it in our conscious mind. We cannot hear John say, "I saw Joe at the airport," and give no rational thought whatsoever to it. If the answer is not immediately obvious, we may decide it is not important enough for us to settle. But that too will be a rational decision.

I have used the illustration above to show how our rational minds are continually at work judging, analyzing, and assessing. It cannot be otherwise. Our decision to deliberately turn off our reason is itself a decision made by reason. Those who distrust reason use it anyway. Those who try to deny reason a place in some areas of knowledge never fully succeed. The very effort to crush the reasoning process in us is painful and creates problems. Our inner being cries out for meaning and purpose in life. We long to see Truth as a unified whole.

One of the most important points to be made in building a case for believing in God is that we must make a choice between alternatives. We do not simply refuse to believe in God. We must choose an alternative. Before we reject our belief in God because of problems, we would do well to examine the alternatives to see what problems they have. We must believe in God, be an agnostic, or be a naturalist. There are many shades of belief, but they would fall into one of these categories. I suppose the postmodernist would say "none of the above" and "any of the above." The image of God *will never be at peace* with such "non-thinking."

In the postmodern paradigm reason does not enter in the question of believing or not believing in God. But as Christians, we do not ditch reason in dealing with postmodernists. That is because *they are not merely postmodernists.* They are made in the *image of God.* It is our responsibility by God's help to rescue the image of God in man from the devastation of postmodernism. In this rescue attempt, we do not depend on cold, dry, abstract, lifeless reason. We speak from our total personality to their total personality. We feel their pain. We do not skip around with oversimplified answers. We do not talk about feeling good all the time. Life is more than a hallelujah good time. But, at the same time that we may experience harsh reality, we can say with the Apostle Paul, "We are troubled on every side, yet not distressed; we are perplexed, but not in despair; Persecuted, but not forsaken; cast down, but not destroyed" (2 Cor. 4:8, 9).

Another factor that we must not forget is that many, even those in the academic world, still function within the modernist's paradigm. They must still be addressed. For that reason we still talk about naturalism and its inadequacies. *Naturalism* is the positive statement while *atheism* is the negative statement of the view. We dare not let the atheist get by with tearing down our view without supporting his own.

I prefer the term "naturalism" to "atheism," though both terms must be used, because naturalism attributes everything to natural causes. We have let the naturalist get by too often by putting us on the defensive and pointing out our problems. We need to put the naturalist on the defensive. We need to expose the inadequacy of naturalism as a worldview.

When we arrive at the conclusion that the Christian worldview passes the test of reasonableness, at the same time we have concluded that belief in God passes the test of being reasonable. While most Christians are not trained to test worldviews in any formal sense, they do think rationally about their faith in God. It is my opinion that most Christians will discover that the tests that I have discussed above already have a familiar ring to them. As Christians, we do not set reason aside when we believe in Christianity. We use reason. Christianity is not anti-rational. It is rational to the core. It is the only rationally consistent worldview. The image of God within cries out for rational consistency.

AN EXAMINATION OF THE ARGUMENTS FOR THE EXISTENCE OF GOD

I have already pointed out that I do not take the approach of using arguments to prove the existence of God. Since others do, I will state the arguments and show why I do not think they prove the existence of God. As I have pointed out above, I do think that much of the data is useful in showing the reasonableness of believing in God. In fact, I do not believe that there is a rationally consistent alternative.

The Cosmological Argument

This is probably the most widely used of all the arguments for God's existence. It argues from *effect* to *cause*. Everything that has a beginning is an *effect* and must have a *cause*. The universe had a beginning. Therefore, it must have a *cause*. That *cause* is God.

The problem is: How do we know the universe had a beginning? Can we prove it? Does not our confidence that the universe had a beginning belong in the category of faith-knowledge? If we work on the assumption that the universe did have a beginning, how do we know that the cause that produced the universe was not itself the product of another cause? This type reasoning could go on endlessly. It is easy enough to know what we believe about whether the universe had a beginning. It is easy to reject the idea of endless causes, but have we proved our point in each case?

Certainly, the most reasonable answer for the origin of the universe and human beings is belief in a Personal Creator.

The Teleological Argument

The teleological argument argues that the presence of design in the universe points to the existence of a Designer. The presence of order, harmony, and signs of purpose in the universe are said to argue for the existence of an intelligent *cause* who is God. This argument presupposes the *effect* to cause argument involved in the cosmological argument. It would, therefore, have all the weakness of the cosmological argument.

While the presence of order and harmony are impressive, one could raise the question: What about the presence of disorder and disharmony? Do they tell us something about the originating cause? We may feel that we have an answer to this question, but we must admit the problem.

Certainly, the most reasonable explanation of the presence of design in the universe is a Personal Designer.

The Moral Argument

This is another *effect* to *cause* argument. The *effect* in this case is the feeling of a moral imperative in man. Since man would like at times to escape this moral imperative, it does not seem adequate to think of it as self-imposed. The existence of God as a Lawgiver is considered the cause of the moral imperative.

Without relying upon divine revelation, can we prove, in the sense of absolute proof, that morality is not the product of culture? Can we prove that moral ideas have not originated from the interaction of people in society? I think the answer of a Moral Creator is far more reasonable, but I do recognize the problem of proving them to be an impossible alternative so far as proving things goes.

The Ontological Argument

This argument requires more thought to be grasped than the previous ones. It is stated thus:

We have the idea of an absolutely perfect being.
Existence is an attribute of perfection.
Therefore, an absolutely perfect being must exist.

This argument is very fascinating. It is harder to cope with from a logical viewpoint than the others. Yet, it seems to be less convincing. It is saying that the only way we can think of an absolutely perfect being is to think of it as existing. The very idea of a perfect being is said to involve the idea of its existence. To think of a perfect being and not think of its existence is to think of something less than a perfect being. The problem in my mind is this: Can we not logically have the idea of an absolutely perfect being and think of its existence as a part of that perfection, and then deny the reality of the whole idea? It seems to me that existence is the attribute of *being* rather than *perfection*. Existence is the attribute of a real being as distinguished from an imaginary being. The difficulty in getting a hold of this argument would mean, to say the least, that it would not be the reason for the faith of many people.

A variation of this argument simply says that since we have the idea of a perfect being, the only adequate explanation of this idea is that God exists and is the cause of our having this idea. It is argued that imperfect beings would not originate the idea of a perfect being. Certainly, the existence of God is a reasonable explanation for the idea of a perfect being, but can we prove that it would be impossible for the idea to have originated from imperfect beings?

There have been variations of these arguments, and other arguments have been given, but what has been given above illustrates the principle involved in the problem of proof. Varying values have been placed on these "so-called proofs."

Concerning the value of the arguments for the existence of God, James Oliver Buswell explains:

> In approaching the theistic arguments we must first of all ask ourselves the purpose of the arguments. . . . Facts are observed and implications of facts are inferred, leading to more or less probability in conclusions, with more or less cogency. There is no argument known to us which, as an argument, leads to more than a probable (highly probable) conclusion. . . . The theistic arguments are no exception to the rule that all inductive arguments about what exists are probability arguments. This is as far as the arguments, qua arguments, claim to go.[9]

Berkhof says concerning their value:

> They have some value for believers themselves, but should be called testimonia rather than arguments. They are important as interpretations of God's general revelation and as exhibiting the reasonableness of belief in a divine Being. Moreover, they can render some service in meeting the adversary. While they do not prove the existence of God beyond the possibility of doubt, so as to compel assent, they can be so construed as to establish a strong probability and thereby silence many unbelievers.[10]

Addison H. Leitch explains with reference to the arguments:

> They have been subjected to much criticism and therefore to considerable refinement in the history of thought. In spite of such criticism, however, they keep cropping up in one form or another, one argument, or one way of stating the argument, appealing to one generation more than another; but none of the arguments ever quite disappears. That these arguments keep reviving is probably a reason for their fundamental strength; men feel under some duress to define what they know must be true about God from the evidence of the external world.[11]

It is usually conceded that the arguments for the existence of God do not prove in the absolute sense of the word. However, they are frequently mentioned without this clarification. Some would take them to prove in the absolute sense.

Why We Believe the Bible to Be the Word of God

THE STARTING POINT OF OUR FAITH IN THE DIVINE ORIGIN OF SCRIPTURE

The Bible identifies itself to us as being a divine revelation. We would certainly expect a revelation from God to so identify itself to us. We could not conceive of a revelation from God not bearing the marks of self-authentication. We do not expect every part to bear the label, but we do expect the whole to be adequately labeled as a revelation from God. It is only then that we will consider any message or book to be a divine revelation.

Why be concerned over a Book that claims to be the Word of God? It has a message for us. It makes demands upon us. Our interest is not kindled simply because it proposes to be a message for us that makes demands upon us. Our interest is kindled because of the *inescapable questions* which represent unquenchable longings. The message of the Bible sounds like what our innermost being needs. In the Bible we see answers to our *inescapable questions*. In the Bible we see provisions for our needed experiences. It speaks to our total personality. We see it as the alleviation of our lostness.

As a person who thinks he or she has a dreaded disease finds a sudden interest in that which claims to be a cure, we find ourselves interested in that which proposes to be a message from God and an answer to our questions and our needs. The person with the disease must be concerned with the validity of the claims of the cure. The claims must be subjected to the proper tests. So it is with that which claims to be the Word of God. It must be subjected to tests.

THE CLAIMS OF SCRIPTURE UNDER TESTING

It is my conviction that in some way God has placed in our constitution certain ideas that are self-evident truths about any book that is truly a divine revelation. These are placed within us by God to help us keep from being led astray. The same data I use to show the reasonableness of believing the Bible to be the Word of God is used by others to construct arguments for believing the Bible to be the Word of God. I will show later the problem with trying to construct proofs from the data.

It is a self-evident truth that any book that would be a divine revelation would also be indestructible. That the Bible has historically withstood severe assaults up to this point means that it passes this test in the only way it can. From this standpoint, the Bible is safe for believing as a divine revelation.

It is a self-evident truth that a book that would be a divine revelation would be characterized by unity and nobility of thought. To me the Bible passes this test. I believe it will for others if they come at it with the right attitude of heart and mind. If they develop a critical attitude toward Scripture that blinds them to this unity and nobility of thought, they will reject it as a divine revelation. They will reject it as a divine revelation because they believe it to be a self-evident truth that a divine revelation ought to be characterized by unity and nobility of thought. There must be a willingness to see the Truth before it can be seen (Jn. 7:17). It is my conviction that those who come at the Scripture with the right attitude do see this unity and nobility of thought. For such people, the Bible passes this test and is safe for believing so far as this test is concerned.

It is a self-evident truth that a book which would be a divine revelation would have a good influence. For me the Bible passes this test. I believe it also does so for others who look at it with the right attitude. The same further elaboration, in principle, could be made about this self-evident truth as for the others. The Bible passes this test.

It is a self-evident truth that a significant amount of fulfilled prophecy would have to have a supernatural source. If it is constantly associated with good and is consistently related to the rest of the worldview, the supernatural source would be God. It is my conviction that to those who approach the Bible with the right attitude, it passes this test.

If anyone wants to raise any objections against calling these self-evident truths by which to test a divine revelation, I would ask, "Would you believe a book to be a divine revelation if it did not pass these tests?"

The reasonableness of our faith in Scripture is also shown by the way in which the Bible fits into a functioning system of Truth (or worldview). When we believe in God, the Bible, Jesus Christ, and man with his needs, it all fits together. There is togetherness, cohesiveness, and interrelatedness. If we were to take the Bible out of this system of thought, it would, in effect, be destroyed. The Bible is integrally related to God, Jesus Christ, and the needs of man. We expect Truth to have this togetherness, cohesiveness, and interrelatedness.

We should single out for separate consideration the testimony of Jesus Christ concerning the Scripture (Mt. 5:17, 18; Jn. 10:35; and others). Jesus Christ bears witness of the divine origin and truthfulness of Scripture. The Bible also bears witness of the truth of the claims of Jesus Christ (Jn. 5:39). In a sense we believe the Bible because of Jesus Christ and Jesus Christ because of the Bible. To believe in one is to believe in the other.

Some immediately charge: "This is circular reasoning." There is nothing wrong with circular reasoning as long as it is not presented as proof. Circular reasoning is all right as long as it is used to demonstrate togetherness, cohesiveness, and interrelatedness. A system will present many opportunities for circular reasoning. It is not circular reasoning that is wrong. It is making wrong claims for circular reasoning that is wrong.

Our belief in the Bible as a part of the Christian system of Truth passes the tests of the criteria we have given for testing a system.

(1) It answers the *inescapable questions of life*. The Bible comes through strong at this point. It meets the needs of our *total personality*. To reject it is to be lost on the sea of reality.

(2) It is internally consistent. There is consistency between believing in the Bible, God, and the other parts of the system. There is consistency in the Bible.

(3) Its *causes* are adequate. The God of the Bible is fully capable of revealing the truth of the Bible and inspiring the writers to write the Bible. The *causes* set forth in the Bible are capable of producing the *effects* ascribed to them.

(4) It conforms to that which is undeniably true. There is no fact of reality which is undeniably true that is contradicted by the Bible. There may be some things that may be questioned, but they do not stand as undeniably true and in contradiction to the Bible.

An Examination of the Arguments for the Divine Inspiration of the Bible

I have already pointed out that building arguments is the proper approach to defending that the Bible is the Word of God. The better way is to show how believing the Bible to be the Word of God passes the test of being a part of a rational worldview. I think it is appropriate, at least, to give a brief description of these arguments. I will also give a brief evaluation of these as arguments. I have used some of the same information above to show that it passes the test of reasonableness to believe the Bible to be the Word of God.

We will first examine the argument based on the indestructibility of the Bible. The Bible has survived in the midst of adversity. Many attempts have been made to destroy it, but all attempts have failed. It is felt that this survival is evidence (some would speak of it as proof) of the supernatural origin of Scripture.

That the Bible is still with us proves it has not been destroyed, but it does not prove it cannot be destroyed. There can be no proof that the Bible cannot be destroyed. We believe that it cannot be destroyed, but that is based on our faith in its own testimony (Mt. 5:18; 24:35). We cannot prove to an unbeliever that the Bible is indestructible and then use it as a base from which to build our case.

Another problem with this argument is: If we found another book that had withstood the same attempts to destroy it, would we believe it to be the Word of God for that reason? Doubtless, that would not convince us.

A second argument that is frequently used is the argument from the character of the Bible. The Bible is characterized by unity and nobility of thought. It is so characterized to those of us who believe it and love it, but unbelievers frequently challenge its unity and nobility of thought. An argument based on the character of the Bible would not be convincing to such a person. The unity and nobility of thought of the Bible is knowledge that is shared by believers, but not by the critics of Scripture.

We can raise the questions at this point: If we discover another book that is characterized by unity and nobility of thought, would we of necessity believe it to be divinely inspired? I think not.

A third argument is based on the influence of the Bible. Wherever the Bible has been, it has had an uplifting influence upon society. It is felt by many that this evidences the divine inspiration of Scripture.

The same problems can be raised about this argument that have been mentioned about the others. Many people do not believe that the Bible has had a good influence. With such people, we could not use this information to prove the divine origin of Scripture. Again, I raise the question: Would we believe some other book to be of divine origin if it had a good influence?

A fourth argument is based on fulfilled prophecy of the Bible, particularly that which was fulfilled within the biblical period. The believer does believe the Bible sets forth much prophecy and its fulfillment. He also believes that any unfulfilled prophecy will be fulfilled in the future. The problem in using this to convince an unbeliever is that some people either explain away the prophetic statements of Scripture or consider them as history instead of prophecy. To such people there would be no proving value from what we call fulfilled prophecy. Another problem is that through satanic influence some predictions are made that come true. We do not grant, then, in every case that a predictive utterance that turns out to be true is of God.

The data used in these arguments are useful in showing the reasonableness of our faith. It is a mistake to use the data to construct arguments and claiming them as proof. We do not prove a system to be true by starting with some commonly accepted major premise or premises and proving that the basic ideas of the system are seen to be a necessary logical conclusion. Rather, we subject a system to certain tests. To test for validity is not the same as proving something to be a logical necessity. Also, we must be concerned with necessity other than logical necessity.

Conclusion

The approach used in this chapter is very satisfying to me. The Christian worldview with its belief in God and the Bible meet every test of reasonableness. My faith in God and the Bible meets my personal needs. I do not feel threatened by any other worldview. To me other worldviews fail woefully both from a rational viewpoint and from the standpoint of meeting the needs of the total personality. I wholeheartedly recommend God, the Bible, and Jesus Christ to every human being.

8

The Creation of Man

One of the *inescapable questions of life* is: Who am I? We know our name, but we need help in knowing our full identity. What is the real nature of man? Knowledge of the full nature of man is tied in with his origin. As those who are committed to the Christian system of Truth, we are committed to what the divine revelation says about the origin of man. This knowledge comes to us as a given in the divine revelation. It is integrally related to the Christian system. Our first obligation is to study the data of revelation to find out what it says about the origin of man.

The Biblical Teaching Concerning the Origin of Man

The Bible clearly attributes the origin of man to a creative act of God. Genesis 1:27 reads: "So God created man in his own image, in the image of God created he him; male and female created he them." Genesis 2:7 reads, "And the LORD God formed man of the dust of the ground, and breathed into his nostrils the breath of life."

There can be no debate over whether God is man's creator according to the Bible. The question is: Does the Bible leave room for theistic evolution? According to theistic evolution, God directed the process of evolution and made use of it in bringing man into existence. Physically, man would have an animal ancestry according to theistic evolution. He would have become man when God breathed into his nostrils the breath of life and he became a living soul.

Many have felt compelled by the findings of science to accept theistic evolution. The problem for the Christian is: What does the divine revelation say? Are the biblical teachings compatible with theistic evolution? He must apply the laws of language to the biblical account and see if it is compatible with theistic evolution. If it is not, he must reject it.

It is my conviction that the biblical account is incompatible with theistic evolution. I shall offer two proofs: (1) The creative days do not allow enough time. (2) The creation of Eve is definitely outside the pattern of evolution.

EXEGETICAL EVIDENCE FOR THE SOLAR-DAY VIEW OF THE DAYS OF THE CREATIVE WEEK

A word should be said here about proof. When discussing our belief in God and the Bible, I pointed out that we should apply the test of reasonableness rather than attempt to prove the existence of God and the divine origin of Scripture. Now, I am speaking of proof that the Bible is incompatible with evolution. Once a system of thought is accepted as true, we can talk about proving things to people who believe the system to be true. In principle, we can prove that the Bible teaches a view by studying its teachings in the light of the laws of interpretation. It will be proved to those who accept the Bible to be the Word of God if they are convinced by our interpretation. It will have no meaning to those who do not accept the Christian worldview as being true. We may not always succeed, but in principle we can prove things to those who believe the Bible to be the Word of God.

It is my conviction that the days of the creative week must be understood as literal days. It is true that the Hebrew word *yôm* (day), like the English word "day," can refer to a period of time longer than a 24 hour day in certain contexts. However, it is my conviction that the case is clear-cut against long days in Genesis 1. Though it is agreed that *yôm* can refer to a period longer than a 24 hour day, it is not agreed by all Hebrew scholars that *yôm* is suitable as an equivalent for the word "age." I will not get involved in this discussion since I think the context is against such usage even if the word is suitable in a proper context to mean "age."

The first reason is that the days are qualified as having *evening* and *morning*. Evening and morning are the phenomena that make up a solar day. The Hebrew is translated literally, "And there was evening and there was morning."

Day with the qualification of evening and morning can mean *nothing other than a solar day*. Some have felt that they could give a figurative meaning to evening and morning.

Edwin K. Gedney says:

> It is natural for us to think of this as meaning ending (evening) and beginning (morning), for so it is in our culture. This was not true of Hebrew age. The beginning of the day was evening and it is logical to think that the writer intended that here . . . Evening and morning then have the sense of "beginning" and "ending" in the passage.[1]

Buswell comments:

> It is obvious that if the word "day" is figurative, the parts of the day would be figurative, as when we say "a new day is dawning," meaning, "a new era is opening." The Hebrews regarded the new day as beginning at sunset. Thus the words, "The evening and the morning were the —th day," would be equivalent to saying in literal modern words, "The epoch had its gradual beginning, and gradually merged into the epoch which followed.[2]

Buswell suggests that if day is taken figuratively it follows that evening and morning must be taken figuratively. I agree that if the day is figurative that evening and morning must be. However, we need to move with caution here. Evening and morning are descriptive of the day. The meaning of evening (*'erev*) and morning (*bōqer*) is what determines the meaning of day (*yôm*). A figurative use of day depends upon a figurative use of evening and morning. If a figurative use of evening meaning "beginning" and morning meaning "ending" cannot be supported the figurative use of the word *day* must be abandoned.

The problem facing us is not whether the word *day* (*yôm*) can refer to a long period of time. It is whether evening (*'erev*) can have the figurative meaning of beginning and whether morning (*bōqer*) can have the figurative meaning of ending. Let us examine the evidence.

The figurative use of the words suggested by Gedney and Buswell is without parallel in the Old Testament. (I base my conclusions upon a study of the occurrences of the Hebrew words for evening and morning listed in *The Englishman's Hebrew and Chaldee Concordance of the Old Testament.*) At no place do we find that evening is used figuratively to mean "beginning" nor that morning is used to mean "ending." In fact, morning did not end the literal day. Morning in the literal day referred to the change from darkness to light, not the last part of the 24 hour day. Morning is *never used figuratively to mean ending.* It *is* used figuratively to mean early. The Hebrew word for morning is translated "early" in the KJV in Psalm 46:5; 90:14; and 101:8. A study of these passages will show that it means early in a figurative sense.

It is of further interest to note that when the Israelites referred to the daylight hours they spoke of them as *from morning to evening* (Ex. 18:13, 14). From a practical viewpoint they looked at morning as "early" and evening as "late" in spite of the fact that from a technical point the 24-hour day began at evening.

Judges 19:9 is very interesting at this point. It reads, "Behold, now the day draweth toward evening, I pray you tarry all night: behold the day draweth to an end" (KJV). The NIV translates, "Now look, it is almost evening. Spend the night here; the day is nearly over."

Concerning the Hebrew for "draweth toward evening," Garnett H. Reid gives the following explanation of how it is developed. "In Judges 19:9, *'ārav* is a diminutive verb 'to become evening,' from the same root as the noun, *'erev,* 'evening.' Here the infinitive construct plus *l* seems to be a time indicator: 'the day declined toward evening.'"[3] It is quite clear that in Hebrew usage the approaching of evening was considered *late, not early.*

Interpreting *evening* figuratively to mean "beginning" and *morning* figuratively as "ending" is contrary to their usage in Scripture. Therefore, the terms *evening* and *morning* cannot be fitted into the day-age interpretation. When evening and morning are used in the same context, they can refer to nothing but a solar day.

Further support is seen for the literal-day view in the reference to the creative week in Exodus 20:8-11. The most natural meaning for "six days" in verse 11 is to understand the meaning to be the same as it is in verse 9. In verse 9, the days are obviously solar days.

Problems for the Solar-Day View of the Days of the Creative Week

THE FOURTH DAY AND THE FUNCTION OF THE SUN

From an exegetical viewpoint, two problems have been raised for the literal-day view. The first is the fact that the sun was not made to function until the fourth day. First, let it be said that this poses a greater problem for the day-age view than the literal-day view. The literal-day view has a problem for only 72 hours. The day-age view has a problem that could extend into millions or billions of years. It is very doubtful that any holder of the day-age view actually believes that the earth existed that long before the sun began to function.

If we take the view about the sun's function during these days that Buswell takes, there is no problem with regard to the first three days. He suggests that the sun functioned during the first three days, but was not visible. The light of the sun was diffused through a cloudy atmosphere.[4] If that be the case, the sun's function would be adequate to cause the transition from darkness to light and light to darkness during the first three days. There would be no problem under such circumstances of thinking of the days as solar days.

Whatever the case might have been during the first three days, the knowledge that the words *evening* and *morning* are used from the fourth day onward helps us interpret the previous references. Whether or not the sun functioned on the first three days, there was a division of light from darkness. We are told in Genesis 1:4, "God divided the light from the darkness." It is clear that the sun had its normal function from the fourth day on. All of the creative days are described, "And there was evening and there was morning." This tells us that all were the same kind of day. There can be no reason for understanding the first three days of the creative week to be different, so far as length is concerned, from the last three.

THE LENGTH OF THE SEVENTH DAY

The other exegetical problem is presented by a reference to the seventh day in Hebrews 4. In verse 4, it is said, "And God did rest the seventh day from all his works." Verse 5 speaks of the rest as having continued until Moses' day (and is still continuing). "And in this place again, If they shall enter into my rest." Since the rest is continuing, it is concluded that the day is continuing. This would make the seventh day a long day. If the seventh day of Genesis 1 and 2 were a long day, it would follow that the first six were also long days.[5]

My answer to this problem is that although the rest is continuing, the day is not continuing. The day is clearly treated as a fact of history. "And God did rest the seventh day" (Heb. 4:4). The seventh day is presented as being already finished in the past. The language of Exodus 20:11 and Genesis 2:2, 3 also treat the seventh day as a completed fact of history. If the seventh day is history, there is no basis for interpreting it as a long day.

H. C. Leupold comments:

> There ought to be no need of refuting the idea that *yôm* means period. Reputable dictionaries like Buhl, BDB or K.W. know nothing of this notion. Hebrew dictionaries are our primary source of reliable information concerning Hebrew words. Commentators with critical leanings utter statements that are very decided at this instance. Says Skinner: "The interpretation of *yôm* as aeon, a favorite resource of harmonists of science and revelation, is opposed to the plain sense of the passage and has no warrant in Hebrew usage." Dillman remarks: "The reasons advanced by ancient and modern writers for constructing these days to be longer periods of time are inadequate."[6]

So far as I am concerned, there can be no doubt that the days were literal days. If the description in Genesis 1 is not of literal days, one wonders how it could have been stated so as to clearly mean a literal day. Suppose God did mean these to be understood as literal days, can anyone say that anything was said that would confuse the issue, or anything left out that would be needed to clarify it?

I appreciate the fact that devout people have struggled with the question of whether the days of the creative week could be understood as long periods of time. Many have accepted the day-age view who have not accepted theistic evolution. Some have accepted what is called progressive creationism. According to this view, God, by several acts of fiat creation, created the phyla and families of animals. Among animals there was evolutionary development, but the development did not step outside the boundaries of "kinds." When it comes to man, the progressive creationists reject the animal ancestry of man. Man was created by a special act of creation.[7] These people accept the view of an old earth, rather than a young earth. While I do not accept this view, I think it is unfair and irresponsible to call it theistic evolution. I would like to challenge those who accept this view to take a hard look at the problems that I present for those who would like to hold to a longer history of the earth, animals, and man than is allowed by the six 24-hour days interpretation of the creative week.

Problems for the Day-Age View of the Creative Week

FAILS TO BRING A HARMONY BETWEEN SCIENCE AND SCRIPTURE

The day-age theory cannot be supported as an interpretation of Genesis, and it raises another serious problem. It fails to really solve the problem of harmonizing scientific opinions on geology and paleontology with Scripture. Carl F. H. Henry, though not an advocate of the literal-day view, in discussing the difficulties of the day-age theory points out that "the Genesis days do not harmonize fully with the chronology, proposed by modern science."[8]

Bernard Ramm, though rejecting the literal-day theory, also rejects the day-age theory because to accept the long-day view and to accept the order in which they appear could not be squared with science. He illustrates the problem by pointing out: "We have a botanical creation with no animals and a mammalian creation with no creation of plants, yet the science of biology tells us how intimately related plants, animals, and insects are in the order of nature."[9]

The only real thing that the day-age theory does is allow for more time, but the order of what happened still fails to fit in with modern science. Therefore, it fails as a means of bringing about harmony.

OFFERS NO HELP ON HOW LONG MAN HAS BEEN ON EARTH

Another observation is that *the day-age theory offers no help at all in the problem of how long man has been on the earth.* The question of the antiquity of man is studied by scientists in connection with fossils. It is obvious that wherever fossils are found death has occurred. It is equally obvious that regardless of the length of the creative days that men did not die until after the sixth creative day. Surely, no one would place Genesis 3 in the sixth day. Death occurred in the human race after Genesis 3. This means that all fossil remains of human beings must be accounted for after the sixth creative day was finished. The person who believes in the day-age theory and the person who believes in the literal-day theory would have to look for a way to scripturally account for the age of man through exactly the same possibilities.

Apparently, Fetzer overlooked the fact mentioned above in making the following observation: "By taking the age-day interpretation of Genesis and by realizing that the genealogical tables of Genesis have gaps in them, we free ourselves from any notion that man was made in 4004 B. C."[10]

The possibility of gaps in the genealogies may help give an earlier date for the origin (this will be discussed later), but the day-age theory cannot be used to *increase the time man has been on earth one iota of time* more than the literal-day view. Again the day-age view is seen to fail to offer any aid.

THE PROBLEM OF CONDITIONS REQUIRED FOR THE CREATIVE WEEK

Another problem that one encounters, when he by the day-age theory or some other view tries to allow enormous lengths of time for the six creative days, is the type of conditions that must have prevailed during this time. The geological strata require catastrophic conditions, and the fossils of animals require death.

Ramm shows an awareness of this when he remarks: "There was disease and death and bloodshed in Nature long before man sinned."[11] He further comments:

> Outside of the Garden of Eden were death, disease, weeds, thistles, thorns, carnivores, deadly serpents, and intemperate weather. To think otherwise is to run counter to an immense avalanche of fact. Part of the blessedness of man was that he was spared all of these things in his Paradise, and part of the judgment of man was that he had to forsake such a Paradise and enter the world as it was outside of the Garden, where thistles grew and weeds were abundant and where wild animals roamed and where life was only possible by the sweat of man's brow.[12]

Many would not be willing to go along with Ramm in ascribing such conditions to earth and animals before man sinned. However, one must admit conditions of this kind before he can hope to get any help from the day-age theory on the length of time that animals have been on the earth.

We may not know what the exact conditions were before man sinned, but one can hardly reconcile most of what Ramm says above with what God said to Adam when He said, "Cursed is the ground for thy sake; in sorrow shalt thou eat of it all the days of thy life; Thorns also and thistles shall it bring forth to thee" (Gen. 3:17, 18).

Also, with regard to this statement: "Part of the blessedness of man was that he was spared all of these things in Paradise, and part of the judgment of man was that he had to forsake such a Paradise and enter the world as it was outside the Garden," Ramm overlooks that man's responsibility to God would have taken him outside the Garden even if he had not sinned. This is seen in that man, before he sinned was commanded to "have dominion over the fish of the sea, and over the fowl of the air, and over the cattle, and over all the earth, and over every creeping thing that creepeth upon the earth" (Gen. 1:26).

We may not know the exact conditions of the earth before man sinned, but we must conclude that the earth is different now as a result of the curse. We must also conclude that man would have gone into all the earth if he had never sinned.

Those who want to resort to a view that seeks to explain animal fossils and geological changes by placing them within the six days of creation must ask if they can reconcile the conditions that would have produced these with the Genesis account. Special attention should be given to the statement at the close of days 3-5, "And God saw . . . that . . . it was good." The pronouncement at the end of the sixth day includes the whole creation. "And God saw every thing that he had made, and, behold, it was very good" (Gen. 1:31).

If the days of the creative week are literal 24-hour days, there can be no harmony between the Bible and evolution. This is true since man was created on the sixth day. Twenty-four hours is not enough time for evolution. In my opinion, the case is clear for the literal-day interpretation; therefore, I see no possibility of evolution.

Other Problems for Those who Wish to Hold to the Bible and Accept Theistic Evolution

THE CREATION OF EVE

As has already been stated, if one accepts the literal-day view he cannot accept evolution. However, theistic evolution has not won its case with those who believe the Bible even if the day-age theory were a proved fact. There are many who accept the day-age view that reject evolution. They reject it on other grounds. The account of the creation of Eve in Genesis 2:21, 22 requires one to believe that the creation of Eve was instantaneous and by a direct act of God that bypassed natural processes. No one can hope to escape by claiming that this is poetic or symbolic. If the language is capable of being understood at all, it means that God took something from Adam and by a direct act made Eve. Those who advocate theistic evolution would not be willing to grant that Eve was created by a special act of God. Those who grant that Eve was created by a special act also grant that Adam was.

THE QUESTION OF A FINISHED CREATION

Another problem with theistic evolution is that it has the same forces at work in the world today that were at work in the creative week. If so, what is meant by, "And on the seventh day God ended his work which he had made" (Gen. 2:2)? There can be no finished creation, nor can there be any ceasing of creative activity in theistic evolution because it fails to distinguish, in essence, between creative activity and the activity of providence.

After examining Genesis 1 and 2, one feels like asking, "If God used the evolutionary process to bring man into existence, why did He make it so hard for one to believe in evolution after studying Genesis 1 and 2?"

Biblical Problems Involved in Accepting the Dates Given by Secular Scientists for the Origin of Man

Bishop Ussher, based on a study of the biblical data, gave 4004 B.C. as the date for creation. Someone else by using the same method might vary some in the suggested date for the origin of man in keeping with the biblical record. Hardly anyone would suggest a date that would be as precise as 4004 B.C.

Anyone would either be ignorant or less than honest to deny that there are problems. On the one hand, the Bible, as I understand it, rules out any possibility of an animal ancestry of man. Man came into existence by a creative act of God. On the other hand, we live in a world when men, competent in their field, insist on the evolutionary hypothesis of man's origin and a time period of several hundred thousand years or more for man's existence on earth. How do we cope with all this?

THE LATITUDE ALLOWED BY SCRIPTURE

The beginning place for the Christian is to examine the Scripture and see how much latitude he has to accommodate himself to contemporary scientific thought. He must operate within the framework of these limitations. To fail to do so would be to be less than honest and would violate his rationality as a person who is committed to the Christian worldview.

A few things have already been decided up to this point that help set the limits of this framework of possibilities. (1) There can be no room for considering the evolutionary view of the origin of man. (2) Any attempt to lengthen the time of man on earth beyond the time of about 6,000 years must be found after the sixth day of creation. It was pointed out that this is just as true of the day-age theory as it is the literal-day theory. This is true since death would have occurred after the sixth day regardless of the length of that day. All fossils of man, therefore, must be placed in the period of history after the sixth day. The day-age theory would offer a possibility of a longer animal history and more time for geological ages, but the conditions that must have existed during that time are, so far as I am concerned, impossible to reconcile with the biblical account in Genesis 1 and 2.

There are two more subjects that need to be discussed that shed light on the biblical limits on how much latitude can be allowed: (1) The possibility of gaps in genealogies. (2) The meaning of "kinds" in Genesis 1.

THE POSSIBILITY OF GAPS IN GENEALOGIES

The only way of allowing any significant amount of time beyond the 4004 B.C., according to Ussher's date, is through the possibility of gaps in the genealogies in Genesis 5 and 11. It is an established fact, determined by comparing different accounts of the same genealogy, that there are some names left out of some genealogies.[13]

That there are gaps in some genealogies only creates the possibility that there are gaps in other genealogies, not the necessity. However, it does mean that the possibility of gaps cannot be ruled out. This gives one the right to speculate about such possibilities. If there were gaps, it would obviously lengthen the time since man's creation. Also, if there were gaps in Genesis 5 the amount of time that would have transpired for each name left out would be greater than would be accounted for by a life span in our day since the people lived to be considerably older then than now.

Some have taken the position that if there were gaps we can consider any date of man's origin that might be conjectured by scientists. Their reasoning is that an unknown number of gaps of unknown duration could possibly account for any number of years. A word of caution needs to be sounded here. It might be granted that the unknowns would keep a person from dogmatically stating the exact limitation of how far back one could go. However, it is a strain upon the elasticity of a reason-controlled imagination to believe that these unknown and unknowable gaps could allow for any imaginable age of the human race short of infinity.

We could *with caution* consider the possibility of *a few thousand years* added to the 4004 B.C. date. But we cannot go hundreds of thousands of years.

THE BEGINNING OF CIVILIZATION

It might be well to bear in mind that while we could consider gaps as a possibility for lengthening the antiquity of man, we must keep in mind facts cited by Ramm as he wrestles with this difficulty.

He seems to be caught in a dilemma between scientific thought and the facts of the Bible at this point. He brings out some of the problems in accepting an early date for the origin of man. He explains:

> The chief problem with an origin of man at 500,000 B.C. is the connection of Genesis 3 and Genesis 4. We might stretch the tables of ancestors a few thousand years, but can we stretch them 200,000 years? In the fourth and fifth chapters of Genesis we have lists of names, ages of people, towns, agriculture, metallurgy, and music. This implies the ability to write, to count, to build, to farm, to smelt, and to compose. Further, these were done by the immediate descendants of Adam. Civilization does not reveal any evidence of its existence till about 8,000 B.C. or, to some 16,000 B.C. We can hardly push it back to 500,000 B.C. It is problematic to interpret Adam as having been created 200,000 B.C. or earlier, with civilization not coming into existence till say 8,000 B.C.[14]

THE LENGTH OF TIME FROM GENESIS 3:15 TO THE COMING OF CHRIST

Another point to keep in mind is that it places considerable strain upon us to believe that between the redemptive promise of Genesis 3:15 and the coming of Christ there would have been hundreds of thousands of years. We expect in some way to be able to interpret biblical history so as to show a movement from Genesis 3:15 to the cross. This problem presents enough difficulty in thinking about a few thousand years. What explanation does one offer for hundreds of thousands of years between the first redemptive promise and the coming of Christ? If we say that human beings have been on earth for 500,000 years, we would be saying there were 498,000 years between Genesis 3:15 and the coming of Christ. We would be saying it was 496,000 years between Genesis 3:15 and the call of Abraham to bring the nation of Israel into existence. The nation of Israel was the channel God chose to bring the Messiah into the world. All of this would make it look like God was asleep!

THE MEANING OF "KINDS"

Now we turn our attention to the problem of the meaning of the word "kinds." The zoological classification into phyla, classes, orders, families, genera, and species was not existent when Moses wrote the Pentateuch. There are no exegetical grounds for equating kind with species. This is true whether they are to be equated in fact or not. The Hebrew word for kind means form or shape. The limits of each kind is set, but there is no way of proving that the limitation is equated with species. There may be a variation within the kind, but each kind would remain within its own boundaries.

The position that the "kinds" of Genesis need not be equated with our term species has been accepted among staunch conservatives. There is coupled with this the admission that new species have arisen since the creation.

John W. Klotz says, "We shall certainly have to admit that there have been new species."[15]

Henry M. Morris states:

> Nothing in the account [Genesis] indicates how many original "species" there were, or what constitutes a "species" . . . The only biological unit identified therein is called a kind . . . the various types of living creatures were to bring forth "after their kind." This states, quite plainly, that there were to be definite limits to possible biological change. . . . But within those limits, it can surely be inferred that variation and speciation [origin of new species] are possible.[16] (Brackets mine)

I am not qualified to speak on the question of whether new species can arise or have arisen. However, when men such as John W. Klotz and Henry M. Morris, who show no desire to give strained interpretations of Scripture to harmonize with scientific opinions, do believe that new species have arisen, I am inclined to believe that new species have arisen. However, one should move with caution at this point since it is doubtful that the literal-day view leaves time for very much development within kinds.

When we talk about the possibility of new species, we are not talking about man, but plants and animals. A limited amount of variation from what was created is permissible, so far as Scripture is concerned, since we have no proof that species and kinds are to be equated.

THE POSSIBILITY OF A GAP BETWEEN GENESIS 1:1 AND 1:2

Some have looked for help in reconciling science and Scripture by suggesting a gap of time between Genesis 1:1 and 1:2. Those who take this position understand Genesis 1:1 to be a description of a perfectly created universe. They take verse 2 to be a description of a cursed earth. Some connect this with the fall of Satan. Others have held to the idea of a pre-Adamic race that fell.

Such a gap would permit time for geological ages, but it would offer no help in allowing for geological ages where fossils are embedded in the rock unless one wants to believe in the creation of plants, animals, and a race prior to the creative week of Genesis that was destroyed. They would take the fossils that have been given extremely old dates to refer to this creation. Beginning in verse 3, they understand the reference to be to a restoration of the earth and a new creation of plants, animals, and man. Personally, I am not impressed by the idea of such a creation prior to the creative week. There is certainly no biblical evidence for it. The gap theory was popular forty or fifty years ago, but has waned in popularity over the years.

THE QUESTION OF THE TIME OF THE BEGINNING OF THE FIRST CREATIVE DAY

There is some problem over the exact point in Genesis 1:1-3 where the first day of the creative week began. It does not appear to have started at verse 1. If it did not, we have no way of knowing how long the earth was in the shape described in verse 2 before the first day began. It could have been a very short time, or it could have been a long time. If it were a long time, it could help in thinking about an older earth, but it would be of no help with regard to the age of fossils.

The Influence of the Theory of Evolution

Note: The influence of the evolutionary philosophy in shaping thought has diminished in scholarly circles since *Biblical Systematics* was published. In retrospect, its influence was already declining in 1975, but that decline was not apparent. Since what I said then adequately summarizes the influence of the evolutionary philosophy and gives a perspective from the 1970s, the following section is essentially unchanged from that which was previously published. After this section, I will comment on the present situation.

One might ask: Why all the concern over evolution? The biggest reason is that it is unscriptural. However, one might ask: In view of all the bad interpretation that has received much lighter treatment, why not be easier on those who feel that evolution is in harmony with Genesis 1 and 2? The problem is that there is a philosophy of life that often accompanies evolution which has had devastating effects on Christianity and that for which Christianity stands.

Of course it could be said that evangelicals who accept evolution do not accept the evolutionary philosophy of life. It could be said in reply that this might be true in particular cases, but it will hardly remain true. Respect for the scholarship of geologists and paleontologists seems to have been one of the chief reasons that most who have accepted theistic evolution did so. Those who set forth the evolutionary philosophy of life or the evolutionary philosophy of the origin of religion are as learned in their fields of study as the geologists and paleontologists are in theirs. Shall we accept the conclusions of one out of respect to his scholarship and reject the conclusions of another though his scholarship is just as respectable?

Those who are motivated by respect for the scholarship of others will eventually accept the total evolutionary view including the philosophy of life. Those who stay with the Scripture will have to do so at the cost of rejecting much of what is called respectable scholarship. This is not intended to cast reflection upon scholarship as such. However, it is intended to make it clear that we cannot accept the Christian system of thought without turning down much of what is known as respectable scholarship in other systems of thought. Are we any worse if we reject the conclusions of geologists and paleontologists than we are when we reject what some other scholars say?

I am well aware that evangelicals who hold to theistic evolution would not go along with most of the things that will be pointed out as the products of evolutionary thinking. However, I do believe that the tide moves in that direction and that many who take the step of theistic evolution will in varying degrees move in these directions.

Carl Henry gives a frank account of the past influence of evolution. He explains:

> This evolutionary speculation challenged not only the dignity of man on the basis of creation; it challenged also the fact of his fall and sinfulness. For both these conceptions, evolutionary philosophy substituted the dogma of human progress and perfectibility. Hence it eliminated the doctrine of man's need of supernatural redemption. The intellectual movement of the past century portrays a loss of faith in the Apostles' Creed simultaneous with a rise of faith in the evolutionary creed. The new importance of change whetted the destructive assault on Holy Scripture as a divinely given revelation, and on Jesus Christ as an absolute divine incarnation.[17]

The theory of biological evolution brought into prominence the principle of change and progress. When this view became deeply embedded in the minds of scholars, they became convinced that every area of life must submit to the principle of change and progress. Religion and morals were not to be exempted.

THE INFLUENCE ON RELIGIOUS THOUGHT

When applied to the realm of religion, detrimental results immediately appeared. The origin and development of religion was to be studied within the framework of an evolutionary philosophy. The beginning of religion was to be found on a very low level such as superstition or ancestor worship. Through a gradual development Christianity finally emerged on the scene. Until this is recognized there can be no intelligent understanding of theological liberalism.

In liberalism the evolutionary principle became the interpretive principle in interpreting the Old Testament. Some of the results of this have been (1) a denial of the Mosaic authorship of the Pentateuch; (2) the view that monotheism had its beginning with Amos; and (3) the dating of the origin of the law after the Babylonian captivity.

There is also a denial of the historicity of the account of sinless Adam and Eve placed in the Garden of Eden, and the account of the fall. The evolutionary philosophy has no place for a sinless state because the earlier state of man is thought to be below the present state. It has no place for a fall because man is on the upward climb. It is easy to see how destructive this could be for Christian doctrine. Neo-orthodoxy, because of its allegiance to evolution, has denied that Adam and Eve were historical persons. It has rejected the optimism of liberalism, but its respect for evolution would not allow an orthodox position on Adam and Eve.

THE INFLUENCE ON MORALS

The application of the principle of change and progress to the realm of morals is quite obvious. There can be no looking back to a set of morals revealed in a Bible that was written in the long ago. There can be no doubt that this has been the greatest reason for the moral decay that has given respectability in many circles to gross immorality.

Henry says:

> Triumph of the evolutionary philosophy actually engendered one of the most staggering moral declensions in the history of the world. Deterioration reached its widest extremes with the speculative dogma that man is an animal only, and with the application of the ancient Greek doctrine of change to all fields of study, religion included.[18]

CONCLUDING OBSERVATIONS

It is true that in the past Christians have rejected, for a time, some of the things we all now accept, for example, the fact that the earth is round. However, there has not been any such viewpoint that has had such a devastating effect on Christianity when it was accepted.

It would be exceedingly strange if God would use a method in creation, that when finally discovered by man, would have such effects in the first century of its acceptance as evolution has had. Should it be thought strange that so many have found evolution unacceptable within the Christian faith?

Observations for the Present

When evolution was given scientific respectability by the publication of *Darwin's Origin of Species* in 1859, it appeared to go hand in glove with the optimism of modernism. Evolution became foundational in modernist thought. When the evolutionary principle was applied to the moral, religious, social, economic, and political areas, to the modernist it became the basis of heightened optimism.

With an understanding of how evolutionary principles work, it was thought that progress could be speeded up. This was followed by a heyday for liberalism. World War I became the hope of a war that would end all wars. This is not what happened.

In less than twenty-five years the world was at war again. World War II was never understood as the war that would end all wars. Even though the Allies won, it was not an occasion for optimism on the world scene. Pessimism was winning the war over optimism. Pessimistic Existentialism emerged.

What happened? What had brought about this drift toward pessimism? What went wrong? Part of the answer is to be found in the negative influence of evolution.

Viewed from one side, evolution was the basis for optimism. But there is also a dark side to evolution. When man could be explained without God, the dignity that goes with being made in the image of God was stripped away. The best that could be said of human beings was that they were the highest of the animal kingdom. That is quite a plunge in human significance. With this lowering of human dignity came a lowering of human hope and a lowering of moral expectation. When man is made in the image of God, the character of God becomes the standard to which a person is to aspire. When man is simply the highest of the animal kingdom, there are no values that transcend human experience.

When the concept of survival of the fittest is accepted, it motivates those who have evil motives to strive for power to bring others under their control. When individuals or masses of people get in the way of their utopian dreams, they meet them with brute force—thus an Adolf Hitler and a Joseph Stalin.

Since evolution emphasized the principle of change and progress, it undercut the concept of absolute Truth. Every thought was subject to change. There was no place for Truth. This trend toward the denial of absolute Truth, for a while, brought to some a false sense of freedom—freedom from the tyranny of God. But this victory was short-lived. There was no basis for hope.

The dark side of evolution was in conflict with the side of modernism that nourished optimism. Instead of promoting high morals, the foundation of high morals was undercut. Instead of high ideals, there was a rejection of any Truth claim for ideals. If there is no basis for moral truth, certainly we cannot insist on any standard for beauty and excellence. There is no basis for hope and optimism. Instead of hastening the move toward the bright hopes of modernism, evolution in reality contributed to the defeat of modernism and the rise of postmodernism.

An Examination of the Scientific and Theological Approaches to a Study of the Origin of Man

A careful examination of the scientific and the theological approaches to the study of the origin of man, I believe, will reveal that the ultimate question in determining whether evolution or creationism is true is a question of whether naturalism or Christian Theism is the correct worldview. The question of the origin of man and the universe cannot be settled as a separate issue. It must be settled in the context of worldview thinking.

ASSUMPTIONS OF THE SCIENTIFIC STUDY OF THE ORIGIN OF MAN

1. The person who makes a scientific investigation assumes that which is the object of his investigation was produced by natural causes.

2. The only kind of data that is allowable is sense data. Biblical statements cannot be considered as data because they do not fall in the category of sense data.

3. The uniformity of nature is assumed for the past, including man's origin. The same system of cause and effect in operation today was in operation and brought man into existence.

In the broad sense, the word "science" would include any field of study whenever it proceeds on principles in keeping with good scholarship. In the restricted sense, science is limited to the realm of nature that can be studied through the five senses. It is science in the restricted sense that proposes to study the origin of man.

All logical thinking requires a person to find one or more unbending principles with which all else must harmonize. The person who makes a scientific study to determine the origin of man has accepted as an unbending principle: "Man's origin can be accounted for by natural causes."

CONCLUSIONS INHERENT IN A SCIENTIFIC STUDY OF THE ORIGIN OF MAN

A few conclusions are now beginning to be obvious:

1. If the answer to man's origin is to be found through science, the answer will not be a divine act of creation. This is true since divine activity is in the category of the supernatural, not the natural.

2. This same observation viewed from the other side tells us that if the answer to man's origin is to be found in a divine act of creation, it is not discoverable by science since science finds answers only among natural causes.

3. If life had a beginning, it must be found on a low level. It is very difficult for anybody to believe that life came into being from lifeless matter by natural causes. If one is going to believe such, it is obvious that he will want to reduce his difficulty as much as possible by thinking the first life to be one-cell life. No one could believe that natural causes could give sudden rise to a human being from lifeless matter.

4. Some form of evolution is presupposed by those who believe man has come into being by natural causes. Natural causes could not suddenly take one-cell life and change it into a fully developed human being.

5. It is obvious that it would take a slow, drawn-out process. An enormously long period of time would have been required.

Eugenie C. Scott, an avowed evolutionist, makes some interesting observations on the limitations of scientific inquiry. Scott is very insightful in explaining:

> By definition, science cannot consider supernatural explanations: if there is an omnipotent deity, there is no way that a scientist can exclude or include it in a research design. This is especially clear in experimental research: an omnipotent deity cannot be 'controlled' (as one wag commented, 'you can't put God in a test tube, or keep him out of one.') So by definition, if an individual is attempting to explain some aspect of the natural world using science, he or she must act as if there were no supernatural forces operating on it. I think this methodological materialism is well understood by evolutionists. But by excluding the supernatural from our scientific turf, we are elimi-

nating the possibility of proclaiming, via the epistemology of science, that there is no supernatural. One may come to a philosophical conclusion that there is no God, and even base this philosophical conclusion on one's understanding of science, but it is ultimately a philosophical conclusion, not a scientific one. If science is limited to explaining the natural world using natural causes, and thus cannot admit supernatural explanations, so also is science self-limited in another way: it is unable to reject the possibility of the supernatural."[19]

Robert T. Clark and James D. Bales in their book, *Why Scientists Accept Evolution* make it clear that a commitment to naturalism is what gave birth to the theory of evolution. In the "Preface" of their book they explain, "If it was decided that all must be explained naturally, then obviously one would have to accept some hypothesis of evolution regardless of whether it was scientifically established."[20] In this well-documented book, they proceed to show that it was this commitment to naturalism before, during, and after Darwin that actually gave rise to and formed the basis of the acceptance of evolution.

NATURALISM BASED ON FAITH

It is important to remember that the above observations are necessary conclusions on the part of the person who seeks the answer to man's origin in science. These conclusions are inherent in the approach before the first bit of evidence is examined. There are only two things left for evidence to do: (1) to describe the pattern of development, and (2) if the evidence is adequate, to give support to the preconceived conclusions inherent in the approach.

Another important observation is that to believe natural causes gave rise to the origin of the universe, life, and the development of life is a conclusion of faith. There is no proof nor can there be any proof that natural causes explain everything within the scope of our experience and observation. This statement is not made on the basis of whether natural causes do or do not explain everything. It is made because it does not lend itself to proof. Those who take the scientific approach cannot get away with the denial that their system is based on faith. If their faith is wrong, their system is wrong.

The only way a person can take the whole package of science on the origin of man and the age of the earth is to accept naturalism as the system of thought that explains the whole of reality. If God has acted, His acts are not the subject of scientific investigation. I am not suggesting that nothing dealing with the length of human history is subject to scientific investigation. I am saying that science cannot settle either for or against creation by a supernatural act. I am saying that if we believe in God we will have to let revelation tell us whether God created and what the limits of scientific investigation are.

Assumptions of the Theological Approach to Study the Origin of Man

A theological approach to the study of the origin of man assumes that:

1. God exists.
2. God has given a propositional revelation of Himself and His plan in the Bible. This revelation can be understood by the grammatico-historical method of interpretation.
3. There is a supernatural realm and a natural realm. These are interrelated, but are distinct.
4. Whatever the Bible sets forth as belonging to the supernatural must be so accepted.

Theologically, the origin of man is accounted for as taking place by a direct act of God in a period of time not longer than 24 hours. The evidence for this position, based on the assumptions stated above, has already been given in this chapter.

THEOLOGY OR SCIENCE?

The point is simply this: If the theological method is a valid approach for studying the origin of man, the scientific method is not. If the scientific method is a valid approach for studying the origin of man, the theological method is not. An individual may choose either one he prefers, but an evangelical Christian must accept the theological approach.

THE CHRISTIAN ATTITUDE TOWARD SCIENCE

This approach is not intended to be anti-science. It only seeks to find proper limits for science. We do accept the uniformity of nature, but we do not place the whole realm of reality in nature. In such realms as medicine, chemistry, physics, etc., we would use the same approach any scientist would. However, when the Bible attributes something to a direct act of God, we dare not consider it an object of scientific investigation. Science ceases to be science when it seeks to enter the sphere of the supernatural.[21]

In its proper sphere, we should have a very high regard for the scientific method. No generation has ever been so blessed by scientific research as ours. It is postmodernism, not Christianity that is posing a threat to the survival of science. Loren Fishman explains:

> Under the Postmodernists regime, there can be no confidence in data-based conclusions, because, it is held, language is incapable of bearing facts or of being used logically. Still less are we to trust reports of investigators; when they come from even the not-too-distant past. . . .

Fishman goes on to say:

If, as Postmodernists would have it, meaning and Truth are inexorably bound to context and historical setting, then the whole point of scientific theorizing would vanish, and science itself would have to be abandoned.[22]

A Christian view of science does not discuss the conclusions of science as its starting point. It simply limits science to the sphere of the natural. This limitation makes it as Christian as any non-biblical field of study can be. Of course, the Christian recognizes the realm of nature as being the creation of God.

After the limitation of science is made, the chief difference between the Christian and the non-Christian is: When the Christian discovers the marvelous wonders of nature, he feels like singing, "How Great Thou Art." The non-Christian feels like singing, "How Great I Am," or "How Great We Are," or "How Great Man Is."

The problem with many efforts to harmonize the Bible and science is that they have started at the wrong place. Science is not Christian because of its conclusions. It is Christian when it lets divine revelation determine what is supernatural, therefore, not an object of scientific investigation. It is very obvious that the ideas on the origin of man that come from scientific investigation will not be the same as those which come from the theological approach. If we accept the conclusions of scientists on the origin of man, it becomes quite obvious that the biblical account must be either rejected or twisted to fit. When the proper limitation is placed on science, there is no difficulty. In the realm of the natural, there is no difference in the approach of a Christian and a modernist in the approach to scientific research.

The Question of the Age of the Earth

Our discussion so far has centered around the problem of the origin of man. It is equally clear that scientific research cannot discover the age of the earth if the theological assumptions are correct.

THREE UNIVERSAL EVENTS NOT CAUSED BY NATURAL CAUSES

According to the Bible there are three universal events which do not fall in the category of events caused by natural causes:

1. The creation
2. The curse
3. The flood

We have no way of knowing what the earth looked like immediately after creation. We have no way of measuring creative activity.

We know that the curse affected the earth, but we know of no way to determine exactly how it affected it.

We know that there was a flood that was very devastating in its results. Those who have the proper scientific credentials can make some helpful observations. But they cannot with absolute precision tell how the flood would affect the question of dating the age of the earth.

THE CREATION, THE CURSE, AND THE FLOOD OVERLOOKED BY NATURALISM

Scientific study, when based on naturalistic assumptions, overlooks all three of the things mentioned above. If these things are true, and if our theological assumptions are true, it is impossible to discover the exact age of the earth because we would not know how to make proper allowances for the three events. Also, if the theological assumptions are true, any attempt to discover the age of the earth which attributes all that ever happened to the earth to natural causes will necessarily give a much older age for the earth than is actually the case.

We may illustrate our point this way. Suppose we had seen some of the water that Jesus turned to wine (Jn. 2), but had not known that it was turned into wine by a miracle, we would have assumed that it was made by natural processes. If anyone had asked us how long it took to make the wine, we would have told them the length of time it takes to make wine by natural processes. We would have been wrong. Why? Because of our failure to take into account that it was miraculously made.

If our theological assumptions are true, it is easy to see why those who do not take creation by a direct act of God, the curse, and the flood into account, will come up with the wrong answer on the age of the earth. We can rest assured that the earth is younger than naturalistic scientists tell us. However, we cannot know the exact age of the earth because the Bible does not tell us.

Morris makes observations along the same line as stated above. He explains:

> The Biblical framework involves three major facts of history, each of tremendous importance with respect to the scientific study of data bearing on these problems. These facts are of such obvious significance that to ignore them means that one is arbitrarily rejecting even the possibility that God could have given a genuine revelation of beginnings in His Book of Beginnings. The three facts are: (1) a real creation; (2) the fall of man and resultant curse on the earth; and (3) the universal deluge in the days of Noah.[23]

With reference to creation, he remarks:

> Now this can only mean that, since nothing in the world has been created since the end of the creation period, everything must then have been created by means of processes which are no longer in operation and which we therefore cannot study by any means or methods of science. We are limited exclusively to divine revelation as to the date of creation, the duration of creation, the method of creation, and every other question concerning the creation necessarily involves creation of an "appearance of age." It is

impossible to imagine a genuine creation of anything without that entity having an appearance of age at the instant of its creation.[24]

THE PROBLEM OF FOSSILS

One of the most vexing problems to the Christian is the problem of fossils. Fossils of men would have come after the curse. Probably the same can be said of animals. Granting that fossils occurred after the creation and curse, only one of the events mentioned above occurred during fossil history, that is the flood. The flood would have something to do with the distribution of fossils, but I am not prepared to say whether it would have affected the aging process of fossils.

Those who have the scientific qualifications to pursue this matter should consider such matters as the flood and fossils; things that affect the aging processes; and the accuracy of dating methods. It must also be kept in mind that while the Christian would like to see a later date for fossils, the scientist is favorable toward the idea of extremely old fossils. This is true because his system requires an extreme antiquity of life on the earth. We have as much right to look for the possibilities of dating fossils late as they do to look for possibilities of dating them early.

THE BIAS OF MOST SCIENTIFIC RESEARCH ON FOSSILS

It is interesting to observe that the vast majority of the scientific studies done on the age of fossils has been done by people who believed in naturalism. They believed that man's origin and development must be accounted for by natural causes. This caused them to look for evidence for a long history of man on the earth. It also caused them to interpret the available data with a favor toward a long history of man on the earth. Is it not reasonable to believe that the bias of naturalism could have caused the scientist to overlook evidence that might have supported a younger date for fossils? Is it not reasonable to believe that if enough people who believed in special creation and a younger history of man and animals had been studying the evidence that they might have more answers to perplexing problems about the age of life on earth?

GAINS MADE IN CREATION RESEARCH SINCE 1970

What I said in the paragraph above in 1975 has proved to be true. An abundance of scientific material has appeared since that time showing tremendous progress in answering the questions that have been raised by naturalistic evolutionists. Many organizations that promote the truth and the scientific credibility of the biblical view of creation have done a great work. The best known of these groups is the Institute for Creation Research headed by Henry Morris. More good materials have been produced since 1970 showing the scientific credibility of the biblical view of creation than were produced in the history of the world before then. It is imperative that we acquaint our people with what Christian creationists have produced.

When we talk about scientific credibility for the biblical view of creation, we are not speaking of scientific evidence for the act of creation by God. We are speaking of a scientific model that interprets the data relating to geology, paleontology, etc. We are talking about a creationist model as opposed to an evolutionary model.

Concluding Observations

It is best for most of us to admit that we do not have a ready answer to all the problems raised by scientists relating to evolution and creationism. Those who are capable may be able to give answers for most problems, but they cannot remove all the difficulty.

Since we cannot readily show the answers to all of these questions, what will we do with our faith in the biblical view of man? One lesson I have learned in life is that we will never believe anything if we cannot believe even though we do not have answers for all the problems.

Lest we let the evolutionist upset us and intimidate us when we admit we believe with problems, let us call attention to some of his problems. First, he must believe in the eternity of matter or energy in some form. He has no proof of this. It is believed out of necessity. It must be a rather embarrassing point because we seldom hear it mentioned.

The spontaneous generation of life out of lifeless matter places a great strain on the intellect. There is no proof for it. There can be no proof for it. Even if scientists created life out of matter, it would not prove life originated spontaneously out of lifeless matter. If men after thousands upon thousands of hours over a period of several years finally created life out of matter, it would not prove that it could have happened without all the minds, equipment, and controlled conditions. Yet, in spite of all the difficulty, those who look to natural causes for the answer must believe that life originated that way.

What about this belief in naturalism? There is no proof for it. There can be none. It must be a matter of faith. The naturalist has a heap of problems, but he believes anyway. He may be able to point to a vast number of learned men and learned works that support his position. This is not much comfort though when such a view introduces him into bankruptcy when it comes to the answers to the basic questions of life. The more the traces of biblical influence are removed from those who believe in naturalism, the more bankrupt they become on basic issues. This is evidenced by the emptiness of postmodernism.

Theism is accepted by faith too. However, it is not embarrassed by it. Neither does it try to cover up the place of faith. It readily admits the place of faith. Many who follow naturalism try to avoid admitting the place of faith in their system.

There are problems in believing the biblical view of creation. However, there are also problems in believing in evolution and explaining life on the basis of natural causes. Naturalism bankrupts a person morally and spiritually. It leaves him on the sea of life without a compass, guide, or North Star. Theism and the biblical explanation of the origin of man and God's relationship to man open the door to riches in the areas that count the most—the moral and the spiritual. Is it not reasonable to believe that the truth about the origin of man and knowledge for life will not be contradictory? Shall we not expect that same source of Truth that tells us how to face life to also tell us the real answer to man's origin?

Truth is for life. All truth must ultimately fit together so as to make a rational worldview. It would be a strange world if Truth left us without answers to the *inescapable questions of life.* Biblical truth meets our needs by answering these questions and giving practical guidance in life.

Would we not also expect it to give an accurate answer regarding man's origin? Yes, there are problems, but the evolutionary answer has problems too. Let us stick with the answer that also prepares us for life.[25]

The concern I expressed in 1975 in *Biblical Systematics* has been greatly lessened by the labors of those whom I referred to above. Many believers have good scientific credentials. In writing today, I would still have to say that there are still a few hard questions, but those who try to give an evolutionary answer have more problems than we do. Many debates have been conducted between biblical creationists and naturalistic evolutionists. The creationists are doing very well. The unbelieving evolutionists have more unanswered questions than those of us who believe in the biblical view of creation.

9

The Nature of Man

The psalmist asks one of the most important questions ever to be raised by a human being in Psalm 8:4: "What is man, that thou art mindful of him?" The answer to this question is not simply an exercise in mental curiosity by those seated at the intellectual round table. Our whole being cries out for an answer.

Proper identification is important. Even a machine requires proper identification. A motor requires proper identification in order that the right fuel may be used, the proper function may be understood, the right adjustments may be made, the right parts may be ordered for replacement, etc. Improper identification can have serious results. The same can be said of plants. What may be fatal to one plant may not be harmful at all to another. The same can be said of animals. Improper identification can be dangerous and even fatal because improper identification can result in an improper prescription.

It seems absurd, in a way, to even talk about improper identification of human beings since we are each human. We observe others and are observed by them. The problem rests in the danger of an improper description of man. There are two conflicting views of human beings that demand our attention. One view describes man as a being related to the animal world. He has an animal history. He has the needs of an animal of his type. The other view describes man as created by God in God's image. He is accountable to God.

It is obvious that the prescriptions written for man's needs will differ greatly according to which of these views a person subscribes. If the wrong prescription can cause malfunction, and even disastrous results for a machine, it should be more obvious that the wrong prescription for a human being can have *the most serious consequences*. We need a proper prescription for our lives. Proper prescriptions can come only after we have proper identification. It is only when we have a prescription based on our design that we can know true happiness.

Special divine revelation takes the guess work out of identification. Identification comes to us as a "given" from the Creator Himself. The real nature of man's personality and what it takes to meet those needs will never be discovered by observation and experience. It must come to us as a "given."

I am not suggesting that the whole picture of man comes so fully amplified that there is no room for study. I am saying, however, that revelation does give us the basics and that all amplification of details must involve reflection upon the data of revelation. Also, we must be constantly subjecting whatever may be known through research and observation to the authority of revelation.

One of the important things to observe about a system is that nothing in a system can be fully identified without reference to other parts of the system. Every part of a system is tied into the system by relationships to other parts. These relationships must be touched on in identifying a part. The matter of relationship in identification is clearly revealed in the statement: "Man is created in the image of God." To identify man without identifying God and then elaborating the meaning of "the image of God" is disastrous.

The Meaning of Being Created in the Image of God

It is a mistake to begin our identification of a human being by saying, "Man is a sinner." That is true, but there is something more fundamental in explaining what a human being is. Human beings are created in the image of God.

If the man at a body shop is going to work to restore a wrecked automobile, he will need to know what it was like before it was wrecked. So it is with human beings. While it is necessary for us to recognize that "All have sinned," we need to know what human beings were like before they sinned. Saying that a human being is a sinner tells you about a serious problem he has, but it does not tell you what a human being is. It is important in identifying man to say that he was created by God, but that still does not tell you what a human being is. Plants and animals were also created by God. We have not told what a human being is until we say that he or she is created in the image of God.

Once we know what it means to be created by God in His image, then we can begin to address the fact that man is a sinner, the problems that presents, and the hope and meaning of redemption. What human personality is and how human personality functions is understood by understanding the meaning of being created in the image of God. The basic needs of human beings are determined by knowing the design of human beings as they came from the hand of the Creator.

That man is created in the image of God is declared in Genesis 1:26, 27. The meaning is that man is patterned after God. In what sense is man patterned after God? That it was not a physical likeness is too obvious to require proof in view of our study of the nature of God.

A RATIONAL LIKENESS

We get clues from Colossians 3:10 and Ephesians 4:24 regarding what is involved in being created in God's image. In Colossians 3:10 we read: "And have put on the new man, which is renewed in knowledge after the image of him that created him." The image of the Creator in man is linked to rationality. Therefore, we conclude that being created in the image of God involves man's rationality. We do not make people rational by educating them. We can educate people because by the design of creation they are rational.

Human beings are created as rational beings, and this makes it possible for us to think, reason, and learn. It is astounding what human minds have been able to accomplish. All of this has been possible because God created human beings with intelligence.

As created rational beings, not only are we able to think and reason, but we also have rational needs. We *need* knowledge and understanding.

People need answers to the *inescapable questions of life:* Is there a God? If so, what is He like? How can I know Him? How do we account for the origin of the universe and man? What is a human being? How do I know what is right and what is wrong? Is there life after death? If there is, how do I get ready for it? Human beings are in desperate need of answers to these questions. Human beings need a worldview. When a person starts answering these questions, he or she is developing a worldview.

If we are going to minister effectively to a generation that has been conditioned by the post-modern mood, it is imperative that we minister to people's rational needs. We must go beyond minimum Christianity (Heb. 6:1, 2). We must strive to give people a comprehensive and meaningful understanding of life and thought. This move must not be limited to college and seminary class-rooms. It must take place in local churches. It was God who determined that human beings need Truth. The image of God within needs knowledge whether the conscious mind recognizes it or not. It is our responsibility to minister to the designed needs of the image of God.

A MORAL LIKENESS

In Ephesians 4:24 Paul wrote: "And that ye put on the new man, which after God is created in righteousness and true holiness." We conclude from this that the image of God in man makes man a moral creature. In thinking of morals at this point we are to think in the broadest sense of the word to include the whole scope of what is involved in holiness, love, wisdom, and ideals. We do not make people moral by teaching them morals. We can teach them morals because by the design of creation they are moral. Paul tells us that every human being has the law of God written on his or her heart (Rom. 2:14, 15).

The need to live according to God's moral standard and to appreciate beauty and excellence is designed in every human being . We cannot decide whether we need to live according to God's moral standard. *God decided that* when He created us. We can decide whether we want to live according to God's moral teachings, but we cannot decide whether we need to. God has already decided that. A human being cannot go contrary to God's moral law without suffering the consequences.

Any society that tries to ignore the morality of the Ten Commandments will be a troubled society. It will have many people who will try to escape the pain of reality by any means available to them. In our society, a refuge from reality might be sought through alcohol, illicit sex, gambling, or drugs. It is especially troubling when people violate the sexual morality of the Bible (1 Cor. 6:18).

One of the favorite questions that is asked today is: "Who's to say that sex outside marriage is wrong?" (or it could be some other basic moral question). The answer to that question is: "Every human being, if he or she will let the image of God within speak!"

Since we all have to deal with our own sinfulness, it helps us when we can see moral issues addressed in the Bible, but general revelation does a good job of informing us on basic morality. At the judgment, no person will be able honestly to say to God, "I didn't know it was wrong to lie. I didn't know it was wrong to steal. I didn't know it was wrong to murder. I didn't know it was wrong to have sex outside marriage." The suppression of the Truth will no longer work. It may be helpful to reread the comments in Chapter 3 on "General Revelation."

Until Jesus Christ returns, we will always have to contend with sin. No sin will be exterminated from the human race prior to His return. But there is a decided difference between the presence of sinful behavior and the idealizing of such behavior. It was this problem that Paul addressed in Romans 1:32, "They not only do the same, but also give hearty approval to those who practice them" (NASB). The word that is translated "give hearty approval to" is *suneudokeō*. The literal meaning is "to think well with." When wrong behavior is approved and idealized we have reached a new low. That is where we are in America when it comes to abortion and sex outside marriage.

LIKENESS SUMMED UP IN THE WORD PERSON

The one word that sums up the idea of rationality and morality is the word "person." God is personal. Man is personal. The basic thrust of the idea of being created in the image of God is that *man is a personal being*. A person is one who thinks, feels, and acts.

THE MEANING OF MIND

We think with our minds. The mind is referred to in Matthew 22:37; Romans 14:5; and Hebrews 8:10. The words "think," "reason," and "understanding" are used too often in Scripture to require a list of proof texts. We think with our minds. We grasp ideas. We reason. We make judgments. We draw conclusions. We size up situations.

THE MEANING OF HEART

The heart is referred to in Matthew 22:37; Romans 10:1, 9; Hebrews 8:10; and many other verses. We feel with our hearts. The heart is the seat of the emotions. With the heart we feel the reality of the truth that we know with our mind. The heart registers the value we place on things. It is with the heart that we feel sorrow and sadness. Sorrow and sadness reflect feelings of negative value or disvalue. Feelings of positive value are joy, happiness, satisfaction, peace, and contentment. Heart involvement represents the involvement of our deepest inner self. The human heart cries out for more than a mere objective grasp of knowledge.

THE MEANING OF WILL

The New Testament does not use the noun form of will to refer to the faculty of choice in man. However, the verb form (*thelō*) is used (Mt. 16:24; 21:29; 23:37; Mk. 8:34; Jn. 7:17; Rev. 22:17; and others). By will we mean power of choice. Every command, every prohibition, every exhortation, and every entreaty in the Bible which is made to people presupposes that they are capable of making choices.

Whether we want to think of the act of willing as the function of a faculty of the person or simply the person making a choice, the fact remains that the ability to choose is part of being a person. That ability of choice is what we call *will*. In his totality, man is a *thinking, feeling, acting being*. He thinks with his mind, feels with his heart, and acts with his will.

THE CONSTITUTIONAL AND FUNCTIONAL LIKENESS OF GOD IN MAN

What has been said about man as a personal, rational, moral creature is frequently referred to as the formal likeness of God in man.[1] I prefer to speak of it as the constitutional likeness of God in man. The image of God in man at creation included more than constitutional likeness; it also included functional likeness (also referred to as material content[2]). The functional likeness means that man, as created, thought, felt, and acted in a way that was pleasing to God.

I think the distinction between constitutional and functional likeness is made clearer if we divide the scope of person into "personhood" and "personality." Personhood would embrace the constitutional likeness of God, i.e., all the elements that go together to constitute a person. Personality refers to the way in which a person thinks, feels and acts. At times "person" and "personality" are used synonymously, but there is usually a difference. In this study, personality will be used as defined above. Man as created was in the likeness of God both with respect to his personhood and his personality.

THE TWO LEVELS OF PERSONALITY

The functioning of personality occurs on two levels: the conscious level and the subconscious level. Man as created and as he developed after creation, up to the time of the fall, functioned both on the conscious and subconscious level in the likeness of God.

The subconscious mind is programmed with ideas, attitudes, and responses. Mind, as it is referred to here, is used in the broad sense to include mind, heart, and will. It is this use of the word mind that we employ when we say, "I have made up my mind to do so and so." Mind in this instance involves more than the reasoning, thinking mind. It involves our total personality: our mind, heart, and will.

Through study, thought, observation, and meditation, we store knowledge or ideas into our subconscious mind. Only a very limited part of our knowledge is at any given moment in our conscious mind. It is stored for recall in our subconscious mind. The storage of ideas is much like the programming of a computer. Our mind is programmed with a vast store of ideas that can be brought to the surface with differing degrees of speed.

In the process of meditation, ideas to which we are committed take on the appropriate attitudes in the heart. We are programmed to think and feel a certain way under certain circumstances. The programming of the subconscious mind of Adam and Eve was constituted with ideas and attitudes which were in the likeness of God before the fall. In their innermost being they were like God. I agree with Berkhof when he says. "The image of God in which man was created certainly includes what is generally called 'original righteousness,' or more specifically, true knowledge, righteousness, and holiness. . . . Man's creation in this moral image implies that the original condition of man was one of positive holiness, and not a state of innocence or moral neutrality."[3]

In theological writings, references are frequently made to "original righteousness" and "original sin." I have been unable to find anyone who comments on the meaning of the word "original" when discussing the meaning of original righteousness and original sin. Most commonly, we think of original as meaning "first" as distinguished from some other place in the order of numerical sequence. Sometimes, we take the meaning to be the original as distinguished from a copy. Neither of these meanings properly modifies righteousness or sin in the terms "original righteousness" or "original sin."

According to the *Oxford English Dictionary*, one of the meanings of original is "innate." That seems to fit the meaning of original righteousness and original sin. When we speak of man, as created, as possessing original righteousness, we mean he was innately righteous. Righteous thoughts, feelings, and actions flowed from the very design of his nature. By original sin, we mean that since the fall of Adam and Eve human beings are born with an innately depraved nature. There is an innate proneness to sin.

DESIGNED FOR RELATIONSHIPS
Inherent in the constitutional likeness of God in man and demonstrated in the functional likeness is the fact that man is designed for relationships. A human being cannot be adequately described apart from these relationships. In fact, a person will die, suffer malfunction, or be less than human according to what relationship (relationships) is involved and depending upon the extent he or she is deprived or deprives himself of these relationships. The relationships are: (1) his relationship to God; (2) his relationship to other people; (3) his relationship to the created order; and (4) his relationship to himself.

DESIGNED FOR A RELATIONSHIP WITH GOD
Human beings are designed for a relationship with God. Man's relationship to God is seen in his fellowship with and his responsibility to God. After we are told of the creation of man by God, we read, "And God blessed them, and God said unto them, Be fruitful, and multiply, and replenish the earth, and subdue it: and have dominion over the fish of the sea, and over the fowl of the air, and over every living thing that moveth upon the earth" (Gen. 1:28). We read also of man's moral responsibility when God said, "But of the tree of the knowledge of good and evil, thou shalt not eat of it: for in the day that thou eatest thereof thou shalt surely die" (Gen. 2:17). From the reference to God walking in the garden immediately after the fall, we would infer that He had done so before and that they had fellowship with God. Before the fall Adam and Eve functioned properly and in a way that was becoming to God in their relationship with Him. We do not make people religious by teaching them about God. We can teach them about God because they are religious by the design of creation. Human beings are in desperate need of a meaningful relationship with God. A quote from Augustine mentioned previously in Chapter 3 also expresses the deep inner sentiments of every human being, "Thou madest us for thyself, and our heart is restless, until it repose in Thee."[4]

DESIGNED FOR INTERPERSONAL RELATIONSHIPS
Human beings are designed for social relationships. In Genesis 2:18, God said, "It is not good that the man should be alone; I will make him an help meet for him." While the direct reference here is to making a wife for Adam, considering a human being is a member of a race, it is obvious that social relationships are a part of the design of God. A person's need for reciprocal social rela-

tionships is no less real than his need for air, water, and food. This need for social relationships was created in our basic design and *cannot be ignored* without serious consequences. It can be inferred from Genesis 2:18 that it is not good for man to be a loner. Loners are troubled people.

Primary in human social relationships is marriage. It is interesting that the first mention of social relationships was tied in with marriage. Jesus gave His blessings to marriage when He attended the wedding at Cana of Galilee (Jn. 2). Jesus confirmed the institution of marriage when he said, "Have you not read, that He who made *them* at the beginning *'made them male and female,'* and said, *'For this reason a man shall leave his father and mother and be joined to his wife: and the two shall be one flesh'?"* (Mt. 19:5, 6, NKJV). Man and wife marriages are the only marriages that the Bible knows anything about.

Research is beginning to recognize that there are some real differences between men and women. However, we did not have to wait for it to be confirmed by research to know that. Our own experience as a member of the human race tells us so. In fact, a person has to work very hard to miss this fact. What we already know finds confirmation in Genesis 1:27 where it reads, "So God created man in his *own* image, in the image of God created he him; male and female created he them." While there is a large area of likeness between men and women, each has his or her unique contribution to make. Men and women complement each other. Men and women are attracted to each other because they are different. If you place the north pole of a magnet near the north pole of another magnet, the magnets will repel each other. The same is true of the south poles. But if you put the north pole of a magnet beside the south pole of another, they come together.

It is important to understand what worldview or anti-worldview a person is coming from when he or she is discussing male and female contributions in life. God did something wonderful when He made man and woman. If we will recognize that men and women are different by divine design, men will do a good job of being male and women will do a good job of being female.

DESIGNED FOR A RELATIONSHIP WITH THE CREATED ORDER

We are designed for a relationship to the created order (Gen. 1:26, 28-30; Ps. 8:6-8). Man was designed for the responsibility of exercising dominion over the earth, plants, and animals. This meant he had a management responsibility over the created order. It was to be used to meet his needs and to serve his purposes. This responsibility has been referred to as the "Cultural Mandate."

Our relationship with the material universe is more than a means of survival. It is for our pleasure and enjoyment. It presents us with a challenge. It is an opportunity for us to put our creative minds to work. The Cultural Mandate sanctifies and elevates to the level of divine service the work of farmers, housekeepers, skilled workers, helpers, scientists, engineers, artists, etc. The list could go on. When done for the glory of God, all that we do is a divine service. The challenge is great. Work was a part of the original plan of God for man. It did not involve the undesirable aspects that it does now, but work has always been a part of the divine plan.

This managerial responsibility must also involve a concern for ecology. We must be concerned about the condition of things as we pass them on to future generations.

In the Cultural Mandate, God is saying to every human being:

I have made you in My image. I have given you a mind. Your mind is capable of taking what I have given you in the physical universe and achieving much that will be for your enjoyment, comfort, deep satisfaction, and My glory. The possibilities of creative achievement are limitless.

I have given you a moral nature. My laws are written in your heart. As you carry out this Mandate your mind is to do its work under the supervision of your moral nature. See what you can do with the challenge that is before you. One day, I will have you to report to Me to see how good a steward you have been of the opportunities that you have had.

The fall of man complicated matters in the fulfillment of this Mandate. But the Mandate still remains in force. Stephen M. Ashby reminds us that "it is our responsibility as stewards of this divine command to educate people to think Christianly with an integrated and unified field of knowledge in regards to their faith with their learning."[5]

DESIGNED FOR AN INTRAPERSONAL RELATIONSHIP

Man was designed for a relationship with himself. Anytime there is responsibility and challenge, there is also a place for self-examination. How did I do? How can I face the challenge that is before me? There were two clear illustrations of responsibility: (1) the responsibility to refrain from eating of the tree of the knowledge of good and evil (Gen. 2:17); (2) to exercise dominion over the earth and its inhabitants.

To eat of the forbidden fruit was to reap the consequences of death. It would also make man guilty. Guilt when recognized by the person becomes self-judgment on the negative side. To refrain from eating would have produced self-acceptance on the positive side. The responsibility to exercise dominion over the earth has the same basic results so far as self-judgment and self-acceptance are concerned. The moral tone may not be as strong, but the same basic principles are involved.

In connection with the responsibility placed upon man and the challenge given to him, we see that man is goal-oriented. Achievement with its rewards, as well as failure with its losses, are inescapable parts of a human being that were designed in him by the Creator.

The Importance of the Fact That Man Was Created in the Image of God

CONTRIBUTES TO A PROPER SENSE OF WORTH

The image of God in man gives dignity and places a sense of worth on man. Psalm 8:5-8 reads:

For You have made him a little lower than the angels,
And You have crowned him with glory and honor.
You have made him to have dominion over the works of Your hands;
You have put all things under his feet,

All sheep and oxen—
Even the beasts of the field,
The birds of the air,
And the fish of the sea
That pass through the paths of the seas (NKJV).

As a result of the fall there is a dark side to human nature, but even in fallen man there are still signs of nobility.

It was fallen man that Jesus was talking about when He said, "Behold the fowls of the air: for they sow not, neither do they reap, nor gather into barns; yet your heavenly Father feedeth them. Are ye not much better than they?" (Mt. 6:26). It was the greater worth of man than animals that Jesus appealed to when He defended His healing of the man with a withered hand on the sabbath day. "And he said unto them, What man shall there be among you, that shall have one sheep, and if it fall into a pit on the sabbath day, will he not lay hold on it, and lift it out? How much then is a man better than a sheep? Wherefore it is lawful to do well on the sabbath days" (Mt. 12:11, 12).

Since sin complicates the way we feel or should feel about ourselves, I will wait until we deal with the subject of sanctification before I deal with the Christian approach to self-worth.

MAKES SIN AGAINST HUMAN BEINGS A SERIOUS MATTER

Sin against our fellow man is viewed very seriously because man is made in the image of God. Genesis 9:6 shows that man being created in the image of God is the basis for capital punishment. The statement in James 3:9, that man is made "after the similitude of God," makes cursing a fellow human being a serious matter.

Fellow human beings, regardless of race, nationality, or sex, must all be viewed as having special worth, as having been created in the image of God. It is this basic respect for one another that forms the starting point of a right relationship between people.

HUMAN BEINGS CHARACTERIZED BY DEPENDENCE, INDEPENDENCE, AND INTERDEPENDENCE

Creation in the image of God means that man is characterized by both *dependence* and *independence*. Because man is created by God, he is dependent upon God. Man is not just an individual; he is a member of a race. People are *interdependent* upon each other. Man is a person, which means he has a measure of independence. The ideal for human attainment on the individual basis involves both independence and dependence. The ideal for social relationships involves interdependence. While an adequate sense of independence is necessary, it is a mistake to make total independence an ideal to achieve. Such a goal places an undue strain on a person and interferes with good interpersonal relationships.

Because human beings are characterized by independence, dependence, and interdependence, the human personality in relationship to others will be characterized by both distance and closeness. To go too far in either direction creates problems. Clinging (holding on to closeness) and pushing away (developing distance) can be seen very early on the part of a baby in the relationship between mother and child. The move toward independence starts early in a child and progresses on until adulthood. The teenage years are difficult, involving a period of transition from the dependence of childhood to the independence of adulthood. The move toward independence sometimes gives rise to rebellion. The ideal for adulthood is not *absolute* independence, but by the time of adulthood, a healthy sense of independence should be achieved.

Horizontal (being approachable) and vertical (looking up to with respect) attitudes should characterize our relationship with others throughout our lives. One of the things involved in the development of interpersonal relationships is the appropriate measure of closeness and distance for each relationship.

Each person will need to work on the proper balance of closeness and distance in his or her life. Too much dependence (closeness) makes a weak person. Too much independence (distance) makes a cold, insensitive person. Some avoid closeness in interpersonal relationships for fear that they will end up getting hurt. When such people sense a closeness developing, they automatically start pushing people away. It is almost impossible to accommodate some people. They push you away almost instinctively. They fear that they might become indebted to someone. They seek refuge in distance. Even when life is falling apart, such a person turns away those who might help. Such an approach proves detrimental to the person needing help, to those who seek to help, and to everyone around him or her.

In some instances, relational distance is very important. Recently, my wife and I saw the biography of General George C. Marshall on television. General Marshall made a good use of distance in his relationship with President Roosevelt. He would not let President Roosevelt call him George. He would not attend social functions at the White House. But President Roosevelt had such respect for him that he appointed him Chairman of the Joint Chiefs of Staff during World War II. At one time Roosevelt offered General Marshall the command of the army in Europe. This was a position he found desirable, but when he sensed that Roosevelt really wished that he would stay in Washington, he declined. President Roosevelt said in relief, "I would not be able to sleep at night without having you in Washington." At an important time in history General Marshall demonstrated the value of distance. Along with his great military abilities, distance won for him a place close to the president.

INFLUENCE AND RESPONSE, NOT CAUSE AND EFFECT

In some sense, an individual's actions are both *his own* and *under his control*. If this be not the case, he or she is *less than a person*. Yet, the fact that he is a relationship creature means his actions cannot be explained as independent in the absolute sense. *Influence* is brought to bear on his actions. *Influence* in personal decisions can never be equated with *cause* as in mechanical cause and effect relationships. *Influence* and *response* are more appropriate terms, where persons make decisions, than the terms *cause* and *effect*.

In many of our decisions, we are both active and acted upon. To have to make a choice between active and passive is to equate personal relationships with mechanical cause and effect relationships. These principles relate both to our relationships to God and our relationship to other human beings. It is only when we distinguish between influence and response and cause and effect that we can begin to understand how God works with us as human beings.

THE FACTOR OF HUMAN DESIGN

When we see the full meaning of the fact that we are designed to be (1) personal, rational, moral beings, and (2) that we are designed for the four basic relationships, then we can determine our needs according to our design. The *design* of human beings represents *not only possibilities, but needs.* It is not only possible for us to be rational and moral and to have functioning relationships, but we need to function rationally and morally, and properly in the framework of the *four basic relationships.* Failure in any of these areas means loss. All rational, moral, and spiritual functions are functions of the personality. A Christian psychology, sociology, and system of ethics must have as a part of its foundation an acquaintance with what it means *to be made in the image of God.* It is utterly impossible for human beings through observation and experience alone (empiricism) to ever arrive at an adequate understanding of human needs and human behavior. It is only when we let special divine revelation inform us about human design and its implications that we can develop an adequate understanding of human need and how to effectively minister to those needs. Then and only then can we help our fellow human beings be what they are designed to be and become what they can by redemption.

We pay very close attention to design and how it determines need in machines. We are very careful when we buy fuel for our automobiles. We get diesel fuel if that is what our car was designed for. We get gasoline if our car was designed for gasoline. Shall we be less careful in finding out what we are designed for? Will we ignore the question of human design and recommend that people create their own meaning and purpose or simply go along with what society is saying? We know better than to pour water in the fuel tank of our car. It is even more important that we live according to the design that the Designer designed into our being when He made us in His own image.

Postmodernism is right. Modernism did not succeed in finding a solution to human need. The score card on postmodernism so far is worse! The human race cannot handle 200 years of postmodernism.

THE REJECTION OF HUMAN DESIGN BY EXISTENTIALISM

Existentialists say that *existence* precedes *essence. Essence* refers to meaning and purpose. This means that a person exists first and then he or she must create his own purpose and meaning.[6] There is no such thing as universal Truth that precedes human existence that ministers to needs and to which he or she must submit. There is no moral authority. Therefore, there are no moral absolutes. As Jean-Paul Sartre says, "Before you come alive, life is nothing; it's up to you to give it a meaning, and value is nothing else but the meaning you choose."[7]

A COMPARISON OF MODERN EXISTENTIALISM AND POSTMODERN EXISTENTIALISM

Gene Edward Veith, Jr., is very helpful in summing up this comparison. He explains:

This postmodern ideology is more than simple relativism. Whereas modern existentialism teaches that meaning is created by the individual, postmodern existentialism teaches that meaning is created by a social group and its language. According to this view, personal identity and the very content of one's thoughts are all social constructions. The old existentialism stressed the alienated individual, dignified in loneliness and nonconformity; postmodern existentialism stresses social identity, group-think, and fashion sense. Postmodern existentialism goes back to Nietzsche to emphasize not only will, but power. Liberation comes from rebelling against existing power structures, including oppressive notions of "knowledge" and "truth."[8]

Postmodernism is not content with a simple denial of Truth. It is hostile toward any serious claim to a possession of Truth. Whether the claim of Truth is made by Christianity or modernism, postmodernists view such a claim with suspicion. Instead of viewing Truth as that which makes people free as taught in Scripture (Jn. 8:32), postmodernists view any claim to Truth as expressive of the desire to bring someone else, particularly those of some other culture, under oppressive control. Postmodernism promotes suspicion of oppression and a venting of anger, but it offers no belief in any universal principles of justice and fairness to guide the process of correction. The solution is to be found in power.

There is some reason to be concerned that some people may use Truth claims to mistreat other people. However, that danger is lessened greatly when the following are true: (1) It is based on an openly accessible divine revelation; (2) That revelation is understood by the same laws of interpretation that the common man uses when he interprets other written documents; (3) It is connected with an all embracing rational worldview; and (4) It is guided by a sense of justice, fairness, compassion, kindness, etc. that all human beings are capable of understanding if they are not controlled by anger, hatred, and distrust. Any approach to Truth that considers itself to be Christian and would not be consistent with these observations has missed what biblical Christianity is all about.

People with Truth claims become oppressive when they: (1) Claim to be in touch with Truth that is not openly available to others; (2) Claim that they alone, or only special ones can interpret the Truth; (3) They move with disregard for the law of non-contradiction (consistency not required); (4) They do not recognize universal ethical and moral values and principles that they and others must submit to and thus have an approach that accommodates itself to "the end justifies the means"; (5) They are obsessed with some special issue or cause without considering the broader picture of human needs and concerns; and (6) Those in leadership are filled with anger and hatred. Any person or movement that claims to fly the Christian banner of Truth and is guilty of any of these has misunderstood biblical Christianity.

THE CHRISTIAN POSITION ON ESSENCE AND EXISTENCE

Christianity believes that *essence* precedes *existence*. There is meaning and purpose for life which has preceded the birth of each human being. Truth is eternal and universal. It has authority over human beings. It is designed to minister to his or her needs. Every human being is designed for Truth. Every human being shares a basic common design. Every person is made in the image of God, and is made for a relationship with God. This design determines his or her needs and what it will take to meet those needs. In the basic sense, every human being has the same needs programmed into his or her being. The Truth of God is designed to meet our needs both as an individual and as a member of society. Though God's Truth is eternal and unchanging, it is designed to meet the needs of every human being who will turn to God through Jesus Christ and seek to live by His Truth. It addresses our needs wherever we are. It addresses our needs that are brought on by our personal uniqueness and the uniqueness of our social environment.

The attempt of modernism to put life together without God failed even by the tests of postmodernism. Postmodernism's social construction of "Truth" (fiction or myth) is a failure. It should not take 200 years to find this out. Fictitious answers to *upper story* questions never meet the needs of the one who has been designed by God for Truth. Such a move exchanges "the truth of God for a lie" (Rom. 1:25, NASB). Fiction is fine for entertainment, but it is not befitting of one made in the image of God to choose fiction as a foundation of hope for this life and the next. America needs to wake up! We cannot mistreat the image of God within us without suffering the consequences. We need to find out what God has designed us for and live in accordance to that design.

THE IMAGE OF GOD AND HUMAN GOVERNMENT

Government, both secular and church government, should allow the degree of freedom that is required for man to develop his personality and prepare to meet God. On the one hand, there must be government. On the other hand, there must be freedom.

Recognition that man is made in the image of God does not require religious conformity in a culture, but it does offer hope of a moral consensus. The founding fathers of our nation did not seem to have a lot of trouble at this point.

The Declaration of Independence of the United States of America makes reference to "the Laws of Nature and of Nature's God." It speaks of "self-evident truths." It reads, "We hold these truths to be self-evident, that all Men are created equal, that they are endowed by their Creator with certain unalienable Rights, that among these are Life, Liberty, and the Pursuit of Happiness."

This document recognizes that human beings are created by God. Human beings "are endowed by their Creator with certain unalienable Rights." These truths were considered to be "self-evident." These self-evident truths were implanted within the human heart and mind when God created man.

On the foundation that man is created by God, and a belief in self-evident truths and unalienable rights, our forefathers founded a nation that has been a champion of freedom, justice, and human rights. It has been a blessing to the world and a refuge for oppressed people.

It is not the purpose of civil government to endorse a plan of redemption, but it cannot carry on its function when it writes off all Truth. While modernism did not recognize general revelation, by recognizing the rational and moral nature of reality it did give a chance for general revelation to convey its moral message. With the aid of general revelation and Christian influence we were able to have an essential moral consensus prior to the rise of postmodernism. Postmodernism denies the rational and moral nature of reality. In so doing postmodernism refuses to allow that which is written within to speak. It has no place for self-evident truths.[9]

THE IMAGE OF GOD IN MAN AND THE INCARNATION

One of the most important facts related to man's being made in the image of God is that it made the incarnation possible. There could have been no incarnation with a non-rational, non-moral, sub-personal animal. The possibility of redemption is closely related to the creation of man in the image of God.

A Comparison of Views on the Image of God in Man

In his treatment of the image of God, Erickson gives three views that have been given in the history of the church on the meaning of being created in God's image. These are (1) the substantive view, (2) the relational view, and (3) the functional view.

According to Erickson, in the substantive view the image of God is "located within man; it is a quality or capacity resident in his nature."[10] He points out that "the substantive view has been dominant during most of the history of theology."[11]

With regard to the relational view, Erickson explains, "Many modern theologians do not conceive of the image of God as something resident within man's nature."[12] He gives Karl Barth and Emil Brunner as adherents of this view. In describing Brunner's view he explains:

> Brunner uses the analogy of a mirror to clarify the distinction between the formal and material aspects of the image of God. When we bear the image of God in the material sense, we are in positive and responsive relationship to him. Brunner likens this aspect of the image to the reflection in a mirror. Keep in mind that the reflection is not permanently imprinted on the surface, for we are speaking of a mirror, not a photograph. When turned toward a light, a mirror reflects that light; the mirror is not the source of the light nor does it possess the light.[13]

Concerning the functional view Erickson explains:

> This is the idea that the image is not something present in the makeup of man, nor is it the experiencing of relationship with God or with fellow man. Rather, the image consists in something man does. It is a function which man performs, the most frequently mentioned being the exercise of dominion over the creation.[14]

The view that I have set forth would be the *substantive* view. The image of God is something that exists within a human being. God is rational and moral. We are rational and moral. Or, to put it in other words, we are personal beings. God is personal. We are personal. The other views pick up on something that is true about man, but, as I see it, fail to come to grips with the heart of the matter. It is true that a human being reflects something of what God is like, but that is a by-product of the image of God, rather than the image itself. If man were not in his very being in the image of God, he could not mirror God's likeness. Fallen man still reflects traces of the image of God, but only those who are redeemed will be transformed into the functional image of God and reflect what it means to be made in God's image.

The relational view contains an important exegetical flaw. If the image of God were to refer to the fact that man mirrors God or should mirror God, "image" in Genesis 1:26 should be a verb. Instead it is a noun.

I used the term "functional likeness," but not in the same way that Erickson referred to it above. My use of it is essentially synonymous to "material content" in the substantive view. As created, man functioned in the likeness of God in his behavior. While there is some likeness that remains in fallen man, it is greatly distorted. It is the purpose of redemption to restore the functional likeness of God. Progress is being made in this life as we grow in sanctification. It will be completed in the next life.

With regard to the view that Erickson called the "functional view," the adherents of this view confuse a responsibility that man, as one created in the image of God, has with the image of God. It is true that man is responsible for exercising dominion over the earth, but that does not tell what he is. Rather, it tells what he is supposed to do. The image of God in Scripture clearly tells us what man is.

Man Created as a Dichotomous Being

There has been much debate over whether man is a dichotomous being or a trichotomous being. To say that man is a dichotomous being is to say that he consists of a body (material part) and spirit (some use soul and spirit interchangeably). To say that man is a trichotomous being is to say that man consists of a material body and two immaterial parts—soul and spirit.

Augustus Hopkins Strong gives the following explanation of dichotomy:

> We conclude that the immaterial part of man, viewed as an individual and conscious life, capable of possessing and animating a physical organism, is called *psuchē* (soul); viewed as a rational and moral agent, susceptible of divine influence and indwelling, this same immaterial part is called *pneuma* (spirit). The *pneuma* (spirit), then is man's nature looking Godward, and capable of receiving and manifesting the *Pneuma Hagion* (Holy Spirit); the *psuchē* (soul) is man's nature looking earthward, and touching the world of sense. The *pneuma* (spirit) is man's higher part, as related to spiritual realities or as capable of such relation; the *psuchē* is man's higher part, as related to body, or as capable of such relation.[15]

As Strong presents it, soul and spirit are different terms referring to the same immaterial substance. These terms each speak of the same immaterial part from a different viewpoint of function. Some trichotomists assign approximately the same functions to *soul* and *spirit,* but use the terms to refer to two different immaterial parts.

THE MEANING OF SOUL

I think the real problem centers around trying to think of the soul in terms of being a "part" of man. An examination of the Hebrew word *nephesh* and the Greek word *psuchē* as used in the Bible does not seem to support the idea that it refers to an immaterial substance of man.

In Genesis 2:7; 14:21; 17:14, *nephesh* means being, individual, or person. The use in these verses would not make sense if *nephesh* referred to a part of man. It is the person, not a part of the person, that is in view. *Nephesh* is translated person several times (Ex. 16:16; Lev. 27:2; Num. 19:18; Jos. 20:3, 9; and others). In Genesis 19:17; Exodus 4:19; 21:23; Leviticus 17:14; and many others, it is translated life. In these passages it would not fit to think of *nephesh* as being the immaterial part of man. In Leviticus 26:11, 15; Psalm 42:2; and other similar uses the reference is to the inner-most being. In these cases it would be possible for *nephesh* to refer to the immaterial part of man, but it is not necessary. Also, one wonders why Psalm 42:2 did not use the word "spirit" if the usual distinctions made between soul and spirit by both dichotomists and trichotomists are valid. The meaning of *nephesh* in Numbers 16:38 is "self." It is translated "yourselves" in Deuteronomy 4:15.

In the New Testament the word *psuchē* at times clearly means individual or person (Acts 2:41; 7:14; 27:37; Rom. 13:1). In Luke 1:46 and John 12:27, *psuchē* refers to the innermost being. Again one wonders why the word *spirit* instead of *soul* did not appear in Luke 1:46 based on the usual distinctions. In Ephesians 6:6, *psuchē* is translated heart. Luke 12:19 is a clear case of where the meaning of the word *psuchē* is self.

A study of the evidence supports the conclusion that *soul* does not refer to an immaterial part of man. *Soul* refers to a self-conscious individual, the innermost being, the self, the life, or the person.

THE MEANING OF SPIRIT

Psalm 31:5; Ecclesiastes 3:21; 12:7; and Zechariah 12:1 are clear references to the Hebrew word *ruach* (spirit) in which the reference is to the immaterial part of man. John 3:6 is a clear reference where the Greek word *pneuma* (spirit) refers to the immaterial part of man. Man's basic nature is in his spirit (Jn. 3:6; Rom. 1:9; 2 Cor. 2:13; and Heb. 12:23). Functions and states that are attributed to man's spirit do not always require it to be a reference to the immaterial part of man, but they are always consistent with that idea (Gen. 41:8; Ex. 6:9; 1 Kg. 21:5; Ps. 34:18; Acts 17:16; 18:5, 25; and Rom. 1:9). These observations, along with the knowledge that angels and evil spirits are called spirits, apparently because of their immaterial make-up, lead to the conclusion that the spirit of man is the immaterial part of man and describes it as being spirit rather than physical.

THE DIFFERENCE BETWEEN THE USE OF THE WORDS *SOUL* AND *SPIRIT*

A contrast of the use of *soul* and *spirit* will help clarify what I mean by my view of dichotomy. Soul is not an immaterial part of man, but spirit is. No occurrence of the word for soul requires it to be a part of man.

The only verses that present a problem are Revelation 6:9 and 20:4 where reference is made to seeing the souls of those who were martyred. I think Alan F. Johnson has properly understood the use of "souls" in these verses. In commenting on Revelation 6:9, he explains, "This is generally understood to mean the disembodied souls of these saints. However, the Greek word *psuchē* has various meanings and probably stands for the actual 'lives' or 'persons' who were killed rather than their 'souls.' They are seen by John as persons who are very much alive though they have been killed by the beast."[16]

Many occurrences of the word cannot be understood as a reference to a part of man. All occurrences of the word *spirit,* unless of course we are talking about the spirit of jealousy, the spirit of wisdom, etc., when referring to man, are capable of being understood as the immaterial part of man. Many occurrences of the word *spirit* must be understood as referring to a part of man. A way of saying it that may be a slight oversimplification is: *I am a soul. I have a spirit.*

It is hard for most of us to think of soul without thinking of a part of our being because we have been accustomed to thinking that way. If we will give *soul* the same basic meaning as *person,* that will help get away from thinking of soul as a part of our being. We do not think of person as an immaterial substance, nor a material substance. We are a person. We have a *body and a spirit.* Also, the words *mind, heart,* and *will* do not refer to different immaterial parts of man's being. In the same way we think of these terms, we can train ourselves not to think of soul as an immaterial substance, but the self-conscious individual, the innermost being, the self, the life, or the personality.

THE DIFFERENCES BETWEEN MY VIEW AND THE TRADITIONAL VIEW

My view of dichotomy differs from the traditional view which sees a high degree of interchangeableness between soul and spirit. It might be true that sometimes a person could accomplish his purpose in a sentence by using either, but he would not be saying identically the same thing. At times the purpose in a sentence could not at all be served by one term as well as the other. A choice must be made between the terms. If it is a part of man, it must be spirit. If it is person or individual, it must be soul. In reading treatments on soul and spirit, I find some treatments that come very close to my view, but are not developed altogether the same.

A human being consists of a body and a spirit. Viewed as a functioning unity as a conscious, thinking, feeling, acting being, a human being is called a soul or person. A human being still remains a soul after the death of the body, but is not complete. He or she awaits the resurrection of the body.

There is a very close relationship between spirit and soul. Without the spirit there would be no soul. In a sense we might think of soul as issuing forth from spirit. To borrow terminology from Berkhof when he explains the difference between nature and person, soul is the terminus to which spirit tends.[17]

THE ADVANTAGES OF MY VIEW

There are some very definite advantages to the approach I am suggesting. The traditional understanding of soul and spirit, both in dichotomy and trichotomy, make the expression "soul-winning" inaccurate since soul is understood to refer to the lower function of man. To be consistent, one should talk about spirit-winning. In my view, soul-winning is appropriate terminology since it refers to winning the person. Soul embraces *all* of a person's experiences, *both the ordinary experiences of life and his or her relationship with God.*

Another advantage is that it does away with the need of trying to decide what functions are to be attributed to soul and what functions are to be attributed to spirit. By distinguishing between the use of soul and spirit, traditional dichotomy engages in this about as much as trichotomy. The problem is that when we get through we find functions attributed to soul that are supposed to be attributed to spirit. When soul is basically equated with person or personality, *any action or attitude can be attributed to it.* When soul refers to the lower functions of man, and spirit the higher functions of man, it comes unexpectedly when we read that Mary said, "My soul doth magnify the Lord" (Lk. 1:46). It is surprising when we read in Ephesians 6:6 "doing the will of God from the heart" and discover that the Greek word for heart in this verse is *psuchē* (soul). We are puzzled when we read in James 1:21 "and receive with meekness the engrafted word, which is able to save your souls." It seems from the usual distinction between soul and spirit that the word spirit should have appeared in these passages, but it did not. However, there is no problem when the meaning I suggest is given to soul.

It is true that the spiritual functions of man are frequently ascribed to the spirit. In such instances, the intention is not to give us the functions of spirit as distinguished from soul, but spirit as distinguished from the body.

THE QUESTION OF THE DIFFERENCE BETWEEN HUMAN BEINGS AND ANIMALS

We run into another problem when we try to make the distinctions usually made between soul and spirit. We might expect animals to have souls but not spirits. Yet Ecclesiastes 3:21 speaks about animals having a spirit. I am inclined to agree with Buswell at this point. He says, "The distinction between man and beasts is qualitative, not substantive. It is not that man has or is a soul, spirit, heart, mind, will, affective being, but that man's non-material being is a person created in the image of God."[18]

VERSES USED TO SUPPORT TRICHOTOMY

Trichotomists appeal to 1 Thessalonians 5:23 and Hebrews 4:12 for support. Since I do not consider soul and spirit to be synonymous, I do not think there is a conflict between my view of dichotomy and these verses.

The Origin of the Immaterial Part of Man

By origin of the immaterial part of man, I am not referring to the original creation by God, but to the origin of the immaterial part as it relates to those who have descended from Adam and Eve. In one sense, this discussion may not belong under the discussion of man as created, but in another sense it does. The design of providing the immaterial part of man is not related to the fall, but was already a part of the divine plan before the fall. The same plan would have been followed if there had been no fall of man into sin.

There are three approaches: (1) The pre-existence theory which teaches that the immaterial part of man existed prior to the creation of the body. Since this view has never been accepted by orthodox Christians, I do not deem it necessary to deal with it. There are no reasons for anyone to even be confused about whether the Bible supports such a view. (2) The creationist theory teaches that God creates the immaterial part of each person and places it in the body sometime between conception and birth. (3) The traducian theory teaches that the immaterial part of man is transmitted through propagation just as the body is.

THE CREATIONIST VIEW

One of the main reasons people have advocated the creationist view is that it is felt this was the only way for Christ to be born without depravity. It is felt that traducianism would result in a depraved nature for Christ. I would suggest that the same divine act of conception that could provide Jesus with a body that did not bear the marks of depravity could also sanctify the immaterial part of man.

The most serious objection to the creationists' view is how the immaterial part becomes corrupt. One thought, which is sometimes associated with the federal headship view of Adam's sin and the race, suggests that God created the immaterial part of man corrupt because Adam violated the covenant God made with him when he sinned. I cannot conceive of God creating anything corrupt. Another view states that God creates the immaterial part sinless, but that it becomes corrupt upon contact with the body. There is a close relationship between the spirit and the body, but to blame the total process of perpetuating the depravity of the race on the body is more than can be justified. The depravity of the spirit is far more basic in our depravity than that of the body.

THE TRADUCIAN VIEW

The traducian theory most easily accounts for the perpetuation of depravity in the human race and its effect on the total person. Some are of the opinion that the Bible does not give a clear-cut case for either creationism or traducianism. I do not think this is the case. In Genesis 5:3 we read, "And Adam . . . begat a son in his own likeness, after his image; and called his name Seth." If the creation of man in God's image included the personhood and personality of Adam, certainly the begetting of Seth in Adam's image included Seth's personhood and personality. Personhood and personality cannot be based upon body alone, but must embrace the spirit also. Traducianism offers the only adequate explanation of Adam begetting Seth in his own image.

THE IMPLICATIONS OF THE TRADUCIAN VIEW

There are some interesting implications of traducianism. According to traducianism the beginning of a human person takes place at conception. This means in the event of a miscarriage that a human being who will live forever has come into existence. There will be a human being who will live with God forever. The implications as they relate to abortion are obvious. Abortion puts to death a defenseless human life. The question of when human life begins is not to be settled scientifically by the medical profession, but theologically by those who subscribe to the Bible as God's revelation.

The Effect of the Fall on the Image of God in Man

Concerning the effect of the fall on the image of God, Henry explains: "The fall of man is not destructive of the formal image (man's personality) although it involves the distortion (though not demolition) of the material content of the image."[19] Berkhof comments: "As created in the image of God man has a rational and a moral nature, which he did not lose by sin and which he could not lose without ceasing to be man. This part of the image of God has indeed been vitiated by sin, but still remains in man even after his fall into sin." Gordon H. Clark says, "Sin has interfered with but does not prohibit thought. It does not eradicate the image but causes it to malfunction."[20]

As was stated previously when discussing the meaning of being made in the image of God, I prefer "constitutional likeness" to "formal image" and "functional likeness" to "material content," but the meaning is the same whichever way it may be stated. I, further, made a distinction between personhood and personality. This distinction will be particularly helpful in explaining the effect of the fall on the image of God in man.

THE EFFECT ON THE CONSTITUTIONAL LIKENESS

With reference to the constitutional likeness, the fall did not change this fact. The personhood of man remains intact. He is still a thinking, feeling, acting being. He is still morally constituted. All of the constituent parts of personhood remain intact after the fall. The parts have suffered damage, but they all remain. The damage reflects itself in the personality.

THE EFFECT ON THE FUNCTIONAL LIKENESS

The effect of the fall is seen in the functional likeness. A basic and drastic change occurred in man's personality. Before the fall, man thought, felt, and acted both on the conscious and subconscious levels in absolute conformity to the likeness of God. After the fall, this was no longer true. Man no longer thinks, feels, and acts in a way that is pleasing to God. This is true both on the conscious and subconscious levels. However, it is not as simple as saying that man is the precise opposite of what he was before the fall. We must avoid oversimplified explanations of how the fall affected the image of God.

THE PROBLEM OF GIVING A SIMPLE DESCRIPTION OF FALLEN MAN

It is clear that man fell from a state of holiness into a state of sin (Is. 53:6; Rom. 3:23). It is clear that sin has placed man under condemnation before God (Rom. 6:23; Rev. 21:8). It is clear that fallen man cannot please God and has no fellowship with God (Eph. 2:1-3; Rom. 8:7, 8). It is clear that man cannot come to God without the drawing power of the Holy Spirit (Jn. 6:44). It is clear that a work so drastic as to be called a new birth is required for man's salvation (Jn. 3:3-7). But we also find areas where the state and condition of man are not so clearly understood.

Henry is grappling with the difficulty of giving a clear statement on the effect of the fall on the functional likeness in man as indicated in the quotation given earlier. He states that while there is a "distortion" there is not a "demolition" of the material content (functional likeness). Berkhof and Clark also indicate the difficulty of making a clear statement. What we are dealing with here is: How depraved is man? What do we mean when we say there is not a demolition of the functional likeness?

I am not raising the question of whether man is totally depraved; but rather, what is meant by *total depravity*. Charles C. Ryrie makes the following observations about the meaning of total depravity:

> The concept of total depravity does not mean (1) that depraved people cannot or do not perform actions that are good in either man's or God's sight. But no such action can gain favor with God for salvation. Neither does it mean (2) that fallen man has no conscience which judges between good and evil for him. But that conscience has been affected by the fall so that it cannot be a safe and reliable guide. Neither does it mean (3) that people indulge in every form of sin or in any sin to the greatest extent possible.[21]

In commenting on Ryrie's three points, Ashby explains:

> (1) There is such a thing as "relative good." But depraved people do not do the right thing, with the right motive, to satisfy the righteous expectations of a holy God.
> (2) I agree that fallen man has a conscience—but it is skewed and judges trivial things as important and monumental things as trivial.
> (3) Total depravity is not ABSOLUTE depravity. Every person is not a Hitler or a Charles Manson. But every aspect of one's being is conditioned by sinful inclinations.[22]

In summary, *total* means that the corruption has extended to all aspects of man's nature, to his entire being; and *depravity* means that because of that corruption there is nothing man can do to merit saving favor with God.

THE EFFECT OF THE PRESENCE OF THE IMAGE OF GOD IN FALLEN MAN ON HUMAN BEHAVIOR

Why is it that every sinner does not exhibit his depravity as thoroughly as he could? Why is it that every sinner does not commit every sin? Why is it that a degree of moral concern can be found among sinners? Why is it that sinners perform some good deeds? The answer goes back to the understanding that sinners still retain personhood. They are still personal, rational, moral beings by constitution and design.

Man did not become non-moral in the fall anymore than he became non-rational. A being must be moral, i.e., morally constituted, to be immoral. He must be rational, i.e., rationally constituted to be irrational. It is the moral constitution of man that Paul is discussing in Romans 2:15 when he speaks about the Gentiles, "Who show the work of the law written in their hearts" (NKJV).

The sinner, still bearing the image of God, is so constituted that he has the categories of right and wrong. Right is considered a plus factor, and wrong is considered a minus factor. No human being does what he knows to be wrong without considering it, to some extent, to be a minus factor. This fact cannot be obliterated.

I do not say this as a person who has been out of touch with the problem side of human nature. I have had considerable experience dealing one on one with troubled people . I have learned to listen when people give clues concerning what is happening in their deep inner self.

I remember one day listening to a talk show when a prostitute called in. She said, "I am a prostitute. I don't like what I am doing. But I don't know anything else to do." Recently, I saw a program on television that was dealing with prostitution in Russia. As one of the women was interviewed, she said, "I don't want my daughter to know what I am doing. I am humiliated. I feel dirty. I receive dirty money."

Some time ago I watched a program detailing one method of dealing with deeply troubled teenagers. A member of the group would sit before the others for a period of very hard questioning which attempted to get to the bottom of what was bothering the person. This was not a religious treatment center. One girl broke down and cried, "I had an abortion. I killed the baby that was within me."

Sin has introduced a foreign element into man's being. Man was made for righteousness. He was not made for sin. A human being can never live in sin and have self-acceptance and full harmony of being. Sin has placed man in conflict, contradiction, and confusion. Sin puts a person at cross purposes with the image of God within from which there is no escape. To whatever extent a person has forfeited the morality of the Ten Commandments, to that extent, he or she is in trouble—not only with God but with himself or herself. No person who lives in gross violation of the morality of the Ten Commandments is happy. If you doubt this statement, start listening and you will gather your own evidence.

Since man cannot totally erase moral concern, he tries to enter into label changing. He tries to place the label "right" on what he or she wants to do. This includes abortion and all kinds of sexual sins. The effort never totally succeeds. Regardless of what may go on in the conscious mind, a person can never accept in his deep inner being the violation of the basic morality of the Ten Commandments. Ten thousand arguments will never make these violations acceptable. Notice the lack of self-respect among those who try this route. Notice the need of alcohol and the need of drugs. Notice the presence of misery, despair, and depression. All of these tell us that the deep inner self is not going along with the attempt to set aside basic human morality. The image of God within cries out for Truth, a right use of reason, moral uprightness, forgiveness for guilt, and an experience of beauty, excellence, and order. The image of God longs to experience what it means to be in the likeness of God. The image of God within can be neglected, but not without a high cost.

Man is in drastic need of approval both from himself and from others. This fact gives rise to worthy deeds among sinners. Every person feels good when he by conscious choice does what he believes to be right. Every person feels good when he by conscious choice accommodates another person.

The categories of right and wrong, with right being a plus factor and wrong being a minus factor, indelibly written in the constitution of man, produces some good in the sinner. This good will never provide acceptance before God, neither will it meet the needs of the person himself. It is the presence of this moral constitution in man that provides a point of contact for the gospel. If fallen man were a moral blank, or had the categories of right and wrong reversed, there would be no point of contact for the gospel. There would be no grounds for conviction of sin.

THE INFLUENCE OF EXTERNAL RESTRAINTS ON CURBING THE EXPRESSION OF HUMAN DEPRAVITY

In addition to the influence of man's own moral constitution in curbing his experience with sin and producing some good, there are external restraints that keep people from being as wicked as they would otherwise be. There are the restraints of parents, government, society, and the church. I can remember well that, at times, I refrained from doing a thing because I was afraid that Mama and Papa would find out about it.

ASSESSING THE TRUE NATURE OF DEPRAVITY

In assessing the seriousness of the power and influence of depravity, we must keep in mind that the truest picture of sin does not always manifest itself in overt acts. Everyone has imagined committing sins that he has not committed. The same capacity that can imagine evil can commit evil. Everyone has kept in check some desire for evil that he has had. With the same capacity we desire evil, we can also commit evil. Sometimes people enjoy seeing sin committed by others. The same capacity that enjoys evil can commit evil.

THE IMPOSSIBILITY OF FALLEN MAN ATTAINING A RIGHT STANDING BEFORE GOD BY HIS OWN EFFORTS

It is possible and sometimes happens that an unconverted person reaches a measure of decency and uprightness in society. He or she may perform humanitarian deeds, but all of these fall far short of meeting divine approval (Rom. 3:23). The presence of sin in his life still renders him unrighteous before a holy God. The power of sin in his life makes him stand in need of the new birth.

The Question of the Freedom of the Will

The real controversy over depravity centers around the will. Does fallen man have a free will? If descendants of Adam do not in some sense have freedom of will, then they have lost their personhood. One of the factors involved in being a person is to have power of choice or the ability to will. The will can only choose and act to the extent that it is free. To deprive will of freedom is to deprive it of being a will. I think the debate between Calvinism and Arminianism should be framed over whether fallen man is a functioning, personal being. Does he have a functioning mind, heart, and will?

THE MEANING OF FREEDOM OF THE WILL

Before proceeding to discuss the effect of depravity on the will, let us make a few things clear about what is and is not meant by freedom of will. The freedom of the will does not mean that forces or influences cannot be brought to bear upon the will. In fact, the very nature of freedom of the will means that forces or influences will be brought to bear upon the will. It does not mean that these forces cannot be a contributing factor in the exercise of the will. It does mean that these influences or forces *cannot guarantee or determine* the action of the will. We are dealing with influence and response, not cause and effect.

THE FRAMEWORK OF POSSIBILITIES AND THE MEANING OF FREEDOM OF THE WILL

Freedom of will is a freedom within a *framework of possibilities*. It is not absolute freedom. Man cannot be God. He cannot be an angel. The freedom of a human being is in the framework of the possibilities provided by human nature. Also, the influences brought to bear on the will have a bearing on the framework of possibilities.

Before Adam and Eve sinned, it was in the framework of possibilities within which they operated to remain in the practice of complete righteousness, or to commit sin. After they sinned, it no longer remained within the framework of possibilities for them to practice uninterrupted righteousness. The same is true for fallen man now (Rom. 8:7, 8). If anyone *freedom of will* to mean that an unconverted person could practice righteousness *and not sin,* he misunderstands the meaning of freedom of will for fallen human beings. Romans 8:7, 8 makes it clear that Scripture does not teach this.

Jesus makes it clear that it does not fall within the framework of possibilities for a sinner to respond to the gospel unless he is drawn by the Holy Spirit (Jn. 6:44). The influence of the Holy Spirit working in the heart of the person who hears the gospel brings about a framework of possibilities in which a person can say yes or no to the gospel. If he says yes, it is his choice. If he says no, it is his choice. To say less than that is to raise serious questions about the existence of real personhood after the fall. If a human being is not in some sense a *self-directed* being, he or she is not a person. The self-direction may have a high degree of dependence at times, but it is still self-direction. As has already been made clear, I am not suggesting that fallen man can choose Christ without the aid of the Holy Spirit. In fact, I strongly reject such an idea. I am saying, however, that no matter how much or how strong the aid of the Holy Spirit may be, the "yes" decision is still a decision that can rightly be called the person's decision. After all, one can say no.

The view that I hold is the same as that which was advocated by Jacobus Arminius. Throughout history, there have been very few individuals who have had so many viewpoints wrongly attributed to them as Arminius. J. Matthew Pinson has done considerable research in order to clarify what Arminius taught and did not teach. Pinson comments:

> Arminius believed that men and women have no ability to seek God or turn to him unless they are radically affected by his grace. Arminius has been assumed by most interpreters (an assumption based on the assumption of semi-pelagianism) to hold a doctrine of free will which makes individuals totally able to choose God or spurn him. However, Arminius's view of human freedom does not mean freedom to do anything good in the sight of God or to choose God on one's own. For Arminius, the basic freedom which characterizes the human will is freedom from necessity. . . .This has sounded to some like semi-pelagianism, but though Arminius states that the human will is free from necessity, he states unequivocally that the will is not free from sin and its dominion:
>
>> . . . the free will of man towards the true good is not only wounded, maimed, infirm, bent, and (*nuatum*) weakened; but it is also (*captivatum*) imprisoned, destroyed, and lost: And its powers are not only debilitated and useless unless they are assisted by grace, but it has no powers whatever except such are excited by grace [Arminius, vol. 2. 193].
>
> Fallen humanity has no ability or power to reach out to the grace of God on its own.[23]

THE DIFFERENCE BETWEEN MY VIEW AND CALVINISM

Faith can be called a gift in the sense that it would not have been possible without divine aid. It is not a gift in the sense that it exists outside the person and is given to him, nor is it a gift in the sense that God believes for the person. The person himself does the believing by divine aid.

I think Calvinism errs in its understanding of "dead in trespasses." Cornelius Van Til explains the Calvinistic interpretation:

> It was only as a creature of God, made in his image, that man could sin. So, when a sinner, and as such "dead in trespasses," unable of himself even to stretch forth his hand to receive salvation, Scripture continues to deal with him as a responsible being. He is called to faith and repentance. Yet faith is a gift of God. Lazarus lay in the tomb. He was dead. Yet Jesus told him to come forth. And he did come forth.[24]

The above interpretation interprets "dead" in "dead in trespasses" (Eph. 2:1) as meaning lifeless. The dead body of Lazarus had no life in it. It was capable of no action until it was made alive by Jesus. If "dead in trespasses" means dead in the same way, the logic of Calvinism follows. The sinner would be both deaf and speechless. He would know nothing about God, sin, and salvation until God made him alive through the new birth. Then and only then would he be able to hear and to speak.

I think "dead in trespasses and sins" or spiritual death means that man is separated from God, dead in relationship to God. There is no communion and no fellowship with God. The principle is similar to that spoken of by Paul when he said, "By whom the world is crucified unto me, and I unto the world" (Gal. 6:14). Both Paul and the world were alive in the sense that they were not lifeless. They were not alive so far as a functioning relationship between them was concerned.

Spiritual death, if this be the correct interpretation, refers to the fact that the sinner is cut off from communion and fellowship with God. This is true both because a holy God demands that it be so until sin is taken care of, and also because the bias of the sinner's heart is against God. The fact the sinner is not in communion with God does not mean he is totally deaf to God's communication. If that were the case, the sinner could not even distort the message of God. You cannot distort that to which you are totally deaf. That a person is a sinner does mean he does not hear well. He tends to resist and oppose the Truth and to distort the Truth. The gospel has to go forth against great opposition. The Holy Spirit must work before there can be a successful communication of the gospel to the sinner and before there will be conviction and response from the sinner. This approach recognizes the seriousness of sin, the necessity of the enlightening and drawing power of the Holy Spirit, and the personhood of the sinner.

I believe that saving faith is a gift of God in the sense that the Holy Spirit gives divine enablement without which faith in Christ would be impossible (Jn. 6:44). The difference between the Calvinistic concept of faith and my concept of faith *cannot* be that theirs is *monergistic* and mine is *synergistic*. In *both* cases it is synergistic. Active participation in faith by the believer means that it must be synergistic. Human response cannot be ruled out of faith. Justification and regeneration are monergistic. Each is an act of God, not man. Faith is a human act by divine enablement and therefore cannot be monergistic.

The Consequences of Adam's Sin Upon the Race

The questions to be answered are: (1) Is Adam's sin imputed to the race? (2) If it is imputed, how and why? (3) How is depravity transmitted?

ROMANS 5:12-19

The key passage in deciding the consequences upon the race of Adam's sin is Romans 5:12-19. How do we interpret, "death passed upon all men, for all have sinned" in verse 12? "Death passed upon all men" is the effect. "All have sinned" is the cause. Concerning the Greek word translated "have sinned," there are two possibilities so far as Greek grammar is concerned. "Have sinned" is a translation of *hēmarton* which is the aorist. If we understand the aorist as a simple aorist, we would translate "all sinned." It would mean that all sinned at some time in the past. This would mean that death passed upon the race because the race sinned at some time in the past.

If we understand the aorist as being a gnomic aorist, we would translate it "all sin." If we understand it to be a culminative aorist, we would translate it "all have sinned." Whether we would understand the Greek to be a gnomic aorist or a culminative aorist, the interpretation would be the same. It would mean that death passes upon all men because all people sin.

If we understand that death passed upon all men because all men sinned at some time in the past, death would pass upon all because all sinned in Adam. If we understand that death passes upon all men because all sin, death would pass upon each person because of his own sins, not the sin of Adam. The context must decide which of these interpretations is right.

I think the chart below will help us see how the context decides the question.

CAUSE	EFFECT
5:12 "All have sinned" or "All sinned"?	"Death passed upon all men"
5:15 "The offence of one"	"Many be dead"
5:16 "By one [person]"	"Condemnation"
5:17 "One man's offence"	"Death reigned"
5:18 "The offence of one" (The Greek means "one offence.")	"Judgment came upon all men to condemnation"

On the "effect" side of the chart, it is obvious that the effect in 5:15-18 is the same as the effect in 5:12. If it is clear what the cause of the effect is in 5:15-18, that should help clarify what the cause is in 5:12. The cause in 5:15-18 is "one person," "one man's offence," and "one offence." Putting that together, it is clear that the cause is the one offense committed by Adam when he ate the forbidden fruit.

If 5:12, 15-18 all give the same effect, it is to be expected that 5:12,15-18 will all give the same cause. The cause is clear in 5:15-19. This interprets the cause in 5:12. While Greek grammar may allow the statement in 5:12 to refer to each individual's sin, the context decides against it and in favor of the other grammatical possibility. It is clear in the total context that 5:12 is to be interpreted, "all sinned in Adam."

Romans 5:12-19 definitely settles the fact that the sin of Adam is imputed or placed on the account of the whole race. The question to be decided now is how and why was this done?

THE APPROACHES USED TO EXPLAIN THE IMPUTATION OF ADAM'S SIN TO THE RACE

One view would say that the answer is found in Adam's natural headship of the race. The other would declare that while Adam is the natural head of the race, the natural headship did not furnish a grounds for imputing the sin of Adam to the race. Adam was appointed federal head of the race and the grounds of imputation are found in the federal headship of Adam.

According to the view that grounds imputation in the natural headship of Adam, sin is imputed to the race because the race by being in Adam was a part of Adam when he sinned, thus identified with him in his sin and the guilt of that sin. This view accepts the traducian view of the origin of the human spirit. Depravity is transmitted by the process of propagation.

According to the federal headship view, Adam became the representative of the race by divine appointment. The reason for Adam's being chosen was his natural headship, but natural headship did not of itself involve the race in Adam's sin. God entered into a covenant with Adam promising to bestow eternal life upon him and his posterity if he should obey God, and corruption and death would pass on to his posterity if he should disobey God. It is the covenant relationship of the race with Adam by virtue of his being appointed as the representative of the race that involves the race in the consequences of his sin. Instead of saying the race sinned in Adam, this view would say, "All are accounted as sinners."

Comparison of Natural and Federal Headship Theories

Natural Headship View	Federal Headship View
1. Traducianist	1. Creationists as a rule, but could be traducianist
2. Adam representative of the race because the race was in him	2. Adam representative of the race because of divine appointment
3. Sin imputed because of identification by being in Adam	3. Sin imputed to the race because Adam, as appointed representative of the race, violated the covenant
4. All sinned	4. All are accounted as sinners
5. Immaterial part transmitted with a depraved nature	5. Immaterial part created by God with corrupt and depraved nature, or created without corruption and corrupted by contact with a corrupt body. (A few would go along with the traducian view, but this is not the usual view.)

THE FEDERAL HEADSHIP VIEW

While a person may be a traducianist and hold to the federal headship view, a creationist must hold to the federal headship view if he believes in the imputation of the sin of Adam to the race. Being in Adam from a physical viewpoint only would not furnish an adequate basis for imputing the sin of Adam to the race as it relates to the total personality.

The federal headship view works on the assumption that the federal headship principle of imputation explains the imputation of the death and righteousness of Christ to the redeemed. It then seeks to build a parallel view of the imputation of Adam's sin to the race.

While there may be some people who accept the federal headship view of Adam that do not accept unconditional election, the federal headship principle fits logically in the Calvinistic system. The covenant made with Adam, because of Adam's disobedience, brought condemnation to all who were in the covenant. In this case, it was the whole race. The covenant made with Christ, because of His obedience in death and righteousness, brought eternal life to all who were in the covenant. In this case, according to Calvinism, it was only those who were unconditionally elected to be parties of the covenant who were in the covenant.

By an act of His own will and based on His own reasons, God chose to include the whole race as the recipient of the guilt and consequences of Adam's sin. He could have chosen to have done otherwise. There was nothing in the nature of things that made it necessary for it to be that way. By an act of His own will and based on His own reasons, God did not choose to elect the whole human race and make them participants in the benefits of Christ's obedience. There was nothing in the nature of the case that required Him to limit the number of the elect. I mention these observations here because in systematic thinking we must see the possible bearing on other parts in a system of the way we interpret principles and their application in a particular place.

Romans 5:12—Support for Federal Headship View or Natural Headship View?

Does the Scripture aid in our choice between the natural headship view and the federal headship view? I think it does. The evidence presented above supports the conclusion that Romans 5:12 is to be interpreted as, "All sinned in Adam."

The language of Romans 5:12 is more appropriate for the natural headship view because the language of Romans 5:12 and of the natural headship view are identical. The "all sinned" of Romans 5:12 must be twisted to mean "all are accounted as sinners" for the federal headship view. "All sinned" is in the active voice. "All are accounted as sinners" would require the passive voice.

THE NATURAL HEADSHIP VIEW

We have some difficulty accepting with our total being the conclusion that the whole race was condemned for Adam's sin. This is made far more acceptable when we see that the nature of things made it necessary that the race be charged with Adam's sin than to think that God made the decision in no relationship to necessity. There are those who say in rebuttal, God can do anything. God cannot be limited by necessity. This is to misunderstand the case. God must act in accord with His nature. As an expression of His own nature, God has built certain principles and guidelines into the nature of reality. He is obligated to abide by these principles and guidelines in order that He may maintain a rational consistency with His creation. The objectionable features of the creationist view of the origin of the spirit and how it becomes corrupt have already been discussed earlier in the chapter and need not be repeated here.

Let us now return to a further discussion of the natural headship view. We have already seen that it best accords with Scripture. Now let us look at the logical defense.

The race was in Adam and has descended body and spirit from him. This means that we were in Adam and were identified with him in his sin. It necessitates our being a partaker with him in his guilt and condemnation. To say otherwise would say that not all of Adam was condemned because that which was in Adam's loins, which was the race potentially, was as much a part of Adam as any other part. No matter how many subdivisions there may be, the parts never lose their real identification as being a part of the original whole. We have never lost our identification with him in his sin.

I would not accept some of the ideas that have usually been associated with this view. In explaining this view, A. H. Strong says, "The powers which now exist in separate men were then unified and localized in Adam; Adam's will was yet the will of the species. In Adam's free act, the will of the race revolted from God and the nature of the race corrupted itself."[25]

It sounds as if Strong may be saying that the will of every human being acted in Adam's will. I do not think this to be the case. The wills did not exist. Only the potential for those wills existed. Our wills came into being only when we came into being as individual persons. To say that all sinned in Adam must not be understood to say that their wills were active in Adam. We could say that his will was the will of the race since the race was in him and descended from him, but we cannot speak of the wills of the race being combined in his will.

The Parallel Between the Principle of Imputation of Adam's Sin to the Race and the Imputation of the Death and Righteousness of Christ to the Believer

The principle involved in imputation of something from one to another is *identification by being in or in union with the person.* This is true whether it be sin or whether it be righteousness. The Scripture knows of no other way that the action of one person can be imputed to another. This is the principle involved in the imputation of the death and righteousness of Christ to the believer.

The Bible knows of no imputation from one to another except in a manner that makes it so the action can in some sense be said to be *the action of the person himself.* Paul said in Galatians 2:20, "I am [or I have been] crucified with Christ." By being in union with Christ, Paul became so identified with Christ that it could be said he was crucified with Christ. Paul was not actually crucified with Christ in the sense of experiencing the sufferings of Christ. By identification with Christ the death of Christ became his so he could get credit for its benefits. (For a more thorough explanation of this see the discussion on the union of Christ in connection with the doctrine of justification.)

In a similar sense that the death of Christ is ours, the sin of Adam is ours. We did not perform the sin by an act of our own will, but we were in Adam when he committed the sin. We were identified with him. We were in Adam at the time of his sin. Our connection with him is maintained by an unbroken continuity between Adam and us. We were not in Christ at the time of His crucifixion, but were placed in Him when we exercised faith. We are now in Him.

I think the federal headship principle misinterprets both the imputation of Adam's sin and the imputation of the death and righteousness of Christ. The Scripture knows of only one principle of imputation of the actions of one person to another and that is identification by union. The *natural headship view*, not the federal headship view, *maintains the parallel between Christ and Adam* in connection with the principle involved in imputation. (If the reader has problems at this point, I would suggest that he skip over and read what is said about union with Christ as it relates to justification. The whole case is better elaborated there.)

THE QUESTION OF THOSE DYING IN INFANCY

A question that always arises in this connection is: What about those dying in infancy? I will reserve the discussion of this until later. Let me just say at this point, I believe in infant salvation. The discussion belongs more properly to the doctrines of atonement and salvation.

Other Views on the Imputation of Adam's Sin to the Race

There are two more views that should be mentioned. The theory of mediate imputation denies that the guilt of Adam is imputed to the race. We receive depravity from him, and depravity forms the basis of guilt and condemnation. The sin of Adam is the indirect cause, not the direct cause of the race being charged with guilt. This imputation of guilt precedes personal acts of sin. This view does not accord with Scripture as we have seen from our discussion above.

Another view that is frequently referred to as the Arminian view does not teach that the race is charged with the guilt of Adam's sin. Depravity is inherited from Adam and causes people to sin. They are not condemned before God until they commit individual sin upon becoming responsible persons. The discussion above shows the inadequacy of this view.

While it is true that some Arminians have advocated this view, it is by no means universally accepted and should not be called the Arminian view. This is especially true since it was not the view held by Arminius himself. It is somewhat puzzling why people with good scholarly credentials would say that Arminius denied the imputation of Adam's sin to the race. This is the position set forth by A. H. Strong under the heading, "The Arminian Theory, or Theory of voluntarily appropriated Depravity."[26] In his book, *With Wilful Intent,* David Smith attributes this view to Arminius and uses Strong as his authority for it.[27]

Pinson sets the record straight. He explains:

> Arminius' views on original sin are summed up in the passage entitled "The Effects of This Sin." It is clear here that Arminius is Augustinian. . . . His position on the effect of Adam's sin upon the race is that "the whole of this sin . . . is not peculiar to our first parents, but is common to the entire race and all their posterity, who, at the time when

his sin was committed, were in their loins, and who have since descended from them by natural propagation" [Arminius, vol. 2, 156].

Arminius believes that all sin in Adam and are guilty in Adam, apart from their actual sins.

In the *Private Disputations,* Arminius echoes the sentiments of his public disputations. In disputation thirty-one, he states that "all men who were to be propagated from [Adam and Eve] in a natural way, became obnoxious to death temporal and death eternal, and [*vacui*] [brackets in the quotation] devoid of this gift of the Holy Spirit or original righteousness [Arminius, vol. 2, 375.] (brackets Pinson's)

An examination of Arminius's confessional beliefs and his writings makes it impossible to believe some of the interpretations of his doctrine of original sin.[28]

One of the chief concerns of Arminians has been to deny that infants go to Hell. Some have sought support for this denial by denying guilt before individual guilt enters the picture. Many others have believed that the guilt of Adam was imputed to the race, but was removed for all in atonement. Arminius, himself, believed in the salvation of all who died in infancy. He did not work on the basis of a non-involvement in Adam's sin as a basis for believing that those who die in infancy go to Heaven when they die.[29]

Man as Affected by Redemption

The basic principles will be stated briefly here. Another thorough development of the ideas will be given in connection with the doctrines of salvation.

Redemption concerns itself with restoring that which was lost in the fall. It is the design of redemption to restore the functional likeness of God in man. It is designed to make man like God in his personality. He is to be made in the likeness of God both on the conscious and subconscious levels in the way he thinks, feels, and acts.

Concluding Challenge

One of the greatest challenges before the church during these times when postmodernism is the main secular force shaping our culture is to declare that man is created by God in the image of God. It needs to be proclaimed and explained. We need to explain how sin has entered into the picture, but that the basic needs of human nature are determined by our creation in the image of God. This discussion must not be limited to the classrooms of our colleges and seminaries and theological conferences. It must be taught in our local churches. It must be taught to our children. The unchurched need to hear about the image of God and how it determines human need.

10

The Incarnation

Christianity is Christ-centered. Jesus Christ is Creator, Redeemer, and Lord. Without Jesus Christ there would be no Christianity. We would all be hopelessly in the bondage of sin and under condemnation. We would be groping in darkness without a light to guide us. Apart from a plan to send Christ into the world, the unveiling of the nature and plan of God for man, which we refer to as special revelation, would have ended with the fall of man. All special revelation of God after the fall presupposes and is in some way related to God's plan of redemption through Christ.

The question that Jesus asked His disciples in Matthew 16:15 is of the greatest importance. After having asked who others thought Him to be and receiving a variety of answers, "He said to them, 'But who do you say that I am?'"(NKJV). Because Jesus Christ is both the center and the foundation of Christianity, it is essential that this question be answered correctly.

Our understanding of the importance of the answer to this question does not depend upon reason alone. God reveals this to us in Scripture. The truth or falsity of a person's answer to this question is one of the basic tests to determine whether a person is proclaiming the gospel or is speaking heresy (1 Jn. 2:22, 23; 4:1-3; and 2 Jn. 7-11). When we discuss some finer points of detail that may not be settled for us by exegesis of Scriptures, we cannot expect unanimous agreement. On the basics that are clearly revealed in Scripture, there must be agreement.

As important as it is, our interest in the doctrine of Christ does not rest solely upon doctrinal soundness. Jesus Christ is not simply central in a system of doctrine (or worldview). He is central to us as persons. He is our Redeemer and Lord. We love Him. We worship Him. We adore Him. We want to understand Him. To understand Him is to appreciate Him more.

A knowledge of Christ satisfies both heart and mind. In a world that is marred by sin, it is He and He alone that forms the foundation for integrating the facts of reality into a pattern of life and thought that gives purpose and meaning to life. He is the only One that can rescue us from the despair of sin and postmodernism's sea of confusion. He is the only Captain who can pilot our ship into the harbor of eternal happiness. It is with the highest appreciation for Him and the deepest sense of responsibility that we proceed into the study of the

The Purpose of the Incarnation

THAT CHRIST MIGHT BE OUR KINSMAN-REDEEMER

The Hebrew word for redeemer is *goel*. The word *goel* is a participle form of the verb *gaal*. Robert B. Girdlestone says, "Perhaps the original meaning of the word is 'demand back,' hence to extricate." In discussing the use of *goel* in Leviticus chapters 25 and 27, Girdlestone explains:

The deliverance was effected in this case by payment or by exchange. In cases of poverty, where no payment was possible, the nearest of kin was made responsible for performing the work of redemption. Hence no doubt it came to pass that a kinsman came to be called by the name Goel, as he is in Numbers 5:8, I Kings 16:11, and throughout the Book of Ruth. Compare Jeremiah 32:7, 8.[1]

Based on the observation made by Girdlestone, we would gather that the word *goel* first meant to deliver. It came to mean a kinsman who had the right of redemption through usage growing out of the right of redemption given to a near kinsman in Leviticus 25 and 27. In order to establish a few principles, let us make a few observations about the case of the brother who sold himself to a sojourner or stranger (Lev. 25:47-55). It is important to observe that only a near kinsman had a right to redeem this one sold (verses 48, 49). The principle of substitution was such that it came as near as possible to being the action of the person himself. It is true that an act of a kinsman should not be equated with the act of the individual. It is, however, as near as possible to the action of the individual without it being his. When, in the chapter on atonement and justification, we look at the principle of substitution involved in atonement and justification, we will be able to see why the attempt was made to make the action as near as possible the action of the person redeemed.

The kinsman-redeemer type was used by God to prepare the way for the coming of Christ, who through the incarnation became our Kinsman that He might have the right to redeem us. After having examined the use of *gaal* and *goel*, Girdlestone concludes:

> In most of the passages above enumerated redemption may be considered as synonymous with deliverance, but always with the idea more or less developed that the Redeemer enters a certain relationship with the redeemed—allies Himself in some sense with them, and so claims the right of redemption. The truth thus set forth was doubtless intended to prepare the mind of God's people for the doctrine of Incarnation.[2]

There could be no redemption from the curse and power of sin apart from the incarnation of deity. The payment price was greater than a mere human could have paid. The full penalty of sin could only be paid by deity. The Redeemer had to be man to have the right to redeem. He had to be God to be able to redeem.

H. Dermot Mc Donald sums up the thought of Anselm, Archbishop of Canterbury on the necessity of the incarnation as it is expressed in *Cur Deus Homo?*:

> God's purpose of perfecting human nature "cannot be done except by a complete satisfaction for sin, which no sinner can make" (2:4). For since the debt is infinite, it can be paid only by God; and since it is man who owes it, it must be paid by man. "There is no one, therefore, who can make satisfaction other than God himself." "But no one ought to make it except man: otherwise man does not make satisfaction" (2:6). Since,

then, no one can but God, and no one ought but man, "it is necessary that One who is God-man should make it"; the one, that is, who is himself at once perfect God and perfect man. In this way Anselm affirms the rationale of the incarnation of God the Son, who as the Son of God come in the flesh is the God-man. He must be man to act as the race, and he must be God to make the immeasurable satisfaction.[3]

That a redeemer had to be a kinsman explains why no redemption was offered to fallen angels. They were created a company of individuals. There is no birth among them. A member of the Trinity could not identify himself with them through birth. They could have no kinsman-redeemer. Therefore, they could have no redemption.

Regardless of whether or not there is life in outer space, one thing is clear. It will not extend our missionary responsibility. The right of redemption through the incarnation only extends to the human race. Jesus is a kinsman only to the human race.

That Christ May Reveal God to Us

The image of God in man at creation embraced both a constitutional likeness and a functional likeness. In the fall, man lost the functional likeness of God. It is the design of redemption to restore the functional likeness of God in man.

The restoration of the functional likeness of God in man requires not only atonement, but also a better view of what God is like. While man is still morally constituted, he is confused and his vision has become blurred concerning what God is really like. One of the purposes of the incarnation was to give us a better view of what God is like. Jesus revealed the likeness of God in terms of experiences and encounters with real life.

The writer of Hebrews speaks of Jesus as "being the brightness of his [God's] glory, and the express image of his person" (Heb. 1:3). The answer to Philip when he said, "Lord, shew us the Father, and it sufficeth us" (Jn. 14:8) was "Have I been so long time with you, and yet hast thou not known me, Philip? he that hath seen me hath seen the Father; and how sayest thou then, Shew us the Father?" (Jn. 14:9).

A demonstration of real life in a real world offers a dimension to our understanding that far exceeds a mere description. The moving examples of love as Jesus had compassion on the sick, the afflicted, the hungry, and those who were as sheep without a shepherd tell us something of the love that characterizes God that no definition could convey. The unparalleled love of Christ as shown by His death to pay the penalty of sin for those who had sinned against Him gives us a dimension of love that the wisest minds and the most gifted with words could never describe.

The example of a sinless life in spite of the cleverest designs of Satan and in spite of the provocative encounters with vile and conniving men, gives a dimension to holiness that cannot be conveyed by the lives of the most saintly among the redeemed. The staunch stand of Jesus when He pronounced judgment upon Chorazin, Bethsaida, and Capernaum (Mt. 11:20-24); the solemn language He used when He pronounced the woes upon the Pharisees (Mt. 23:13-36); and the determined stand against the desecration of the Temple when He ran the money changers out of the Temple (Jn. 2:13-16) show the righteous demands of His holiness, i.e., an intolerance of sin that doctrinal treatments cannot convey. The satisfaction of the holiness of God by the sufferings and death of the Son of God gives the highest possible revelation of God's attitude toward holiness and sin.

We needed all of the moral instruction of Scripture, but instructions alone were not enough. We needed a model that demonstrated for us in the encounters with real life in a real world. Jesus Christ is that model. He has revealed to us and for us what it means to be in the functional likeness of God.

Jesus Christ demonstrated for us the true likeness of God as the substance of that likeness would have been lived out in the form of the culture of a first century Jew living in Palestine. In that culture, He lived out the timeless, universal, and unchanging truth of the likeness of God. Jesus did not view culture as value-neutral. When the pattern of that culture was acceptable, He demonstrated the likeness of God in the pattern of that culture. When the pattern of that culture was unacceptable by divine standards, He confronted it and became a transforming influence on it. This is particularly evidenced when the culture produced by the oral tradition of Pharisaism was in conflict with divine truth.

We were in desperate need of a model for living out God's truth in a culture contaminated by sin. We needed to know how to live in the likeness of God in a society out of line with divine values. Jesus became a model for all people in all cultures and in all time periods.

The Humanity and Deity of Christ

THE HUMANITY OF CHRIST

Since the controversy about Christ usually has focused on His deity rather than His humanity, there has been a tendency to fail to emphasize the human nature of Christ and the implications of His humanity. His humanity is usually taken for granted. In view of the preceding discussion relating to Jesus as our Kinsman-Redeemer, it was no less essential for Him to be human to be our Redeemer than it was for Him to be divine.

The birth of Christ attests the genuineness of His human nature (Mt. 1:18-25; Lk. 2:11). It is true that He was miraculously conceived (Mt. 1:18-25; Lk. 1:26-35), but at the same time it was a human birth. He possessed a human body (Heb. 2:14; Jn. 2:21; Mt. 26:12) and a human spirit (Lk. 23:46). He experienced human growth and development (Lk. 2:40, 52). He experienced human needs. He became hungry (Mt. 4:2; 21:18). He experienced thirst (Jn. 19:28). He became tired (Jn. 4:6). He slept (Mt. 8:24). He died and was buried (Mk. 15:43-46).

There is never the slightest hint in the New Testament that Jesus was not human. He referred to Himself as a man (Jn. 8:40). He is called a man by others (Jn. 1:30; Acts 2:22; 13:38; 1 Cor. 15:21, 47; Phil. 2:8; and others).

THE DEITY OF CHRIST

(See the discussion on the deity of Christ in chapter 6, "The Trinity," page 82-85.)

Erroneous Views Concerning the Two Natures and the Person of Christ

In getting a clear understanding of the truth, it sometimes helps to contrast the truth with error. We will take a brief look at some of the errors in the history of the church to help us see the truth more clearly. For those who are interested in a more thorough treatment of these erroneous views than will be presented here, such a treatment can be found in most systematic theology books, books on the History of Doctrine, and Church History books.

THE EBIONITES

The Ebionites arose around the early part of the second century. They were a Jewish group that gave Jesus a place of importance in their beliefs, but denied that He was deity. They felt that monotheism was incompatible with attributing deity to Jesus.

THE GNOSTICS

Full blown Gnosticism appeared about the same time the Ebionites did. However, it is generally felt that an incipient form of Gnosticism was afoot around the middle of the first century. An early form of Gnosticism was addressed in Colossians which was written about A. D. 60. The basic principles of Gnosticism can be found in the latter part of the first century as is evidenced by some of the statements of John in combating heretical views of Christ (1 Jn. 4:1-3; and 2 Jn. 7).

The gnostics worked on the assumption that matter is inherently evil. For this reason, they either denied the reality of Jesus' human nature or denied sthere was any real incarnation. Concerning the last form of Gnosticism, Alexander M. Renwick explains, "This heavenly Christ acted in the man Jesus but was never incarnate."[4]

THE ARIANS

Arius denied the integrity of the divine nature of Christ. Christ was the first of created beings. Through Him the rest of creation was created. He could be called God, but not in the full sense of the word.

Arianism was condemned at the Council of Nicea in 325. Arius taught that Jesus was *like* substance (*homoi-ousia*) with the Father. The opposition which finally prevailed after a long struggle was led by Athanasius who taught that Jesus in His divine nature had the *same* substance (*homo-ousia*) with the Father. The modern group known as Jehovah's Witnesses has a view that is similar to the views of Arius.

THE APOLLINARIANS

While the Arians denied the integrity of the divine nature of Christ, the Apollinarians denied the integrity of the human nature of Christ. Apollinarians held to the view that man consists of body, soul, and spirit. The human nature of Jesus had a body and soul, but not a human spirit (mind). The intelligence of Christ was supplied by His eternal Logos. This view was condemned at the Council of Constantinople in 381.

With reference to the controversy surrounding the Appollinarian error, McDonald comments:

In the fourth century Gregory of Nazianzus repudiated the abridged humanity of the Christ of Appollinarius with the observation that that which is unassumed is unhealed. If only half Adam fell, he argues, then that which Christ assumes and saves must be half also; but if the whole of his nature fell it must be united to the whole nature of Him who was begotten and so be complete as a whole. Let them not begrudge us, he concludes, our complete salvation and clothe the Saviour with bones and nerves and the portraiture of humanity.[5]

THE NESTORIANS

Nestorius was accused of an improper teaching regarding the union of the human and the divine natures in Christ. He was condemned at the Synod of Ephesus in 431. What is called Nestorianism sets forth the view that the union of the human and divine natures in Christ is somewhat analogous to the indwelling Holy Spirit in the believer. The difference is a matter of plenitude and control. The result was the existence of two persons.

Some scholars are of the opinion that Nestorius was misunderstood. McDonald explains:

Although Nestorius was condemned for heresy by the excessive zeal and vindictiveness of Cyril [of Alexander], the question of his actual unorthodoxy has persisted. The discovery of Nestorius' The Bazaar of Heracleides in a Syriac translation in 1910 reopened the issue. Opposing verdicts have returned. J. F. Bethune-Baker declares that Nestorius was no Nestorian; while F. Nau upholds his condemnation.[6]

From the research that I did on Nestorius for a paper while in seminary, I am inclined to believe that Nestorius was falsely accused. But it helps in our understanding of the true view when we contrast it with what is called the Nestorian view.

THE EUTYCHIANS

Eutyches was caught up in an overreaction against Nestorianism. He taught that the divine and human natures combined to make a third nature. Concerning this mingling of the natures to make a third nature, A. H. Strong explains:

Since in this case the divine must overpower the human, it follows that the human was really absorbed into or transmuted into the divine, although the divine was not in all respects the same, after the union, that it was before. Hence the Eutychians were often called Monophysites, because they virtually reduced the two natures to one.[7]

Charles Hodge raises some important questions with regard to this view:

> But what was the nature which resulted from the union of the two? The human might be exalted into the divine, or lost in it, as a drop of vinegar (to use one of the illustrations then employed) in the ocean. Then Christ ceased to be a man. . . . Where then is his redeeming work, and his bond of union or sympathy with us? Or the effect of the union might be to merge the divine into the human, so that the one nature was after all only the nature of man. Then the true divinity of Christ was denied, and we have only a human saviour. Or the effect of the union of the two natures was the production of a third, which was neither human nor divine, but theanthropic, as in chemical combinations an acid and an alkali when united produce a substance which is no longer either acid or alkaline. Then Christ instead of being God and man, is neither God nor man.[8]

Eutychianism was condemned at the Council of Chalcedon in 451. It was this same council that set forth the view that we speak of as the orthodox view.

The Orthodox View Concerning the Two Natures and the Person of Christ

THE CHALCEDON INTERPRETATION

The basic thrust of the decision of the Council of Chalcedon in 451 was to affirm two basic truths about Christ: (1) He had two natures—a human nature and a divine nature. Each of these exists in its completeness and integrity. (2) Jesus Christ is one person.

At the Council of Constantinople in 681 the Monothelite doctrine, which teaches that Jesus had only one will, was rejected and the doctrine of two wills and two intelligences was added to the orthodox doctrine.

The Union of the Two Natures in One Person

H. C. Thiessen explains:

> The person of Christ is theanthropic but not His nature. That is, we may speak of the God-man when we wish to refer to the person; but we cannot speak of the divine-human nature, but say the divine and the human nature in Christ.[9]

If we were to use the words "God-man" or the words "Divine-human" to refer to the natures of Christ, we would in effect be suggesting a cross between the two natures. We would be advocating Eutychianism.

The Evidence That Christ Is One Person

We can speak of *theanthropic* (made up of two Greek words meaning "God-man") or God-man person or personality of Christ. That He was only one person is clear. When we meet Jesus in the gospels, we get the impression that we are meeting only one person. Jesus refers to Himself as "I," not "We." He is addressed as "Thou." He is referred to as "He."

The Meaning of Theanthropic Personality

What is involved in the recognition of Jesus' person or personality as being theanthropic? We are not to think of the personality of Christ as being a cross between a divine personality and a human personality. The personality of Christ involved all the attributes of both human and divine personality, but was not a cross between the two.

Theologians speak about the impersonal human nature of Christ being united with the divine nature of Christ. While the divine personality of Christ existed prior to the incarnation, the human personality did not. The incarnation did not involve the union of a human personality and a divine personality. In the incarnation the human nature found personal awareness in the theanthropic personality. Without alteration to the divine personality, the personality of Christ took on the attributes of human personality and became a theanthropic personality.

We might find somewhat of a parallel when we use the center of a circle that is already drawn and draw another circle using the same center. The center which was at one time the center of only one circle becomes the center then of another circle. We have one center and two circles. The two natures of Christ find personal awareness in the one personality. The divine nature had personal awareness in this personality before the incarnation when this personality took on the attributes of human personality and gave personal awareness to a human nature that had had no prior and no separate personal awareness.

The Omnipresence of the Theanthropic Personality

The human nature of Christ is restricted to the limits of the human body. The theanthropic personality of Christ is omnipresent. The personal presence of Christ is always theanthropic at all times and at all places.

A Union of the Two Natures, Not an Enclosure of the Divine Nature in the Human

There is a mistaken idea that easily develops around the word incarnation which means "in flesh." We are not to think, as some do, of the divine nature being shrunk to the size of a human sperm and being placed in the womb of the Virgin Mary. Following through with this idea is the idea that deity, in the incarnation, was enclosed within the confines of a human body.

With regard to these observations, let it first be said that deity will not shrink. The incarnation is the union of the divine and human natures, not the enclosure of the divine nature within the confines of a human body.

One Will or Two?

Let us now turn our attention to a discussion of whether Christ has one or two wills. As was pointed out previously, the one will doctrine (Monothelite doctrine) was rejected and the position of two wills in Christ was adopted at the Council of Constantinople in 681. I agree with Strong when he says: "The theory of two consciousnesses and two wills, first elaborated by John of Damascus, was an unwarranted addition to the orthodox doctrine propounded at Chalcedon."[10]

I think the real question is this: Is will an attribute of personality or an attribute of nature? If will is an attribute of nature, Christ had two. If will is an attribute of personality, He had one.

In deciding whether Jesus had one will or two, I think it will be helpful to see how the implications of our thinking would affect our thinking on the Trinity. In the Trinity, there are three persons and one nature. If will is related to nature, there is only one will in the Godhead. If will is related to personality, there are three wills in the Trinity.

Sometimes we have become so accustomed to thinking of will as "plan," as when we think of "God's will," that we read that meaning where it does not belong. Surely, there is one plan in the Trinity. That is not what we are talking about here. We are talking about the capacity to say, "I will." As I see it, that capacity clearly belongs to personality as distinguished from nature. If so, there are three wills in the Trinity, but only one in Christ. If will belongs to nature, there are two wills in Christ, but one in the Trinity.

What I am saying is this. The same conscious awareness that is aware of a divine nature in Christ is aware of a human nature in Christ. The same conscious awareness of determination (will) that directs the divine nature also directs the human nature. In directing the divine nature, it is consciously aware of the divine nature and all the attributes of divine personality. In directing the human nature of Christ, it is aware of the human nature and all the attributes of human personality.

POINTS OF ESSENTIAL AGREEMENT ON THE NATURES AND PERSON OF CHRIST

In my estimation, to fathom the mysteries of the incarnation is more difficult, in so far as we can understand either, than it is to fathom the mysteries of the Trinity. In trying to fathom the mysteries of the incarnation, we should keep the following truths firmly fixed in our minds: (1) We must adhere to two natures in Christ, the divine and the human, both in their completeness and their integrity. (2) These two natures are in union, but are distinct and are in no way mingled one with another. (3) Christ is only one person. (4) The personality of Christ has the attributes of divine personality and human personality, but is not a cross between divine personality and human personality. These truths must not be denied by statement or implication. When these truths are maintained, we may err on details, but not on basic truths.

A CONTRAST OF THE TRUE VIEW WITH THE FALSE VIEWS

It would be helpful to show the contrast between the true view of Christ and the false views. In contrast to the Ebionites, we believe in the deity of Christ. In contrast to the gnostics, we believe in the real humanity of Christ and in a real incarnation. In contrast to the Arians, we believe in the completeness and integrity of the deity of Christ. In contrast to the Apollinarians, we believe in the completeness and integrity of the human nature of Christ. In contrast to the Nestorians, we believe Christ is one person, not two. In contrast to the Eutychians, we reject the idea of a mingling of the natures in Christ. Each nature, the human and the divine, maintained its completeness and integrity.

The Relationship of the Two Natures of Christ in His Earthly Life

THE PROBLEM STATED

The basic problem centers around the omniscience, omnipotence, and omnipresence which are attributes of the divine nature. The question is: Did Jesus set aside these attributes during His life on earth? Or was some limitation placed upon their exercise? Some have answered by saying yes to the first question. Others have said no to the first question, but yes to the second question.

AN EXAMINATION OF THE BIBLICAL DATA

Philippians 2:7

Philippians 2:7 has been a key verse in the debate over what Jesus gave up in the incarnation. The key word is the word *kenoō* which may be translated "to empty." The KJV translates, "But made himself of no reputation." A better translation would be, "But he emptied himself."

The question is: Of what did Jesus empty Himself? There is nothing in the passage to suggest that He emptied Himself of any of His attributes. The theme of the passage is humility. Paul is challenging the readers to, "Let this mind be in you, which was also in Christ Jesus" (verse 5). He who had existed from eternity with all the privileges and glory of deity took on Himself the "form of a servant, and was made in the likeness of men: And being found in fashion as a man, he humbled himself, and became obedient unto death, even the death of the cross" (verses 7, 8).

There are two basic observations: (1) Prior to coming to earth, Jesus had experienced the *full glory of God* (Jn. 17:5). When He came to earth, as He was viewed by men, the glory of His deity was veiled. His deity was not apparent at all except to those who believed in Him. Even they did not see the glory of His deity. (2) *He was a servant.* As a servant He was obedient to the Father. Philippians 2:5-8 does not elaborate the nature of this submission to the Father other than that He "became obedient unto death, even the death of the cross."

I would conclude that while the passage is very helpful in our understanding of the humility and submission demonstrated in the Incarnation, it offers no solution to the problem related to His omniscience, omnipotence, and omnipresence. The fact of submission to the Father may be of help, but how it relates to these attributes and their use must be settled by other data.

THE QUESTION OF OMNIPRESENCE

Before proceeding further, I want to comment on the problem of omnipresence. If we consider immensity to refer to the infinity of the essence of God as distinguished from omnipresence, it is impossible to think of surrendering His immensity. The immensity of the essence can in no way be subjected to voluntary limitation. If Jesus did not share the essence of God, He would not be God. The infinity of the essence is not subject to change.

Omnipresence, when distinguished from immensity, refers to personal presence. The fact of the personal presence of Christ would not be subject to limitation. The action of the person is subject to voluntary submission to the Father, but not the fact of His omnipresence.

THE QUESTION OF OMNISCIENCE AND OMNIPOTENCE

The problem centers around omniscience and omnipotence. With regard to His omniscience, He did not always exercise it. He stated that He did not know the time of His second coming (Mk. 13:32). Does this mean that He had set aside His omniscience? The evidence is to the contrary. Jesus saw Nathanael under the fig tree, though Jesus was not there. This fact when declared to Nathanael caused him to acknowledge Jesus to be the Son of God (Jn. 1:47-50). Jesus "knew all men, And needed not that any should testify of man: for he knew what was in man" (Jn. 2:24, 25).

As it relates to Jesus' omnipotence, He never tried to perform any act without success. His miracles attest that His divine nature did not set aside omnipotence. It is a mistake, as some do, to have His miracles and His whole life lived out in the strength of the Holy Spirit in the same manner that the Holy Spirit works in us. If the miracles of Christ had been performed solely in the power of the Holy Spirit, they would not attest to His deity (Acts 2:22). A view that places the total success of Jesus' life on dependence upon the Holy Spirit would have a dormant divine nature during His life on earth. The evidence is too strong to the contrary for such a view to be taken seriously. I am not denying that He had a relationship to the Holy Spirit, but I am saying that much of what He did reflected the action of His divine nature.

THE MAIN PROBLEM: OMNISCIENCE

There is no problem in seeing the exercise of omnipotence being subjected to the will of the Father. There is a problem with omniscience. It is difficult to conceive of a member of the Trinity as not being in the full exercise of omniscience at all times. However, in Mark 13:32 Jesus seems to clearly state that He did not know the time of His second coming. In the face of this difficulty, some have sought other ways of explaining the verse. In spite of the problems, it seems to be best to take the obvious interpretation and conclude that there was some limitation placed on Jesus' exercise of omniscience during His earthly life. The suggestion that He did not know in His human nature, but did in His divine nature is unsatisfactory. Jesus did not say that His human nature did not know. Rather, He said the Son did not know.

John 6:38

That Jesus did live His life in submission to the Father is evident. The evidence is too obvious in the gospels to require repeating here. Jesus states this truth clearly when He said, "For I came down from heaven, not to do mine own will, but the will of him that sent me" (Jn. 6:38).

A SUBORDINATE, RATHER THAN COORDINATE, EXERCISE OF THESE ATTRIBUTES

A common way of stating the voluntary limitation on the exercise of omniscience and omnipotence is: Jesus gave up an independent exercise of these attributes for a dependent exercise of these attributes. In the exercise of these attributes He was in submission to the Father's control during His life on earth. Warren Young prefers to speak of Jesus as giving up the coordinate exercise of these attributes for a subordinate exercise. He says that Jesus never made an independent use of these attributes.[11] It is probably best to speak of the coordinate and subordinate use of these attributes rather than the independent and dependent use. The same is meant of either choice of terms, but coordinate and subordinate seem to be better terms to express the ideas involved.

The Problem of the Peccability or Impeccability of Christ

THE PROBLEM STATED

The view of peccability is that Jesus could have sinned. The view of impeccability is that Jesus could not have sinned. There have been devout Christians who have taken each position. There is no direct teaching of Scripture that speaks to the point of the question. The Bible clearly teaches that He did not sin. That does not tell us whether He could have. I will give a case for the impeccability of Christ.

The Result of the Union of the Two Natures in One Person

In the union of the two natures in one person, *I do not believe it is possible to impute moral guilt to His humanity without imputing it to His Divinity.* When we distinguish nature and person, moral responsibility belongs to person. Nature is morally responsible only as it manifests itself in personality. Jesus had only one personality. It is clear that deity cannot sin (Tit. 1:2). Moral guilt could not be experienced by the theanthropic personality of Jesus without deity sinning. Since deity cannot sin, Jesus could not have sinned.

I am not saying that the human nature of Christ could not have sinned if it had not been in union with the divine nature. But human nature in union with divine nature cannot sin. If I could see how His human nature could have sinned without imputing guilt also to the divine nature, I would believe that He could have sinned. But since nature is morally responsible only as it manifests itself in personality, I do not believe that Jesus could have sinned. If He had sinned, guilt would have been imputed to the theanthropic personality. Human personality can sin. But theanthropic personality cannot sin.

The Reality of the Temptation

Some have charged that if Jesus could not have sinned, His temptation was not real and He cannot be our sympathetic High Priest. The first point we need to clarify is that there are two sources of temptation. (1) Temptation can be from within. This is what James spoke of in James 1:14 when he said, "But every man is tempted, when he is drawn away of his own lust, and enticed." He is referring to temptation by our depraved nature. (2) Temptation can be from without. This is what happens when another person tries to get us to do wrong.

Jesus was tempted in the second way. He was tempted by the devil. Jesus did not have a sinful nature. He had no inner urges to sin. The inner urge to sin is already sin. Jesus was hungry and desired to eat, but He did not desire to eat if eating involved obeying Satan. He had not the slightest inclination to want to obey Satan. Such inclination is in and of itself sin.

The principle is well illustrated by Jesus' prayer in the garden of Gethsemane. He prayed, "O my Father, if it be possible, let this cup pass from me: nevertheless not as I will, but as thou wilt" (Mt. 26:39). Jesus dreaded drinking the cup of condemnation for our sins. He would have preferred not to do it if it were consistent with the plan of God. He shows not the slightest desire to refrain from drinking the cup if refraining involves disobedience to God. It is a mistake to understand Jesus as being on the brink of disobedience and about to back out of the whole arrangement. *His commitment was completely unwavering.*

Jesus felt the weight of temptation. He felt the pressures of life. He could easily sympathize with the problem of a hungry man who is struggling with the possibility of getting food in a wrong way. A person of principles and conviction in a depressed mood might not have any difficulty in refusing illegal drugs or alcohol, but he would, as a result of that experience, be able to better understand the person who does have difficulty. Jesus' encounters with life were real. His own inner needs were real, but His commitment to right never wavered. He never needed cleansing from an evil thought.

The Reason for the Temptation

Some say, "If Christ could not have sinned, there was no reason for the temptation." I think there was. A statement saying that Jesus could not have sinned would never have been as meaningful to us as a real encounter with the devil in which the devil failed to make Him sin. A statement saying He could not have sinned would have been good for rational arguments, but it would not have met the needs of our total personality as well as actual victory over temptation.

Another purpose that was served in the temptation is that it closes the mouth of the devil. He can never say, "I did not have a chance to make Him sin. If I had I could have made Him sin."

The Resurrection of Christ

The resurrection is treated here for two reasons: (1) It is appropriate if we want to continue our discussion of the incarnation to make observations about the incarnation of Christ as He is now. (2) The discussion of atonement, as will be made in the next chapter, should be followed by a study of the application of salvation without interrupting the thought to study the resurrection.

THE INCOMPATIBILITY OF NATURALISM AND CHRIST'S RESURRECTION

For the naturalist who does not believe in God, and for the person who believes in a "god," but restricts his activities to the framework of the laws of nature, there can be no bodily resurrection of Christ from the dead which has been performed by God. Such thinking is not allowed within the naturalist's system of thought or worldview. He has ruled out such a conclusion before he examines the data. Even if he were convinced that Jesus became alive after being killed, he would not believe that God raised Him from the dead. His system has no room for such. He will not believe that God raised Jesus from the dead until he rejects naturalism and believes in divine revelation. Something must happen that will bring him to the point of seeing and feeling the inadequacy of his worldview (or lifeview). At that point, he will be more interested in hearing and considering the evidence for the resurrection of Christ. Once our system of thought allows the possibility of the resurrection of Christ, we have a right to appeal to the divine revelation and to the witnesses mentioned therein.

THE BIBLICAL EVIDENCE FOR THE BODILY RESURRECTION OF CHRIST

For those who believe in God and the biblical revelation, there is proof. The tomb was empty. Only a bodily resurrection needs an empty tomb. Jesus had prophesied that His body would be raised (Jn. 2:19-22; Mt. 27:62-66). He showed His body to Thomas (Jn. 20:26-28). He declared to His disciples that He had a body of flesh and bones (Lk. 24:39).

THE HISTORICAL EVIDENCE OF THE BODILY RESURRECTION OF CHRIST

Few people will challenge the fact that Jesus actually lived as a historical person. The evidence supports the conclusion that He was crucified and actually died (Jn. 19:31-37). Witnesses attest that He was seen alive after He died (Mt. 28:9, 16, 17; Lk. 24:39-51; Jn. 20:11-29; Acts 1:21-26; 2:32; and 1 Cor. 15:3-8.) There is historical, empirical evidence that Jesus died and that after He died He was seen alive in the same body that was crucified. There is more historical, empirical evidence for the resurrection of Christ than exists for many major events from the same time period. Josh McDowell has given extensive treatment to this subject.[12] There can be no empirical evidence that God raised Him from the dead. The divine act of resurrecting the body of Christ did not fall within the view of the five senses. The fact that "God hath raised him from the dead" comes only by special divine revelation. Those who received that revelation have passed it on to us in the Bible (Rom. 10:9). The empirical evidence supports the conclusion that Jesus Christ died and came back to life. The only reasonable explanation of His restoration to life after being crucified is that God raised Him from the dead.

THE QUESTION OF WHETHER OR NOT JESUS' RESURRECTION BODY WAS A MATERIAL BODY

The question is frequently raised: Was Jesus' resurrection body a physical, material body? There is certainly no biblical evidence to the contrary. That His body went through closed doors shows it was not subject to the same laws as it was previously, but this is not an argument against a physical body. When Jesus fed the 5,000, the fish and loaves were multiplied by a process not natural, but this is no reason to deny that what Jesus fed them was real material food. The burden of proof that Jesus' body was not material rests with those who make the claim. Unless we labor under some influence of the gnostic view, there is no reason for denying that Jesus' resurrection body was material. Matter is not inherently evil.

Differences and Likenesses as Compared With His Body Prior to the Crucifixion

The resurrection body was a body of flesh and bone (Lk. 24:39). We would judge from 1 Corinthians 15:50 that it did not possess blood. His body bore the marks of the crucifixion (Jn. 20:24-28). It was not bound by the same limitations as before (Jn. 20:19, 26). It is no longer subject to death (Rom. 6:9; and Rev. 1:18).

The Significance of Christ's Resurrection

Without the resurrection of Christ, the whole system of Christian truth would crumble. The resurrection assures us of the truth of Jesus' divine claims (Rom. 1:4). It assures us of our justification (Rom. 4:25). The atonement wrought at the cross could not have been applied by a dead Christ. Only a living Christ can bestow the benefits of His death. The bodily resurrection of Christ assures us of our own bodily resurrection (1 Cor. 15:13-23; and 1 Th. 4:14). His resurrection is the ground of victorious living for us (Rom. 6:4, 5, 8).

THE APOLOGETIC VALUE OF THE RESURRECTION OF CHRIST

In Romans 1:4 Paul tells us that by His resurrection from the dead, Jesus Christ was declared to be the Son of God with power.

> Miracles in the N. T. had a sign value; i.e. they had theological significance. The miracles of Christ were a sign of the fact that God stamped His approval on Jesus Christ. His claims and His teachings were thereby confirmed as being true (Acts 2:22; Jn. 20:30, 31). The miracle of the resurrection is the miracle of miracles. By the resurrection of Christ, God gave Him the clearest possible stamp of approval. If Jesus had remained in the tomb, all of His claims would have been voided. When God raised Him from the dead, He declared in no uncertain terms that He is the Son of God.[13]

In the New Testament, the apologetic value of the resurrection of Christ was not to atheists to get them to believe in God. It was primarily to Jews who already believed in God. The apologetic value of both Christ's miracles and His resurrection was to stamp God's approval on Jesus Christ, His claims, and His teaching. To believe in Jesus Christ would of course mean that a person would also believe in the Old Testament and the God of the Old Testament. Paul makes it clear in 1 Corinthians 15:12-19 that to reject the resurrection of Christ would mean to reject our resurrection and the Christian hope. Without the resurrection of Christ, the Christian message falls apart.

Paul referred to the resurrection of Christ in His message to the pagans at Mars Hill (Acts 17:18, 31). In verse 31 he said, "He hath given assurance unto all men, in that he raised him from the dead." At Mars Hill Paul was dealing with those who believed in false gods. In this case Paul was not trying to convince atheists that God exists. Rather, he was trying to convince those who believed in false gods that the Judeo-Christian God was the true God and the only hope we have is to be found in Jesus Christ.

The apologetic value of the resurrection of Christ does not come from a dispassionate, impersonal, objective, cold, legal approach to the evidence for the resurrection of Christ directed to an objective disinterested person. Certainly, showing the legal credibility of the resurrection of Christ is important. But the highest potential of the apologetic value of the resurrection of Christ is realized when we speak and write out of deep personal concern for those who are made aware of the inadequacy of life and thought without Christ. The person who has allowed the *inescapable questions of life* to do their work is a ripe candidate to hear and listen to the evidence for the resurrection of Christ. It will also help if he understands that the question of the resurrection of Christ is a part of the total process of testing the Christian worldview for validity. In such a case, a person is not simply trying to settle some academic point. He or she is in a life or death struggle. Such a person must think honestly. This is no time for deception. But they enter such a study in a desperate hope of finding answers for their deep inner longings for meaning for this life and the next.

The Ascension and Exaltation of Christ

THE CONTINUITY OF THE NATURES OF CHRIST

Jesus will forever remain the incarnate Son of God. He will forever be fully human and fully God. His body is now a resurrected and glorified body, but it is still a body. Buswell explains:

> Our Lord Jesus Christ continues to be a man and ever will be a member of our race. This, of course, does not mean that He is subject to the material limitations which characterize our life upon this earth, but it does mean that He has a bodily tangible form such as was manifested to His disciples after His resurrection, and such as will appear to us all in His glorious second coming.[14]

We are told in Acts 1:11, "This same Jesus, which is taken up from you into heaven, shall so come in like manner as ye have seen him go into heaven."

THE EXALTATION OF CHRIST

Paul tells us: "Wherefore God also hath highly exalted him, and given him a name which is above every name: That at the name of Jesus every knee should bow, of things in heaven, and things in earth, and things under the earth; And that every tongue should confess that Jesus Christ is Lord, to the glory of God the Father" (Phil. 2:9-11).

Jesus will never die again. He will never be jeered or spit upon again. He is King of Kings and Lord of Lords. He sits in glory at the right hand of the Father (Heb. 10:12). He is coming again in triumphant power (Rev. 19:11-16).

11

Atonement and Justification

Of all the events in the experience of Christ, His birth, His life, His death, His resurrection, and His return, His death stands central. As important as the other events are both in themselves and in relation to His death, the death of Christ remains central because apart from atonement there would be no forgiveness of sins. Christianity would be nonexistent. It is the birth that makes the death of Christ possible, but it is the death that makes the birth important. It is the resurrection that makes possible the application of the benefits of His death. It is the death that makes His resurrection important and makes the one who has been restored to life the Redeemer.

It is of utmost importance that we maintain a sound doctrine of atonement. The study of atonement must be done with the whole personality, not just the rational mind. While a study of atonement is fascinating in its logical consistency, it must go much deeper than that to be comprehended. It must grip the heart also. There is nothing that sheds light on the seriousness of holiness and sin like the atonement that God provided to bring forgiveness of sin. A proper view of atonement puts seriousness into the whole study of theology. Any system of ethics that does not read from atonement the seriousness of sin and the understanding of God's holiness and God's love that is seen in atonement will be grossly inadequate. Any view of grace that is not grounded in the understanding of sin, holiness, and the high regard for law that is manifested in atonement will be empty, shallow, and shot through with the tendencies of antinomianism.

It is not enough to proclaim the statement: "Jesus died to save sinners." That statement must be grasped in its essential meaning before it is the gospel. That statement could be made by either a liberal or a fundamentalist, but with drastically different interpretations growing out of drastically different views of the authority of Scripture.

Most preaching falls short of giving a developed view of atonement. I hope this will be corrected. We need preaching and teaching that give a developed view of the need and the nature of atonement and how it is applied in justification. We need to preach and teach this truth often enough that our hearers will have an intelligent understanding of what Jesus Christ did on their behalf. Underdeveloped views of atonement run the risk of being replaced by false views. It is with a realization that our task is serious that we enter our study of atonement and its application in justification.

The major attention of this chapter will be taken up with contrasting the satisfaction view of atonement and the governmental view of atonement and the resulting views of justification. Some attention will be given to the moral influence of atonement as advocated by liberalism. For those who are interested in a study of the various views of atonement that have arisen in the church, I would recommend the treatment given by H. Dermot McDonald.[1]

The Penal Satisfaction View of Atonement

BASIC ASSUMPTIONS

There are five basic assumptions upon which the penal satisfaction view of atonement rests: (1) God is sovereign. (2) God is holy. (3) Man is sinful. (4) God is loving. (5) God is wise. It is from a development of the inherent principles that are in these basic assumptions that we see the necessity, the provision, and the nature of atonement.

Lest we fall into the trap of mechanical versus personal reasoning, it is important for us to remind ourselves that atonement is designed to settle a conflict between persons—God and man. We must see sovereignty as personally administered by one who thinks, feels, and acts. God is capable of feeling joy, satisfaction, sorrow, and holy wrath. To deny God the ability to feel is to deny the integrity of His personality. Henry C. Thiessen explains:

> Philosophers frequently deny feeling to God, saying that feeling implies passivity and susceptibility of impression from without, and that such a possibility is incompatible with the idea of the immutability of God. But immutability does not mean immobility. True love necessarily involves feeling, and if there be no feeling in God, then there is no love of God.[2]

Holiness is not an abstract principle, but an attribute of personality. It is not simply an attribute. It is an experience of the divine personality. It involves the principles and attitudes by which the divine personality operates. The same observations that have been made about holiness can also be applied to love and wisdom. These are experiences of the divine personality.

Man is personal. Sin is an experience of the human personality in conflict with a personal God. Atonement is designed to resolve this conflict and to form the foundation for restoring holiness as the experience of the human personality.

THE NECESSITY OF ATONEMENT

The necessity of atonement draws upon the first three of the previously given basic assumptions. God as Sovereign is both Lawgiver and Judge of the universe. This places man in a position of accountability before God. God cannot lay aside His responsibility as Judge, and man cannot escape his accountability before God—the Supreme Judge of the universe.

If there were no responsibility on God's part and no accountability on man's part, there would be no need of atonement, but this relationship is inescapably bound up in the nature of the case. Having established this responsibility-accountability relationship, there is still no necessity of atonement except as that necessity grows out of the holy nature of God. It is the holy nature of the One who is Sovereign, Lawgiver, and Judge that makes atonement necessary to resolve the conflict between man and God, since God has placed man under condemnation.

THE NECESSITY FOR SIN TO BE PUNISHED

From the forewarned judgment against sin in Genesis 2:17 to the Great White Throne Judgment in Revelation 20:11-15, the Bible repeatedly reminds us of God's attitude toward sin. The culmination of God's attitude toward sin is seen in the eternal condemnation of the wicked (Mt. 25:45; Mk. 9:43-48; Rom. 6:23; Rev. 21:8).

Why is there such a dreadful penalty against sin? No principle of expediency for divine government could ever justify taking such a strong measure against sin apart from absolute necessity. Our whole being abhors the idea that God would take such a drastic step as eternal punishment apart from an absolute necessity existing within the nature of God. Such a step would be a violation of both the holiness and love of God. Our confidence in God tells us that He would not have taken such a step as eternal punishment if it had not risen from a necessity in the divine nature.

God's law issues from and is an expression of His holy nature. For holiness to be holiness, it not only differs from sin, but it is intolerant of sin. This intolerance manifests itself in a penalty against the violation of the moral law of God. As J. Oliver Buswell, Jr. remarks:

> The punishment of all that violates, or is contrary to the holy character of God is a logical implication and a necessary consequence of God's holiness. If God is holy, it must follow that He will vindicate His holiness as against all sin and corruption which is contrary thereto.[3]

The holy law of God pronounces a penalty upon the person who violates that law. It is the work of divine justice to execute the penalty of the law and thus protect the holiness of God. The justice of God will not tolerate any attempt to set aside or diminish the penalty of the broken law of God. There can be no forgiveness of sin without a full satisfaction of the justice of God in the payment of the penalty.

Romans 3:26 declares that the design of propitiation was to make it possible for God to maintain His justice, while at the same time justifying the sinner who comes to God believing in Jesus. The implication is that for God to justify sinners without atonement would compromise the justice of God. This cannot be. It is clear that in this passage Paul is telling us that justice required atonement before there could be forgiveness.

A proper of view of both the necessity and the nature of atonement arises out of the absolute necessity for God to punish sin. This necessity comes from His holiness.

THE NECESSITY FOR ABSOLUTE RIGHTEOUSNESS

In Romans 2 and 3, Paul builds a strong case that our justification before God demands nothing less than absolute righteousness. In 2:1–3:8, Paul is particularly concerned with the Jews who have not believed in Jesus as their Messiah. He wants them to understand that they are not prepared to stand justified before God. He wants them to understand that merely being a descendant of Abraham through Jacob will not prepare a person to stand before God and receive the eternal inheritance promised to the seed of Abraham in Genesis 13:14, 15 and 17:8.

The general consensus holds that Paul is addressing Jews in Romans 2. There are different opinions on what Paul is trying to say in verses 6-13. The problem centers around what Paul is trying to tell us will happen in "the day of wrath and revelation of the righteous judgment of God" (verse 5). He speaks of judgment according to deeds (verse 6). Patient continuance in "well doing" is what will be rewarded. Those who do not obey the truth will be under the wrath of God (verses 8, 9). Those who do good will receive "glory, honor, and peace." In verse 12 he says that those who have sinned without the law (Gentiles) will perish. Those who have the law (Jews) and sin will be judged by the law (verse 12). In verse 13, he says emphatically that to have been the recipients of the law, as the Jews were, would carry no weight at the righteous judgment of God. Only those who are doers of the law will be justified.

These words have puzzled commentators. Thus, a variety of interpretations have been given. Most have concluded that verses 6-13 refer to the good works of Christians. This passage would be telling us that good works are essential evidence of being a Christian.

There are two problems with this interpretation. The first problem is that it does not fit the context. In Romans 1:18–3:20, it is clear that Paul is building a case for the argument that the whole world, including both Jews and Gentiles, stands condemned before God. No good reason can be given why Paul would depart from that theme in Chapter 2 to talk about Christians doing good works as evidence of salvation. The second problem is that the works of which Paul speaks are absolute. In building his case, Paul states it from both the positive side and the negative side. On the positive side, he speaks of continuing in well doing. On the negative side, the presence of sin means judgment. In verses 12 and 13 there is no room for interpreting the "doing" to be anything less than "doing without exception."

Another view interprets the good works as "faith." Support for this interpretation has been sought from Jesus' words when He said, "This is the work of God, that ye believe on him whom he hath sent" (Jn. 6:29). The problem with this view is that it does not fit the context.

A third view is that Paul is speaking hypothetically. If it were possible for a person to render absolute obedience to God, such a person would be justified. But, of course, such obedience is impossible for human beings.

In giving my view, I will quote from my Romans commentary:

> I agree with those who hold the hypothetical view in saying that Paul's aim is to get the unbelieving Jew to see that as a law violator he is under condemnation. Where I differ is that I do not see it as hypothetical. Paul is not simply telling the law violator that he is condemned; he is telling him what is required of anybody who will ever be justified in God's sight.
>
> The only way that any person can ever be justified before God is to have absolute righteousness (or to say it another way is to be considered a doer of the law). Briefly put, in 2:6-13 Paul is saying that a person must have absolute righteousness. In 3:10 he points out, "There is none righteous." In 3:20 he points out that "by the deeds of the law shall no flesh be justified in his sight."

We must have absolute righteousness (2:6-13). We do not have absolute righteousness (3:10). We cannot produce absolute righteousness (3:20). The only hope of justification for either Jew or Gentile is to have absolute righteousness provided for us.[4]

There are two things that the justice of God will not permit a departure from: (1) Sin can under no circumstances go unpunished. (2) Under no circumstances will a person stand justified in God's presence without absolute righteousness.

THE NATURE OF ATONEMENT

Sinful man is in a predicament for which he has no remedy of his own. He is under the condemnation of eternal death. The justice of God requires that the penalty be paid. Nothing less will be accepted.

I am not suggesting that an actual council, as I will describe, took place, but I am saying that what follows illustrates the principles involved. The justice of God demanded that the penalty of sin be paid. The love of God was interested in saving man, but it had to submit to the justice of God. The wisdom of God came forth with a plan that would satisfy both holiness and love. Through the incarnation of Christ and the substitutionary death of Christ, love could fulfill its desire to save, and holiness could hold to its insistence that sin be punished.[5]

There are two aspects of atonement: (1) active obedience, and (2) passive obedience. Active obedience of Christ refers to the idea that He lived a life of absolute obedience to the Father. He lived an absolutely righteous life. Passive obedience refers to the death of Christ. He submitted to the wrath of God for our sins. Most of the discussion centers around passive obedience because it involved the payment of the penalty for our sins. A complete accounting of atonement also embraces the righteous life Christ lived on our behalf which was His active obedience.[6]

THE PASSIVE OBEDIENCE OF CHRIST

What happened in the passive obedience of Christ? The Bible is quite clear on the basic principles involved. Isaiah 53:6 tells us, "The LORD hath laid on him the iniquity of us all." First Peter 2:24 reads, "Who his own self bare our sins in his own body on the tree." Galatians 3:13 tells us, "Christ hath redeemed us from the curse of the law, being made a curse for us." Second Corinthians 5:21 says, "For he hath made him to be sin for us, who knew no sin."

When Jesus Christ went to the cross, all the sins of all the world that ever had been committed, were being committed, and ever would be committed were laid on Him. With our sins upon Him, He took our place under the righteous wrath of God. God poured out His wrath upon Him as if He were guilty of all the sins of the whole race. We read in Isaiah 53:10, "Yet it pleased the LORD to bruise him; he hath put him to grief." In a very real and literal sense, Jesus took the place of every sinner.

It is a mistake to restrict the sufferings of Jesus Christ to that which was inflicted upon Him by the Roman soldiers. The death Jesus Christ suffered by crucifixion was the least part of His suffering. The greatest suffering that was inflicted on Him was inflicted by His own Father. He took the place of sinners before God and drank the cup of wrath that was due sinners. He suffered as much on the cross as sinners will suffer in an eternal Hell. He experienced separation from the Father. He who had enjoyed unbroken fellowship with the Father in eternity past uttered these words on the cross, "My God, my God, why hast thou forsaken me" (Mt. 27:46). This was a cry of agony rather than a cry from lack of understanding.

When Jesus finished suffering for the sins of the world, He said, "It is finished" (Jn. 19:30). When these words were uttered, He was telling us that He had finished paying for our sins. The same One who had a short time before uttered the words, "My God, my God, why hast thou forsaken me?" was now able to say, "Father, into thy hands I commend my spirit" (Lk. 23:46).

When Jesus uttered the words, "Father, into thy hands I commend my spirit," this was the greatest reunion the universe has ever known. The One whose fellowship with God had been interrupted by having our sins placed upon Him had paid the penalty and removed the obstacle that separated Him from the Father. The way for His reunion was open. In opening it for Himself, He opened it for us. He identified Himself with our broken fellowship that we might be identified with His fellowship. He identified Himself with our sin that we might be identified with His righteousness.

Payment of the penalty through a qualified substitute was the only way God could save man. As William G. T. Shedd explains:

> The eternal Judge may or may not exercise mercy, but he must exercise justice. He can neither waive the claims of the law in part, nor abolish them altogether. The only possible mode, consequently, of delivering a creature who is obnoxious to the demands of retributive justice, is to satisfy them for him. The claims themselves must be met and extinguished, either personally, or by substitution. . . . And this necessity of an atonement is absolute not relative. It is not made necessary by divine decision, in the sense that the divine decision might have been otherwise. *It is not correct to say, that God might have saved man without a vicarious atonement had he been pleased to do so. For this is equivalent to saying, that God might have abolished the claims of law and justice had he been pleased to do so.*[7] [italics mine]

How was Christ able to pay the full penalty of our sins in a short time on the cross? It will help to elaborate on the penalty of sin. As the penalty of sin is related to man, it is called eternal death. The sinner will be paying it forever. Why is this so? I will suggest the following explanation. The penalty for sinning against a holy and infinite Person is an infinite penalty. Man is infinite in only one dimension of his being, i.e., his duration. Man will exist forever. The only way a human being can pay an infinite penalty is to pay it forever. Therefore, Hell must be eternal.

As this relates to Christ, because of His divine nature He is infinite in capacity. He can suffer an infinite penalty without it going into infinite time. Apart from this fact, there could have been no salvation. The only qualified redeemer is one who is the incarnation of deity. Our Redeemer had to be *man* to have the *right* to redeem. He had to be *God* to be *able* to redeem.

I am not saying that Jesus suffered the identical penalty that man would have suffered. I am saying that He suffered an equivalent penalty. If we say that Jesus went to Hell for us when He paid our penalty, we are not meaning that He went to the lake of fire. We are meaning that He was subjected to equivalent punishment.

THE ACTIVE OBEDIENCE OF CHRIST

In the discussion on the necessity of atonement above, I pointed out that up through Romans 3:20 Paul had developed a case for saying that if we were going to stand justified before God it was necessary for us to have absolute righteousness. For us, that was bad news. We did not have absolute righteousness (Rom. 3:10), nor could we produce absolute righteousness (Rom. 3:20). So far as our own standing on our own merits is concerned, the trial was over. We were condemned. We were helpless, but not hopeless.

> Just as surely as Paul, up through 3:20, sets forth our need, in 3:21-26 he proclaims a provision of absolute righteousness by Christ to meet our need.
> As human beings we must be "doers of the law." In Christ we have His righteousness which, so far as our justification is concerned, makes us "doers of the law." Christ's obedience becomes our obedience. It can be seen that to be doers of the law (or to have absolute righteousness) is not a requirement that is set aside by grace. Rather, the requirement, which we could not meet, was met for us by Jesus Christ.[8]

Romans 1:18–3:20 paints a very dark picture. In 3:21 the picture changes. The same God who declared the whole world as fallen short of the standard required by His holiness has made a provision that will stand under the scrutiny of the Supreme Judge of the universe. Paul says, "But now." Now at this point in human and divine history, "the righteousness of God without the law has been manifested" (3:21). This righteousness is a "God-provided righteousness." This righteousness is "without works." It in no way takes into account our law-keeping or our failure to keep the law. It is the righteousness of Christ.

THE PROPITIATORY WORK OF CHRIST IN ATONEMENT

The word "propitiation" is the most inclusive term in the New Testament denoting atonement. The key passage for understanding propitiation is Romans 3:25, 26. It is not necessary to become involved in all the controversies about how to translate the word. Personally, I think propitiation or propitiatory sacrifice translates the word properly.[9]

The word *propitiation* means, in the biblical setting, to turn away the wrath of God and restore a person to favor with God. The word for propitiation is translated "mercyseat" in Hebrews 9:5 (KJV), where it refers to the lid on the Ark of the Covenant. The lid on the Ark of the Covenant was the place of propitiation in the Old Testament Tabernacle. An understanding of what happened at the place of propitiation in the Tabernacle will help at this point.

The Ark of the Covenant was located in the Holy of Holies where the High Priest went only once a year on the day of atonement. The Ark of the Covenant had within it the tables of the law (the Ten Commandments). The tables of the law represented the demands of the law which were: (1) absolute righteousness and (2) a penalty against sin in case of disobedience. When the High Priest slew the goat on the day of atonement and took his blood into the Holy of Holies and sprinkled it on the mercyseat, it was as if he were saying to the Law, "This symbolizes the meeting of the demands that you require from sinners."

The animal *without spot or blemish* symbolized righteousness. The *slain* animal symbolized the payment of a penalty through a substitute. The satisfaction of the law was symbolized. This satisfaction included both the payment of the penalty and the provision of righteousness.

From the above discussion, we would observe that at the place of propitiation the law is satisfied. This, of course, tells us what the design of propitiation was. It was designed to satisfy the penal demands of the law, thus making it so God can turn away His wrath from the sinner who believes in Christ, and at the same time maintain His justice. It was also designed to satisfy the demand for righteousness, thus giving positive grounds for God to view favorably the sinner who believes in Jesus and at the same time maintain His justice.

What the Old Testament sacrifice did in symbol on the day of atonement, Jesus Christ did in reality. He lived a completely holy life, thus fulfilling the demand for absolute righteousness. He paid the full penalty for sin, thus fulfilling the demand for a penalty. Propitiation, to sum it up, is the full satisfaction of the demands of the law, for righteousness and the payment of a penalty, by Jesus Christ. This makes it possible for God to turn His wrath from the sinner who believes in Jesus, and to view him with favor, yet remain a God of justice.

THE REVELATION OF THE HOLINESS AND THE LOVE OF GOD

In the atoning work of Jesus Christ, we have the highest revelation of God's holiness and God's love. The holiness of God is seen in its refusal to approve a way of forgiveness that did not meet every demand of the moral law of God. The highest honor ever paid to God's holiness was paid by the Son of God, when He fully satisfied the demands of the law to make possible our salvation. The highest possible regard for God's holiness is manifested in the atonement.

The love manifested at the cross is the highest possible manifestation of love. It will forever remain the unparalleled example of love. The sinless Son of God, on behalf of those who had sinned against Him, suffered the full wrath of God for their sins that they might be forgiven of their sins. The cross as no other point in history or in the future demonstrates the supremacy of holiness and the submission of love to holiness. While the cross is the foundation of grace, it is also the foundation of the highest interest in holiness on our part.

As McDonald explains: "In the atonement God's holiness is present in penal action and God's love is present in paternal grace. The cross is the place of a judgment on sin that God cannot withdraw and of a divine love for sinners that he will not withhold."[10]

Justification According to the
Penal Satisfaction View of Atonement

The full view of atonement cannot be developed without also embracing the doctrine of justification. It is for this reason that I am treating justification here rather than in a later chapter.

THE NATURE OF JUSTIFICATION

There are two aspects of justification. There is the negative aspect which deals with the remission of the penalty for sin. There is the positive aspect which deals with restoration to favor with God.

THE GROUND OF JUSTIFICATION

Our justification is based on the imputation of the atoning work of Christ to our account. The chart below will help us see what takes place in justification.

DEBITS	The Sinner	CREDITS
Absolute Righteousness		No payment
Eternal Death		No payment
	CONDEMNED	

DEBITS	The Believer	CREDITS
Absolute Righteousness		Christ's Righteousness
Eternal Death		Christ's Death
	PAID IN FULL	
	JUSTIFIED	

We have already looked at how atonement was accomplished. Now the question: How does the death and righteousness of Christ come to be placed on our account? The condition for having the death and righteousness of Christ placed on our account is faith in Christ (Rom. 3:28; 4:1-25; Gal. 2:16; 3:1-18). Since there will be an elaboration on faith as the condition of salvation in a later chapter, I will not elaborate further at this time.

While *faith in Christ alone* is all that is involved on our part to receive the death and righteousness of Christ, there is more involved in the imputation of the death and righteousness of Christ to our account. The *ground* of the imputation of Christ's death and righteousness is the union of Christ and the believer. The substitutionary work of Christ for us was not substitution pure and simple. It was a substitution of the kind that in its application made it so that the believer can say, "I am" or "I [have been] crucified with Christ" (Gal. 2:20).

UNION WITH CHRIST AND THE IMPUTATION OF THE DEATH OF CHRIST TO THE BELIEVER

The Scriptural evidence is clear that it is through union with Christ that the benefits of Christ's atonement, by which we are justified, are applied to us. Paul tells us: "Likewise reckon ye also yourselves to be dead indeed unto sin, but alive to God through Jesus Christ our Lord" (Rom. 6:11). "Through" in this verse translates the Greek preposition *en*. It is better to translate "in." It is "in Christ Jesus" that we are to consider ourselves to be dead to sin and alive to God. Again Paul says, "There is therefore now no condemnation to them which are in Christ Jesus" (Rom. 8:1). The grounds for "no condemnation" is being "in Christ Jesus."

Romans 6:1-11

In Romans 6:3, 4 and Galatians 3:27, baptism is used as a metonymy. A metonymy is a figure of speech in which one word is used for another which it suggests such as the cause may be given for the effect or the effect for the cause. An example of this is, "For he [Christ] is our peace" (Eph. 2:14). The meaning is that Christ is the cause or source of our peace. The container may be given for that which is contained. An example of this is referring to the contents of the cup as the cup in the Lord's Supper (1 Cor. 11:25). The symbol is given for the thing symbolized. I believe an example of this is baptism in the verses under study.

In Romans 6:3, Paul says, "Know ye not, that so many of us as were baptized into Jesus Christ were baptized into his death?" This verse is designed to tell us how the believer's death to sin referred to in verse 2 was accomplished. By being baptized into Jesus Christ, we were baptized into His death. It was in this manner that His death became our death. It also tells us what kind of death is referred to. It is Jesus' death. The only kind of death that He died to sin was a penal death.

In saying that baptism is a metonymy in this passage, we are saying that the wording credits water baptism with what actually belongs to that which is symbolized. Water baptism does not baptize a person into Christ. It only symbolizes baptism into Christ. It is baptism by the Holy Spirit (1 Cor. 12:13) that baptizes the believer into Christ. In this baptism we are united with Christ. In this union, His death becomes our death.

That Paul is saying that a union with Christ is accomplished by this baptism into Christ is made clear in verse 5. The word *sumphutos* which is translated "planted together" is a horticultural term. It is better translated "grown together." Conybeare and Howson give the translation, "For if we have been grafted into the likeness of his death." In a footnote they explain, "Literally, have become partakers of a vital union [as that of a graft with the tree into which it was grafted] *of the representation of his death* [in baptism]."[11] The NASB and the NIV translate "united with." The meaning is that by union with Christ we have the likeness of His death. As a rule it is simply said that we died with or in Christ. In this case likeness is used to stress that we have the credit for His death, but did not experience the pain and agony of it.

That we received Jesus' death as our death in this union is further developed in this passage. In verse 6 which is given to explain verse 5, we are told, "Our old man is [or "was" based on the

Greek] crucified with him." Our old man here is our pre-salvation self or person, not our sinful nature. When we became a new man in conversion, what we were before that time became our old man because we are now a new person.

That the crucifixion of our old man was the penal death we died with Christ is clear from verse 7 where this death results in justification. The word that is translated "freed" is *dikaioō* and should be translated "justified." Only a penal death justifies. The only penal death that can justify us is the death of Christ.

Death by identification is further developed in verse 8, "Now if we be dead [or "died" based on the Greek] with Christ." If there has been any lack of clarity about having died by our union with Christ, verse 11 should remove all doubt. Paul plainly tells us that it is "in Christ Jesus" that we are to consider ourselves to be dead to sin and alive to God."

Three things are very clear in this passage: (1) Paul talks about union with Christ. (2) This union identifies us with Christ's death. (3) This death is a penal death.

I am aware that most people understand the death to sin in this passage to be ethical rather than penal. In research for a thesis dealing with the believer's death to sin I became firmly convinced that Paul was referring to a penal death. Support for this position was found in commentaries on Romans by David Brown, Thomas Chalmers, Robert Haldane, James Morrison, H. C. G. Moule, and William G. T. Shedd.[12] Some would insist on the ethical interpretation since Romans 6 deals with sanctification. I will show how the penal death relates to sanctification in the chapter on sanctification.

Galatians 2:19, 20

We are not dependent upon Romans 6:1-11 alone. The penal death interpretation fits the context of Galatians 2:20. This death becomes the believer's death by being "in Christ." With reference to Galatians 2:19, 20, Shedd quotes Ellicot:

> The meaning is: "I died not only as concerns the law, but as the law required." The whole clause, then, may be thus paraphrased: "I, through the law, owing to sin, was brought under its curse; but having undergone this curse, with, and in the person of, Christ, I died to the law, in the fullest and deepest sense: being both free from its claims, and having satisfied its course."

Shedd in making his own comment on the passage explains:

> Some commentators explain St. Paul's crucifixion with Christ, to be his own personal sufferings in the cause of Christ. But St. Paul's own sufferings would not be the reason he is "dead to the law." Christ's atoning suffering is the reason for this.

Other Passages

After referring to 2 Corinthians 5:15, 16 and 2 Timothy 2:11, Shedd concludes:

These passages abundantly prove that the doctrine of the believer's unity with Christ in his vicarious death for sin is familiar to St. Paul, and is strongly emphasized by him.[13]

Shedd on Union With Christ

Shedd calls the union between Christ and the believer a spiritual union. In speaking about this union, he explains:

> Upon this spiritual and mystical union, rests the federal and legal union between Christ and his people. Because they are spiritually, vitally, eternally, and mystically one with him, his merit is imputable to them, and their demerit is imputable to him. The imputation of Christ's righteousness supposes a union with him. It could not be imputed to an unbeliever, because he is not united with Christ by faith.[14]

Walvoord on Union With Christ

John F. Walvoord says concerning the union of Christ and the believer:

> Important theological truths are related to the doctrine of identification [he explained elsewhere in the article that union is commonly taken as a synonym for identification] in Scripture. The believer is identified with Christ in his death (Rom. 6:1-11); his burial (Rom. 6: 4); his resurrection (Col. 3:1); his ascension (Eph. 2:6); his reign (2 Tim. 2:12); and his glory (Rom. 8:17). Identification with Christ has its limitation, however. Christ is identified with the human race in incarnation, but only true believers are identified with Christ. The identification of a believer with Christ results in certain aspects of the person and work of Christ being attributed to the believer, but this does not extend to possession of the attributes of the Second Person, nor are the personal distinctions between Christ and the believer erased. Taken as a whole, however, identification with Christ is a most important doctrine and is essential to the entire program of grace.[15]

Summary Comments

Identification by union makes that which was not actually a part of a person's experience his by identification. For example, prior to the time that Hawaii became a part of the United States, a citizen of Hawaii could not have said, "We celebrate our day of Independence on July 4." Immediately upon their becoming a state, the same person who formerly could not make the statement could say, "We celebrate our day of Independence on July 4." What happened on July 4, 1776, became a part of their history. The history of the United States became the history of Hawaii, and the history of Hawaii became the history of the United States.

Prior to the union of Christ on the condition of faith, a person could not say, "I died with Christ." Immediately, upon union with Christ a person can say, "I died with Christ." The history of the cross became his history, not in the experiential sense, but by identification so that he received full credit for that death. At the same time, the history of our sins became Jesus' history, not in the sense that His character was affected, but so they would come in contact with the penalty He had already paid for them. He took the responsibility for them, but it was a responsibility He had already assumed on the cross. It is this side of the truth which Shedd was addressing in the quotation given earlier when he said, "And their [believers'] demerit is imputable to him."

UNION WITH CHRIST AND THE IMPUTATION OF THE RIGHTEOUSNESS OF CHRIST TO THE BELIEVER

Attention has been given thus far to the imputation of the death of Christ to the believer; let us now turn our attention to the imputation of Christ's righteousness. Loraine Boettner comments:

> Throughout the history of the Church most theological discussions have stressed Christ's passive obedience (although not often calling it by that name), but have had little to say about His active obedience. The result is that many professing Christians who readily acknowledge that Christ suffered and died for them seem altogether unaware of the fact that the holy, sinless life which He lived was also a vicarious work in their behalf, wrought out by Him in His representative capacity and securing for them title to eternal life.[16]

In speaking of the righteousness of Christ that is imputed to us, it may be that we should understand righteousness to mean "that which is required to make one right or righteous before God." And, that would include both the penal death (passive obedience) and the righteous life of Christ (active obedience). I am inclined to agree with Robert Haldane when he says:

> No explanation of the expression, "The righteousness of God," will at once suit the phrase and the situation in which it is found in the passage before us [Rom. 3:21], but that which makes it that righteousness, or obedience to the law, both in its penalty and requirements, which has been yielded to it by our Lord Jesus Christ. This is indeed the righteousness of God, for it has been provided by God, and from first to last has been effected by His Son Jesus Christ, who is the Mighty God and the Father of eternity.[17]

Whether the righteousness of God that was provided for us includes the death of Christ or not, it would most certainly include the righteous life of Christ.

Paul says in 2 Corinthians 5:21, "That we might be made the righteousness of God in him." In Philippians 3:9, Paul says, "And be found in him, not having mine own righteousness, which is of the law, but that which is through the faith of Christ, the righteousness which is of [from] God by faith." Both the NASB and the NIV translate *ek* as "from." In these verses, righteousness is ours "in Christ." Philippians 3:9 makes it clear that Paul is talking about a righteousness that is not his own in the sense of having personally produced it, but a righteousness that is from God.

In Romans 1:18–3:20, Paul had talked about man's need for righteousness. In and of himself, man did not and could not have righteousness. In Romans 3:21, Paul came through with a message of hope for those who were helpless. He spoke of a God-provided righteousness which was apart from personal law-keeping. It was provided by God on the condition of faith (3:22). In Romans 4:6, Paul spoke about the imputation of righteousness without works. In Romans 5:17, he spoke of the gift of righteousness. In Romans 10:3, he spoke of a righteousness that is not established by our own efforts but is submitted to. By taking all of this evidence together, we conclude that the righteousness which justifies is the righteousness of Christ placed on our account, given as a gift on the condition of faith.

JUSTIFICATION BASED ON REAL RIGHTEOUSNESS, NOT SIMPLY DECLARED RIGHTEOUS

On the condition of faith, we are placed in union with Christ. Based on that union we receive His death and righteousness. Based on the fact that Christ's death and righteousness became our death and righteousness, God as Judge declares us righteous.

Some give great stress to the word "declare." They say that we are declared righteous, but we are not righteous. I beg to differ. Based on the death and righteousness of Christ becoming ours, we are righteous. The righteousness upon which this declaration is made is a real righteousness. It is true that in our own persons we are not absolutely righteous, but we are not declared to be righteous in our own persons. We are declared to be righteous on the basis of a real righteousness, the righteousness of Christ. As will be seen later, the stress on the word "declared" belongs not to the satisfaction view but the governmental view.

JUSTIFICATION, THE WORK OF GOD AS JUDGE

It is important to observe that justification is the work of God as judge. God, as judge, will not justify us in any way other than that which protects His own holiness and shows an interest in our holiness. The moral concerns of God are fully protected and are clearly manifested in God's provision of atonement and justification.

A shallow look at an account balanced by a gift of the death and righteousness of Christ leads to a cheap view of grace and has serious moral consequences. It has traces of antinomianism which lacks appreciation for the moral responsibility of the believer.

It is true that justification is by grace which is an unmerited favor. That fact must never be compromised. It must never be corrupted. There is a right way and a wrong way to approach grace. Grace must be understood in *the context of moral law,* not moral law in the context of grace. By this I mean that we start with law, and *grace conforms to the requirements and interests of law.* We do not begin with grace and make law conform to grace. We do not begin with the gospel and then move on to law. Rather, we begin with law and then proceed to the gospel. It is only when people see how they stand before God's law that they are ready to give proper attention to the good news of God's grace. In the last half-century or so, much harm has been done in the evangelical church world by preaching grace in such a way that the interests of law and holiness are not properly dealt with. The most open example of this has been those who have advocated the view that a person can receive Jesus as Savior without receiving Him as Lord.

In Romans 3:31, Paul says, "Do we then make void the law through faith? God forbid: Yea, we establish the law." The provision of grace operates within the framework of the highest regard for law. Man was condemned by the holy law of God because of his sin. The holiness of God would not tolerate a plan of redemption that did not pay full respect to the law of God. We are not talking about arbitrary law. We are talking about law as the expression of the holy nature of a personal God. We are not talking about playing around with a legal technicality like sometimes goes on in our legal system. We are talking about truth. The only plan of atonement that God would approve was one that gave full satisfaction to the holiness of God by meeting all the demands of the law. Justification must be the work of God as Judge. As Judge He sees to it that the fullest interest of the law is maintained. No person is justified apart from the complete satisfaction of the law. The full protection and the sure manifestation of God's moral concern is clearly seen by the way in which God provided atonement and justification. For God to be so determined to protect the interest of His holiness in atonement and then, by justification, to open the way for a Christian experience in which holiness is something we can take or leave would be absurd.

When we begin with grace or try to build grace on a weak moral foundation, we corrupt both grace and law. The hasty conclusions that are drawn in such a manner are both false and dangerous. It is reasoned that while moral responsibility might be good, it is optional. Since Jesus satisfied the demands of the law and the only condition of salvation is faith, it is felt by some that it is conceivable that a person can be a Christian and at the same time live in any degree of sin. We need to be careful in combating this error *lest we corrupt grace;* at the same time we must combat it *lest we corrupt both law and grace.* We combat it not by changing the nature of atonement and justification, but by having a view of sanctification that is an appropriate accompaniment of justification. This we will propose to do in the chapter on sanctification.

RECONCILIATION, THE RESULT

Atonement and justification were designed to resolve a conflict between God and man. The guilt of man closed the door of fellowship with man from God's side. Justification opened that door. It prepares the way for reunion and fellowship with God.

Full reconciliation involves reconciliation on our part. This involves repentance and regeneration which will be discussed later. As a result of all of this we are restored to fellowship with God. The functioning personal relationship with God that we so drastically need becomes a reality in salvation. The foundation for it all rests upon atonement and justification. The logical consistency and adequacy of atonement and justification meet the needs of our mind. The forgiveness of sins and restoration to favor and fellowship with God meet the needs of our hearts.

The Governmental View of Atonement

The majority of theologians who view the Bible to be an objective divine revelation have adhered to the basic ideas of the penal satisfaction view of atonement. There have been some who have held to the governmental view. This view was first introduced by Hugo Grotius (1583-1645). Adherents of this view since Grotius have included Charles Finney, James H. Fairchild, John Miley, and H. Orton Wiley. In order to avoid some of the criticisms that have been given to this view, some have modified the governmental view, but have still held to most of the essentials.

BASIC ASSUMPTIONS

The basic assumptions are: (1) God is sovereign. (2) Man is sinful. (3) God is loving. (4) The end of God's sovereignty is the happiness of man.

THE NECESSITY OF ATONEMENT

One of the basic principles of the governmental view is the rejection of the absolute necessity that sin be punished. Miley says:

> While thus asserting the intrinsic evil of sin, Grotius denies an absolute necessity aris-
> ing therefrom for its punishment. The punishment of sin is just, but not in itself an
> obligation.[18]

Sin requires punishment only as it is necessary to secure the ends of God's government. Fairchild explains the interpretation of the end of government as it is perceived by those who advocate the governmental view:

> And when we speak of detriment to God's government, we should mean harm to the
> great interests of his rational and dependent universe. We sometimes speak of the
> necessity of protecting God's honor as a ruler, or of magnifying the law of God, and or
> meeting the claims of justice. These terms have a limited significance; but all essential
> facts implied are summed up in the comprehensive idea of securing the wellbeing of
> God's rational creatures, the subject of his government. This is the sole end of gov-
> ernment; and when this is secured the honor of God, and of the law, and of justice, will
> all be safe. Atonement is adopted to secure these ends.[19]

Since it is not an absolute necessity that sin be punished, the penalty can be set aside and never be paid either by the person or a substitute as long as another means can be provided which will protect the interests of government. It is concluded that atonement is necessary to protect the interests of government since forgiveness too easily granted would present problems.

Miley explains concerning Grotius' view:

Forgiveness too freely granted or too often repeated, and especially on slight grounds, would annul the authority of the law, or render it powerless for its great and imperative ends. Thus he finds the necessity for an atonement—for some vicarious provision—which, on remission of penalty, may conserve these ends.[20]

The necessity of atonement rests in the need of a means by which sin can be forgiven without loss of respect for government. When this is achieved, the penalty can be set aside and sins can be forgiven.

THE NATURE OF ATONEMENT
It can be seen that there is a drastic difference between the necessity of atonement in the satisfaction view and the governmental view. That difference in the necessity of atonement results in drastically different views on the nature of atonement.

THE SUPREMACY OF PUBLIC JUSTICE
In the governmental view of atonement, public justice, not retributive justice, is satisfied. It is not *the holy nature of God* that is satisfied, but *the public good.* Charles G. Finney explains:

> Public justice, in its exercise, consists in the promotion and protection of the public interests, by such legislation and such an administration of law, as is demanded by the highest good of the public. It implies the execution of the penalties of the law where the precept is violated, unless something else is done that will as effectually serve the public interests. When this is done, public justice demands, that the execution of the penalty shall be dispensed with, by extending pardon to the criminal. Retributive justice makes no exceptions, but punishes without mercy in every instance of crime. Public justice makes exceptions, as often as this is permitted or required by the public good.[21]

THE PLACE OF A PENALTY IN PUBLIC JUSTICE
In serving the need of public justice a penalty is *a moral force to discourage disobedience.* The death of Jesus Christ is not a penalty for sin. Occasionally some who hold to the governmental view use the word "penalty" in a loose sense but never in a technical sense. The death of Jesus Christ is a substitute for a penalty. It takes the place of a penalty and serves the same purpose as a penalty.
According to Miley, Grotius viewed the death of Christ as a penal example.

> And he makes a very free use of the term penal substitution. Yet he does not seem to regard the sufferings of Christ as penal in any very strict sense—certainly not as a substitutional punishment of sin in the satisfaction of a purely retributive justice.[22]

Fairchild explains concerning the governmental view of the death of Christ:

The theory presented does not present that Christ suffered the penalty of the law....
In a very proper sense *the death of Christ takes the place of the penitent sinner's punishment, as a moral force in the government of God;* and thus it is that the Scriptures represent that Christ died for us; that "he bore our sins in his own body on the tree." The suffering of Christ made the punishment of the penitent unnecessary.[23] [italics mine]

THE MORAL FORCE OF THE DEATH OF CHRIST

It may be asked what is it that constitutes this moral force in the death of Christ and thus makes atonement possible? Fairchild explains:

> *It is an exhibition of God's estimate of sin,* in that no arrangement less significant than the coming of the Emmanuel, and his patience and obedience unto death, could be devised, to counteract the mischief of sin, and deliver men from ruin....
>
> Again, it is to be observed that *in the death of Christ sin has made an exhibition of itself....* Sin never so displayed its malignity and hatefulness, as in that infamous deed; and the sight of the cross from that day to this, has tended powerfully to make the world ashamed of sin....
>
> *It exhibits the beauty of holiness,* even more impressively than the odiousness of sin. The character and consecration of the Savior is the highest exhibition of goodness and unselfish devotion that the world has seen....
>
> Again, *the cross is an exhibition of the love of God,* in the sense of sympathy and compassion for sinners.... *The goodness and the severity of God are united in the great lesson of the cross.*[24] [italics mine]

The value of Christ's death in the governmental view is revelational. It reveals God's attitude toward sin, that sin is odious, the beauty of holiness, and the love of God.

JUSTIFICATION ACCORDING TO THE GOVERNMENTAL VIEW OF ATONEMENT

Just as there is a drastic difference between the satisfaction and governmental views of atonement, there is also a drastic difference in the views of justification that grow out of these differing views of atonement.

NO IMPUTATION OF EITHER THE DEATH OR THE RIGHTEOUSNESS OF CHRIST TO THE BELIEVER

Fairchild comments:

> Theologians who hold to the imputation of our sin to Christ, and of his righteousness to us, treat justification as a judicial act, a pronouncing of the sinner just before the law.... The simpler and more reasonable view is, that *there can be no transfer, or imputation, either of guilt or of righteousness.*[25]

FAITH IMPUTED FOR RIGHTEOUSNESS

In the governmental view the penalty is set aside in the light of atonement when the sinner exercises faith in Christ. The chart below will help us see what takes place in justification according to this view.

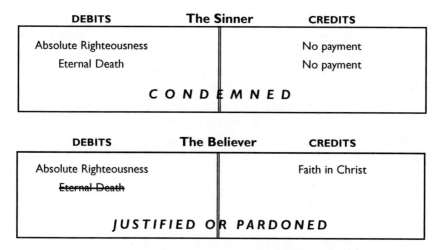

DEBITS	The Sinner	CREDITS
Absolute Righteousness		No payment
Eternal Death		No payment
	CONDEMNED	

DEBITS	The Believer	CREDITS
Absolute Righteousness		Faith in Christ
~~Eternal Death~~		
	JUSTIFIED OR PARDONED	

Those who hold the governmental view agree that absolute righteousness is what God required of the sinner, and eternal death is the penalty for disobedience. However, in view of faith in Christ, God sets the *penalty aside*. The same consideration that would have been given to *absolute righteousness* is given for *faith*. Faith is not absolute righteousness, but it is counted "for" or "as" righteousness. Fairchild says, *"Faith is another word for the righteousness which the law requires."*[26] The exact meaning of "faith counted for righteousness" is understood with some variations among governmentalists, but all concur in denying that there is any imputation of the death or righteousness of Christ to the believer. These variations do not have any essential effect on the view.

Since justification, in the governmental view, declares the person to be righteous without this declaration being based on an absolute righteousness, it can be seen that it is appropriate to give stress to the word "declare." The believer is declared to be righteous, but he is not righteous. This is supposed to be the way grace works. The satisfaction view does not admit this interpretation of "declare." The believer is declared righteous because the righteousness of Christ, which is a real righteousness, is his.

JUSTIFICATION, THE WORK OF GOD AS SOVEREIGN

The judge must go by the law and uphold the law. He can declare a person righteous only as he is righteous by the standard of the law. A ruler has more latitude. This can be seen in the right of a governor to pardon.

In the governmental view, God as Ruler declares the believer righteous not by the strict standard of law but in a manner that is designed to protect the public good. This is what allows Him to set the penalty aside. The justice administered is not *retributive* justice but *public* justice. Finney explains:

> Courts never pardon, or set aside the execution of penalties. This does not belong to them, but either to the executive or to the lawmaking department. Oftentimes, this power in human governments is lodged in the head of the executive department, who is generally at least, a branch of the legislative power of government. But never is the power of pardon exercised in the judicial department. . . .
>
> It consists not in the law pronouncing the sinner just, but in his being ultimately governmentally treated as if he were just; that is, it consists in a governmental decree of pardon or amnesty—in arresting and setting aside the execution of the incurred penalty of law— . . .[27]

THE ANALOGY BETWEEN THE GOVERNMENTAL VIEW OF ATONEMENT AND HUMAN GOVERNMENT

It is interesting to note that Hugo Grotius, the founder of the governmental view of atonement, was a lawyer. In fact, he holds the distinction of being the father of International Law. Charles Finney was also a lawyer. The governmental view of atonement and justification is developed by drawing an analogy between the way a governor of a state works in granting a pardon and the way God works.

THE TECHNICAL USE OF THE WORDS "PARDON" AND "JUSTIFY"

If we would be technical in the use of language, the governmental view should speak of "pardon" and the satisfaction view would speak of "justification." In the satisfaction view God, as Judge, declares the believer *justified* because, in Christ, all of the requirements of the law have been met. In the governmental view, God, as Sovereign Ruler, declares the believer righteous and pardons the believer because, in view of the revelational influence of Christ's death, no violence is done to the interest of God's government.

Since we are not always technical in our use of language, *justification* and *pardon* will continue to be used interchangeably. Another factor that will keep the word "pardon" alive is that it lends itself more easily to use in poetry than the word "justify."

Criticism of the Governmental View of Atonement and Justification

While the governmental view has many important differences that distinguish it from the moral influence theory of liberalism,[28] it has some dangerously close parallels. (1) Both views deny that there is any principle in the divine nature that requires satisfaction in atonement. (2) Both deny that it is absolutely necessary to inflict a penalty on sin. (3) Both views consider the value of Christ's death to be revelational.

Those who have believed in the governmental view have historically believed in the doctrine of Hell for those who do not receive Christ by faith. Liberalism believes in universalism. There is no penalty against sin in the strict sense of the word. In liberalism, the emphasis in the revelational value of the death of Christ stresses the love of Christ. It is God's love on the one hand assuring the sinner that there is no obstacle to his return. On the other hand, God's love is a moral force to bring about moral transformation in the sinner. The great love of God manifested in sending Jesus to die is meant to show us that God loves us and serves as a heart-moving revelation designed to bring about moral change. In the governmental view, the death of Christ reveals the holiness of God, the seriousness of sin, the love of God, and God's interest in maintaining His government.

In the discussion of the satisfaction view, I set forth the reason for believing that it is an absolute necessity for sin to be punished. God's holy nature requires it. If the holy nature of God requires that sin be punished, it is a very serious matter to deny that truth. The governmental view proposes to emphasize the importance of holiness and the seriousness of sin. As weighed against the importance of God's holiness and the seriousness of sin in the satisfaction view, the governmental view falls far short. In the satisfaction view, holiness is so important and sin is so serious that nothing short of a full satisfaction of God's law can make atonement for sin. Nothing less would permit God in His capacity as Judge to declare the believer to be righteous. In the governmental view, God in His capacity as Ruler can set aside the penalty of sin and declare the believer to be righteous, who is in fact not righteous.

All of the valid principles that the governmental view proposes to uphold are done better by the satisfaction view. The satisfaction view more successfully shows the importance of holiness and the seriousness of sin. It gives a much higher view of the love of God. It creates a more solid foundation for respect for God's government.

While the satisfaction view does reveal the importance of holiness, the seriousness of sin, and the wonder of God's love, what it reveals is *not* what makes atonement. Atonement is based on full satisfaction of the demands of the law. God uses atonement as an instrument of revelation, but revelation is not a means of atonement. This revelation of God is used by God to bring people to Christ and promote holiness and love among believers.

While important differences can be pointed out in the revelation principle in the governmental view and the liberal view, I do not believe these differences are adequate to give the needed protection against liberal influence. Though I have not researched the subject to see, I am inclined to believe, that history would show there had been a loss among governmentalists in this direction.

The most important thing that can be said for the governmental view is that its advocates have held to a serious view of Scripture. They have proposed their view to be the Scriptural view. The advocates of the moral influence view have had a low view of Scripture. Whatever protection the governmentalists have from taking up the liberal view rests far more upon their respect for Scripture than upon logical arguments to maintain the governmental view as opposed to the moral influence view.

One of the important distinctions between the satisfaction view and the governmental view is the ends they propose to serve. The governmental view is *man-centered*. It seeks to protect the welfare of mankind. The satisfaction view is *God-centered*. It seeks to vindicate the divine nature.

In my opinion, the governmental view is seriously inadequate. It is dangerously close to liberalism's view. Once a person denies the absolute necessity of the punishment of sin, there is no logical barrier which prohibits the slide into the moral influence theory. Whatever safety there is lies in the commitment to Scripture rather than a safety in the logic of the case.

Objections to the Penal Satisfaction View as Raised by the Governmental View

PENAL SATISFACTION NOT NECESSARY

For a general development of the necessity for penal satisfaction, see my treatment of "The Necessity of Atonement" on page 184. At this point I want to discuss the importance of having a proper view of the necessity of atonement in order to maintain the integrity of Christian thought.

THE IMPORTANCE OF A PROPER VIEW OF THE NECESSITY OF ATONEMENT

A person's view of the *necessity* of atonement determines his *view* of atonement. When we speak of the necessity of atonement, we mean atonement was necessary if a way of salvation were to be provided. The provision of atonement is not a necessity. There was no provision of atonement for fallen angels.

A person's view of atonement and his view of Hell must be consistent with each other. If eternal punishment is an absolute necessity, it follows that penal satisfaction by one who is both God and man would be the only means of making the forgiveness of sin possible. If penal satisfaction did not occur in atonement, *eternal punishment in Hell* (the only way a *finite* person can pay an *infinite* penalty) is not a divine necessity.

In particular individuals, ideas may be held without adhering to systematic coherence. But in the community of human experience, ideas have a way of moving toward logical consistency. A particular person may believe that eternal punishment of sinners in Hell is an absolute necessity and yet not believe in the penal satisfaction view of atonement. However, when minds join together to promote that approach, given enough time the inconsistency will surface. It will be seen that you cannot speak consistently of the necessity for the punishment of sin on the one hand, and on the other hand deny penal satisfaction in explaining atonement. Belief in the absolute necessity of the punishment of sin will move in the direction of the penal satisfaction view of atonement.

A particular person may not believe in the penal satisfaction view of atonement, and may believe that eternal punishment of sinners in Hell is an absolute necessity. However, in the community of Christian experience the inconsistency of such an approach will surface. If rejection of the penal satisfaction view persists, in time, there will also be a rejection of the *absolute necessity* for the punishment of sin. If there is an absolute necessity that sin be punished, it follows that if Jesus Christ made atonement for our sins, it was necessary for Him to pay the penalty of sin.

There can be no satisfactory way to *maintain* the doctrine of an eternal Hell while at the same time *rejecting* the absolute necessity of the punishment of sin in atonement. Some may want to suggest that the problem would be eased if we would take the approach of the annihilation of the wicked rather than the view of eternal punishment. My first answer is that it is not our responsibility to look for ways that are more acceptable than that which is given in the divinely inspired Word of God. I would also say annihilation would not be an act of kindness. It could be tolerated morally only if it were an absolute necessity. If it were an absolute necessity, how could Jesus Christ, as our substitute, make penal satisfaction? Whatever else we might say, He certainly was not annihilated!

Emil Brunner believed in annihilation, and also believed in the penal satisfaction view of atonement.[29] However, he makes no attempt to explain how Jesus Christ satisfied the penal demand for annihilation. I can understand how infinite suffering by the One who was both God and man could be equivalent to eternal suffering on the part of a finite person. I cannot understand how anything that Jesus did would be considered equivalent to annihilation. If there was any absolute necessity of any kind of punishment for sin, it would be an absolute necessity for satisfaction to be made by *a qualified substitute*. Otherwise it would not be an absolute necessity to punish sin. Our deep inner being will not tolerate the idea that God would pronounce the penalty of eternal death on any other basis than that it was an absolute necessity growing out of His holy nature

The power with which postmodernism conditions individuals today seriously diminishes the way people feel about sin. Even Christians do not feel as deeply about sin as they did prior to the rise of postmodernism. Relativism and deep feelings about sin do not go together.

Even people who would check the right answers on a questionnaire on basic matters about right and wrong do not feel as deeply about sin as people did forty or fifty years ago. This makes it harder for the Holy Spirit to bring conviction over sin to people's hearts. It makes it much harder for people to think of sin as being so serious that it deserves the penalty of an eternal Hell. If people do not feel deeply about sin, judgment, and Hell, they certainly will not feel deeply about the need of an atonement for sin that would require Jesus Christ to suffer the full wrath of God for sin. All of this makes it much harder than it once was to convince people that they need a salvation that can be provided only by Jesus Christ.

Postmodernism has contributed to a troubled and mixed up society. That problem is a deep Christian concern. But as important as it is to help people with mixed-up lives, that is not what made it necessary for God to require atonement. It was the guilt of our sins that demanded a holy God require atonement before He could forgive sin. Atonement is of tremendous importance for those whose lives are filled with hurting, but Jesus did not have to go to the cross because we were hurting. Rather, He went to the cross because we were guilty.

If people were hurting, and there was no problem of guilt before a holy God, a case might be made for the helpfulness of the incarnation. But there would be no case for the need of atonement. The *need* of atonement rests on human guilt and the necessity of the divine nature to punish sin— *that and that alone.*

PENAL SATISFACTION THROUGH A SUBSTITUTE NOT POSSIBLE

There are two types of punishments meted out by the judicial system—pecuniary punishment and penal punishment. Pecuniary punishment is the punishment that takes the form of a fine. It is possible for a substitute to pay a fine for a person. Penal punishment involves a punishment of the person. The person goes to jail, to prison, or is put to death. In our judicial system there is no substitution in the area of penal punishment. The punishment of sin is not pecuniary, but penal. Therefore, it is argued that there can be no substitution for us.

This objection does bring up a valid concern. *Substitution* pure and simple, whereby one person does something for or in the place of another, *would be invalid in atonement.*

The answer to this objection is found in the union of Christ and the believer as was discussed in connection with the satisfaction view. By identification with Christ the believer can say, "I died with Christ." The action can be considered to be his, not simply an action that was performed for him. As a result of this union with Christ, God can view the death and righteousness of Christ as *being the death and righteousness of the believer.*

In our judicial system, we cannot have penal substitution because there is no way it can be said that a person went to jail without actually going. In Christ, we can say we died with Him without actually going through this experience. Therefore, penal substitution is possible. For a more thorough discussion of how union with Christ makes it so Christ's death and righteousness are made a part of the believer's history, see the discussion on "The Ground of Justification" (p. 191).

UNIVERSAL SALVATION OR LIMITED ATONEMENT A NECESSARY RESULT

It is argued that all for whom Christ died must of necessity be saved since His death settles their account and therefore forms the necessary basis for their forgiveness. Either Christ died for everybody and everybody would be saved, or He died only for the elect and only the elect will be saved, the objection states.

Again the answer is found in the kind of substitution involved. Christ died for the whole world in a *provisionary* sense. He suffered the penal wrath of God for sin, but that fact alone does not place His death on everybody's account. It can be efficacious only as it is placed on a person's account. It can be placed on a person's account only as a result of a union with Christ. Union with Christ is conditioned on faith.

The Calvinist may want to insist that the objection is valid and that Christ died only for the elect. The only way this argument could have any validity would be to deny the possibility of provisionary atonement. If there can be no provisionary atonement, it *does follow* that if Christ died for a person, his justification is *never provisionary* but always *real.*

In explaining the view of limited atonement, Louis Berkhof comments: "The Calvinist teaches that the atonement meritoriously secured the application of the work of redemption to those for whom it was intended and their complete salvation is certain."[30]

A close look at what Berkhof said will show that it does not rule out the provisionary principle in atonement. He says that the atonement "makes certain" the salvation of those for whom it was intended. He did not say that the atonement automatically saved everybody for whom it was intended. Calvinists do not teach that the elect are justified before they experience faith. They teach that the person for whom Christ died will of a certainty be justified, but they do not consider a person justified until he experiences faith as the condition of justification. Thus, atonement is provisionary until the time it is applied. The *only way* to deny the provisionary nature of atonement is to consider all people for whom Christ died to be justified *before* they experience faith.

Once it is accepted that atonement is *provisionary,* the objection, which states that penal satisfaction leads to either universalism or limited atonement, is seen to be invalid. Atonement is provisionary until it is applied. It can be applied only on the condition of faith and on the grounds of union with Christ. When applied, atonement becomes efficacious. Then and only then is atonement efficacious. The objection that the penal satisfaction view requires either universalism or limited atonement fails.

Considerable biblical evidence supports the truth that Christ died for every person, thus provisionary atonement was made for all people. Hebrews 2:9 makes it clear that Jesus tasted death for every man. John tells us that "He is the propitiation for our sins: and not for ours only, but also for *the sins of* the whole world" (1 Jn. 2:2). In 1 Timothy 2:6 Paul tells us that Christ Jesus "gave himself a ransom for all." In 1 Timothy 4:10, Paul tells us that Jesus "is the Saviour of all men, specially them that believe." This provisionary atonement is applied to whosoever will meet the condition of faith (Jn. 3:16; Acts 17:30; Rom. 10:13; 1 Tim. 2:4; 2 Pet. 3:9; and Rev. 22:17). The fact that Calvinists have accepted the view of unlimited atonement tells us that the biblical case for unlimited atonement must be strong and convincing.[31] More attention will be given to the extent of atonement in a later chapter when I deal with decrees and election.

DOUBLE PAYMENT WITH REGARD TO SINNERS WHO GO TO HELL

The discussion above about provisionary atonement and union with Christ answers this objection. The death of Christ is not on the sinner's account who goes to Hell. His account does not show a double payment. It is true that his sins were paid for provisionally, but there is no double payment as long as there is no double entry on the person's account. No person will go to Hell with the death and righteousness of Christ on his account.

ANTINOMIANISM, THE LOGICAL RESULT

It is argued that if we receive the death of Christ and the righteousness of Christ, the way is open for license to sin. If the account has been completely settled by Christ, it is argued that a person can live as he pleases.

If we think of justification *apart* from sanctification, we have *antinomianism*. However, when we understand that justification is always accompanied by sanctification, we see that the antinomian charge is invalid. It is the nature of sanctification that *disallows* antinomianism. The evidence that sanctification nullifies the charge of antinomianism will be seen in the development of the doctrine of sanctification in the next chapter.

We should not be surprised when our doctrine of atonement and justification causes us to be accused of giving license to sin. Paul was accused of the same thing (Rom. 3:8; 6:1). We should be concerned if we cannot answer the charge. We do not answer the charge by tampering with the doctrine of justification, but by setting forth the doctrine of sanctification.

NECESSARILY LEADS TO THE CONCLUSION: "ONCE SAVED, ALWAYS SAVED"

It is not hard to see why this objection would be raised, but it is easily answered. If we had actually experienced what Jesus did on the cross, it would follow that we could never be called upon to pay the same price again. It is true that *as long as we have the death and righteousness of Christ we are saved.* As long *as we are in union with Christ, we are* as *safe* from the wrath of God as He is.

Is it possible for us to forfeit our salvation and be lost again? The death and righteousness of Christ are ours by identification. They remain ours only as we remain identified with Him. The identification with Christ is ours as long as we remain in union with Him. The union is ours conditionally. It is conditioned on faith in Christ. If we make shipwreck of our faith, the union will be broken. We will lose our identification with Christ. His death and righteousness will no longer be ours.

John 15:2 teaches that we can be taken out of Christ. It is the branch "in me" that "he taketh away." I will give further discussion of this subject in the chapter on perseverance. It was mentioned here only to answer the objection raised against the satisfaction view.

Infant Salvation

In the history of the church, there have been those who have thought that infants who died without being baptized were lost. But the tendency has been for theologians to look for some hope that those dying in infancy are spared from eternal condemnation. An article entitled "Infant Salvation" in *The New Schaff-Herzog Encyclopedia of Religious Knowledge* states that "with the Calvinist the heart is stronger than logic. Dr. Charles Hodge teaches emphatically the salvation of all infants who die in infancy, and asserts that this is the 'common doctrine of Evangelical Protestants' (*Systematic Theology*, I, 26)."[32] Arminians have always taken the position that those dying during infancy went to be with Christ. The tendency is for most people to believe that those dying in infancy are either safe or saved.

SCRIPTURAL GROUNDS FOR BELIEVING IN INFANT SALVATION

The Bible does not address the subject of infant salvation directly. We go on the basis of implications. When the young son of David died, in explaining to his servants why he ceased to fast after the child died, David said, "But now he is dead, wherefore should I fast? Can I bring him back again? I shall go to him, but he shall not return to me" (2 Sam. 12:23). It is inferred that David and the child would meet each other after death. The implication is that the child will be with God in eternity.

In Matthew 18:10, Jesus said, "Take heed that ye despise not one of these little ones; for I say unto you, That in heaven their angels do always behold the face of my Father which is in heaven." The reference to "their angels" implies that they are in a favorable relationship with God. To me the implications involved in these passages give a solid foundation for rejecting the idea that infants will go to Hell.

While I believe in infant salvation, I do not believe as Summers, Fletcher, Pope, and Wiley do that infant salvation is taught in Romans 5:18, 19.[33] Romans 5:18 says *"the free gift came* upon all men unto justification of life." Romans 5:19 says, "By the obedience of one shall many be righteousness." If the "all" of 5:18 is taken to refer to all who would make up the human race, it would be teaching universal salvation, which is not what these men taught. I think the "all" would refer only to those who are identified with Christ.

There is no hint in the context that Paul would be specifically dealing with the question of infant salvation. Up to this point Paul had said that the action of One Person formed the basis of salvation of all who would believe. That sounded too good to be true. An objector might ask: How could the righteousness of one person be the basis for salvation for many (all who would believe)?

> When the occasion calls for it, Paul makes use of the *a fortiori* argument. This argument seeks to move from something that is harder to believe to the easier to believe. This is the kind of argument used in 5:8-10. In vv. 12-29, Paul shows that it is easier to believe that Christ, one Person, can be the cause of the justification for many than it is to believe that Adam could be the cause of condemnation for many.[34]

If a case can be made for the view that infants are identified with Christ, that would form a basis for infant salvation. In such a case, it would be an inferred meaning, not the direct meaning of the passage. These verses do not address the question of infant salvation.

SUGGESTED EXPLANATION OF HOW INFANTS ARE SAVED

It should be restated here that the position I am taking is *infant salvation*. I disagree with those who base the safety of the infant on the innocence of infants. According to such a view, infants are *safe*, not *saved*.

THE PROBLEM OF FAITH AS THE CONDITION OF SALVATION

The reason there is a problem in thinking about infant salvation is that faith is the condition of salvation. Infants are not capable of exercising faith. If they cannot exercise faith, how can they be saved?

The requirement of the condition of faith is God's way of dealing with us as persons—those who think, feel, and act. God will not transgress our personality. In requiring faith, God treats us as persons and requires a response from us. Failure to require a response in which we choose Christ would be a failure to treat us as persons. This problem does not exist with the infant. He or she is a person, but is not fully developed so as to enable the individual to exercise all the rights and privileges nor to assume all the responsibilities of being a person. There is no transgression of the individual's personality or will if God should remove his racial guilt since he is not capable of saying either yes or no. This approach may be all that needs to be said, but I will give more thoughts on the subject in the following discussion.

THE DIFFERENCE BETWEEN RACIAL GUILT AND PERSONAL GUILT

Racial guilt belongs to us simply by our being members of the human race—descendants of Adam. Personal guilt is ours because of our own personal sins. It should not seem strange if the application of atonement would be approached somewhat differently for forgiveness of racial guilt than from forgiveness of personal guilt.

Our personal sins were laid on Jesus on the cross. We receive forgiveness for them when we exercise faith in Christ and are placed in union with Him on an individual basis.

THE IDENTIFICATION OF CHRIST WITH THE RACE IN THE INCARNATION AND INFANT SALVATION

When Jesus Christ became incarnate, He became a member of the race. He identified Himself with a race that was under racial condemnation because of Adam's sin. In the incarnation, He became man and became identified with our racial guilt. Identification by union is a two way street.[35] In our personal union with Christ, our guilt was transferred to Christ and His death and righteousness were transferred to us.

The identification of Christ with the race in the incarnation[36] is a two way street. Racial guilt was transferred to Christ. When He died and paid for racial guilt, there was an automatic transfer of that payment to the account of the race. This could be done because He was identified with the race. Personal guilt could not be taken care of automatically because the incarnation, as such, did not identify Him with our personal guilt. The transfer of personal guilt to Christ and the transfer of His death and righteousness for personal guilt requires a union between Christ and the individual person.

Certain points need to be made clear. (1) Jesus did not have a depraved nature. The miraculous conception of His human nature sanctified His human nature. (2) Jesus did not actually sin in Adam. He simply became identified with Adam's sin. It did not change His character any more than it did when our personal sins were laid on Him. He no more actually sinned in Adam than we actually died in Christ. (3) The identification of Christ with the race, while not changing His character, did place Him in a position that He could assume the responsibility for racial sin and pay the penalty for it.

If we accept this view, we believe that guilt and condemnation passed on the race from Adam. If it had not been for Christ, the whole human race would have been lost, including infants. Because of the atoning work of Christ, racial guilt has been lifted from everyone. If a person goes to Hell, he will go because of his own personal failure to measure up to God's standard of absolute holiness. Those who die in infancy will not escape Hell because the guilt of Adam was not imputed to them, but because the atoning work of Christ is applied to them.

THE AGE OF ACCOUNTABILITY

This approach to infant salvation does not open the way for a person to reach the age of accountability having lived a righteous life and not need to be saved. Depravity (or original sin) is not static. The operational base of the depravity is the subconscious mind. While the subconscious mind operates below the level of consciousness, it is not passive. It is characterized by attitudes, inclinations, dispositions, drives, and passions. These traits are active. They are ready to manifest themselves in overt acts of sin. They are culpable before God. These traits stand condemned by God as *traits* before they are manifested in *actions*. Romans 8:7, 8 assures us that depravity will manifest itself in acts of sin.

I am inclined to believe that racial guilt involves more than the guilt imputed from Adam. Depravity or original sin is not passive in those who have not reached the age of personal accountability or responsibility. Depravity manifests itself even in infants. A temper tantrum on the part of an infant is not consistent with the holiness of God. Depravity manifests itself in sinful activity before a child reaches the age of personal accountability. All sin that precedes the time of personal accountability is racial sin. All racial sin is covered because the One who went to the cross was identified with the race. The transfer of His death and righteousness was automatic. It was built into the nature of the case.

When the child reaches the age of accountability, he or she reaches that point in life as one who is already sinful. The one who is already sinful racially immediately becomes one who is sinful personally. From that moment, the only hope is from a personal union with Christ conditioned on personal faith in Christ.

THE MEANING OF THE AGE OF ACCOUNTABILITY

The Bible is addressed to those who are personally accountable. It does not deal with the question of the age of accountability. Whatever we say in this regard is in some measure speculative.

Children have some sense of right and wrong before they reach the age of accountability. In my opinion, we must distinguish between the feeling of guilt on the part of the child in relation to his or her parents and guilt in relation to God. The age of accountability is reached when the child has some realization that he or she has sinned against God.

I am of the opinion that while general revelation alone is adequate to bring an individual to the age or time of accountability that point is reached more quickly where children are taught from the special revelation of God in the Bible. Adequate teaching of the Bible to children, I would think, would bring a child more quickly to the time of accountability than would be the case where there is little or no biblical knowledge. The gospel would be involved in bringing the child to the time of accountability. In such a case, it would be possible for the child to be saved at that time. Those who do not have these opportunities would reach the age of accountability at a later point in life.

Those who are severely retarded mentally would be dealt with the same way infants would. There is good reason to believe that the people who never have anything but general revelation would not reach the age of accountability as soon in life as those who have the benefit of special revelation. However, in the light of Romans 1:18-32, especially verses 19 and 20, we must believe that at some point along the way those who reach adulthood do become accountable.[37]

ERICKSON'S VIEW ON THE STATUS OF INFANTS
In his *Christian Theology*, Millard J. Erickson commented:

> The current form of my understanding is as follows: We all were involved in Adam's sin, and thus receive both the corrupted nature that was his after the fall, and the guilt and condemnation that attach to his sin. With this matter of guilt, however, just as with the imputation of Christ's righteousness, there must be some conscious and voluntary decision on our part. Until this is the case, there is only a conditional imputation of guilt. Thus, there is no condemnation until one reaches the age of responsibility. If a child dies before he or she is capable of making genuine moral decisions, there is only innocence, and the child will experience the same type of future existence with the Lord as will those who have reached the age of moral responsibility and had their sins forgiven as a result of accepting the offer of salvation based upon Christ's atoning death.[38]

Erickson goes on to explain what happens when we reach the age of responsibility and how we become guilty of Adam's sin. He explains:

> We become responsible and guilty when we accept or approve our corrupt nature. There is a time in the life of each one of us when we become aware of our own tendency toward sin. At that point we may abhor our sinful nature that has been there all the time. We would in that case repent of it and might even, if there is an awareness of the gospel, ask God for forgiveness and cleansing. At the very least there would be a rejection of our sinful makeup. But if we acquiesce in that sinful nature, we are in effect saying that it is good. In placing our tacit approval upon the corruption, we are also approving or concurring in the action in the Garden of Eden so long ago. We become guilty of that sin without having to commit a sin of our own.[39]

It will be observed that Erickson does not use the term "infant salvation." The term used in his "Author and Subject Index" is "Infants, status of." He sets forth the position of a conditional imputation of Adam's sin. At the age of responsibility, when a person approves or takes sides with the corrupt nature that he or she received from Adam each person becomes guilty of Adam's sin. That act of approval would cause each of us to be guilty before God "without having to commit a sin of our own." If a child dies prior to that time, "there is only innocence, and the child will experience the same type of future existence with the Lord as will those who have reached the age of moral responsibility and had their sins forgiven as a result of accepting the offer of salvation based upon Christ's atoning death."

EVALUATION OF ERICKSON'S VIEW

Deep within, we cannot bear the thought that those dying in infancy will spend eternity in Hell. Even Calvinists try to avoid such a conclusion. At the same time, we speak with hesitation when we try to explain why we think that is the case. We do not want to leave the impression that we have a weak view of sin or the fall of man into sin. We certainly do not want to be labeled Pelagian or Semi-Pelagian. We almost find it easier to pass over the subject and say nothing about it rather than to invite misunderstanding and accusations that may grow out of misunderstanding. It is obvious that Erickson was struggling with his thoughts and his words when he sought to set forth his view on the status of infants. This is evidenced when he introduced his discussion with these words: "The current form of my understanding is as follows." Whatever we may say about Erickson's view, he did not back off the subject.

Erickson's hope of eternal life for the one who dies before reaching the age of responsibility is "innocence." Based on this innocence, the one dying before the age of responsibility has the same future with God as those have who have placed faith in the atoning work of Christ. Adam's guilt is not imputed to the one who dies before reaching the age of responsibility. The imputation of Adam's guilt to the individual is conditional. It is imputed when the individual at the age of responsibility acquiesces and approves the corrupt nature inherited from Adam. At that point the individual becomes guilty of Adam's sin and his or her own acts of sin that are committed from that point on.

It seems to me that since the race was in Adam when he sinned that the very nature of the case means that his sin was necessarily imputed to the race, including infants. Erickson sets forth a conditional imputation of Adam's sin. Through that means he seeks to protect the innocence of infants and insure their eternal life that way. It seems to me much better and more in keeping with Scripture to recognize that the nature of the case required the imputation of Adam's sin and then believe in infant salvation as I explained it above. Erickson tries hard to distance himself from the view that says we inherit depravity from Adam, but not Adam's guilt. But when he resorts to the conditional guilt to be imputed only upon approval of the corrupt nature at the age of responsibility, it seems that he has, in fact, distanced himself from the natural headship view of the imputation of Adam's sin to the race. While that seems to be the logic of the case, on the page prior to the one the quotations above come from he clearly commits himself to the natural headship view. In summarizing, he explains:

> We have, further, espoused the Augustinian view (natural headship) of the imputation of original sin. We were all present in undifferentiated form in the person of Adam, who along with Eve was the entire race. Thus, it was not merely Adam but man who sinned. We were involved, although not personally, and are responsible for the sin.[40]

When we look at all of Erickson's thoughts on the subject of Adam's sin and the race and the question of whether those who die in infancy are lost, we are convinced that he does not believe that those who die in infancy are lost. We are sure he believed that we inherit a corrupt nature from Adam. However, we are left a little bit confused on the question of the imputation of Adam's guilt.

On one page, he says, "We were actually present within Adam, so that we all sinned in his act. There is no injustice, then, to our condemnation and death as a result of original sin."[41] On another page, he speaks of conditional imputation of Adam's guilt. We become guilty of Adam's sin only after we approve of the sinful nature that we receive from Adam.[42] That happens when we reach the age of responsibility. In such a case, it seems that Adam's sin is not imputed to us because we were in Adam, as taught by the natural headship view, but because we personally choose sides with the sinful nature received from Adam.

James Leo Garrett concludes that though Erickson "espoused" the natural headship view, by the way he dealt with the question of infants he "abandoned realism [the natural headship view] and instead opted for . . . the Placean theory of the imputation of depravity."[43] The Placean theory is the theory of the mediate imputation of Adam's sin as distinguished from the immediate imputation of Adam's sin.

Erickson supports his conclusion with regard to infants by suggesting that there is a "parallelism between our accepting the work of Christ and that of Adam."[44] I think we can understand why he makes this suggestion. But I think there is an important difference which makes his suggestion invalid. We were in Adam at the time of his sin. It is the fact of being in Adam that forms the basis for the imputation of Adam's sin. Being *in Adam* makes it so the imputation of his sin was required. If it was required, it could not be conditioned on some personal approval that we would give upon reaching the age of responsibility.

As it relates to our personal sins, we were not in Christ at the time of His death. The union with Christ, that identifies us with Christ and makes His death ours, took place at the time we placed our faith in Jesus Christ as our Lord and Savior. Being in Christ does not just make it *merely possible* for His death and righteousness to be imputed to us. Being in union with Christ *requires that His death and righteousness be imputed to us.* It cannot be otherwise as long as we are in union with Christ. If that be true, if we were in Adam at the time of his sin, it was necessary that the guilt of his sin would be imputed to us. When identification by union is present, imputation is not optional with God. In "Chapter 9: The Nature of Man," I pointed out:

> The principle involved in imputation of something from one to another is *identification by being in or in union with the person.* This is true whether it be sin or whether it be righteousness. The Scripture knows of no other way that the action of one person can be imputed to another. This is the principle involved in the imputation of the death and righteousness of Christ to the believer.[45]

The nature of the case means that we were in Adam when he sinned. It also means that the incarnation has identified Christ with the race. In the incarnation, there was an automatic identification of Christ with racial guilt. That identification meant that when Christ made atonement, since He was identified with the race, there was an automatic application of the benefits of atonement for racial guilt to the race.

As it relates to our personal sins, it was different. They were laid on Christ (Is. 53:6). The benefits of atonement for personal sins can be applied only when there is a personal union with Christ. When a person places his faith in Jesus Christ as Lord and Savior, he is baptized into Christ by the Holy Spirit. At that point, he or she has the death and righteousness of Christ placed on his account.

12

Sanctification

The two aspects of sin are *guilt* and *depravity*. Sin as guilt makes a person liable to punishment. Sin as depravity is a power in a person's life that causes him to commit sin.

Two aspects of salvation are designed to deal with the two aspects of sin: *justification* and *sanctification*. Justification settles the problem of guilt. It changes our standing before God. Sanctification deals with the problem created by depravity. It changes our experience with God and with sin.

It is very helpful in understanding the doctrine of salvation to get a clear understanding of the difference between justification and sanctification and the relationship between the two.

Contrast Between Justification and Sanctification

JUSTIFICATION	SANCTIFICATION
1. Positional (Standing)	1. Experiential (State)
2. Objective	2. Subjective
3. Right Standing with God	3. Conformity to the Image of Christ
4. Always Full and Complete	4. Moving Toward Completion
5. Christ's Righteousness	5. Personal Righteousness
6. Absolute Righteousness	6. Relative Righteousness Now— Absolute in the Life to Come

A review of this chart after studying this chapter will make it more meaningful. Presenting it here puts the mind on the alert so we can avoid confusing justification and sanctification. Let it be said here that while there are *clear distinctions between justification and sanctification,* the Bible knows of *no separation of the two.* We cannot receive justification without also receiving sanctification.

The Relationship Between Justification and Sanctification

At conversion, we receive justification and sanctification simultaneously. While both are received at the same time, justification is logically prior to sanctification and makes sanctification possible. Sanctification is *dependent* upon justification. Justification is *not dependent* upon sanctification. Justification is dependent upon the death and righteousness of Christ.

FINNEY'S VIEW OF THE RELATIONSHIP BETWEEN JUSTIFICATION AND SANCTIFICATION

Charles Finney's view, on this point, is an illustration of the errors that can grow out of the governmental view of atonement and justification. He remarks:

> Present sanctification, in the sense of present full consecration to God, is made another condition, not ground of justification. Some theologians have made justification a condition of sanctification, instead of making sanctification a condition of justification. But this we shall see is an erroneous view of the subject. . . . Sanctification is sometimes used to express a permanent state of obedience to God, or of consecration. In this sense it is not a condition of present justification, or of pardon and acceptance. But it is a condition of continued and permanent acceptance with God. It certainly cannot be true, that God accepts and justifies a person in his or her sins. The Bible everywhere represents justified persons as sanctified, and always expressly, or impliedly, conditionates justification upon sanctification, in the sense of present obedience to God.[1]

Sanctification—an Essential Accompaniment of Justification

I can appreciate Finney's concern for not separating justification and sanctification and thus allowing a person to be justified who is not sanctified. However, his approach confuses the doctrine of justification and places it in jeopardy.

Sanctification is always an *accompaniment* of justification, but it is *not a condition* or *ground* of justification. It is simply that the salvation "package" includes both, and the package cannot be broken to separate the two. We can no more have justification without sanctification than we can sanctification without justification.

The ultimate concern of God in redemption is to restore fallen human beings to favor and to a functional relationship with God. Justification is an absolutely essential step in the process of redemption. To bypass justification or to ground it on anything other than the death and righteousness of Christ is to do violence to the holiness of God and to grace. To break the package and allow justification without sanctification is to commit the following errors:

1. It is a serious misunderstanding of Scripture. I will deal with this later in this chapter.
2. It is to ground the satisfaction of the holiness of God in atonement and justification in a technical necessity in God rather than a *personal necessity* in God. If the satisfaction of holiness is a *technical necessity,* that interest can be set aside when the technicality is settled. It would be a formality required to uphold the letter of the law. If the satisfaction of holiness is grounded in God's personal experience of holiness and His attitude toward sin, that interest is just as strong once a person is justified as it was before. Justification is a step in the process of redemption that makes sanctification possible. A holy God will most definitely pursue His interest in holiness with the believer.
3. It opens the door to cheap easy-believism which promises justification without sanctification—forgiveness without change. Such a view is not the gospel. It is another gospel. For

years, we have operated with the rightful assumption that grace would become corrupted through a wrongful involvement of law—that it would in effect become another gospel; but the reverse danger received, in most cases, no attention. It is true that a wrong involvement of law can corrupt grace so that we would be preaching another gospel. This is what Paul taught in Galatians (Gal. 1:8, 9). It is also true that we can so abuse grace and void its interest in law that we would be preaching another gospel. This is what Paul was warning against in 1 Corinthians 6:9-11; Galatians 5:19-21; and Ephesians 5:3-7. The Book of James exposes this error. Particular interest is given to it in James 2:14-26. First John gives a clear warning against this error (1 Jn. 1:6; 2:3, 4, 9-11; 3:3-10, 14, 15; 4:20). The correction of this error does not change the nature of the doctrine of justification, but the correction must insist that justification is always accompanied by sanctification. *Forgiveness and change always go together.*

THE INFLUENCE OF PSEUDO-CALVINISM

A corruption of the Calvinistic doctrine of perseverance has been largely responsible for the spread of cheap easy-believism. It has talked about people being eternally secure who show no evidence of sanctification. This is a corruption of Calvinism. Historic Calvinism has taught the perseverance of the saints, not eternal security whether they persevere or not.

James Oliver Buswell, Jr. who is a Calvinist, calls this corruption of Calvinism *pseudo-Calvinism.* He explains:

> I have heard several pseudo-Calvinistic speakers in Christian college chapel exercises say, "Dear young people, there are two ways to go to heaven: The spiritual way and the carnal way. It is so much better to take the spiritual way!" I knew a certain young person who believed this false doctrine and said to the Dean, "I am a Christian, but I do not mind sitting in the bleachers. I choose to go to heaven the carnal way!"
>
> No! The carnal way is the way to eternal punishment. Those who practice things of this kind are not going to inherit the kingdom of God. (Galatians 5: 21)[2]

As has already been observed in earlier chapters, I am not a Calvinist, but I do think it is important that both non-Calvinists and Calvinists be aware of the difference between historic Calvinism and the corruption of Calvinism by pseudo-Calvinists. The pseudo-Calvinist reminds me of Ahimaaz. When Absalom was killed, he prevailed upon Joab to let him go and tell David. At first Joab denied the request and sent Cushi. Ahimaaz again prevailed upon Joab to let him go. With reluctance, Joab consented. With great zeal, Ahimaaz overtook Cushi and was the first to get to David. When Ahimaaz gave his report, he said, "I saw a great tumult, but I knew not what it was" (2 Sam. 18:29).

The pseudo-Calvinist has heard that salvation is free. It is a gift. It is by grace. Without thinking things through and getting things in perspective, he concluded that it meant that sanctification was optional. Off he goes with his half-truth. It is true that salvation is free, but it is not true that sanctification is optional. He goes off half-cocked having a misunderstanding of both Calvinism and

Scripture. The harm that this has done to the Church of Jesus Christ is beyond estimate. A morally drained society is being confronted by a morally anemic church.

It would be unfair to lay the spread of cheap easy-believism altogether at the feet of the pseudo-Calvinist. Many non-Calvinists have picked up the chant of cheap easy-believism with no significant modifications and have preached it. Cheap easy-believism is inherent in all weakening of the moral thrust of Christianity.

The tragedy of cheap easy-believism is that it leads to many false professions. It offers assurance to people who have never been saved. It is not the gospel. It is another gospel. It is as much a corruption of the gospel as is a wrong emphasis on law. There is less hope of leading people out of cheap easy-believism than there is from a corruption of the gospel by a wrong emphasis on law. The wrong emphasis on law corrupts grace but does not corrupt law. Cheap easy-believism corrupts both law and grace. By understanding neither law nor grace, it has weakened all points of appeal that could be used to bring about correction.

It is not easy to correct the view that corrupts grace through a wrong emphasis on law, but there is a possibility. By leaving law intact and in good shape, law can be used as a starting point from which to show a person that a proper understanding of grace satisfies, honors, and upholds the law.

How Justification Contributes to Sanctification

We need to elaborate now on how justification contributes to sanctification. Justification makes both a negative and a positive contribution to sanctification.

THE POWER OF SIN BROKEN

On the negative side, the power of sin is broken. Paul says, "For sin shall not have dominion over you: for ye are not under the law, but under grace" (Rom. 6:14). As we observed in the previous chapter, Romans 6:7 should be translated, "For he that died is justified from sin." The death referred to is the penal death of Christ which belongs to the believer by union with Christ. Justification based on the identification of the believer with the penal death of Christ is given by Paul as the grounds for his statement "that henceforth we should not serve sin" (verse 6).

How does the penal death of Christ received in justification break the power of sin? David Brown explains:

> As death dissolves all claims, so the whole claim of sin, not only to "reign unto death," but to keep its victim in sinful bondage, has been discharged once for all, by the believer's penal death in the death of Christ; so that he is no longer a "debtor to the flesh, to live after the flesh." (chapter 8:12)[3]

Before the guilt problem is solved by the death of Christ, there is nothing to check the power of sin. Sin reigns unchecked. When the believer has the guilt problem settled by the death of Christ, the power of sin is broken. The believer is delivered from the sphere where sin reigned and is transferred into the sphere of grace. "That as sin hath reigned unto death, even so might grace reign through righteousness unto eternal life by Jesus Christ our Lord" (Rom. 5:21).

THE ENTRANCE OF GOD'S SANCTIFYING GRACE

On the positive side, the penal death of Christ received in justification opens the way for the entrance of God's sanctifying grace. Paul says, "For if we have been planted together [grown together or united] in the likeness of his death, we shall be also in the likeness of his resurrection" (Rom. 6:5). To be in the likeness of Christ's death is to have His death become our death so we receive the benefits of it. This involves justification.

To be in the likeness of Christ's resurrection is to live a life of triumphant power over sin. In verse 4, Paul explains "like as Christ was raised up from the dead" as being that which involves the "walk in newness of life." The likeness of Christ's resurrection manifests itself in newness of life. This involves sanctification. The likeness of Christ's death (justification) opens the way for likeness of Christ's resurrection (sanctification).

Our guilt stood as a barrier between us and the sanctifying power of God. God's holiness would not allow Him to enter into a personal relationship with us as long as our guilt was still upon us. When the guilt was removed by the justifying grace of God, the way was open for the entrance of God's sanctifying grace. As Robert Haldane explains:

> So long as the sinner is under the guilt of sin God can have no friendly intercourse with him; for what communion hath light with darkness? But Christ having canceled his people's guilt, having redeemed them from the curse of the law, and invested them with the robe of his righteousness, there is no longer any obstacle to their communion with God, or any barrier to the free ingress of sanctifying grace.[4]

As the justifying grace of God is effective in forgiving our sins and restoring us to favor with God, so the sanctifying grace of God is effective in changing our experience with God and sin. It guarantees a change in our lives.

JUSTIFICATION FOUNDATIONAL FOR SANCTIFICATION

It can be seen that justification is foundational for sanctification. To interpret sanctification on the one hand to be a condition or ground of justification, or on the other hand to interpret justification as contributing to a weak view of sanctification, is to grossly misunderstand the biblical teaching on salvation.

GOD'S PERSONAL INTEREST IN HOLINESS MAINTAINED IN BOTH JUSTIFICATION AND SANCTIFICATION

In interpreting principles that apply to persons and to personal relationships, we tend to become mechanical. We cannot totally avoid the treatment of principles this way at times. We can and must offset the influence of this tendency, nonetheless, by constantly putting things in perspective by reconstructing the context in terms of persons and personal relationships. The requirements that holiness makes in atonement is grounded in God's personal concern for holiness. He is not simply protecting the letter of the law or some legal technicality. When the demands of holiness are put into the context of God's personal concern for holiness, that concern can neither be stopped nor depreciated by the satisfaction of the law involved in justification. It will manifest itself in a concern for sanctification that is consistent with the holy nature of God. The redemptive process is designed to restore us to favor with God and to restore the holiness that was lost in the fall. Justification is a step in that process by a personal God who is intensely interested in holiness. That interest will never be diminished.

The Meaning of Sanctification

To sanctify is to make holy. Holiness is more than a moral term. It also speaks of a relationship with God. There can be a measure of morality without dedication to God, but there can be no holiness without dedication to God. The person whom we refer to as a "good moral" person, who is not dedicated to God, is unholy.

The first Table of the Law begins with "Thou shalt have no other gods before me," and goes through "Remember the sabbath day, to keep it holy" (Ex. 20:3-11). The second Table of the Law begins with "Honor thy father and thy mother," and goes through "Thou shalt not covet" (Ex. 20:12-17). Obedience to the first Table of the Law constitutes *godliness.* Obedience to the second Table of the Law constitutes *righteousness. Holiness* embraces godliness (reverential living before God) and righteousness (conformity to God's moral standard). Disobedience to the first Table of the Law constitutes ungodliness. Disobedience to the second Table of the Law constitutes unrighteousness. Disobedience to any of the Ten Commandments constitutes a failure to be holy.

It is interesting in studying the prophetic writings to see which Table of the Law is receiving attention. For example, Hosea's main concern is with the violation of the First Table of the Law, while the main concern of Amos is with the violation of the Second Table of the Law.

The primary meaning of holiness is dedication to God, but we cannot think of the primary meaning as existing apart from the secondary meaning which is separation from sin. To move toward God is to move away from sin as surely as to go north means to go away from south.

POSITIONAL SANCTIFICATION

Positional sanctification means to be positionally set apart for God. Positional sanctification has as its goal experiential sanctification. The thought here is similar to that of electing a person to be president of an organization. He is elected to serve. At the moment the former president's term expires, he is president positionally on the basis of being elected. He is president in experience only as he functions in the capacity for which he was elected. We are positionally set apart by God at conversion. We are experientially sanctified only as we practice holiness.

We can distinguish in fact between positional sanctification and experiential sanctification for purposes of definition, but we are not to think of the believer as being positionally sanctified without being experientially sanctified. From now on, all use of the word *sanctification* in this study will refer to experiential sanctification unless otherwise indicated.

EXPERIENTIAL SANCTIFICATION

We not only study the subject of sanctification where the word and related words are found, we also study it anywhere the concept is found whether the word or related words appear or not.

Sanctification begins with conversion (2 Cor. 5:17). It is at that very moment that a person begins to experience holiness. A changed life is the essential fruit of conversion.

Sanctification continues to progress in this life by the process of growth (2 Pet. 3:18). Every challenge to dedication or separation from sin that is addressed to Christians is evidence that the New Testament treats sanctification as being progressive and involving growth.

Sanctification will not be completed until the resurrection. The spirit will be completely sanctified at death. At the resurrection, however, sanctification will be completed so far as the body is concerned. After death, we will be completely holy. We will never again have anything in our personality that will not be compatible with God and acceptable to God.

The Goal of Sanctification

RESTORATION OF THE FUNCTIONAL LIKENESS OF GOD

This brings up again the subject of the image of God in man. As was observed earlier, at creation the image of God embraced the *constitutional likeness* which embraced personhood and the *functional likeness* which embraced personality. All of the constituent parts of personhood remained after the fall, though they suffered damage. This damage reflects itself in man's personality. Man lost his functional likeness of God in the fall. He no longer thinks, feels, and acts in the likeness of God. It is the design of redemption to restore the functional likeness of God to man's personality. As Paul tells us in Romans 8:29, we are to be "conformed to the image of his Son [Christ]."

It is very important that our concept of the Christian life take into account that man is a person. God has made us persons who think, feel, and act. We are never more personal than when we are the closest to God—when our personality is most closely conformed to His likeness.

THE LIMITATIONS OF ILLUSTRATIONS IN EXPLAINING
OUR RELATIONSHIP WITH GOD

Mechanical terms and expressions can be used to illustrate as long as we do not take them too far. The control of a machine, the use of an instrument, the filling of a vessel, the molding of clay, and the control of a puppet may all be used to illustrate our dependence upon God. However, we should recognize the limitations of these illustrations. There is one drastic difference. A person is one who thinks, feels, and makes choices. If this observation is not taken into account, the error can be serious. A puppet cannot refuse to obey the directions of its master; a person can. The actions of a person must reflect his or her own basic nature before they are his in the truest sense of what it means to be a person. If the actions of a being are not in some sense his own, he is not a person.

INFLUENCE AND RESPONSE, NOT CAUSE AND EFFECT

We need to say again that we must not interpret the relationship between persons in terms of mechanical cause and effect. Influence and response are more appropriate terms. Also, the choice is not to be made between being either active or passive. Such a choice fits mechanical relationships but not personal relationships. In many decisions we are both active and acted upon. We are dependent, independent, and interdependent in our personal relationships.

SANCTIFICATION AND THE SUBCONSCIOUS MIND

If we are to truly be in the likeness of Christ, we must be in His likeness both on the conscious and subconscious levels of our personality. Thoughts, words, and actions take place on the conscious level, but they are expressions of our inner basic nature which exists on the subconscious level.

It is the design of sanctification to change our thoughts, words, and actions into the likeness of Christ and to so change our basic inner nature that these thoughts, words, and actions represent a real attitude of heart. Anything less than this fails to recognize the implications involved in the fact that man is personal.

The view of redemption that makes man, in his highest dedication, a surrendered instrument or machine to be controlled by God, to the point that a Christian's decisions are in no real sense his own, fails to understand what is meant to be changed into the image of Christ. Such a view fails to fully reckon that man is a personal being.

The church has always been plagued with the idea that there is no real redemption of the personality in this life. Man is pictured by some as being so totally wrecked by sin that he is beyond repair in this life, even by God. Salvation becomes a divine towing service for the wrecked human being. Nothing can be done to restore him in this life. Everything will be made all right when we are finally towed into the heavenly garage, but that will be in the next life.

The best thing, according to this view, is for a person to dwell on the idea of his or her own nothingness and worthlessness. He is to believe that he is doing nothing and cannot do anything worthwhile. God is doing everything. The best he can do is to keep from being a hindrance while God is towing His wrecked humanity into the heavenly garage. To despise himself would seem to be his highest virtue. To respect himself or to have anything like self-confidence is a sin.

Biblical Evidence for the Transformation of the Subconscious Mind

I appreciate the problems that many sincere Christians have that move them, to whatever extent, along the line of thought described above. However, the Bible clearly teaches that there is a basic change in the personality of redeemed people both on the conscious and subconscious levels that makes our actions in a real sense our own and a reflection of our inner nature.

In Romans 8:29, the word for "conformed" is the Greek word *summorphos*. Sanday and Headlam explain that this word "denotes inward and thorough and not merely superficial likeness."[5]

In 2 Corinthians 3:18, when Paul speaks about the process of being changed (NASB and NIV translate "transformed") into the image of the glory of the Lord, he uses a very interesting word. He uses a verb that is kin to the word used in Romans 8:29. It is the word *metamorphoō*. The word is made up of two words meaning "after" and "to form." The noun which comes from the same root is the word *morphē*. R. C. Trench calls attention to an interesting contrast between *morphē* and another Greek word *schēma*. He explains that *morphē* "signifies the form as it is the utterance of the inner life."[6] *Schēma* refers to outward appearance or fashion and can be superficial.[7] *Suschē matidzō* is a verb which is made up of two words "with or together" and the verb form from the same root as *schēma* which means " to fashion." *Metamorphoō* refers to an internal change rather than a mere external change. *Suschēmatidzō* refers to an outward, superficial change.[8]

The choice of the word *metamorphoō* in 2 Corinthians 3:18 shows us that when Paul speaks of being changed into the image of the Lord, he is speaking about a deep, basic change in the inner nature of the Christian. It is a change of our personality on the subconscious level that manifests itself in conscious actions that are true reflections of the person.

In Romans 12:2 Paul says: "And be not conformed to this world: but be ye transformed by the renewing of your mind."

The Greek word for conformed is *suschēmatidzō*. The Greek word for transformed is *metamorphoō*. Trench explains:

> "Do not fall in," says the apostle, "with the fleeting fashions of this world, nor be yourselves fashioned to them (*mēsuschēmatizesthe*), but undergo a deep abiding change (*alla metamorphousthe*) by the renewing of your mind, such as the spirit of God alone can work in you" (cf. 2 Corinthians iii.18).[9]

It is clear from the words used in Romans 8:29; 12:2; and 2 Corinthians 3:18 that Paul is referring to the fact that as Christians we experience a deep, basic, inner change.[10] The life of the believer is brought into the likeness of the life of Christ. The outward life is to be a manifestation of an inner reality.

SANCTIFICATION AND THE TOTAL PERSONALITY

The New Testament teaches that conformity to the image of Christ extends to each area of the personality. It affects the way we think, feel, and act. Romans 12:2 proves to be very interesting at this point. Paul speaks about a basic, inner change taking place "by the renewing of your mind." Concerning the meaning of this expression, Barclay M. Newman and Eugene A. Nida explain:

> The meaning is that the Christian confession demands that the entire bent of one's mind be changed. The entire clause may be rendered as "permit God to change your inside by giving you a completely new mind" or ". . . by making your mind and your heart completely different."[11]

As I understand it, the renewing of the mind is not a process that somehow stands outside the basic inner change that brings it about. Rather, it is involved in the change. The renewing of the mind is involved in the basic inner change.

The important question here is: What is the mind? In the English language, the word "mind" means: (1) that with which we think and reason, (2) the mind (in the limited sense just referred to) plus the heart and the will. It is this use of the word mind that is reflected in the statement: "I have made up my mind to serve the Lord." We mean by this that our whole being—mind, heart, and will is involved in the decision.

I believe the Greek word *nous* as Paul is using it embraces mind, heart, and will. Concerning the meaning of *nous,* J. H. Thayer gives as one of its meanings: "The mind, comprising alike the faculties of perceiving and understanding and those of feeling, judging, determining."[12] This use of the word mind is closely related to person or personality. We would be correct in saying that in Romans 12:2 when Paul speaks of a change in our basic inner nature by the renewing of our mind that he was referring to a basic inner change in our total personality.

Persons, Not Puppets

We are told in Scripture that God said with reference to the New Covenant, "I will put my laws into their mind" (Heb. 8:10). The evidence that we have examined up to this point, the challenge to use our minds and our hearts in our relationship with God, and the challenges that are made to our will leave no doubt that in a very real sense as Christians our actions are to spring from the inner realities of our personality.

It is a misunderstanding of Scripture for us to reduce ourselves to instruments for God to use or channels for God to work through. These metaphors are all right if we do not press them too far. When we press them to the point that we are to passively yield ourselves to God with the idea that we are to do nothing and let God use us like a puppet, we are overlooking the truth that God has made us as persons and treats us accordingly in His dealings with us.

In our relationship with God, we are both *dependent* and *independent.* We are dependent in the sense that we need His help and cannot be what we should be without His help. We are independent in the sense that even though we cannot be what we should be without God's help, in a real sense, our actions are our own. God does not treat us like puppets. We have latitude for obedience and disobedience.

The Fruit of the Spirit: An Expression of our Transformed Inner Nature

Let me illustrate by applying the basic principles of our discussion to the fruit of the Spirit in Galatians 5:22, 23. Dependence is seen in that the various virtues listed are called the fruit of the Spirit. But when we talk about love, joy, peace, longsuffering, etc., we are not simply talking about divine activity in which we are used as channels. It may sound good to talk about God loving through us, but what about God having joy through us, or God having peace through us, and so on through the list? The Holy Spirit is helping us to be the kind of person who loves, experiences joy, peace, longsuffering, etc. As the Holy Spirit produces fruit in us, these virtues begin to characterize us and express our inner nature. In this work of the Holy Spirit, we are both active and passive. He is working in us as active *persons,* not as passive *puppets.*

I am not suggesting that our inner being is completely transformed in this life. I am not suggesting that there are no inner conflicts. I am, however, suggesting that though there be inner conflicts there are also inner realities.

Sanctification and a Proper View of Self-worth

A proper view of redeemed man gives a foundation for a proper sense of self-worth, self-respect, and a good self-image. We were created in God's image. This gives a sense of self-worth. Sin made us unworthy of God's favor, but it did not render us worthless. God considered man worth (not worthy) what it cost to redeem him. Because of that, we are now sons of God. We belong to the family of God. This gives a sense of self-worth. We are being transformed into the image of God in our personality. All of this runs counter to the idea of downgrading ourselves. We dare not downgrade the redemptive work of God in our lives.

It is no compliment to God for a Christian to grind himself or herself into the dust of nothingness so he can claim no credit for what he is and so he can give all the glory to God. It is no compliment to God for us to thank Him for making us "nothing." I think it brings far more glory to God for us to recognize the positive good He has done for us, to us, and in us and to thank Him for it and to give Him the glory for it. In a proper view of self-worth, a Christian is always cognizant that he or she owes his existence and everything that is worthwhile to God as Creator and Redeemer. This recognition gives rise to gratitude and humility.

Sanctification and the Self

Along the same line of thought there seems to be a widespread confusion about "self." I can appreciate the difficulty of being exact and precise. Frequently, wrong terminology may be used, though one understands the right meaning, but to speak of crucifying self and to condemn loving oneself is wrong terminology and leads some people into confusion.

Let us reflect on the idea that a person should not love himself and see where such thinking would lead. Jesus said, "Love thy neighbour as thyself" (Mt. 22:39). If I am to love my neighbor *as myself,* but I am not to love myself, that is a poor standard for loving my neighbor. It is all right for a person to love himself (see Eph. 5:28, 29). But it must be done in the context of loving God and our neighbor. That is not the same as being in love with yourself. It is not narcissism.

The Bible does not speak of "crucifying self" nor "dying to self." The self is the real you. The only way to crucify self would be to bring about the annihilation of the self. This is impossible.

Jesus taught self-denial, but that is not crucifixion of self; neither is it self-torture. In Luke 9:23, Jesus said, "If any *man* will come after me, let him deny himself, and take up his cross daily and follow me."

In the history of the church, there have been those who have been so obsessed with self-denial that they could not see that broader picture of Christian responsibility. They became ascetics. Such an approach to self-denial misses the focus of the verse. If an undue amount of time is spent in self-examination, the person has become self-centered regardless of what his or her motives are for this inward search. We need to be Christ-centered, not self-centered. The focus of the verse is on Jesus' words "follow me," not on "deny himself."

Self-denial is necessary to the extent that it requires us to set aside all plans and all personal interests that interfere with following Jesus. When self-denial causes us to set aside all of our desires and plans that would interfere with following Jesus, it has fulfilled its purpose. Self-denial is a tough assignment, but it does not call on a person to grind himself or herself into the dust of nothingness. A person who is truly following Jesus has practiced and is practicing self-denial, but this kind of self-denial is not an obsession.

"Self" is not some aspect of our being that gives us trouble. Self is the real you—the real person. Selfhood embraces our personhood and personality. A person does not need to crucify the self. He needs to surrender self and develop self. He or she needs self-improvement, not self-crucifixion.

I am sure many people mean essentially the same thing by the expression "crucifixion of self" as I suggest by my interpretation of self-denial, but many take it much further. It becomes a hindrance to the development of the personality of the Christian.[13]

Both Earthen Vessels and Vessels of Honor

It will help at this point if we will keep in mind that there are several different aspects or angles of the truth. If we develop our view from just one aspect or angle of a particular subject, we will fail to see it in proper perspective. Our thinking will not be properly balanced by the different angles of the truth.

In 2 Corinthians 4:7 Paul says, "But we have this treasure in earthen vessels, that the excellency of the power may be of God, and not of us." In contrast to God, we see our weakness. We see our utter dependence upon Him. We give Him honor, glory, and praise. We see that without Him we would be nothing and could do nothing (Jn. 15:5). Paul refers to us as "earthen vessels" to stress this side of the picture.

If our total thinking of a Christian as a vessel is taken from 2 Corinthians 4:7, we can see the direction it would take us in our thinking. This is not all that Paul said about us as vessels. In 2 Timothy 2:21 he explains, "If a man therefore purge himself from these, he shall be a vessel unto honour, sanctified, and meet for the master's use, and prepared unto every good work." Here we see Paul talking about the Christian who separates himself or herself from iniquity as being a "vessel unto honour. . . meet [or fit] for the master's use, and prepared unto every good work." This represents true value. We must take both 2 Corinthians 4:7 and 2 Timothy 2:21 into account in arriving at a proper estimate of ourselves as Christians.

To have a sense of value carries with it a sense of responsibility. If a person has a sense of value, he wants to dress and act in a manner that is appropriate for that value. The practical application of the Christian value system is affected by whether we downgrade ourselves or whether we recognize a value that is given to us by creation and redemption.

True Humility

True Christian humility is not based on having a low sense of self-worth. It is based on a recognition that the Christian is indebted to God for his or her self-worth. When he or she recognizes this dependence upon God, he is thankful. He is not filled with a haughty spirit. He also recognizes a sense of debt and gratitude to other people. Recognition of dependence and the feeling of gratitude leave no room for false pride.

Humility is not a marvel when expressed by a person who is characterized by self-degradation and poor accomplishments. It is a marvel when exercised by those who have achieved success and have a sense of self-worth. For such a person to recognize his or her dependence upon God and upon others and to express his gratitude to God and to others, we call this virtue. This is true humility.

The Righteousness of Sanctification

The righteousness in justification is the righteousness of Christ which becomes ours. It was not acted out or lived out by us. The righteousness of sanctification is our personal righteousness that is worked out in us by the Holy Spirit as we avail ourselves of the grace of God. This righteousness is sometimes called *imparted* righteousness as contrasted with the *imputed* righteousness of justification. The word *imparted* is misleading. It sounds as if righteousness were a substance that exists outside of us and is imparted to us. It is better to speak of it as a righteousness that is worked out in us or produced in us.

The Scope of Sanctification

THE FOUR BASIC RELATIONSHIPS

Sanctification is to extend to all of life's experiences. All of life's experiences involve one or more of the *four basic relationships:* (1) a person's relationship with God, (2) a person's relationship with other people, (3) a person's relationship with himself, and (4) a person's relationship with the created order. In sanctification, these relationships are to be lived out in subjection to God's authority as revealed in the Bible, the Lordship of Christ, and the leadership of the Holy Spirit.

THE FOUR BASIC VALUES

All morals and ideals are reducible to *four basic ethical values* (or virtues). The four basic values are the foundation for the guiding moral and ethical principles as we function within the framework of the four basic relationships. The four basic values are: (1) holiness, (2) love, (3) wisdom, and (4) ideals. Holiness is concerned with the question: Is it right or is it wrong? Love is concerned with the question: How can I show my concern? Wisdom is concerned with the practical side of truth. It asks the question: What is the best judgment? Ideals are concerned with the question: What is good, beautiful, and excellent? Because of holiness, we have convictions. Because of love, we are concerned. Because of wisdom, we exercise common sense, or good judgment. Because of ideals, we are challenged toward excellence.[14]

The influence of sanctification is to manifest itself in our total experience. It embraces our experiences both as a member of the church and a member of society. To believe in a unified view of knowledge, we must believe that our belief in God and Christian values have implications for the whole of life.

THE IMAGE OF GOD IN MAN AND THE SCOPE OF OUR SANCTIFICATION

In determining the scope of sanctification, we need to go back to the meaning of being created in the image of God. We were designed to be in the functional likeness of God. This should be seen in the entire scope of human experience. All our experiences in every area of life are to be affected by the divine likeness that we are to manifest. The design of sanctification is to restore the functional likeness of God that was lost in the fall. We were designed to be in the moral likeness of God. When we speak of the moral likeness of God in this context, we are using the word moral in its broadest meaning. We are to be holy, loving, and wise because God is holy, loving, and wise. We are to be concerned about ideals, beauty, and excellence because God is the quintessence of the high and the lofty. This likeness of God is to be highly evident as we carry out the divine mandate to exercise dominion over the earth and its inhabitants, and as we obey the Great Commission.

DEALING WITH THE INFLUENCE OF POSTMODERNISM

We cannot take our cue on ethical values and virtues from postmodernism. We cannot settle for relativism. We must go to the Word of God as the revelation of the nature of God. We must aim to be like God both in our church life and in our life as a member of society. When we settle for less than what it means to be like God, we do it to our own loss and the loss of others.

The conditioning power of the Postmodern Mood has been sapping the moral strength of the church. A few voices, but not enough, are being heard on the moral front. But it seems that far fewer know what to say or whether to say anything at all about ideals, beauty, and excellence. The barbarians are taking over and this is deemed to be perfectly fine. After all, it is all a matter of private taste.

IDEALS, BEAUTY, AND EXCELLENCE AND THE SCOPE OF OUR SANCTIFICATION

We dare not forget that God is a God of *beauty, majesty,* and *excellence.* He calls on us to be concerned about the noble, the beautiful and the excellent. Paul tells us in Philippians 1:10, "That ye may approve things that are excellent" (KJV). The NIV reads, "That you may be able to discern what is best." The meaning of the Greek is "that you may approve things that make a difference." This tells us that all things are not of equal value. We need to be able to make distinctions. We should strive for the best. We cannot as Christians accept the postmodern rejection of the distinction between higher and lower.

We are in desperate need of heeding the admonition given by Paul in Philippians 4:8. To be sure that we get the full import of this verse I will quote from the KJV, NASB, and the NIV.

> Finally, brethren, whatsoever things are true, whatsoever things are honest, whatsoev-
> er things *are* just, whatsoever things *are* pure, whatsoever things *are* lovely, whatsoev-

er things *are* of good report; if *there be* any virtue, and if there be any praise, think on these things (KJV).

Finally, brethren, whatever is true, whatever is honorable, whatever is right, whatever is pure, whatever is lovely, whatever is of good repute, if there is any excellence and if anything worthy of praise, let your mind dwell on these things (NASB).

Finally, brothers, whatever is true, whatever is noble, whatever is right, whatever is pure, whatever is lovely, whatever is admirable—if anything is excellent or praiseworthy—think about such things (NIV).

There is certainly a wide range of forms that can demonstrate ideals, beauty, and excellence. There will certainly be room for individual taste. But that is not the same as saying that we may rightly call anything beautiful or excellent. We must not set aside the aim to be in the likeness of God in all areas of our being. We dare not for the sake of evangelism or any other high and worthy goal declare a truce in any of these areas.

Nothing reflects the spirit of the age as much as people's attitude about the areas covered by ideals, beauty, and excellence. It is reflected particularly in the way people dress and the kind of music they listen to. When these areas are explained as a mere happenstance of culture, people let down their guard.

People cave in on these areas before they do on the moral areas. But once a surrender has been made in the area of ideals, beauty, and excellence, participation in the culture of the times serves as a moral anesthesia. Once a person's moral sensitivity has been numbed by the spirit of the age, the stage is set for a moral downfall.

A Call for a Revival of Christian Humanism

I would like to make a plea for a revival of Christian Humanism. The association of the word "humanism" with secular humanism has caused many Christians to develop a negative attitude toward the word humanism. However, there is a drastic difference between the meaning of humanism when it is modified by the word "secular," and when it is modified by the word "Christian."

As I am using the word, humanism recognizes that every human being has a potential, and that potential should be developed to its fullest and highest level of achievement. When we add the word "Christian" to humanism, an explanation is given for why human beings have this potential and why it should be developed to its highest and fullest level of achievement.

Human beings have this potential because they are created by God in His image (Gen. 1:26). Human beings are in the rational likeness of God (Col. 3:10). The creative potential of human minds when seen both individually and collectively staggers the imagination.

Being created in the image of God, also involves a moral likeness (Eph. 4:24). Our moral and ethical ideals are to reflect the likeness of God. This means that the guiding ideal for our goals should be high. The aim to be in the likeness of God means that we should be in the likeness of God as it relates to the ideals of beauty, excellence, and order.

In Genesis 1:26, God commands us to exercise dominion over the created order. This command to exercise dominion over the earth has been called the "Cultural Mandate."[15] Our responsibility is far-reaching. In carrying out this mandate, we are to aspire to the high ideals that are set for us by our responsibility to be in the likeness of God. We are to aspire to bring the entire scope of life under the Lordship of Christ.

If sin had not entered the picture, there would be no problem in living the whole scope of our lives in complete conformity to God's likeness. Sin changed things. The only way we can live our whole life in the likeness of God is through the redemption that is ours through Jesus Christ. In this life, living up to this challenge is not without complications.

While it is true that fallen man cannot bring all of life into conformity to the likeness of God, that does not mean we must reject everything that is or has been done by unsaved people. There is a dark side of human nature. But not all traces of nobility are eradicated from human experience. The image of God is not completely silent in fallen human beings. For that reason, there have been remarkable achievements by unsaved people. As Christians, we study these achievements and critique them in the light of the revealed truth in the Bible. The challenge before us is to bring our own achievements into conformity to the high ideals required by the likeness of God and the Lordship of Christ.

Usually, when we speak of Christian Humanism, we are thinking of that branch of studies known as the humanities. The main areas in the humanities that come to our minds when we are thinking about humanism's emphasis on excellence are architecture, art, music, and literature. My aim in calling for a revival of Christian Humanism is to include these areas, but also to extend the concern for beauty, excellence, and order to every area of life.

In the carrying out of our responsibilities to fulfill the Cultural Mandate and the Great Commission, there are many opportunities for us to manifest genuine concern for excellence, the high, the lofty, and the beautiful. These are all legitimate concerns for Christian Humanism. Philippians 1:10 and 4:8 (cited above) set the challenge before us. It is the decline of the manifestation of these concerns that David Wells is speaking of when he explains:

> Western culture once valued the higher achievements of human nature—reasoned discourse, the good use of language, fair and impartial law, the importance of our collective memory, tradition, the core of moral axioms to which collective assent was given, those aesthetic achievements in the arts that represented the high-water marks of the human spirit. These are now all in retreat. Reasoned discourse has largely disappeared; in a nation of plummeting literacy, language has been reduced to the lowest common denominator, to the vulgar catch phrases of the youth culture; the core of values has disintegrated; the arts are degraded; the law is politicized.[16]

There was a time (prior to 1960) when it was assumed that when a person pursued advanced education that he or she would move forward in his or her aesthetic appreciation. Now we can no longer count on this. There is a strong possibility that a student may go backwards rather than forwards in these areas. Colleges and universities have become the most unlikely places for a person to develop appreciation for good taste, manners, and refinement. Even Christian institutions are at a loss about how to deal with the problem. Ideals are considered by many to be in a neutral area where only personal opinion and preference prevail. As perceived by some, the problem seems to be those who still believe that churches and Christian institutions should promote beauty and excellence.

The Broad Application of Ideals, Beauty, and Excellence

When we look around at the great works of artists and musicians, we may feel that we do not have anything to offer in the area of ideals. However, opportunities for the demonstration of beauty, excellence, and order are available for all people in every strata of society.

My early memories take me back to the Great Depression. Our family knew what poverty was. But poverty did not silence the concern for ideals at our house.

My mother and my father would not let poverty deny us the experience of beauty. Every year they had a flower garden. When it came to farming, my father had a touch of perfectionism. The crops were kept clean from weeds and grass, the hedgerows were cut, and the farming equipment was kept in good condition.

My mother was a good seamstress. She took what she was able to buy and made dresses for herself and my sisters that would help them look nice, especially on special occasions. We went through some tough times, but there never was a time when I did not have what we called in those days a Sunday outfit. In that limited society, special occasions were events such as church, funerals, the first and last days of school, and graduation.

To give touches of beauty to our home my mother and my sisters would take tin cans and make decorative ornaments for the house. At Christmas time, we would cut a tree from the woods and they would decorate it with whatever they could get. I remember that one of the decorations was popcorn strung on a string and wrapped around the tree.

I am of the opinion that my parents' emphasis on ideals in my childhood made a difference in my life. The experience of ideals lifts your sights. It causes you to aim higher. If it had not been for the emphasis on ideals (though simple) by my parents when I was growing up, I do not believe that I would have been where I am today.

Regardless of your lot in life, you can experience beauty, excellence, and order. Beauty applies to the artistic side of life. Excellence is involved in beauty, but it is not restricted to beauty. Excellence calls for doing your reasonable best in whatever you do. Order deals with developing an ordered mind and working toward giving order and organization to your life.

There are some things that any of us can do to express our concern for beauty, excellence, and what is appropriate. Women can work on being ladies. A trip to the beauty shop demonstrates concern in this area. Men can work on being gentlemen. We can polish our shoes. We dress appropriately for the occasion if our wardrobe affords it. We can mow our grass. We can clip our hedges. We can give our best to our occupation. We can broaden our interests. We can enjoy the beauty of nature. We can enjoy the beauty and excellence produced by others.

A Special Appeal to Women

Our sons Jon and James recognize a special debt to their mother as it relates to broadening their horizons and their interests. In a Mother's Day address in 1993, among other things, James said this about his mother:

> One of the greatest contributions that was given to me, mainly by my mother, was the expansion of my horizons. She read to me in her lap as a baby and toddler until I basically learned to read at home before I went to school. The first couple of years of school were boring because she had taught me how to read without actually trying.
>
> She felt like it was her responsibility to pass the heritage of our families to us. Much time was spent talking about our family and our spiritual heritage.
>
> I wish I had a dollar for every museum, historical landmark, and exhibit that we saw. Our exposure to music, good music, was very broad. I learned to love the arts, flowers, and beauty in general because of the continual influence of my mom. I would be a boring soul indeed had she not added color to my life.[17]

While the challenge for beauty and excellence is made to both men and women, women play a particularly important role. Someone has said, "Women are the bearers of civilization." I want to challenge women. Rise to the occasion! Do not let the barbarians continue to destroy all that is beautiful and noble in our culture. Help us to get back to a concern for manners, politeness, poise, dignity, and charm for ladies.

The Need for Balance

Life is not always simple. The complication presented by sin, the shortage of time, money, ability, help, etc. limit what we can do. We cannot do everything that we would like to do. Frequently, we need to look at a situation from several different angles, and then make a decision. We are pulled at from many directions. We experience tension. The best is not always possible. We have to prioritize in the light of reality. Proverbs 26:4, 5 illustrate for us what I call: "the principle of tension and counterbalance." The first verse reads, "Answer not a fool according to his folly, lest thou be like unto him." The next verse reads, "Answer a fool according to his folly, lest he be wise in his own conceit."

One verse tells you not to answer a fool. The other verse tells you to answer a fool. Obviously you cannot do both of these in every situation. If that be the case, how do you obey these two verses? What you have to do is to consider what the greatest risk is. If the greatest risk is that you will be like him, you do not answer him. If the greatest risk is that he will be wise in his own eyes, you do answer him. It will not always be easy to decide which of these to do, but you must do one of them. It is a serious mistake to choose one of these and adopt it as your approach to every situation.

These verses help us develop an important principle of interpretation: There are some truths that cannot be set forth in one principle alone, but must be set forth in two or more principles which counterbalance each other. Here we see tension. There is tension between the different sides or angles of truth. This tension is needed to keep balance. This principle of interpretation guides us in areas where we are dealing with what we might call *general truth* instead of *absolute truth*. As is illustrated in Proverbs 26:4 and 5, there is no absolute truth about whether and when to answer fools. This principle is similar to the principle, "There are two sides to the same coin," or "There are many facets of truth." I will call this principle of interpretation: the *principle of tension and counterbalance*.

It is important to remember that there are absolute truths such as the moral teachings of the Ten Commandments. These we must obey. But there are some areas of life for which we have general principles rather than absolute truths to guide us. In these cases we are by the help of God to make wise choices. It is important to remember that on some subjects the truth cannot be set forth in a single statement or principle. We must hear or read a broad range of thoughts on the subject lest our thinking should get out of balance.

I am well aware that on the scale of priorities that beauty and excellence do not rank as high as holiness. But we dare not prioritize beauty and excellence out of existence. There may be some very devout Christians who neglect some areas while they give an unusual amount of attention to other important areas. But in the community of Christian experience the full implications of what it means to be in the likeness of God needs to be worked out. To use an illustration: It may be acceptable that some people would play only a few keys on the piano keyboard, but the broader community of believers should play the whole keyboard.

Regeneration and Sanctification

REGENERATION IN CALVINISM AND ARMINIANISM

In traditional Calvinism, regeneration precedes faith. Calvinists consider it to be impossible for a sinner to believe unless he or she is first regenerated. Arminians believe that it is absolutely necessary for the Holy Spirit to work in the heart of the person who hears the gospel in order for faith to be possible (Jn. 6:44). But to Arminians this work of the Holy Spirit is not regeneration. In Arminianism, faith precedes regeneration. In Calvinism, only the regenerate believe. In Arminianism, only believers are regenerated. Both believe that believers are justified.

Classical Arminianism believes in *conditional monergism* with regard to justification and regeneration. Justification and regeneration are solely the acts and the provisions of God. This means justification and regeneration are effects. God is the cause.The condition for justification is faith in Christ. Faith is a human experience that can take place only with divine aid. Justification is solely an act of God, as the Supreme Judge of the universe, in which the person who has the death and righteousness of Christ is declared righteous. Justification is the ground of sanctification. Regeneration is the first step in sanctification and forms the foundation for all growth and development that takes place in the process of sanctification. Without regeneration there could be no sanctification. Regeneration is solely the work of the Holy Spirit.

In making *regeneration* precede faith, Calvinism makes *sanctification* precede *justification*. By anybody's definition, regeneration is a life changing experience. Regeneration is the first step in sanctification. When Calvinism has regeneration preceding justification, it is on a collision course against its own theology. Calvinism correctly understands that sanctification is dependent on justification. Louis Berkhof, a major Calvinistic theologian, tells us that "regeneration is the beginning of sanctification." Only a few lines down on the same page he says, "Justification precedes and is basic to sanctification in the covenant of grace. . . . Justification is the judicial basis of sanctification."[18]

I think it is in order to restate a quotation given earlier in this chapter from Robert Haldane. Haldane, whose Calvinism is not in question, explains:

> So long as the sinner is under the guilt of sin God can have no friendly intercourse with him; for what communion hath light with darkness? But Christ having canceled his people's guilt, having redeemed them from the curse of the law, and invested them with the robe of his righteousness, there is no longer any obstacle to their communion with God, or any barrier to the free ingress of sanctifying grace.[19]

It can be seen that what both Berkhof and Haldane say puts their theology in conflict with the concept that regeneration precedes faith. Calvinism, correctly observes that sanctification is grounded in justification. This creates a problem when they say that "regeneration is the beginning of sanctification" and yet, they place regeneration before justification.

THE NECESSITY OF REGENERATION

Paul tells us that "the carnal mind is enmity against God: for it is not subject to the law of God, neither indeed can be. So then they that are in the flesh cannot please God" (Rom. 8:7, 8). For a person who is so enslaved by his or her inherited depravity, there can be no conformity to the image of Christ apart from regeneration. The Christian life would be impossible apart from regeneration.

THE MEANS AND AGENCY OF REGENERATION

Peter says that God "hath begotten us again unto a lively hope by the resurrection of Jesus Christ from the dead" (1 Pet. 1:3). Regeneration is involved in partaking of the benefits of Christ's resurrection. By union with Christ, we share the benefits of His resurrection. We are identified with His life as well as His death (Rom. 6:4, 5, 8, 11).

The Word of God as a life-giving Word is an instrument in our regeneration. James said, "Of his own will begat he us with the word of truth" (Jas. 1:18). Peter speaks of "being born again, not of corruptible seed, but of incorruptible, by the word of God, which liveth and abideth for ever" (1 Pet. 1:23).

The Holy Spirit is the agent who performs the work of regeneration (Jn. 1:33; 3:5, 6; Tit. 3:5; Eph. 2:10). This means that regeneration is solely a divine work. Since it is solely the work of God it is monergistic. God is the cause. Regeneration is the effect.

THE NATURE OF REGENERATION

In regeneration we are made new creatures or a new creation (2 Cor. 5:17). We are given a new direction in life (2 Cor. 5:17 and Eph. 2:10). We have a different attitude toward sin and Jesus Christ. We have a basic desire in our heart to do right and to be right with God. This change is a basic change, not an *absolute* change. It puts a person on the side of God and right, but it does not eradicate all traces of sin.

THE RESULTS OF REGENERATION

As a result of the new birth we become children of God. We are restored to fellowship with God and have the ability to function morally and spiritually. To enter into the kingdom of God (Jn. 3:3, 5) does not refer to entering the kingdom of God after death. It refers to entering it now as a functioning citizen of that kingdom. We have to enter the kingdom of God now to be in it after death.

The new birth results in victorious living. John tells us, "For whatsoever is born of God overcometh the world: and this is the victory that overcometh the world, even our faith" (1 Jn. 5:4). Since this will receive further development when I discuss the guaranteed results of sanctification, I will not give further development to it at this time.

The Holy Spirit and Sanctification

An understanding of the ministry of the Holy Spirit should begin with the recognition that He is named "Holy" Spirit. His name should reveal that the primary thrust of His ministry toward us is to produce holiness. Holiness is to be lived out seven days a week, not just demonstrated in worship services and special moments.

THE FRUIT OF THE HOLY SPIRIT IN OUR LIVES

The major thrust of the Holy Spirit's ministry deals with the way we live. Jesus demonstrated this when He said: "And when he is come, he will reprove the world of sin, and of righteousness, and of judgment" (Jn. 16:8). Also, notice what is said about the fruit of the Holy Spirit in Galatians 5:22, 23, "But the fruit of the Spirit is love, joy, peace, longsuffering, gentleness, goodness, faith, meekness, temperance." In Ephesians 5:9 Paul says, "For the fruit of the Spirit is in all goodness and righteousness and truth." In Galatians 5:16, 17 Paul reminds us: "This I say then, walk in the Spirit, and ye shall not fulfil the lust of the flesh. For the flesh lusteth against the Spirit, and the Spirit against the flesh: and these are contrary the one to the other: so that ye cannot do the things that ye would." The presence of the Holy Spirit is a restrictive relationship that keeps us from doing things we would do without His presence. Also, pay attention to the context of the words of Paul when he said, "For as many as are led by the Spirit of God, they are the sons of God" (Rom. 8:16). In verse 15 he had said, "If ye through the Spirit do mortify the deeds of the body, ye shall live." The leading that Paul spoke of in verse 16 is the mortifying of the deeds of the body. In this case it is not leadership into the unknown. The leading enables us to live the way we already know we should live. It is righteous living that Paul is talking about.

Stated negatively, the Holy Spirit is working in us to give us victory over sin. Stated positively, the Holy Spirit works in us to produce virtue that is expressive of Christian values. The Holy Spirit is not satisfied by our simply laying aside sins. He wants us to put on Christian virtue. The Christian virtues mentioned as the fruit of the Spirit are constituent elements in the functional likeness of Christ in us.

Christianity is virtue (moral and ethical values) oriented through and through. This value orientation permeates the whole fabric of the Christian system of life and thought. It is not our right to diminish or tone down this emphasis on virtues. It is our responsibility to experience and proclaim these virtues.

THE EVIDENCE THAT A PERSON IS FILLED WITH THE HOLY SPIRIT

If you want to know if a person is filled with the Holy Spirit, you see if he manifests the fruit of the Spirit. It is his seven-day-a-week lifestyle that tells the story, not just the way he behaves in worship services or when he is praying or talking about God. There is a place for excitement. We need more of it, but excitement apart from the fruit of the Spirit in a person's walk is of the flesh, not the Holy Spirit.

THE HOLY SPIRIT AND THE HUMAN PERSONALITY

The relationship of the Holy Spirit and the Christian is a relationship between persons. This means we are talking about *influence* and *response,* not mechanical *cause* and *effect.* When we speak of love as being the fruit of the Holy Spirit, we are not to interpret this in terms of mechanical cause and effect but rather in terms of influence and response. When we think in terms of influence and response, we are safeguarding the fact that we are talking about a personal relationship. The response of love is an experience for which we are dependent upon the Holy Spirit, but at the same time we actually love. The action is our own. We are not just talking about action. We are talking about action that is expressive of our inner nature. The Holy Spirit is helping us to become the kind of person who loves.

In speaking about dependence upon the Holy Spirit, some have said, "We are to *trust* not *try.*" This would be appropriate if we were talking about mechanical cause and effect relationships. Since we are talking about influence and response, we both *try* and *trust.* We set ourselves in action trusting the Holy Spirit to help us. We do not wait for Him to do it for us. Regardless of how much divine aid we receive, it will be our personality acting when we love, and the same is true when we practice other Christian virtues.

Some have understood Paul to advocate passivity on our part when he said, "By the grace of God I am what I am." He concluded the verse by saying, "Yet not I, but the grace of God which was with me" (1 Cor. 15:10). In the same verse Paul said, "I laboured more abundantly than they all." "Yet not I, but the grace of God which was with me" is not intended to mean that in no sense were Paul's actions his own. If so, it would cancel out the statement, "I laboured more abundantly than they all." By attributing His efforts to the grace of God, Paul was expressing gratitude and dependence.

The truth is set forth in proper balance in Philippians 4:13 where Paul said, "I can do all things through Christ which strengtheneth me." "I can" denotes personal involvement and capability. "Christ which strengtheneth me" shows dependence. We can depend upon divine aid, but it is divine aid to help us be persons, functioning in the likeness of Christ. It is not a divine aid that reduces us to puppets.

The Word of God and Our Sanctification

In His prayer in John 17, Jesus said, "Sanctify them through thy truth: thy word is truth" (verse 17). In John 8:32 He said, "And ye shall know the truth, and the truth shall make you free." Knowledge is closely related to truth. Peter says:

> Grace and peace be multiplied unto you through the knowledge of God, and of Jesus our Lord. According as his divine power hath given unto us all things that pertain unto life and godliness, through the knowledge of him that hath called us to glory and virtue (2 Pet. 1:2, 3).

Truth is experienced as knowledge. Truth is grasped and understood by the mind, experienced or felt in the heart, and acted upon by the will. Truth must be grasped and understood in order for there to be growth and stability in the Christian life. When we truly believe an idea, that idea produces the appropriate attitude in our heart. What we know and feel is what guides our behavior. Our will is influenced by our ideas and attitudes.

In Philippians 4:8, after having called attention to truth, honesty, justice, purity, loveliness, things of good report, virtue, and praise, Paul said, "Think on these things." Why did Paul say, "Think on these things"? It is because thinking transforms behavior. To think on those things was to meditate upon them. There are several references where the Bible speaks about meditation (Jos. 1:8; Ps. 1:2; 19:14; 63:6; 103:4; 119:15; 143:5; and 1 Tim. 4:15).

Why meditate? In meditation, ideas take on depth and become richer, but the main purpose of meditation is for ideas to produce proper attitudes in the heart. In meditation our subconscious mind becomes programmed[20] with ideas and attitudes. This programming of the subconscious mind changes our basic inner nature. The actions that arise out of this programming are expressions of the real self. Our subconscious mind needs to be programmed with the Word of God. It is then that it will become a sanctifying influence in our life to transform our personality into the likeness of Christ.

One of the greatest challenges of the church is to help Christians overcome the conditioning power of the postmodern mood. No acquaintance with the word *postmodernism* or the postmodern paradigm is required to be conditioned by postmodernism. The postmodern mood permeates the atmosphere. Relativism is in the air we breathe. There is no problem in differing with other people on moral and religious matters as long as you do not say that what the other person believes is untrue or is wrong. The influence of privatizing moral and religious thought is not altogether outside the church. The thinking on the subject of Christian liberty on the part of many is not free from the taint of moral relativism. It is not just unbelievers who ask the question, "Who's to say whether so and so is wrong?" Christian liberty is equated, in the minds of many, with the right of preference.

We must not let the influence of our culture rob us of our belief in truth. We must learn how to help those who are conditioned by postmodernism and the postmodern mood to come to a clear recognition of God's truth. In 2 Peter 1:2, 3 which is quoted above, Peter makes it unquestionably clear that we are saved and we advance in godly living through "the knowledge of God, and of Jesus our Lord" and "through the knowledge of him that hath called us to glory and virtue." Knowledge comes through believing, understanding, and experiencing truth.

The Ministry and Our Sanctification

In Ephesians 4:11, 12, Paul said,

> And he gave some, apostles; and some, prophets; and some, evangelists; and some, pastors and teachers; For the perfecting [equipping] of the saints, for the work of the ministry, for the edifying of the body of Christ.

In these verses we see that God has called people and has given them a variety of gifts for ministering to believers. Ministers with a different gift and a different emphasis help in one way while those with another gift and a different emphasis help in another way. It is the plan of God for Christians to benefit from different types of ministries. The work of ministers is designed to help equip the saints for the work of the ministry (verse 12) and to help Christians move toward maturity (verses 13, 14).

The preaching ministry is designed to contribute to our moral sanctification. Paul said to Timothy, "Preach the word; be instant in season, out of season; reprove, rebuke, exhort with all longsuffering and doctrine" (2 Tim. 4:2).

In the New Testament, the sanctification of the members was not only the responsibility of the leadership in the church but the whole body. The writer of Hebrews said:

> Let us consider one another to provoke unto love and to good works: Not forsaking the assembling of ourselves together, as the manner of some is; but exhorting one another: and so much the more, as ye see the day approaching (Heb. 10:24, 25).

Prayer, the Mediatorial Work of Christ, and Sanctification

In time of temptation we are invited to come boldly to the throne of grace. There we will find a compassionate High Priest who can be touched by the feeling of our infirmities. He faced temptation in the real encounters of life. He understands and cares. He is able to help (Heb. 4:14-16). When we come to Him with a desire to overcome sin and a desire to be holy, we can be sure that that is the kind of prayer He wants to answer.

The Guaranteed Results of Sanctification

The design of God to make us righteous is not a design that may or may not be effective. A measure of success is guaranteed. First Corinthians 6:9, 10; Galatians 5:19-21; and Ephesians 5:3-5 make it clear that those who are characterized by gross immorality can lay no claim to salvation.

First John makes it abundantly clear that only those who are basically righteous have any right to claim to be a Christian. On the positive side, he says, "And hereby we do know that we know him, if we keep his commandments" (2:3). On the negative side, he says, "He that saith, I know him, and keepeth not his commandments, is a liar, and the truth is not in him" (2:4). In 3:10 he says, "Whosoever doeth not righteousness is not of God."

First John 3:9 is an unusually strong and clear verse on this subject. This verse refers to "whosoever is born of God." This means every Christian because every Christian is born of God. Concerning one who is born of God, John says he "doth not commit sin . . . and he cannot sin." The meaning here based on the Greek tense is: "He does not go on sinning and he cannot go on sinning." It does not mean that he never sins; but it does mean that sin is not the habit of his life, and it cannot be the habit of his life as long as it can be said he is born of God. I am inclined to believe that in order to understand the meaning of this verse we need to understand the distinction made between *sins of ignorance* and *presumptuous sins* discussed in Numbers 15:27-31. I am inclined to believe that the reference here is not to repeated failures that grow out of weakness, but a defiant, deliberate choice of sin. More attention will be given to this subject when I deal with the subject of perseverance.

It is quite clear that John would have had no hesitancy in saying that those who do not practice righteousness are not saved (1 Jn. 2:3, 4, 15, 16; 3:2, 3, 10; 5:4). There can be no doubt about it. The Bible says that salvation changes the life (2 Cor. 5:17 and Eph. 2:10). There is an interest in righteousness in the heart of a Christian.

A Christian is one who has recognized his or her moral guilt and unworthiness. He has come to Jesus Christ desiring to be forgiven of his sin and wishing to have his experience with sin changed. He has received a new nature through the new birth. This new nature is interested in righteousness. He has declared war on sin. He may not win every battle, but he is a soldier fighting against sin. When he sins, it is the sin of one who is defeated in battle, not the sin of one who had not declared war on sin. When he does sin there is a process that begins within him to work repentance.

The Christian is not and cannot be morally indifferent or unconcerned about sin. There is room for moral growth, but his or her heart is cultivable soil. Man fell from a state of holiness into a state of sin. Redemption is designed to bring man from the state of sin into a state of holiness. If there is no holiness, there is no redemption.[21]

I am fully aware that salvation is by grace, and that it is free and thus a gift. To insist that it must have the results that the Bible unquestionably ascribes to it is in no way to confuse or corrupt grace. We need simply to understand what it is that is free. It is salvation which consists of justification and sanctification. Justification guarantees forgiveness to the person who has it. Sanctification guarantees a changed life to the person who has it.

The fact that a thing is free has nothing to do with whether or not it will work. "Free" simply means that it does not cost anything. The giver of our free salvation has said that it will work. First John 3:9 says that the presence of the new birth prohibits the practice of sin. Galatians 5:17 says that because we have the Holy Spirit we cannot do the things that we would.

In the chapter on the nature of man, I point out that the freedom of the will is a freedom within the framework of possibilities. Unsaved persons and Christians do not have the same framework of possibilities. According to 1 John 3:9 and Galatians 5:17, it is not in the framework of possibilities for the Christian to practice sin. It is within the framework of possibilities for him to please God and to live right.

There is some latitude within this framework of possibilities. There is room for disobedience but not on an unlimited scale. Since there is room for disobedience, Christians must be challenged, exhorted, and admonished. There is also room for variations of growth and progress. Here, there is the need for challenge, exhortation, and encouragement.

Sanctification and Perfection

It is not my purpose here to involve myself in the controversies surrounding the subject of perfection. I will just set forth what I believe the New Testament teaches on the subject and support my case.

The Meaning of the Greek Word *Teleios*

In the majority of places in the New Testament where the word "perfect" is found, it is a translation of the Greek word *teleios* which has as its basic meaning "complete." This is obvious in 1 Corinthians 13:10. Paul says, "But when that which is perfect is come, then that which is in part shall be done away." In this verse, the "perfect" is contrasted with the "part." It is obvious that the perfect is the whole or the complete.

In most cases the completeness referred to is the completeness that is achieved through growth. Thus, the perfect is the mature. This meaning is obvious in Hebrews 5:14 where the Greek word for perfect is translated by the words "of full age." Both the NASB and the NIV translate "mature." The writer of Hebrews is telling us that strong meat belongs to those who through growth and development have reached maturity.

Maturity is obviously the meaning of perfect in Ephesians 4:13. A reading of verses 13 and 14 together shows that the "perfect man" of verse 13 is contrasted with "children" of verse 14. Both the NASB and the NIV translate "mature." The perfect or mature man has the steadfastness that goes with maturity in contrast to the instability that goes with immaturity.

In 1 Corinthians 14:20 the Greek word for perfect (*teleios*) is translated "men." The NASB translates "mature." The NIV translates "adult." Paul is telling us that in malice we should be like children. We are, in understanding, to be mature or adult. In the KJV "men" is used to mean adult.

The thrust of completeness seems to be a little different in Matthew 5:48. Jesus said, "Be ye therefore perfect, even as your Father which is in heaven is perfect." Let us read the word complete in each of the places where the word perfect occurs. This will raise the question: In what way are we to be "complete, even as our Father which is in heaven is complete?" In the previous context beginning with verse 43, Jesus has been talking about two kinds of love. One was a love that only loves those who love us. This would be an incomplete love. The other was a love which embraced both those who love us and those who do not. This would be a complete love. The Father showed His love to both the just and the unjust by sending the rain and sunshine to both. This illustrates the complete or perfect love of the Father. We, like the Father, are to have a complete or perfect love that loves both those who love us and those who do not.

The Meaning of the Greek Words *Artios* and *Katartizmos*

In Ephesians 4:12 and 2 Timothy 3:17 Greek words with a different connotation are used. In 2 Timothy 3:17 the Greek word is *artios*. The meaning of the word for perfect is explained by the last part of the verse. The perfect man is "throughly [thoroughly] furnished unto all good works." He is a prepared person. He is equipped for service.

In Ephesians 4:12 the Greek word is *katartizmos*. The KJV translates "perfecting." The NASB has "equipping." The NIV has "to prepare." This word is closely related to *artios* which was used in 2 Timothy 3:17. The meaning is "the equipping or preparing of the saints for the work of the ministry."

SUMMARY OF THE NEW TESTAMENT VIEW OF PERFECTION

The idea of flawlessness is not the meaning of the Greek words for perfect. The reference in most places is to the complete in contrast with the incomplete, or the finished with the unfinished. An unfinished building would not be perfect even if the workmanship were flawless. The person who is mature physically is perfect even though he is not flawless. The child would not be perfect even if he were flawless in his physical body. It is also obvious that when perfect refers to "equipping," flawlessness is not the point of emphasis.

When we are challenged to be perfect in the New Testament, we are challenged to be mature, complete, and equipped. Certainly, this would call for moral concern and progress, but it does not entangle us with the depressing goal of moral perfection.[22]

Sanctification and Christian Liberty

In Galatians 5:1, Paul says, "Stand fast therefore in the liberty wherewith Christ hath made us free, and be not entangled again with the yoke of bondage."

It will help us understand what Paul has in mind by "liberty" if we will keep in mind what he was trying to accomplish in Galatians. Paul was warning the Galatian Christians against attempts that were being made to lead them back under the Mosaic law. He warns them against two types of legalism: (1) soteriological legalism, and (2) ethical legalism.

Legalism is the wrong dependence on law. Soteriology deals with the doctrine of salvation. Soteriological legalism is a dependence, at least, in some measure on keeping the law as a requirement for justification. Paul deals with soteriological legalism in 3:1-18.

Ethical legalism is a wrong dependence on law to set forth moral and religious responsibility. Ethical legalism seeks to spell out religious responsibility in the form of a detailed set of laws. Paul deals with ethical legalism in 3:19-4:31. It is ethical legalism that Paul is concerned about when he admonished the Galatian Christians to, "Stand fast therefore in the liberty wherewith Christ hath made us free."

THE LAW AS THE *PAIDAGŌGOS*

In Galatians 3:23–4:7, Paul points out that if the Galatian Christians would go back under the law it would be a backward move. To go back under law would be to go back under a "school-master" (KJV). The NASB has "tutor." The Greek word is *paidagōgos*. This word is made up of *pais* (child) and *agō* (to lead). It literally means "child-leader." The literal use of the word *paidagōgos* referred to a trusted slave who was over Greek and Roman boys from about six to sixteen. He gave physical protection, helped instill the values of the family, and watched over the young boy as he went to school. The work of a *paidagōgos* was similar to that of a guardian, tutor, nursemaid, or an English nanny.

Paidagōgos is a carefully chosen metaphor. Whoever is under a *paidagōgos* is considered to be in a state of immaturity. Paul chose that word to tell us that just as the boy who was under the *paidagōgos* was a child, so God's people were viewed as children from Mount Sinai to Calvary. By referring to the law as a *paidagōgos*, Paul was telling us that the Mosaic Law was a method of treatment adapted to the immaturity of God's people when they were under its administration.

DELIVERANCE FROM THE LAW AS THE *PAIDAGŌGOS*

Paul hastens to tell the Galatian Christians that they were no longer under the Mosaic Law as a *paidagōgos*. In verse 25 we read, "But after that faith is come, we are no longer under a "school-master" (*paidagōgos*). The Greek reads literally, "But the faith having come." Just as "the law" was frequently a synonym for the Mosaic Law, "the faith" was also frequently a synonym for the New Covenant. The meaning is that since the faith (the New Testament or New Covenant) has been established by Christ, God's people are no longer under a *paidagōgos* (child-leader). God's people are no longer dealt with through a childhood method of treatment. They are dealt with by an approach that is appropriate for adulthood.

In giving a reason for this deliverance, Paul explains, "For ye are all the children of God by faith in Christ Jesus" (verse 26). The word for children (*huioi*) refers to heirs of legal age or mature sons. Both the NASB and the NIV translate *huioi* as "sons." This verse is not telling us how we became a Christian. It is telling us how we became adult sons. Paul is saying, "For you are all adult sons of God through the faith (the New Covenant) in (in union) with Christ."

Paul continues this line of development through 4:7. The adoption to which Paul refers in 4:5 is not speaking of the way a sinner becomes a Christian. It is telling us how God's people were delivered from a childhood method of treatment and placed under a method of treatment appropriate for adulthood. To be adopted as Paul is using the term is to be delivered from the *paidagōgos* and to be placed in the position of an adult son. In connection with the establishment of the New

Covenant by Jesus Christ, God's people were delivered from the *paidagōgos* and given the status of adult sons.

To give a full development of how Paul develops this line of thought is beyond the purpose of this chapter. For a more thorough treatment, see the appendix entitled, "Legalism in the Book of Galatians," page 489.

The Meaning of Deliverance From the Law as a *Paidagōgos*

When most people think about deliverance from the law they think of deliverance from the curse of the law. That is not the thrust of Galatians 3:23–4:7.We may avoid a lot of confusion if we understand there are two ways that we are delivered from the law: (1) We are delivered from the curse of the law, and (2) We are delivered from the law as the *paidagōgos* (child-leader).

We experience deliverance from the curse of the law the moment we are saved. Believers have always been delivered from the curse of the law when they were saved. This includes all who were saved before the coming of Christ.

Deliverance from the law as a *paidagōgos* was a historical event that took place when the New Covenant was established. It happened for all of God's people at the same time. As I have pointed out above, it is this deliverance that Paul is talking about in Galatians 3:23–4:7.

To go back under law would be to go back under a *paidagōgos*. It would be to trade the superiority of an adulthood method of treatment for the inferiority of a childhood method of treatment. It would be to trade an approach to being taught moral and religious truth on the adult level for an elementary approach fitted for childhood. That would be trading freedom for bondage (or slavery). The childhood method of treatment is appropriate for children, but if adults are treated that way it becomes bondage. Paul was appealing to these Christians to see the absurdity of such a move. This is what he was driving at when he said, "How turn ye again to the weak and beggarly elements, whereunto ye desire again to be in bondage?" (Gal. 4:9). That would be ethical legalism.

The most thoroughgoing ethical legalism that the world has ever known was Pharisaism. In its oral tradition or oral law, it went far beyond what was written in the Mosaic Law.[23] While the Mosaic Law was not nearly as binding as the legalism of the Pharisees, it was a form of ethical legalism when compared to the liberty of the New Testament.

Christian Liberty

Christian liberty is not a liberty to do as you please. It is a liberty to cease to be incumbered with the more detailed approach of a childhood method of treatment. It is an opportunity to grow up and act responsibly.

ROMANS 14:5

In recent years, the confusion of Christian liberty with moral relativism has greatly weakened the way the church thinks and feels about sin. A misunderstanding of Romans 14:5 has contributed to this problem. Paul said, "One man regards one day above another, another regards everyday *alike*. Let each man be fully convinced in his own mind" (NASB).

A misreading of this verse has left many with the viewpoint that unless there is a direct command in the Bible against the matter in question each person can have whatever opinion he or she chooses about it. That is not what the verse says.

Paul is not saying that one person's opinion is as good as another's. He is speaking of the individual's right to apply *the principles of Scripture* to the areas of life that are not specifically spelled out in the New Testament. It is the individual Christian's responsibility to draw principles from what is taught in the Bible and to apply those principles to life. There is no kinship between being "fully convinced in his own mind" of Romans 14:5 and the right of opinion in moral relativism.

The Greek word for "fully convinced" is *plērophoreō*. It calls upon a person, in deciding on the matter under question, to make a full use of his or her mind. He is to study the teachings of the Bible that seem to be pertinent to the matter and make the decision which he is fully convinced best accords with the Bible. He is to abide by his integrity, and respect the decision of another person who follows this same procedure, but arrives at a different conclusion. Paul is not giving validity to preferences that are based on mere feelings or cultural trends that have no regard for God or the Bible.

Personal Reflections

When it comes to the subject of sin, there have been a lot of changes in the church world in the time covered by my memory. Let us take a look at what has happened within the church in the last fifty or sixty years on the subject of legalism and Christian liberty.

While I was brought up in a very conservative background in the 1930s and the 1940s, I was not brought up on a long list of things that were right and wrong. But it seemed as if everywhere I went, right and wrong, honesty, integrity, purity, modesty, responsibility, duty, diligence, faithfulness, loyalty, self-control, respect for age, respect for authority, concern for others, thoughtfulness, kindness, courtesy, politeness, manners, dignity, beauty, and excellence were emphasized and extolled. This made a tremendous impression on me. I would not trade that heritage for any amount of material wealth.

Substance deals with basic ideas, concepts and principles. It deals with truth on the foundational level. It deals with universal truth. *Form* deals with how we manifest the concern expressed by substance. Form can vary, but it must always be appropriate.

The virtues given above deal with substance. The way you manifest the concern set forth in the substance is form. Some attention was given to form. But far more attention was given to substance than form. Form was seen to be rooted and grounded in substance.

When I came to Free Will Baptist Bible College in 1948, I was introduced to rules, teaching on etiquette, and various experiences that were designed to help maintain and promote the virtues mentioned above. This same thing was happening in many other Christian schools during that time.[24]

Many who were trained under this system decided to take a shortcut. It seemed to be a lot easier to bypass the substance and go straight to the form. It was easier to simply give people a list than it was to show that the form was rooted and grounded in substance. There was an attempt to give *form* an absolute status.

By the time of the 1960s, it was very obvious the virtues that had been extolled in the culture of 1930s and 1940s were losing support in society. What we now know to be postmodernism was challenging the very *substance* which many conservative Christian colleges and churches had sought to maintain and promote through the form of the rules they had put in place. All of this was very disturbing. It was disturbing to those whose roots took them back to the time when the virtues had been extolled in the society. It was disturbing to those who had chosen the short cut of relying on lists. There was a tendency to meet the challenge of the change in the culture by producing more intense and stronger preaching about the things on the list.

I was very concerned at what was taking place. The substance involved in the virtues that I have been discussing was losing ground in the culture. Much of the attention that was given to expressing concern over what was happening sought to solve the problem by giving heavy emphasis to form. Form came across in terms of a list.

In 1968, I started teaching a course called "Biblical Ethics." In this course, I tried to show that we must major on substance and principles. It is not as simple as having a good list to show to people. In 1973, my book *Biblical Ethics* was published.[25] While the terms *form* and *substance* do not appear in the book, I think anyone who reads the book will agree that the concepts of form and substance permeate the book. Major attention in the book deals with the concept of substance. I was having to come to grips with what was happening during that time in the culture, the churches, and how to carry out my responsibilities as a student dean.

LONG-LIST LEGALISM AND SHORT-LIST LEGALISM

There was some just criticism that could be brought against the attempt on the part of many to take the shortcut of letting *form* do the work. To bring correction, the doctrine of Christian liberty received a renewed interest. There is a valid doctrine of Christian liberty. But there is a serious fault in much that is called Christian liberty.

The problem is that in many cases one form of legalism has been exchanged for another form of legalism. An over-dependence upon law to express moral or ethical responsibility is ethical legalism. There are two kinds of ethical legalism: *long-list legalism* and *short-list legalism.*

A person is not a legalist simply because he has deep convictions or because he may have a list. What makes it legalism is when he attempts to turn his list into laws and tries to let the laws do the work. He does not ground them in substance.

Moral and ethical values cannot be maintained unless the form is grounded in and is an expression of substance. We must recognize that even when people are deeply committed to substance there will not be unanimous agreement on form. A healthy amount of tension on the differences in the form that best preserves the substance is necessary and helpful.

There can be some justification in calling people "legalists" who give undue attention to lists of do's and don'ts. Some have given too much attention to form and not enough attention to substance.

At the same time, I think more recent times have produced a trend toward short-list legalism. Much of what is called Christian liberty is short-list legalism. When the only thing that can be recognized as sin is what is specifically called a sin in the Bible, that is not Christian liberty. It is short-list legalism. It is legalism because it *only* recognizes a thing to be a sin if there is a law against it in the Bible. Christian liberty recognizes the responsibility to apply the principles of the Bible and recognize that some things are sins that are not named in the Bible.

THE IMPORTANCE OF IDEALS

I know we would not believe that all of the virtues mentioned above have equal value. Certainly, it is worse to violate morals than it is ideals. At the same time, we cannot vacate our responsibility in the area of ideals. We must give serious thought to the difference between the impact of postmodernism on ideals and the impact of Christianity on ideals. I understand that we must be able to meet people where they are. The question is where do we go from there. We must have as our aim to lead people into the full experience of what it means to be made in the image of God.

We must learn to challenge people to higher ideals and do it in such a way that those who do not measure up to these ideals will not feel alienated.

I am afraid that we underestimate the damage that postmodernism has done to the cause of Christ when it undermines ideals. I will illustrate with young people. It is very difficult to be a young person in today's culture. The rejection in our culture of the traditional concern for ideals is a manifestation of the spirit of the age. This rejection is seen in matters like music and dress. It is through matters like this that young people get caught up in the spirit of the age. It is not as easy as saying that these things do not matter. This negative attitude crosses over into the non-negotiable moral areas.

We are not going to solve the problem for them or for ourselves by simply negating particular things that young people want to do. Particulars grow out of universals. Universals deal with substance. Particulars deal with form. Universals are embedded in worldviews. If we do not want young people to be conditioned by postmodern thinking, we must provide the opportunity for them to be conditioned by Christian worldview thinking. Christian ideals flow from Christian worldview thinking.

THE NEED FOR AGREEMENT ON SUBSTANCE

We may not be able to agree on matters of form, but there should be agreement on substance. Would we not agree that there should be a strong emphasis on right and wrong, honesty, integrity, purity, modesty, responsibility, duty, diligence, faithfulness, loyalty, self-control, respect for age, respect for authority, concern for others, thoughtfulness, kindness, courtesy, politeness, manners, dignity, beauty, and excellence? We need to promote these virtues among both the old and the young. How can we do less?

Both the long-list legalists and the short-list legalists have failed to give proper emphasis to substance. Let's give more attention to virtues. Surely, we can agree at that level. To give proper emphasis to substance will not erase all differences about form, but it will make it easier to discuss the question of appropriate form.

Sanctification for Those With a Difficult Past

Ever since the fall of Adam and Eve, depravity has been a powerful force at work in human beings. Vile sins are nothing new. However, there have been times when there were more effective restraints in society than there are at the present time. When modernism recognized that there was a moral nature to reality and held to moral ideals, and Christianity gave a strong emphasis to teaching morals, things were different. It did not produce an ideal society. But it did make a difference in the moral climate of the nation. The influence of postmodernism has been in the direction of moral relativism and nihilism. This has led to more of a moral breakdown than existed when modernism was the predominate secular influence.

We are living in dark days as far as alcohol, illegal drugs, sexual immorality of every imaginable kind, abortion, violence, and crime are concerned. Many young people have traveled the route of sin by the time they are 15 or 16 years of age (some even earlier than that). This means that by the time these people are first confronted with the gospel their lives bear the scars of deep sin. Many are mixed-up, confused, enslaved, tattered, and torn.

We have a message of hope for those whose lives have been ruined by sin. God is not only in the business of forgiving sin, He is also in the business of changing lives.

I do not have an oversimplified view of what this involves, but I refuse to believe that there are lives too complicated to be transformed by the grace of God. I believe it is possible for the grace of God to take the dishonest and make them honest, to take the impure and make them pure, to take the unrighteous and make them righteous, and to take the unholy and make them holy.

If you have had a past that has not been complicated by the type of sins that I have mentioned, you have much to be thankful for. If the same can be said for your family, you need to count your blessings.

If there is no one in your church that comes from a background like I have described, you need to rethink what you are doing. If your church does not have people who were saved out of deep sin, it is not because you are doing a good job, it is because you are not ministering to today's world.

1 CORINTHIANS 6:9-11

First Corinthians 6:9-11 is the best passage in all of the Bible to use to give people hope who been involved in deep sin. Paul says:

> Know ye not that the unrighteous shall not inherit the kingdom of God? Be not deceived: nether fornicators, nor idolaters, nor adulterers, nor effeminate, nor abusers of themselves with mankind, Nor thieves, nor covetous, nor drunkards, nor revilers, nor extortioners, shall inherit the kingdom of God. And such were some of you: but ye are washed, but ye are sanctified, but ye are justified in the name of the Lord Jesus, and by the Spirit of our God.

Corinth was a very wicked city. From Paul's words we can assume that there were people in the church at Corinth who had been saved out of a background of involvement with the sins that he had mentioned in verses 9 and 10. That is implied by Paul's words, "And such were some of you."

When Paul said "Such were some of you," he was telling these people that God had written past tense on their sins. They had not only been forgiven; they had been changed. They had become new creatures in Christ (2 Cor. 5:17). They were no longer the kind of person they used to be. That is the hope God gives to those who have explored the depth of sins.

When the man who once practiced dishonesty turns from his sin and turns to Christ and practices honesty, that person is no longer a dishonest person but an honest person. When the woman who once practiced impurity turns from her sin to Christ and practices purity, she is no longer an impure person but a pure person. I do not think that any of us would like to view ourselves as a combination of all of the bad things that we ever did or thought about doing. We are what we have become in Christ. God offers every human being the opportunity to become a new person. The devil tries to tell some people who lived sordid lives before they were saved that because of their past they have no right to speak out against sin and for righteousness. Who is in a better position to speak out against sin and for righteousness than the person who knows from experience the devastating effects of sin and by experience what it means to be set free and transformed?

When I think of God's amazing grace and how it takes a sinner and makes him righteous, the unclean and makes him clean, the impure and makes him pure, the ungodly and makes him godly, and the unholy and makes him holy, my mind goes to the poem, "The Touch of the Master's Hand."[26]

'Twas battered and scarred, and the auctioneer
Thought it scarcely worth his while
To waste much time on the old violin,
But he held it up with a smile.
"What am I bidden, good folks," he cried,
"Who'll start the bidding for me?"
"A dollar, a dollar"; then, "Two! Only two?
Two dollars, and who'll make it three?
Three dollars, once; three dollars, twice;
Going for three—" But no,
From the room, far back, a gray-haired man
Came forward and picked up the bow;
Then, wiping the dust from the old violin,
And tightening the loose strings,
He played a melody pure and sweet
As a caroling angel sings.

The music ceased, and the auctioneer,
With a voice that was quiet and low,
Said: "What am I bid for the old violin?"
And he held it up with the bow.
"A thousand dollars, and who'll make it two?
Two thousand! And who'll make it three?
Three thousand, once; three thousand, twice,
And going, and gone," said he.
The people cheered, but some of them cried,
"We do not quite understand
What changed its worth." Swift came the reply:
"The touch of a master's hand."

And many a man with life out of tune,
And battered and scarred with sin,
Is auctioned cheap to the thoughtless crowd,

Much like the old violin.
A "mess of pottage," a glass of wine;
A game—and he travels on.
He is "going" once, and "going" twice,
He's "going" and almost "gone."
But the Master comes, and the foolish crowd

Never can quite understand
The worth of a soul and the change that's
   wrought
By the touch of the Master's hand.

—Myra Brooks Welch

THE CASE OF MARY MAGDALENE

In many cases those who are saved out of a difficult past feel that even though they will go to Heaven when they die that they can make no worthwhile contribution to the cause of Christ. Let's look at some cases in the New Testament. Mary Magdalene was a woman out of whom Jesus had cast seven demons (Lk. 8:2). How would that look on a person's resume? Every time after this occasion, except one, where we see the name of Mary Magdalene (Mt. 27:55, 56, 61; 28:1; Mk. 15:40, 41, 44-47; 16:1, 2, 9, 10; Lk. 24:10; and Jn. 20:1-18) her name is mentioned first. This indicates that she was the leader of the women who followed Jesus. The only exception is John 19:25. In this case Jesus' mother is mentioned first, then her sister, and then Mary the wife of Cleophas before mentioning Mary Magdalene. The probable reason for not mentioning Mary Magdalene first is out of respect for Jesus' mother. In John 20, we learn that Mary Magdalene was the first person to whom Jesus revealed himself after the resurrection (verse 11-16). She was the first person ever to tell about the resurrection of Christ. She was the one who told the disciples about the resurrection (verse 18). Mary Magdalene was a worthwhile follower of Jesus. When we consider what she was before she met Jesus and what she became through knowing Jesus, it should be a source of encouragement to those whose lives suffered severe damage from sin before they came to know Jesus.

THE CASE OF THE APOSTLE PAUL

Paul spoke of himself as one "Who before was a blasphemer, and a persecutor, and injurious" (1 Tim. 1:13). It would have been understandable if the Apostle Paul had spent the rest of his life beating himself over the head for his part in persecution of believers. It would have been understandable if God had not chosen him to be an apostle. However, God chose one who had persecuted the church to be the apostle to the Gentiles. He wrote more books in the New Testament than any other person. He is considered by many to be the best Christian who ever lived. Paul's words in 1 Timothy 1:15, 16 are filled with hope that God can save anybody and make that person useful in His service. The NIV captures the spirit of what Paul is telling us when it translates:

> Here is a trustworthy saying that deserves full acceptance: Christ Jesus came into the world to save sinners—of whom I am the worst. But for that very reason I was shown mercy so that in me, the worst of sinners, Christ Jesus might display his unlimited patience as an example for those who would believe on him and receive eternal life (1 Tim. 1:15, 16, NIV).

When we get a glimpse of the holiness of God and see our sin for what it really is, all of us feel like saying with Isaiah, " Woe is me! For I am undone; because I am a man of unclean lips, and I dwell in the midst of a people of unclean lips: for mine eyes have seen the King, the LORD of hosts" (Is. 6:5). For all who feel this sense of being undone and unworthy, Paul cries out, "God's grace is sufficient!" He can forgive and He can transform. Jesus calls out, "Come unto Me all you who labor and are heavy laden, and I will give you rest" (Mt. 11:28, NKJV).

13

The Condition of Salvation

I have chosen to discuss the nature of salvation first and then come to a discussion of the condition of salvation. As a rule it is done the other way around. I have chosen to do it this way because I believe we can get a better understanding of the condition of salvation this way.

Repentance and Faith: One Condition or Two?

THE PROBLEM SET FORTH

As a rule, we say that there is only one condition of salvation. That condition is faith. However, we frequently say that repentance is a condition of salvation. In discussions of repentance and faith, it frequently sounds as if there are two conditions of salvation. How many conditions of salvation are there?

Numerous times in the New Testament, faith is presented as the only condition of salvation (Jn. 1:12; 3:16, 18, 36; Acts 16:31; Rom. 3:22, 28; 4:1-25; 5:1; Gal. 2:16; 3:1-18; Eph. 2:8, 9; and 1 Jn. 5:13).

There are also places where repentance, without the occurrence of the word faith, is mentioned as the condition of salvation (Lk. 24:47; Acts 2:38; 3:19; 5:31; 11:18; 17:30; 26:20; 2 Tim. 2:25; Heb. 6:6; and 2 Pet. 3:9).

What conclusion do we draw from this? If we draw the conclusion that repentance and faith make up two conditions of salvation, there would be only three places in the New Testament where both conditions would be mentioned in the same passage (Mk. 1:15; Acts 20:21; and Heb. 6:1). Would we conclude that these are the only three places where a person is told how to be saved in one passage? Would we have to pick up one condition in one place and one in another if we did not use one of these verses?

If we want to make repentance and faith two conditions of salvation, what do we do with the fact that the words "repent" and "repentance" do not occur in the Gospel of John nor in 1, 2, and 3 John? Do we conclude that these books do not have the complete requirement for salvation?

I think it would be strange if the condition(s) of salvation were found in only three places in the Bible. The preferred conclusion is to believe that there is only one condition of salvation if we can support that conclusion. There is a problem involved in trying to make a choice between repentance and faith for the condition because both are presented in the Scripture as the condition of salvation.

I believe the answer is found in looking at repentance and faith as one condition because both are presented in the Scripture as the only condition of salvation. They both speak of the same experience.

THE MEANING OF REPENTANCE

The Greek word *metanoeō* which is translated "repent" means to change one's mind. So far as the Greek word is concerned, in its usage, it could refer to a change of mind whether for good or for bad. R. C. Trench says, "Plutarch (Sept. Sap. Conu. 21) tells us of two murderers, who having spared a child, afterward 'repented' (*metenoēsan*), and sought to slay it."

Trench goes on to say:

> It is only after *metanoia* has been taken up into the uses of Scripture, or of writers dependent upon Scripture, that it comes predominantly to mean change of mind, taking a wiser view of the past.[1]

To change the mind in repentance refers to the change of the mind, heart, and will. One viewpoint is exchanged for another viewpoint. There is an appropriate change of attitude and behavior to go along with the exchange of viewpoint. It is a reference to a change of attitude and behavior that Paul has in mind in Acts 26:20. He preached "to the Gentiles, that they should do works meet [fit] for repentance" (see also Mt. 3:8 and Lk. 3:8).

In repentance there is a change of mind. There is a change of opinion, viewpoint, or conviction. In the repentance related to salvation, the question is: On what does the change focus? This question will be answered by an examination of the passages where repentance is used in connection with salvation.

The passages where the context clarifies the area of change in repentance are found in Acts. If we read these passages and translate repent "to change one's mind," it will help us to see what areas of thought the speakers had in mind. On the day of Pentecost when Peter said to the Jews, "Repent" (Acts 2:38), in the context they were to repent of their unbelief toward Jesus Christ (Acts 2:23, 36). This would involve not only a change of opinion but of attitude and behavior. The same basic thought is seen in Acts 3:19 and 5:31. In Acts 17:30, on the negative side, they were to change their mind regarding idolatry (verses 22-29). On the positive side, they were to believe in Jesus Christ (verse 31).

THE RELATIONSHIP BETWEEN REPENTANCE AND FAITH

In repentance, there is a "from" and a "to." The exact nature of the "from" may vary from one person to another. Some need to change from a simple case of unbelief. Others need to change from false religion or paganism. Whatever the case may be about the nature of what a person may need to change his or her mind from, the "to" for all is the same. All are to change to faith in Jesus Christ.

While repentance includes a "from" and a "to," the stress of repentance is on the *to* instead of the *from.* Repentance is a forward moving word. This is not to diminish the importance of the from It is to place primary focus on the to. The "to" of repentance is identical with faith. In Acts 20:21 Paul speaks of "repentance *toward* God." In 2 Timothy 2:25, he speaks of "repentance *to* the acknowledging of the truth." [Italics in these verses mine.]

Faith and repentance are involved in each other. To exercise faith implies a change from unbelief, whatever the form of unbelief may be. Repentance terminates in faith. If we tell a person to repent, or if we tell him to believe, we are telling him to do the same thing. Repent stresses that change is involved. Faith stresses the end to which change is directed.

We can illustrate the difference between repentance and faith this way. If we tell a man in Atlanta to leave Atlanta and go to New York, that would illustrate repentance. If we should tell the man in Atlanta to go to New York, that would illustrate faith. We would be telling the person to do the same thing no matter which approach we might choose.

A word needs to be said about sorrow and repentance. Some equate sorrow for sins with repentance. Sorrow is not repentance. It leads to repentance. Paul tells us that "godly sorrow worketh repentance to salvation" (2 Cor. 7:10).

Faith is the primary term because it is faith that describes the positive response in which repentance terminates. Repentance speaks of a change *from* something *to* something. Faith explains what the something is to which repentance is directed.

When we speak of repentance and faith in salvation, we are talking about one condition for salvation, not two. To experience repentance and to experience faith is to experience the same thing. Since faith is the primary term, we will now turn our attention to a discussion of saving faith.

The Nature of Saving Faith

THE MEANING OF SAVING FAITH

Saving faith is the abandonment of all trust in self or anything else and a complete, confident trust in Christ for salvation.

The problem that plagues us is: How do we avoid leaving the impression that salvation can be a superficial experience if faith is the only condition for salvation? Some try to cope with this problem by the way they explain the nature of faith. They try in some way to explain that faith, by definition, involves obedience. But at the same time they explain that faith is distinguished from works.

As I see it, we do not avoid the impression that salvation is a superficial experience by the way we define faith. Faith is not complicated. There are two elements of faith: (1) acceptance of redemptive truth, and (2) trust.

In the history of God's people, the content of saving faith involved the redemptive truth with which God had confronted people at a given time in history. They were to accept this revelation to be true. For us, we are to believe the redemptive revelation of God as it is revealed in Jesus Christ. I can see how a person may have saving faith and have some misunderstanding of what the Bible says about Christ. I cannot see how a person can have saving faith and not believe what the Bible says about Jesus Christ. Faith believes what the Bible says about Jesus Christ to be true.

In the trust element of saving faith, there is dependence upon God for salvation. In the New Testament, this is dependence upon Jesus Christ for salvation.

We do not safeguard ourselves from superficial Christianity by the way we define faith. It does not take some special knowledge of Hebrew or Greek to define faith so the safeguards can be built in our definition. What we need is a correct definition of salvation.

We believe "for salvation." Salvation is the goal for faith. There will be no superficial experience for the person who experiences salvation unless salvation is superficial.

Salvation consists of justification and sanctification. The whole study of sanctification, especially the guaranteed results of sanctification, made it clear that sanctification cannot be superficial. We cannot believe for the forgiveness of sins without believing for a change in our experience with God and sin. If we receive salvation, we will receive forgiveness of sin and a change in our experience with God and sin. That will not be superficial.

Where the problem comes is when we tell people they can be forgiven and leave the impression that a change in experience is optional. This opens the way for a lot of professions in which there is no salvation. The tragedy is not that such people receive Jesus as Savior, but not as Lord. The tragedy is that they neither receive Jesus as Lord nor Savior.

There can be no exercise of saving faith without at least some understanding of what salvation is all about. Saving faith is exercised by a person who realizes that salvation is designed to forgive people of sin and restore them to the experience of holiness. Such a person realizes that he or she is a sinner. He sees sin as serious. He sees himself as unworthy and condemned. He is under conviction. The problem of sin is real in his or her mind and in his heart. He wants something done about sin in his life. He wants to be forgiven. He wants to be changed. He understands that Jesus Christ has suffered on the cross and died to save him. He believes what God has said in the Bible about Jesus as Savior. He trusts in Jesus as Savior. In so doing, he trusts in Jesus to forgive his sins and to change his life. According to Christian theology, upon this act of faith, based on the atoning work of Christ, the person is justified and sanctified.

There is no saving faith except where a person has become aware of his or her sins and has a changed attitude toward sin and Jesus Christ. The termination of that change, we call faith. The process of change including the termination of the process, we call repentance. Both terms need to be used. Faith needs to be used to explain the real nature of the condition of salvation. Repentance needs to be used to make people aware that a deep change of mind, heart, and will is involved in the exercise of saving faith.

I like the way it is done among the Baptists in the Former Soviet Union. When someone makes a profession of faith, they say, "He repented." When I asked Oleg, the interpreter who traveled with my wife and me when we were in the FSU, when he was saved, he said, "I repented in 1988." Christians are regularly referred to as believers. But they speak of the initial act of faith as repentance.

FAITH AND THE PERSONALITY

The mind, heart, and will are involved in saving faith. With the mind, the truth about sin, Jesus Christ, and salvation is comprehended objectively. The content of the truth is grasped and understood.

With the heart, what is grasped objectively by the mind is grasped subjectively. The truth about sin becomes real. Conviction takes place. The truth about Jesus Christ and salvation becomes real. The reality of the truth conditions the heart for action to follow.

The emotions are definitely involved in the experience of faith and the total Christian experience. We feel what we believe. We are not emotional blanks. Emotions are a part of the human personality by creation. Emotions need to be based on Truth and disciplined by Truth, but emotions must not be downgraded.

With the will there is the commitment of the personality to Jesus Christ. We receive Jesus Christ. The will can act only where there is a prepared mind and a prepared heart. The will, out of the prepared mind and heart, sets in action the response of faith. What is objectively perceived by the mind is subjectively felt by the heart, and subjectively appropriated by the will.

FAITH AS A GIFT

Jesus said in John 6:44, "No man can come to me, except the Father which hath sent me draw him." There must be a move toward man on God's part before there will be any response on man's part. Not only is there a need for a divine invitation, but there is also a need of a divine drawing. The Holy Spirit must take the Word of God and work in the human heart and mind to prepare the heart and mind before there can be the response of faith from a sinner.

It does not belong within the framework of possibilities of the unsaved person for him to be able to respond to Jesus Christ apart from the work of the Holy Spirit. The Holy Spirit works as the Word is preached. The human heart can resist this work of the Holy Spirit, but where the Holy Spirit is allowed to work He enlightens the mind concerning sin, Jesus Christ, and salvation. He produces conviction in the heart. The preparation of the mind and heart by the Word of God and the Holy Spirit creates a framework of possibilities in which a person can respond in faith to Jesus Christ. The response of faith is not guaranteed, but it is made possible. The person can say, "Yes," or he or she can say, "No."

Faith is called a gift because it cannot be exercised without the work of the Holy Spirit. At the same time, it is a response of the person in such a way that it is a response of his or her personality. It is in a real sense his own action. If a human being is to be treated as a person, in some real sense the action must be the person's own regardless of how much divine aid may be given. Otherwise, a human being has been reduced to a subpersonal being.

Some have understood "the faith of the Son of God" in Galatians 2:20 and similar references to mean that saving faith is Christ's faith given to the person. It is a gift in that it is taking Christ's faith and giving it to the person.

In the expression "the faith of the Son of God," the genitive case in the Greek could be considered a subjective genitive and thus be understood as "faith belonging to Christ." It can also be considered an objective genitive and would mean "faith in Christ." While either interpretation would be possible so far as Greek grammar is concerned, only one is possible in the light of Scripture. The Bible addresses us and tells us to believe. We are nowhere told that Jesus is to believe for us. It is clear that "the faith of the Son of God" is not Jesus' faith, but it is our faith in Jesus.

Faith is not some substance that exists outside of us that is to be given to us. It is an experience that must take place within us. That is the only way we can have faith. Faith is a gift in the sense that

God gives to us the aid that is necessary, without which, we could not exercise faith. It is not a gift in the sense that it is not an exercise of our own personality.

FAITH THE CONDITION, NOT THE GROUND OF OUR SALVATION

The difference between condition and ground could be illustrated this way. The condition for a chair supporting me is for me to sit in the chair. When I am sitting in the chair, the chair is the ground of my support.

The ground of our salvation is Jesus Christ and His atoning work. The condition of our salvation is the response of faith.

Sometimes people make the mistake of focusing more on the condition than the ground. In looking for assurance, they examine their faith instead of Christ. If I want to have confidence that a chair will hold me up, I will examine the chair, not my confidence in the chair. As I examine the chair, if it is well built, my confidence will be made sure.

If I want my assurance of salvation to be strong, I should examine Christ—the ground of my salvation. In so doing, I will have a strong faith and confidence. If I examine my faith, I will tend to have doubts. It is not faith in faith that is the condition of salvation. It is faith in Christ.

FAITH AND DOUBT

Sometimes, we get caught up in the reasoning that if salvation is by faith, a Christian cannot doubt his or her salvation because faith rules out doubt. At first thought, the definition of saving faith would seem to make it sound as if there is no room for doubt. Saving faith is a complete, confident trust in Christ for salvation. Doubt is not exactly consistent with a complete, confident trust.

How do we harmonize the possibility of doubt with saving faith? Definitions describe a thing in its ideal, healthy state. For example, a definition of a dog would include that a dog is a four-legged animal. Yet, I have seen dogs that had only three legs. A dog could be a dog with fewer than four legs, but it would not be a normal dog in full health. Saving faith in its healthy state does not include doubts. However, saving faith can and does exist where doubts also exist. As a rule, these doubts will clear up with a better understanding of doctrines of salvation. However, in some cases the difficulty is not cleared up this way. The problem is related to complications in the person's background.

The Difference Between Classical Arminianism and Classical Calvinism on Faith as a Gift

I make the reference here to Classical Calvinism because there are some trends in Calvinistic thought that would approach the question somewhat differently. I will deal with that kind of Calvinism later. Herein lies the bottom line difference between Classical Arminianism and Classical Calvinism. Calvinism insists that regeneration, which is irresistible grace, precedes saving faith. Regeneration makes the "yes" answer of faith in Christ a guaranteed result. The "no" answer is not an option for the person who has been regenerated by the Holy Spirit. In such a case, we are dealing with *cause* and *effect*. Regeneration is the *cause*. Faith is the *effect*. R. C. Sproul, in explaining the view of Augustine points out:

> When Augustine says grace is irresistible, he means it is effectual. It is a monergistic work of God that accomplishes what he intends it to accomplish. Divine grace changes the human heart, resurrecting the sinner from spiritual death to spiritual life. Formerly the sinner was unwilling and not inclined to choose Christ, but now he is not only willing but eager to choose Christ. . . .

Sproul rejects the concept that the sinner is "dragged to Christ against his will." He goes on to say:

> This view is clearly monergistic *at* the initial point of the sinner's movement from unbelief to faith. The whole process, however, is not monergistic. Once the operative grace of regeneration is given, the rest of the process is synergistic. That is, after the soul has been changed by the effectual or irresistible grace, the person himself chooses Christ. God does not make the choice for him. It is the person who believes, not God who believes for him. Indeed the rest of the Christian life of sanctification unfolds in a synergistic pattern.[2] [italics his]

REGENERATION: MONERGISTIC IN BOTH CLASSICAL ARMINIANISM AND CLASSICAL CALVINISM

While there is an important difference between my view of regeneration and the view of Calvinism, the difference is not *monergism*. In both views regeneration is solely the work of God. In Calvinism, the order is regeneration, faith, justification, and sanctification. In my view the order is faith, justification, regeneration, and sanctification.

THE WORK OF THE HOLY SPIRIT IN FAITH

I repeat here what I said in "Chapter 9: The Nature of Man":

> Jesus makes it clear that it does not fall within the framework of possibilities for a sinner to respond to the gospel unless he is drawn by the Holy Spirit (Jn. 6:44). The influence of the Holy Spirit working in the heart of the person who hears the gospel brings about a framework of possibilities in which a person can say yes or no to the gospel. If he says yes, it is his choice. If he says no, it is his choice.[3]

The work of the Holy Spirit in this case is solely a work of God and would thus be *monergistic*. It is not regeneration. It can be resisted.

In Calvinism, the only work of God that is capable of resulting in saving faith is regeneration. Regeneration so transforms the person that he or she will freely believe. It is irresistible. The "No" answer is ruled out.

THE QUESTION OF SYNERGISM

It is my contention that faith is *synergistic* in both Calvinism and Arminianism. Sproul says in the quotation given above, "Once the operative grace of regeneration is given, the rest of the process is synergistic. That is, after the soul has been changed by the effectual or irresistible grace, the person himself chooses Christ. God does not make the choice for him."

It seems to be evident that *Sproul considers faith to be synergistic.* If there is any doubt in anyone's mind, Sproul removes the doubt. In another source he says, "Faith is not monergistic."[4] Sometimes it sounds like Calvinists are saying that faith is *monergistic.* But the nature of the case makes that impossible. By definition, faith is a human act of believing. Active participation in faith on the part of the believer means that it cannot be otherwise than *synergistic.* In my view we are dealing with influence and response. The person can say, "Yes" only by the aid of the Holy Spirit. But under this circumstance, he can say, "Yes" or "No." Human participation *cannot* be ruled out of faith in *either* Calvinism or Arminianism.

AN INCONSISTENCY IN CALVINISM

In Calvinism it is impossible for a person to believe unless he or she is first regenerated. There is also another impossibility. It is impossible for sanctification to take place *prior to* justification. Let me repeat a quotation given from Robert Haldane in the previous chapter. He explains:

> So long as the sinner is under the guilt of sin God can have no friendly intercourse with him; for what communion hath light with darkness? But Christ having canceled his people's guilt, having redeemed them from the curse of the law, and invested them with the robe of his righteousness, there is no longer any obstacle to their communion with God, or any barrier to the free ingress of sanctifying grace.[5]

Following through with this reasoning, justification must be *prior to* regeneration. This is true since regeneration is the initial work of sanctification. In support of this conclusion, I will give again a quotation used in the previous chapter from Louis Berkhof. Berkhof tells us that "regeneration is the beginning of sanctification."[6] He goes on to quote A. H. Strong with approbation. Strong says, "It (sanctification) is distinguished from regeneration as growth from birth, or as the strengthening of the holy disposition from the original impartation of it."[7]

In his discussion on justification, Berkhof points out that there have been those who advocated the idea that the elect were justified from eternity. He would place antinomians and some Reformed theologians in this category. He goes on to give a thorough refutation of this view.[8] He explains, "The elect are not personally justified in the Scriptural sense until they accept Christ by faith and thus appropriate His merits."[9]

One of the arguments, according to Berkhof, that has been used in support of eternal justification is:

The sinner receives the initial grace of regeneration on the basis of the imputed right-eousness of Christ. Consequently, the merits of Christ must have been imputed to him before his regeneration.

Berkhof's response is:

> But while this consideration leads to the conclusion that justification logically precedes regeneration, it does not prove the priority of justification in a temporal sense. The sin-ner can receive the grace of regeneration on the basis of a justification ideally existing in the counsel of God and certain to be realized in the life of the sinner.[10]

Berkhof recognizes the problem of having regeneration prior to justification. He does not reject the conclusion that regeneration is dependent on justification. He recognizes that justification is logically prior to regeneration. But he says that "it does not prove the priority of justification in a temporal sense." His only answer is, "The sinner can receive the grace of regeneration on the basis of a justification ideally existing in the counsel of God and certain to be realized in the life of the sinner."

If indeed it is true that regeneration is "the beginning of sanctification" (Berkhof, a major Calvinist theologian), and if indeed it is true that God cannot enter with His sanctifying grace until the guilt problem is solved by justification (Haldane, one whose Calvinistic credentials are not in question), Calvinism is in trouble with its view of having regeneration prior to justification.

Unless someone can come up with a better answer, the validity of Calvinism's insistence that regeneration precedes faith hangs on the fragile thread of the suggestion that Berkhof gave of "jus-tification ideally existing in the counsel of God and certain to be realized in the life of the sinner." That fragile thread will not hold!

I have no quarrel with the idea that in some sense all of God's decisions are eternal. But His decisions are based on a prior knowledge of what He will do. He has not performed an act until He actually does it. I have no quarrel with the idea that whatever God knows He will do He will certainly do. However, such knowledge was a knowledge of what God would do. He knew from eternity who would believe and whom He would justify and when He would justify them. In both Calvinism and Arminianism, a person is not justified in the sight of God until he believes.

To speak of "justification ideally existing in the counsel of God and certain to be realized in the life of the sinner" is not the same as saying that the person is already justified. There can be no divine actions that require justification as a grounds until the person is in fact justified. If that is the case, Calvinism is in trouble with its own theology when it places regeneration prior to justification.

In his refutation of "the doctrine of justification from eternity," Berkhof makes it clear that jus-tification cannot be considered a reality until it takes place in time. One of the arguments used by the advocates of justification from eternity that Berkhof cites is, "Justification is an immanent act of God, and as such must be from eternity." His response is:

It is hardly correct, however, to speak of justification as an *actus immanens* in God [an immanent act, or an act inherent in God Himself]; it is rather an *actus transiens* [a transitive act, or an act originating in God but acting upon an object, an act which is not complete until the object exists], just as creation, incarnation, and so on. The advocates of justification from eternity feel the weight of this consideration, and therefore hasten to give us the assurance that they do not mean to teach that the elect are justified from eternity *actualiter* [actually or really], but only in the intention of God, in the divine decree. This leads us back to the usual distinction between the counsel of God and its execution. If this justification in the intention of God warrants our speaking of a justification from eternity, then there is absolutely no reason why we should not speak of a creation from eternity as well.[11]

Later on Berkhof explains: "Justification is one of the fruits of Christ's redemptive work, applied by the Holy Spirit. But the Spirit did not and could not apply this or any other fruit of work of Christ from eternity."[12]

Berkhof would be in agreement with my statement: "He [God] has not performed an act until He actually does it." I think Berkhof has successfully refuted the validity of his own statement, "The sinner can receive the grace of regeneration on the basis of a justification ideally existing in the counsel of God and certain to be realized in the life of the sinner."

There can be no divine action based on justification that has not already occurred. If this be true, regeneration cannot precede faith.

Regeneration is not an act of God that prepares the way for redemption. It is a redemptive act. I commend Calvinism for upholding the satisfaction view of atonement and the imputation of the death and righteousness of Christ as the ground of justification. I believe that they need to reexamine the question of whether the redemptive act of regeneration can be performed on a person before the death and righteousness of Christ is actually imputed to his account.

THE QUESTION OF SOVEREIGN GRACE

Classical Calvinists have been champions of the satisfaction view of atonement. But they speak of election as being based on sovereign grace. Sovereign grace would be a divine right growing out of God's sovereignty rather than a provision made possible by atonement. This seems to be what John Piper, in his book on Romans 9, is saying when he remarks:

We can say God's glory and his name consists fundamentally in his propensity to show mercy and his sovereign freedom in its distribution, or to put it more precisely, it is the glory of God and his essential nature mainly to dispense mercy (but also wrath, Ex 34:7) on whomever he pleases apart from any constraint originating outside his own will. This is the essence of what it means to be God. This is his name [underlining his].[13]

The question that I am concerned about is not whether some constraint is imposed on God outside His will. I do not believe that is the case either. The question is whether His own holy nature forbids him to choose anyone for salvation apart from Christ. Does not His own holy nature forbid Him to choose a person for salvation apart from the application of atonement? Will not His holy nature forbid Him from performing a redemptive act on a person before the death and righteousness of Christ is imputed to him? I think it will.

The Difference Between Classical Arminianism and Erickson's View

Erickson agrees with Calvinism on unconditional election, but differs with Classical Calvinism on the logical order of regeneration and faith. Erickson points out:

> The biblical evidence favors the position that conversion is prior to regeneration. Various appeals to respond to the gospel imply that conversion results in regeneration. Among them is Paul's reply to the Philippian jailer (we are assuming that regeneration is part of the process of being saved): "Believe in the Lord Jesus, and you will be saved, you and your household" (Acts 16:31).[14]

Erickson correctly observes that faith must precede regeneration because regeneration is a part of salvation which is conditioned on faith.

While Erickson rejects the view that regeneration precedes faith, he sides with Calvinism on the view that God's call is irresistible. He observes:

> The special calling is simply an intensive and effectual working by the Holy Spirit. It is not the complete transformation which constitutes regeneration, but it does render the conversion of the individual both possible and certain. Thus the logical order of the initial aspects of salvation is special calling—conversion—regeneration.[15]

Earlier in his treatment of the subject, Erickson compared his view with the Arminian view. He explains:

> Special or effectual calling, then, involves an extraordinary presentation of the message of salvation. It is sufficiently powerful to counteract the effects of sin and enable the person to believe. It is also so appealing that the person will believe. Special calling is in many ways similar to the prevenient grace of which Arminians speak. It differs from that concept, however, in two respects. It is bestowed only on the elect, not upon all humans and it leads infallibly or efficaciously to a positive response by the recipient.[16]

I think Erickson has correctly analyzed the difference between his view and the Arminian view as I hold to it. R. C. Sproul's description of Lewis Sperry Chafer would suggest that Chafer's view is similar to Erickson's.[17]

Since Erickson has God electing people to be in Christ rather than electing people in Christ as taught in Ephesians 1:4, it follows that the divine choice of election was based on sovereign grace rather than grace made possible through atonement. In any view of unconditional election, the divine decision to elect the person of necessity preceded the divine decision to apply the benefits of atonement and justification to the person. The person is elected to have the benefits of atonement applied. I am referring here to those divine decisions as they were made in eternity past. More will be said about this issue in the chapter on "Decrees and Election."

Faith Not a Work

Arminians believe that faith is the condition of justification. Calvinists also believe that faith is the condition of justification. The problem comes as we have seen in Calvinists' claim that regeneration must precede faith and give birth to faith. Since Arminians believe the sinner can believe without first being regenerated, the Calvinists tend to view faith in Arminianism as being a work. Thus they have charged that Arminians believe people are justified by works.

Based on the place of faith in justification in the governmental view of atonement and justification, it can at least be understood why this charge would be made against the Arminians that hold this view. Let me reproduce here the chart from Chapter 11 on the governmental view of justification:

DEBITS	The Believer	CREDITS
Absolute Righteousness ~~Eternal Death~~		Faith in Christ
JUSTIFIED OR PARDONED		

In this view of justification, it is recognized that faith in Christ is not absolute righteousness, but it gets the same consideration before God that absolute righteousness would receive. Faith in Christ is counted as righteousness. It can be seen why this approach could be accused of considering faith as a work. I am sure that those Arminians who believe in this approach to justification by faith would deny that this means they believe in justification by works. They would deny that faith is a meritorious act that earns their salvation. They would say that for God to treat faith in Christ as if it were absolute righteousness would be a gracious act of God. Calvinistic works that have criticized Arminianism have been based on this approach to Arminianism rather than the kind of Arminianism that I have set forth in this book. I am persuaded that my views are in essential agreement with those of

Jacob Arminius. But that is not the reason I believe my view. It is because I believe it is based on Scripture.

In Classical Arminianism, the ground of justification is the imputation of the death and righteousness of Christ to the believer's account. The condition of justification is faith in Jesus Christ. Faith in no way whatever gets any consideration as any form of merit that would form the smallest part of the ground of my justification. The only ground of my justification before God is the penal death of Christ and His life of absolute obedience to the Father.

If when I stand before God He should ask me, "What is your hope of acceptance based on?" I would not mention anything that I have ever done or not done. I would say, "My hope is built on nothing less and nothing more than the death and righteousness of Christ." I would not even say, "I had faith in Christ." When I declared that I was basing my hope of acceptance on the death and righteousness of Christ—that and that alone—would be a manifestation of my faith. Until the time when I stand before God, my song is to be found in the words of that great hymn written by Edward Mote:

My hope is built on nothing less
Than Jesus' blood and righteousness;
I dare not trust the sweetest frame,
But wholly lean on Jesus name.

On Christ, the solid Rock, I stand;
All other ground is sinking sand,
All other ground is sinking sand.

When darkness seems to hide His face,
I rest on his unchanging grace;
In every high and stormy gale,
My anchor holds within the vale.

On Christ, the solid Rock, I stand;
All other ground is sinking sand,
All other ground is sinking sand.

His oath, His covenant, His blood,
Support me in the whelming flood;
When all around my soul gives way,
He then is all my hope and stay.

On Christ, the solid Rock, I stand;
All other ground is sinking sand,
All other ground is sinking sand.

When He shall come with trumpet sound,
Oh, may I then in Him be found;
Dressed in His righteousness alone,
Faultless to stand before the throne.

On Christ, the solid Rock, I stand;
All other ground is sinking sand,
All other ground is sinking sand.[18]

The words of the Apostle Paul destroy forever the possibility that faith can rightly be called works. He says:

For what saith the scripture? Abraham believed God, and it was counted unto him for righteousness. Now to him that worketh is the reward not reckoned of grace, but of debt. But to him that worketh not, but believeth on him that justifieth the ungodly, his faith is counted for righteousness (Rom. 4:3-5).

The Meaning of "Faith Counted for Righteousness"

Those who believe the governmental view of atonement believe that in the statement, "Faith is counted for righteousness" (Rom. 4:3, 5, Gal. 3:6), they find solid support for their position. I dealt with that question in my commentary on Romans. I will quote that treatment here.

It must be admitted that, so far as this expression is concerned, the governmental view is grammatically possible. (See 2:26 where uncircumcision is counted "for" circumcision.) The big question is: Does it fit the context of Scripture as it relates to atonement and justification? Of immediate concern is: How does such an interpretation fit what Paul has already said in Romans? To answer this question, we must go back to what Paul said about the necessity of atonement.

There are three very important truths set forth in Rom. 2:1–3:20. (1) God's requirement for justification is absolute righteousness (2:1-16: see notes on 2:13). (2) No human being has produced righteousness (3:10). (3) No human being by his own activity can produce absolute righteousness (3:20).

The big question before us now is: Is it universally and unchangeably true that "God requires absolute righteousness for justification?" If this is true, the governmental view and all similar views cannot be considered valid interpretations of atonement and justification. *The same principle that eliminates the governmental view establishes the satisfaction view.* What God requires has been provided by Christ. He provided for us and offers to us nothing less than absolute righteousness (see notes on 3:25, 26).

If the satisfaction view is true, how do we understand "his faith is counted for righteousness?" There are two possibilities. The first is to keep the translation as it is and to understand it to mean "faith, embracing its object which is Christ," is counted as righteousness (Lenski, 290). The meaning would be similar to Jesus' statement to the woman in Luke 7 when He said, "Thy faith hath saved thee" (Lk. 7:50). It is quite obvious that it was Christ who saved the woman. This being true, it was faith embracing its object. The One embraced by faith saved her. In this instance, faith would be a metonymy.

There is another view that seems more likely. A distinction is made between "the imputation [or counting] of faith" (v. 5) and the "imputation of righteousness" (v. 6). A further point of clarification comes from the meaning of "for" (Greek *eis*). While "for" is a proper translation, there are other possibilities. A very common translation is "unto." It is also translated "toward."

By translating it as "toward," it would read, "his faith is counted toward righteousness." Faith, then, is counted (or imputed) toward the receiving of righteousness" (see Alford 347, 348; Black 76; Haldane 162, 163; Hodge 110; and Plumer 160).[19]

Some of what has been dealt with in this chapter about Arminianism and Calvinism will receive further treatment in Chapters 15, 16, and 17.

Conclusion

I believe that I can say, "Justification is by faith alone" with as much conviction and as much confidence as any Calvinist or Lutheran can. But I would like to go further and make a distinction between the condition of justification and the ground of justification. When it comes to the ground of justification, I would say, "Justification is by Christ alone." My hope in built on nothing less and nothing more than the death and righteousness of Christ—that and that alone. The death and righteousness of Christ are placed on my account on the condition of faith alone. By God's help, I believed and He freely justified. To put it briefly, "Justification is grounded in Christ alone. It is bestowed on the condition of faith alone."

14

Perseverance

The concern before us in this chapter is: Is it possible for a person who has once experienced the saving grace of God to once again be lost? I am going to take the position that it is possible for a person who has been saved to commit apostasy and become once again lost and under the wrath of God. While I will take the position that it is possible for a person to be lost after he has experienced the grace of God, the position that I will set forth, I believe, will stand up against any charge of salvation by works.

In order for us to develop a strong case for our position, we must understand why those arriving at the opposite conclusion do so. In dealing with their views, it is incumbent upon us to be fair and honest in our treatment of their views.

There are basically two very different approaches used by those who take the position "once saved, always saved." *The first view,* and the one that has a longer history, *claims that those who are truly saved will continue in faith and holiness.* This is the view that is held by traditional or Classical Calvinism.

The second view is that once a person is saved, nothing that he or she could ever do would cause him to be lost again. If a person should deny his faith, or if he should live in any imaginable degree of sin, he would never cease to be a child of God. While those who take such a view would admonish saved persons not to live in such a manner, they would admit that such could happen and that it would never alter a person's justification before God. Most of the people who hold this view would not likely hold to the other points of Calvinism,[1] especially unconditional election and irresistible grace. This view is, what I would call, the popular view. It is held more by popular preachers than by scholars.

As a point of clarification, I need to make it clear that there are those who accept only this point of Calvinism, but do not accept the position that saved people could be in, and continue in, any imaginable degree of sin. They believe that those who are living such a lifestyle were never saved.

Classical Calvinism's View of "Once Saved, Always Saved"

We need to give a brief treatment of Classical Calvinism. There are five major points in Classical Calvinism's soteriology: (1) total depravity, (2) unconditional election, (3) limited atonement, (4) irresistible grace, and (5) perseverance of all those who are saved.

The first point, total depravity, puts forth the idea that the entirety of the human personality is permeated by sin. The Calvinistic view of depravity is that the sinner is under the power of sin to such a degree that in order to exercise faith he or she first must be made alive. A spiritually dead person could not believe—only one who is made alive by regeneration could believe. How this fits into the Calvinistic system will be clearer as we explain the other points of Calvinism.

The most fundamental of all the points of Calvinism is its view of unconditional election. It is the Calvinist's view that in eternity past, for reasons known only to God, that God chose certain ones to be saved, and He chose not to save others. God will see to it that those whom He chose or elected will come to faith in Christ and be saved.

While there are some who believe in unconditional election and take the position that Christ died for everybody, the traditional position is that Christ died only for the elect. Thus, it is referred to as limited atonement. The intent and thereby, the extent of atonement was only for the elect.

When Calvinists speak of irresistible grace (some prefer to speak of effectual grace), they mean that all whom God moves upon to bring to saving faith will certainly believe and be saved. In Classical Calvinism, the effectual call (or irresistible grace) of God is regeneration.

In Calvinism, regeneration precedes faith. The person is regenerated and then he believes and is justified. In Arminianism, the person believes, then he is justified and is regenerated.

In Calvinism, a sinner cannot believe unless he is first regenerated. When Calvinists speak of faith as a gift, they mean that God is totally responsible for the person having saving faith. It was all of God.

It can be seen that the first four points of Calvinism logically lead to the last point: the final perseverance of all who are saved.

THE CASE FOR CLASSICAL CALVINISM'S VIEW OF PERSEVERANCE

The basic foundation of the traditional Calvinistic view of "once saved, always saved" is their interpretation of God's sovereignty. Lewis Sperry Chafer says:

> The failure of one soul to be saved and to reach glory whom God has ordained to that end means the disruption of the whole actuality of divine sovereignty. If God could fail in one feature, be it ever so small, He could fail in all. If He could fail in anything, He ceases to be God and the universe is drifting to a destiny about which God himself could know nothing.[2]

As perceived by the Calvinist, their view of unconditional election is the logical outgrowth of the doctrine of sovereignty. The doctrine of unconditional continuance in salvation is the logical result of unconditional election. As James Oliver Buswell Jr. explains:

> If God has unconditionally elected to save people, and if He has provided atonement which makes their salvation certain, it follows by inevitable logic that those whom God has elected to eternal salvation will go on to eternal salvation. In other words, a denial of the doctrine of the perseverance of the saints is a denial of the sovereign grace of God in unconditional election.[3]

Millard J. Erickson comments:

Since God has elected certain individuals out of the mass of fallen humanity to receive eternal life, and those so chosen will necessarily come to receive eternal life, it follows that there must be a permanence to their salvation. If the elect could at some point lose their salvation, God's election of them to eternal life would not be truly effectual. Thus, the doctrine of election as understood by the Calvinist requires perseverance as well.[4]

Chafer, Buswell, and Erickson—all Calvinists, show the connection between unconditional election and final perseverance. It is unthinkable that God would unconditionally elect a person and draw him by irresistible grace, and not guarantee that he would remain in a state of grace.

The Popular View of "Once Saved, Always Saved"

As I said above, this view is held more so by popular preachers than by scholars. For a view to be held more so by popular preachers than by scholars does not make that view either right or wrong. But it does help us to know who it is that holds the view.

Again, according to this view, once a person is saved he could never do anything that would cause him to be lost again. If a person should deny his faith or if he should live in any imaginable degree of sin he would never cease to be a child of God.

One of the proponents of this view is Charles Stanley. Stanley comments:

> If abandoning the faith or falling into sin short-circuits salvation, I have the ability to demonstrate unconditional love to a greater extent than God. If there is a condition—even one—to God's willingness to maintain a relationship with His children, it is not unconditional. On the other hand, I know people who have demonstrated pure unconditional love to family members who were incredibly undeserving.[5]

In another place, Stanley asks:

> *Does the Scripture actually teach that regardless of the consistency of our faith,* our salvation is secure? [Italics his]

He then answers:

> Yes, it does, through both proposition and illustration.

> ### "If We Are Faithless..."
> The clearest statement on this subject is issued by Paul's second letter to Timothy:

> > If we died with Him, we shall also live with Him;
> > If we endure, we shall also reign with Him;

> If we deny Him, He also will deny us;
> If we are *faithless*, He remains *faithful;*
> for He cannot deny Himself.
> —2 Timothy 2:11-13[6] [Italics his]

My main purpose at this point is to explain what Stanley and others are saying and why it is that they believe it. My answer to their thinking will come later. But since it will not fit in at a later point to deal with 2 Timothy 2:11-13, let me say a few words about it now. Stanley does not deal at all with the statement, "If we deny Him, He will also deny us." In fact Stanley is saying that a person who is a Christian could deny Him, and He will not deny that person.

With regard to the last part of verse 13, "If we are faithless, He remains faithful, for he cannot deny Himself," I would give the following explanation: If we become faithless, Christ will remain faithful to His character and will deny us. What I have said is in agreement with the explanation given by M. R. Vincent:

> True to his own nature, righteous character, and requirements, according to which *he cannot accept as faithful one who has proved untrue to him.* To do so would be to deny himself.[7] [Italics mine]

The Case for the Popular View of "Once Saved, Always Saved"

As we can see, this view is quite different from the view held by Classical Calvinists. It is also built on a different doctrinal foundation. Those who advocate the popular view think it is *a necessary consequence of their view of atonement and justification.* Stanley remarks: "If Christ took upon Himself every single one of your sins, what is going to cause God to reverse His verdict of not guilty? Hallelujah, not a thing."[8]

In order to understand this view, we need to understand the view of atonement and justification that it is built on. While I differ strongly with this view, it is not because I have a different view of atonement and justification. To put it briefly, the view of atonement is what is called the penal satisfaction view. I have explained this at length in Chapter 11 of this book and in my Romans commentary.[9]

The satisfaction view of atonement is based on the idea: (1) that Jesus Christ suffered the full wrath of God for our sins thus paying its penalty and (2) that Jesus lived a completely righteous life thus rendering to God perfect obedience on our behalf. In so doing, Jesus completely satisfied the holy demands of God for us.

On the condition of our faith in Christ, God placed on our account the death of Christ and the righteousness of Christ. Christ's death and Christ's righteousness legally applied to our account fully satisfies God's requirement for our guilt (because of His death) and restores us to favor with God (because of His righteousness). Those who take this popular view believe that the nature of Christ's payment for our sins requires that nothing we could do could ever alter that fact. While I differ very strongly with this, I can see why some people believe it. When I present my view, I will explain why I think "once saved, always saved" is not a necessary result of the satisfaction view of atonement and Justification.

In about the last twenty years or so, a position has received a lot of attention that would tend to go along with this approach. Its proponents are involved in the "Lordship Controversy." One side insists that at salvation we must receive Christ as Lord and Savior. The other side insists that a person can receive Christ as Savior without receiving Him as Lord. Those who insist that a person can receive Christ as Savior without receiving Him as Lord would admit to the possibility of such things as Stanley suggests. Some scholars have taken this position. Among these is Zane Hodges.[10]

I should also point out that there are those who accept the logic of the popular view, but try to avoid its abuses. They would accept the idea that nothing a person could ever do would cause him to cease to be saved, but they would insist that if a person is saved he would show evidence of salvation. They would tend to believe that those who did not show evidence were never saved. On the one hand, they believe that verses like John 10:28-30 teach that once a person is saved he or she will never be lost again. On the other hand, they believe that the change spoken of in 2 Corinthians 5:17 rules out the idea that a person could be saved and show no evidence of salvation.

The Conflict of Opinion Among Those Who Believe "Once Saved, Always Saved"

It is very important that we keep in mind that the view I have just presented as the "Popular View" is rejected by many Calvinists. In speaking of extreme views on the doctrine of continuance in salvation, William Wilson Stevens explains:

> One [view] is held by those who say they believe in the doctrine (eternal security of the believer) but who have really perverted it, maintaining that one is justified and is eternally safe regardless of what he may become in his person and character.[11]

Buswell comments:

> In a young people's conference I once heard a Christian layman speak as follows: "I was once a member of a young people's gospel team. We were all saved, and we had some success in preaching the gospel. But one member of the team got into worldly company. He married a very worldly girl. He denied his Christian profession of faith, and he died a drunkard. Now you see, young people, he was a Christian; he went to heaven; but he was a "carnal Christian" and he did not have the reward of a "spiritual Christian." No wonder the Arminians are scandalized by what is falsely called Calvinism.[12]

Much of the popular preaching on this subject perverts Calvinism rather than setting forth the historic Calvinistic position. Such preaching has done great harm to the church. Both the traditional Calvinist and the Arminian are disturbed by this kind of preaching. I appreciate much of what some of these people do, but this area of their thought causes me great concern.

The historic position of Calvinism has held to the perseverance of the saints, not to a guarantee of their future salvation whether they persevere or not. As John H. Gerstner explains concerning the Calvinistic view, "Perseverance not only does not, but cannot, lead to antinomianism because, by definition, it means persevering in holiness and not unholiness."[13] Berkhof explains concerning this doctrine, "It is maintained that the life of regeneration and the habits that develop out of it in the way of sanctification can never entirely disappear."[14]

Arguments for "Once Saved, Always Saved" Based on Scripture

The cases given above are doctrinal in nature. Let us now turn our attention to passages of Scripture that are used to support the view "once saved, always saved." The exegetical proof would be about the same for most of these verses no matter which of the views set forth above are used. I will not make an exhaustive list of verses, but I will deal with the primary verses. Up to this point, I have given the views and why the proponents of these views believe them. At this point, I will give my reasons for believing that the verses do not require the conclusion "once saved, always saved." Later, I will explain why the cases given earlier are not valid.

JOHN 10:28, 29

There are three arguments found in these verses: the first, the words "eternal life"; the second, the words "they shall never perish"; the third, "neither shall any man pluck them out of My hand."

I do not need to show that these verses teach that a person can be lost after he is saved. They do not. I will give support for that position later from other passages. The only thing I need to do is to show that to accept what these verses teach does not contradict the viewpoint that a person can be lost again after he or she has experienced saving grace.

Let us examine these arguments and see if they state a truth that contradicts the idea that it is possible for a Christian ever to be lost again

Let us consider the first one. It must be admitted that eternal life can be possessed only in the sense of potential. The believer certainly does not possess eternity. Some have taught that there is no past and future with God, but no one has ever said that of the believer. The eternal life of the believer is in the Son as is taught in 1 John 5:11, "God hath given us eternal life, and this life is in his Son." This life is the believer's by identification with Christ. Should that identification be broken (Jn. 15:2, 6), he would be severed from this eternal life, yet it would not alter the fact that he had possessed it. It should also be pointed out that Adam possessed the potential for eternal life before he fell, but he lost it with the fall. It is seen then that the loss of salvation does not contradict the words, "eternal life."

The second argument is based on "they shall never perish." John 3:36 teaches that the converse is true of unbelievers when it says, "He that believeth not the Son shall not see life." No one says that, since it is said of the unbeliever that he shall not see life he is permanently bound without hope in that condition. It is a fact that, as an unbeliever, he shall not see life, but if he becomes a believer, he will see life.

Now, if the words "shall not see life," which describe the unbeliever, are not contradicted when the unbeliever becomes a believer and sees life, where is the contradiction when it is said that a believer "shall not perish," but if he becomes an unbeliever he will perish? The fact is that a believer, as long as he remains a believer, "shall not perish."

The third argument is based on the statement, "Neither shall any man pluck them out of My hand." The next verse adds a similar thought concerning the Father's hand. The teaching is simply this: The believer's relationship with God is a personal one between him and God. Though all of the powers of the universe were to combine against the believer, they could not take the believer away from God. Some would add, "Neither can the believer take himself out of the body of Christ." Yes, that is true. But, it is also true that he could not have placed himself into the body of Christ. However, upon his faith in Christ, the Holy Spirit placed the believer into the body of Christ (1 Cor. 12:13). If the believer renounces his faith, God will take him out (Jn. 15:2, 6). There is no contradiction between the statements "No one can take us out of Christ" and the statement "God the Father takes those people out of Christ who turn from Christ in unbelief."

ROMANS 8:35-39

It is my opinion that this passage does not deal with the question of whether a saved person can ever be lost again. Rather, it teaches that a person who is a child of God can never, at the same time, be separated from God's love. In other words, the believer is never to interpret hardship as meaning that God does not love him. Instead, he should recognize that God's love is still with him and should say with Paul, "Nay, in all these things we are more than conquerors through him that loved us" (Rom. 8:37). It was because of God's abiding love that Paul could say, "I have learned in whatsoever state I am, *therewith* to be content" (Phil. 4:11).

While I think Paul was telling the believers in Romans 8:35-39 that the trials and tribulations of life do not mean that God does not love us, I do not take that position as a means of escaping the view that the passage teaches "once saved, always saved." It presents no problem to me to say that the passage deals with the security of the believer.

Suppose the passage does deal with the matter of security. It would be explained the same way as the statement of Jesus when He said, "Neither shall any man pluck them out of My hand" (Jn. 10:28). Paul would be saying as emphatically as human language can make it that our personal salvation is a matter between the individual believer and God. He would be saying that neither tribulation, distress, persecution, famine, peril, sword (verse 35), death, life, angels, principalities, powers, things present, things to come (verse 38), height, depth, nor any other creature viewed collectively or singularly can take a believer away from Christ. I believe that. What Paul says in these verses in no way contradicts the viewpoint that if a believer turns away from God in defiant, arrogant unbelief that God will take him out of Christ (Jn. 15:2, 6).

When I was in Russia, on more than one occasion when speaking on this subject, I said, "Communism put many in prison because of their faith and killed many because of their faith. But

Communism did not take one person out of Christ." If all of the governments of the world voted that a person should be taken out of Christ that would not and could not make it happen.

For Russian Baptists, the possibility of losing salvation is very important. In the past, many of them could have avoided prison if they had been willing to deny their faith. Many of them filled a martyr's grave rather than deny their faith. When my wife and I were there in 1996, we could still feel the pain of the Stalin years as we moved across Russia.

ROMANS 11:29

Romans 11:29 reads, "For the gifts and the calling of God are without repentance." This means that if God has made an *unconditional* promise, it will forever remain an *unconditional* promise. On the other hand, if He has made a *conditional* promise, He will never change the condition of that promise. This is the line of reasoning used by Paul in Galatians 3:15-18. The Abrahamic Covenant that had already promised justification on the condition of faith could neither be set aside nor have the condition changed when the law came. There is certainly no argument to prove that a promise could not be *irrevocable* and *conditional* at the same time.

PHILIPPIANS 1:6

In this verse Paul says, " Being confident of this very thing that He which hath begun a good work in you will perform it until the day of Jesus Christ." This is a confidence that we can have as believers. God will perform the work of salvation until the day of Jesus Christ in those who continue in faith. This is not a promise made to unbelievers. There is no contradiction if one who is a believer becomes an unbeliever and the promise no longer applies.

I have not dealt with every verse that is used by those who believe in "once saved, always saved," but the major verses have been given attention. I believe that what I have said about these verses will help a person understand other verses that may be introduced.

A Case for Believing It Is Possible for a Person to Be Lost Again After He Is Saved

THE DOCTRINAL FOUNDATION

What I have presented above shows the doctrinal foundations upon which the different approaches to "once saved, always saved" are based. Let us now turn our attention to the doctrinal foundation for believing that it is possible for a person who is saved to turn again to unbelief and again be lost.

The theological foundation that supports the possibility of becoming lost again after a person is saved is found in what it means to be made in the image of God. (See Chapter 9, "The Nature of Man.") Being made in the image of God means that we are personal beings. We think, feel, and act.

A person makes decisions or choices. Regardless of how much influence is brought to bear upon the will or how much assistance is given, a person's actions are in a very real sense his own. That is what it means to be a person. While there is divine aid for the Christian, it is possible for him to resist this aid and make wrong choices. Among these wrong choices is the possibility of turning back to unbelief. God made us persons. In His relationship with us, He never violates our personhood. While I do not think the likelihood is high that a person who is saved will become an unbeliever again, I do believe that because we are persons, the possibility remains open.

The terminology usually used in explaining what I have just said is "freedom of the will." While that is appropriate terminology, I think the real issue is whether a Christian is a genuine, personal being. Does he think, feel, and make choices (both good and bad)? Freedom of will is involved in what it means to be a person. This subject will be dealt with more thoroughly in the next chapter.

THE TEACHING OF SCRIPTURE

The ultimate question is what does the Scripture teach? I will now turn my attention to a biblical defense of the view that it is possible to be lost again once a person has been saved. Then I will show how this position is consistent with other doctrines.

It will not be my purpose to see how many verses I can set forth to support my position. Rather, I will deal with those that are most helpful and the ones that, so far as I am concerned, must be interpreted so as to fit the idea that a saved person could be lost again. *To say that a saved person could never be lost again would place us in contradiction,* I believe, *with what these verses irrefutably teach.*

HEBREWS 6:4-6

Had these people been saved?

In this passage, those under consideration have the following characteristics: (1) "once enlightened"; (2) "have tasted of the heavenly gift"; (3) "were made partakers of the Holy Ghost;" (4) "have tasted the good word of God"; (5) have tasted "the powers of the world to come"; (6) have repented. (It is definitely implied that they had repented because it is said that it is impossible to renew them *again* to repentance.)

It would certainly seem obvious that the characteristics given above are descriptive of a saved person. However, some say this describes those who had *only* professed faith in Jesus, but had not actually received Him as Savior. Herman Hoeksema takes this position. In commenting on Hebrews 6:4-6, he explains:

> But the author has in mind their former state, as they *appeared,* as they were known by men, as they used to be members of the church visible in the world. They were baptized. And they went through the *outward show of repentance,* and for a time walked in that repentance. But now they have definitely *fallen away even from the outward show.* They have become unbelievers. They have become wicked. They have become a part of the Antichrist. And the text says that it is impossible that those who so fall can ever again be renewed unto repentance. The case of these people is therefore hopeless. Their falling away is final. They can never return.[15]

Since there are those who take the position that this passage is dealing with individuals who made a profession of faith, but were never saved, we will take a careful look at the passage to see whether it refers to those who had been saved or to those who had merely professed to have faith in Jesus Christ.

The word that is translated enlightened in verse 4 is *phōtidzō*. In Hebrews 10:32, it is translated "illuminated." The writer says, "But call to remembrance the former days, in which, after ye were illuminated, ye endured a great fight of afflictions." It sounds here as if he is referring to the conversion experience. Thayer says concerning this word that it means "to enlighten spiritually, imbue with saving knowledge . . . with a saving knowledge of the gospel: hence *photisthentes* of those who have been made Christians, Heb. vi. 4; x. 32."[16]

Some have argued that since the word *taste* is used, they approached the very threshold of salvation, even to the extent of having partial acquaintance with what it is like to be a Christian, but they were not saved. Such an experience is without scriptural support; either a person is saved or he is not.

By comparing the use of the word *taste* in other parts of the Scripture, we see that it can mean an experience. Examples are Matthew 16:28, Hebrews 2:9, and 1 Peter 2:3. We shall take particular notice of Hebrews 2:9 where it says, speaking of Jesus, "that he by the grace of God should taste death for every man." Surely this is referring to an actual experience with death.

It is my position that the word *taste* is one of the strongest words that could have been used. In tasting, there is always a *consciousness* of the presence of that which is tasted. There is always an *acquaintance* with the distinctive characteristics of that which is tasted. This is evidenced by 1 Peter 2:3. By tasting, the believer learned that one of the distinctive characteristics of the Lord is that He is gracious. There is also a matter of contact in tasting. In other words, tasting may be called *conscious acquaintance by contact.*

When we apply the previous observations to the subject under consideration, we learn that those mentioned here have had an experience in which they become *consciously acquainted by contact* with the heavenly gift. The heavenly gift either means Christ or salvation. In either case, it would mean that the person would be saved, because only a saved person has such an acquaintance with Christ or with salvation.

Now we go to the third expression: "were made partakers of the Holy Ghost." In Hebrews 3:14, we find a reference in which the same Greek word that is translated *partake* in Hebrews 6:4 is used. It reads: "For we are made partakers of Christ." This would certainly refer to a close relationship. The Greek word for partaker could be translated a *companion* or *one who goes along with*. When used of being made a partaker of the Holy Ghost, it carries with it the idea of a companion relationship—a going along with. *To go along with* means to be *in agreement.* The person is taught by and led by the Holy Spirit.

The fourth characteristic is: "have tasted the good word of God." These persons had gone further than the original enlightenment of the way of salvation, as mentioned in the first expression. They had an acquaintance with the Word of God. Such an understanding belongs only to Christians.

The fifth expression is that they had tasted "the powers of the world to come" and seems to mean that they had entered into the joys of knowing that they were going to Heaven because of their faith in Christ.

The sixth characteristic is that they had repented. Repentance[17] and faith both refer to the same experience, but from different angles. Therefore, we must conclude that they had experienced saving faith (See my discussion on the relationship between repentance and faith in the previous chapter).

Concerning the description of those referred to in the passage under study, J. D. O'Donnell says:

> If one of such an experience is not saved, it is hard to imagine what it would take to describe a true believer. Even many securitists admit that a saved person is described but try to diminish the meaning of the passage by interpreting the full passage as a hypothetical situation that will never take place.[18]

Robert E. Picirilli comments:

> There is absolutely no doubt those lives refer to genuine Christian experience. If you wanted a better way to describe conversion, you could not find it! Any one of the four expressions cannot fail to represent real salvation. Take the third phrase for example: A "partaker," one who partakes of, one who is in fellowship with. Now, only a real Christian is a partaker of the Holy Spirit of God.[19]

What had these people done?

In interpreting these verses, we must remember that these Jews were in danger of forsaking Christ and going back into Judaism. These warnings were given to keep them from making this mistake.

In 6:6 it is said "they crucify to themselves the Son of God afresh." Let us note that this is a crucifixion in relationship, that is, to themselves. An example of crucifixion in relationship is found in Galatians 6:14 where Paul says, "By whom the world is crucified unto me, and I unto the world." So far as reality was concerned, both Paul and the world were living and active; but so far as relationship was concerned, they were dead to each other. They had no relationship existing between them.

The relationship of Christ to the unsaved is that of a dead Christ; but to the saved, He is a living Christ. A person could not crucify to himself the Son of God afresh unless he were in a living relationship to Him; therefore, such could be committed only by a saved person.

If we will compare this verse with Hebrews 10:29, we shall get a more complete picture of what is discussed. In this verse, the person has "counted the blood of the covenant, wherewith he was sanctified, an unholy thing." This would be the case of the Jewish believer who came to the point that he said that Christ's blood was no more than any other man's blood; it was not that blood which was typified by the sacrifices in the Old Testament; it possessed no saving power; Christ was not the Savior.

When the person came to this point, he denounced his faith in Christ; he drove Christ out of his life; in relationship Christ became a dead Christ; thus, he had crucified Christ to himself.

When this person denounced his former faith in Christ, he was saying that there was nothing to the experience he thought he had had with Christ. In so doing, he put Him to an open shame.

What is the condition of the person who has fallen away by unbelief?

The writer of Hebrews says that it is impossible to renew such a person again unto repentance. It is my understanding that this means that he cannot be restored to faith. He cannot be saved again. Not everyone who interprets this passage to teach that loss of salvation is possible accepts the position that it is impossible for such a person to be saved again. It seems to me that "For it is impossible . . . to renew them again unto repentance" admits to no other interpretation than that it is impossible for such a person to be saved again.

Some would say that it is impossible with man, but not impossible with God. There is nothing in the passage that would suggest this. The comments of I. Howard Marshall are insightful here. He observes:

> The point at issue is not the question as to who might be able to restore the lapsed, but the fact that the lapsed cannot be restored. This is important because the passage gives us no right to assert that there may be a special intervention of God to restore those whom men cannot restore."[20]

Some have suggested that it means that it is impossible to renew them to repentance "while they are crucifying to themselves the Son of God afresh." They would suggest that they could repent and be saved again if they would quit crucifying the Son of God. That is about the same as saying that it is impossible to repent as long as they remain unrepentant. Or, they can repent if they repent. This kind of thinking reduces the statement to a mere truism.

Others agree that apostasy is without remedy, but a person could forfeit his salvation by an accumulation of sins (usually a vague concept) and could repent and be saved again. Some would object to saying he would be saved again (repeated regeneration). But if he or she did not repent, he would be lost if he died that way. I am of the conviction that the only thing that brings loss of salvation is apostasy or unbelief. The conviction that apostasy is without remedy does not depend upon this passage alone. It is taught by other passages also as we will see when we look at some of these other passages.

Once it is seen that apostasy is without remedy, we will be more cautious about what we think would cause a person to forfeit his or her salvation. Marshall speaks to this point when he says, "It is agreed on all hands that, if the passage does teach the impossibility of repentance, this is only in the case of a definite attitude of apostasy and not in the case of individual sins."[21]

HEBREWS 10:26-29

Had the person been saved?

In this passage, the person is qualified as having been sanctified (verse 29). The other references in the epistle in which the word *sanctify* is used are: 2:11; 9:13; 10:10, 14; 13:12. If the reader will examine these verses, he will find that each of these except for 9:13 has reference to sanctification that accompanies salvation in the New Testament. If the writer of the epistle were going to use sanctification in an entirely different sense here, does it not seem reasonable that he would have made it clear when using it in connection with such a drastic warning? Also, keep in mind that the sanctification referred to here was effected by the blood of Christ. Regardless of what the warning is in these verses, we must admit that it is to saved people. Verse 26 refers to the state of wilful sin (or apostasy) that the person is in. Verse 29 explains how all of this got started. It refers to the initial act of apostasy which set in motion this state of apostasy.

What had this person done?

The person referred to here had "counted the blood of the covenant, wherewith he was sanctified, an unholy thing" (verse 29). To count the blood of Christ as being no different than that of any other person constitutes unbelief. It is apostasy or shipwreck of faith. As Marshall explains, "Such a sin is an act of total rejection of God. The sinner has become an adversary of God (Heb. 10:27), and he has rejected the very things which were the means of his salvation, the atoning blood of Christ and the Spirit of grace."[22]

What is the condition of the person who has fallen away by unbelief?

In verse 26 we see that he is sinning "wilfully." The Greek indicates that the reference is not to an act of wilful sin, but a *process* of wilful sin. Such wilful sinning is not possible as long as a person is born of God. Verse 26 describes the state of the apostate, while verse 29, which is past tense, describes the first act of sin that started this state.

As a further point of clarification, verse 26 says of such a person, "There remaineth no more sacrifice for sins." There is no longer a sacrifice for sins. The apostate has sins but no available sacrifice for his sins. Having rejected the sacrifice made by Jesus Christ, there is no other sacrifice to which to turn.

Robert Shank has a concern at this point. He raises the question, "Is apostasy without remedy?" He then says, "Several passages of Scripture seem to affirm this."[23] After that he goes to great lengths to build a case for saying that there is a remedy for apostasy. "Chapter XIX: Is Apostasy Without Remedy?" is devoted entirely to an attempt to prove that apostasy is remedial. Shank's basic approach is to show that even though there are some verses that seem to teach that apostasy is without remedy, in a number of other places, the New Testament seems to teach otherwise.

He illustrates with the case of the Apostle Peter. He explains:

> On the mount, with James and John, he beheld His glory—the glory of the only begotten of the Father—and heard the Voice out of the cloud, "This is my beloved Son" (Matt. 17:5). And yet, in the hour of trial, he denied even the remotest acquaintance with Jesus: "I do not know the man!"—as though He were quite an ordinary person, thus conceding that the judgment of His enemies was, in his opinion, entirely correct. How persistent he was in his denial—three times! And how deliberate and emphatic

his denial! He cursed and swore under oath, "I know not the man."

And yet, Peter found forgiveness. Is that not encouraging for us all, as we think of the many times and many ways we have so shamefully denied our Holy Saviour? Have we not sworn by deed and life, if not in word, "I know not the man"? Have we no need to go out and weep bitterly with Peter? But still He comes—the man of Sorrows, forever scarred—and gently asks, "Lovest thou me?"[24]

We cannot read Shank's words above without empathizing with the deep feeling of concern that he conveys. Shank conveys a sense of humility before God that we should deeply appreciate. However, I do not believe he has proved his case. I cannot, in this present treatment, give an in-depth critique of Shank's view. But I believe I can show that his view is flawed.

I believe he overlooked the connection between the sin of apostasy in Hebrews 10:26-29 and the presumptuous sins of Numbers 15:30, 31. I do not think there is any doubt that the writer of Hebrews meant to say that the "wilful sin" of Hebrews 10:26 was the same kind of sin as the presumptuous sin in Numbers 15:30, 31. There was no sacrifice for the presumptuous sin. There is an obvious connection between the words "There remaineth no more sacrifice for sins" (verse 26) and the fact that there was no sacrifice for sins in the case of presumptuous sins in Numbers 15:30, 31. In supporting his view, Shank ruled out the idea that there was any sin beyond forgiveness. Surely, we cannot keep Numbers 15:30, 31; Hebrews 6:4-6; 10:26-29; and the teachings of Jesus on the unpardonable sin in mind and still sustain the position that there is no sin for which there is no remedy.

I have done extensive research which shows that the wilful (*hekousiōs*) is to be equated with the presumptuous sin of Numbers 15:30, 31 and Psalm 19:13. This material will be found in Appendix 1.[25] I will give a brief treatment here to the ideas that are pertinent to our present concerns.

The LXX does not use *hekousiōs* to refer to presumptuous sins. However, *akousios* and *akousiōs* which mean "unwilling" are used several times to refer to sins of ignorance. *Akousios* is used to translate the Hebrew for sins of ignorance in Numbers 15:25, 26; and Ecclesiastes 10:5. *Akousiōs* is used in Leviticus 4:2, 22, 27; 5:15; Numbers 15:24, 27-29; 35:11, 15; and Joshua 20:3, 5, 9. It can hardly be doubted that *hekousiōs* as it is used in Hebrews 10:26 was deliberately chosen as being in contrast with *akousiōs*.

The Old Testament makes a clear distinction between sins of ignorance and presumptuous sins. Sins of ignorance (also called "unintentional sins"[26]) were basically sins of weakness. The person who committed such a sin had better desires, but these desires were defeated. The one committing such a sin was to offer a sacrifice (Num. 15:27-29). Presumptuous sins were committed with a "high hand." They came from an attitude of arrogant, defiant, unbelief. According to Numbers 15:30, 31, there was no sacrifice for presumptuous sins. If, in fact, the sin of apostasy mentioned in Hebrews 6:4-6 and 10:26-29 is to be equated with the presumptuous sin of Numbers 15:30, 31, that should settle forever the question of whether apostasy is without remedy.

It is important to observe that the writer of Hebrews is not introducing a new idea when he speaks of a sin for which there is no sacrifice. He is simply placing the sin of apostasy in the category of the presumptuous sin of the Old Testament. Those who are in a state of saving grace, do commit sins, but they are the kind referred to in Numbers 15:27.

Once we see the distinction between presumptuous sins and sins of ignorance in the Old Testament, it is clear that this distinction comes over in the New Testament. It is evident that when Jesus said, "Father forgive them; for they know not what they do" (Lk. 23:34), He was considering the sins of those who crucified Him to be in the category of sins of ignorance. In Acts 3:17, Peter said that the Jews had crucified Jesus through ignorance. For that reason they could be forgiven (Acts 3:19). In describing himself before his conversion, Paul said, "Who was before a blasphemer, and a persecutor, and injurious." In explaining how it was that he could be forgiven, he said, "But I obtained mercy, because I did it ignorantly in unbelief" (1 Tim. 1:13). It is clear that Paul was placing his sins of blasphemy and his persecution of the church in the category of sins of ignorance. It was for that reason that they could be forgiven.

I believe that if Paul's persecution of the church could be considered a sin of ignorance that surely Peter's denial of Christ on the night of the betrayal of Christ should be considered a sin of ignorance (or weakness). If that be true, the case of Peter would have no bearing on the question of whether there is or is not a remedy for apostasy. If we keep the Old Testament teaching on presumptuous sins in mind, and the teaching of Hebrews 6:4-6 and 10:26-29 in mind, I do not think we will have any serious problems in maintaining the view that apostasy is without remedy.

A Matter of Concern

Any discussion of unpardonable sin runs the risk of causing some people ungrounded concern. Over the years, I have had a number of people to talk with me about their fears that they had committed the unpardonable sin. In my opinion, none of those who talked to me about their fears had come close to committing the unpardonable sin. Usually, these people were undergoing an extended period of some form of unhappiness. In their search for what may be the cause for this unhappiness, they came up with the idea that if they had committed the unpardonable sin that would be a big enough reason to explain their problems. Then, they became afraid that they might have committed the unpardonable sin.

My first observation is if a person is concerned about whether he or she has committed the unpardonable sin, I believe that we can confidently say that such a person has not committed apostasy or the unpardonable sin. When the Holy Spirit works a concern in a person's heart, it is to bring repentance, not to tantalize him. That being true, if the Holy Spirit produces a concern in a person, that person has not committed apostasy. Also, it is very important to realize that it is not just the act itself that makes the kind of sin mentioned in Numbers 15:30, 31 a presumptuous sin. It is the attitude of arrogant, defiant, unbelief that is manifested in the sin.

The words of Peter will help us understand the finality of the apostate's situation, and will help us to see that those who come to us with their fears have not committed apostasy. He tells us:

For if after they have escaped the pollutions of the world through the knowledge of the Lord and Saviour Jesus Christ, they are again entangled therein, and overcome, the latter end is worse with them than the beginning. For it had been better for them not to have known the way of righteousness, than, after they have known it, to turn from the holy commandment delivered unto them (2 Pet. 2:20, 21).

Verse 10 of 2 Peter 2 sheds more light on the subject. In this verse Peter describes these apostates teachers as *tolmētēs*. The KJV translates *tolmētēs* as "presumptuous." The NASB renders it as "daring." The NIV translates it as "arrogant." *Tolmētēs* occurs only here in the New Testament. Concerning its use here, J. A. Motyer explains, "The single occurrence of the noun (*tolmētēs*) is clearly in the bad sense. . . , the arrogant man of 2 Peter 2:10 who brooks no restriction on self-will and recognizes no authority to which he will be answerable."[27]

It is clear that Peter is considering these false teachers to be guilty of the presumptuous sin of Numbers 15:30, 31. The arrogant, defiance of these apostates gives a finality to their action. Before they were saved they did not have this finality about their lost condition. The presumptuous, daring, arrogant decision with which they committed apostasy means that it was done with finality. This puts them in worse condition than they were before they were saved.

I believe we can rest assured that the person who come to us to talk about his or her fears of having committed the unpardonable does not fit the description of the people described in 2 Peter 2:20, 21; Hebrews 6:4-6; and 10:26-29. If there is concern to be restored to a right relationship with God, such a person has not committed apostasy.

The people in the U.S. who have come to me with their fears have not said that, in their past, they had made a decision to denounce their faith in Christ. The situation in Russia presented a different problem. When I spoke on this subject there, some real concerns were expressed. In a discussion period, someone said that he had known someone who under persecution had renounced his faith in Christ. Later on the person had repented.

In order to evaluate a case like that we need to keep in mind the distinction between presumptuous sins and sins of ignorance. It is not simply what a person does or says that determines the case. Attitude is a decisive factor. In explaining how he was able to get forgiveness for persecuting the church, Paul is certainly implying that if he had done what he did "presumptuously," there would have been no forgiveness.

We cannot imagine the suffering inflicted, in times past, upon some people in Russia to get them to deny their faith. Death was merciful in the light of the severe torture to which some were subjected. I think we would have to say that it was certainly possible for the lips to utter the words of a denial of faith that did not represent an arrogant, defiant, unbelief toward God. If that be the case, the words of denial that the person uttered would not be equivalent to apostasy or shipwreck of faith. It appears that there were some who spoke words of denial that did not in fact commit apostasy. But I do not believe that we can explain all cases that way.

We must be faithful to the teaching of the Bible. If we are convinced the Bible teaches that apostasy is without remedy, we must teach it. The same would be true of whatever we believe it teaches on the unpardonable sin. However, we should do so with compassion and caution. We should not choose to speak on it to draw a bigger crowd. We need to keep in mind the problems that such topics cause for some people. Also, based on my experience in talking with people, I would caution preachers about jumping too quickly to the conclusion that the person who talks with them about having committed apostasy has, indeed done so. I think it would be better to take it as a plea for help.

A View Held by Many Calvinists

I pointed out above that Hoeksema takes the position that the people referred to in these passages were not saved. Probably, most Calvinists take the position that they were saved. A proponent of this view is Millard J. Erickson: He explains:

> While Hebrews 6 indicates that genuine believers *can* fall away, John 10 teaches that they *will not*. There is the logical possibility of apostasy, but it will not come to pass in the case of believers. Although they could abandon their faith and consequently come to the fate described in Hebrews 6, the grace of God prevents them from apostatizing. God does this, not by making it impossible for believers to fall away, but by making it certain that they will not. Our emphasis on *can* and *will not* is not inconsequential. It preserves the freedom of the individual. Believers are capable of repudiating their faith, but will freely choose not to.
>
> At this point someone might ask: If salvation is sure and permanent, what is the point of the warnings and commands given to the believer? The answer is that they are the means by which God renders it certain that the saved individual will not fall away. . . . It is not that God renders apostasy impossible by removing the very option. Rather, he uses every possible means of grace, including the warnings contained in Scripture, to motivate us to remain committed to him. Because he enables us to persevere in our faith, the term *perseverance* is preferable to *preservation.*[28]

In supporting his interpretation of Hebrews 6:4-6, Erickson explains:

> The meaning in cases like this must be determined on the basis of the context. The key element in the present context is found in verse 9. "Though we speak thus, yet in your case, beloved, we feel sure of better things that belong to salvation. . . ." Verse 9, however, is a statement that they will not fall away. They could, but they will not! Their persistence to the end is evidence of that truth. The writer to the Hebrews knows that his readers will not fall away; he is convinced of better things regarding them, the things that accompany salvation.[29]

It is important to observe that Erickson and those who say that these passages describe something that is only theoretically possible are admitting that the possibility of losing salvation is consistent with every doctrine except the sovereign, keeping power of God. Erickson actually says, "There is the logical possibility of apostasy." This approach is admitting that there are no logical arguments that prohibit the possibility that a person could commit apostasy and be lost after he is saved. The position that a person who is saved will in no case ever commit apostasy and be lost again would depend solely on a commitment on God's part in which God says that He will keep such from ever happening. For this to be a necessary conclusion would require: (1) a promise from God that He would not allow a person who is saved to apostatize, or (2) that the doctrine of unconditional election would be true. In the case of unconditional election, the guarantee that apostasy would not happen would be implicit in the doctrine of unconditional election. If God gives a promise that He will not allow a Christian to commit apostasy, where is it? I will deal with the subject of election in the next chapter. I will build a case for conditional election in Chapter 17.

Erickson's view is also dependent on the view that the only way that John 10:28, 29 can be understood is as denying the possibility that a person can lose his salvation. I think I have shown in my treatment of these verses above that that is not the required interpretation of John 10:28, 29.

Another important point in Erickson's case is his view that Hebrews 6:9 affirms the position that the writer was telling his readers that the danger he was describing had not and would not happen to them. I think we can safely say that the recipients of the epistle had not committed apostasy. But that is not the same as saying that no one had. The ones who had committed apostasy would have already left the church. Verse 9 is a statement of what was true of the recipients of the epistle at the time of the writing of the epistle, not a guarantee about the future.

The translation of the NASB of the first part of Hebrews 6:6 is, "And *then* have fallen away." This translation suggests that some had fallen away. It is a better translation of the Greek than the "if" translation of the KJV and the NIV. The "if" translation requires that *kai* (the Greek for "and") be left untranslated. The *kai* is translated in the NASB as "and." That gives us a more accurate picture of what the Greek is saying.

I believe that Robert Shank's comments are to the point concerning the view that these are only warnings to help the believer avoid an apostasy that he most certainly will not commit. He explains:

> The folly of their contention is seen in the fact that, the moment a man becomes persuaded that their doctrine of unconditional security is correct, the warning passages immediately lose the very purpose and value which they claim for them. . . . How can there be any "earnest warning" to the believer who is sufficiently "instructed" to understand that the "warning" is directed against an impossibility?[30]

2 PETER 2:20-22

Had these people been saved?

The ones under consideration are qualified by two expressions: (1) "They have escaped the pollutions of the world." (2) They did it "through the knowledge of the Lord and Saviour Jesus Christ."

In the same epistle, in 1:4, the following expression occurs: "having escaped the corruption that is in the world through lust." It is associated with being made a partaker of the divine nature which is a privilege only for Christians. The expression in 1:4 is practically the same as in 2:20. Surely they refer to the same thing. It is the only other such expression in the epistle. On what grounds does a person say that one text is referring to a saved person and the other text to one who has made a false profession of Christianity?

Let us examine the second expression: "through the knowledge of the Lord and Saviour Jesus Christ." It will be observed that this knowledge was the basis of their having escaped the pollutions of the world. It will also be noted that, in 1:3, 4, the following things are obtained through the knowledge of Christ:

1. "All things that pertain unto life and godliness" (verse 3).
2. "Partakers of the divine nature" (verse 4).
3. "Escaped the corruption that is in the world through lust" (verse 4).

A careful study of 1:3, 4 and 2:20 will show that, in both instances, the corruption of the world had been escaped through the knowledge of the Lord and Savior Jesus Christ.

When such evidence occurs within the bounds of the same epistle for considering those in 2:20 as being saved on the same grounds as those in 1:3, 4, the question must be asked, "For what reasons can a person deny that those referred to in 2:20 were saved while affirming that those in 1:3, 4 were saved?" Also, keep in mind that every expression such as "through the knowledge of our Lord and Saviour Jesus Christ" found in the epistle, without exception, refers those who are saved. Regardless of what we may interpret the warning to be, we must accept the fact that it refers to people who have been saved.

What is the warning about in this passage?

In 2 Peter 2:20-22, it is made plain that the warning here is against forsaking the truth that is in Christ for a false system. This is made clear when we read the entire second chapter. The first part of the chapter makes mention of false teachers, and the last part warns against being led astray by them and tells what the consequences will be.

What will be the result if they fail to heed the warning?

In this passage it is said, "The latter end is worse with them than the beginning . . . it had been better for them not to have known the way of righteousness." The only way these statements could be true would be that they describe the same condition as the verses in Hebrews; therefore, we conclude that these could not be saved again.

Other Passages

The passages just treated, I think, are the basic passages, but they are by no means the only ones that exist. Let us examine a few more.

COLOSSIANS 1:21-23

In this passage, Paul is laying down a stipulation of continuance in the faith as a condition of one's being presented holy, unblamable, and unreprovable in His sight. Here it is definitely implied that to fail to continue in the faith would mean loss of salvation. It is also worthy of note that Paul is warning his readers not to become entangled with false teachers who were teaching things contrary to the true view of Christ.

JOHN 15:2, 6

In verse 2, it is said the branch that bears no fruit is taken away. It has been objected that you cannot press an analogy too far. Therefore, this passage must not be taken as proving that a person can be lost again after having been saved. The only thought that is being taught here is that of fruit bearing. I also believe in exercising great caution against pressing analogies too far. I believe that much injustice is done to the interpretation of Scripture by overworking analogies and figures. But we must keep in mind that Jesus Himself is drawing all of the analogies in this allegory;[31] therefore, when He says, "Every branch in me that beareth not fruit he taketh away: and every branch that beareth fruit, he purgeth it," I must make a distinction between "being taken away" and "being purged." Also, "being taken away" requires an interpretation because Jesus draws the analogy Himself and says that there is a work which the Father does of taking away the unfruitful branches.

It is important to observe that there are two kinds of branches spoken of in verse 2: (1) one that bears no fruit, and (2) one that does not bear as much as it should.

A branch is not taken out because it fails to bear as much as it should. Such a branch is pruned so it will bear more fruit. The believer is not taken out of Christ because he or she is not bearing as much fruit as he should. Rather, God works with him to get him to bear more fruit. It is the one who bears no fruit that is taken away.

I think it will be very helpful if we tie this in with Hebrews 6:7, 8. The result of the apostasy that is described in verses 4-6 is seen in verse 8. The apostate is bearing thorns and briers.

It is a point of interest here to note that verses 7 and 8 are speaking of the same piece of ground. At first it brought forth herbs, and later it brought forth thorns and briers. *The Amplified Bible* makes it clear that verse 8 is speaking about the same piece of ground as verse 7. It reads, "But if [that same soil] persistently bears thorns and thistles, it is considered worthless and near to being cursed, whose end is to be burned."[32] [Brackets by translators].

By comparing our findings to John 15:2, we see the apostate as one who does not bear fruit; instead, he bears thorns and briers. Therefore, he is taken out as one who does not bear fruit.

John 15:6 is referring to the same things as verse 2, only looking at it from a different point of view. Here we see that, if a man abides not in Christ, he is cast forth as a branch.

I think 1 John 2:22-24 is helpful in determining just what is meant by *abiding* and *abiding not*, as used in John 15. In 1 John 2:22, 23, John warns against those who have false views concerning Christ. In 2:24, he says, "Let that therefore abide in you, which ye have heard from the beginning." In other words, instead of taking the view of Christ as is presented to you by false teachers, continue to believe the correct doctrine of Christ which you have heard from the beginning.

Then he goes on to say, "If that which ye have heard from the beginning [the correct doctrine of Christ] shall remain in you, ye also shall continue in the Son, and in the Father."

The same Greek word that is translated *abide* in John 15 is translated *continue* in the verse just cited. In 1 John 2:24, the condition for continuing (abiding) in Christ is to abide in the true doctrine concerning Christ. It is definitely implied that, if the reader of 1 John should choose to forsake the true doctrine of Christ, he would not remain in Christ.

Second John 9 gives proof of what we have just said, "Whosoever transgresseth, and abideth not in the doctrine of Christ, hath not God." This verse definitely proves that a person who does not believe in the true doctrine of Christ is not saved. Taken in its context, it seems to be a warning to the saved person not to be led astray by false teachings concerning Christ. To forsake the true doctrine in favor of the false would mean that the person would not have God.

Upon considering these references, it seems clear that for a person not to abide in Christ, as in John 15:6, would mean that he forsook the true teachings of Christ. Is it not also taught in the other references mentioned that to fail to continue in the true doctrine of Christ would mean rejection by God, which John 15:6 describes as being cast forth as a branch? The result of being cast forth is to be withered and burned. The same thing happens to the apostate of Hebrews 6 as is seen in the figure set forth in verse 8.

Up to this point, the following conclusions have been established: (1) The Bible teaches that a saved person can lose his salvation.[33] (2) Salvation continues on the condition of faith but will be forfeited by unbelief. (3) As long as a person remains saved, he has both justification and sanctification. (4) When a person does lose his salvation, he cannot be saved again.

The Consistency of the Possibility of Loss of Salvation
With Other Doctrines

There are several questions that are yet to be answered in developing and defending the doctrine. The first problem is to show the consistency of this doctrine with other doctrines.

CONSISTENT WITH GOD'S SOVEREIGNTY

The Calvinistic view of continuance in salvation is the logical outgrowth of their interpretation of God's sovereignty. To show this connection, I will repeat a quotation given earlier in this chapter from Lewis Sperry Chafer. He explains:

> The failure of one soul to be saved and to reach glory whom God has ordained to that end means the disruption of the whole actuality of divine sovereignty. If God could fail in one feature, be it ever so small, He could fail in all. If He could fail in anything, He ceases to be God and the universe is drifting to a destiny about which God himself could know nothing.

Their interpretation of divine sovereignty is the foundation principle and the guiding principle in the thought of thorough going Calvinism. There can be no question that "God must accomplish what He sets out to do if He is to be Sovereign." I fully concur with this statement. The question is *what has God set out to do.* Has He set out to include all divine activity in a *cause* and *effect* relationship as distinguished from an *influence* and *response* relationship? Does God have the same sort of cause and effect relationship with persons that He has with the material universe?

If God works with *cause* and *effect* relationships in His relationship with human persons, the Calvinistic system has much to commend itself. By applying the *cause* and *effect* relationships to persons, I do not mean to infer that the nature of the object in personal relationships may not be taken into account, but it is *cause* and *effect* as long as *the cause guarantees the effect.* It cannot be otherwise. This must be true in both redemptive and nonredemptive matters. If not, God is not sovereign on Calvinistic premises. At least this would be true in Classical Calvinism. Those who choose the name Calvinist, but are not willing to follow through with the logical implications set forth above probably need to rethink whether they should call themselves Calvinists. The burden of proof is on them as to whether or not they can legitimately designate themselves as Calvinists.

The ultimate question in all of this is: What has God revealed to us in His Word concerning His sovereignty? The problem is that if a person goes to the Bible with the preconceived notion that the only way for God to be sovereign is for Him to perform all of His activity in the framework of cause and effect relationships, he will force that interpretation on all Scripture passages, regardless of what they say. Therefore, we need to give some attention to whether this is the only way in which an absolute Sovereign may act.

Is it impossible, in principle, for God to direct His sovereignty within the framework of *influence* and *response* when it comes to His relationship with persons? Is He incapable of working within this framework? Does He have to restrict Himself to cause and effect relationships to keep from losing His sovereignty? My answer to all these questions is no. I would think any person would think long and hard before he gave a yes answer to any of these questions. Yet, if the answer to these questions is no, there is no logical necessity for a person to believe that all of God's activity toward persons must be with the intent of a guaranteed effect. We do not have to study the Word of God with the predisposition that divine sovereignty demands a guaranteed effect.

I believe God accomplishes *all of His purposes.* He achieves *all of His goals.* The choice to create human beings as personal beings was His own choice. That choice meant He would deal with us as persons. He would work with us in the framework of *influence* and *response.* This meant man's responses could include both *obedience* and *disobedience.* God does not lose His sovereignty when man disobeys. We are not to assume that God desires man's disobedience. We should assume however that God desires that disobedience would be a real option for man, created as he is with personality. In the *cause* and *effect* relationship approach to sovereignty, it is rather difficult to see how disobedience ever entered the universe without either destroying God's sovereignty, if He disapproves of sin, or corrupting His holiness if He does not. It does not help very much to say that God's ways are inscrutable to us.

In the *influence* and *response* approach, God does not depend upon omnipotence alone to execute His sovereignty. He depends upon wisdom. It takes far more wisdom for God to be sovereign within the framework of influence and response than it does within the framework of cause and effect. I think the *influence* and *response* approach exalts the sovereignty of God far more than does the *cause* and *effect* approach. If we grant that God's sovereignty must work within the framework of *cause* and *effect*, unconditional election, irresistible grace or effectual call, and unconditional continuance in salvation all follow through with absolute precision of thought and logical necessity. It is a very simple system. It may be hard to believe, but it is not hard to understand. If we grant that God's sovereignty *could* work within the framework of influence and response whether it does or not, the Calvinistic system does not follow through as a logical necessity. We would be dependent upon revelation to tell us how God chooses to operate.

If we grant that God's sovereignty works within the framework of influence and response, Calvinism is either ruled out or one would be using influence and response simply as a disguised form of cause and effect. It requires more thought to comprehend personal relationships than it does *cause* and *effect* relationships. The simplicity of *cause* and *effect* relationships is not found in influence-response relationships. The operation of God's sovereignty within the frame work of influence and response requires more thought to be appreciated and understood. This should not be surprising since we are dealing with personal relationships. There is much that is hard to explain about the function of personal relationships, even when speaking of exclusively human relationships.

A more thorough treatment of Calvinism will be given in the next chapter. My purpose in these observations has been to show that there is no logical necessity which requires that the Calvinistic system be true. I am quite certain that it is within the *framework of logical possibilities* for God to choose to use the approach of *conditional continuance in salvation* in dealing with man. There is *no logical necessity* for God to lose His sovereignty and the universe either fall apart or run on an uncertain course if a person should lose his salvation. This would be true only if God chose to operate within the framework of unconditional continuance in salvation, but failed to achieve His purpose.

If God says that every Christian is eternally secure and can under no circumstance ever lose his salvation, we would certainly judge God to be less than sovereign if anyone did lose his salvation. However, there is nothing in the nature of God's sovereignty to forbid Him to be able to work in a plan whereby He used the approach of conditional continuance in salvation rather than unconditional continuance. As Picirilli explains, "We believe in a Sovereign God; but a Sovereign God is just as free to make salvation conditional as any other way. And our God is big enough to handle a real contingency in His universe."[34]

COMPATIBLE WITH ATONEMENT AND JUSTIFICATION
Berkhof comments:

In His atoning work Christ paid the price to purchase the sinner's pardon and acceptance. His righteousness constitutes the perfect ground for the justification of the sinner, and it is impossible that one who is justified by the payment of such a perfect and
efficacious price should again fall under condemnation.[35]

It is true that as long as a person has the death and righteousness of Christ he is justified. He
cannot be lost and at the same time have the death of Christ. However, since he has the death and
righteousness of Christ only by identification conditioned on faith, on the condition of unbelief the
identification can be broken and the person would no longer have the death and righteousness of
Christ. (For a more thorough explanation of this point, see the discussion under objections to the
satisfaction view of atonement in Chapter 11, "Atonement and Justification.")

A Choice to Be Made by Calvinists

The Calvinist, to be logical, must decide between basing his view of unconditional continuance
on *atonement* or *upon the keeping power of God.* If atonement seals the security of the believer
so that it cannot be undone, there is no place for being kept by the power of God, at least so far as
justification is concerned. By the nature of the case, it could not be forfeited. The only place for the
keeping power of God for those who base unconditional continuance in salvation on the nature of
atonement and justification would be in the area of sanctification. The keeping power of God would
have no bearing on continuance in justification since by the nature of the case justification could
not be forfeited.

Either choice that the Calvinist makes is not without consequences for him. To ground unconditional continuance on atonement and justification means that it cannot be grounded in the power
of God that is related to His sovereignty. To take the ground for unconditional continuance away
from the keeping power of God creates a real problem for those who say the passages used to support conditional continuance are, instead, warnings that God uses as a means of helping those who
are saved to persevere. Berkhof explains concerning the warnings:

> There are warnings against apostasy which would seem to be quite uncalled for if the
> believer could not fall away, Matt. 24:12; Col. 1:23; Heb. 2:1; 3:14; 6:11; 1 John 2:6.
> But these warnings regard the whole matter from the side of man and are seriously
> meant. They prompt self-examination, and are instrumental in keeping believers in the
> way of perseverance. They do not prove that any of those addressed will apostatize, but
> simply that the use of means is necessary to prevent them from committing this sin.[36]

To interpret these warnings, as Berkhof and many other Calvinists do, to be real warnings used
to prevent apostasy on the part of believers means that, in principle, a person could lose his salvation were it not for the power of God. For this to be true, the loss of salvation would have to be consistent with every other doctrine except the promised keeping power of God. Yet, Berkhof, as quoted above, grounds unconditional continuance also in atonement and justification. It cannot be both

ways. If the Calvinist chooses to ground unconditional continuance in atonement and justification rather than the power of God, he *cannot* interpret the passages referred to as warnings used by God to help the believer persevere. This would be true because, in principle, there would be no possibility of losing his salvation. There must at least be the *possibility* in principle, if not in fact, of a person losing salvation before warnings can be said to be used in helping a person to keep from losing his salvation. The warning is not a warning if it does not say to the person that he would lose his salvation if a certain thing were to take place.

Those who ground unconditional continuance in salvation on atonement and justification must come up with some other interpretation of the "warning verses." The other interpretation that is given for these passages is that they are warnings to professing Christians. Herman Hoeksema in dealing with Hebrews 6:4-6 in a quotation given earlier in this chapter does not believe that these people had been saved. He takes the position that "they went through the outward show of repentance, and for a time walked in that repentance. But now they have definitely fallen away even from the outward show." Wayne Gruden takes the position that while it is possible to take what is given in this passage as a description of a saved person, the case is not decisive.[37]

My own treatment, and why I believe the people referred to in this passage had been saved, appears earlier in this chapter. I will not restate my case here. I will simply say that if we knew some who had made a false profession, I think we would spend our time trying to get them to make a genuine decision for Christ. We would do that rather than tell them that if they fall from that profession, they can never be renewed to that profession again. What those who merely profess need to know is that they are not saved. They need to be told how they can tell that their profession is empty. They need to examine themselves in the light of the guaranteed results of salvation.

When a person chooses to ground unconditional continuance in salvation in the power of God rather than grounding it in atonement and justification, he is admitting that in principle a person could lose his salvation, if not in fact. This means that unconditional continuance must either relate: (1) to logical necessity growing out of a *cause* and *effect* relationship view of sovereignty, or (2) God's promise of unconditional continuance. Either way, we expect to find a Scriptural basis for unconditional continuance that would take the form of a *promise*. I have already given my reasons for believing the Scripture teaches the contrary. Earlier in this chapter I have dealt with the verses thought by some to make such a promise.

CONSISTENT WITH THE IMPUTATION OF CHRIST'S DEATH AND RIGHTEOUSNESS

While the satisfaction view of atonement and Justification are consistent with the possibility of losing salvation, it is not consistent with some patterns of thought in connection with the possibility of losing salvation. If we believe in the imputation of Christ's death and righteousness as the ground of our justification, we do not have room for a halfway state between being saved and being lost. If we are in union with Christ, we have His death and righteousness and are justified. If we are not in union with Christ, we are not justified.

We can be in danger of losing our salvation, but we have lost it only when the union is broken and we no longer have the death and righteousness of Christ.

CONSISTENT WITH THE UNION WITH CHRIST
Berkhof explains:

> They who are united to Christ by faith become partakers of His Spirit, and thus become one body with Him, pulsating with the life of the Spirit. They share in the life of Christ, and because He lives they live also. It is impossible that they should again be removed from the body, thus frustrating the divine ideal. The union is permanent, since it origenates in a permanent and unchangeable cause, the free eternal love of God.[38]

There can be no question that as long as a person is in union with Christ he is saved. To be in union with Christ is to be saved. For one not to be in union with Christ means he is not saved. The question of whether this union can be broken is for God to decide. Our knowledge should come from His revelation. It is not for us to decide on the basis of what we think is logical necessity or what we consider to be unthinkable. Jesus has answered the question for us in clear terms, "Every branch in me that beareth not fruit he taketh away" (Jn. 15:2). I pointed out above that those who base their view of unconditional continuance upon the keeping power of God are admitting, in principle, that their view of union with Christ would not preclude believing a person could lose his salvation.

According to John 15:2, 6, if one turns back to unbelief, God will take that one out of Christ. Such a person will no longer be in union with Christ. He or she will no longer have the death and righteousness of Christ on his account. If what I am saying here is true, there are no grounds on which to build the popular view of "once saved, always saved" that is advocated by Stanley and others.

CONSISTENT WITH SALVATION BY GRACE THROUGH FAITH
Salvation by grace means that it comes by unmerited favor. It is a gift bestowed upon us that we do not deserve. It is something for which we in no way pay. Our justification is a gift from God. In no way did we participate in the ground of our justification. It is the death and righteousness of Christ that forms the grounds of our justification—not our obedience. This fact always remains unchanged. The act of baptizing us into Christ, regenerating us, and the indwelling of the Holy Spirit are all gifts of God grounded in the atoning work of Christ. These have all been applied to our account. Every loving move of God toward us is based on His grace which is grounded in Christ's atonement. Nothing that I have said about conditional continuance in salvation has at any point contradicted these observations.

There is nothing whatsoever about the nature of a gift that either keeps it from being rejected when offered or keeps it from being returned if received. It is inherent in the nature of a gift that as long as it remains a gift the recipient of the gift can in no way participate in the payment of the gift. The very nature of the requirement of justification along with the qualifications of a human being who has sinned, means that a human being can never participate in the payment for his own justification. He can provide neither absolute righteousness nor infinite sufferings.

The Bible plainly conditions salvation on faith. To insist that salvation is *kept on the condition of faith* no more contradicts the notion of free salvation than saying that it is *received on the condition.* It is surprising that anyone would think so. It is folly to charge that to require the continuation of faith for the continuation of salvation makes faith a work and thus puts salvation on the basis of works. The Bible, itself, clearly removes faith from the category of works (Rom. 4:3-5).

Faith would be a work if it were to be considered the *ground* of our justification instead of the *condition.* Faith contributes *absolutely nothing* to the ground of our justification. The ground of our justification is the death and righteousness of Christ on our account—nothing more and nothing less! When this distinction is made between *ground* and *condition,* there is no way that continued faith serving as the condition of continued justification could make a *work* out of faith.

Picirilli comments:

> Any time the Bible talks about believing for salvation, the verb *"believing"* is always in the tense in the Greek that means continuing belief. . . . Verses like John 5:24, "he that . . . *believeth"* always have the verb in the tense that denotes the action in process. In other words, we could well interpret John 5:24: "He that goes on believing in me shall not come into condemnation." So in this way too, the *conditional* nature of such promises is made clear.[39]

It would be helpful at this point to elaborate on what it means to say that a person has saving faith in Jesus Christ. It means more than saying that he maintains correct doctrine about Jesus, although it certainly involves that. When a person exercises faith in Jesus, he is recognizing Jesus as a Redeemer from sin. This includes both justification and sanctification. Faith in Jesus as Redeemer always implies that the person who is exercising this faith also wants redemption. He is trusting in Jesus both to forgive him and to make him the kind of person he should be. There is the desire and the expectation that God will be working to make the person into the likeness of Christ. We are not to suppose that people who are basically indifferent to moral and spiritual concerns have saving faith. This would contradict both the nature of saving faith and the nature of salvation.

Roads to Apostasy

HERETICAL DOCTRINE

One of the main roads to apostasy is through false doctrine. This is one of the reasons that the New Testament takes such a strong stand against heresy (Gal. 1:8, 9; 1 Jn. 4:1-3; 2 Jn. 7-11; Jude 3-19; and others) and gives so much attention to grounding Christians in the faith.

This danger may be presented to the Christian by cults as well as various forms of liberal doctrine within many denominations. One of the tragedies of born again Christians attending liberal seminaries has been that many have lost their faith. As strange as it may seem, this was more of a problem fifty years ago than it is today.

THE INFLUENCE OF MODERNISM

In secular education, modernism seeks to build a worldview based on natural causes and effects. It has no place for divine revelation. The problem here centers to a large extent on the fact that many believers encounter naturalism when confronted by teachers who are far better trained than they are. In many instances, they do not know of anyone to whom they can turn who can explain the difficulties they are facing. They run the risk of being overcome by naturalism when they are unable to defend themselves. This is one of the reasons that Christian colleges should be provided for Christian young people where their faith will be strengthened rather than undermined. The greater danger now is from postmodernism. I mention modernism here because there are still many functioning according to the modernist paradigm.

THE INFLUENCE OF POSTMODERNISM

The danger of postmodernism does not come from powerful rational arguments against Christianity. Postmodernism spells the death of Truth, the death of reason, the death of morals, and the death of a rational worldview. In Christian thought, belief in Truth, the proper use of reason, moral conviction, and a rational worldview are all foundational to the survival of Christian thinking. The conditioning power of postmodernism creates a postmodern mood which desensitizes people and undermines the concern in these areas that is necessary to Christian conviction. The brand of bigotry which is leveled against anyone who dares to believe that his or her view is true and someone else's view is wrong is more than some are prepared to cope with.

TAMPERING WITH SIN

A third road that leads to apostasy is tampering with sin. This can lead to a spirit of defeat and place one under the chastising hand of God (Heb. 12:7-11). God has determined that His people will be holy; thus, He places His people under chastisement when they sin. God's determination to make His people holy will bring a sinning Christian to a point in which he or she will either have to repent or forsake God altogether. If he should turn from God, this will mean turning from faith. He will make shipwreck of faith (1 Tim. 1:18, 19).

A PROLONGED EXPERIENCE WITH SEVERE UNRESOLVED PROBLEMS

When a person goes through a period of severe difficulty, and he seems to find no answers to the problem he or she is facing, whatever belief-system (or worldview) he acknowledges will be seriously challenged. People are at higher risk of changing their belief-system when the view that they trust in proves to be inadequate to deal with the problems of life that they are facing.

I have made the above statement many times in classes that I have taught. I remember one occasion when, after I said that, a young man gave the class an illustration of what I had said. He said that he and his wife had lost a five-year-old daughter. His wife's father was an atheist. His atheism was unable to support him in his time of grief at the loss of his granddaughter. He gave up his atheism, which was inadequate for his need, and became a Christian. His daughter who was a Christian almost lost her faith. The pain she was experiencing placed a strain on the view that she had believed and was trusting in. The student said that his wife had been able to find answers for her needs and that she had been able to deal with her doubts.

We will do well to keep in mind that the Book of Hebrews was written to believers who were suffering persecution. The writer refers to the book as "a word of exhortation" or "a word of encouragement" (Heb. 13:22). It was during a time of severe discouragement that some had chosen to forsake Christ and go back to the Old Testament sacrifices.

SUFFERING FROM SEVERE PERSECUTION

With many of us in America, our belief in the possibility of apostasy is somewhat an academic matter. We have not been given the choice of prison or freedom if we would deny our faith in Christ. We have not been given the choice of life or death if we would deny our faith. As I traveled across Ukraine and Russia in 1996, I saw those who had chosen prison rather than deny their faith. In Kiev, Ukraine I had the privilege of meeting Georgi Vinns who spent eight years in prison for his faith before President Carter arranged for his release in connection with the release of two Russian spies.[40] I met those who had family members who chose death rather than to deny their faith. I saw those whose children were denied the right of higher education because they were Christians. I saw those who suffered all kinds of harassment from the KGB. To the Baptist in the Former Soviet Union, the doctrine of the possibility of shipwreck of faith is very real. Those living in areas of continued persecution need our prayers that they will keep the faith.

A Word of Caution to Arminians

When the impression is given that it would be very easy for a person to lose his or her salvation, many live their lives in the bondage of fear. Jesus said, "I am come that they might have life, and that they might have it more abundantly" (Jn. 10:10). There is no abundant life in living in the bondage of fear.

Any view of a biblical teaching that makes one live in the bondage of fear is faulty. It is not God's intent for people to be obsessed with the fear of losing salvation. An unhealthy fear leads one into over-introspection. As Christians, we are not to be given over to continuous introspection. Continuous introspection makes a person self-centered. As Christians, we are to be Christ-centered.

We need to have a healthy concern about the possibility of us losing our salvation. But it is not healthy when it causes people who are nowhere close to losing their salvation to be robbed of the joy of the Christian life.

We need to help people see that they are saved by Christ alone, on the condition of faith alone. They need to see that they are justified by the death and righteousness of Christ. They are justified by Christ's righteousness, not their own. They need to understand that the only thing that would cause them to lose their salvation would be a deliberate choice to turn from Him. That is my doctrine. I have assurance of salvation. I do not live in fear of losing my salvation.

Assurance of Salvation

No writing on perseverance is complete unless it is also discussed from the standpoint of assurance. Certainly the grounds of assurance are strong enough in the Scriptures that a child of God can enter into the blessings of assurance and not be constantly worried by the fear of falling.

When we stop and think what the new birth does for a person, surely we have strong grounds to believe that he will continue in the faith. By the new birth a person is made a new creature (2 Cor. 5:17) and possesses a new nature. This new nature within him is thirsting and hungering for the things of God. There is also a distaste for the things of sin. With this change wrought in his heart, the person who is born again will never be satisfied apart from a close walk with God.

The relationship which the indwelling Spirit has with the believer is another ground of assurance that the believer will continue in the faith. The Holy Spirit has a vital interest in us and works patiently and untiringly with the believer to get him to be an obedient child. He does this by producing a consciousness and conviction of sin in the heart of the Christian. He chastises the believer (Heb. 12:7, 8, 11), making it so that he cannot enjoy life except when living in harmony with God. He teaches the Christian many wonderful truths about Christ that encourage him to live for Christ. Along with all else He does, He gives strength to the believer in his warfare against the flesh (Gal. 5:16, 17). Thus, we see that the Holy Spirit seeks to lead the believer away from that which would ensnare him; He enables him to walk in this way and keeps him from enjoying walking any other way.

John 10:28, 29 gives the Christian strong grounds on which to stand. In Christ he has eternal life and will never perish. When a person is saved, he is baptized into Christ's body; and as long as he is in Christ, he has eternal life and will never perish. This is what we have in Christ, and we are also promised that no one can take us out of Christ. Salvation is a personal matter between the believer and Christ. No outsider can take the believer out of Christ. If he is ever taken out, it will be an act of God the Father as husbandman, as is set forth in John 15:2, and that only on the grounds of not abiding in Christ (Jn. 15:6). To be in Christ means to have eternal life, and no outside force nor combination of forces can take us out of Christ.

Another ground of security is that God will not cast us out at the least little thing we do. We are saved by faith and kept by faith. We are lost, after we are once saved, only by turning from faith in Christ to unbelief.

The view, as we have given it, gives a person all the assurance he needs to have joy. It does not keep him in constant fear of falling; yet, at the same time, he is aware that it is possible to fall. It also keeps salvation on a faith basis instead of mixing it with works. This is not just a line of reasoning; it has the support of the Scriptures.

Some who hold to unconditional continuance in salvation seem to think that conditional continuance makes the continuation of salvation a matter that is so totally of man that God is out of the picture. This is not the case. God is working with the person to help him or her continue in faith and to grow in grace. The continued response of faith is not in a context where the Christian is totally independent. It is in a context where he is dependent upon God. God is working in and through him. Yet, there is a sense in which his decisions are his own. It is possible for him to go contrary to God's leading not only before he is saved, but also afterward. Nevertheless, those who love God and understand the positive grounds for assurance do not live with fear that they will go contrary to God's leading and depart from the faith.

To warn Christians against apostasy is not intended to make people live in great fear. Let me illustrate. Suppose you were traveling down a road after a severe rain storm and you discovered that a bridge was out and you put up a sign to warn people. You would not do that to create fear in people. You would do that to increase their safety. The warning signs on a road give me assurance as I travel. Since I know what the dangers are, I can avoid them.

As I travel the road of the Christian life, if there are warning signs along the way it helps me to know what the dangers are. It helps me avoid apostasy if I know what it is and what the result would be.

When many Calvinists interpret Hebrews 6:4-6, they say the same thing that I have just said (See the quotation given from Erickson earlier in this chapter). Calvinists, who take this approach, think it is a warning to help a Christian avoid something that he will not do. I think it is a warning to help a Christian avoid a sin that he could commit and in rare instances some people do commit. When I see these warning signs, they help me follow Peter's advice when he said, "Wherefore the rather, brethren, give diligence to make your calling and election sure: for if ye do these things ye shall never fall" (2 Pet. 1:10).

It also helps our assurance when we see that a Christian is not lost every time he commits a sin. Christians do commit sins of the kind mentioned in Numbers 15:27. The Christian desires to do right, but he does not always succeed. But Hebrews 6:4-6 and 10:26-29 are talking about something drastically different. When Christians commit the kind of sins referred to in Numbers 15:27, they feel bad about what they are doing and the Holy Spirit works to produce repentance. We have no right to offer assurance to people who sin and do not have any concern about it. Such people do not show evidence that they have been made new creatures as is spoken of in 2 Corinthians 5:17. In most cases like this, the people have never been saved. However, when people are chastised for their sins, that is evidence of salvation (Heb. 12:7, 8).

Let me say here that assurance is not guaranteed by a person's theology. A person may believe any of the various forms of the doctrine of "once saved, always saved" and still doubt his or her salvation. It is possible for a person to believe that he cannot lose salvation and still not be sure that he has it. One of my professors told about a leading Calvinist theologian who lost the assurance that he was one of the elect and went insane. It is important for all of us to give attention to the assurance of salvation.

Justification and Sanctification Always Together

We must not conclude this study without stressing that salvation includes both justification and sanctification. To speak about continuing in salvation is to speak about continuing in both justification and sanctification. The package cannot be broken. We cannot have one without the other. The viewpoint that offers continued justification, whether conditional or unconditional, without sanctification has no support whatsoever in the Bible. It is also impossible to reduce sanctification to the point that it has no results in the believer's experience.

I have already dealt with this point in the chapter on sanctification. Let me give a summary restatement that holiness is not optional but is a guaranteed result of salvation. (1) Paul emphatically states that those who live in gross sin will not inherit the kingdom of God (1 Cor. 6:9-11; Gal. 5:19-21; and Eph. 5:3-7). (2) The writer of Hebrews says that without holiness no man shall see the Lord (Heb. 12:14). (3) From both a positive and a negative viewpoint, 1 John makes it clear that for a person to fail to practice righteousness means that he is not saved (1 Jn. 2:3, 4, 9-11; 3:3-10, 14, 15; 4:20; and 5:4, 18).

These verses do not say that for a person to practice these sins would cause him or her to lose his salvation. That is not the reason given for saying that those practicing sin are not saved. The reason given for denying that people who practice sin are saved is that those who are born of God cannot practice sin (1 Jn. 3:9).[41] Practicing righteousness is neither the condition of receiving salvation nor is it the condition for its continuation. It is a result of salvation, or we might say it is a part of salvation.

The loss of salvation cannot come as a result of practicing sin, because a person who is born of God does not have practicing sin in the framework of his possibilities. (See "The Guaranteed Results of Sanctification," pp. 241-42.) This does not mean that he cannot commit acts of sin. The fact that acts of sin are an open possibility for the believer means that it is an open possibility that a person could commit an act of apostasy. This is so only if apostasy is a sinful act rather than being a process of practicing sin. While the initial act of apostasy is a single act, it will be followed by a practice of wilful or defiant sin (Heb. 10:26). The single act of apostasy propels a person into the practice of sin.

Before Adam and Eve sinned, it was not in the framework of possibilities that they could practice sin, but it was within the framework of possibility for them to commit an act of sin. When they committed that act of sin, their nature was changed. With their change of nature they could practice sin. The sinner does not have it within the framework of possibilities for him to practice righteousness and to be able to please God. By the help of the Holy Spirit, it is within the framework of possibilities for the sinner to respond to the gospel and be saved. If he does respond, this introduces him to a framework of possibilities wherein he can practice righteousness and please God. Having done so he can no longer practice sin.

It is within the framework of possibilities for a person to lose his salvation if the cause for it can be summed up in an act of departure. There would, of course, be some things that lead up to the act of departure. From the standpoint of reason, it is just as logical that a saved person could make this departure, so far as his own will is concerned, as it was for Adam and Eve to sin or for a sinner to respond to the gospel. It is also just as logical to believe that a Christian can depart from his faith, in the light of God's sovereignty, as it is to believe that Adam and Eve sinned in the light of God's sovereignty. The only thing that could make it more logical to believe that Adam and Eve could sin, in the light of God's sovereignty, but that the Christian cannot depart from faith, would be to believe that God wanted Adam and Eve to sin while He does not want the Christian to depart from his faith.

Some Practical Problems

Some people are hard for us to identify in the light of our theology. It seems as if they have definitely been saved at some time in the past. It seems that they have not committed apostasy or turned from their faith. Yet, it seems that they are living in sin or practicing sin. I would say that obviously one of our judgments is wrong. Either, the person never was saved, has lost his faith, or is not living in sin. I may not be able to decide what his real case is. I would certainly not offer assurances to such a person. I would not propose to give an official diagnosis of his case. I am sympathetic with those who may feel obligated to consider such people as neither exactly in nor exactly out, but I think the position that I have set forth which says that a person must be either in or out is more tenable.

I believe a person is either saved or unsaved, but I cannot pass judgment on all cases. It is my opinion that a similar position will have to be adopted in some cases regardless of what a person's view may be.

Some people prefer to limit their use of the word *apostasy* to a departure from the faith on theological grounds, i.e., trading the truth for heresy. I use the term *apostasy* to refer to shipwreck of faith in the broad sense. It is what a person leaves, not what he goes to that counts. Some may go to a clearly defined system of unbelief. Others may simply turn to unbelief.

There is a problem about the use of the word *backslider.* The question is often asked: Is the backslider saved? It depends on how the word *backslider* is used. The word does not appear in the New Testament. In the Old Testament, it is a very strong word. In every instance except one, the Hebrew word means to turn away or to turn back. The exception is Hosea 4:16 where it means stubborn or rebellious. If by backsliding, we mean a person has turned away from God, such a person is not saved. He has made shipwreck of faith.

In the common use of the word *backslide*, it has a variety of meanings. Some use it only of serious cases. Others use it to refer to lesser degrees of drifting. I prefer not to use the word *backslide* because of the various interpretations that people give to it. They invariably understand me according to their meaning of the word, not mine. To say that a backslider is *not* lost means to some people that a person could be saved and then fall into the worst conceivable state of sin and still be saved. This is absolutely false, whether a person believes in conditional or unconditional continuance in salvation.

Many careless words are spoken on the subject of security—sometimes in stating our own view and at other times stating the views of other people. A well-formulated doctrine of security requires much careful thought and study. The same is true if we are going to understand the other person. The subject of continuance in salvation is an important subject and should receive some of our most careful thought.

15

Introducing the Study of Election

I realize that it is not customary to treat decrees and election after treating the doctrine of perseverance. However, my choice of dealing with it here is deliberate. I believe that a discussion of decrees and election should draw from a thorough study of the doctrines of Scripture, God, man, and salvation both in its provision and application. While Arminians and Calvinists share much common ground, there are major points of difference. Nothing calls attention to that difference like a study of decrees and election.

In this chapter, I will call attention to several terms, ideas, and concepts that I have dealt with before. It will make it easier reading to restate things than it would to refer back to earlier treatments to be read. Another reason for treating material more than once is, I think it is good for some subjects, especially those which require more thought, to receive repeated treatment in a book. In a few cases, I will simply refer back to an earlier treatment.

My plan in this chapter is to first survey Calvinistic and Arminian thought on decrees and election. I will deal with the main concepts that are involved in treating these subjects. I will show what I consider to be problems in Calvinistic thought, and I will build a case for the Arminian position on these subjects.[1] In Chapter 16, I will show what I believe to be the proper interpretation of the passages that Calvinists use to support unconditional election. In Chapter 17, I will give the biblical support for conditional election.

The Calvinistic View of Unconditional Election

Unconditional election says that God, in eternity past, chose to elect certain ones from the fallen race of men for salvation. This election was in no way related to God's foreknowledge of faith on the part of the individual. Those who were thus elected will in due time be saved. God has provided the death and righteousness of Christ for their justification. In the course of time, those who have been chosen will be called. This call is an irresistible call (or an effectual call). It cannot fail to result in saving faith. This salvation is an absolute gift. Man did not in anyway do anything to merit it or receive it. The elect are in no way responsible for having faith. That faith is his or hers as an absolute gift of God.

The Order of Decrees in Calvinism

The wording for the decrees given below is from Millard Erickson.[2]

SUPRALAPSARIANISM
1. The decree to save (elect) some and reprobate others.
2. The decree to create both the elect and the reprobate.
3. The decree to permit the fall of both the elect and the reprobate.
4. The decree to provide salvation only for the elect.

INFRALAPSARIANISM
1. The decree to create human beings.
2. The decree to permit the fall.
3. The decree to elect some and reprobate others.
4. The decree to provide salvation only for the elect.

SUBLAPSARIANISM
1. The decree to create human beings.
2. The decree to permit the fall.
3. The decree to provide salvation sufficient for all.
4. The decree to save some and reprobate others.

Most Classical Calvinists are Infralapsarian. Supralapsarianism, in making the decree to elect some and to reprobates others precede the decree to create, is what is sometimes referred to as Hyper-Calvinism. While in a minority, Supralapsarians have been accepted among Classical Calvinists. Many theologians do not list Sublapsarianism as a separate category. The particular significance of Sublapsarianism is that in making the decree to provide atonement to precede the decree to elect it takes the position of unlimited atonement—thus, four-point Calvinism. All of the above approaches to decrees are in agreement on unconditional election.

Calvinism, Determinism, and Free Will

I must confess that it is not simple to answer the question: "Do Calvinists believe in free will?" Some seem to reject the concept of free will. Others claim to believe in free will. Then, there is the problem of how they define free will. In order to get a clearer picture of how Calvinists deal with the concept of free will, we must first examine their concept of determinism.

THE QUESTION OF DETERMINISM IN CALVINISM
There are various forms of determinism. Our concern is with theistic determinism. Norman L. Geisler explains:

This is the view that all events, including man's behavior, are caused (determined) by God. One of the more famous advocates of this view was the Puritan theologian Jonathan Edwards. He maintained that the concept of free will or self-determinism contradicted the sovereignty of God. If God is truly in control of all things, then no one could act contrary to his will, which is what self-determinism must hold. Hence, for God to be sovereign he must cause every event, be it human or otherwise.[3]

J. A. Crabtree gives a concise definition. He explains: "By 'divine determinism' I mean to denote one who believes every aspect of everything that occurs in the whole of reality is ultimately caused and determined by God."[4]

John S. Feinberg points out, "The fundamental tenet of determinism (and the various forms of Calvinism are forms of determinism) is that for everything that happens, in the light of prevailing conditions, the agent could not have done other than he did. For determinists, there are always sufficient conditions that decisively incline the agent's will to choose one option or another."[5]

These comments about determinism bring up the question: "What about the scope of determinism?" Let us take a look now at how Calvinists deal with this problem.

The Scope of Determinism: The Whole of Created Reality (Unlimited Determinism)

It is obvious that Jonathan Edwards would take his stand with those who make the scope of determinism coextensive with the whole of reality. Gordon H. Clark makes divine determination cover everything including the sinful acts of men. In commenting on Proverbs 21:1 and Ezra 7:6, he explains:

> God controls all governmental policies and decisions. Not only did God cause Pharaoh to hate the Israelites, he caused Cyrus to send the captives back to build Jerusalem. He also caused Hitler to march into Russia and he caused Johnson to escalate a war in Viet Nam. God turns the mind of a ruler in whatever direction he wants to.[6]

In commenting on the action of Joseph's brothers when they sold him to slavery, Clark remarks:

> If Joseph's brothers had killed him as they first thought about doing, then God would have been mistaken. The sale had to take place. Does this mean that God foreordained sinful acts? Well, it certainly means that these acts were certain and determined from all eternity. It means that the brothers could not have done otherwise.[7]

Most Calvinists who make determinism coextensive with the whole of reality are not looking for opportunities to makes statements like Clark makes. If they had to make a comment they would try to soften their comments, but they cannot deny what Clark said.

The Scope of Determinism: Soteriology (Limited Determinism)

Richard A. Muller gives a different perspective on determinism than Clark gives. This rather lengthy quotation will be given so his point will be clear. He explains:

> It is not the case, as the proponents of Arminianism allege, that the use of biblical examples by Calvin and other Reformed theologians to argue their case for predestination indicates "a divine determinism of all human actions." The issue debated between the Arminians and the Reformed was not philosophical determination but soteriology. The biblical examples drawn from the Reformed typically point to the bondage of human beings in sin, to the inability to choose salvation, and, therefore, to the necessity of grace in salvation—not a determination of human actions in general and, especially, not a determination of human beings to commit individual transgressions. It was never the Reformed view that moral acts of human beings are predetermined, any more than it was ever the Reformed view that the fall of Adam was willed by God to the exclusion of Adam's free choice of sin. The divine ordination of all things is not only consistent with human freedom; it makes human freedom possible. As J.S.K. Reid has argued of Calvin's theology, the divine determination so belongs to the ultimate order of being that it cannot be understood as a philosophical determinism in and for the temporal order of being: human responsibility is assumed and God is not the author of sin. This overarching providential determination (which includes the divine ordination of and concurrence in freedom and contingency) is, moreover, distinct from predestination: predestination is the specific ordination of some to salvation, granting the inability of human beings to save themselves. Again; this is not a matter of philosophical determinism, but of soteriology.[8]

Muller also says:

> Reformed doctrine in no way denies that some events are genuinely contingent, having a "cause that could by its nature could have acted differently," that others result from divine persuasion, and that still others are the result of human free agency or deliberation. Reformed theology only insists that the beginning of the redeemed life is solely the work of God, and therefore distinguishes between the general decree of providence that establishes all things, whether necessary, contingent, or free, and the special decree of predestination that establishes salvation by grace alone. Far from being a rigid metaphysical determinism of all human actions, a form of necessitarianism (which was never Reformed doctrine in any case), predestination applies only to the issue of salvation. And the Reformed exegesis of biblical passages related to predestination, far from indicating a determinism of all human actions, indicates the ultimate determination of God in matters pertaining to salvation.[9]

Muller further comments and includes a quotation from the strict Calvinist, William Perkins (1558-1602):

> Human beings move about with a natural freedom, can eat and drink; they can also exercise their humanity freely in the arts, trades, and other occupations; they can practice "civill vertue, justice, temperance, liberalitie, chastitie"; and they may freely exercise the ecclesiastical duties of outward worship.[10]

Muller should not think it strange when Arminians interpret Calvin and other Reformed theologians to mean that "predestination indicates 'a divine determination of all human actions.' "

Well known Calvinists interpret divine determination to be coextensive with the whole of reality. Calvinists, as well as Arminians, need to be aware that there is not unanimous agreement among Calvinists on this point.

THE QUESTION OF FREE WILL IN CALVINISM

It is not a simple matter to find out where Calvinists stand on the subject of free will. It is denied, affirmed, defined, and ignored.

The Denial of Free Will

In a chapter entitled "Free Will," Clark launches an attack on the concept of free will for human beings. One clear statement is found in connection with a comment on Ephesians 1:11. He comments, "This verse states in particular that God works our own willing. It is clear therefore that man's will is not free, but is directed by the working of God."[11]

R. K. McGregor Wright leaves no doubt where he stands on the question of free will. He comments, "The Arminian form of the freewill theory is behind every important issue in evangelical apologetics today. However unpopular and threatening this type of probing may be, evangelical freewillism cannot be allowed to remain unquestioned. Too much is at stake."[12]

The Acceptance of Free Will

J. Oliver Buswell, Jr. remarks:

> As for me, the denial of free will seems to be purely arbitrary philosophical dogmatism, entirely contrary to reasonable evidence and to the biblical view. There is no reason—no psychological, philosophical, or biblical reason—why we may not accept the view that a personal being may be free to choose between certain motives, and having chosen, is personally responsible for his choice. If God is angry with sin, then it follows that the sinner is blameworthy, cosmically, ultimately, absolutely. [13]

In support of his position, Buswell points out:

The answer to question thirteen of the Westminster Shorter Catechism tells us, "Our first parents, being left to the freedom of their own will, fell from the estate wherein they were created by sinning against God." Thus the Westminster Standards repeatedly and emphatically answer the question of the possibility of free will in the affirmative.[14]

The Acceptance of Freedom, but Unclear About Free Will

It is hard to see where Boettner stands on the issue of free will. He comments, "Human nature since the fall retains its constitutional faculties of reason, conscience and free agency, and hence man continues to be a responsible moral agent."[15] Later in his book where he deals with "Objections Commonly Urged Against the Reformed Doctrine of Predestination" he explains what he means by free agency and foreordination. He points out, "By a free agent we mean an intelligent person who acts with rational self-determination; and by Foreordination we mean that from eternity God has made certain the actual course of events which takes place in the life of every person and in the realm of nature."[16]

He gives further confirmation of his belief in free agency when he says, "Predestination and free agency are the twin pillars of a great temple, and they meet above the clouds where human gaze cannot penetrate."[17]

Boettner seems willing to use the term free agent, but he shies away from using the term free will with affirmation. He remarks:

Furthermore, if we admit free will in the sense that absolute determination of events is placed in the hands of man, we might as well spell it with a capital F and a capital W; for then man has become like God,—a first cause, an original spring of action,—and we have as many semi-Gods as we have free wills. Unless the sovereignty of God is given up, we cannot allow this independence to man. It is very noticeable—and in a sense it is reassuring to observe the fact—that the materialistic and metaphysical philosophers deny as completely as do Calvinists this thing that is called **free will.**[18] [bold print his]

Boettner leaves us wondering what the difference is between *free agency* and *free will.* What he says about free will is not supported from any source. It is a caricature of free will. The way it is described, no one would claim it. I must confess that I find Boettner's use of "self-determination" surprising when he gives his definition of "free agency" in the quotation given above. I am surprised that he would affirm *any* use of the term "self-determination" in referring to human beings.

Feinberg speaks of a freedom which he thinks is compatible with determinism. He explains:

Like many other determinists, I claim that there is room for a genuine sense of free human action, even though such action is causally determined. This kind of freedom cannot be indeterministic, of course. Instead, determinists who hold to free will distinguish two kinds of causes which influence and determine actions. On the one hand, there are constraining causes which force an agent to act against his will. On the other hand there are nonconstraining causes. These are sufficient to bring about an action, but they do not force a person to act against his will, desires, or wishes. According to determinists such as myself, an action is free even if causally determined so long as the causes are nonconstraining. This view is often referred to as *soft determinism* or *compatibilism,* for genuine free human action is seen as *compatible* with nonconstraining sufficient conditions which incline the will decisively in one way or another.[19]

Later in this same treatment, in commenting on human responsibility, Feinberg explains:

People are morally responsible for their actions because they do them freely. I agree that no one can be held morally accountable for actions that are not free. But as has already been argued, compatibilism allows the agent to act freely. The key is not whether someone's acts are causally determined or not, but rather *how* they are determined. If the acts are constrained, then they are not free and the agent is not morally responsible for them.[20]

An Observation

Let us take a look at what Feinberg is saying. He says, "Like many other determinists, I claim that there is room for a genuine sense of free human action, even though such action is *causally determined.*" Later he comments, "The key is not whether someone's acts are causally determined or not, but rather *how* they are determined. If the acts are constrained, then they are not free and the agent is not morally responsible for them." [emphasis mine] (See quotations above from Feinberg.)

Feinberg's determinism is coextensive with the whole of reality. The determinism of Muller that is referred to above is restricted to soteriology. Feinberg and Muller would be in essential agreement when it comes to election. However, they differ sharply when it comes to other matters.

It is important to observe that for Feinberg and those who make determinism coextensive with the whole of reality, *all human acts are caused by God.* When he talks about the agent being responsible, he is particularly talking about sin. This is true since there would be no question about action that is acceptable to God. The *only cause* that he has in mind in his determinism is God. This is true since the determinism under consideration is *divine determinism.* That means that God is the cause not only of faith on the part of those who believe, but also for the sins of *dishonesty, murder, rape,* etc. The reason the person is responsible for such action, though it is "causally determined," is that he did what God caused him to do freely, not by constraint. In *unlimited determinism,* God causes people to lie, steal, murder, and to commit rape, but they are not constrained to do so, according to those who advocate this view.

Since Muller limits his determinism to soteriology, all acts that are not related to soteriology *are not causally determined.* This would mean that in these areas there would be no essential reason that his view would have to differ from Arminianism.

I will wait until I present my own thinking before I make any critical observations.

The Question of Foreknowledge and Free Will in Calvinistic Thought

Foreordination, for most Calvinists, takes the mystery out of foreknowledge. As Boettner explains:

> The Arminian objection against foreordination bears with equal force against the foreknowledge of God. What God foreknows must, in the very nature of the case, be as fixed and certain as what is ordained; and if one is inconsistent with the free agency of man, the other must be also. Foreordination renders the events as certain, while foreknowledge presupposes they are certain.

He goes on to say:

> The Arminian doctrine, in rejecting foreordination, rejects the theistic basis for foreknowledge. Common sense tells us that no event can be foreknown unless by some means, either physical or mental, it has been predetermined.[21]

Feinberg, in arguing for his position of "soft determinism," says, "If indeterminism is correct, I do not see how God can be said to foreknow the future. If God actually knows what will (not just might) occur in the future, the future must be set and some sense of determinism applies."[22] Crabtree also sees a problem of divine foreknowledge of free human events. He explains, "No one, not even God, can know the outcome of an autonomous decision that has not been made, can he? To assert the possibility of such knowledge is problematic."[23]

Buswell does not see a problem with God having a knowledge of free acts of human beings. He remarks:

> To the question then how God can know a free act in the future, I reply I do not know, but neither do I know how I can have knowledge by analysis, by inference from reason or from causes, or from statistical data reported by intuition, or (if it is insisted upon) by innate ideas. Knowledge is a mystery in any event, and God's knowledge of free events in the future is only one more mystery, revealed in Scripture. We have good and sufficient grounds to accept, and no valid ground to reject, what Scripture says on this subject.[24]

The Strength of Calvinism in Theological Scholarship

The strength of Calvinism in the world of scholarship is evident. An examination of commentaries on Romans will reveal that about 80 percent of the commentaries on Romans will support the concept of unconditional election. This observation is based on an examination of about 40 commentaries when I wrote my commentary on Romans. For those who are interested in treatments on unconditional election, I recommend the comments on Romans 8:29, 30 and Romans 9 in the following commentaries: Haldane, Harrison, Hendriksen, Hodge, Murray, Olshausen, Plumer, and Shedd. For treatments that support the position of conditional election see the following commentaries on Romans 8:29, 30 and Romans 9: Clarke, Godet, Greathouse, Lenski, Meyer, Picirilli, and Sanday and Headlam. It should be pointed out that though Lenski and Meyer in their comments support the concept of conditional election, as Lutherans, they would not use the term "conditional election."

One may wonder why Calvinists have produced so many more scholarly writings than Arminians. A significant factor is that the emphasis on scholarship among Presbyterians has resulted in the production of scholarly works greater in proportion than their numerical strength.

The tendency among Arminians is to be more inclined to activity than to scholarly pursuits. Also, Arminians are inclined to think that common sense would direct people to take the Arminian approach. The list is short when you look for good works on conditional election. On the popular level, there exists a host of people who believe in "once saved, always saved," but believe in conditional election. These people have not come forth with outstanding works on conditional election. For many years there existed a widely used book written by the respected theologian, Henry C. Thiessen that taught conditional election.[25] When this book was revised by Vernon D. Doerksen it was changed so that the book now teaches unconditional election.[26] In this move, a book that had been widely used to voice the position of conditional election became a voice for unconditional election.

A Debt of Gratitude to Calvinism

Calvinists work on the assumption that unconditional election is necessary in order to maintain the doctrines of the sovereignty of God, the total depravity of fallen man, and that salvation is absolutely free. The theological world owes a debt of gratitude to Calvinism for its insistence that salvation is the free gift of God. I am sure that Arminians have needed this reminder. However, I am in sharp disagreement with those Calvinists when they make the claim that unconditional election is necessary if salvation is to be free. Calvinists have not hesitated in criticizing Arminians. I am sure they will be understanding if some criticism is returned. My advice to fellow Arminians is that if we expect to be treated with seriousness, then we must give time and effort to producing some well-thought-out treatments of our doctrine.

An Introduction of Classical Arminian Thought on Decrees and Election

THREE BASIC ASSUMPTIONS OR CONVICTIONS OF CALVINISM

I will be giving my answer to Calvinism as I explain and build my case for Classical Arminianism. The unconditional election taught in Calvinism seems to rest on three basic assumptions: (1) That the sovereignty of God requires unconditional election and thus precludes conditional election. (2) That total depravity precludes the response of faith from a sinner unless he is first regenerated by the Holy Spirit. (3) That salvation is free precludes conditional election. If these three assumptions are true, then Calvinism has made its case. If these three assumptions are not true, then Calvinism is in trouble.

An Answer to the First Assumption of Calvinism

The first and probably the most foundational of these assumptions of Calvinism is: That the sovereignty of God requires unconditional election and thus precludes conditional election. Calvinistic thought rests on two great pillars in the history of theological thought: that of Augustine of Hippo and John Calvin. It appears to me that Augustine's doctrine grew out of his thought that depravity was so strong it could only be dealt with by unconditional election. It appears that Calvin's view grows more out of the idea that unconditional election is the only view of election that is consistent with the sovereignty of God.

In Calvinism, the central truth to be reckoned with is that *everything else must harmonize with the sovereignty of God.* The Calvinistic concept of the sovereignty of God, as I see it, is developed along the lines of *cause* and *effect.* This is why Calvinists have a special difficulty dealing with the origin of sin. It is hard to find good discussions on the origin of sin in Calvinistic writings. Also, this is why some Calvinists are unlimited determinists. This stress on a *cause* and *effect* approach to interpreting the sovereignty of God is also the reason that those who want to restrict determinism to matters relating to salvation when discussing theology on its broader points sound like they are unlimited determinists. In fact, it is hard to find out where many Calvinists stand on whether determinism is unlimited or limited.

The answer to Calvinism's assumption that the sovereignty of God requires unconditional election and thus precludes conditional election will be lengthy. It must deal with the following concerns: (1) Influence and response vs. cause and effect, (2) The meaning of freedom of will, (3) The need of a theology of personality, (4) The question of divine determinism, and (5) The question of the foreknowledge of God in relation to the free acts of human beings.

Cause and *Effect* or *Influence* and *Response?* An Arminian Answer

Calvinism has oversimplified the way God carries out His sovereignty. In so doing they have oversimplified the relationship of God to man in the application of redemption. As I see it, it is very important to distinguish between *cause* and *effect* relationships and *influence* and *response* relationships.

In the relationship of the physical to the physical, or the relationship of the parts of a machine to one another, we are dealing with *cause* and *effect* relationships. The concepts of active and passive apply in their simple meaning. When a hammer hits a nail, the hammer is active and the nail is passive. The hammer *causes* the nail to be driven into the wood. The nail had no choice. A force outside the nail caused the nail to be driven into the wood.

Interpersonal relationships do not submit to such a simple analysis. *Influence* and *response* provide more appropriate terms. A person is one who thinks with his mind, feels with his heart, and acts with his will. In the simple sense of the terms *cause* and *effect,* one person cannot *cause* another person to do anything. This does not depend upon the lack of ability that one person has to influence another. Rather, the inability of one person to *cause* another person to do something grows out of the nature of what it means to be a *person.* When an appeal is made to a person, it is inherent within the nature of a person to consider the appeal and then make a decision. There is no such thing as a person doing or not doing something *without having made a decision.* This is true regardless of how strong the influence may be upon him or her.

Calvinism's approach to irresistible grace (or effectual call) sounds more like cause and effect than influence and response. When the appropriate time comes with regard to the elect, God regenerates him or her. As a regenerated person, he or she is caused by God to have faith in Jesus Christ as Lord and Savior. In such a view, faith is considered to be a gift. It is problematic for faith to be considered his choice, his act, or his response. The possibility of a negative response does not exist. It was a guaranteed response. The fact that it was guaranteed makes the terms cause and effect appropriate. All of this is considered by Calvinism to be necessary if salvation is to be a gift.

In explaining the gift of faith that way, the Calvinist is thinking along the lines of *cause* and *effect.* The only problem is that if being a person means anything beyond being a smoothly operated puppet with conscious awareness, it is impossible to describe the experience of a person in such a manner. We must keep in mind that a human being is a personal being because God has made him or her that way. This is necessary to the very notion of being made in the image of God. Can anyone really deny that faith is a personal response to the working of God with that individual? At least in some sense, the response of faith is a decision in which the person who believes actively participates. Even Calvinism must admit this. (See "The Question of Synergism," p. 260.)

In my opinion, it has been a mistake over the centuries to focus the conflict between Calvinists and Arminians on whether fallen or redeemed man has a *free will.* The real question is: Is fallen man a personal being, or is he sub-personal? (The same question can also be asked concerning redeemed man.) Does God deal with fallen man as a person? If He does, He deals with him as one who thinks, feels, and acts. To do otherwise undercuts the personhood of man. This, God will not do; not because something is being imposed on God to which He must submit, but because God designed the relationship to be a relationship between *personal beings.* Human beings are personal beings by God's *design* and were made for a *personal relationship* with a personal God. God will not violate His own plan. The nature of the case does not demand that God work in a *cause* and *effect* relationship with human beings.

We dare not take the position that God is unable to work with human beings within the framework of *influence* and *response*. Are we going to settle for the thinking that the inability of *fallen man* results in the *inability of God*, i.e., the *inability of God* to work with fallen man and redeemed man in an *influence* and *response* relationship? I hope not! Are we going to say that the very *nature* of God's *sovereignty* requires Him to work in a *cause* and *effect* relationship and prohibits Him from working in an *influence* and *response* relationship? I hope not!

I am sure that Calvinists would want to say that they do not believe in "mechanical" *cause* and *effect* as it relates to the way God deals with human beings. While they would object to the word "mechanical," if they opt for any form of *determinism* they cannot successfully reject the words *cause* and *effect*. My reading of Calvinistic writings suggests that a Classical Calvinist would not object to these terms. If anyone doubts this observation, I would suggest that he reread the quotations above that are taken from Calvinistic writings. I think the description of God's relationship to man that Calvinists would give would be much like my description of *influence* and *response*. However, the result is thought to be *guaranteed*. When the result is guaranteed, they would simply have a softened form of cause and effect. Any time the result is guaranteed, we are dealing with *cause* and *effect*. When the *guarantee* is gone, *Calvinism is gone*.

From a Calvinistic viewpoint, it will not do to say that *cause* and *effect* describes God's relationship to us, but *influence* and *response* describes our relationship to one another. The entirety of that which falls within the scope of determinism falls within the scope of cause and effect. There is no influence and response. Yet, I get the impression when I read Calvinistic writings that they are trying to persuade me. Persuasion is a form of *influence*. I get the impression that they think I could and should agree. I do not think they have any different idea about persuasion than I do. I have a statement that I make sometimes, "Calvinists are Arminian except when they are making Calvinistic statements."

I need to point out that in common speech, we frequently tend to use influence and response and *cause* and *effect* somewhat interchangeably. We may say, "He caused me to do it." To be technical, we should say, "He influenced me to do it, and I chose to do it." Though the terms may be to a certain extent interchangeable in common speech, I do not believe any confusion will develop from my using them the way I do in a theological writing.

The Meaning of Freedom of the Will

The discussion of *cause* and *effect* and *influence* and *response* sets the stage for a discussion of the meaning of the freedom of the will. I am going to restate here what I said about the meaning of free will in Chapter 9.

The New Testament does not use the noun form of "will" to refer to the faculty or organ of choice in man. Instead, the verb form (*thelō*) is used (Mt. 16:24; 21:29; 23:37; Mk. 8:34; Jn. 7:17; Rev. 22:17; and others). By "will" we mean power of choice. Every command, every prohibition, every exhortation, and every entreaty made in the Bible to human beings presupposes that they are capable of making choices.

Whether we want to think of the act of willing as the function of a faculty of the person or simply the person making a choice, the fact remains that the ability of choice is part of being a person. That ability of choice we call will. In his totality, man is a thinking, feeling, acting being. He thinks with his mind, feels with his heart, and acts with his will.

Let us make a few things clear about what is and is not meant by freedom of will. The freedom of the will does not mean that forces or influences cannot be brought to bear upon the will. In fact, the very nature of freedom of the will means that forces or influences will be brought to bear upon the will. It does not mean that these forces cannot be a *contributing factor* in the exercise of the will. It does mean that these influences or forces cannot *guarantee* or *determine* the action of the will. We are dealing with *influence* and *response,* not *cause* and *effect.*

THE FRAMEWORK OF POSSIBILITIES AND THE MEANING OF FREEDOM OF THE WILL

Freedom of will is a freedom within a framework of possibilities. It is not absolute freedom. We cannot be God. We cannot be an angel. The freedom of a human being is in the framework of the possibilities provided by human nature. Also, the influences brought to bear on the will have a bearing on the framework of possibilities.

Before Adam and Eve sinned, it was in the framework of possibilities within which they operated to remain in the practice of complete righteousness, or to commit sin. After they sinned, it no longer remained within the framework of possibilities for them to practice uninterrupted righteousness. The same is true for fallen man now (Rom. 8:7, 8). If anyone reads the meaning of freedom of will to mean that an *unconverted person* could practice righteousness and not sin, he misunderstands the meaning of freedom of will for fallen human beings. Romans 8:7, 8 makes it clear that Scripture does not teach this.

Jesus makes it clear that it does not fall within the framework of possibilities for a sinner to respond to the gospel unless he or she is drawn by the Holy Spirit (Jn. 6:44). The influence of the Holy Spirit working in the heart of the person who hears the gospel makes possible a framework of possibilities in which a person can say yes or no to the gospel. If he says, "yes," it is his choice. If he says, "no," it is his choice. To say less than that is to raise serious questions about the existence of real personhood after the fall. If a human being is not in some sense a *self-directed* being, he or she is not a person. The self-direction may have a high degree of dependence at times, but it is still self-direction. As has already been made clear, I am not suggesting that fallen man can choose Christ without the aid of the Holy Spirit. In fact, I strongly reject such an idea. I am saying, however, that no matter how much or how strong the aid of the Holy Spirit may be, the "yes" decision is still a decision that can rightly be called the person's decision. Also, he could have said no.

When I say that human beings have a free will, I mean that they can rationally consider a matter and make a choice. In bringing a person to the point of saving faith, the Holy Spirit makes it possible for a person to give the response of faith. At the same time this work of the Holy Spirit can be resisted. The person can say no. What puts Arminians at odds with Calvinists is that in Calvinism when God works with a person to bring him to faith, he or she *cannot say no.* Yes is the only answer he can give. Calvinists believe that apart from irresistible grace nobody could be saved. Irresistible grace is not simply the way God chooses to work in saving people, it is the only option open to God to save lost people. Total depravity, according to Calvinism, makes it impossible for a human being to respond apart from irresistible grace. The sovereignty of God, as viewed by Calvinism, is incompatible with a no answer. Thus, resistible grace, according to Calvinism, is ruled out.

TERMS USED IN DEFINING FREE WILL

I have run across the terms: spontaneity, indifference, libertarian, and self-determination. No Calvinists would deny that human beings have a will. However, as we have seen, some Calvinists out right deny that human beings have a free will. Others want to use the term "free will," but define it in a way that will be consistent with their version of Calvinism. While a few others want to maintain real freedom of the will.

LIBERTY OF SPONTANEITY AND *LIBERTY OF INDIFFERENCE*

It would appear from what I have read that thoroughgoing Calvinists, who affirm a belief in the freedom of the will, would concur that there is *liberty of spontaneity,* but not the *liberty of indifference.* Crabtree gives the following explanation of these terms, "One exercises the liberty of spontaneity when what he does is done in accordance with his own will and desires. One exercises the liberty of indifference when what he does is such that he could have done otherwise."[27]

Ronald H. Nash gives the following explanation of these terms:

> Human beings may be said to be free in two quite different senses. The *liberty of indifference* explains human freedom as the ability either to do something or not. . . . In order to be genuinely free in the sense of indifference, a person must have the ability either to do something or not. The *liberty of spontaneity,* on the other hand, explains human freedom as the ability to do whatever the person wants to do. On this second view, the question of the person's ability to do otherwise is irrelevant. The key question is whether he is able to do what he most wants to do.[28]

In searching for some light on the historical use of the terms *liberty of spontaneity* and *liberty of indifference,* I turned to the *Oxford English Dictionary* (*OED*). One of the meanings given for spontaneity is:

> Spontaneous, or voluntary and unconstrained, action on the part of persons; the fact of possessing this character or quality. 1651 C. CARTWRIGHT *Cert. Relig.* 1.181 Thus we see how Bernard doth agree with Calvin in making the freedome of mans will to consist in a spontaneity and freedom from coaction [constraint, coercion]. 1702 *Le Clerc's Prim. Fathers* 348. Freedom in his opinion, is only a meer Spontaneity, and doth not imply a Power of not doing what one would. [sic][29]

The help in the *OED* on the *liberty of indifference* was found under "indifferency." One of the meanings for indifferency is "Indetermination of the will; freedom of choice; an equal power to take either of two courses, *Liberty of Indifferency,* freedom from necessity, freedom of will. Obs."

These references given in the *OED* make it clear that at one time the *liberty of spontaneity* was used to mean that the will was free in that it was not coerced. It was not speaking of a freedom to make a different decision. *Liberty of indifference* was freedom to choose a different course of action. Crabtree's and Nash's definition of these terms is consistent with what we learn from the *OED*.

Determinism rules out the *liberty of indifference.* The way the *liberty of indifference* is defined by Crabtree and Nash and the way it is used in the *OED*, I would accept it. However, I am not happy with adding the words, "an equal power to take either of two courses," as seen in the *OED* definition. I think that oversimplifies the matter. Also, there may be more than two options.

If we could stick to this distinction between "spontaneity" and "indifference," I think they would be very useful in helping us distinguish between an Arminian view of free will and a Calvinistic view of free will. Most Calvinists would accept the *liberty of spontaneity* and reject the *liberty of indifference.* Arminians would accept both the *liberty of spontaneity* and the *liberty of indifference* as these terms are defined above.

However, there is a problem in using the term *liberty of indifference.* It is loaded with other possible connotations. It could also mean unconcerned or disinterested. Unconcerned or disinterested is not what I mean by freedom of the will. Even Berkhof, usually a careful scholar, fails to grasp the historic meaning of *liberty of indifference.* In raising the question of whether "the predetermination of things was consistent with the free will of man," his response was:

> And the answer is that it certainly is not, if the freedom of the will be regarded as, indifferentia (arbitrariness), but this is an unwarranted conception of the freedom of man. The will of man is not something altogether indeterminate, something hanging in the air that can swing arbitrarily in either direction.[30]

I do not know of anyone who would define free will that way. These kinds of comments complicate discussion between Calvinists and Arminians.

Freedom of the will does not mean that a person is free from being influenced or even being pressured. People are pressured frequently in their daily experiences. The whole point of what it means to be a person is that a person is presented with options. Influences are brought to bear upon the person seeking to influence him or her to choose one of these options. The person rationally considers the options and makes a choice. The problem is that if he is reasoning from faulty premises the conclusions will be invalid. Bias and prejudice can blind a person to the truth. This blindness especially works on the level of premises.

If we will use the terms *liberty of spontaneity* and *liberty of indifference* with their original intended meaning, I think they will be very helpful in establishing meaningful communication between Arminians and Calvinists.

LIBERTARIAN

Libertarian is a term that is used to describe a person who believes in free will. The dictionary meaning of libertarian is, "An advocate of the doctrine of free will." But it also means, "A person who upholds the principles of absolute and unrestricted liberty esp. of thought and action."[31] I would qualify as a libertarian by the first definition. But the term libertarian conjures up too many objectionable ideas in people's minds for me to want to be identified by the term.

SELF-DETERMINED

Self-determined is sometimes used in a discussion of determinism and free will. Norman Geisler advocates this view. He points out that both Thomas Aquinas and C. S. Lewis hold to this view. In commenting on this view, Geisler explains:

> Representatives of moral self-determinism sometimes speak of free will as though it were the efficient cause of moral actions. This would lead one naturally to ask: what is the cause of one's free will? But a more precise description of the process of the free act would avoid this problem. Technically, free will is not the efficient cause of a free act; free will is simply the power through which the agent performs the free act. The efficient cause of the free act is the free *agent,* not the free will. Free will is simply the power by which the free agent acts. We do not say that humans are free will but only that they *have* free will. . . . So it is not the power of free choice which causes a free act, but the *person* who has the power.[32]

Later on in this treatment Geisler comments:

> God is the cause of the fact of freedom, and humans are the causes of the acts of freedom. God made the agent, but the agents cause the actions. God gives people power (of free choice), but they exercise it without coercion. Thus God is responsible for bestowing freedom, but human beings are responsible for behaving with it.[33]

John Miley, a Methodist theologian whose *Systematic Theology* appeared near the end of the nineteenth century, would be in agreement with Geisler's statement, "The efficient cause of the free act is the free *agent,* not the free will. Free will is simply the power by which the free agent acts." Miley explains:

> We find the higher meaning of the term [agent] only in personality. There we reach the power of rational self-energizing with respect to ends. There is no such power in the will itself. It is simply a faculty of the personal agent.

He goes on to say:

> The freedom of the will, therefore, cannot be the true question of freedom. The fact means nothing against the reality of freedom, but points to its true location in our own personal agency, and in the result will make it clearer and surer.[34]

Placing the real freedom in the personal agent is to place it in the person or personality. I think this has much to commend itself. But the term "free will" is so firmly fixed in theology as a theological term to express freedom that we cannot escape using and defining the term.

I think Geisler's view has much to commend itself. There is a technical turn in what he is saying that most people will not want to work through, but I think he is on the right track. The term *self-determinism* by itself could be subject to gross distortion. It could picture a person as a loose canon out of control. No one who reads what Geisler says will get such an idea. But apart from a context it could suffer such distortion.

Properly understood, my view would be self-determinism, though I prefer to speak of human beings as *self-directed.* Self-determination of human beings must be understood in the context of their relationship with a sovereign God who is bringing influences to bear on them, granting them freedom (permission) of choice, and carrying out His purposes. Anything less will fail to measure up to biblical Christianity.

My problem with Geisler is how he combines his view of self-determinism with "soft determinism."[35] The problem with determinism whether it is called "hard determinism" or called "soft determinism" is that it is still determinism. When Geisler speaks of soft determinism it is divine determinism.

In the following quotation, Geisler explains his approach to the relationship between foreknowledge and determinism:

> But granting that God does not pass through temporal successions, then what he thinks, he has forever thought. . . . So from God's vantage point he simply knows (not foreknows) what we are doing with our free choices. For what we have, are and will choose is present to God in his eternal NOW. This being the case, there is no problem of how an act can be truly free if God has determined in advance what will take place. God's foreknowledge is not foreordaining anything which will later occur to him. All of time is present to God's mind from all eternity. Hence, God is not foreordaining from his vantage point, but simply ordaining what humans are doing freely. God sees what we are freely doing. And what he sees, he knows. And what he knows he determines. So God determinately knows and knowingly determines what we are doing freely.[36]

The key words in understanding Geisler's view as I see it are, "And what he sees, he knows. And what he knows he determines." Geisler's divine determinism is based on *what God knows.* In genuine determinism, knowledge is based on *what is determined.* Bringing up the concept of Eternal Now, does not change that. I will deal with this problem later in this chapter under the heading, "The Question of How God Could Have Foreknowledge of Free Human Choices" (p. 329).

It seems to me that Geisler does a better job in building his case for self-determinism (free will) than he does linking self-determinism with divine determinism.

The Consistency of the Influence and Response Model
With the Teachings of Scripture

I think anyone who does not come with philosophical presuppositions that would prevent agreement would agree that influence and response is the way human beings deal with one another. Those who have not already made up their minds, to the contrary, would also most likely accept the idea that God would work with us, as human beings, within the framework of an influence and response relationship. The question for the Christian is: Will it stand the test of Scripture?

PHILIPPIANS 2:12, 13

Gordon Clark remarks concerning this passage:

> Now, among the many biblical passages that deny free will, there is one so clear and so pointed that I do not see how anyone could possibly misunderstand it. In Philippians 2:12-13 the Apostle Paul tells us to "work out your own salvation with fear and trembling, for it is God which worketh in you both to will and to do his good pleasure."[37]

As we have already noted, not all determinists reject free will as Clark does. But any consistent, *unlimited determinism* would interpret these verses within a cause and effect framework. I can see why they would do this. However, these verses present no problem when interpreted in keeping with the *influence* and *response* model.

In Romans 5:3 Paul says, "Tribulation worketh patience." What Paul is saying is that it is the design of tribulation to work patience. The design does not come to fruition in every case. Some people become very impatient in times of tribulation. There is no reason whatever that the work of God to get us to will and to do of His good pleasure could not be interpreted in terms of *design* and *purpose* in a manner in keeping with *influence* and *response*. The meaning would be that God works in us to influence and to enable us to will and to do His good pleasure.

We are not to think of human beings as operating outside the realm of divine influence. At the same time, we know that they do not always respond properly to this divine influence. This is true of both the saved and the unsaved. We do, of course, insist that there is a compliance that makes a difference between the saved and the unsaved. To say that human beings *always* respond properly to divine influence would say something about God, as the One who does the influencing, that I do not think we want to say. We cannot attribute all that is happening in the world to the influence of God. Nor, can we make Him the cause or the determiner of all that is happening. This is the kind of thinking that inclines many to atheism. It is unthinkable that a sovereign, holy, just, fair, and loving God would be the determining cause of everything that is happening in our world. There is something within us that rebels against such a thought.

The *influence* and *response* model has room for disobedience. It does not require divine determinism as the bases of all that happens. While there is room for obedience or disobedience, we are not to limit human freedom to mere obedience or disobedience. We are not to think of God as giving a list of minute details requiring yes or no answers for every move we make. Human freedom leaves room for creativity in obedience to the divine commandment—to human beings exercising dominion over the earth and its inhabitants (Gen. 1:26). Christians are given freedom and are encouraged to exercise stewardship over their gifts and callings (1 Pet. 4:10 and Tit. 1:7), the mysteries of God (1 Cor. 4:1, 2), and the gospel (1 Cor. 9:17 and Eph. 3:2). Stewardship involves a creative thinking and planning responsibility. It is not possible to harmonize *divine determinism* and *stewardship responsibility* to God.

The Need for a Theology of Personality

Human freedom is a freedom to function as persons. It is the freedom to think, plan, and act. I would invite you to examine several books on systematic theology. Turn to the index in each set and find the word "personality." Over and over again you will find references to divine personality, but no reference to human personality. It will be a very rare find, when you discover one that makes any reference to "human personality." One of the rare finds where a theologian develops the meaning of human personality is found in, Arminian theologian, John Miley's *Systematic Theology.*[38]

Why is it so hard to find a theology book that defines and expands the treatment of human personality? I think it is because there is not much place for it in deterministic thinking. Calvinists do not have much place for a development of thought on the function of human personality. Calvinists are afraid that if they say very much about the function of human personality they will take something away from God. Calvinists have produced most of the outstanding works on theology. Arminians have tended to follow the Calvinist model. However, they merely give an Arminian interpretation. Since Calvinists do not usually deal with the meaning of human personality in their writings, most Arminians do not either. I think I can safely say that a person will find more references to human personality in this book than in all of the others systematic theology and doctrine books combined. Treatments are given to mind, heart, and will. But it will be rare to find where the term personality is used in connection with these treatments. Christian ministry is in great need of an understanding of human personality in reaching lost people and in ministering to the needs of Christians. The foundational thinking of human personality, how it functions, and how personality change is made should be done by *theologians*. While library research is essential, our understanding of human personality needs to be hammered out in the arena of life.[39]

God's Foreknowledge and Human Freedom

Classical Calvinism has problems with the idea that God can have foreknowledge of the actions of those who have free will in the Arminian sense of free will. In unlimited determinism, the fact that God has determined everything that will happen is considered to be the foundation for God's foreknowledge. There is no need of foreknowledge of free acts in unlimited determinism because free acts do not exist. Calvinists who have a place in their thought for free will in the sense of *liberty of indifference,* would have to acknowledge that God has foreknowledge of free acts of human beings. The reader may want to review the material given above under, "The Question of Foreknowledge and Free Will in Calvinistic Thought."

ARMINIANISM ON FOREKNOWLEDGE AND HUMAN FREEDOM

In Classical Calvinism, there is agreement that God has absolute knowledge of the future down to the smallest detail. There is not agreement on how to deal with the question of human freedom or whether human freedom exists. In Arminianism there is agreement that human beings have freedom of choice. This includes the freedom to place their faith in Christ upon hearing the gospel, or conversely they can refuse to place their faith in Christ.

On the current scene there is not agreement among Arminians on the question of foreknowledge as it relates to free acts of human beings. Classical Arminianism agreed with Calvinism that God has absolute knowledge of the future down to the smallest detail. This, of course, would require that God has foreknowledge concerning the free acts of human beings. In recent years, some Arminians have rejected the view that God has foreknowledge of the free acts of human beings.

A DENIAL OF DIVINE FOREKNOWLEDGE OF HUMAN FREE CHOICE

Clark Pinnock is the best known of those who do not believe that God has foreknowledge of the acts of free agents. In an autobiographical account entitled, "From Augustine To Arminius: A Pilgrimage in Theology," Pinnock describes how he changed from being a Calvinist, rooted in Augustinian thought, to becoming an Arminian. He explains:

> I had to ask myself if it was biblically possible to hold that God knows everything that can be known, but that free choices would not be something that can be known even by God because they are not yet settled reality. Decisions not yet made do not exist anywhere to be known even by God. They are potential—yet to be realized but not yet actual. God can predict a great deal of what we will choose to do, but not all of it, because some of it remains hidden in the mystery of human freedom. Can this conjecture be scriptural?[40]

Pinnock goes on to say:

> Thus it has become increasingly clear to me that we need a "free will" theism, a doctrine of God that treads the middle path between classical theism, which exaggerates God's transcendence of the world, and process theism which presses for immanence.[41]

At the heart of what Pinnock is concerned about is how God's sovereignty is administered in the light of man's free will. He explains:

As Creator of the world God is sovereign in the fundamental sense. He has chosen to bring into existence a world with significantly free agents. In keeping with this decision, God rules over the world in a way that sustains and does not negate its structures. Since freedom has been created, reality is open, not closed. God's relationship to the world is dynamic, not static. Although this will require us to rethink aspects of conventional or classical theism, it will help us relate sovereignty and freedom more coherently in theory and more satisfactorily in practice.[42]

Another advocate of "free-will" theism is Richard Rice. He comments:

The idea that God interacts with a world where there is genuine creaturely freedom does not require us to deny divine foreknowledge. It requires only that we define the scope of foreknowledge with care. In some respects the future is knowable, in others it is not. God knows a great deal about what will happen. He knows everything that will ever happen as the direct result of factors that already exist. He knows infallibly the content of his own future actions, to the extent that they are not related to human choices. Since God knows all possibilities, he knows everything that could happen and what he can do in response to each eventuality. And he knows the ultimate outcome to which he is guiding the course of history. All that God does not know is the content of future free decisions, and this is because decisions are not there to know until they occur.[43]

In further elaborating on his view, Rice points out "that God is dynamically involved in the creaturely world."[44] In commenting on God as a loving parent, Rice explains:

Further evidence for the portrait of God as a loving parent comes from its impact on personal religious experience. It provides us with a view of God who is genuinely personal and lovable. It presents us with a God who is vulnerable, who can take risks and make sacrifices, a God who is momentarily delighted and disappointed, depending on our response to his love.[45]

The driving concern of Pinnock and Rice seems to be: (1) That we have a view of God and His foreknowledge that allows for genuinely free acts on the part of human beings, and (2) That our view of God be such that it contributes to a warm personal relationship with God while we experience the real encounters of life.

AFFIRMATION OF ABSOLUTE DIVINE FOREKNOWLEDGE

Arminius makes it unquestionably clear where he stands on the question of God's foreknowledge. He comments, "I am most fully persuaded that the knowledge of God is eternal, immutable and infinite, and that it extends to all things, both necessary and contingent, to all things which He does of Himself, either mediately or immediately, and which He permits to be done by others."[46]

On the contemporary scene Jack Cottrell speaks out for absolute divine foreknowledge. He explains:

> While acknowledging that non-Calvinists disagree on this point, I affirm that God has a true knowledge of future free-will choices without himself being the agent that causes them or renders them certain. Such knowledge is grounded in—and is thus conditioned by—the choices themselves as foreknown. This is how God maintains sovereign control over the whole of his creation, despite the freedom he has given his creatures.[47]

In another place Cottrell comments:

> To say that God has foreknowledge means that he has real knowledge or cognition of something before it actually happens or exists in history. This is the irreducible core of the concept, which must be neither eliminated nor attenuated. Nothing else is consistent with the nature of God.[48]

To make it emphatically clear, he remarks, "Surely God foreknows everything about the life of every individual. He cannot help but foreknow, just because he is God."[49]

Robert E. Picirilli makes it very clear where he stands on God's foreknowledge when he says, "All things that occur are *certainly* foreknown by God. Every happening is certain and known as such from all eternity."[50]

In summing up an excellent chapter, "God's Knowledge of the Present, Past, and Future," William Lane Craig comments:

> Thus, in the New Testament as well as the Old, God is conceived as knowing not only all past and present events, but all future events as well. This foreknowledge would seem to extend to future free acts, events which could not possibly be inferred from present causes and which in any case are not so represented by the biblical authors. We have seen examples throughout Scripture of God's foreknowledge of such events, including even the thoughts which individuals shall have. It does not, therefore, seem possible to deny that the biblical conception of God's omniscience includes foreknowledge of future free acts.[51]

A Critical Evaluation of Calvinistic Approaches
to the Basis for God's Foreknowledge

HARD, UNLIMITED DETERMINISTS

Calvinists who are hard, unlimited determinists solve the problem by eliminating free acts. Everything is determined by God down to the most minute detail. God knows the future because He determines what the future will be. God is the cause of all that happens. The logic of this view is easy to follow. Unconditional election and unconditional reprobation fit logically into unlimited determinism. The problem is when you try to harmonize it with the biblical view of God and man.

If God has determined everything that will be, He is the cause of everything. This cannot be harmonized with the biblical view of the holiness of God. A holy God did not and will not determine and cause all of the lying, stealing, hatred, bitterness, depression, mental anguish, pain, suffering, alcoholism, drug addiction, divorce, child sex abuse, rape, abortion, murder, etc. The law of non-contradiction means nothing if the sin that we are experiencing and seeing can be harmonized with causal determination of a holy and loving God. No retreat to the inscrutable wisdom of God is acceptable to justify such obvious contradiction.

If God is the cause of everything, why would He cause James Arminius, John Wesley, Adam Clarke, Richard Watson, John Miley, H. Orton Wiley, the Arminians that I have mentioned in this chapter, and a host of others to be Arminian? Why did He also cause Augustine, John Calvin, Augustus Toplady, John Gill, Charles Spurgeon, Jonathan Edwards, Charles Hodge, Benjamin Warfield, those referred to in this chapter, and a host of others to be Calvinists? Would a rational God cause devout believers to arrive at conclusions that are diametrically opposed to one another? He did if unlimited determinism is true.

When it comes to sin, guilt, judgment, and punishment for sin, in deterministic thinking, the problem is not solved by saying the person did what he wanted to do—he or she was not coerced.

The point is that in determinism the "want to" is determined by God. Yet, we see God punishing people for doing what He causally determined that they would do if unlimited determinism is true.

SOFT, UNLIMITED DETERMINISM

Soft determinists are compatibilists. They believe in both determinism and free will. Their concept of free will would be the *liberty of spontaneity* as distinguished from the *liberty of indifference* (see the treatment of these terms earlier, pp. 325, 326).

The key to understanding the *liberty of spontaneity* is the kind of influences that can be brought to bear upon a person to influence him or her to make a choice. It will help in understanding soft determinism if we use again some material quoted from Feinberg earlier. He explains:

> On the one hand, there are constraining causes which force an agent to act against his will. On the other hand there are nonconstraining causes. These are sufficient to bring about an action, but they do not force a person to act against his will, desires, or wishes. According to determinists such as myself, an action is free even if causally deter-

mined so long as the causes are nonconstraining. This view is often referred to as *soft determinism* or *compatibilism,* for genuine free human action is seen as *compatible* with nonconstraining sufficient conditions which incline the will decisively in one way or another.[52]

Feinberg speaks of "constraining causes which force an agent to act against his will." From his standpoint, causes that would force an agent to act against his will can exist only in theory. In the real world there could be no such thing because God has determined all causes. The causes that are determined by God, according to Feinberg would never force a person to act against his or her will. Since all causes in unlimited determinism are determined by God, there would be no room for real causes or influences in our world that would coerce a person.

Let me repeat another quotation from Feinberg. He points out:

> The fundamental tenet of determinism (and the various forms of Calvinism are forms of determinism) is that for everything that happens, in the light of prevailing conditions, the agent could not have done other than he did. For determinists, there are always sufficient conditions that decisively incline the agent's will to choose one option or another.[53]

What makes Feinberg's view determinism is, as can be seen from the last quotation, that no decision that is ever made could be different from what it was. Every action is determined by God. Feinberg makes this clear in other places. He remarks, "God decides what will happen in our world and then sees that his decisions are carried out."[54] Later on he refers to Calvin's thought with approbation, "For Calvin, then, God's sovereignty means he governs all things according to his will. This means God not only overrules in the affairs of men, but also determines what will happen in their lives. This providential determination extends to every area of our lives."[55]

Soft determinism clearly denies freedom of choice in the sense that a person could have done differently. I agree with Picirilli when he says, "A choice that actually can go but one way is not a choice, and without this 'freedom' there is not personality."[56]

While soft determinism seeks to come across as being milder than hard determinism, as long as it remains "unlimited determinism" it cannot escape the criticism that I made above against hard determinism. The basis for the criticism that I made was the fact that it is *unlimited* determinism, not that it was *hard* determinism. Changing from "hard" to "soft" determinism brings no relief at all from the criticism that is directed toward determinism qua determinism. For example, if a person believes that capital punishment is wrong, changing the method of execution from electrocution or hanging to lethal injection does not make capital punishment acceptable. It may be that if capital punishment will take place in spite of his best efforts to stop it, that the person who opposes it would prefer lethal injection rather than some other form of execution. But it would not make capital punishment acceptable to the person. It may well be that a person who is opposed to unlimited determinism would prefer that a person promote soft determinism rather than hard determinism, but he would still have all the objections that he had against unlimited determinism, qua unlimited determinism.

LIMITED DETERMINISM

As we have seen earlier in this chapter, Richard Muller believes in limited determinism. He limits determinism to soteriology. I will use part of a quotation used earlier to show how he limits determinism. He explains:

> Reformed theology only insists that the beginning of the redeemed life is solely the work of God, and therefore distinguishes between the general decree of providence that establishes all things, whether necessary, contingent, or free, and the special decree of predestination that establishes salvation by grace alone. Far from being a rigid metaphysical determinism of all human actions, a form of necessitarianism (which was never Reformed doctrine in any case), predestination applies only to the issue of salvation. And the Reformed exegesis of biblical passages related to predestination, far from indicating a determinism of all human actions, indicates the ultimate determination of God in matters pertaining to salvation.[57]

It appears that Muller restricts determinism to "the beginning of the redeemed life." He not only states that determinism is limited to soteriology in his own thinking, he insists that it is the Reformed or Calvinistic position. It is obvious that many Calvinists would not agree with him on this limitation of determinism.

Before I evaluate Muller's position, I will give a quotation from him that gets to the heart of his objection to Arminianism. He comments:

> The Arminian God is locked into the inconsistency of genuinely willing to save all people while at the same time binding himself to a plan of salvation that he foreknows with certainty cannot effectuate his will. . . . Reformed doctrine, on the other hand, respects the ultimate mystery of the infinite will of God, affirms the sovereignty and efficacy of God, and teaches the soteriological consistency of the divine intention and will with its effects.[58]

It would appear that outside of the beginning of salvation that Muller would believe in the *liberty of indifference*. What he says certainly points to such a conclusion. If that is the case, he would apparently believe that God has perfect foreknowledge of the free acts of human beings that He has not determined.

Muller's major criticism of Arminianism is the Arminian view that God has a genuine desire for the salvation of all human beings while at the same time His foreknowledge tells Him that His desire for the salvation of all will not be fulfilled. That would be a failure. Sovereigns do not fail to accomplish their goals or purposes. In Calvinism, God's desire to save is only toward those He has elected. God's desires will be effectuated.

It appears, that as it relates to the rest of mankind and the decisions of believers besides those related to the beginning of salvation, that Muller's concept of free will would not be essentially different from the view that I would hold. The questions that I would like to have an answer to are: Does God have any kind of desires regarding the mass of unbelievers who are left out of God's elective plan? Are all of these desires met? Or, should we say that God has no desires at all for those who are unbelievers? Are they totally beyond God's concern so that no matter what they do it does not matter to God?

The reason that I ask these questions is that if those who take Muller's view can admit that there is any incompatibility whatever between what a Sovereign God desires and what actually happens, the question still remains: "Would that mean that God has forfeited His sovereignty?" If the answer is no, it should help us (and them) to understand that if God desires the salvation of all and it does not take place, then neither does it mean that God has forfeited His sovereignty. If Muller's view of free will for the non elect and many of the decisions of the elect is what it appears to be, those who take such a position could make some meaningful contributions to our understanding of the relationship between God's sovereignty and the free will of man.

Another point to be made is that when determinism is limited to unconditional election, the person who takes such a view must accept the position that God can have foreknowledge of free acts of human beings. That is the only way God can know that those individuals that he would choose to elect would exist. It is impossible for a particular individual to exist apart from having a certain set of parents, grandparents, great-grandparents, etc. all the way back to Adam and Eve. In that chain of events, there would be numerous free acts that God must have knowledge of before He could know that a particular individual would exist. Once it is admitted that God can have knowledge of free human acts, there is no reason so far as the exercise of foreknowledge is concerned that God could not have used the approach of conditional election.

AN OBSERVATION

I think it would be very helpful if Calvinist theologians would declare themselves on whether they believe in unlimited determinism or limited determinism. It would help if we knew whether they believe only in the *liberty of spontaneity* or whether they believe that the *liberty of indifference* applies to some areas of human experience. If the liberty of indifference applies to some areas, what are these areas? If the *liberty of indifference* applies to any areas at all, in these areas it would be helpful if Calvinists and Arminians could engage in discussion on: (1) The question of God's foreknowledge of free acts of human beings, (2) How the failure of free agents to obey God does not mean that God has forfeited His sovereignty, and (3) The problem of limiting God's sovereign control to the area of soteriology.

The Question of How God Could Have Foreknowledge of Free Human Choices

As we have observed above, many Calvinists work on the assumption that it is impossible for God to have foreknowledge of free choices and free acts of human beings. Since these Calvinists also believe that God has foreknowledge of all that will ever take place, they believe that the only basis that God can have of foreknowledge is for God to be causally related, by divine determinism, to all that will ever happen in the future. God knows the future because He determines the future. Since everything that has happened, is happening, or ever will happen is determined by God, these Calvinists deny free will in the sense of the *liberty of indifference.* Some Arminians, as we have seen, also deny that God can have foreknowledge of the free choices and acts of human beings. They end up limiting the omniscience of God. Most Arminians believe that the foreknowledge of God includes the free choices of human beings.

We will now turn our attention to some of the attempts that have been made to explain how God has foreknowledge of free human choices and acts.

GOD'S FOREKNOWLEDGE OF FREE ACTS BASED ON GOD'S BEING TIMELESS

The most common way theologians describe God's eternity is to refer to it as timelessness. It is said that God has no past and no future. Everything with God is one eternal now. Time is said to be a creation of God and will be terminated by Him. Time is characterized by past, present, and future and has succession of events. Eternity has only the present, thus no succession of events.[59]

This approach to God's timelessness has been used by some to explain how God could know what the free acts of human beings will be before they occur. Geisler, as one who holds to this view, explains:

> For what we have, are and will *choose* is *present* to God in his eternal NOW. This being the case, there is no problem of how an act can be truly free if God has determined in advance what will take place. God's foreknowledge is not foreordaining anything which will *later* occur to him. All of time is present to God's mind from all eternity. God does not really foreknow it; he simply knows it in his eternal presence. Hence, God is not foreordaining from his vantage point, but simply ordaining what humans are freely doing. And what he sees, he knows. And what he knows, he determines. So God *determinately* and *knowingly determines* what we are freely deciding.[60]

Those who hold this view explain that from a technical viewpoint, God does not have foreknowledge of free acts since all knowledge to God is Now. However, it would be viewed as foreknowledge by us.

This view has problems. This view gives God a *direct perception* of all that is happening. This direct perception of what is happening is God's way of knowing human events whether they be past, present, or future to us. But what about contingencies that never happen? In explaining the inadequacy of this view to explain how God knows the free acts of human beings, Arminius astutely observes:

> That reasoning, however, does not exhaust all the difficulties which may arise in the consideration of these matters. For God knows, also, those things which may happen, but never do happen, and consequently do not co-exist with God in the Now of eternity, which would be events unless they should be hindered, as is evident from 1 Sam. xxiii, 12, in reference to the citizens of Keilah, who would have delivered David into the hands of Saul, which event, nevertheless, did not happen.[61]

There is another problem in trying to use the Eternal Now view of God as a basis for His foreknowledge of free human acts. The question is: Is this a valid view of God's relationship to time? There is one big problem. How can events be eternally now to God (like my writing this book—if that is so, it has taken longer than I thought) when in fact they have not always existed? I do not have any trouble seeing that God can see the past, the present, and the future with equal vividness. But He sees the past as past. It does not have present objective reality to God. He sees the future with equal vividness to the present, but He sees it as future. The future does not have objective reality to God. If these observations are correct, the Eternal Now view is without merit. (See my more thorough treatment in Chapter 5, pp. 67-70.)

GOD'S FOREKNOWLEDGE OF FREE ACTS BASED ON GOD'S MIDDLE KNOWLEDGE

One of the chief proponents of this view, on the current scene, is William Lane Craig. In his promotion of middle knowledge, Craig has a twofold purpose: (1) He desires to show how God does, in fact, have foreknowledge of free acts of human beings, and (2) He wishes to present a view that will be acceptable to both Calvinists and Arminians. In doing so he hopes to bring Calvinists and Arminians closer together.

The founder of this view was the Spanish Jesuit Luis Molina (1535-1600). Craig says concerning Molina, "By means of this doctrine he proposed to avoid the Protestant error of denying genuine human freedom, yet without thereby sacrificing the sovereignty of God."[62] Craig calls attention to Molina's error in soteriology. Then he goes on to say:

> But we should be short-sighted, indeed, if our repugnance to Molina's soteriology blinded us to his insights in resolving the tension between the doctrines of divine sovereignty and human freedom. He claimed to be able to affirm both of these doctrines, and he boldly asserted that had the doctrine of middle knowledge been known to the early church, then neither Pelagianism nor Lutheranism would have arisen. The resolution of the tension between God's sovereignty and man's freedom is an admirable objective that ought to interest any Christian.[63]

In following Molina, Craig asserts that there are three types of divine knowledge. He gives the following table in explaining his view:

The Three Logical Moments in God Knowledge
[logical as distinguished from chronological]

1. Natural Knowledge: God's knowledge of all possible worlds. The content of this knowledge is essential to God.
2. Middle Knowledge: God's knowledge of what *every* possible free creature would do under any possible circumstances and, hence knowledge of those possible worlds which God can make actual. The content of this knowledge is not essential to God.

God's Free Decision to Create a World
---

3. Free Knowledge: God's knowledge of the actual world. The content of the knowledge is not essential to God.[64]

God's natural knowledge is innate. God must have natural knowledge or He would not be God. According to Craig, natural knowledge includes the laws of logic. In getting to the point of how this line of thinking helps us to understand how God has foreknowledge of free events, he explains:

> God's natural knowledge includes knowledge of all possibilities. He knows all possible individuals that he could create, all the possible circumstances he could place them in, all their possible actions and reactions, and all the possible worlds or orders which he could create. God could not lack this knowledge and still be God; the content of natural knowledge is essential to him.[65]

Natural knowledge gives God the knowledge of every person who would make up all possible worlds. Middle knowledge gives God a knowledge of how each person would respond to each hypothetical encounter. As Craig points out, "Middle knowledge is the aspect of divine omniscience that comprises God's knowledge, prior to any determination of the divine will, of which contingent events would occur under any hypothetical set of circumstances."[66]

Both natural knowledge and middle knowledge are logically prior to God's decision to create one of these possible worlds. Craig tells us, "Indeed, God's decision to create a world is based on his middle knowledge and consists in his selecting to become actual one of the possible worlds known to him in the second moment."[67] After (logically after, not temporally after) God's decision to create, God possessed foreknowledge of the world that he would actually create.

In all of the possible worlds that God could create, the individuals were free. This would mean that the individuals in the one that God did choose to create were free. Those who hold this view believe they have an explanation for believing in human free will and God's foreknowledge of the free acts of human beings. Since God chose to create this world rather than one of the other worlds that He could have created, it is concluded that this world and *the individuals and their free acts were predestinated (or predetermined)*—thus preserving the concerns of both Calvinism and Arminianism.

AN EVALUATION OF THE MIDDLE KNOWLEDGE APPROACH

As I see it, there is a fatal flaw in this approach. The problem is found in the explanation of natural knowledge. In a quotation given above, Craig explains:

> God's natural knowledge includes knowledge of all possibilities. He knows all possible individuals that he could create, all the possible circumstances he could place them in, all their possible actions and reactions, and all the possible worlds or orders which he could create.[68]

A careful look at this explanation of God's natural knowledge will reveal that it already presupposes God's foreknowledge of free human choices and acts. Let us limit our discussion to "He knows all possible individuals that he could create." The only individuals that God could have foreknown of the human race without having foreknowledge of free human choices and acts, if human beings were to have true free will, would have been Adam and Eve. From that point on free choices were involved in every conception and every birth. For God to know that I would exist would require a knowledge of all the free acts from Adam and Eve to me that were involved in every marriage, every conception, and every birth of my endless number of grandparents, and my parents. If He knew that, He already had knowledge of free human choices and acts.

If my observations are correct, this view would not be the grounds of an explanation of how God has foreknowledge of free acts of human beings because it already assumes such foreknowledge in the definition of God's natural knowledge. Also, I contend that the only individuals that have free will are real persons. Fictitious individuals (only theoretically possible individuals) do not have free will. They are moved about, not by a will of their own, but the will of the one who imagines their existence.

GOD'S FOREKNOWLEDGE OF FREE ACTS A MYSTERY

The majority of those who have believed in God's foreknowledge of free human choices have not attempted to give an explanation of how God was able to have this kind of foreknowledge.

Arminius makes the concession, "I do not understand the mode in which He knows future contingencies, and especially those which belong to the free-will of creatures, and which He has decreed to permit, but do not of Himself."[69]

Let me repeat a part of a quotation given earlier in this chapter, where Buswell, a Calvinist, says that he saw no problem in foreknowledge of free acts of human beings. He explains:

> To the question then how God can know a free act in the future, I reply I do not know, but neither do I know how I can have knowledge by analysis, by inference from reason or from causes, or from statistical data reported by intuition, or (if it is insisted

upon) by innate ideas. Knowledge is a mystery in any event, and God's knowledge of free events in the future is only one more mystery, revealed in Scripture. We have good and sufficient grounds to accept, and no valid ground to reject, what Scripture says on this subject.[70]

I cast my lot with those who do not understand the way God is able to foresee future free acts. The Bible makes it quite clear that God does possess foreknowledge of all future events, including free acts. Berkhof reminded us in a quotation used above, "It is perfectly evident that Scripture teaches divine foreknowledge of contingent events, I Sam. 23:10-13; II Kings 13:19; Ps. 81:14, 15; Isa. 42:9; 48:18; Jer. 2:2, 3; 38:17-20; Ezek. 3:6; and Matt. 11:21."[71]

As we can see, the Bible makes it clear that God has foreknowledge of free human choices and acts. I believe God's foreknowledge of free acts is also necessarily implied from God's foreknowledge of His own actions. It would have been impossible for God to have had foreknowledge of sending Jesus Christ into the world apart from a knowledge of the free acts of human beings, that is, unless a person takes the position of unlimited determinism. For God to have foreknowledge of the exact identity of the human nature of Jesus Christ required that He have foreknowledge of His exact ancestry. For God to have this knowledge required that He have a foreknowledge of free acts of human beings.

I cannot explain how God created the universe *ex nihilo* (from nothing), but I believe it. I do not know how Jesus worked His miracles, but I believe He did. Why should I be concerned if I do not know how He has foreknowledge of free human choices and acts? As Buswell reminds us, there is much about our own ability to gain knowledge that we do not understand. I have sometimes made the statement that our knowledge of God is more adequate for our needs than our understanding of human personality. We cannot reach a consensus about whether human beings have a free will, what free will means, whether human beings are trichotomous or dichotomous or unitary beings, what human personality is, and how human personality is changed.

There are many things about God that we do not understand. I cannot comprehend that God had no beginning. Yet, I believe it. I cannot think of God in any other way. Though I cannot understand how God has foreknowledge of free events, yet, I believe it. I cannot think of God in any other way. I can identify with Cottrell when he said "Surely God foreknows everything about the life of every individual. He cannot help but foreknow, just because he is God.[72]

We must all agree that there are some things about God that are inscrutable!

DIVINE FOREKNOWLEDGE NOT TO BE EQUATED WITH DIVINE CAUSALITY

It is important for us to realize that causality cannot be ascribed to foreknowledge. Nor can divine cause be required for foreknowledge. These conclusions are necessary if there is to be the possibility of real contingencies in human experience. Picirilli, who acknowledges a debt to James Arminius and Richard Watson, has an excellent treatment on this subject. He explains:

The Arminian insists that there are things that actually can go either of two ways, and yet God knows which way they will go. He knows all future events perfectly. This means that they are all *certain*, else He would not know what will be.[73]

He goes on to say:

The Arminian insists that there is no conflict between "certainty" and true "contingency," although explanation of this requires a careful and technical discussion of three important terms: certainty, contingency, and necessity. The distinction between these plays an important role in the issues related to predestination. I would venture that, in this matter alone, there is more room for misunderstanding and more to be gained from clarity than almost any other point in dispute.[74]

In explaining the terms "contingency" and "necessity," Picirilli comments:

The free acts of morally responsible persons are *contingent*. A contingency is anything that really can take place in more than one way. The freedom to choose does not contradict certainty. Certainty relates to the "factness" of an event, to *whether* it will be or not; contingency relates to its *nature* as free or necessary. The same event can be both certain and contingent at the same time.[75]

In explaining the term "necessary," he points out that

Events that can transpire in just one way, that must inevitably be the way they are, are said to be *necessary*. For such events there were causes leading to the event that allowed no freedom of choice, causes that necessarily produced the event. Whenever God, for example, "makes" something happen the way it does without allowing for any other eventuality, that event is a necessity.[76]

He goes on to say:

God foreknows everything future as certain. That certainty of future events does not lie in their necessity but in their simple factness. They will be the way they will be, and God knows what they will be because He has perfect awareness, in advance, of all facts. But that knowledge *per se*, even though it is *fore*knowledge, has no more causal effect on facts than our knowledge of certain past facts has on them.[77]

Further on he says:

The Calvinist errs, on this subject, in suggesting that God knows the future certainly only because He first unconditionally foreordained (predestinated) it. But that is to confuse knowledge with active cause and so in effect take away contingency. God's foreknowledge, in the sense of prescience, is part of His omniscience and includes all things as certain, both good and evil, contingent, and necessary. It is not in itself causal.[78]

I think Picirilli has made his case. God's foreknowledge of events means that it is certain that they will occur, but it does not make the events necessary. Reference has already been made in this chapter to God's knowledge of hypothetical contingencies. If divine cause had to be the basis for knowledge of that which is neither past nor present, that would rule out knowledge of hypothetical contingencies. That would mean that any reference to hypothetical cases in Scripture by God would be only educated guesses. Such a view of God is unthinkable.

DIVINE FOREKNOWLEDGE OF FREE HUMAN CHOICES AND ACTS NOT BASED ON A SPECTATOR ROLE

It is important to keep in mind that in eternity past God did not observe the future as a mere spectator any more than He occupies the position of a mere spectator now. At the present time, God is deeply involved in what is taking place. As a holy, loving, caring, personal, omnipotent, omniscient, wise, and sovereign God, He is deeply concerned about and is deeply involved in what is happening in the human race. There is a consistency between all of God's attributes and His actions as a divine Sovereign.

God is not an impassive Being who cannot be moved by the concerns of human beings. He cares deeply about people. He cares deeply about people because it is His nature to care. He cares deeply about people because He created them for His glory in His image. He wants us to care deeply about people. He feels the pain and suffering of people. He wants us to feel the pain and suffering of people as well.

It is the kind of God that I have just attempted to describe who foresaw the future from all eternity. As He foresaw the future, He saw it as it would progressively unfold from: (1) The result of His creative activity and His divine influence. (2) The result of the devastating influence of sin. (3)The result of the response that human beings would give as a result of the redemptive work of Jesus Christ, the ministry of the Holy Spirit, the ministry of the Word of God, and the ministry of the redeemed. (4) The result of all of the influences that would come from all sources outside Himself. (5) The result of all the influence that He would bring on people through His power and His infinite wisdom. He saw then, everything that He sees and is doing now. He is the same God now that He was then. Everything that He is doing now is just as real as it would be if He had not known it in advance.

The Consistency Between the Sovereignty of God and the Influence and Response Model

Up to this point in this chapter, I think I have been able to raise some serious objections to the *cause* and *effect* model of how God plans and carries out His plan for the human race. The question before us now is: Is the *influence* and *response* model consistent with the sovereignty of God? I believe it is. I may not be able to answer all of the questions that I may be confronted with about this model, but I think it will have considerably fewer problems than the *cause* and *effect* model.

A Point of Clarification

Are the following two questions the same? (1) Is free will in the sense of *the liberty of indifference* consistent with the sovereignty of God? (2) Is free will in the sense of the *liberty of indifference* consistent with divine determinism? If the only way that a sovereign God can maintain His sovereignty in dealing with human beings is through a *cause* and *effect* approach, these questions are essentially the same, and the answer to both questions is no. However, if a sovereign God can maintain His sovereignty through an influence and response approach, the questions are not the same. The answer to the first question is yes. The answer to the second question is no.

THE QUESTION OF LIMITING THE SOVEREIGNTY OF GOD

It is usually assumed that if God is going to grant free will to human beings in the sense of the *liberty of indifference* that it would impose a limitation on the sovereignty of God. Arminians frequently make this concession. My first question to the suggestion of a limitation is: What kind of limitation? Does the use of the word "limitation" mean to make God weaker? If so, my response is that a God who can grant true freedom of will and still retain His sovereign control is a much greater God than a God who must limit His approach to sovereign control to determinism. I am in agreement with Cottrell when he says:

> We must not think that God's control varies according to the degree that he causes things or the degree of freedom bestowed on his creatures. Unless God is in *total* control, he is not sovereign. The issue is whether such total control requires a predetermination or causation of all things. I contend that it does not; God's sovereignty is *greater* than that![79]

My next question with regard to whether free will imposes a limitation on God is: A limitation in comparison to what? Why is it a limitation on God if He should choose to govern human beings through an *influence* and response model rather than a *cause* and *effect* model?

The two models do have some significant differences. If God had chosen to make man a machine with conscious awareness, His sovereign control could have been carried out with absolute precision. There would have been an absolute correlation between divine *cause* and *effect* as it would have been experienced by human beings. Certainly, no one would claim that all we see happening in today's world is in exact conformity to the desire of a holy and loving God! This is the fatal flaw of unlimited determinism whether hard or soft.

According to the *influence* and *response* model, it would have been possible for Adam and Eve and the human race to have lived a life of absolute obedience. This would comport with a *liberty of indifference.* But, as we know, it did not actually work out that way. This did not spell the end of God's sovereignty. It did mean that He had to follow through on the warning that He gave to Adam and Eve when He said, "But of the tree of the knowledge of good and evil you shall not eat, for in the day that you eat you shall surely die" (Gen. 2:17, NKJV).

In the *influence* and *response* model, once sin entered the picture, there would not be an exact correspondence between divine desire and human response. Divine sovereignty took on a new direction. God placed human beings under the sentence of death and cursed the earth. In Genesis 3:15, He made a promise to Adam and Eve that we know in the light of further revelation involved the promise of redemption through Jesus Christ. He is carrying out that plan with the human race. It is being done through the influence and response model.

THE INFLUENCE AND RESPONSE MODEL AND THE FULFILLMENT OF GOD'S SOVEREIGN PURPOSES

One of the most important questions for theologians to answer is: Is the *cause* and *effect* model the only way that a sovereign God can carry out His purposes? Or, can God work effectively in carrying out His purposes through the *influence* and *response* model?

There is absolutely no reason that a sovereign God cannot carry out His sovereign purposes while using an *influence* and *response* model. Once sin entered the picture, there would not be a precise, exact correlation between God's desires and human action. To say what I am saying is not the same as saying that God will not accomplish what He plans to do. *God's plan will not be thwarted!*

If God is going to be sovereign, and I cannot imagine God not being sovereign, He must be able to make plans and carry them out. It cannot be otherwise. However, if God works with human beings through an *influence* and *response* model in accordance with both the *liberty of spontaneity* and the *liberty of indifference,* we would necessarily use different criteria for judging His effectiveness as sovereign than we would if He operated through cause and effect.

The *cause* and *effect* model would expect an exact correlation between God's desire and what follows. Determinism is required for the *cause* and *effect* model. The smallest failure between God's desire and what follows would mean the collapse of God's sovereignty.

In *influence* and *response,* there is an exact correlation between what God sets out to do and what follows. If God says something will happen, it will happen. But that is not the same as saying that there is an exact correlation between what God desires and what follows. I think we can safely say that God does not desire for lying, hatred, murder, rape, and thievery to occur. At the same time, this does not mean that God will not accomplish the purposes He sets before Him.

The purposes that God set before Himself, as they relate to human beings, are best explained by the *influence* and *response* model. God purposed to create human beings with a free will. He purposed that they would be free to obey Him or disobey Him, to please Him or displease Him. It turned out that Adam and Eve disobeyed God. God obviously did not desire that they disobey Him. Such an attitude would be prohibited by His holiness. Their disobedience did not mean that God had ceased to be sovereign.

God was not caught off guard. He knew what would happen. He set in motion the processes that would bring about the plan of redemption through Jesus Christ. This plan was to be based on the fact that Jesus Christ would pay in full the penalty for the sins of human beings. He would provide absolute righteousness to meet the demand for absolute righteousness. He would offer this free salvation to all who would believe in Jesus Christ. He would have this message preached. He would have the Holy Spirit work to draw people to Christ as the gospel is preached. All of this would be done in keeping with the *influence* and *response* model. The end result of all of this would be "That in the dispensation of the fulness of times he might gather together in one all things in Christ, both which are in heaven, and which are on earth; even in Him" (Eph. 1:10). All of this is being done "according to the purpose of him who worketh all things after the counsel of his own will" (Eph. 1:11).

Many seem to think that God would be helpless when it comes to carrying out His sovereign purpose if He did not work through *cause* and *effect*. That this is not a necessary conclusion is seen by the way human beings work. The way human beings work with one another is through *influence* and *response*. Many things are accomplished this way. Contractors sign contracts and build buildings. For them to accomplish this goal, they have to influence people to work for them.

They have to influence them to do what they ask them to do. They may not always get the ones to work that they ask. But they get others. They succeed with the project.

Human contractors can deal with those who are free in the sense of the *liberty of indifference* through the *influence* and *response* model. If they can, cannot a sovereign and wise God accomplish His purposes with those who are free in the sense of the *liberty of indifference* through the *influence* and *response* model?

I believe that in the last several pages I have made my case for the position that a sovereign and wise God is not required to use the cause and effect model in order to maintain His sovereignty and accomplish His purposes. I believe that God can and does work through the influence and response model. That being true, there is no reason that a sovereign God could not use the approach of conditional election.

We will now turn our attention to the second assumption of Calvinism.

An Answer to the Second Assumption of Calvinism

The second assumption of Calvinism is that total depravity precludes the response of faith from the sinner unless he is first regenerated by the Holy Spirit. As I pointed out earlier, the view that the nature of depravity requires that the sinner be regenerated before he or she can respond with faith had its origin with Augustine.

To place regeneration before faith, poses some serious problems for Calvinism. This was dealt with in Chapter 13. I will restate this problem below. For a more thorough treatment please refer back to "An Inconsistency in Calvinism" (pp. 260-62).

Calvinism is faced with two important assumed impossibilities. (1) It is impossible for a person to believe unless he or she is first regenerated. (2) It is impossible for sanctification to take place prior to justification. A Classical Calvinist will not argue against either of these statements. In Chapter 13, I gave support for these two assertions from Robert Haldane and Louis Berkhof. The Calvinistic credentials of these men are not in question.

In Classical Calvinism, the order is regeneration, faith, justification, and sanctification. *In placing regeneration before justification Calvinism has a problem.* By anybody's definition, regeneration is a life-changing experience. Berkhof tells us that "regeneration is the beginning of sanctification."[80] If regeneration is the beginning of sanctification, this means that Classical Calvinism has the process of sanctification beginning before justification occurs. This cannot be!

Calvinists have, by and large, adhered to the satisfaction view of atonement and justification. If a person is consistent in developing the implications of the satisfaction view of atonement, it is clear that God cannot perform the act of regeneration (an act of sanctification) in a person before he or she is justified. God can move in with His sanctifying grace only after the guilt problem is satisfied by justification. To think otherwise is to violate the law of non-contradiction. I realize that when we talk about the *ordo salutis* (order of salvation) we are talking about logical order instead of chronological order. But that logical order is inviolable!

Regeneration is not an act of God that prepares the way for redemption. It is a redemptive act. I commend Calvinists for upholding the satisfaction view of atonement and the imputation of the death and righteousness of Christ as the ground of justification. I believe they need to reexamine the question of whether *the redemptive act of regeneration* can be performed on a person before the death and righteousness of Christ is actually imputed to his account.

THE NECESSITY OF THE DRAWING POWER OF THE HOLY SPIRIT

It is evident that it is no simple matter for a person who is under the bondage of sin to be brought to an exercise of saving faith. Jesus drives that point home when He said, "No man can come to me, except the Father which hath sent me draw him" (Jn. 6:44).

We dare not take the depravity of human beings lightly. Apart from the drawing power of the Holy Spirit, none would come to Christ. If a person cannot exercise faith in Christ unless he or she is *first* regenerated by the Holy Spirit, those who believe in the satisfaction view of atonement and justification are in trouble as we have seen above. For a person to be regenerated *before* he or she is justified contradicts the logical priority of justification to sanctification. To avoid this contradiction, a way must be found that will place justification before regeneration. I believe that in the influence and response model we can maintain a strong view of depravity and at the same time maintain the *ordo salutis* to be faith, justification, regeneration, and sanctification.

We know that Adam and Eve were created with original righteousness. They had a righteous and sinless nature. By a satanic attack through the serpent, Eve responded in a way that *contradicted* her righteous nature. She disobeyed God and obeyed the serpent. Then Adam, following the example of Eve, responded in a way that contradicted his righteous nature. All of this happened through an *influence* and *response* relationship. Satan influenced Adam and Eve and they responded.

It is a matter of historical fact that Adam and Eve by the influence of Satan acted contrary to their nature. Satan did not perform some transforming act on them to give them a depraved nature, making it possible for them to sin. We grant that Adam and Eve, through Satanic influence, an influence which did not first change their nature, were brought to sin. Will we say that God cannot, without first regenerating sinners, influence sinners through the Word of God and the Holy Spirit, so that some of them will contradict their sinful nature and be brought to Christ? How can a person acknowledge the factualness of what happened to Adam and Eve and deny the possibility that a person could exercise saving faith by the aid of the Holy Spirit without first being regenerated?

God made human beings in His image. He made them personal beings. He made them to live in an *influence* and *response* relationship with Himself. While depravity puts human beings in a state of being that requires divine aid before they can respond to the gospel, there is no reason to believe that God cannot continue to work with human beings in keeping with the *influence* and *response* model. That is the only way that is consistent with the personhood of human beings.

The image of God still remains in fallen creatures and can be appealed to by the moral teachings of the Bible; by the message of sin and guilt; by God's provision of atonement through Jesus Christ, and by the offer of salvation through Christ alone through faith alone. When sinners are confronted with this message, the Holy Spirit can and will work to draw sinners to Christ. They can be brought to that point in which they are enabled to say either yes or no.

To make it clear that I have a very serious view of sin and depravity, let me quote here what I said in Chapter 9 under the heading, "The Problem of Giving a Simple Description of Fallen Man" (p. 155).

> It is clear that man fell from a state of holiness into a state of sin (Is. 53:6; Rom. 3:23). It is clear that sin has placed man under condemnation before God (Rom. 6:23; Rev. 21:8). It is clear that fallen man cannot please God and has no fellowship with God (Eph. 2:1-3; Rom. 8:7, 8). It is clear that man cannot come to God without the drawing power of the Holy Spirit (Jn. 6:44). It is clear that a work so drastic as to be called a new birth is required for man's salvation (Jn. 3:3-7). But we also find areas where the state and condition of man are not so clearly understood.

I think I have shown that Calvinists are in deep trouble when they place regeneration, which clearly includes sanctification, ahead of justification in the *ordo salutis*. That problem alone should spell a death blow to Classical Calvinists insistence that regeneration must precede faith and justification. I think I have shown that there is no reason to believe that God cannot use the influence and response model in working with sinners to lead them to Christ.

An Answer to the Third Assumption of Calvinism

The third assumption of Calvinism is that the only way salvation could be free is by unconditional election. My treatment of atonement and justification in Chapter 11 should make it unquestionably clear that I believe justification is a gift. It is by grace. Not one thing that I have ever done or ever will do is placed on my account with God as part of the price of my redemption. The only way God, as Supreme Judge of the universe, can justify a member of the fallen human race is to have Christ's righteousness and Christ's death placed on his account. That and that alone is the ground for justification. That is it and nothing else. Justification is by *Christ alone* by (conditioned on) *faith alone*. That is pure and uncorrupted grace!

Is anyone really going to insist that for God to require faith in Christ *as a condition for receiving* the death and righteousness of Christ would mean justification by works? Does not Paul insist in Romans 4 that to be justified by faith (faith as a condition, not ground) is in contradiction to justification by works? Even a Calvinist believes that faith is a condition of salvation.

Earlier in this chapter, I pointed out that the unconditional election taught in Calvinism seems to rest on three assumptions. These assumptions are: (1) That the sovereignty of God requires unconditional election and thus precludes conditional election. (2) That total depravity precludes the response of faith from a sinner unless he is first regenerated by the Holy Spirit. (3) That salvation is free precludes conditional election. I pointed out that if these three assumptions are true, Calvinism has won its case. I also pointed out that if these three assumptions are not true, Calvinism is in trouble. I believe I have shown that these assumptions do not rest on solid ground.

Now I want to turn our attention to the question of decrees in Arminian thought.

Types of Decrees Consistent with Arminian Theology

The decrees of God are His eternal purpose or purposes. Decrees could be called God's eternal will or His eternal plan. I will consider three basic types of decrees: efficacious decrees, decrees to influence, and decrees to permit.

EFFICACIOUS DECREES

Efficacious decrees are decrees in which God decrees that certain things will come to pass. In these decrees, God Himself will be responsible for their fulfillment. There are two types of efficacious decrees: unconditional efficacious decrees and conditional efficacious decrees.

UNCONDITIONAL EFFICACIOUS DECREES

Unconditional efficacious decrees are not dependent upon any conditions for their fulfillment. The work of creation would be an example of this kind of decree. The provision of Hell for the wicked and the provision of atonement through Jesus Christ would also be examples of this kind of decree.

Because of God's foreknowledge of sin, by the necessity of His holy nature, He decreed to prepare Hell for the wicked. On the occasion of God's foreknowledge of sin, God was moved by His love to decree the provision of atonement.

Note: It can be seen by the use of foreknowledge in these two unconditional efficacious decrees how foreknowledge was used in the "determinate counsel" of God in Acts 2:23. It is not necessary to consider foreknowledge in this case to be causal. It is possible to consider foreknowledge to be instrumental in the decree to predestinate the crucifixion of Christ. In this case foreknowledge would furnish God with the information that would be necessary for Him to make the plans for the provision of atonement through the death of Christ. By the help of His foreknowledge, God could decree the death of Christ in a way that would not violate the freedom of choice of the persons who would be involved.

CONDITIONAL EFFICACIOUS DECREES

In conditional efficacious decrees, God efficaciously decreed that certain things would take place when certain conditions were met. These decrees were made because God, on the basis of His foreknowledge, knew that these conditions would be met. An example of this kind of decree would be the justification and regeneration of a person when he believes. It is for this reason that I can say that a believer's justification and regeneration were efficaciously decreed. Justification and regeneration are monergistic. They are solely the work of God.

DECREES TO INFLUENCE

Decrees to influence refer to the action of God through which He would work with His responsible creatures to bring about desired responses. While there is a desired response on the part of God, that response is not guaranteed by the influence of God. The drawing power of the Holy Spirit upon the unsaved when they read or hear the gospel would be an example of this kind of decree. I have not seen this terminology (or any synonym) used elsewhere. I do not believe that we can successfully understand the workings of God with man apart from this decree or one by another name that says the same thing. It is the lack of tolerance for an idea of this kind that puts Calvinism into an awkward position in trying to explain the origin of sin without making God responsible for sin.

DECREES TO PERMIT

These decrees have reference to the action of God in permitting certain things, but not efficaciously bringing them about. All events that God foreknows (which embraces all that ever will happen) are either efficaciously decreed or are permitted. All acts of human beings (or free agents) come under this permission *whether evil or good.*

While the *permission* and the *events* which follow, whether evil or good, are decreed, both are not decreed in exactly the same sense. The permission, itself, is a divine act. The events that follow, which are our present concern, are human acts—some in obedience and some in disobedience. As it relates to those acts which are good, God has the relationship of both influence and permission. As it relates to those acts which are evil, God's relationship to its occurrence is permission only.

William G. T. Shedd says, "The permissive decree relates only to moral evil. Sin is the sole and solitary object of this species of decrees."[81]

It is a mistake to limit permission to disobedience. The decrees to influence and the decrees to permit are God's way of dealing with persons made in His own image. They are permitted to either obey or disobey. They are permitted to be good stewards or bad stewards. In this arrangement, some things happen that please God and some things happen that displease God. It pleased God to make man in His own image and give him a choice in matters. The plan pleased God. But He is not pleased with the sinful deeds of human beings.

An Order of Decrees Consistent with Arminianism

In the first edition of his *Systematic Theology*, Henry C. Thiessen adopted a modified form of Sublapsarianism. He explains:

> We believe that the decrees are in this order: 1. The decree to create, 2. The decree to permit the fall, 3. The decree to provide salvation for all, and 4. The decree to apply that salvation to some, to those who believe.[82]

Thiessen modified the fourth point of Sublapsarianism to conform to his doctrine of conditional election. This modification of Sublapsarianism would be compatible with Arminianism.

Conclusion

I believe that I have shown in this chapter that there are no a priori reasons that would prohibit God from working through the approach of conditional election. The remaining question is: What is the biblical teaching on election? That will be the subject of the next two chapters.

16

A Challenge to the Exegetical Support for Unconditional Election

In the last chapter, I dealt with the theological problems that must be dealt with in a study of election. The views on unconditional election and conditional election were set forth. Attention was given to decrees, determinism, the sovereignty of God, the meaning of free will, etc. I set forth two differing models for the way God carries out His sovereign purposes with human beings: the *cause* and *effect* model and the *influence* and *response* model. Unconditional election is best served by the *cause* and *effect* model. Conditional election is best served by the *influence* and *response* model. I believe that the *influence* and *response* model best maintains theological consistency.

The big question before us is: what does the Bible teach? The ultimate test of a theological viewpoint is: Will it stand the test of biblical exegesis?

If unconditional election is true, there must be at least one passage of Scripture that irrefutably teaches unconditional election. I believe Calvinists would agree that they would consider Romans 9 to be that passage that unquestionably and irrefutably teaches unconditional election. Romans 9 is considered to be the bedrock of Calvinism. [1]

The question for us to decide is: "Does Romans 9 teach unconditional election?" Once that question is decided, we will examine other passages.

When I wrote my commentary on Romans, [2] which was published in 1987, I examined about 40 commentaries on Romans 9. As a result of that study, I concluded that about eighty percent of the commentaries set forth the view of unconditional election. If conditional election is going to stand, those who believe it must be able to deal with Romans 9 adequately and with integrity.

The case for unconditional election in Romans chapter 9, stands or falls on the meaning of the question that Paul raises in verse 14.

Calvinism on Romans 9:14

In Romans 9:14, Paul asks: "What shall we say then? There is no injustice with God is there ? May it never be!" (9:14). If we miss the meaning of Paul's question in verse 14, we will likely come away from Romans 9 with a wrong view of what Paul is meaning to convey. It is absolutely necessary for us to understand why Paul asks the question in verse 14, if we are going to be able to understand the contribution that Romans 9 gives to our understanding of election.

It is assumed by those who believe in unconditional election that Paul is raising the question of whether God was unrighteous or unjust in unconditionally choosing Jacob while rejecting Esau. Robert Haldane explains, "The Apostle anticipated the objection of the carnal mind in this doctrine. Does not loving Jacob and hating Esau before they had done any good or evil, imply, that there is injustice with God?"[3] Everett F. Harrison observes, "God's dealings with Jacob and Esau might be challenged as arbitrary, on the ground that Esau was the object of injustice."[4] William S. Plumer says, "The meaning is this: Does God's treatment of Isaac and Jacob display injustice to Ishmael and Esau?"[5] William G. T. Shedd explains. "The objection is raised that in such discrimination as that between Jacob and Esau, God acts unjustly."[6] John Piper comments, "When Paul said that God chose to bless Jacob over Esau apart from any basis in their actions but simply on the basis of his choice (*ek tou kalountos*, Rom. 9:12), his opponent objected that this would call God's righteousness into question (9:14).[7]

It is obvious that these commentators are of the opinion that in setting forth the choice of Jacob and the rejection of Esau (verses 10-13), Paul has established the doctrine of unconditional election. They take the question that Paul raises in verse 14 to be dealing with an objection to the doctrine of unconditional election.

The Context of the Question in Romans 9:14

The question before us is: Is Calvinism's interpretation a proper assessment? If Paul is, in fact, raising the question of whether God is unrighteous in unconditionally electing Jacob for salvation while not extending the same privilege to Esau, Calvinism has won the debate. This is true because unconditional election would already be implied in the question in Romans 9:14. I do not concede to Calvinism. I believe that Calvinism has *wrongly interpreted* the question in verse 14. They have wrongly interpreted the question in verse 14 because they have wrongly interpreted verses 6-13, particularly verses 11 and 12. A proper understanding of verses 6-13 should help us understand why Paul posed the question of whether there is injustice in God in verse 14.

Three Views of Verses 6-13 as Related to Election

There have been basically three views given of this passage (verses 6-13) as it relates to election. Major attention has been given to how this passage climaxes in verses 10 and 11.

(1) Most who believe in conditional election have taken the position that this passage has nothing to do with election or rejection with regard to individual salvation. Rather, it is understood to refer to the election of Jacob as the third of the patriarchal ancestors (the other two being Abraham and Isaac) of the nation of Israel. Thus, the Covenant Seed of Abraham were chosen through Jacob rather than Esau. Jacob was elected as the third patriarch. Esau was rejected with the result being that his descendants were not a part of the Covenant Seed of Abraham. (See Clarke,[8] Godet,[9] and Sanday and Headlam.[10])

(2) Some who believe in unconditional election agree that the passage deals with the election of Jacob as the third patriarchal head of the Covenant Seed of Abraham and that Esau was rejected for the position. However, this position goes on to view Jacob and Esau as types. Shedd explains:

> Jacob and Esau, like Isaac and Ishmael, are *types* of two classes that have been spoken of: viz: the "children of the promise," and the "children of the flesh" (v. 8). The

theocratic election of Isaac and Jacob illustrates the spiritual election of individuals; and the theocratic reprobation of Ishmael and Esau illustrates the spiritual reprobation of individuals."[11]

Hodge also takes this position.[12]

(3) The more common view among those who support unconditional election would be to understand the passage as being directly concerned with unconditional election rather than to support it by analogy. This view is held by Hendricksen,[13] Murray,[14] and Piper.[15]

Let's take a serious look at verses 6-13 and see what the context is for the question in verse 14.

The Jewish Problem

A BELIEF THAT GOD UNCONDITIONALLY PROMISED ALL JEWS ETERNAL LIFE IN THE ABRAHAMIC COVENANT

Note: Recent translations usually translate *sperma* as "descendant" or "offspring." These are valid and helpful translations. However, since the terminology "Abraham's Seed" has so fixed itself in eschatological literature, I will use the term "Abraham's Seed" in this treatment except when I quote other sources.

To find out why Paul raised this question in verse 14, we need to review the context. In verses 1-3, Paul expressed his deep concern over the many Jews who were not saved. This created a serious problem for the Jews. The unbelieving Jews were not prepared for such an observation. That large numbers of Jews, who were the Covenant People of God, would be lost and under God's wrath was for them unthinkable.

Observations on the Jewish Understanding of Salvation

We are confronted with two seemingly contradictory concepts in the New Testament concerning the Jewish viewpoint on their own salvation. The first is the concept of unconditional salvation of all Jews as the seed of Abraham. It was this viewpoint that caused John the Baptist to say, "Therefore bring forth fruit in keeping with your repentance; and do not suppose that you can say to yourselves, we have Abraham for our father; for I say to you, that God is able from these stones to raise up children to Abraham" (Mt. 3:9; see also Jn. 8:33-40).

The other viewpoint is that they were depending on their own works. This viewpoint is set forth by Paul when he said. "But Israel, pursuing a law of righteousness, did not arrive at *that* law. Why? Because *they did* not *pursue it* by faith, but as though *it were* by works" (Rom. 9:31, 32).

It appears that even their thinking about salvation by works was not referring to the salvation of an individual Jew by works. Rather, the reference seems to be to a corporate righteousness. That a strong sense of corporate righteousness was prevalent among the Jews can be seen from the apocryphal book 2 Esdras in which the writer expresses his bewilderment over what appeared to be the preferred treatment given to Gentiles. He was desperately concerned about why God had delivered

Israel over to Babylon. In his prayer he expressed his bewilderment over the matter. In 3:27-36, he complains:

> 27 So thou didst deliver the city [Jerusalem] into the hands of thy enemies. 28 Then I said in my heart, Are the deeds of those who inhabit Babylon any better? Is that why she has gained dominion over Zion? 29 For when I came here I saw ungodly deeds without number, and my soul has seen many sinners during these thirty years. And my heart failed me, 30 for I have seen how thou dost endure those who sin, and hast spared those who act wickedly, and hast destroyed thy people, and hast preserved thy enemies, 31 and hast not shown to anyone how thy way may be comprehended. Are the deeds of Babylon better than those of Zion? 32 Or has another nation known thee besides Israel? Or what tribes have so believed thy covenants as the tribes of Jacob 33 Yet their reward has not appeared and their labor has borne no fruit. For I have traveled widely among the nations and have seen that they abound in wealth, though they are unmindful of thy commandments. 34 Now therefore weigh in a balance our iniquities and those of the inhabitants of the world; and so it will be found which way the turn of the scale will incline. 35 When have the inhabitants of the earth not sinned in thy sight? Or what nation has kept thy commandments so well? 36 Thou mayest indeed find individual men who have kept thy commandments, but nations thou wilt not find.[16]

It appears that these two observations about salvation among the Jews are mutually exclusive. However, from all I can gather, Jews were not as concerned with harmonization as some of us are. They were more content to let some loose ends dangle in their thought.[17] E. P. Sanders astutely observes, "The Rabbis were not concerned with the internal systematic relationship of their statements."[18]

Their concept of unconditional corporate election of all Jews was by far the more basic of the two thoughts. All the rest of their thoughts must be weighed in the light of that foundational thought.

As Charles Hodge in commenting on Romans 3:3 explains:

> It is plain that the whole first part of this chapter is an answer to the objections of the Jews to the apostle's doctrine that they were exposed to condemnation. This is clear as to the first verse, and the fifth and those that follow it. . . . Their great objection to Paul's applying his general principles of justice to their case was that their situation was peculiar: "God has chosen us as his people in Abraham. If we retain our relation to him by circumcision and the observance of the law, we shall never be treated or condemned as the Gentiles." Traces of this opinion abound in the New Testament, and it is openly avowed by the Jewish writers. "Think not," says the Baptist, "to say within yourselves, We have Abraham to our father," Matt. iii.9. "We be Abraham's seed," John 8:33. Comp. Rom. 2:17; 9:6; and other passages, in which Paul argues to prove that being the natural descendants of Abraham is not enough to secure the favour of God.

That such was the doctrine of the Jews is shown by numerous passages from their writings. "If a Jew commit all manner of sins," says Abarbanel, "he is indeed of the number of sinning Israelites, and will be punished according to his sins; but he has, notwithstanding, a portion in eternal life." The same sentiment is expressed in the book Torath Adam, fol. 100, in nearly the same words, and the reasons assigned for it, "That all Israel has a portion in eternal life. . . ." Justin Martyr, as quoted by Grotius on chap. ii.13, attributes this doctrine to the Jews of his day: "They suppose that to them universally, who are of the seed of Abraham, no matter how sinful and disobedient to God they may be, the eternal kingdom shall be given."[19]

Douglas J. Moo raises the question:

Who constitutes the "Israel" to whom God's promises of salvation have been given?

He goes on to say:

The standard view among Paul's Jewish contemporaries was that this Israel was made up of all those physically descended from Jacob, the heir of Abraham and Isaac, who was himself named "Israel." Only those who had refused their inheritance by outright apostasy would be excluded from Israel to whom the promises belonged.[20]

This Jewish thinking was based on the promise of the eternal possession of the land to Abraham and his seed (Gen. 13:14, 15 and 17:8). The eternal possession of the land meant, to them, the promise of eternal life in the next life. Since the Jews are the Covenant Seed (descendants, or offspring) of Abraham, they took this to mean that in the Abrahamic Covenant an unconditional promise was given to them of eternal life. Paul's suggestion that some of them were not saved ran counter to their understanding of the Abrahamic Covenant.

The Jews believed in the unconditional corporate election of all Jews based on the promises of the Abrahamic Covenant. In this case, corporate election means more than the election of a group of people who came to be known as Jews. It embraced each individual who descended from Abraham through Jacob. Hodge sees their interpretation of the Abrahamic Covenant as the foundation of their thinking in terms of the corporate salvation of all Jews. He explains:

It should be remembered that the principal ground on which the Jews expected acceptance with God, was the covenant which he had made with their father Abraham, in which he promised to be a God to him and to his seed after him. They understood this promise to secure salvation for all who retained their connection with Abraham, by the observance of the law and the rite of circumcision. They expected, therefore, to be regarded and treated not so much as individuals, each being dealt with according to his personal character, but as a community to whom salvation was secured by the promise made to Abraham.[21]

Having in mind the Jewish viewpoint of the unconditional corporate election of all Jews as the seed of Abraham, we can see why Paul's suggestion that many Jews were not saved (verses 1-3) would not be received by the Jews. The claim that only those Jews believing in Christ would be saved was totally unacceptable in their thinking. To them, it was an attack on the promise that God had made to Abraham. It was an attack on the veracity, righteousness, or justice of God.

Additional Information on Jewish Thought About Salvation

As we have seen, the prevailing thought among Jews in New Testament times appears to have been that all Jews were unconditionally saved. However, it does seem that there was some modification of opinion and some variety of views. I will call brief attention to this problem. The article "Resurrection" in *The Jewish Encyclopedia*, gives us insight into Jewish thought. It reads:

> It became a matter of dispute between the older school of the Shammites, represented by R. Eliezer, and the Hillelites, represented by R. Joshua, whether or not the righteous among the heathen have a share in the future world, the former interpreting the verse, "The wicked shall return to Sheol, even all the Gentiles that forget God" (Ps. ix. 18 [R. V. 17]), as condemning as wicked among the Jews and the Gentiles such as have forgotten God; the latter interpreting the verse as consigning to Sheol only such as have actually forgotten God (Tos Sanh. xiii. 2). The doctrine "All Israelites have a share in the world to come" (Sanh. xi. i), based upon Isa. ix. 21 (Hebr). "The people all of them righteous shall inherit the land," is therefore identical with the Pharisaic teachings as stated by Josephus (Ant. xviii. 1. § 3; "B. J." ii. 8 § 14), that the righteous will rise to share in the eternal bliss. It is as deniers of the fundamentals of religion that heathen, Samaritans, and heretics are excluded from future salvation (Tos. Sanh. xiii.; Pirke R. El. xxxviii.; Midr. The. xi. 5). Regarding plurality of opinions in favor of the salvation of righteous non-Jews, and the opinions those who adhere to the national view, see Zunz, "Z. G." pp. 371-389. Related to the older, exclusive view also is the idea that the Abrahamic covenant releases the Israelites from the fire of Gehenna (Gen. R. xlviii; Midr. The. vii. I; 'Er. 19a).[22]

Another factor to keep in mind in trying to understand Jewish thought is that it also appears that they held to a remote possibility of loss of salvation. While the quotation that I will give came from the eighteenth century it probably represents the thinking of some in biblical days. "Rabbi Israel Baal Shem Tov, founder of Hasidism, is reported to have said: 'Every Jew is an organ of the *Shekhinah*. As long as the organ is joined to the body, however tenuously, there is hope; once it is cut off, all hope is lost.' "[23]

It appears that some thinking might have already existed before the time of Christ that might have been in conflict with the view that all Jews were saved. In 2 Esdras 7:47, 48 the writer says:

> 47 And now I see that the world to come will bring delight to few, but torments to many. 48 For an evil heart has grown up in us, which has alienated us from God, and has brought us into corruption and the ways of death, and has shown us the paths of perdition and removed us far from life—and that not just a few of us but almost all who have been created (See also 7:59-61, and 8:1-3)

The Development of My Thinking
on the Jewish Understanding of Salvation

My comments must be brief. But I think it is incumbent upon me to address this problem, at least, briefly. My thinking on the way Jews looked at the basis for their salvation has gone through some changes over the years. For a while, I went along with the popular view that Jews believed in salvation by works. By the time I wrote my commentary on Romans, published in 1987, I had given considerable attention to the Abrahamic Covenant. In the light of Genesis 13:14, 15 and 17:8, I could see why the Jews, as implied in Matthew 3:9 and John 8:33-39, believed that the Abrahamic Covenant promised them that they would have eternal life and the land of Canaan would be their eternal inheritance. In the study that I did for writing the commentary, the greatest help that I received came from Charles Hodge's comments in his *Commentary on the Epistle to the Romans*.

In 1970, I wrote a Th. M. thesis entitled "Jesus and the Pharisees" for Chicago Graduate School of Theology. That helped me to have a better understanding of Jewish thinking at the time of Jesus. The emphasis in that thesis was on Oral Tradition. In writing that thesis, I became convinced that there was a considerable amount of misunderstanding about the Pharisees. The knowledge that I gained about the Pharisees has been useful to me as I have tried to understand their view of election or salvation, but I did not address that issue in the thesis. The conflict that Jesus had with the Pharisees dealt with the issue of *ethical legalism* rather than *soteriological legalism*.

The Pharisees correctly worked on the assumption that the whole of life should be lived out in submission to God. Their problem came from the conviction that this responsibility to God could be spelled out in minute detail in terms of laws. These laws were to be spelled out by the properly recognized Jewish authorities. This was passed along to the people in the form of Oral Tradition or Oral Law. It is referred to in the KJV as the Tradition of the Elders. The individual did not have the freedom to use on-the-spot judgment to go contrary to these laws. There was no room to use common sense and to be extemporaneous in showing mercy if it went contrary to the prescription of the Oral Tradition (See Mt. 15:1-20, Mk. 7:1-23).

It is possible for a person to be an *ethical legalist* (a heavy reliance on laws to express moral and ethical responsibility), and not be a *soteriological legalist* (a dependence on obedience to laws as a way to be saved). A failure to make this distinction has contributed and continues to contribute to a lot of confusion. Just because a person has strict convictions and seeks to get other people to live by them, does not necessarily mean that he or she believes in salvation by works (*soteriological legalism*).

I think that, beyond doubt, the prevailing opinion among the Jews of Paul's day was that in connection with the call and the covenant that God made with Abraham, He unconditionally promised salvation to all Jews. That does not mean that all of the rest of Jewish thought worked itself out logically in the same pattern that we might expect of a systematic theology today. It is our responsibility to recognize that the Jews did believe in the unconditional salvation of all Jews, and then see, to the best of our ability, how the rest of the pieces of the puzzle fit together. These other pieces of the puzzle include statements made in the New Testament that seem to connect Jews to salvation by works and the statements from Jewish writings that seem to imply that salvation is by works.

If, in our study to understand the Jewish view of salvation, we do not begin with the Jewish concept of a covenant relationship between God and Israel and how that covenant relationship is perceived by the Jews, we will be hopelessly confused. That covenant relationship was instituted by God when He established the covenant with Abraham and His seed. The Jews understood that they were the Covenant Seed of Abraham. Through the Abrahamic Covenant, God elected or chose Israel to be His people. This relationship was to be an eternal relationship. All Jews were considered saved. They believed in corporate salvation or corporate election. This election included each individual Jew, but they were not chosen individually. Election applied to them as individuals because they were members of the group.

While the Jews believed in the unconditional election or salvation of all Jews, in the arena of life this presented them with real problems. What place does merit have in a person's relationship with God? What about the descendant of Abraham who becomes an apostate and turns against God and the Law of Moses? They did not want to ignore these problems. But they did not want to reject the conviction that all Jews are saved. If we start with what they say about works and merit, we will conclude that at least in some measure they thought that salvation is by works. If we take this approach, we will never understand the place that their concept of a covenant relationship with God had in their thinking. It seems that is where most people have started. With such an approach, it will be impossible to understand Romans 9.

It seems to me that if we get to the bottom of Jewish thinking it would be summed up like this: God unconditionally elected all Jews as a group. It is to be expected that individual Jews will manifest an interest in serving God. If they do not, it puzzles Jews in a way similar to the way it bothers us as Christians when other Christians do not take their relationship to God as seriously as we think they should. But the Jews assume that such people are in the covenant. Though they assume that these people are safely in the covenant, what they say may not always sound consistent with that conclusion. It may sound like that for an individual Jew to keep his place in the covenant he must maintain obedience. But at the same time, it seems that his place in the covenant is unconditionally secure. It seems that the more fundamental aspect of their thinking is that the covenant is unconditional.

It seems to me that the only way Jewish thinkers are, in any way, willing to alter the "all" in "all Jews are saved" is the elimination of those who are guilty of apostasy. Such cases would be rare. I have quoted from sources above that will support the fact that such thinking has existed in Jewish thought. It is not that Jews must do something to be saved or remain saved. They are saved and will remain saved unless they commit apostasy. That there is such a thing as apostasy for Jews seems to be a rather reluctant conclusion, but one that they cannot dismiss.

Though it seems that apostasy would be the only way, in Jewish thinking, that a person would be eliminated from the blessings of the covenant, some things that they say would sound as if obedience to the covenant is required to remain in the covenant. That type of inconsistency prevails in Jewish thought. I do not think that this means that they had no concern about the law of non-contradiction.

They lived knowing that with the information available to them, they could not remove the apparent contradiction. I would say that a systematic harmony of the doctrines of a sovereign, holy, and loving God, and sin, guilt, grace, and forgiveness can be developed only in the light of the incarnation, atonement, and the resurrection of Christ. At best, Jewish theology without Jesus Christ would, of necessity, fall short of a harmonious, consistent systematic theology. This would be true of their theology before Jesus came. It would also continue to be true of their theology after the coming of Jesus if they leave Him out of their thinking.

If the position that I have described is the true understanding of the Jewish approach to salvation, what about the passages in the New Testament that would suggest that Jews had a problem with salvation by works? Before I respond, let me say again that the Jews were not as concerned as we are about bringing a systematic harmony to their thinking.

In trying to answer the question of why we get the impression in some places that the Jews believed in salvation by works, I would make the following observations. My first observation is that pastors and teachers face many problems in their personal encounters with people that are not found in scholarly treatments. For example, among those who believe that loss of salvation is possible, there are some who take the position that if a Christian commits one sin he is lost until he confesses that sin. Though a person may encounter that as he works with people, I doubt that there has ever been a scholarly treatment that set forth that view. Yet, it must be dealt with because there are people who think that way.

Paul was not just dealing with the members of the Sanhedrin. He was not just dealing with famous Rabbis. He was dealing with the Jews who attended the synagogue and wherever else he might meet them. I do not think it would have been uncommon for Jews to have referred to the corporate superiority of the Jews to the Gentiles. It would not be hard at all to see how the question of works could get into the picture. When Paul drew the discussion away from corporate salvation to individual salvation, it is not hard to see how particular individuals would defend themselves on the grounds of moral superiority—particularly as compared with Gentiles.

E. P. Sanders' View of the Jewish Understanding of Salvation

My introduction to Sanders came after most of my thinking had been developed. Sanders has made a significant contribution to our understanding of the thinking of the Jews of Paul's time. His conclusions have been shocking to many, and have given rise to a lot of controversy. Sanders sums up his thought about the way the Jews looked at salvation as follows:

> The pattern is this: God has chosen Israel and Israel has accepted the election. In his role as King, God gave Israel commandments which they are to obey as best they can. Obedience is rewarded and disobedience punished. In case of failure to obey, however, man has recourse to divinely ordained means of atonement, in all of which repentance is required. As long as he maintains his desire to stay in the covenant, he has a share in God's covenantal promises, including life in the world to come. The intention and effort to be obedient constitute the condition for remaining in the covenant, but they do not earn it.[24]

Sanders chooses to call his view "covenantal nomism." In defining covenantal nomism, he explains:

> Briefly put, covenantal nomism is the view that one's place in God's plan is established on the basis of the covenant and that requires as the proper response of man his obedience to its commandments, while providing a means of atonement for transgression.[25]

In another place, he says:

> The all-pervasive view is this: all Israelites have a share in the world to come unless they renounce it by renouncing God and his covenant. All sins, no matter of what gravity, which are committed within the covenant, may be forgiven as long as a man indicates his basic intention to keep the covenant by atoning, especially by repenting of transgression.[26]

Sanders is sharply critical of the fact that so many Christians have understood the Jews of New Testament times to be obsessed with a rigid, legalistic approach to salvation.[27]

AN ASSESSMENT OF SANDERS' VIEW

It seems to me, as I have emphasized up to this point, that the Jews of Jesus and Paul's day worked on the assumption that all Jews were saved. They started in life as being one of God's chosen, covenant people. The only thing that could change that would be an act of outright apostasy. If they worked on that assumption, they had to believe in unconditional salvation. If that be true, they did not believe in salvation by works. Sanders has a right to be perturbed about this.

I agree with Sanders that in making a study of Jewish thought that we must start with their concept of their covenant relationship with God. It is hopeless to understand Jewish thought any other way. Whatever they say about works and merit must always be understood in that light. At least, we should attempt to understand it in that light. We cannot force an absolute harmony on Jewish thought. We may say that some of their statements sound like works salvation. But when understood in the context of an unconditional covenant, we must back off the charge.

When Sanders says, "The intention and effort to be obedient constitute the *condition for remaining in the covenant*, but they do not *earn it*," he is struggling with trying to be fair and as near as possible accurate in describing Jewish thought. Even that must be understood in the context of the conviction that all Israel will be saved. The idea that intention and effort constitute a condition for remaining in the covenant, but do not earn remaining in the covenant may sound contradictory to us. But the Jews chose to live with such seeming conflict of ideas.

It seems to me that the bottom line is that the Jews did not exactly look at obedience as a condition for remaining in the covenant. They viewed that as an unconditional blessing of God. They did not have to do anything to stay in the covenant. But if they renounced God and Judaism, they would lose their place in the covenant. At the same time they would say things that made it look like they did believe that obedience was a condition of remaining in the covenant.

The problem with the Jews in the New Testament was not that they thought they were saved by works. It was that they did not need to be saved, each on an individual basis, but that they were saved collectively and corporately. Paul's aim is to get them to see that this was a mistaken idea. They needed to be saved as individuals, and that was on the condition of faith in Jesus as the Messiah.

A CHALLENGE

Extensive research and writing (perhaps a doctoral dissertation) needs to be done on the Jewish concept of the unconditional salvation for all Jews, the possibility of apostasy, the question of salvation by works, the question of whether few or many will be saved, and the Jewish thinking about the salvation of Gentiles, and how all of this affects our interpretation of the Gospels and the rest of the New Testament.

Paul's Burden in the Book of Romans

While Paul was the Apostle to the Gentiles, he had a heavy burden for the Jews who were unsaved. I am convinced that *the burden of Paul in the Book of Romans was his deep concern that so many of his own kinsmen, the Jews, were not saved*. While the most intense statement of the burden is found in 9:3, Paul's burden for the Jews comes across before we get to chapter 9.

PAUL'S APPEAL TO THE JEWS TO GET THEM TO SEE THAT THEY WERE UNDER THE WRATH OF GOD

The evidence of Paul's burden for the Jews comes early in the book. In showing that the Gentiles who had only general revelation were lost in 1:19-32, Paul took only 14 verses to make his case. In trying to show the Jews that they were lost in 2:1–3:8, he took 37 verses.

That should get our attention. We consider it much harder to show people that the heathen who have only general revelation are lost than we do to show that those who have been confronted with special revelation are lost apart from Jesus Christ. It was harder for Paul to show the Jews, who had received special revelation, that they were lost, than it was for him to show the Gentiles, who had only general revelation.

Paul was intensely interested in getting the Jews to see that the only way to be saved was by Jesus Christ on the condition of faith alone. This was true of both Jews and Gentiles. Paul's concern for the Jews could not be dealt with in isolation from the fact that a host of Gentiles were being saved while many Jews, according to Christian thought, were lost. If he was going to make any headway with his desire to reach Jews, he had to give the Jews an explanation of why so many Gentiles were being saved, while so many Jews were lost.

PAUL'S APPEAL TO THE ABRAHAMIC COVENANT

The appeal to Abraham and the Abrahamic Covenant in Romans 4 had a threefold purpose: (1) To show that in the covenant that God made with Abraham, faith and faith alone was the condition of justification. (2) To show that Gentiles who have faith in Christ are also justified by faith alone. (3) To show that it was God's plan in the Abrahamic Covenant for Gentiles who believe to become Abraham's seed and thus heirs with him and the Jewish believers.

PAUL'S ANSWER TO THE JEWISH CONCERN ABOUT THE LAW

The major concern of Romans 7:7-25 was to deal with Jewish concerns. In verse 7, Paul asks the question, "Is the law sin?"

> Why would Paul raise the question, "Is the law sin?" Because the emphasis up to this point is on what the law cannot do. The law cannot justify (3:20). The law works wrath (4:15). The law tended to make sin abound (5:20). To be out from under the law was supposed to be a plus factor so far as righteous living was concerned (6:14 and 7:6). The law stirred the passions of sins in us into activity (7:5).
>
> We need to keep reminding ourselves how important the law was to the Jewish people of that day, especially in Phariseeism. Law to them was supreme. Even a converted Jew would have difficulty understanding the removal of law from the center of the picture. It is not hard at all to see why a Jew would raise the question, and why he would need an answer.[28]

THE DEPTH OF PAUL'S BURDEN FOR THE JEWS

In chapter 8, Paul speaks of the glorious blessings of the one who has placed his faith in Jesus Christ. "Chapter 8 ended on a triumphant note. While in this emotion-filled state, Paul suddenly thought of his kinsmen—the Jews. When he did, the deep compassion and concern which he had for his kinsmen was activated within him. It is out of this deep concern that he speaks."[29] In anguish of heart he said, "For I could wish that I myself were accursed, *separated* from Christ for the sake of my brethren, my kinsmen according to the flesh" (Rom. 9:3).

In this state of deep concern, Paul reviews the unique position of Israel in the history of redemption. They were uniquely blessed. All of the redemptive covenants were made with Abraham and the Covenant Seed. The redemptive promises were made to them. It was to Israel that the Messianic prophecies were given. The Gentile believers were indebted to the Jews. It was through Israel that God gave the world, as it comes to us from Hebrew the "Messiah," and as it comes to us from Greek the "Christ" (9:4, 5).

PAUL'S APPEAL TO THE JEWS TO GET THEM TO SEE
THE FALLACY OF THEIR REASONING

Against the background of thought that God had unconditionally promised eternal life to all Jews, Paul said, "But *it is* not as though the Word of God has failed" (9:6). If God had unconditionally promised eternal life to all Jews through the Abrahamic Covenant, His promise would have failed if large numbers of Jews, as Paul taught, were unsaved. On the other hand, as John Piper explains, "If Paul can show that God's ultimate 'purpose according to election' never included the salvation of every individual Israelite, then the situation described in Rom. 9:1-5 would not so easily jeopardize God's reliability."[30]

Jewish thought assumed that if masses of Jews were unsaved, that would mean that God's promise had failed. That would mean that God would be unrighteous or unjust because He would be failing to live up to His promise of eternal life to all Jews, as it was given in the Abrahamic Covenant.

With great concern, Paul attempted to show the Jews that God's promise had not failed. He revealed that God had never promised to save all Jews.

ROMANS 9:6

Paul's first step in trying to convince the Jews that God had not promised salvation to all Jews was to say, "For they are not all Israel who are descended from Israel" (9:6). In this verse, Paul is saying that the name "Israel" has a broad and a narrow use. In the broad use it refers to all of those who have descended from Abraham through Jacob. These are the Covenant Seed of Abraham. It is true that the promises of the Abrahamic Covenant were made to all of those who descended from Abraham through Jacob. But the question is: *Does this mean that all are saved?*

Paul is saying we are not to understand that all who have descended from Abraham through Jacob are saved. This suggests that there is a second use of the name "Israel." This use of the name "Israel" refers to the those who descended from Abraham through Jacob who will actually be the beneficiaries of the promises of the Abrahamic Covenant. According to Paul, these are the ones who believe in Jesus Christ for salvation. These are "True Israel."

We could illustrate Paul's point this way. We could say that all who descended from Abraham through Jacob are "A." Those who descended from Abraham through Jacob and are also the ones who will actually be the beneficiaries of the promises of the Abrahamic Covenant are "B." The diagram will illustrate this for us:

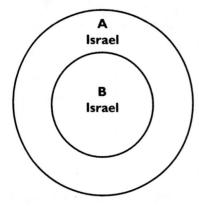

"A" represents all of the Covenant Seed who descended from Abraham through Jacob. "B" represents those who are the part of the Covenant Seed who will actually receive the eschatological promises made in the Abrahamic Covenant. All "B" are "A," but not all "A" are "B." In Jewish thought all "A" would be "B." In their thinking "A" and "B" would be coextensive. Paul's aim in Romans 9 is to show the Jews that such thinking is wrong. If he can get them to see that, it will greatly increase the possibility that they will place their faith in Jesus as the true Messiah and Lord and Savior.

ROMANS 9:7-13

It takes more than a mere statement on Paul's part to convince the Jew. So what follows is designed to get the Jew to come to an understanding of the truth that God did not unconditionally promise eternal life to all who descended from Abraham through Jacob.

The basis for the Jewish misunderstanding was that in Genesis 13:14, 15 and 17:8, the everlasting promise of the land, which implies resurrection and eternal life, was offered to the seed of Abraham. No mention is made of the fact that not all of the seed (offspring or descendants) of Abraham would be saved. However, Paul is going to show that even the Jews do not believe in the unconditional promise of eternal life to *all of the descendants of Abraham*.

In verse 7 Paul observes, "Neither are they all children because they are descendants, but: 'THROUGH ISAAC YOUR DESCENDANTS WILL BE NAMED.'" The Jews understood well that though Ishmael and the descendants of Abraham through his children by Keturah were *Abraham's descendants*, they were not considered a part of *the Covenant Seed of Abraham*. They were also well aware that not even all of *the descendants of Isaac* were a part of this *Covenant Seed*. They understood that the descendants of Isaac through Jacob *were* the Covenant Seed of Abraham, while the descendants of Isaac through Esau *were not* the Covenant Seed of Abraham.

The Jews recognized that though the descendants of Ishmael and Esau were the seed [descendants] of Abraham, they were not the Covenant Seed of Abraham. This meant that the Jews were already admitting that the blessings promised in Genesis 13:14, 15 and 17:8 did not apply to all of the descendants of Abraham. This being true, there was nothing inherent in the promise made to Abraham that required that all who made up the Covenant Seed of Abraham would be saved. This was the point that Paul was calling to their attention in verses 7-12.

The language of Genesis 13:14, 15 and 17:8 did not spell out the limitation of who among the descendants of Abraham would make up the Covenant Seed of Abraham. That clarification came later in the Book of Genesis (21:12 and 25:23). These verses did not spell out who would be or who would not be the ones who would actually inherit the eschatological promise of eternal life. That was the clarification that Paul was desperately trying to make.

If there is no contradiction between the promise made in Genesis 13:14, 15 and 17:8 and the limitation of the Covenant Seed of Abraham to those who descended from Isaac through Jacob, there is no contradiction between Genesis 13:14, 15 and 17:8 and a further limitation of Israel to a true Israel which is made up of believers only.

ROMANS 9:10-13

Since these verses have been a mainstay of Calvinism, I will give special attention to them. It is important to observe that these verses are in a context which has as its purpose to show that there is no reason to believe that all of the Covenant Seed of Abraham (those who descended from Abraham through Jacob) are saved. This means that verses 10-12 are used by Paul to show that not all of the natural descendants of Abraham were saved. If this consideration of the context is not taken into account, the meaning of these verses will be missed.

Verses 10-13 are of particular importance because they point out that even though God had said, "THROUGH ISAAC YOUR DESCENDANTS WILL BE NAMED" (verse 7), not even all of Isaac's descendants made up the Covenant Seed of Abraham. In view of their importance, I will quote these verses:

> **10** And not only this, but there was Rebekah also, when she had conceived *twins* by one man, our father Isaac;
> **11** for though the *twins* were not yet born, and had not done anything good or bad, in order that God's purpose according to *His* choice [election] might stand, not because of works, but because of Him who calls,
> **12** it was said to her, "THE OLDER WILL SERVE THE YOUNGER."
> **13** Just as it is written, "JACOB I LOVED, BUT ESAU I HATED."

The words "And not only this" in verse 10, tell us that Paul is developing the same line of thought that he had been in verses 7-9. He had shown them that in selecting the Covenant Seed of Abraham, God had chosen Isaac rather than Ishmael. He had one more step to make. He showed that God chose Jacob rather than Esau. Abraham was the first patriarch, Isaac was the second patriarch, and Jacob was chosen as the third patriarch. The Covenant Seed would be called through Jacob, the third patriarch. This final limitation of who would make up the Covenant Seed of Abraham was made. All of the descendants of Jacob are the Covenant Seed of Abraham. But this does not mean that all of the descendants of Jacob are saved. If God could determine that the descendants of Ishmael and Esau would not make up the Covenant Seed of Abraham, He could also determine that not all of the Covenant Seed of Abraham through Jacob would be saved. That is Paul's case with the

Jews. Paul was not debating this part just to win a debate. He was trying to win people—his kinsmen according to the flesh.

Before saying more about my thinking regarding verses 10-13, I will examine John Piper's view of verses 6-13.

John Piper's Approach to Romans 9:6-13

I am choosing Piper's treatment to deal with because I think he has given the most thorough and most able treatment of this passage from the side of unconditional election. To get Piper's thinking before us, I will quote his own summary of his understanding of what Paul was trying to accomplish in Romans 9:1-13. He explains:

> The basic problem described in 9:1-5 is that many Israelites, to whom, as a nation, saving promises had been made, are now accursed and cut off from Christ (9:1-3). The condemnation of so many Israelites to eternal destruction raises the question whether God's word has fallen. Paul denies it (9:6a) and defends his denial in 9:6b-13. In defense of God's faithfulness to his word, in spite of many Israelites being accursed, Paul argues that God's "purpose" from the beginning of Israel's history was a purpose "according to election" (9:11), that is, a purpose not to save every individual Israelite, as though descent from Abraham guaranteed that one would be a child of God, but rather a purpose to "call" a true Israel (9:6b) into being by choosing some Israelites and not others "before they were born or had done anything good or evil" (9:11). It is this Israel for whom the promises are valid. The unconditional election of Isaac and Jacob over Ishmael and Esau (whether to eternal destinies or only to historical roles) reveals the *principle of God's freedom in election* which is the ultimate explanation why many of Paul's kinsmen according to the flesh are accursed and cut off from Christ. As he says in Romans 11:7, "the elect obtained it [salvation], but the rest were hardened." For this reason it cannot be said that God's expressed purpose has fallen (9:6a).[31]

Piper, more than anyone else I have read, emphasizes that Paul is dealing with the Jewish thinking that by being a member of the Covenant Seed of Abraham through Jacob they were guaranteed the unconditional promise of eternal life. If a person does not keep this in mind when he studies Romans 9, he will not be able to get to the heart of what Paul is arguing in this chapter.

In the summary of Paul's thought in Romans 9:1-13 given above, it is obvious that Piper thinks the answer is found in the view that God unconditionally elects individuals for salvation. The Jews believed in unconditional election too. The difference was that the Jews believed in the unconditional election for salvation of all of the Covenant Seed of Abraham through Jacob. This election was corporate election, but it guaranteed the salvation of each individual member of the Covenant Seed of Abraham.

This meant that there was a serious conflict, up front, with Paul and the Jews. The Jews thought that all Jews were saved. Paul thought that a large portion of the Jews were lost. The only ones who were saved were those who believed in Jesus as their Messiah, Savior, and Lord. He also thought that was the only way those who were lost could be saved.

According to Piper, Paul's approach to showing the Jews that not all Jews were saved was to show them that only those who are unconditionally elected as individuals are saved. Paul did this by showing that God unconditionally chose Isaac rather than Ishmael and Jacob rather than Esau. The major part of Piper's argument that Paul was advocating unconditional individual election is based on the choice of Jacob rather than Esau. On this subject Piper comments:

> Paul's purpose in referring to God's choice of Jacob over Esau is to show that there is no way to evade the implications of God's unconditional election here. Unlike Isaac and Ishmael, Jacob and Esau had the same parents who were both Jews ("From *one* man Rebecca became pregnant," (Rom. 9:10c). Also unlike Isaac and Ishmael, when the determining promise was made concerning Jacob and Esau (Rom. 9:12c = Gen. 25:23), both were yet unborn and had done nothing good or evil (Rom. 9:11ab). Moreover they were twins in the same womb at the same time and by all human standards the elder Esau should have received the blessing of headship over his brother. Here there are no loopholes. God's choice of Jacob over Esau cannot be due to any human distinctive possessed by birth (like Jewishness) or action (like righteousness). It is based solely on God's own free and sovereign choice.[32]

Having concluded that 9:12 settled, in no uncertain terms that God chooses individuals by an unconditional election, Piper considers that he has shown the fallacy of Jewish thinking that all Jews were guaranteed salvation simply by being the Covenant Seed of Abraham through Jacob. Verse 12, in Piper's thinking supports the unconditional election of Jacob and the unconditional rejection of Esau. He supposes that this would have been met with an objection from the Jews. He supposes that the Jews would have thought that the unconditional election of Jacob and the unconditional rejection of Esau would have shown God to be unjust. This would particularly be true of the unconditional rejection of Esau. This understanding of what Paul had said up through verse 13 sets the stage for Piper's understanding of the rhetorical question that Paul raises in verse 14.

AN EVALUATION OF PIPER'S VIEW

I have pointed out above that Piper understands the Jewish problem. The question is: Does he have the right answer? He finds the answer in the unconditional election of each individual for salvation and the unconditional rejection of others. While he thinks that the choice of Isaac over Ishmael illustrates unconditional election, he thinks that the wording of verses 11 and 12 in setting forth the choice of Jacob and the rejection of Esau makes unconditional election irrefutable.

I do not think that he has made his case for unconditional election. To support my position, I give the following reasons:

1. Even if verse 11 were seen as dealing with election for salvation, the case is still not decided for unconditional election. There is certainly no problem with the election occurring before birth. I think it does. Individual conditional election by God in eternity past does not involve a logical contradiction.

2. To say that election is not being based on works presents no problem for conditional election. Conditional election does *not* mean election based on works. I think that I have made it clear beyond question that nothing the Christian ever does is considered a part of the payment for his justification.[33] If what I have said (in points one and two) is true, even if these verses speak of individual election, there is no conflict between verses 11 and 12 and conditional election.

3. The Calvinist would be wrong to claim that my view makes faith a human work and thus is to be considered as merit. This is true for two reasons: (1) Paul specifically contrasts faith with works in Romans 4:1-8. (2) Faith is a human act in both Calvinism and Arminianism. Faith is synergistic in both Calvinism and Arminism.[34] If the exercise of saving faith is a human work and thus must be considered as merit for salvation, both Calvinism and Arminianism would be indicted. In both cases the human personality exercises faith by divine aid. In Calvinism, the divine aid is regeneration by the Holy Spirit. In Arminianism, the divine aid is the drawing and assisting power of the Holy Spirit.

Conclusions Established by This Study of Romans 9:6-13

There are two things about this passage which seem to me to be unquestionably clear:

1. Paul was showing that not all of the descendants of Abraham were a part of the Covenant Seed. He gives two choices that were made by God that confirmed this observation: First, Isaac was chosen as the one through whom the Covenant Seed would descend while Ishmael was set aside. Second, Jacob was chosen as the one through whom the Covenant Seed would descend while Esau was set aside. These conclusions were readily accepted by the Jews. These observations make it unquestionably clear that no case, based on the Abrahamic Covenant, can be made for the viewpoint that every individual member of the Covenant Seed is saved.

2. This observation meant that no case could be made for the conclusion that because the Jews were the seed of Abraham all were given an unconditional promise of eternal life.

Paul's point was simply this. If there can be a *broad* and a *narrow* use of the expression "the seed of Abraham," there is no reason to reject the idea that in a similar way there can be a broad and a narrow use of the name Israel.

It must be remembered that the Jewish problem grew out of the significance that they gave to the claim that they were the seed of Abraham rather than that they were the descendants of Jacob (Mt. 3:9 and Jn. 8:33-40). Why? Because it was to the seed of Abraham that promises were made (Gen. 13:14, 15 and 17:8).

I think we can safely conclude that the election referred to in verse 11 is not Jacob's election to salvation. My reason for saying so is not because I could not be comfortable with the idea that verse 11 could be speaking about election for salvation. Rather, it is because the context will not support it. I have shown that above.

What, then, is the bearing of verses 6-13 on the subject of election? It is simply this. The Jewish concept of *unconditional personal election* of all Jews as the Covenant Seed of Abraham *must be discarded.* That means that, so far as Israel is concerned, election must shift from the *corporate election* of all Jews to *individual election* or salvation for Jews.

Up to this point in the passage, the question of conditional or unconditional election has not been decided.

It is my understanding that up through verse 13 Paul argued that the choices of Isaac rather than Ishmael and of Jacob rather than Esau should help the Jews see that they are not to interpret the promise of eternal life given in Genesis 13:14, 15 and 17:8 to guarantee the salvation of every individual Jew. Paul feels that he has adequately dealt with this concern. So, in verse 14 Paul gets to the heart of the matter as this would affect the righteousness or justice of God.

The Question Concerning God's Justice in Verse 14

In verse 14 Paul says, "What shall we say then? There is no injustice with God, is there? May it never be!"

My Interpretation of Romans 9:14

As we continue our interpretation of Romans 9, it is important that we keep in mind that Paul is dealing with Jewish concern. He is striving with his whole being to get them to see that believing and trusting in Jesus as Messiah, Lord, and Savior was the only way for them as individuals to be saved. No one ever put his whole being into anything more than Paul did in this chapter.

Paul is *not* trying to settle a Calvinist-Arminian debate on election. What he says may make a contribution to the question of whether election is conditional or unconditional, but that is not the aim and burden of Paul's heart in this chapter.

It is important we realize that in this verse Paul is harking back to verse 6 where he said, "But it is not as though the word of God has failed." If God had promised the salvation of all the Jews as the Covenant Seed of Abraham, God would have failed if all Jews had not been saved. If God had failed to keep His promise, He would have been unrighteous or unjust. That cannot be!

Paul has shown that there is no basis for the idea that all Jews, as the Covenant Seed of Abraham, are saved. God has never made such a promise. Therefore, He cannot be charged with being unrighteous by not bringing it to pass.

CALVINISM AND ROMANS 9:14

Those who believe in unconditional election take this verse to be dealing with an objection to the unconditional election of Jacob and the reprobation of Esau with the emphasis being on the suggestion that God was unjust in the way He treated Esau. (See earlier quotations from Haldane, Harrison, Plumer, and Shedd.) The question is: Does this view fit the context?

First, let me say that I have already shown that Paul did not settle whether individual election for salvation was conditional or unconditional in verses 6-13. If that is true, Paul could not be dealing with objections to unconditional election of individuals in verse 14.

Piper, as I said above, has a good grasp on the fact that Paul is dealing with a Jewish concern. Whose concern is Paul dealing with in verse 14? Let me give again a quotation used earlier from Piper. He explains, "When Paul said that God chose to bless Jacob over Esau apart from any basis in their actions but simply on the basis of his choice (*ek tou kalountos*, Rom. 9:12), his opponent objected that this would call God's righteousness into question (9:14)."[35]

The opponent to which Piper refers would have been a Jew. In Piper's view, in answering the Jew Paul would have explained that the Jews were mistaken in their thinking that all Jews were saved. In God's choice of Jacob over Esau, God was saying that election was on an individual basis, not corporate election. Also, in his choice of Jacob over Esau before they were born and before they had done anything either good or bad God was saying that the choice was unconditional. The concern of the Jewish opponent was supposed to be that it was unrighteous or unjust for God to unconditionally accept Jacob and to unconditionally reject Esau. Special concern was supposed to be on the rejection of Esau.

I would make four observations:

1. The Jews had no difficulty with unconditional election as such. They believed in their own unconditional election.
2. There is no evidence that the Jews had any difficulty with the rejection of Ishmael and Esau. This is true whether the concern was with the unconditional election of the individual for salvation, or with the exclusion of Ishmael, Esau, and their descendants from the Covenant Seed of Abraham.
3. The Calvinistic interpretation of verse 14 is based on a Jewish concern that the Jews did not have.
4. Paul's concern at the beginning of the chapter was to get the Jews to see that God had not promised salvation to all Jews. His burden was to get them to see that the only way a Jew could be saved would be for him or her to have faith in Jesus as the Messiah, Savior, and Lord. It would have brought no relief to Paul for him to be able to get the Jews to exchange belief in unconditional election for all Jews for a view that: (1) God had unconditionally elected certain Jews, and (2) God had unconditionally chosen the others for eternal damnation.

THE JEWISH CONCLUSION

The only trouble the Jews of Paul's day had with unconditional election was that, according to Paul, God had not unconditionally elected all Jews as they had thought. If God did unconditionally elect all Jews and Christianity denied that this was the case, Christ and Christianity would be written off without further investigation.

The concern that the unbelieving Jew would have with God's righteousness or justice was that for God to fail to follow through with the unconditional election of all Jews meant that God had not kept His word. For God to fail to keep His word would mean that He would be unrighteous or unjust. Such a conclusion was unthinkable.

The only hope of getting them to acknowledge Jesus as the Messiah must be connected with evidence that God had never said that all Jews were unconditionally elected. If they could see this, then they could look at the question of their own salvation in the light of the reality that not all Jews are saved. If, in fact, God never said that all Jews would be saved, then Christ and Christianity should not be written off without a hearing.

Paul had, from a brief look at their patriarchal history, shown them that no case could be built for the idea that God had unconditionally chosen all of them for personal salvation.

M. R. Vincent manifests good insight into Paul's question in verse 14 when he said:

> If it be asked therefore, "Is there unrighteousness with God? Does God contradict Himself in His rejection of unbelieving Israel?—it must be answered, "No!" If there was no unrighteousness in the exclusion of Ishmael and Edom from the temporal privileges of the chosen people, there is none in the exclusion of the persistently rebellious Israelites from the higher privileges of the kingdom of heaven. If not all the physical descendants of Abraham and Isaac can claim their father's name and rights, it follows that God's promise is not violated in excluding from His kingdom a portion of the descendants of Jacob. Descent cannot be pleaded against God's right to exclude, since He has already excluded from the messianic line without regard to descent. This choice Israel approved and cannot, therefore, repudiate it when the same choice and exclusion are applied to unbelieving Israel.[36]

Paul had shown that no case could be built for the idea that God was unrighteous in not saving every Jew because He had never made such a promise. He had done this by reviewing their patriarchal history with them. He will now proceed in his appeal to "his kinsmen according to the flesh" by showing that election is individual, not corporate. If Paul can get the Jews to see that election is individual instead of corporate, it will make it much easier for him to help individual Jews to see that the only way to be saved is by faith in Jesus as the Messiah, Savior, and Lord.

PAUL'S APPEAL TO THE JEWS TO SEE THAT ELECTION IS INDIVIDUAL, NOT CORPORATE

I do not think that verses 6-13 deal with individual election, neither do they settle the question of whether election is conditional or unconditional. The way had been prepared for the focus to change beginning in verse 15. Before Paul finishes this chapter, he will deal with both the question of individual election and the question of whether election is conditional or unconditional. It will be shown that election is of individuals and that it is conditional. It is important to keep in mind that Paul is dealing with a question of Jewish concern, not a Calvinist-Arminian debate. Since he deals with universal truth, we will find that what he says is helpful in dealing with the questions raised by Calvinists and Arminians.

Romans 9:15 and Individual Election

Since verse 15 is introduced by "for," we naturally expect a reason or proof to follow. However, such is not the case here. It is obvious that what follows does not take on the form of an argument defending the righteousness (or justice) of God in not saving all Jews. As Lenski explains, "The *gar* is not to prove the statement that there is no justice [The author obviously meant "injustice."] on the part of God in these promises; for what follows is not proof. . . . *Gar* is at times used simply to confirm; it does so here: 'yea.'"[37]

The question of whether God could be unrighteous (or unjust) was not debatable between Paul and the Jew. One would reject such an implication as quickly as the other. The difference came in applying the truth of the righteousness of God to the question of whether all Jews were saved.

What follows in verse 15 is not evidence that God is not unrighteous. That was settled by an emphatic denial. What follows is an illustration from Scripture of how the action of God, who can do no wrong, supports the principle that some, but not all, from among Israel are chosen for salvation. That Paul is appealing to the authority of Scripture rather than building an argument in verse 15 finds broad agreement.[38]

In the quotation from Exodus 33:19, God said to Moses, "I WILL HAVE MERCY ON WHOM I HAVE MERCY, AND I WILL HAVE COMPASSION ON WHOM I HAVE COMPASSION."

My first observation is that the Greek for "whom" (*hon an*) is singular. This places the emphasis on the choice of the individual rather than on corporate election as the case would be if God had chosen to save all of the Covenant Seed of Abraham.

As Picirilli explains:

> Even in the wilderness, when we might think all the nation was automatically entitled to His favor, he said: "I will show mercy on whom I will show mercy." In other words, He wanted it clearly established that neither Moses nor Israel had any special claims on Him that took away His sovereign right to act as He chose. Nor will He show mercy to all of them just because they were Israelites in the flesh.[39]

As it relates to Paul's treatment of individuals in Romans 9:15-21, Thomas R. Schreiner calls attention to the use of the singular in these verses. He explains:

> The word *whom (hon)* is singular, indicating that specific individuals upon whom God has mercy are in view. The singular is also present in the reference that Paul draws from Romans 9:15, in 9:16. God's mercy does not depend on "the one who wills, nor the one who runs." The conclusion to all of 9:14-17 in 9:18 utilizes the singular once again: "God has mercy on whom he wants to have mercy, and he hardens whom he wants to harden." In the same vein 9:19 continues the thought: "Who *(tis)* resists his

will?" And Paul uses the singular when he speaks of one vessel being made for honor and another for dishonor (9:21). Those who say that Paul is referring only to corporate groups do not have an adequate explanation as to why Paul uses the singular again and again in Romans 9.[40]

I strongly agree with Schreiner that the election in these verses is speaking of individual election. I agree with all that he says in the quotation given above. However, I do not join him on unconditional election. But I do not think that that question is settled up to this point in the chapter. It will not be settled until we get to verses 30-33.

Romans 9:15 and Whether Election Is Conditional or Unconditional

Since verse 15 tells us that God shows mercy and compassion to whomever He chooses, it is taken by some as proof of unconditional election. It seems to me to be involved in the very concept of God that He would be the one who decides who will be saved and who will not be saved. However, I do not believe that such an observation decides on the side of unconditional election.

In Jeremiah 18:1-4, Jeremiah observed the work of the potter. The potter had control over the clay to make it into a vessel as it seemed good to the potter to do so. After he made this observation, God said, "'Can I not, O house of Israel, deal with you as this potter does?' declares the LORD. 'Behold, like the clay in the potter's hand, so are you in my hand, O house of Israel' " (18:6).

God was saying to Israel, "You are in my hands. I can do with you what I choose." The exercise of this right on the part of God did not mean that He would not take into consideration anything done by Israel in deciding what He would do with Israel. That He would take Israel's action into account in deciding what to do with Israel is clear in the context of Jeremiah 18:6; see verses 7-10.

It should be obvious from Jeremiah 18:1-10 that the divine prerogative to exercise His right to do as He chooses with people does not mean that His decisions must always be unconditional choices. When we read that God will do as He chooses, it will help if we ask a simple question: What does God choose to do? When God told Jeremiah that He could do with Israel what He chose just as the potter could with the clay, He followed that observation by telling them what He wanted to do.

When we read in Romans 9:15 that God will have mercy and compassion on whomever He wills, it behooves us to ask: On whom does God will to show mercy and compassion? Once it is decided that the mercy and compassion under consideration is that shown in salvation, the answer is easy.

We certainly do not have to list an array of references from the New Testament in order to identify those to whom God wishes to give the mercy of salvation. Consider, for example, the answer given by Paul and Silas to the question: "Sirs, what must I do to be saved?" They said, "Believe in the Lord Jesus, and you shall be saved and your household" (Acts 16:30, 31).

God is choosing whom He wills when He chooses to show His mercy in salvation toward the one who believes in Jesus as his Lord and Savior. Such decision can in no way be viewed as a decision that God is forced to make. The whole idea of salvation was God's idea from the outset. He could have chosen to have left the whole human race in sin without offering salvation. Rather, He planned to provide and offer salvation to lost mankind long before (in eternity past) man felt the pangs of being lost. It was not even in response to man's pleading (much less demanding) that God chose to offer redemption.

The whole plan of salvation from beginning to end is the work and plan of God. God is in charge. When salvation is offered on the condition of faith in Christ, that in no way weakens the words, "I WILL HAVE MERCY ON WHOM I HAVE MERCY, AND I WILL HAVE COMPASSION ON WHOM I HAVE COMPASSION." God's sovereignty is fully in control in this view. I have given extensive attention in the previous chapter to the viewpoint that God is free to exercise His will and that He does it according to the influence and response model.

THE QUESTION OF WORKS

Paul explains, "So then it does not depend on the man who wills or the man who runs, but on God who has mercy" (verse 16).

In order to see the meaning of this verse, we must see what the converse would be. What would it mean if it were of him that wills and runs rather than of God who shows mercy? It would mean that a person would merit or earn salvation. It would mean that his merit would obligate God to save him.

Such a concept is foreign to all Christianity stands for. Man was shut off from God by his own sin. God was under no obligation to save him or even provide a way of salvation.

It was out of God's love that He sent the Holy Spirit to woo us to Christ. It was out of God's love that He has commissioned believers to tell unbelievers about Christ.

God has offered salvation on the condition of faith. We must distinguish between the "condition" and the "ground" of salvation. Salvation is *grounded* solely in the death and righteousness of Christ provided by atonement (as indicated in the satisfaction view of the atonement) and imputed to the believer's account in justification. It is *conditioned* on the response of faith in Christ alone.

God has taken the initiative in providing what man needs for salvation. He has set the condition for salvation. He sends the messenger with the gospel. He woos through the Holy Spirit. The personal response of faith as the condition for salvation can in no way be considered in conflict with or in violation of "So then it does not depend on the man . . . who runs, but on God who has mercy."

Romans 9:16 and Whether Election Is Conditional or Unconditional

Those who believe in unconditional election seem to be quite certain that this verse strikes a death blow to conditional election. Piper sees a parallel between the "willing" and the "running" and "working" of Philippians 2:13. He explains:

> God's mercy determines man's willing and working (Phil. 2:13). And since the "willing and working" referred to in Phil. 2:13 is not evil "works" but the obedience of faith, it follows that the assertion of Romans 9:16 cannot be limited to only some kinds

of willing and running. For these reasons Rom. 9:16 should be construed so as to sweep away forever the thought that over against God there is any such thing as human self-determination in Pauline anthropology."[41]

I think the real question that Piper needs to face is: How is he using the expression "self-determination"? If he means that man's action is not the *cause* or *ground* of his salvation, I could not agree more. On the other hand, if he means that man's action in believing cannot be a deciding factor in God's bestowal of salvation on the one who believes and the withholding of salvation from the one who does not believe, I cannot agree. Such a view is in conflict with the obvious and direct teaching of Scripture (Jn. 3:16, 18, 36; Acts 16:31, etc.).

Faith as a *condition* (as distinguished from a *cause* or a *ground*) does determine on whom God bestows salvation. God is the one, not man, who has decreed that faith is the condition of salvation. When a person responds in faith, it is not *he* who is obligating God to save him. Rather, it is *God* who *has obligated himself* by His very righteous commitment to His promises, *to save the person who believes.* When properly understood, there is not the remotest possibility that such a view can rightly be understood as salvation by works.

Piper is aware of the place of faith in salvation but attempts to make it fit with his concept of unconditional election. He observes, "Faith is indeed a sine qua non [the necessary] condition of salvation; Rom. 9:16, therefore, necessarily implies that the act of faith is ultimately owing to the prevenient grace of God."[42]

I have no quarrel with his statement, "The act of faith is ultimately owing to the prevenient grace of God." The problem is how it is interpreted. If we say that without the work of the Holy Spirit (Jn. 6:44) no man will ever believe in Christ, I would agree. However, such a statement, as I understand it, still leaves room for the individual's response of belief or unbelief.

As I perceive it, this is not Piper's interpretation of the statement. The work of the Holy Spirit "guarantees" or "causes the response of faith. For a person to be *caused* to believe violates what it means to be a person. Faith is a personal experience. *It is a choice.* Divine *assistance* and *influence,* yes. Divine *cause,* no.

I have given considerable attention to the fact that the words *cause* and *effect* are not appropriate in describing personal relationships. *Influence* and *response* are the words to use in describing interpersonal relationships. There is no such thing as a person doing something without having a genuine involvement in the action. (See my discussion under *"Cause* and *Effect* or *Influence* and *Response?* An Arminian Answer" on page 312.)

THE JEWISH CONCERN

To this point, our look at verse 16 has dealt more with current concerns as it relates to election. However, the concern that Paul was dealing with was a Jewish concern. As I stated earlier, in the New Testament we see two seemingly contradictory views concerning the Jewish concept of their own salvation: (1) They were unconditionally saved because they were the Covenant Seed of Abraham. (2) They were depending on their own righteousness.

Up through verse 15, Paul had dealt with their view that all Jews were unconditionally elected. In verse 16 he turns attention to their idea that they were saved by their own righteousness. Such a view is denied. The divine choice for salvation is not based on any merit growing out of the "willing" or "the running" of the Jew. This would rule out any appeal to corporate righteousness on the part of the Jews.

Romans 9:18 and the Problem of Divine Hardening

Having given such extensive treatment to the positive side of election, I must be brief in my treatment of divine hardening. However, I do want to make a few comments.

Paul says, "So then He has mercy on whom He desires, and He hardens whom He desires."

My first observation is that "mercy" and "hardening" are not exact opposites. Mercy in this context refers to the bestowal of salvation. "Hardening" in this context *does not* refer to the infliction of penal wrath. If it did, it would simplify matters for my position. All I would need to do would be to ask, On whom does God desire to inflict penal wrath? The answer is, on those who do not believe in Jesus Christ (Jn. 3:18, 36).

In my opinion the word "harden" is carefully chosen in this context. Those who were saved among the Jews were already experiencing the saving mercy of God. Those who were lost were not already experiencing the penal wrath of God. That is reserved for the eschatological future.

I think there would be general agreement that "blinded" in 11:7 would have essentially the same meaning as "harden" in 9:18. At the moment of Paul's writing the Jews who had not already received the saving mercy of God would be considered "hardened" or "blinded."

It is important to observe that Paul did not consider all Jews who were at that time hardened or blinded to be hopelessly locked by God in that state. The burden of Paul's heart was for their salvation (9:1-3; 10:1; 11:11-14, 28-32).

Some Calvinists seem aware that the word "harden" is not well suited to their purposes. The following quotation from Hendriksen shows how he is struggling to make "harden" suit his purpose. He explains, "There is no reason to doubt that the hardening of which Pharaoh was the object was final. It was a link in the chain: reprobation—wicked life—hardening—everlasting punishment. This does not mean that divine hardening is always final. See on 11:7b-11."[43]

Piper is dealing with the same difficulty when he says, "Must we not conclude, therefore, that the hardening in 9:18 has reference, just as the hardening in 11:7, to the action of God whereby a person is left in a condition outside salvation and thus prepared for destruction."[44] Piper acknowledges in note 31 of chapter 9, "This does not imply that the condition sometimes called hardness of heart (Eph. 4:18) or mind (2 Cor. 3:14) cannot be altered by the merciful revivifying act of God (Eph. 2:1-4)."[45]

John Brown, in defense of the Calvinistic position shows the problem even more clearly. He explains:

The introduction of the idea of judicial hardening seems to destroy the antithesis. *Hardening* is not the natural antithesis of showing mercy. Had it been, "whom He wills He melts into penitence, and whom He wills He hardens into impenitence," the antithesis would have been complete; but the one time in the antithesis, being showing mercy, the other must correspond to it—He does not show mercy; He relents in reference to one, He does not relent in reference to another.

I am therefore disposed to concur with those interpreters (and they are distinguished both for learning and judgment) who consider, the word rendered "harden," as equivalent to "treat with severity" in withholding favors and inflicting deserved punishment.[46]

I think it should be quite obvious that the concept of divine hardening in verse 18 does not aid the cause of those who believe in either unconditional reprobation, or those who say that God simply failed to include some in His plan of unconditional election. However, the word does require some explanation and it does not submit to easy explanation.

That God does work in such a way that spiritual blindness or hardness results is clear. That this is a judicial work is clear. What we do not know is how to explain this, to our fullest satisfaction, in keeping with human responsibility or the nature of God. Yet we know that from God's perspective these concepts are consistent with one another.

The unbelieving Jews in Paul's day were blinded or hardened. When they were encountered by the message of God's grace, the majority resisted and were hardened. God could not reward this attitude. In a sense, it can be said that God hardened them. In a sense it can be said that they hardened themselves.

Hardness, while not to be taken lightly, does not necessarily imply that a person is in a hopeless condition. Paul himself was hardened before his conversion. Many other Jews were saved out of hardness. A proper understanding of how Romans 9 relates to election begins with a proper grasp of the problem Paul is dealing with. That problem is the Jewish concern mentioned above—that Paul does not go along with the Jewish belief in the corporate salvation of all Jews as the Covenant Seed of Abraham.

Election: Individual and Eternal (Rom. 9:19-24)

The material on verses 19-29 comes from my commentary on Romans.[47] Some minor changes and additions will be made to suit the purpose of this chapter. The KJV is used in this commentary.

19 Thou wilt say then unto me, Why doth he yet find fault? For who hath resisted his will?

If God chooses whom He wills for salvation and if He hardens whom He wills, and if Pharaoh was unable to interfere with God's purposes, the question arises, "Why doth he yet find fault [or charge with blame]? For who hath resisted his will?" The word for "will" (Greek *boulemai*) means purpose.[48]

The verse does not suggest that a person cannot resist in the sense of *opposing* God's purpose. Rather, no one can *defeat* God's purposes. A person can disobey God and will be held responsible for his disobedience. However, God has purposes that are carried out in spite of disobedience (Gen. 50:19, 20).

> **20** Nay but, O man, who art thou that repliest against God? Shall the thing formed say to him that formed *it*, Why hast thou made me thus?

The maker has rights over that which he has made (See Is. 29:16 and 45:9). This does not mean the rights of the Creator include arbitrary rights or rights that ignore right and wrong. Rather, the very nature of God is such that He cannot do otherwise than right. Henry C. Thiessen has well said:

> In God we have purity of being before we have purity of willing. God does not will the good because it is good, nor is the good good because God wills it; else there would be a good above God or the good would be arbitrary and changeable. Instead, God's will is an expression of his nature, which is holy."[49]

God is absolutely sovereign. For that reason, we need to find out what He has said and submit to it rather than argue with Him.

> **21** Hath not the Potter power over the clay, of the same lump to make one vessel unto honour, and another unto dishonour?

There can be no doubt that Paul had in mind Jeremiah 18:1-10. (See also Wisdom of Solomon 15:7.) In my comments above on verse 15, I think I made it very clear that if we ask the simple questions, "Who does God want to save?" and Who does God choose to condemn that we will find that God wants to save those who believe in Jesus Christ as Lord and Savior. He chooses to condemn those who do not believe in Jesus Christ as Lord and Savior. For a more complete development of these thoughts see the comments under "Romans 9:16 and Whether Election Is Conditional or Unconditional" (page 368).

> **22** *What* if God, willing to shew *his* wrath, and to make his power known, endured with much longsuffering the vessels of wrath fitted to destruction:
> **23** And that he might make known the riches of his glory on the vessels of mercy, which he had afore prepared unto glory.

What if God, willing? We have two points of concern: (1) How is Paul using the word "willing" (Greek *thelō*)? (2) What is the significance of the form of the verb he uses (a Greek participle)? Concerning the meaning of "willing," Shedd is on the right track when he says:

> The mere permission of God is not meant; nor the purpose of God: which would require *Bouleuon*; but the deep and strong desire: a will that was so profound and intense as to require that self-restraint which is denominated the patience and long-suffering of God (2:4). The phrase [willing to shew his wrath] denotes the spontaneity of the divine holiness, "the fierceness and wrath of Almighty God" against sin (Rev. xix.15), which is held back by divine compassion, upon the ground of the *hilastērion* [3:25].[50] (Brackets mine)

The participle "willing" or "desiring" might be rendered either "because desiring" (Greek: causal participle) or "*although* desiring" (Greek concessive participle). "Although desiring" seems to be preferred.

Although God was strongly desiring to show His wrath toward those who were "vessels of wrath fitted to destruction," He "endured with much longsuffering" these "vessels of wrath" (objects of wrath, not instruments of wrath) "that he might make known the riches of his glory." If God had released his wrath immediately, the human race would have been taken immediately into eternal punishment. In this case, there would have been no vessels of mercy (those who are saved by God's grace). However, instead of immediately releasing His wrath, God through longsuffering withheld His wrath to give people time to repent (Rom. 2:4 and 2 Pet. 3:9). This was done so that there would be those who respond to the gospel; thus God can *"make known the riches of his glory on the vessels of mercy, which he had afore prepared unto glory."*

It is generally agreed in Calvinistic commentaries that the language of the expression "vessels of wrath fitted to destruction" does not imply unconditional reprobation. (See Harrison[51], Hodge[52], Murray[53], and Shedd.[54])

Piper, however, would interpret the reference to an unconditional *fitting* for destruction of the vessels of wrath by God. He develops his argument from the point of view that Paul has been dealing with double predestination in chapter 9. He explains:

> It seems to me that, after the clear and powerful statements of double predestination [unconditional election or predestination of who was to be saved and unconditional predestination to reprobation of who would be lost] in Rom. 9, it is grasping at a straw to argue that the passive voice of *katertismena* proves that Paul denied divine agency in fitting men for destruction. . . . And since Paul's inference from the Pharaoh story is that "God hardens whom he wills" (9:18), the most natural suggestion from the context is that "fitted for destruction" (9:22) refers precisely to this divine hardening.[55]

I think it has been conclusively shown, in commenting on Chapter 9 up to this point, that it is misconstruing what Paul is saying to interpret it to support either unconditional election or unconditional reprobation. So far as verses 22 and 23 are concerned, I am not acquainted with anyone who would insist that these two verses apart from the rest of that chapter must be interpreted in the Calvinistic framework.

I might say with reference to Piper's double predestination, I am not averse to double predestination as such. What I reject is *unconditional* double predestination. I believe in conditional double predestination. On the condition of foreknown faith in Christ, God has predestinated believers to eternal life. He has on the condition of foreknown sin and unbelief predestinated unbelievers to eternal damnation. Apart from such predestination, we cannot assure the believer of eternal life or the unbeliever of eternal damnation. I do not reject predestination. I reject the Calvinistic interpretation of predestination.

The words "afore prepared" (Greek *proetoimazō*) mean to prepare beforehand. In one sense all of God's decisions are eternal. Based on his foreknowledge He knows who will believe in Christ and has chosen them in Christ (Eph. 1:4). The *condition* for being chosen for the application of the benefits of atonement is faith in Christ. The *ground* for being chosen is being in Christ. Those who were foreknown have been prepared in eternity past for glory. For them, things have been prearranged. As Picirilli says, "They are headed for Heaven, 'prepared for glory.'"[56]

24 Even us, whom he hath called, not of the Jews only, but also of the Gentiles?

While God is through longsuffering withholding His wrath from the vessels of wrath, He is withholding it to give an opportunity for salvation for both Jews and Gentiles. It is important to keep in mind that while Paul is deeply concerned that there were so many of his fellow Jews who were unsaved, he was keenly aware and wanted others to know that Jews were being saved.

Verse 23, along with verse 24, clearly shows that election is *eternal* and *individual.*

Old Testament Evidence That Not All Jews Are Saved
(Rom. 9:25-29)

25 As he saith also in Osee, I will call them my people, which are not my people; and her my beloved which was not my beloved.
26 And it shall come to pass, *that* in the place where it was said unto them, Ye are not my people; there shall they be called the children of God.

There is almost unanimous agreement that while in Hosea the "not my people" who are called "the children of the living God" refers to Israel (directed by Hosea to the ten northern tribes), Paul is using it to refer to the Gentiles. If this were demanded by the context, I could accept it, but it appears that such is not the case.

It is very clear that verses 27-29 refer to Israel and call attention to the fact that Scripture should prepare Jews to understand that not all of them are saved. To Paul, the position that not all Jews were saved was not merely academic preservation of theological accuracy. It tore at his heart. He wanted the Jews to know that their belief in unconditional election of all Jews in connection with Abraham was false. That was the only way they would entertain the idea of being saved through faith in Jesus Christ.

It is true, of course, that Paul, as the apostle to the Gentiles, was deeply concerned about the conversion of Gentiles. It is also true that he had just indicated that there were Gentiles as well as Jews among the vessels "afore prepared unto glory" (verses 23, 24). However, that is not the burden of chapter 9.

The burden of chapter 9 is to get the Jews to see that they had misunderstood God's promise to Abraham. They were not unconditionally saved. Salvation was conditioned on faith in Jesus as the Messiah.

Out of this burden, Paul calls attention to the words of Hosea. These references clearly show that Hosea emphasized that there were Israelites who would come from an unsaved state into a saving relationship with God. This reference should put away once and for all the idea of the unconditional election of all Israelites.

Of all the commentaries that I have researched, Lenski's comes the nearest to the position that I have set forth. He applies the fulfillment to the ten tribes rather than the Gentiles.[57]

> **27** Esaias also crieth concerning Israel, Though the number of the children of Israel
> be as the sand of the sea, a remnant shall be saved:
> **28** For he will finish the work, and cut *it* short in righteousness: because a short work
> will the Lord make upon the earth.

It is evident that Isaiah would not have been surprised (disappointed, but not surprised) that large numbers of Jews were not saved (verse 27).

Verse 28 sheds light on why only a remnant would be saved. The longsuffering that Paul mentioned in verse 22 will not be extended forever. The Lord will finish His work. He will "cut it short in righteousness." This means that many will have waited until it is too late.

> **29** And Esaias said before, Except the Lord Sabaoth had left us a seed, we had been as
> Sodoma, and had been like Gomorrha.

The Scripture is saying that only by the mercy of God was a remnant of Israel even surviving. Certainly, the Old Testament is opposed to the concept of the unconditional election of all who descended from Abraham through Jacob!

The Reason Many Jews Were Not Saved (Rom. 9:31-33)

30 What shall we say then? That the Gentiles, which followed not after the law of righteousness, have attained to righteousness, even the righteousness which is of faith.
31 But Israel, which followed after the law of righteousness, hath not attained to the law of righteousness.
32 Wherefore? Because *they sought it* not by faith, but as it were by the works of the law. For they stumbled at the stumbling stone;
33 As it is written, Behold I lay in Sion a stumblingstone and a rock of offence: and whosoever believeth on him shall not be ashamed.

Up to this point in Chapter 9, Paul had made it clear that the Jews as a whole could not lay claim to salvation by claiming they were unconditionally elected as the Covenant Seed of Abraham. He did not give as his reason that God had unconditionally elected *some* rather than *all*. Based on Exodus 33:19 he was telling the Jews that salvation was *individual* rather than *corporate*.

When Paul brought the unbelieving Jews face to face with why so many were not saved, he said that it was, "Because *they sought it* not by faith, but as it were by the works of the law. For they stumbled at the stumbling stone." That stumbling stone was Jesus the Messiah.

The reason that so many Jews were not saved is not based on the idea that God unconditionally elected *some* rather than *all* Jews. Rather, it is because they had failed to meet the condition of faith in Christ. If salvation is conditional, there is every reason to believe that election is conditional.

This is one of the primary passages that is thought to teach that the Jews believed in salvation by works. As I have pointed out in my discussion above, there is not a complete harmony in Jewish thought. Some statements can be found in Jewish writings that may sound as if Jews believed in salvation by works. However, the theme that God had unconditionally saved all Jews is so strong in their thinking that it overrides their thinking about works as a condition for remaining in the covenant. The only exception to "all Jews being saved" would be rare cases of apostasy.

Another factor that must be kept in mind in assessing Jewish thought is their belief in corporate salvation. For that reason, the works that would be under consideration would be corporate works, not individual works.

A Review of the Way Paul Develops His Case in Appealing to the Jews

Paul's viewpoint on election is seen in how he develops his case for the idea that not all Jews are saved:

1. Step one is to show that since not all of the descendants of Abraham make up the Covenant Seed of Abraham (verses 6-13), there is no reason to believe that all of the Covenant Seed are saved.
2. Step two, Paul appeals to Exodus 33:19 to show that election is individual rather than corporate.

3. In step three, Paul gives the reason that not all Jews are saved. It is "Because *they sought it not by faith, but as it were by the works of the law*" (verse 32). In other words, not all Jews are saved because salvation is conditioned on faith and not all Jews have met the condition. This is the bottom line: *salvation is conditioned on faith. And conditional salvation calls for conditional election.*

This is grounded in the Abrahamic Covenant. It was said of Abraham, "And he believed in the LORD; and it was counted unto him for righteousness" (Gen. 15:6). The Abrahamic Covenant is the basic redemptive Covenant.

The hope of the Jew and the hope of the Gentile is the same hope. Paul cries out to them: "For the scripture saith, Whosoever believeth in him shall not be ashamed. For there is no difference between the Jew and the Greek: for the same Lord over all is rich unto all that call upon him. For whosoever shall call upon the name of the Lord shall be saved" (Rom. 10:11-13).

I started with Romans 9 since it is the major passage used to support unconditional election. I believe that in my treatment of Romans 9:1-29 I have shown that it does teach that election is *individual* and that it is eternal. But it does not settle the question of whether election is conditional or unconditional election. However, the most natural interpretation of 9:31-33 is that justification is *conditional.* It is conditioned on faith in Jesus Christ as Messiah, Lord, and Savior. If justification is *conditional,* election is *conditional.*

The only hope left for unconditional election is to find another passage (or passages) that will unquestionably and irrefutably teach unconditional election. If that should be the case, the Calvinists could go to Romans 9:30-33 and say that the "whoever" of verse 33 is limited to those whom God has unconditionally chosen and regenerated. They are the only ones who can give the faith response to God's offer and be saved. If such an approach is taken, Romans 9 could be shown to be consistent with unconditional election. But, by such an approach, Romans 9 would no longer be *foundational for unconditional election.* I believe that Calvinism is in trouble *in* Romans 9. Calvinism is in trouble *without* Romans 9.

I will now turn attention to other passages that are thought, by Calvinists, to teach or support unconditional election. I do not think that it will be necessary for me to be as thorough with these other passages as I have been with Romans 9. The main thing that I need to do is to show that these passages do not contradict conditional election. Attention will first be given to the other passage in Romans that Calvinists use to support unconditional election.

Romans 8:30

The material on these verses comes from my commentary on Romans.[58] Minor changes and additions will be made to suit the purposes of this chapter.

> Moreover whom he did predestinate, them he also called: and whom he called, them he also justified; and whom he justified, them he also glorified.

"Whom he did predestinate" is a reference to those whom "he also did predestinate to be conformed to the image of his Son" (verse 29). I will wait until it fits into the discussion in the next chapter before I deal with verse 29. Verse 30 refers to the order of events as they occur in the ministry of redemption. This is generally agreed upon in commentaries. Therefore, we need not give further attention to this fact.

Calvinists make a point of saying that whenever the call is mentioned in the epistles, it only refers to believers. But that is because believers are being addressed. Paul likes to use the word "called," in referring to believers, to stress that our personal redemption owes its existence to God, who took the first initiative. We are not intruders into this salvation which is ours through Jesus Christ.

On the Calvinist's limitation of the word "called" I would make two observations: (1) To refer to believers as being "called ones" does not mean that the call has not been extended to any one else. A speaker at a special occasion may address the audience as "invited guests." The only thing that he is affirming is that those who are present have been invited. They are not intruders. It does not mean that no one else was invited. When believers are referred to as called, it is not necessary to conclude that others have not been called. (2) While the word "called" may not be used in the epistles to refer to those who have not responded, the concept of a call is seen where the word is not used. There is no plainer reference to this than Paul's statement when he says, "And the times of this ignorance God winked at; but now commandeth all men everywhere to repent" (Acts 17:30). Paul's use of "whosoever" in Romans 10:11-13 implies a call that extends to all men. It makes no difference whether a reference to God's calling sinners to salvation appears in the epistles in connection with the word "call." The concept is undeniably there.

No one is justified who was not first called. There can be no question that Paul is referring to those cases where the call has had its desired effect. That is not the same as saying that the call is irresistible, nor that it has succeeded in every case. This simply cannot be read out of the language.

When the person responds in faith, God justifies him. In due time the one who is justified will be glorified.

It will be observed that called, justified, and glorified are all in the past tense (the Greek aorist tense). The believing recipients of Paul's epistle had been called and justified, but not glorified. There has been some question about the use of the past tense with reference to "glorified" since glorification is yet future. The explanation commonly given is that it refers to the certainty of this future glorification. (See Bruce,[59] Hedriksen,[60] and Meyer.[61])

Murray points out that calling, justification, and glorification are solely the acts of God. He explains, "It is contrary to this emphasis to define any of these elements of application of redemption in any other terms than those of *divine actions*."[62] I find no problem with Murray's statement. The very nature of a call means that it is the activity of the one who extends the call. Justification is a divine act in which God declares us righteous based on the death and righteousness of Christ. The foundation of our justification is solely the merits of Christ rather than our own. But if Murray wants to insist that there is no involvement of the human personality in meeting the condition of faith as it relates to justification, I must differ with him. However, this verse says nothing about faith. I concur with Godet when he says, "If his intention had been to explain the *order of salvation* in all of its elements divine and *human*, he would have put *faith* between calling and justification and glorification."[63]

I certainly have no quarrel with the statement that future glorification will be bestowed on us by divine action. It is quite clear that verse 30 speaks only of divine action. At the same time it is quite clear that it is not an exhaustive treatment of the doctrine of salvation. Paul approached the verse in terms of divine action because he was still giving reasons for believing that God will be with us under any and all circumstances as set forth in verse 28.

Concerning why Paul moved from justification to glorification without mentioning sanctification, I think Bruce is on the right track when he says:

> The difference between sanctification and glory is one of degree only, not one of kind. Sanctification is progressive conformity to the image of Christ here and now (cf. II Cor. 3:18; Col. 3:10); glory is perfect conformity to the image of Christ there and then. Sanctification is glory begun; glorification is sanctification completed.[64]

Calvinists have sometimes thought that this verse guarantees that everyone who is called will respond, everyone who is called will be justified, and everyone who is justified will be glorified. I find myself in agreement with John Wesley when he says:

> St. Paul does not affirm, either here or in any other part of his writings that precisely the same number are called, justified, and glorified. He does not deny that a believer may fall away, and be cut off between his special calling and his glorification, Romans 11:22, neither does he deny that many are called who are never justified. He only affirms that this is the method whereby God leads step by step toward heaven.[65]

There is a parallel with words of Jesus when He said. "For the earth bringeth forth fruit of herself; first the blade, then the ear, after that the full corn in the ear" (Mk. 4:28). The process that is followed from the appearance of the blade until the grain is fully developed is stated, but Jesus does not guarantee that, once the blade appears, in every case all of the other steps follow. In some cases the stalk of grain dies before reaching full development.

While the wording of Romans 8:30 could fit the idea of an effectual call followed by justification of all the called and glorification without exception of all who are justified, it is not necessary to interpret it so. Such a view would require support from some other source. I do not believe that such a source can be found.

The Question of Unconditional Election and the Gospel of John

In deciding between unconditional election and conditional election, a biblical, systematic theologian must find what he considers to be irrefutable biblical proof of one position or the other.

When, to his satisfaction, he has accomplished that, his next responsibility is to show how he would interpret passages of Scripture that would be used by those who have chosen otherwise.

In actual experience, I established my position of conditional election and then worked my way through how I would deal with the passages thought to teach unconditional election. However, in this treatment, I have thought it was better to first show how I would deal with passages thought to teach unconditional election. I deemed it wise to start with Romans 9.

I gave a rather thorough treatment to Romans 9. I believe that Calvinism is in trouble in Romans 9. If that is the case, I do not think it will be necessary for me to be as thorough with the other passages.

If I agreed that unconditional election was taught in Romans 9, I would give a Calvinistic interpretation to several verses in the Gospel of John. Or, if there was some other passage that I thought unquestionably taught unconditional election, I would feel like unconditional election was behind much of what Jesus said in the Gospel of John. I do not believe that unconditional election is taught elsewhere in Scripture. I will show in the next chapter that the Bible teaches conditional election. The only obligation that I have in John is to show that what is said could fit in with conditional election and the *influence* and *response model* of God's sovereign relationship with human beings.

THE JEWISH CONTEXT

While dealing with Romans 9, I pointed out that the prevailing view among Jews was that in connection with the call and the covenant that God made with Abraham, He unconditionally saved all Jews. In support of that position, I gave quotations from, John Piper, Charles Hodge, and Douglas J. Moo. Support was also given from *The Jewish Encyclopedia*. In Jesus' ministry, He would have encountered the same viewpoint. It will be very interesting to keep this in mind when we examine the teachings of Jesus. I am not aware of anyone who has stressed this point in interpreting the Gospels. If anyone has done it, it has not been given the visibility that it deserves.

John 1:12, 13 and the Question of Election

12 But as many as have received him, to them gave he power [*exousia*, authority or the right] to become the sons [*teknon*. The plural is better translated children.] of God, *even* to them that believe on his name.
13 Which were born, not of blood, nor of the will of the flesh, nor of the will of man, but of God.

On verse 13, the NIV gives an interpretive reading that helps us understand the verse. It reads, "Children born not of natural descent, nor of human decision or a husband's will, but were born of God."

Robert W. Yarbrough, in defense of unconditional election says:

Divine election receives sharp emphasis in John 1:13, the identity of "all who received him" in 1:12. That, is those who savingly received the Messiah for who he truly was (1:12) did so because they were "born of God" (1:13)—and not vice versa. More specifically, they cannot ultimately attribute their saved status, if they possess it, to "natural descent," their Jewishness or descent from Abraham (cf. John 8:33).[66]

I agree that regeneration is a work of God. It is *monergistic,* not *synergistic.* However, there is nothing in verses 12 and 13 that would make them suggest that the "regeneration" of verse 13 took place prior to the "believing" in verse 12. The natural reading of the verses suggests that the "believing" of verse 12 precedes the "regeneration" of verse 13. The only person who would read it otherwise would be a person who comes to these verses with a prior commitment to unconditional election.

The Teachings of Jesus in the Gospel of John and the Question of Election

The teachings of Jesus that we will examine were directed to the Jews. It is important that we keep in mind that the prevailing view among the Jewish audiences that Jesus was addressing would have been that all of the Jews were already saved because of their relationship with Abraham. They would have believed in corporate election (or salvation). This presented a special challenge to Jesus.

There is a place for questions to be settled by detailed exegesis. It is especially incumbent upon us to use that approach at times. However, Jesus, as the God-man, avoided that kind of conflict with His Jewish audience. The Pharisees specialized in quibbling over minute details. Jesus did not want to quibble. He did not need to quibble. He spoke as "one that had authority, and not as the scribes" (Mk. 1:22). The authority of the scribes was a documented authority. They passed on the Oral Tradition. They quoted the famous Rabbis. Jesus had authority. He spoke from Himself. His miracles were signs showing that He had the Father's stamp of approval (Acts 2:22, Jn. 20:30, 31). Jesus, in speaking to the Jews said, "But I have greater witness than *that* of John [the Baptist]: for the works which the Father hath given me to finish, the same works that I do, bear witness of me, that the Father hath sent me" (5:36). The "works" that Jesus spoke of were His miracles.

Another thing that we must keep in mind is that some of the Jews that heard Jesus had been saved as Old Testament saints, and were saved prior to the time that they met Jesus. These people would have believed in Jesus when they were confronted with His miracles and His teachings. They became His followers.

With these observations in mind, we can move on and examine the teachings of Christ regarding their bearing on the subject of election. Since God is the same yesterday, today, and forever, we can assume the decisions God made in eternity are in perfect agreement with the decisions He makes in time. Based upon that, we can reason back from what we learn in time to the kind of decisions that God made in eternity.

Since the audience in John was Jewish, we need to see what Jesus was trying to get across to His Jewish audience.

SALVATION (ELECTION) CORPORATE OR INDIVIDUAL?

Those of us who have been brought up in a church where the Bible was taught and preached, automatically look at people as saved or lost. That is not the way, in which, the Jews being addressed by Jesus were accustomed to thinking of themselves as Jews. Jesus had to address them in such a way that they would recognize that salvation was *individual*, not *corporate*. It was necessary for Him to get them to see the truth of His words, "I am the way, the truth and the life; no man cometh unto the Father, but by me" (14:6). Keeping in mind the things that I have mentioned about the Jewish concept of corporate election will not change our understanding of the universal truth taught in the Gospel of John. But it will give us a different understanding of how Jesus was seen and understood by His Jewish audiences.

The first encounter recorded in John emphasizing that salvation must be experienced by each individual is Jesus' meeting with Nicodemus. Nicodemus had seen the miracles that Jesus had performed (verse 1). They had got his attention. He knew that there was something different about Jesus. He knew that God was with Him. His deep desire to see Jesus was apparently coupled with fear—so he went at night to see Him.

Jesus did not discuss the subject of corporate election of Jews. But what He said dealt with the problem in a way that could not be missed. He said to Nicodemus, "Except a man be born again, he cannot see the kingdom of God." Again He says to him, "Except a man be born of water and *of the Spirit*, he cannot enter into the kingdom of God" (verses 3 and 5). It is clear that Jesus is telling Nicodemus that salvation must be experienced *individually*. It is impossible for us to imagine what this ruler of the Jews must have felt when he heard these words. He had not only heard these words; He had seen Jesus' miracles. He also heard Jesus say:

> **14** And as Moses lifted up the serpent in the wilderness, even so must the Son of man be lifted up:
> **15** That whosoever believeth in him should not perish, but have eternal life.

There is a question over whether John 3:18 was spoken by Jesus, or whether it was added by John. John was still battling the problem of corporate election, just as Paul had in Romans 9. What is said in this verse is clearly in conflict with the corporate election of all Jews. "He that believeth on him is not condemned: but he that believeth not is condemned already, because he hath not believed in the name of the only begotten Son of God." Verse 36 carries the same message. In John 5:24, Jesus said:

> Verily, verily, I say unto you, He that heareth my word, and believeth on him that sent me, hath everlasting life, and is passed from death unto life, and shall not come into condemnation; but is passed from death unto life.

Later in this chapter, we read the words of Jesus, "And ye will not come to me, that ye might have life" (verse 40).

These words have a message of hope, for anybody, anywhere, at any time who will turn to Him. There is also a message of judgment for those who will not. But they had a special significance to the Jewish audience. We could add John 4:14; 6:25-29, 35, 51; 7:37-39; 10:7-11, 27-30, and 14:6.

I would like to call attention to one more passage. One of the times when Jesus used the strongest language in talking with the Jews is in chapter 8. There were apparently some who thought they believed in Jesus, but when He said, "If ye continue in my word, *then* are ye my disciples indeed; and ye shall know the truth, and the truth shall make you free" (verses 31, 32). They did not like the suggestion that they were not already free. "They answered him, We be Abraham's seed and were never in bondage to any man: how sayest thou, Ye shall be made free?" (verse 33). Jesus said to them:

> **37** I know that ye are Abraham's seed; but ye seek to kill me, because my word hath no place in you.
> **38** I speak that which I have seen with my Father: and ye do that which ye have seen with your father.
> **39** They answered and said unto him, Abraham is our father. Jesus saith unto them, If ye were Abraham's children, ye would do the works of Abraham.
> **40** But now ye seek to kill me, a man that hath told you the truth, which I have heard of God: this did not Abraham.
> **41** Ye do the deeds of your father. Then say they unto him, We be not born of fornication; we have one Father, *even* God.
> **42** Jesus said unto them, If God were your Father, ye would love me: for I proceeded forth and came from God; neither came I of myself, but he sent me.

In verse 44, Jesus went on to tell them, "Ye are of *your* father the devil, and the lusts of your father ye will do." These Jews went on in verse 48 and charged Jesus with being a Samaritan and being demon possessed. It was extremely clear that Jesus rejected any concept of the corporate election of all Jews. It was also clear that salvation was experienced on an individual basis. If salvation is experienced on an individual basis, it follows that since God is the same yesterday, today, and forever that election in eternity past would have been on an individual basis.

In the discussion above, along with showing that salvation for the Jews is individual rather than corporate, a lot of evidence was given that would show that faith in Jesus as Messiah (or Christ), Lord, and Savior is the condition of salvation. I do not need to go into any depth on this point. I will just say that a reading of the verses used above under "Salvation (Election) Corporate or Individual?" leaves no doubt that salvation is conditioned on faith in Jesus Christ as Lord and Savior.

Calvinists do not deny that justification is conditioned on faith in Christ. Is not justification required for election? If faith is the condition of justification now, why would it not be viewed that way in eternity past?

The Occurrences of the Word *Eklegomai*

Eklegomai occurs five times in John (6:70; 13:18; 15:16, 19). Each of these times, it is translated "chosen." It is the verb form of the word for "elect." In each of these cases the reference is to the Twelve Apostles. The reference is to the fact that Jesus had chosen them to be His apostles. There is no problem for conditional election if it did include election to salvation.

A problem might be supposed by some from the reading of "Ye have not chosen me, but I have chosen you." It seems apparent that this is a reference to being chosen to be an apostle. But the wording presents no problem if it applies to salvation. The provision of salvation, the offer of salvation, the drawing to salvation all originated with God. Any response on the part of any individual is a response to divine initiative. The only difference between unconditional election and the view of conditional election set forth by Classical Arminianism is *the difference in the divine activity that makes faith possible.* In both Calvinism and Arminianism *the individual does make a choice.*[67] There is no such thing as human personality changing from unbelief to faith without making a choice. Calvinism has not won its case by the wording of verse 16.

The wording of verse 19, "I have chosen you out of the world," while referring to the apostles, may embrace election for salvation since they were chosen out of the world. What I have said in the previous paragraph will show that if it is election to salvation, there is no necessary conflict with conditional election.

Didōmi and *Helkuō* in Regard to Salvation

Yarbrough takes the position that the Gospel of John gives strong support for unconditional election. In opening his treatment of "Divine Election in the Gospel of John," he explains, "Divine election in this chapter refers to God's determinative initiative in human salvation."[68] By tying election to "God's determinative initiative" Yarbrough is, of course, taking the position of unconditional election. In commenting on the Hebrew word *bāhar* which is used in the Old Testament for choose or elect, he explains, "The word 'indicates God's prerogative in deciding what shall happen, independent of human choice.'"[69] Having made it clear that his use of the word election is to be understood as a reference to unconditional election, he avows, "John's Gospel implicitly and explicitly asserts God's choosing, his election, of lost sinners to eternal life."[70] While he sees his support in other verses in John, he sees nine verses in 1:19–12:50 as being key verses. To get these before us, I will quote the pertinent part of these verses. In some cases it may be the whole verse. I will use the NASB for these verses. The key Greek words in the verses in question are *didōmi* and *helkuō*. I will indicate where these words occur. To make it simpler to deal with, instead of taking each verse in the order in which it occurs in the book, I will group them together according to the problem they present.

Eklegomai

In 6:70, Jesus said, "Did I Myself not choose you, the twelve, and yet one of you is a devil?" I have already dealt with this verse above under the previous heading "The Occurrences of the Word *Eklegomai*." I need not say more about it here.

Helkuō

No man can come to Me except the Father who sent Me draws [*helkuō*] him (6:44).

And I, if I be lifted up from the earth , will draw [*helkuō*] all men to Myself (12:32).

It is important for us to keep reminding ourselves of the audience that Jesus is addressing. The clash between the concept of corporate election and salvation on an individual basis presented Jesus with a unique challenge. The challenge before Jesus was to get the Jews to see that salvation was on an individual basis and that it required faith in Him as the Messiah. This was not going to take place simply by making statements and giving explanations.

There were two big problems. One of the problems was the power of depravity which works to keep people away from God. This problem is common to all human beings. The other problem was unique to the Jewish people as a result of the way their thinking had developed by the time of Jesus. As they understood it, they did not come into salvation by individual decision. This was decided for them when God called Abraham and made the Abrahamic Covenant with him.[71] For them, salvation was *automatically* bestowed on them as the Covenant Seed of Abraham.

The burden of Jesus' ministry was to show those who thought that salvation was automatically bestowed upon them that such was not the case. It is bestowed on individuals one at a time. God, who is sovereign, decides who will be saved. He has decided that those who place their faith in Jesus as Messiah, Savior, and Lord are the ones whom He wills to save (Jn. 3:16, 18; 5:24; 6:35, 37, 39-40; 8:51, 52; 10:27-29; and 14:6). Those who do not place their faith in Jesus as Messiah, Savior, and Lord are the ones whom God decides to condemn (Jn. 3:18; 6:40; 8:24; and 14:6).

Even though Jesus made salvation available for everyone on the condition of faith in Jesus Christ, it was necessary for God to go a step further. He must send the Holy Spirit to draw them to Christ. Depravity is of such a nature that no one will come to Christ unless he is drawn by the Holy Spirit. While this is true of all human beings, it was particularly important for this point to be driven home to the Jews. They needed to see that they did not have automatic salvation. There was no corporate salvation for them to experience. Salvation happened to people as individuals. Each person had to experience salvation or remain under condemnation. In John 6:44, Jesus was talking about individuals. No individual could come to Christ without being drawn.

There is certainly no contradiction between the drawing spoken of in John 6:44 and the drawing spoken of in Classical Arminianism. Classical Arminianism recognizes that a strong work of the Holy Spirit is necessary before any person can respond to Jesus Christ in faith.

Yarbrough thinks that the word *helkuō* describes an irresistible drawing. He explains:

Outside of the Gospel of John it appears in the New Testament only at Acts 16:19: "they seized Paul and Silas and dragged them into the market place. . . ." John's Gospel uses the word to speak of persons being drawn to Christ (12:32), a sword being drawn (18:10), and a net full of fish being hauled or dragged to shore (21:6, 11). The related form *helkō* appears in Acts 21:30 ("they dragged him from the temple") and James 2:6 ("Are they not the ones who are dragging you into court?"). It is hard to avoid the impression that John 6:44 refers to a "forceful attraction" in bringing sinners to the Son."[72]

I think the evidence Yarbrough presents does suggest that the drawing of John 6:44 is strong. I have no problem with the idea that the drawing spoken of in John 6:44 is a "strong drawing." But I do have a problem with speaking of it as a "forceful attraction." A word used literally may have a causal force when dealing with physical relationships. However, we cannot require that that word have the same *causal* force when it is used metaphorically with reference to an *influence* and *response* relationship. John 6:44 speaks of a personal *influence* and *response* relationship.

For John 6:44 to aid the cause of unconditional election, it must be understood in terms of *cause* and *effect*. The verse plainly says that no one can come to Christ without being drawn by the Father. But there is nothing in the word *helkuō* that would require that it be interpreted with a causal force. In fact, if we keep in mind that the relationship between God and man is a personal relationship, the use of *helkuō* in this verse is best understood in terms of *influence* and *response* rather than *cause* and *effect*.

When we go to John 12:32, the natural meaning of the verse is to understand *helkuō* in terms of *influence* and *response* rather than *cause* and *effect*. When Jesus said, "And I, if I be lifted up from the earth , will draw [*helkuō*] all men to Myself "(12:32), He definitely did not mean that He would drag every human being to Himself. He meant that there would go out from Him a drawing power that would make it possible for any person who hears the gospel to come to Him. It is strained exegesis to suggest as Yarbrough does that the likely meaning of "'all men' in John 12:32 refers to all—both Jew and Gentile—that the Father has given to the Son."[73]

If a person is going to interpret *helkuō* in John 6:44 and 12:32 to be an irresistible drawing, he must first find a passage elsewhere that irrefutably teaches that there is such an irresistible drawing. Then, he might suggest that as the meaning in John. These verses cannot be used as a part of a person's arsenal of irrefutable proof of an irresistible calling.

Didōmi

All that the Father gives [*didōmi*] to Me will come to Me, and the one that comes to Me I will certainly not cast out (6:35).

No man can come to Me, unless it has been granted [*didōmi*] from the Father (6:65).

And I give [*didōmi*] eternal life to them, and they shall never perish; and no one shall snatch them out of My hand" (10:28).

My Father, who has given [*didōmi*] *them* to Me, is greater than all; and no one shall snatch them out of the Father's hand (10:29).

I am separating my treatment of John 10:28 from the rest of the verses because the others refer to *those given to the Son by the Father*. This verse refers to the fact that the *Son* gives eternal life to those who are His. There is no way that this verse can have any bearing one way or the other on the question of whether election is conditional or unconditional.

It seems to be obvious that the use of *didōmi* in John 6:37; 6:65; 10:29 refers to the end result of the Father's "drawing." Those who come as a result of the Father's drawing are considered to be "given to Jesus by the Father." This point seems to be very clear when we take John 6:44, "No man can come to Me except the Father who sent Me draws [*helkuō*] him" and compare it with, "No man can come to Me, unless it has been granted [*didōmi*] from the Father (6:65). "Granted" here could be translated "given." *Didōmi* (granted or given) in 6:65 is interpreted by comparison with 6:44 to be the same as *helkuō* (draw). If that is the case, what I said above about drawing shows that there is no way that the word "given" in John's Gospel lends any support to unconditional election.

In one sense all sinners are being held hostage by sin. It takes a work of God to break through, convince them of their sins, convince them that Jesus can save them, convince them that Jesus is the only way, and, then lead them to Christ. However, there are different approaches that sin takes in holding sinners captive. For some, it has been the allurements of sin, for others it has been the outright unbelief of secular modernism. Many today are held hostage by the moral, cultural, and religious relativism of postmodernism.

The situation that Jesus was facing, and the early church continued to face, was the Jewish misunderstanding of the idea that they were corporately and automatically saved as a result of the call and the covenant that God made with Abraham. Many of the Jews were held hostage by the false assurance that they were automatically and corporately saved. If we are going to understand the way Jesus dealt with the Jews as it is set forth for us in the Gospel of John, we will have to keep these observations in mind when we study the passages we have been looking at. I believe Classical Arminianism is on solid ground in the Gospel of John.

THE QUESTION OF WHY MANY JEWS DID NOT BELIEVE JESUS

He who is of God hears the words of God; for this reason you do not hear *them*, because you are not of God (8:47).

But you do not believe, because you are not of My sheep (10:26).

Perhaps the best way to answer this question is to first answer the following question: "Why did many of the Jews believe in Jesus?" As I said up above, many who were living when Jesus came were already saved. Their heart was right with God. They were submissive to God. When they met Jesus, saw His miracles, and heard His teachings they believed in Him. It was this kind of people that Jesus had in mind when He said in John 7:17, "If any man is willing to do his [the Father's] will, he shall know of the teaching, whether it is of God or *whether* I speak of Myself." There were those who already were of that disposition. These people responded and believed. Others as they saw the miracles and heard the teachings of Jesus responded to the drawing power of the Holy Spirit and believed (7:40-43).

Those who were referred to in John 8:47 and 10:26 were those who were not in a right relationship with God before they met Jesus. At the time these words were spoken to them they were still resisting. There is nothing to suggest that it was impossible for them to believe and be saved at a later date. There is no indication that God had made an unconditional choice to leave them out of His plan.

AN ARGUMENT BASED ON ANALOGY

For just as the Father raises the dead and gives them life, even so the Son also gives life to [or makes alive] whom He wishes (5:21).

Concerning this verse, Yarbrough remarks, "Here is a powerful analogy: As corpses depend on God's vivifying voice to resurrect them, so recipients of 'life,' or salvation, depend on the Son's good pleasure to give it."[74] True, this is a "powerful analogy," but within itself it sheds no light on whether the Son gives life *conditionally* or *unconditionally*.

A PRELIMINARY CONCLUSION

I believe our examination of the evidence in the Gospel of John shows that there is no conclusive or foundational support in the Gospel of John for unconditional election. Any tying of the Gospel of John with unconditional election, depends upon finding it somewhere else first. I think I have shown that such foundational support cannot be found in Romans 9. Before concluding this chapter, I will examine Acts 13:48.

Acts 13:48

And when the Gentiles heard this, they glorified the word of the Lord: and as many as were ordained to eternal life believed.

Of all of the verses in the Bible, this is the one that has taken me the longest to discover what, to me, provides a satisfactory interpretation, corresponding with conditional election. On the surface, it sounds as if these people had been elected to believe. Then, it seemed to follow that all who had been elected to believe believed on that occasion.

As I pointed out in the study of John above, there were those who were already saved prior to the coming of Jesus Christ. They believed in the redemptive message revealed in the Old Testament. They had a personal, trusting relationship with God. Probably most of these true believers lived in Palestine. Since Jews had migrated to others parts of the world some of these true believers would have lived in other parts of the world as well. Since our concern in this passage is with what took place in Antioch in Pisidia, I think we could safely say that there were some in Asia Minor that were saved by believing the Old Testament redemptive revelation prior to Paul's first missionary journey. They were already saved by faith, but they had not come in contact with the message of Jesus Christ.

Along with the spread of the Jews there was the spread of the influence of Jewish monotheism, the way of life set forth in the Old Testament, and the redemptive revelation that was intended to be a message of hope for all mankind. Many Gentiles were influenced by the Jews as they went forth. Proselytes (Acts 2:10 and 13:43) were Gentiles who embraced the Jewish faith including circumcision of the males.[75]

F. F. Bruce tells us that

> Many Gentiles in those days, while not prepared to enter this Jewish community as full proselytes were attracted by the simple monotheism of Jewish synagogue worship and by the ethical standard of the Jewish way of life. Some of them attended synagogue and were tolerably conversant with the prayers and Scripture lessons, which they heard read in the Greek version; some observed with more or less scrupulosity such distinctive Jewish practices as sabbath observance and abstinence from certain kinds of food. . . .
>
> That the first Gentile to hear and accept the gospel should be a God-fearer is the more significant because, as we shall see later in Acts, it was such God-fearers who formed the nucleus of the Christian community in one city after another in the course of Paul's missionary activity.[76]

These Gentiles who were influenced by Jewish thought, but chose not to become proselytes are referred to as *devout men* or *God-fearers*. If some of the Jews were saved by faith before the coming of Jesus, it follows that some of the Gentile proselytes and God-fearers were also saved by faith. I think that any serious study of Acts must keep this observation in mind. I am not suggesting that all of these God-fearers were saved prior to hearing that Jesus the Messiah had come. There would have been some who would not have taken matters that seriously. However, I do believe that some were saved by believing the redemptive revelation of God given in the Old Testament before they heard the gospel message. That possibility no longer exists. But it did exist during this transition period.

The Gentiles who had been influenced by the Jews as they had migrated to different parts of the Roman Empire would not have found the concept of individual salvation as distinguished from corporate salvation as objectionable as the Jews did. I think this could account for much of the early success in reaching Gentiles with the gospel.

Now, let us see how this viewpoint helps us understand Acts 13:48. In verse 43 mention is made of "proselytes." They were among those who were persuaded by Paul and Barnabas "to continue in the grace of God." On the next sabbath day "came almost the whole city together to hear the word of God" (verse 44). The Jews were envious of the success that Paul and Barnabas were having and spoke against them (verse 46). Paul and Barnabas, then, turned to the Gentiles. When this move was made to the Gentiles, it is said, "And as many as were ordained to eternal life believed" (verse

48). The Greek word for "ordained" is *tassō*. It means "to ordain," "to appoint," "to allot," or "to assign." The form of the word that appears in verse 48 is *tetagmenoi*. It is a perfect passive participle form of *tassō*. It is preceded by *ēsan* which is the imperfect form of the Greek word *eimi (to be)*. The expression *ēsan tetagmenoi* is what is called in the Greek a periphrastic pluperfect construction. The literal meaning would be "as many as were having been appointed to eternal life believed." Or in a less literal way, it would be "as many as had been appointed to eternal life believed."

The "had been appointed to eternal life" or the "appointment to eternal life" had occurred before they heard and believed the gospel that was presented by Paul and Barnabas. However, the wording does not require that this appointment to eternal life must be a reference to eternity past. I think what the verse is telling us is that all of those who had been saved prior to their hearing the New Testament gospel subsequently believed when they heard the gospel being presented by Paul and Barnabas. At the moment of their salvation in the past, they were appointed unto eternal life. When they heard about the redemptive work of Jesus the Messiah, they believed and became a New Testament believer.

I believe that what I have given is the most likely interpretation of this passage. If this is the case, this passage would present no problem for the position of conditional election. I would also like to point out that, in so far as the wording is concerned, it could be possible for Acts 13:48 to refer to an appointment made in eternity past. However, there is a problem for those who hold that position. The verse says, "As many as had been appointed to eternal life believed." If it is a reference to an unconditional appointment in eternity past, it would then mean that of the group present that day "as many as" or "all among them" that would ever be saved were saved on that occasion. I would doubt that those who believe in unconditional election believe that. It is hard to believe that, of that group, from among those who did not get saved on that occasion no one ever got saved later.

MY FINAL CONCLUSION

Except for Ephesians 1, I have dealt with the verses most commonly used to support unconditional election. I believe have shown that *none of these passages require unconditional election to be true.* In fact, I think *Romans 9 supports conditional election.* The reason I did not deal with Ephesians 1 in this chapter is I cover it in the next chapter when building my case for conditional election. I will show that it also does not support unconditional election.

17

Scriptural Support for Conditional Election

In chapter 15, I dealt with the theological problems that must be dealt with in a study of election. Unconditional election and conditional election were defined. Attention was given to decrees, determinism, the sovereignty of God, the meaning of free will, etc. Two differing models for understanding the way God carries out His sovereign purposes with human beings were explained. These were the *cause* and *effect* model and the *influence* and *response* model. Unconditional election is best served by the cause and effect model. Conditional election is best served by the *influence* and *response* model.

The ultimate question for a biblical, systematic theologian to try to answer is: Which view of election is taught in the Bible? I think I have shown in the previous chapter that the passages that have been thought to teach unconditional election do not require that interpretation. In fact, Romans 9, which has been considered to be the bedrock of Calvinism, is best understood as teaching election that is *individual, eternal,* and *conditional*. The first problem that I need to deal with in this chapter is the meaning of predestination in the New Testament.

The New Testament Use and Meaning of Predestination

The Greek word for predestinate is *proorizō*. It means to predetermine that a particular thing will take place. It is found six times in the New Testament (Acts 4:28; Rom. 8:29, 30; 1 Cor. 2:7; Eph. 1:5, 11).

ACTS 4:28

> For to do whatsoever thy hand and thy counsel determined before to be done.

In this verse, *proorizō* refers to what happened at the cross as having been predetermined by God. God had predetermined that Jesus Christ would be crucified, and in connection with that event He would suffer the full wrath of God and make atonement for the sins of the human race.

1 CORINTHIANS 2:7

> But we speak the wisdom of God, *even* the hidden *wisdom,* which God ordained before the world unto our glory.

In this verse, it is the revelation of the New Testament gospel ("the wisdom of God in a mystery") which Paul speaks of as being determined by God. God had predetermined that at the appropriate time, which to God was a specific time, the New Testament gospel would be revealed.

While Acts 4:28 and 1 Corinthians 2:7 do indeed indicate that God has predestinated or foreordained that certain things will take place, they do not address the subject of the election of believers. The remaining verses where *proorizō* occurs are pertinent to the question of individual election. The question that demands our attention is: "Does the use of *proorizō* in any of these verses tell us that God has predetermined or predestinated that a particular person will believe?"

ROMANS 8:29, 30

> 29 For whom he did foreknow, he also did predestinate *to be* conformed to the image
> of his Son, that he might be the firstborn among many brethren.
> 30 Moreover whom he did predestinate, them he also called: and whom he called,
> them he also justified: and whom he justified, them he also glorified.

It is obvious that the aim of predestination in verse 30 is the same as it is in verse 29. In verse 29, the aim of predestination is for those whom God foreknew "to be conformed to the image of Christ."

I understand there is a problem surrounding the meaning of *foreknow* and *foreknowledge* in the New Testament. I will address that later when I look at the occurrences of the words for foreknowledge. It is quite clear that these verses do not say that the people under consideration were predestinated to believe. Rather, it is saying that those who do believe are predestinated to be conformed to the image of Christ.

EPHESIANS 1:5

> Having predestinated us unto the adoption of children by Jesus Christ to himself,
> according to his good pleasure of his will.

The "us" of the verse is a reference to those who had been chosen in Christ. I will comment on that verse later when I look at the verses where the Greek word for election occur. The word that is translated "adoption of children" is *huiothesia*. The literal meaning of the word is "son placing." The defining passage for the meaning of *huiothesia* is Galatians 3:19–4:10. It is in Galatians 4:5 that the word occurs. But a study of 3:19–4:10 is necessary in order to grasp what is meant.

In this passage Paul is telling us that in the Old Testament God viewed His believing children as being in a state of immaturity. The Mosaic Law with its civil and ceremonial laws was adapted to immaturity. Paul is telling us that in connection with the coming of Christ that God has placed His believing children in the position of adult sons.

Paul spoke of the Law as being a *paidagōgos* (Gal. 3:24). In wealthy Greek and Roman families, a young boy was placed under a *paidagōgos* from ages 5 or 6 until 16 or 17. The *paidagōgos* was a trusted slave. This slave would go with the young boy for his protection and to instill the family values in the young boy. The KJV translates *paidagōgos* as schoolmaster. That translation might have been useful when the KJV was translated,[1] but that is not the case now.

We do not have an exact parallel in our culture to the *paidagōgoss* of Paul's day. Probably, the nearest parallel would be a *nanny*. The words *tutor* or *guardian* pick up the meaning somewhat. It is impossible to understand what Paul is saying about the *paidagōgos* without being assisted by a knowledge of the Greek and Roman culture of Paul's day.

An understanding of the word *paidagōgos* is necessary before we can understand Paul's use of the word *huiothesia*. The time of *huiothesia* (adoption) refers to the time when the parents released the young man from the *paidagōgos*. This took place when the young man was about 16 or 17. It was the time when he was released from a childhood method of treatment to one in keeping with the maturity of adulthood. Galatians 3:19–4:7 teaches us that in connection with the coming of Christ, God released His children from the *paidagōgos*. The use of *paidagōgos* in Galatians 3:24 is a metaphorical reference to the Mosaic Law with its civil and ceremonial laws.

Adoption *(huiothesia)* in the New Testament does not refer to the legal process of taking one who was not born to parents and making him or her a member of the family. Rather, it refers to taking one who is a member of the family and making him or her a *huios*. *Huios* is the Greek word for son. It refers to one who is a legal heir of legal age. The one so adopted has the privileges of an adult heir. The first privilege to be bestowed is the release from the *paidagōgos*. That means the release from the responsibility of living by the civil and ceremonial laws of the Mosaic Law.

The predestination Paul spoke of in Ephesians 1:5 was the predestination of us as New Testament believers to *huiothesia* (adoption) as explained above. Again, we see that it does not say that certain ones are predestinated to believe. Rather, this predestination was that of New Testament believers who would be adopted and, thus, delivered from the Mosaic Law as the *paidagōgos*. I realize that the meaning of adoption needs much more explanation than I have given here. See a more complete explanation in Appendix 2, "Legalism in the Book of Galatians."

EPHESIANS 1:11

> In whom also we have obtained an inheritance, being predestinated according to the purpose of him who worketh all things after the counsel of his will.

"We have obtained an inheritance" is a translation of *eklērōthēmen* which is the first person plural, aorist passive indicative of *klēroō*. The question to be decided is whether believers were "made an inheritance of God" or whether believers were "given an inheritance." Were we predestinated to be God's inheritance or we were predestinated to receive an inheritance from God? Either of these would be true statements. For support for the idea that believers may be viewed as God's

THE QUEST FOR TRUTH

inheritance see Deuteronomy 32:8, 9. The only pertinent question then is: "What is the meaning here?"

For our present purposes, we do not need to decide which of these is meant. No matter which of these meanings is the true meaning, it will not present a problem to conditional election. It is clear that it is not saying that people are predestinated to believe.

CONCLUSION

This study of *proorizō*, the Greek word for *predestinate*, has not settled for or against either conditional election or unconditional election. While it has not settled the question, it has not done damage to conditional election. Those who believe in conditional election have as much right to the word *predestinate* as those who believe in unconditional election. We do have a different understanding of the terminus of *predestination* as it relates to the act of faith. But as it relates to believers, we see predestination as having the same terminus that Calvinists do.

Those who believe in unconditional election believe that God has unconditionally chosen certain ones to believe and be saved. He predestinates those whom He has chosen to believe. In this case *faith* is the terminus of predestination. The Classical Calvinist approach works on the *cause* and *effect* model in producing faith in the individual. In the Classical Arminian approach, God works on the *influence* and *response* model in getting the response of faith from the individual. This difference in the understanding of the nature of the divine contribution in bringing a person to saving faith is the great continental divide between Classical Calvinists and Classical Arminians.

As it relates to the terminus of predestination in the verses that I have examined, the terminus, as it is believed by Classical Arminians and Calvinists, would be the same. There would, of course, be a difference in how God would achieve these goals.

The terminus of predestination in Romans 8:29 is clearly *that believers would be conformed to the image of Christ.* Classical Arminians and Classical Calvinists would agree that God has predestinated believers to be conformed to the image of Christ.

In Ephesians 1:5 the terminus of predestination is *adoption.* Classical Calvinists and Classical Arminians would agree that God predestinated New Testament believers to be adopted. Differences on the interpretation of adoption would have nothing to do with whether a person is a Calvinist or an Arminian.

In Ephesians 1:11, if the true meaning is that believers are predestinated *"to be God's inheritance,"* that would not present a problem to either Calvinism or Classical Arminianism. If the true meaning is that believers are predestinated *"to have an inheritance,"* that would not present a problem to either Calvinism or Classical Arminianism.

Predestination is just as essential for Classical Arminianism as it is for Calvinism. If there is no predestination, there is no gospel. Our gospel says that God has predestinated salvation for everyone who believes in Jesus Christ and He has predestinated that all who do not believe in Jesus Christ will be condemned to eternal death (Jn. 3:16, 18, 36; 5:24; 14:6; Acts 4:12; 16:31; Rom. 6:23; Rev. 21:8; and others). It is the fault of Arminians that we have almost forfeited the word *predestination* to the Calvinists. As Arminians we need to reclaim the word *predestination.*

The New Testament Use and Meaning
of Foreknow and Foreknowledge

The Greek word *proginōskō* (to foreknow) occurs five times in the New Testament. It is found in Acts 26:5; Romans 8:29; 11:2; 1 Peter 1:20; and 2 Peter 3:17. The Greek word *prognōsis* (foreknowledge) is found only twice in the New Testament—Acts 2:23 and 1 Peter 1:2.

2 PETER 3:17

> Ye therefore, beloved, seeing ye know *these things* before, beware lest ye also, being led astray with the error of the wicked, fall from your own steadfastness.

In this verse, *proginōskō* refers to human knowledge. Peter was saying that since they know the damage that has been done by these false teachers, they should be on their guard lest they be led astray. They already knew (knew beforehand) the end result of those false teachers.

ACTS 26:5

> Which [the Jews who accused Paul] knew (Greek, *proginōskō*) me from the beginning . . .

In this verse, *proginōskō* refers to the knowledge that a person has before the present moment which is *fore[before]knowledge*. We would say "prior knowledge." In 2 Peter 3:17, a person is in possession of a knowledge that makes him aware of the consequences that a particular thing will bring.

Divine foreknowledge as we will see it used in the other verses is different from what is mentioned in Acts 26:5 and 1 Peter 3:17. It refers to a knowledge that God had of events in eternity past. This kind of knowledge is knowledge of an event before it occurs.

ACTS 2:23 AND 1 PETER 1:20

> Him [Jesus of Nazareth], being delivered by the determinate counsel and foreknowledge of God, ye have taken, and by wicked hands have crucified and slain (Acts 2:23).

Calvinists believe these verses confirm their idea that the Greek words for *predestination, election,* and *foreknowledge* are essentially synonymous. They take the use of the word "foreknowledge" (*prognōsis*) in "being delivered by the determinate counsel and the foreknowledge of God" to be *efficacious.*

I believe as strongly as any Calvinist that the crucifixion of Jesus Christ was prearranged and predetermined. The determinate counsel of God and the foreknowledge of God prearranged and predetermined the crucifixion of Christ. I do not believe that this verse requires us to understand the word *prognōsis* (foreknowledge) to be *efficacious* thus making it synonymous with *predetermined* or *predestinated.*

I believe that the proper understanding of *prognōsis* in Acts 2:23 is *instrumental.* The foreknowledge of God enabled Him to see the future as if it were present. I do not believe that everything was or is *present* to God. But He saw the *future* as fully and completely as He does the present.

It is important we realize that God did not foresee the future as a passive observer. He did not simply raise the curtain of time and look at a future that was already fixed before He looked. He planned the future. But when He planned the future with regard to human beings who were made in His image and thus were personal beings with a mind, heart, and will, He chose to work with them in accord with the *influence* and *response* model. He has a *cause* and *effect* relationship with the material universe, but such is not the case with human personality.

The cross of Christ was a predestinated event. At the same time, numerous human beings were involved in one way or another in the effecting of the event. Since human beings with free will were involved, in the crucifixion event, we must understand the role of God's foreknowledge in predestinated events. It is important for us to keep in mind the observations made in the previous paragraph as well as what was stated in Chapter 15.

It is the kind of God that I have just attempted to describe [a God who was not a mere spectator] who foresaw the future from all eternity. As He foresaw the future, He saw it as it would progressively unfold from: (1) The result of His creative activity and His divine influence. (2) The result of the devastating influence of sin. (3)The result of the response that human beings would give as a result of the redemptive work of Jesus Christ, the ministry of the Holy Spirit, the ministry of the Word of God, and the ministry of the redeemed. (4) The result of all of the influences that would come from all sources outside Himself. (5) The result of all the influence that He would bring on people through His power and His infinite wisdom. He saw, then, everything that He sees and is doing now. He is the same God now that He was then. Everything that He is doing now is just as real as it would be if He had not known it in advance.[2]

God's omniscience and wisdom furnished Him with all the information and the "know how" that was needed for Him to arrange the death and suffering of Jesus Christ as the means of atonement for the sins of the world. With the aid of His infinite knowledge and wisdom, the determinate counsel was able to predetermine the crucifixion of Christ in eternity past. In this arrangement *foreknowledge* was aiding, but *foreknowledge* as *foreknowledge* did not bear a causal relationship to the plan for the crucifixion to occur. Without *foreknowledge,* the determinate counsel could not have prearranged and predetermined the plan.

I think I have shown that there is no necessity whatever to give *foreknowledge* in Acts 2:23 a *causal* force with the result that it would be synonymous with *predestination.* I have read the comments on the use of *proginōskō* and *prognōsis* in several commentaries on Acts 2:23 and 1 Peter 1:20. I have tried to understand the reason that Calvinists consider it a valid and necessary conclusion to understand *predestination, election,* and *foreknowledge* to be essentially synonymous. I have also read the explanations given in several lexicons and theological dictionaries on these words. Most of what they say is based on the usage of *proginōskō* and *prognōsis* in Acts 2:23 and 1 Peter 1:20.

The verb *proginōskō* occurs three times in the Septuagint (Wisdom 6:13; 8:8; and 18:6). The meaning of *proginōskō* in the apocryphal Book of Wisdom is "to foreknow" or "to know in advance."

The noun *prognōsis* is found in the apocryphal book, Judith in 9:6 and 11:9. The use in 11:9 is understood as foreknowledge. The only use of the word *prognōsis* outside the New Testament that I have found is used to support the view that foreknowledge is an equivalent of predestination is found in Judith 9:6. Paul Jacobs and Hartmut Krienke give the meaning "of God's foreknowledge decreeing the fall of the Egyptians."[3] They take "foreknowledge" in Judith 9:6 to be the equivalent of "decreeing." *The Theological Dictionary of The New Testament* would be in agreement. On *prognōsis,* it reads, "It is found in the LXX at Jdt. 9:6 with reference to the predeterminative knowledge of God."[4]

It will be helpful to look in Judith 9:5, 6:

> **5** For thou hast done these things and those that went before and those that followed; thou hast designed the things that are now, and those that are to come. Yea, the things thou didst intend came to pass, **6** and the things thou didst will presented themselves and said, 'Lo, we are here'; for all thy ways are prepared in advance, and thy judgment is with foreknowledge (*prognōsis*).[5]

I have found no defense given for the understanding that in Judith 9:6 *foreknowledge* is synonymous with *predestination.* It is true that predestination is spoken of in verses 5 and 6. But there is no reason to believe that *foreknowledge* has the same meaning as *predestination.* I think the meaning is that God's judgments were made in eternity past with the aid of His foreknowledge.

> Who [Christ as a lamb without blemish and without spot] verily was foreordained before the foundation of the world, but was manifest in these last times for you (1 Pet. 1:20).

The word that is translated "foreordained" in 1 Peter 1:20 is *proginōskō.* The RSV translates it as "destined." The NIV has "chosen." The NEB translates "predestined." The NASB settles for "foreknown." I believe that the words *foreordained, destined, chosen,* and *predestined* are all appropriate words to apply to the fact that the atoning work of Christ on the cross was *prearranged, preplanned,* and *predetermined* in eternity past. God was not caught off guard by the fall of the race into sin. The plan of redemption was already made and determined before the fall of Adam and Eve took place in the chronological order of events. What was planned and determined in eternity past took place when Jesus died on the cross. What was in the mind of God in eternity past, was "manifested for us in these last times."

When properly understood, I do not have any trouble with the words *destined, chosen, pre-arranged, preplanned, predestined,* and *predetermined.* Not only do I not have trouble with these words; I am as convinced of their truth as any Calvinist is. I do have a problem with translating *proginōskō* "predestined," or "chosen," or any words with a similar meaning.

Even if the true meaning in 1 Peter 1:20 is "predestined," it should be translated "foreknown." "To foreknow" is the proper translation of *proginōskō.* To give it the meaning "foreordained," "destined," "chosen," or "predestined" is an interpretive translation. The Greek word *proginōskō* and the English word "foreknow" have exactly the same possibilities of meaning foreordained. When *proginōskō* is translated as "foreordination" or some word that is equivalent, the translator has become an exegete He is giving a debatable meaning of *proginōskō* as the translation. Exegesis should be found in commentaries, not translations. If *proginōskō* means foreordained, it is the responsibility of the exegete to defend the interpretation with evidence. I am not aware of any strong defenses of the idea that "predestined" is one of the established meanings of the word *proginōsko* The translation "foreordained" shows an influence of Calvinism to make *foreknowledge* synonymous with *predestination.* When this twist is given to *foreknowledge,* in the end *predestination* becomes the foundation for *foreknowledge.* God knows the future because He has *predestinated* it.

Whatever should be taken from 1 Peter 1:20 can be properly understood by taking *proginōskō* to mean *foreknown.* The plan of God to provide atonement through the death of Christ was foreknown by God in eternity past. For this to have been *foreknown* meant, of course, Jesus was chosen for the purpose of providing atonement by His death and that it was *preplanned, predetermined,* and *prearranged.* All of these concepts, while true, are true by necessary inference from the nature of God and from the direct teachings of Acts 2:22 and 4:28, not by the meaning and use of *proginōskō.*

Calvinism's insistence that *proginōskō* and *prognōsis* are to be taken as synonymous with predestination is without foundation both from biblical usage and from use outside of the Bible.

ROMANS 8:29

> For whom he did foreknow, he also did predestinate *to be* conformed to the image of
> his Son, that he might be the firstborn among many brethren.

The ones that are referred to by "for whom he did foreknow" are "them who are called according to his purpose" in verse 28. Those who have now been called according to his purpose were foreknown by God in eternity past. The explanation that I will give of "foreknow" (*proginōskō*) on this verse is taken from my commentary on Romans.[6]

From the standpoint of conditional election, there are two possible ways to understand foreknowledge as it is used in 8:29. Meyer explains: "God has fore-*known* those who would not oppose to his gracious calling the resistance of unbelief, but would follow its drawing; thereafter He has fore-*ordained* them to eternal salvation; and when the time had come for the execution of His saving counsel, has called them, etc." (ver. 30).[7]

Godet offers the same view, worded somewhat differently, "There is but one answer: foreknown as sure to fulfill the condition of salvation, viz. *faith;* so foreknown as His by *faith*.[8]

Lenski takes a somewhat different approach concerning the word know (Greek *ginōskō*). The meaning is "'to know with affection and with a resultant affect.'" He goes on to say that to add the prefix 'fore' (Greek *pro*) "dates this affectionate knowing back to eternity."[9]

If there is any doubt where Lenski stands on election, the following statement from him should settle the issue: "If it be asked why God did not foreknow, foreordain, call, justify the rest, the biblical answer is found in Matt. 23:37 and similar passages: God did not exclude them, but despite all that God could do *they* excluded themselves."[10]

Lenski's view is probably the correct view. "Whom he foreknew" speaks of knowing persons rather than simply knowing something about them. God foreknew the elect with affection, or He foreknew them as being His. There is no conflict whatsoever with this understanding of foreknowledge and conditional election.

What Meyer and Godet say about foreknowledge as referring to foreknowledge of faith is a necessary inference. To know a person implies a time of getting acquainted with that person. If God foreknew the elect as being His, it is necessarily inferred that this foreknowledge presupposes the person's belief in Jesus Christ as his Lord and Savior.

ROMANS 11:2

God has not cast away his people whom he foreknew.

In this verse, the reference is to the *affectionate foreknowing* of Israel as the Covenant People of God. The emphasis in this verse is the knowledge of corporate Israel as the people of God.

It would be interesting to develop foreknowledge in this verse further, but that would involve a discussion of the place of Israel in the redemptive plan of God. That would lead us away from our present concern, which is how God's foreknowledge fits in with individual election and predestination.

Romans 11:2 illustrates for us the use of foreknowledge as God's affectionate *foreknowing*. But it does not add additional light on foreknowledge and individual election.

1 PETER 1:2

Elect according to the foreknowledge of God the father. . . .

If we were to understand *prognōsis* (foreknowledge) as meaning predestination here, that would mean that election would be grounded in predestination. I think I have shown up to this point that there are no grounds for believing that foreknowledge is synonymous with predestination. This verse merely tells us that election is according to foreknowledge. It does not tell us what in foreknowledge formed the basis of election. It does not settle whether election was conditional or unconditional.

The New Testament Use and Meaning of Election

The word *eklegomai* occurs twenty-one times in the New Testament. *Eklektos* occurs twenty-three times. *Eklogē* occurs seven times. Many of the occurrences when we find these words do not have any bearing on the New Testament doctrine of election. However, I will examine every occurrence which has a bearing on this study.

The Word *Eklegomai*

IN THE GOSPEL OF JOHN

This word is found in John 6:70; 13:18; 15:16, 19. I have already dealt with these verses in Chapter 16 under the heading "The Occurrences of the Word *Eklegomai*."[11] *Eklegomai* is the verb form of the word for "elect." In the occurrences in John, it is translated "chosen." In each of these cases the reference is to the Twelve Apostles. The reference is that Jesus had chosen them to be His apostles. There is no problem for conditional election if it did include election to salvation. For additional comments, see the treatment referred to above in the previous chapter.

Of the occurrences of this word in the New Testament, the only other place that would help shed light on the doctrine of election is Ephesians 1:4.

EPHESIANS 1:4

> According as God hath chosen us in him before the foundation of the world, that we should be holy and without blame before him in love.

This verse is probably the most important verse in the Bible on the subject of election. It makes very clear that believers were chosen in Christ before the foundation of the world. In no uncertain terms, it puts election in eternity past.

From the context of Scripture, it seems to me that the "us" is to be taken as a group of individuals who were chosen *individually*. I think Paul makes it very clear that election is *individual*, not *corporate* in Romans 9. For a more thorough discussion, I would refer the reader to my comments in Chapter 16 under the Heading, "Paul's Appeal to the Jews to See That Election Is Individual, Not Corporate." To support my case that election is individual, I will once again give the quotation that I gave in Chapter 16 from Thomas R. Schreiner which relates to Paul's treatment of individuals in Romans 9:15-21. He calls attention to the use of the singular in these verses. He explains:

> The word *whom (hon)* is singular, indicating that specific individuals upon whom God has mercy are in view. The singular is also present in the reference that Paul draws

from Romans 9:15, in 9:16. God's mercy does not depend on "the one who wills, nor the one who runs." The conclusion to all of 9:14-17 in 9:18 utilizes the singular once again: "God has mercy on whom he wants to have mercy, and he hardens whom he wants to harden." In the same vein 9:19 continues the thought: "Who *(tis)* resists his will?" And Paul uses the singular when he speaks of one vessel being made for honor and another for dishonor (9:21). Those who say that Paul is referring only to corporate groups do not have an adequate explanation as to why Paul uses the singular again and again in Romans 9.[12]

What is of particular importance in Ephesians 1:4 is that Paul says, "He has chosen us in him." We are chosen in Christ. He does not say that we were chosen *to be in Christ*. At this point I believe that Calvinism is in trouble. In Calvinism, the elect were chosen by God as His very own *before* the decree to provide atonement. They were His at that very moment. In both Supralapsarianism and Infralapsarianism, the decision to elect some and reprobate others *precedes* the decree to provide atonement.[13]

Calvinism says, "Chosen by God as His very own before the provision of atonement." Following this election, according to Calvinism, God decreed to provide atonement for those who were elected. Then He decreed that those who were elected would be regenerated. This would guarantee that they would be efficaciously brought to exercise faith in Christ. It was decreed that upon the experience of this efficaciously guaranteed faith the person would be justified and placed in Christ.

This puts Calvinism in serious contradiction with Paul. Calvinism says that the elect were chosen by God as His very own before the decree to provide atonement. Paul says, "The elect were chosen in Christ."

I believe that Arminius was right when he said, "God can 'previously love and affectionately regard as His own' no sinner unless He has foreknown him in Christ, and looked upon him as a believer in Christ."[14]

Arminius goes on to make a statement which I think is very insightful. He explains, "For, if God could will to any one eternal life, without respect to the Mediator, He could also give eternal life, without the satisfaction made by the Mediator."[15]

I believe that Arminius puts his finger on what is probably *the most serious problem in Calvinism*. For the most part, Calvinists have been advocates and defenders of the satisfaction view of atonement. For election to precede, in God's plan, the provision of atonement violates the foundation on which the satisfaction view of atonement rests.

The satisfaction view of atonement insists that the holiness of God requires that *the guilt problem must be solved* before God can enter into fellowship with a fallen member of the human race. The only way that can happen is for a person to have the death and righteousness of Christ applied to his or her account. That takes place when a person places his faith in Jesus Christ and is placed in union with Christ.

It is not the prerogative of Sovereign grace to enter into a personal relationship with a person *apart from the application of the death and righteousness of Christ* to his account. If that is the case, it was not the prerogative of sovereign grace in eternity past to efficaciously and affectively know or elect a member of the human race apart from foreknowing him or her to be in Christ.[16] Calvinism is harmed rather than helped by Ephesians 1:4.

The Word *Haireomai*

2 THESSALONIANS 2:13

> But we are bound to give thanks alway to God for you, brethren beloved of the Lord, because God hath from the beginning chosen you to salvation through sanctification of the Spirit and belief of the truth.

Haireomai occurs only three times in the New Testament. The other two places (Phil. 1:22 and Heb. 11:25) refer to choices by human beings. The related word *haritizō* is used only one time in the New Testament. It is found in Matthew 12:18 in a quotation from Isaiah 42:1. In this use it is said by God the Father to the Son, "Behold my servant, whom I have chosen."

There does not seem to be any special significance in the use of *haireomai* rather than *eklegomai* in 2 Thessalonians. There is some thought given to the view that "from the beginning" refers to "the beginning of Paul's ministry among them." Others take "from the beginning" to refer to eternity past. Whichever view is taken will present no problem to conditional election. The salvation spoken of was experienced by "belief of the truth."

The Word *Eklogē*

This is the noun form. It refers to those who are chosen or elected. It is important that we remember that election refers both to our election by God in eternity past and to the election of God in time. When the New Testament speaks of a person (or persons) as being among the "elect" or "chosen," it means that they have been chosen by God already. People whom God foreknows to be people who will be saved in the future are not referred to as elect.

The use of the word *eklogē* in the following references assumes that the people under consideration have already been saved: Matthew 24:22, 24, 31; Mark 13:20, 22, 27; Luke 18:7; Romans 8:33; 16:13; Colossians 3:12; 2 Timothy 2:10; Titus 1:1; 1 Peter 1:2; 2:9; and Revelation 17:14. It is true that those who are saved in time were chosen by God in eternity past. But no person is designated as being "elect" or "chosen" unless he has already been saved.

The only use of the noun *eklogē* that is helpful in formulating the doctrine of election in eternity past is 1 Peter 1:2. It occurs in the plural form. The meaning is "elect ones" or "chosen ones." Peter goes on to tell us that this election took place in accordance with *foreknowledge*. While it clearly tells us that this election took place in eternity past, it does not address the subject of whether this election was conditional or unconditional.

The Question of Whether Election Was Conditioned on Faith

It is true that the Bible does not specifically say that foreknown faith was the condition of election in eternity past. The Calvinist is correct when he says that the Bible does not tell us why God chose the elect. However, silence on why God chose the elect gives no support for unconditional election. To recognize that God did not spell out for us in the Bible why He chose the elect is not the same as saying that we cannot know whether there was a condition and what that condition was. Since God is the same yesterday, today, and forever means that if we know why God chooses people now, we can reason back to why God chose the elect in eternity past.

I think Arminius has said it well:

> Hence, God acknowledges no one, in Christ and for Christ's sake, as His own, unless that person is in Christ. He who is not in Christ, can not be loved in Christ. But no one is in Christ, except by faith; for Christ dwells in our hearts by faith, and we are ingrafted and incorporated in him by faith. It follows then that God acknowledges His own, and chooses to eternal life no sinner, unless He considers him as a believer in Christ, and as made one with him by faith.[17]

In commenting on "the conformity to Christ" that is predestinated in Romans 8:29, Arminius explains:

> Therefore, no one is predestinated by God to that conformity, unless he is considered as a believer, unless one may claim that faith itself is included in that conformity which believers have with Christ—which would be absurd, because that faith can by no means be attributed to Christ, for it is faith in him, and in God through him; it is faith in reference to reconciliation, redemption, and the remission of sins.[18]

It is abundantly clear that salvation is by faith now. I do not think I need to give further development for the case that if salvation is conditional now, it necessarily leads to the conclusion that election in eternity past was conditional. The burden of proof is upon those who think otherwise.

A Clarification on the Question of Ground and Condition

In our study of atonement and justification, difference was made between the *ground* of justification and the *condition* of justification.[19] The same distinction must be made in election. The *ground* of election is that God foreknew us as being in Christ (in union with Christ). Thus, He chose us *in Christ*. That is what Ephesians 1:4 tells us. Since the condition for being in Christ is *faith in Christ*, it is necessarily implied that God foreknew that the person would meet the *condition* of faith in Christ.

The Extent of the Offer of Salvation

WHERE THE WORD *CALLED* IS USED OR IMPLIED

In Matthew 22:14, Jesus said, "For many are called, but few are chosen." In Acts 17:30, Paul said, "And the times of this ignorance God winked at; but now commandeth all men everywhere to repent." It is generally agreed, even by Calvinists that there is a general call that makes the gospel available to all people.

Some attention needs to be given to the use of the word "called" in the epistles. I will borrow from what I wrote in my Romans commentary. Calvinists make a point of saying that whenever the call is mentioned in the epistles, it only refers to believers. My response is that to refer to believers as being "called ones" does not mean that the call has not been extended to anyone else. A speaker at a special occasion may address the audience as invited guests. The only thing that he is affirming is that those who are present have been invited. They are not intruders. It does not mean that no one else was invited. When believers are referred to as "called," it is not necessary to conclude that others have not been called.[20]

THE APPEAL TO WHOEVER (KJV, WHOSOEVER) WILL

To understand the thrust of "whoever will," we need to remind ourselves again that among the Jews in New Testament times the prevailing view was that all Jews were automatically saved by the Abrahamic Covenant. We must keep this in mind when we consider how a Jewish audience (Jn. 3:15, 16) would have understood an appeal to "whoever will believe in Jesus." It certainly means more than a simple, "Salvation is offered to anyone and everyone who will believe and receive it." The design is to break through the concept of corporate election or salvation and let them know that salvation is on an individual basis. It is for whoever will and only whoever will. The emphasis on only is strong because it is intended to bring an end to the concept of unconditional corporate election or salvation. The aim is to show that salvation is on an individual basis instead of a corporate basis.

John 4:13, 14 is spoken to the Samaritan woman. In view of the conflict between the Jews and the Samaritans, the "whoever" in this verse is meant to assure the Samaritan woman that the life-giving water Jesus was offering was for her too.

Romans 9:33 comes at the end of a chapter in which Paul had poured out his heart to the Jews who had been blinded by the idea of a corporate election wherein all Jews were automatically saved. He desperately wanted to see his kinsmen saved. The "whoever" of this verse is intended both to show that the salvation offer was for the Jews, but also to emphasize that it was made only to whoever would believe in Jesus as Messiah, Lord, and Savior.

In Romans 10:11-13, the "whoever" is intended to make known that the offer extends to Greeks (All Gentiles are implied.) as well as Jews. But when the reference is made to Jews the intent is to make known that while it was a genuine offer of salvation it was also intended to emphasize that only "whoever," among the Jews, would believe in Jesus Christ as Messiah, Lord, and Savior would be saved. It was also making the claim that there was no difference between the way the Gentiles would be saved and the way of salvation for the Jews.

The contexts of these passages do not give the slightest hint that this "whoever will" is only offered to a "select few." Neither Jesus nor Paul inferred that though this offer was to everyone, it had no real possibility of being received by anyone except those whom God had already unconditionally chosen. There is no suggestion that the only hope of a positive response rested on a person first being regenerated.

The Extent of the Atonement

Classical Calvinists are either Supralapsarians or Infralapsarians. Both Supralapsarians and Infralapsarians believe in limited atonement. They believe that the decree to elect preceded the decree to provide atonement. The decree to provide atonement was made specifically for the purpose of providing atonement for the elect. From their viewpoint it is better to speak of the *intent* of atonement than to speak of the *extent* of atonement. But either way you put it, Jesus died only to make atonement for the elect.

Sublapsarian Calvinists believe that God decreed the provision of atonement for all mankind.[21] This was followed by the decree to elect some unconditionally for salvation. Calvinists who believe this would reject that point of Classical Calvinism referred to as limited atonement. These are referred to as Four Point Calvinists. Some who have advocated this position say that God provided salvation for everybody. Nobody responded. Then, God decreed to unconditionally elect some.

In the first edition of his theology text, Henry C. Thiessen adopted a modified form of Sublapsarianism. He explains:

> We believe that the decrees are in this order: 1. The decree to create, 2. The decree to permit the fall, 3. The decree to provide salvation for all, and 4. The decree to apply that salvation to some, to those who believe.[22]

Thiessen's "modified form of Sublapsarianism" I find to be consistent with Arminianism. I accept it as my own.

I find it interesting that many who believe in unconditional election think that the case for unlimited atonement is so compelling that they accept it. However, it seems to me that limited atonement fits more logically with unconditional election and the Calvinistic scheme.

I do not deem it necessary to give a thorough defense of the doctrine of unlimited atonement. The case must be strong and obvious since there are many who believe in unconditional election and yet they part with Classical Calvinism and adopt unlimited atonement. This is the position of Augustus Hopkins Strong,[23] and Millard J. Erickson.[24] Henry C. Thiessen[25] is one who believes in both conditional election and unlimited atonement. He did join the Calvinists on the doctrine of perseverance. Robert E. Picirilli, a Classical Arminian, gives thorough and excellent treatment of the subject of the extent of atonement in his unpublished manuscript, *God's Decrees, Our Faith: Calvinism, Arminianism, and the Theology of Salvation.*[26]

Another reason I will not give an extensive treatment of unlimited atonement is that no one will ever become a Calvinist because he was first convinced of limited atonement and then embraced the other points of Calvinism. Even when he is convinced of other points, he will have some difficulty with limited atonement.

I will now give a brief defense of unlimited atonement.

JOHN 3:16

For God so loved the world that he gave his only begotten Son, that whosoever believeth in him should not perish, but have everlasting life.

The only way anyone would ever question that "world" in this verse meant anything other than every human being is that he comes to the verse with a theological conviction that will not allow him to believe that. In this case the burden of proof is on the person who wants to place a restriction upon the scope of the word "world."

1 TIMOTHY 2:6

Who gave himself a ransom for all, to be testified in due time.

The only possible reason for understanding "a ransom for all" any other way than that Jesus' death was a ransom paid for the sins of the whole race is that the person has a conflict between that interpretation and some other doctrine. This verse occurs in a context where Paul says, "Who [God] will have all men to be saved" (Verse 4). The ransom was provided for "all." The "all" of verse 6 is the same as the "all" of verse 4.

HEBREWS 2:9

But we see Jesus, who was made a little lower than the angels for the suffering of death, crowned with glory and honour; that he by the grace of God should taste death for every man.

The burden of proof is upon the person who would place a restriction upon "every man." The only natural reading of Hebrews 2:9 is that Jesus died for every human being.

1 JOHN 2:2

> And he is the propitiation for our sins: and not for our's only, but for *the sins* of the whole world.

No one should deny that the most natural way to understand this verse is to reckon that the propitiatory sacrifice was intended to make atonement for the sins of the whole world. The only people who would think otherwise are those who believe in either Supralapsarianism or Infralapsarianism. The only reason for taking a verse whose meaning is apparent, and applying a strained interpretation (i.e., trying to make it fit the idea of limited atonement) would be their belief that the decree to elect preceded the decree to provide atonement. In such thinking, God decided whom He would save. Then, He decided to make atonement for those He had elected.

Theological Arguments Against Unlimited Atonement

It is thought by Classical Calvinists that to hold to the satisfaction view of atonement precludes the possibility of unlimited atonement. They claim there are two insurmountable problems for those who believe in a satisfaction view of atonement if they at the same time reject limited atonement: (1) The only logical alternative to limited atonement for one who believes in the satisfaction view of atonement would be universal salvation. (2) If, as described by the satisfaction view of atonement, Christ died for those who are never saved, it would mean double payment with respect to those who spend eternity in Hell. I dealt with this in Chapter 11.[27] For the convenience of the reader I am using that treatment with modifications made to suit the use here.

UNIVERSAL SALVATION OR LIMITED ATONEMENT A NECESSARY RESULT

It is argued that if Jesus paid the full penalty for the sins of the whole race, then all for whom Christ died must of necessity be saved. This is true since His death settles their account and therefore forms the necessary basis for their forgiveness. Either Christ died for everybody and everybody would be saved, or He died only for the elect and only the elect will be saved, or so the argument goes. It is thought that for one who believes in the satisfaction view of atonement that the only way to escape universal salvation is to believe in limited atonement.

The answer is found in the kind of substitution involved. Christ died for the whole world in a *provisionary* sense. He suffered the penal wrath of God for sin, but that fact alone does not place His death on everybody's account. It is effectual for the individual only as it is placed on a person's account. It can be placed on a person's account only as a result of a union with Christ. Union with Christ is conditioned on faith.

The Calvinist may want to insist that the objection is valid and that Christ died only for the elect. The only way this argument could have any validity would be to deny the possibility of provisionary atonement. If there can be no provisionary atonement, it does follow that if Christ died for a person *his justification is never provisionary but always real.*

In explaining the view of limited atonement, Louis Berkhof comments: "The Calvinists teach that the atonement meritoriously secured the application of the work of redemption to those for whom it was intended and their complete salvation is certain."[28]

A close look at what Berkhof said will show that it does not rule out the provisionary principle in atonement. He says that the atonement "makes certain" the salvation of those for whom it was intended. He did not say that the atonement automatically saved everybody for whom it was intended. Calvinists do not teach that the elect are justified before they experience faith. They teach that the person for whom Christ died will of a certainty be justified, but they do not consider a person justified until he experiences faith as the condition of justification. Thus, atonement is provisionary until the time it is applied. The only way to deny the provisionary nature of atonement is to consider *all* people for whom Christ died to be justified *before* they experience faith.

Once we accept that atonement is *provisionary,* we invalidate the objection that penal satisfaction either leads to universalism or limited atonement. Provisionary atonement applied on the condition of faith and on the grounds of a union with Christ answers this objection and sustains the penal satisfaction view.

DOUBLE PAYMENT WITH REGARD TO SINNERS WHO GO TO HELL

The discussion above about provisionary atonement and union with Christ answers this objection. The death of Christ is not on the sinner's account who goes to Hell. His account does not show a double payment. It is true that his sins were paid for *provisionally,* but there is no problem with justice which forbids collection of double payment as long as there is no double entry on the person's account.

The Desire of God and the Salvation of Sinners

I believe we are to conclude that God deeply desires His message of salvation to go out to all people, and He desires a positive response from all who hear this message. There are two passages that speak particularly of this concern of God. These are 1 Timothy 2:1-4 and 2 Peter 3:9.

> I exhort therefore, that, first of all, supplications, prayers, intercessions, and giving of thanks, be made for all men:
> 2 For kings, and for all that are in authority; that we may lead a quiet and peaceable life in all godliness and honesty.
> 3 For this is good and acceptable in the sight of God our Saviour;
> 4 Who will have all men to be saved, and to come unto the knowledge of the truth (1 Timothy 2:1-4).

I think it is obvious that the only limitation on how many and which people are saved is: (1) Our failure to confront people with the gospel, and (2) The failure of people who hear the gospel to respond properly to the gospel. Verse 4 is not telling us that God has *planned* that all people be saved. Rather it tells us that it is His *desire* that all men be saved. The thought that it means anything other than that God has a desire for all people to be saved would never come up unless a person approaches these verses with a theological bias against this view. Nothing in these verses suggests that God does not desire that all people be saved.

> The Lord is not slack concerning his promise, as some men count slackness; but is longsuffering to us-ward, not willing that any should perish, but that all should come to repentance (2 Pet. 3:9).

In verses 3 and 4, Peter reminds us that there would be scoffers who would say, "Where is the promise of his coming? For since the fathers fell asleep, all things continue as *they were* from the creation." These scoffers misunderstand the delay of Christ's return. In verse 9, he tells us that we are not to consider that this delay means that Jesus is not coming again. Rather, the delay is an indication that God is giving sinners time to repent. When Peter says that God is "not willing that any should perish," the word for "willing" (*boulomai*) means "to intend," or "to purpose." It is not God's purpose to plan to *unconditionally* bring about the eternal death of anybody. He does not unconditionally and sovereignly choose some for damnation.

Conclusion

I recognize that there are many Calvinists who are very strongly committed to evangelism and worldwide missions. I respect them for this and I appreciate it. At the same time, I think Calvinism most surely dulls the concern of many. Clearly, in the teaching of unconditional election, obedience or lack of obedience to the Great Commission will not change who or how many people are saved.

As Arminians, we should feel rebuked by those Calvinists who are faithful in their obedience to the Great Commission. If conditional election is correct, and I believe it is, we must get under the burden of reaching lost people for Christ. We must feel deeply about it. We must feel convicted about it. And we must do better.

18

Communicating the Christian Message in a Postmodern Culture

While works on systematic theology would not usually have a chapter on "Communicating the Christian Message in a Postmodern Culture," I believe that, in this book, the stage has been set for such a treatment. I feel compelled to address the subject. As an aid in accomplishing this purpose, I will review what has been said earlier in the book, particularly in Chapters 2 and 3, about modernism and postmodernism. I do this for two reasons: (1) I assume that some will read this chapter who have not read the rest of the book. For that reason, this chapter must be capable of standing alone. (2) For those who have read the rest of the book, this review of the material will refresh his or her mind as to my understanding of the current scene.

It is hard for a young adult to imagine the changes that have occurred in the last three quarters of a century. As I said earlier in this book, my memory takes me back to the 1930s and the 1940s. It is nothing new for a person who has passed seventy to stress how much change has taken place in his lifetime. People have always talked that way. As Robert H. Bork tells us: "Regret for the golden days of the past is probably universal and as old as the human race. No doubt the elders of the prehistoric tribes thought that the younger generation's cave paintings were not up to the standard that they had set." While this kind of thinking on the part of senior citizens is not new, I think what has taken place in my lifetime is unique. In continuing his comment, Bork points out the fallacy of thinking that everything always gets worse. He explains, "Given this straight-line degeneration for so many millennia, by now our culture should be not merely rubble but dust. Obviously it is not." Then he makes a very telling statement about our times. He comments, "Until recently our artists did better than the cave painters."[1]

Bork's comment on recent art brings to my mind the privilege that my wife, Fay, and I had when we were in Russia in 1996. We had toured many art museums throughout Russia and marveled at the paintings of many master painters, including Rembrandt.

At the Russia Museum in St. Petersburg, we saw a display of art from Great Britain produced in the 1990s. One of these works was simply a canvas painted white. Some were given titles, but several were simply referred to as "untitled," obviously because the artists thought no name could describe reality. The message was that life has no meaning and purpose. One painting was titled "Abandoned." This artist must have thought that human beings were abandoned in the universe and that there is no truth that sets people free. His was a picture of despair. Compared to the great classical works of art, these recent British works were pitiful.

Instead of ridicule for these artists and their works, we should have compassion. These works of art, or we might say "non-art" are a commentary on the times. They tell us of the despair of the human heart. We cannot simply condemn this kind of art out of existence. As long as post-modernism gives rise to expressions of art there will be no significant change in art. We must learn to address the despair and hunger in people's hearts with the Truth that sets people free (Jn. 8:32).

What happened in the last half of the twentieth century cannot be explained as a simple phenomenon of culture. We are talking about the most fundamental kind of change that a culture can go through. We are talking about a paradigm shift. The secular culture has experienced a paradigm shift in my lifetime. Few generations of people have had the *privilege* or the *problem* of being aware that they have lived through a *paradigm* shift.

There have been only a few paradigm shifts in the Western world that have had a major influence on the grass roots of society. It would take someone whose knowledge of history is better than mine to make a complete list of paradigm changes. I do not think it is necessary for the list to be complete to help us see that what has happened during my generation's sojourn on this planet is unique in the history of thought.

The Paradigm Shift from the Old Covenant to the New Covenant

The change from the Mosaic Covenant to the New Covenant represents a paradigm shift. In Galatians 3:19–4:7, Paul likens the experience of Israel under the tutelage of the Mosaic Law to that of the Greek or Roman boy under a *paidagōgos*. In Paul's thinking, God viewed His people as immature when they were under the Mosaic Law. Under the New Covenant, we are delivered from the *paidagōgos* (Gal. 3:25). God now deals with us as with adult sons (Gal. 4:1-10). There were some Jewish people who lived during the time that this paradigm shift occurred.[2]

We are not to understand that there was enmity between the Old Covenant approach to the New Covenant approach. However, there were complications that accompanied this transition. A reading of the Book of Acts and the New Testament epistles testifies to the deep struggles and conflicts that existed during the time this paradigm shift occurred.

Paradigm Shifts in the History of Christendom

The church went through a subtle paradigm shift when it moved away from the simple approach that grew out of the New Testament to the more complicated and complex approach of the Medieval church. The Protestant Reformation on the Continent and the English Reformation in England represented a major paradigm shift.

THE PARADIGM SHIFT FROM THE GEOCENTRIC TO THE HELIOCENTRIC VIEW OF THE UNIVERSE

The shift from the Aristotelian-Ptolemaic (geocentric) to the Copernican (heliocentric) view of the universe had a major impact on both the church and the non-church world. The main figures in this shift were Nikolaus Copernicus (1473-1543), Johannes Kepler (1571-1630), Galileo Galilei (1564-1643), and Isaac Newton (1642-1727). All of these men operated within the framework of the Christian worldview.

These men did not intend to undermine Christianity. However, by the time of Newton, some were beginning to feel that, in the light of the scientific explanations of the universe, they no longer needed God to explain the universe. A trend was set in motion that would lead many toward eliminating God from their thinking. The end result of this paradigm shift was a division between the theological world and the secular world. Or, we could say there was a division between the church world and the non-church world. The church no longer had a monopoly on education. Secularism exerted itself in the university. Autonomous reason had no obligation to either the church or the Bible. Reason without the aid of divine revelation could answer all of the questions of human beings. Autonomous reason was all that was needed.

THE CHRISTIAN PARADIGM VERSUS THE MODERNIST PARADIGM

My main interest is in how this drama was played out on the grass roots level of society. For a long time the tendency among the masses was to look at philosophers as strange people. It was thought they were so far removed from reality that they would have no significant influence on society.

I can remember that sometime back in the 1940s I read an article in a newspaper in which some professor in a university somewhere was advocating free love (sex outside of marriage). I knew, at the time, there were those who were guilty of sex outside marriage, but I never dreamed there would ever be a mass movement that would stamp its approval on sex outside marriage. It has happened. I was proved wrong. The thinking of the professor and his ilk have triumphed. *Thinkers do have an impact on the way the average person thinks, feels, and acts.*

It will be beneficial for us to trace the steps of the influence of thinkers on the grass roots of society. By the time of Newton's contribution, in the thinking of many, science had become autonomous. Empiricism was emerging as a challenger to the Christian worldview. The battle lines were being drawn. Soon, secularism would challenge Christianity's claim of having the true worldview. Reason would seek to triumph over the authority of revelation. Reason had made great gains in science. It was thought that reason would eventually find the answer for all human need.

Many in England and America were not willing to completely abandon all religious concerns. They became Deists. Eventually, deism faded as a viable worldview. People with these leanings tended to go to either a complete secularism or some form of theological liberalism.

With the demise of deism, modernism no longer felt the need to find a place for God in its worldview thinking. Modernism became completely secular. A person might believe in a "god" of sorts. That would be all right as long as that belief was completely divorced from his or her worldview thinking.

To understand the effect that the conflict between modernism and Christianity had on the grass roots level we need to review the areas of common ground and the areas of difference between Christianity and modernism.

THE QUESTION OF TRUTH

Both Christianity and modernism believed that Truth existed. They were in serious disagreement with each other about what the Truth was.

THE PLACE OF REASON

Both Christianity and modernism believed in the validity and the importance of reason. Both were strongly committed to the law of non-contradiction. The difference was in the data that was admissible for rational reflection. Christianity believed that the data of divine revelation was admissible for rational reflection. Modernism did not believe in divine revelation. The only data needed was the data supplied by observation and experience. Reason was autonomous. Reason was adequate. Reason could and would find the answers. We were on our way. The coming of utopia seemed inevitable, and all barriers that had not yet been removed would surely be removed in time.

THE PLACE OF MORALS

Christianity believes that the holy nature of God who is our Creator and Sovereign Lord lays the foundation for a moral nature to reality. Special divine revelation gives us authoritative moral teachings. Every human being has general revelation. General revelation writes the moral law of God on the heart of every human being (Rom. 2:14, 15). Those who have the Old and/or the New Testament have special revelation.

Modernism believed there was a moral "nature" (character or constitution) to nature. Since it believed there was a moral "nature" to nature, modernism was able to benefit from the light of general revelation. Modernism was able to read the moral revelation of God from nature, but it did not give credit to God in its credit line. Since modernism read the moral message from nature, there was not a strong conflict between modernism and Christianity on basic morality. Modernism and Christianity parted ways when it came to moral guilt and judgment. But they were not at war with each other on basic morality.

No mass movement challenged the moral ideals of the Ten Commandments prior to 1960. To speak figuratively, you might say there were some brush fires here and there before, but the fire was not blazing through the whole society before 1960. There were many vile and wicked people before 1960, but lying and adultery were not viewed with approbation. The challenge to the moral ideals of the Ten Commandments did not permeate the fabric of society before 1960.

THE PLACE OF BEAUTY, EXCELLENCE, AND IDEALS

God is the epitome of that which is beautiful and excellent. Therefore, Christianity is strong in its emphasis on beauty and ideals. Modernism scored high marks on beauty, excellence, and ideals. There is something instinctive in human nature that grows out of being made in the image of God that points in the direction of beauty, excellence, and ideals. Since modernism did not deny that nature had a "nature," it was able to hear what God had written into human nature about the high, the lofty, and the beautiful. Again, though it denied divine revelation, modernism was still able to draw from the well of general revelation because it recognized that nature had a "nature."

THE PLACE FOR A RATIONAL WORLDVIEW

While the worldviews of Christianity and modernism were worlds apart, there was agreement on the possibility of constructing a rational worldview. Though modernism believed it was possible to construct a rational worldview, it never quite succeeded. The place given to doubt meant that whatever they came up with was always subject to revision. The one thing they were sure of was that there was no place for God and divine revelation in their worldview.

The Influence of the Conflict Between Modernism and Christianity on the Culture

My concern here is with the influence that modernism had in weakening or defeating Christianity. Until about 1960, the two major forces that were trying to shape and influence the culture were Christianity and modernism. Since I am writing from a Christian viewpoint, I am interested in seeing what kind of challenge modernism gave to Christianity and how Christianity responded to this challenge.

THE INFLUENCE OF THE VALUE PLACED ON TRUTH AND REASON

Both modernism and Christianity hold to the law of non-contradiction. The law of non-contradiction depends upon the existence of objective Truth that can make statements true or false. Both Christianity and modernism believed in the existence of objective Truth. Both also agreed that words had meaning. It was possible for a modernist and a Christian to carry on a discussion and understand one another. It was possible, in principle, for them to decide who was wrong.

If a modernist said to a Christian, "I believe in evolution," the Christian understood what he meant. Both believed that evolution was either true or false. If the Christian said, "I believe in the bodily resurrection of Christ," the modernist understood what he meant. Both believed that the bodily resurrection was either true or false. It was possible, in principle, that the Christian could show the modernist that the resurrection was true.

Many college students had questioning minds. They were not questioning whether Truth existed. Rather, they were questioning whether the particular position that was presented was true, or whether the position needed to be modified. It was not uncommon for lively discussions to go on in classrooms. There was a strong interest in debates. The interest was not to win by ridicule and intimidation, but by building a strong rational case based on reasoning and evidence.

THE INFLUENCE IN THE ACADEMIC WORLD

Modernism and Christianity were both strongly committed to the conviction that Truth existed. With the common man, it went without saying that Truth existed. Such statements as, "There is a God," or "There is not a God" were either true or false. The truth or falsity of a statement depends upon the existence of objective Truth. To believe that Truth existed seemed to be so obvious to the average person that he or she never thought about the need of proof, or that anybody would ever think otherwise. That was the way I thought when I was growing up in a "not so highly academic" setting. I realize now that a part of the explanation why no one among the masses was challenging the question of whether Truth existed was that both Christianity and modernism agreed that Truth existed.

When modernism and Christianity were locked in fierce conflict in the classroom and in print, Christianity at times suffered losses. However, what took place in academic circles was not, seemingly, reflected on the grass roots level. Now and then, among the common people, a person who claimed to be an atheist or an agnostic would be found. But they were small in number. From my childhood, I can remember only two people who classified themselves as atheists or as infidels. The place where modernism made its greatest gains was in the universities. One of the areas where the greatest losses occurred was in the battle over evolution. The famous Scopes trial took place in Dayton, Tennessee in 1925. For a while, only a few were prepared to answer the attacks brought on the biblical doctrine of creation by evolutionists. Many lost their faith over this issue. By 1970, the creationists were making good progress in producing good materials in defense of Creationism. Even in the secular community, many now see problems with evolution.

Many who attended secular universities during the time that modernism reigned in secular culture held on to their Christian faith though they did not always have answers. They were convinced that somewhere in the greater picture of things there were answers. Maybe, they thought somebody with better training had answers. Their faith has been rewarded.

Others held to their faith but acceded to a philosophy of life that was not greatly different from that of modernism. The only time they saw a problem was when they heard or read a statement that was in direct and obvious conflict with their Christian faith. They seemed to be able to hold to conflicting views without knowing it. These people did not tend to have a very vibrant and contagious Christian testimony. But they did not leave the church.

Others who attended secular universities maintained a strong faith and testimony. They were able to come out with their Christian faith intact and were able to hold to a Christian worldview. In most cases, those who maintained a strong faith were in contact with some strong and informed Christians who were available to help as they wrestled with the difficult questions.

THE INFLUENCE OF MODERNISM ON THEOLOGICAL EDUCATION AND SCHOLARSHIP

The area of theological education and scholarship was the area where Christianity was hardest hit by modernism. After the fundamentalists suffered defeat in the votes among Northern Baptists and Northern Presbyterians in 1926, liberals were in control of most theological seminaries in America. This was a devastating blow to conservative Christianity. There quickly developed a rush to establish new seminaries and Bible colleges to meet the need of the hour.

There was a dearth of well written conservative theological literature. When I was a student at Free Will Baptist Bible College in 1948-1952, this fact made an indelible impression on me. I remember going to the library and looking over commentaries and theology books. With few exceptions, the scholarly works were written in the nineteenth century. The contemporary scholarly works were written by liberals. It seemed that all that was great among conservative Christians happened in the past.

With the abundance of theological schools and the almost unlimited supply of conservative scholarship today, it is hard to understand where we were just forty years ago. I am not averse to wholesome criticism. I expect what I write to be criticized. But when it comes to those who, from about 1920 to 1960, blazed the trail and made it possible for us to be where we are today, I think we should first offer a prayer of thanksgiving before we criticize them.

THE INFLUENCE ON MORALITY

On the grass roots level there was no major conflict in the area of moral ideals. Modernism heard the moral voice of general revelation that is written in the human heart by God. Their problem was that they did not give God the credit for what they heard.

I am not suggesting that there were no differences between the way modernism and Christianity viewed morality. Those who subscribed to modernism would not have considered everything a sin that more conservative minded Christians would. However, modernism did not attack the basic morality of the Ten Commandments.

On the grass roots level, there was not a serious war raised against the ideals of Christian morality. In fact, it was generally conceded that the moral ideals of the culture and the moral ideals of Christianity were the same. There were violations of these moral ideals, but that was attributed to depravity. This behavior was not attributed to a rejection of Christian morals. There was no serious problem in developing a working consensus of proper moral and ethical conduct.

THE INFLUENCE ON BEAUTY, EXCELLENCE, AND IDEALS

On the grass roots level, there was no serious conflict between modernism and Christianity on what constituted beauty, excellence, and ideals. There was no problem in developing a working consensus in this area. Even during the dire poverty of the Great Depression, those who were hit the hardest by the depression were able in one way or another to show that they cared. People could show that they cared, in so far as it was possible, by dressing up for special occasions. They could take pride in the way they did their work. Even when they lived in make-do living arrangements, women would try to keep things clean and looking neat.

They would make decorations out of tin cans or whatever they could find. They would grow flowers in their yard. Parents would teach basic manners to their children. Times were hard, but that did not annihilate concern for beauty, excellence, and ideals. It was understood that if a person went to college he or she would experience cultural refinement. There was, for many, an appreciation of the fine arts.

I am not suggesting that everybody manifested a concern for beauty and excellence. However, they certainly did not idealize their failure to show concern in these areas. They would tend to be apologetic. No one was saying that the failure to manifest concern was as good as manifesting concern.

When parents manifested a concern for the appearance of their children, taught them basic manners, the importance of having good character, the importance of sexual purity, to have a sense of duty, to be thankful, to be thoughtful, to be faithful to marriage vows, and to have a concern for others, it made a difference. It has been fifty years since I lived in my boyhood home area around Greenville, North Carolina. This allows me to see contrast. I can remember a family that, in addition to experiencing poverty, was also hit by two major tragedies. But the children were taught the values that I have mentioned above. The children were trained so that when they were presented with opportunities for improvement and advancement they were able to move ahead in life. The last time I saw this widowed mother, she gave the appearance of a dignified, successful woman. Her children showed the benefit of being trained in the values that I mentioned above. They have moved ahead in life.

THE INFLUENCE OF MODERNISM ON EVANGELISM

In understanding the influence of modernism on evangelism, we need to look at the influence on two different segments of the population: (1) The general population, and (2) The academic community.

THE GENERAL POPULATION

The general population was aware that some viewed science as a hindrance to belief in God. But that level of unbelief did not permeate the general population. Here and there a few hard core unbelievers could be found. But the general population was not influenced by hard core unbelief. So far as what people believed deep down is concerned, there was a Christian consensus. This consensus involved what they believed and the way they should act.

The moral consciousness made it so preaching could appeal to people's feeling of guilt. Sin, guilt, judgment, Hell, and life after death were issues that were real to people. Most people planned to get saved before they died. It was the preacher or soul-winner's responsibility to remind people of the danger of delay and to make the plan of salvation clear to them. This approach was fruitful in reaching many lost people.

THE ACADEMIC COMMUNITY

Those who were in the academic community had their roots in the general population. The difference was that in college or in the university they were more in touch with the impact of modernism. Many times they heard things that were in conflict with Christianity. The presentation they heard in class was on a much higher academic level than what they had heard in church. If what they heard was convincing, the problem of the law of non-contradiction popped its head up. In many cases they were not in contact with anyone who could give a good defense of the Christian position.

Popular use was made of evidential apologetics to make the case for the truth of Christianity. Arguments were given for the existence of God. The historical accuracy of the Bible and the case for the preservation of the biblical manuscripts were given to reconfirm the faith of Christians and help doubters come to faith. One of the most powerful weapons was the evidence of the resurrection of Christ. To be convinced of the resurrection of Christ was to be convinced of the truth of the Christian worldview.

It is important to realize that prior to 1960 there was no widespread attack on the existence of Truth, the importance of reason in discovering Truth, and the validity of the law of non-contradiction. When the case was compelling for the truth of Christianity, the Holy Spirit worked to bring many in the academic community to salvation.

The Paradigm Shift to Postmodernism

FROM 1960 TO 1990

The shift from modernism to postmodernism took place during a time of transition of about thirty years. It was evident in the 1960s that something drastic was taking place. But at that time few, if any, realized we were in the throes of a paradigm shift. We did not realize that the overthrow of modernism was in process. Few people were calling what was happening "postmodernism" in the 1960s and 1970s. Even a thinker as insightful as Francis Schaeffer (1912-1984) never used the term postmodernism in his writings. What was happening was spoken of as secular humanism. But "secular humanism" is too noble a term to apply to what is taking place now.

From 1960 to 1990 was a very troubling time for Christians. Christian leaders were confused. They knew that something was wrong, but they did not know what it was. Whether in Christian schools or in local churches, what used to work was not getting the same results. Those in Christian ministry, who worked hard, seemed to do reasonably well in the 1960s and the 1970s. But by the 1980s it was obvious that things were getting harder. Some pockets of the culture were not as affected by what was happening as others. But everybody knew that things were different.

SINCE 1990

By 1990 modernism was dethroned as the greatest secular force affecting our culture, and postmodernism had ascended to the throne. A paradigm shift of mammoth proportions had occurred. It was only in the 1990s that most of us were able to get a perspective on what had happened. When we did, it gave us insight into what we had been experiencing since 1960. By reading what others were saying about the paradigm shift from modernism to postmodernism and by thinking through what we had experienced, the picture of the last forty years fell into place. We knew something about moral relativism, religious relativism, and cultural relativism. Francis Schaeffer had talked about the escape from reason and the irrational upper story. Later we discovered that what had taken place was the overthrow of modernism by postmodernism.

In Chapters 2, 3, and 4, I gave considerable attention to explaining modernism and postmodernism. What I say here will have to be brief. My main purpose in this chapter is to deal with the problem of how we communicate the Christian message in a postmodern culture. I do need to take time explain the main ideas of postmodernism and how it differs from modernism and Christianity.

THE QUESTION OF TRUTH

Christianity and modernism believed that objective Truth existed. As a result of the failure of modernism, postmodernism does not believe that objective Truth exists. There is no truth that makes anything either true or false. To say that something is "true" for me, or "true" for you is to say that we find it helpful, or it works for you or for me. *There is the death of Truth.*

THE QUESTION OF REASON

The most fundamental law of reason or rationality is the law of non-contradiction. Both Christianity and modernism believed in the law of non-contradiction. Postmodernism rejects any definitive commitment to the law of non-contradiction. A person may believe contradictory things. *There is the death of reason.*

THE QUESTION OF NATURE

Both Christianity and modernism believed that there was a "nature" to nature. There was something about human experience that made it possible for us to have a common understanding of some basic things. Christianity believes that God created human beings to be rational and to have a moral constitution. Modernism believed that reality had a moral and rational nature. Postmodernism denies that there is a "nature" to nature. *There is the death of nature.*

THE QUESTION OF COMMON SENSE

Common sense works on the assumption that there are some things that are too obvious for a person to miss. The nature of reality makes it that way. Both Christianity and modernism believed in common sense. The death of nature also means that there is no foundation for common sense. *There is the death of common sense.*

THE QUESTION OF MORALS

Both Christianity and modernism believed that there was a moral "nature" to nature. This made it possible for there to be a consensus on basic morality. There was universal Truth. In postmodernism, there is no universal Truth that judges actions to be right or wrong. It goes beyond a simple denial of divine revelation about moral issues. By denying that there is a "nature" to nature, postmodernism is denying the existence of innate moral knowledge that is written in the human constitution by any means whatever. There is no moral voice within. By announcing the death of nature, postmodernism works to silence the voice of general revelation.

It is important for us to see the difference between modernism and postmodernism as it relates to general revelation. Both modernism and postmodernism would reject the concept of general revelation. However, there is an important difference in the practical results that follow. Since modernism did believe that nature had a "nature," it made it possible for general revelation to speak. That meant they could learn moral truth from nature. They denied that God was the source, but they got the message. Christians believed in both general revelation and special revelation. General revelation communicates basic moral concepts. Since the modernist learned basic morality from that which is written in nature, there was a moral consensus in society.

The picture changes with the paradigm shift to postmodernism. Postmodernism undercuts the possibility of a moral consensus. It goes beyond a simple denial of general revelation. It denies that Truth exists. There is no moral "nature" to nature. Postmodernism says there is no moral truth to be learned. There is no common sense. There is no moral voice to be heard. Morals have been privatized.

As it relates to society, the denial of a moral "nature" to nature and the consequent quenching of the voice of general revelation has been very devastating. *There is the death of a moral consensus.* Nihilism has arrived.

THE QUESTION OF BEAUTY, EXCELLENCE, AND IDEALS

Both Christianity and modernism believed in giving an emphasis to beauty, excellence, and ideals. There was a distinction made between the good and the bad, the noble and the ignoble, the lovely and the unlovely, and the appropriate and the inappropriate. Postmodernism rejects all of that. Since there is no "nature" to nature, there is no universal Truth. There is no higher and lower. There is no place for propriety. *There is the death of a consensus on beauty, excellence, and ideals. There is the death of propriety.* The classical and the low-grade may be a part of the same service. It is all a matter of personal taste. Those whose developmental years took place before 1960 are supposed to leave tradition behind and adjust.

I do not think it has dawned on very many what is at stake in the death of high ideals. This seems to be an area where there are legitimate differences. But that is not the same as saying that we can so privatize ideals that we give our sanction to the death of ideals.

THE QUESTION OF THE HOPE FOR A RATIONAL WORLDVIEW

Christianity and modernism believe in the possibility of a rational worldview. It is obvious that postmodernism has no room for a rational worldview. It has no room for an overarching view that gives a true explanation of the whole of reality. *There is the death of a rational worldview.*

An Assessment of the Current Situation

Our culture is in trouble. Hardly anyone doubts that assessment. This state of deterioration has not gone as far as it will if nothing is done to change the direction we are headed. However, in assessing the current situation, it is important to remember that postmodernism is not the only force that is shaping our culture.

The influence of modernism on morals and ideals is severely weakened, but not totally destroyed. It still lives on in the memories of many whose ideas and ideals were shaped when modernism was a significant force in the culture. It does not seem likely that there will be a revival of modernism as an influence in the area of morals and ideals.

THE QUESTION OF THE HARD SCIENCES

It will be interesting to see what happens in the hard sciences. In the universities, science classes are still taught in accord with the modernist paradigm. The only two paradigms in Western thought that would support science are modernism and Christianity. In rejecting the "nature" of nature, postmodernism undercuts scientific inquiry and research. It offers no foundation or motivation for scientific research

Some who are involved in the hard sciences are aware of this problem. *The Flight From Science and Reason* was published in 1996. This book is a compilation of papers read at a conference in 1995 sponsored by the New York Academy of Sciences also entitled "The Flight From Science and Reason."[3]

Some may want to resort to modernism to support science, but follow postmodernism as it relates to the issues of culture. Such a marriage will not last. When postmodernism denied that there was a "nature" to nature, it undercut the foundation of science. When a person can, in his or her thought, accept the violation of the law of non-contradiction, that person is no longer qualified to do scientific research. Such a person cannot be trusted to do scientific research.

I am not announcing the demise of science. Considering the strength and momentum that science has, it would take a long time for it to die. I make no claim to being able to predict the changes that will take place in the future. However, I will say that if science depends for its survival on postmodernism, it will die. If postmodernism gains complete control in our society, given time there will be a "New Dark Ages."

It may appear, for a while, that science, morals, ideals, and religion may exist without a foundation. I am reminded of a song from yesteryear that went something like this, "You push that middle valve down, and the music goes around and round, di di o ho, di di o, and it comes out here." I use that to describe my knowledge of computers. I am able to make a limited use of computers that way. Even a postmodernist can make use of a computer. But being computer scientist requires a conviction that nature has a "nature," a rational, consistent order. The same causes must always produce the same results. Postmodernism denies that there is this reliable order to nature. It will dawn on postmodernists that they have no basis for computer science. They will lose interest in other scientific pursuits.

THE FAILURE OF MODERNISM

Since modernism believed there was a moral and a rational "nature" to nature, it was able to meet with limited success. It was able to make progress in the area of empirical science. It was able to contribute to basic morality because it did not quench the voice of general revelation. Also, since Christian influence was present in its operational context, it was influenced by the moral ideals of Christianity. The problem with modernism in these areas was that it had no real explanation about why nature had a "nature." From a philosophical viewpoint, this was a major factor in the overthrow of modernism, as reigning king, in the secular world.

It is important to realize that the failure of modernism was not just academic. It was a failure to meet human need. Modernism had promised that reason would meet the total need of human beings. It would do this without dependence upon God. It declared that human beings were basically good. After the assessment of two World Wars, the gassing of the Jews by Hitler, the slaughter of the Russians by Stalin, the dropping of the atomic bombs on Hiroshima and Nagasaki, and other atrocities, the thinking that human beings were basically good was no longer a tenable view. There was no longer any basis for the utopian optimism of modernism. Pessimism replaced optimism. Modernism put up a struggle for a while. By the 1960s, it became evident that modernism was in trouble.

From the standpoint of advances in scientific achievement, modernism was in good shape when it was challenged in the 1960s. Great progress had been made and the promise was for much more. No charges could be brought against the progress of empirical science in the hard sciences.

The problem was that empiricism had not been able to meet the total needs of human beings. It had failed to meet the needs of human personality. It had not been able to meet the needs of the human soul. It was the failure to meets the needs of human personality, not a failure in the hard sciences that removed modernism from the throne in secular thought.

THE POSTMODERN MOOD

If postmodernism were explained, probably only a few people in America would subscribe to its tenets. In spite of that, postmodernism is the main force shaping our culture. But it is not the only force. Modernism is not dead; it still influences many people. However, I do not believe those who subscribe to modernism are making any considerable effort to stem the tide of the breakdown of our culture by postmodernism.

There are those who do have concern about the moral deterioration of our culture. There are some outspoken voices trying to stem the tide toward moral ruin. Dr. James Dobson, a conservative evangelical Christian, is speaking out. He is particularly concerned with family values. He is heard by several million listeners. Dr. Laura Schlessinger, an orthodox Jewess, has a listening audience that goes into the millions. She preaches, teaches, and nags about honesty and purity. William Bennett, a Roman Catholic, is well known for speaking out on moral issues.

I think it is generally understood that Christianity stands for character and for right against wrong. However, that voice is not as strong as it used to be. The church, as I was acquainted with it in my youth, had a clearer message about character, right and wrong, guilt, judgment, and Hell than it did on the gospel of grace. Or, you could say that the church had a clearer message of law than it did grace. If the church world today were charged with overemphasizing law, I do not believe it would be found guilty. I think the problem today is the other way around.

In the last 50 to 75 years the conservative, evangelical, and fundamentalist churches have found it difficult to uphold moral law while upholding grace. The origin of this problem was not connected with the rise of postmodernism. Christian leaders failed to wrestle with maintaining proper regard for the high ideals of Christianity while recognizing that justification is absolutely free. It is based totally on the imputation of the death and righteousness of Christ. Few know how to drive home the point that salvation includes both justification and sanctification. Sanctification results in holy living. Holy living involves living by the morality of the Ten Commandments.

Once we talk about the practical implications of the moral teachings of the Ten Commandments, all sorts of questions arise. This brings up the question of Christian liberty. When you leave the most literal meaning of the moral teachings of the Ten Commandments, and get into the practical application, there is a tendency, on the part of many, to privatize moral concerns. Even if things are not condoned they are tolerated.

It has been exceedingly unfortunate that soon after this problem arose within the church world, postmodernism began to promote moral relativism, nihilism, and the privatization of moral values in the general culture. This kind of thinking began to permeate the atmosphere, as if it is in the very air that we breathe. Television brings it into our dens. Even when people say they do not agree with these ideas, they are affected. They are desensitized.

Almost everyone who is fifty or older, and many who are younger, can remember how he or she has been desensitized about some things. We do not have the same feelings about sin that we used to have. When it comes to matters like politeness, manners, and propriety, we have been hit very hard. We see very little deep concern manifested over these areas. It is practically impossible to find a working consensus in these areas. One of the worst places to hope to find a concern or a consensus is institutions of higher learning. They were among the first places to capitulate in these areas. Our society is permeated with the influence of barbarism. It seems as if nobody knows how to deal with the problem. The favorite question that seems to be asked is, "Who's to say whether one way of doing things is any better than other ways?" "Who's to say which way is best?" Those questions are not asked with the expectation that some names could be given. These questions imply there is no one qualified to give answers. When these questions are asked, it usually closes the conversation.

The Future

I make no claim to having insights that are not available to others. But I believe we can make some observations about what the future may be like.

While we have seen great progress in the material world, when it comes to science and technology, we have suffered deterioration in the area of morals and ideals. There is no prevailing, working consensus in these areas. The result is that most of the time anything goes. The person who wants to suggest that there are some specific things that constitute civil behavior will encounter strong resistance both in the non-church world and the church world. In the general culture, concerns for character and purity are less important than economic success.

In the general culture, it took a failure of massive proportions for the diagnosticians to announce that modernism had failed. It took about 200 years of experimentation before it was seen that modernism was bankrupt so far as meeting human need was concerned.

It will likely not be 200 years before those in the secular world realize that postmodernism is a loser. It will require a lot of hurting before the doom of postmodernism will be announced. It took the devastation of two world wars, Hitler's atrocities to the Jews, Stalin's slaughter of millions of his own people, the inhumane conditions of prisons in Siberia, and the dropping of the atomic bomb on Hiroshima. Apart from the question of whether the atomic bombs should have been dropped, this massive killing shows that modernism's dream was falling apart before the diagnosis was made that would eventually lead to the downfall of modernism.

Postmodernism will not likely be overthrown until much more devastation and hurt occur. If the overthrow of postmodernism takes place within secularism, what form of secularism will replace it? It is not likely there will be any serious attempt to restore modernism to the throne. It does not appear that there are any steps below postmodernism to which a person could descend. When a person denies that Truth exists, denies that there is a rational and moral "nature" to nature, denies the distinctions between higher and lower in matters of culture, and denies that there is any rational worldview or metanarrative, how much lower can he go? From the negative side, how much further can one descend? What else can secularism offer?

It seems to me that if we look in the negative direction, it will be fertile ground for an authoritarian ruler. If things get bad enough, someone will likely step up to the bat and take charge. This may or may not tie in with end-time events. If Jesus should come soon, it would likely be shaping up for end events. Since we do not know when Jesus is coming, we have to be careful about dogmatic interpretations.

If secularism (including an authoritarian secular leader) is not the direction the culture takes, it will likely be some form of religion. Let us hope that it will be Christianity. In the meantime, we need to do our best to meet the need of the hour with the Christian message.

Understanding the Challenge of Communicating the Christian Message in a Postmodern Culture

As we take a look at the challenge before us in communicating the Christian message in a postmodern culture, I am reminded of the words of Jesus when He saw that great multitudes were following Him.

> If anyone comes to Me and does not hate his father and mother, wife and children, brothers and sisters, yes, and his own life also, he cannot be My disciple. And whoever does not bear his cross and come after Me cannot be my disciple. For which of you, intending to build a tower, does not sit down first and count the cost, whether he has enough to finish it—lest, after he has laid the foundation, and is not able to finish it, all who see it begin to mock him, saying, 'This man began to build and was not able to finish.'" Or, what king, going to make war against another king, does not sit down first and consider whether he is able with ten thousand to meet him who comes with twenty thousand? Or else, while the other is still a great way off, he sends a delegation and asks conditions of peace. So likewise, whoever of you does not forsake all that he has cannot be My disciple (Lk. 14:26-33, NKJV).

If we want to be used of God in communicating the Christian message in a postmodern culture, we need to give serious thought to these words of Jesus. We cannot ignore these words if we want to make a difference for God in our times.

Jesus said that the one who would be His disciple must "hate his father and mother, wife and children, brothers and sisters." Jesus meant that the one who would follow Him must not let the members of his family come between him or her and following Jesus. Beyond that we must give these family members the love and respect that we are taught to give in the rest of the Bible. I cannot explain why Jesus chose this exact wording, but I know what He meant.

I do not think that Jesus' comment about the king who finds himself severely out numbered by enemy troops finds application in our responsibility to minister to those who are under the influence of the postmodern paradigm. We are not to send a delegation and ask the "conditions of peace" (verse 32).

We do not need to make a distinction between being saved and being a disciple. It is assumed in the gospels that a saved person is a disciple. The only question is with regard to the quality of his discipleship.

The words of Jesus in Luke 14:26-33 tell us that the price we must pay is great. It was true when Jesus was on earth. It is true today. If we want to have a fruitful ministry in a postmodern culture, we must pay the price. We must assess the situation. This means we must assess postmodernism and decide how to deal with it. Then we must follow through, paying the price.

An illustration comes to my mind. I was reared on a farm in eastern North Carolina. If it was decided that a well was needed, it could be dug by hand with a shovel. At eighteen feet, the person would strike water.

When I moved to Nashville, Tennessee, I found out that the situation was quite different. You do not *dig* a well. You *drill* a well. You drill through rock to depths much greater than eighteen feet. If a man tried to dig a well with a shovel around Nashville, he could wear out an endless number of shovels, but he would never dig a well.

It is possible for a person to have a well around Nashville. But it takes more knowledge, different equipment, and more money than it did where I came from. A person has to decide whether he wants a well. If he is willing to pay the price, he can have a well.

From 1930-1960, reaching people for Christ was like digging a well in eastern North Carolina. Reaching people now is more like drilling through rock around Nashville. The same approaches that brought good results then do not work now. There is a lot of frustration among pastors. Some are doing what they have always done. Some are experimenting with new ideas. Some view culture as value-neutral and have sought to make peace with postmodernism, except when it is a direct violation of the morality of the Ten Commandments.

If we are going to come to grips with what we are up against, we must realize that the paradigm shift from modernism to postmodernism has greatly increased the difficulty of communicating the Christian message. The general population is being held captive by depravity and postmodernism. Those of us who live in the Western world are commissioned to be a part of Jesus' rescue team to free people from the power of sin and postmodernism. I am of the opinion that no other paradigm shift in the history of the church in the Western world gave the church as great a challenge as the paradigm shift from modernism to postmodernism in our secular culture. Pastors who want to have fruitful ministries must come to grips with the problem and learn to deal with it. A serious attempt must also be made to prepare the people in the pew.

THE UNIQUENESS OF THE PARADIGM SHIFT FROM MODERNISM TO POSTMODERNISM

The shift from the Aristotelian-Ptolemaic to the Copernican view of the universe had a major impact on both the church and the non-church world. This move, along with the progress of science in other areas of thought, paved the way for the division between Christian and secular thought. This form of secular thought we call modernism. In the Western world, modernism rivaled Christian thought for the next two centuries. Modernism proved to be a formidable foe.

The problems involved in dealing with modernism and postmodernism are very different. When a Christian confronted a modernist, the two could understand each other. Both believed that Truth existed apart from the knower. They believed that words had meaning. They believed in the law of non-contradiction. Modernism and Christianity were in agreement on basic morality. Both promoted high ideals.

In the grass roots population, as distinguished from the academic elite, the success rate of modernism was not as high in converting people to a godless view of life. In my early memories there was a consensus on basic morality and the promotion of high ideals. Both Christianity and modernism contributed to this prevailing consensus. For those who did not follow the godlessness of secularism, one might say that there was a Christian consensus.

As we have seen, things are drastically different in the 1990s. In the universities, full-blown postmodernism is strongly entrenched in the humanities and the social sciences. When we speak of the death of Truth, the death of reason, and the death of a rational worldview with the effect of all of this on morals and high ideals, we are thinking about full-blown postmodernism.

On the grass roots level, it is a postmodern mood that prevails. When I speak of the postmodern mood, I mean that the grass roots population, or the general culture is conditioned by postmodernism without necessarily subscribing to the full tenets of postmodernism. This influence is seen more in the area of morals and ideals.

The conditioning power of postmodernism has had a *desensitizing* effect on those who would still subscribe to the existence of Truth that makes actions either right or wrong. People do not feel as deeply about sin as they used to. This is true of both Christians and non-Christians. Our feelings have been numbed. We have become accustomed to things being the way they are. William Bennett makes this point in his book, *The Death of Outrage.*[4] The church has been affected. There is not as much preaching on sin, guilt, judgment, Hell, and the need of atonement as was the case before the transition to postmodernism. The preaching done on these issues does not get the results that it once did.

The culture has deteriorated even more in the area of beauty, excellence, and high ideals than in the area of morals. Many who have tried to stand for morality have thrown in the towel in the area of ideals. They are too weary to take on the battle for high ideals. Even though they may be concerned about the decay in the area of ideals, they do not give them a high enough rating on the scale of priorities to enter the fray. They suffer internally over the deterioration of music, dress, and civility. They may say something about it to someone who has a kindred spirit, but they do not speak up. They long for a return of the days when there was a concern for high ideals. But it appears hopeless.

Many try to pass off the whole matter in the area of ideals as just a matter of culture. Culture is viewed as value-neutral. The thing for the church to do is to adapt to this harmless change in the culture. It is all a matter of taste. The saints should be willing to make these changes for the sake of reaching more people. It is thought that the key to reaching today's people is to make changes in the style of music and a few other things in the way that the service is conducted before the pastor brings the message. Regardless of what value there may or may not be in these suggestions, I think that the matter of reaching people who have been conditioned by postmodernism is much deeper than that. It is a tragic underestimation of what is involved in rescuing those who are held captive to postmodernism or the postmodern mood to think that the major factor involved in reaching these people is a change in worship styles.

How Long Do We Have?

When we are given an assignment, the way we go about it is to a large extent determined by how much time we have in which to get it done. The way we go about reaching and dealing with those who have been conditioned by postmodernism is also determined by our thinking about how much time we have to get the job done. The ultimate answer to that question is determined by how long it will before Jesus come again.

I believe all of us must admit that we do not know when Jesus will come. It may be soon or it may be a few hundred years. Some of us may feel very strongly that Jesus is coming soon. Those who do could be right. But they could be wrong. I must admit that I do not know when Jesus is coming. I hope He comes before I finish writing this book. But, so far as I know, it could be another 100 years or more.

Does when we think Jesus will return have any impact on how we go about our work in serving God? If we are convinced that Jesus is coming very soon, I think we will be more prone to taking a shallow, surface approach to things. We would not want to take on many in-depth, long-lasting projects. We would give more time to evangelism than we would to edification. It would dampen our zeal for Christian education. We would build cheaper buildings because we would assume that we would not be using them long.

If we thought it could be a long time before Jesus comes again, we would do more long-range planning. We would be more interested in in-depth pursuits. We would focus our attention on building works that would last.

In the last 100 years, I believe that in many cases people have consciously made their plans on the assumption that Jesus *would* be coming very soon. I think many others have been influenced in this direction, subconsciously, by ideas that they had programmed into their subconscious minds. I believe that Jesus is coming again. I believe it *could be today.* But I believe it *could* be a long time. Since I do believe it *could be a long time,* we should lay the kind of foundation and build the structure of Christian thought and experience that will last. We need to build churches that will stand the test of time. We need to prepare them to face anything that the devil may throw at them.

If Jesus comes in my lifetime, I want to be at my post of duty. It may be that I will be reading my Bible or praying. I may be sharing the gospel with some lost person. I may be helping some troubled person learn how to deal with the pressures of life. I may be preaching a sermon. I may be teaching a class. I may be writing another book. I may be cutting grass. I may be asleep. I want to be faithful to my normal duties. Since I do not know when He is coming, I need to be preparing for a longer stay on this earth. I need to be preparing those who will be here long after I am gone. I need to be making my contribution to preparing them to face postmodernism, an authoritarian leader, or whatever may come.

We do not need to be looking for short-cuts.

Sizing Up Our Assignment to Minister to a Postmodern Culture

Jesus said to Peter and Andrew, "Follow Me, and I will make you fishers of men" (Mt. 4:19, NKJV). I am not much of a fisherman, but I do know enough about fishing to know that you use different kinds of bait for different kinds of fish. You fish at different depths for different kinds of fish. God has designed each kind of fish to have its own unique nature. The person who wants to be a good fisherman must come to an understanding of how the design of each kind of fish works itself out in its own unique habits. When a person has come to an understanding of the unique habits of the different species of fish, he or she can catch fish when amateurs are not having much success.

Just as the fisherman must do a study of fish in order to be a good fisherman, we must make a study of human beings to effectively win them and minister to them. The first thing we need to do is to understand the *design* that God has programmed into human beings.

WHAT IS MAN?

In Psalm 8, the psalmist asks a very important question, "What is man?" (Verse 4). If we are going to become fishers of men, we must be able to answer that question. It would seem that since we are human beings, we would automatically know what a human being is.

It seems like a useless question. But it is far from being a useless question. I have dealt, at length, with the nature of man both as a result of the *design* of creation and the result of the fall in Chapter 9. I will be brief here.

It is a mistake in identifying a human being to start by saying that he is a sinner. We must first start by saying that a human being is created in the image of God. Then, we can say that this one who was created by God in His image has sinned. He is a sinner and stands guilty and condemned by God.

Human beings are a product of divine *design*. We are *designed* in God's image (Gen. 1:26). That means we are in the rational likeness of God (Col. 3:10) and the moral likeness of God (Eph. 4:24). Our *design* also includes the fact that we are *designed* for a personal relationship with God (1 Jn. 1:3). We are also *designed* for interpersonal relationships with other human beings (Gen. 2:18). The nature of our *design* means that we have rational needs, moral needs, a need for a personal relationship with God, and a need for social relationships.

The Importance That We Are Designed Beings

The concept of *design* is very important. Even with machinery, we dare not ignore the element of *design*. Needs are determined by *design*. Most automobiles are designed to run on gasoline. Some are designed to run on diesel fuel. The *design* of the engine determines the kind of fuel that is needed. We dare not put diesel fuel into an automobile designed for gasoline. A few people have done this unintentionally. It spells trouble.

When we recognize that human beings are designed by God in His image, a lot of things will begin to make sense. If we are designed by God in His image, that design determines what our needs are. If we deny or ignore that human beings are designed by God in God's image, serious consequences will follow.

Man as Fallen

The fall of man had drastic effects. Sin as both guilt and depravity became a part of human experience. Sin as guilt placed human beings under the sentence of eternal death (Rom. 3:23; 6:23; Rev. 20:10; and 21:8). Sin as depravity turned each human being against God and against himself.

It is being made in the image of God, not sin, that determines a person's basic needs. The fall did not change our basic needs as human beings. Our *design* determines our need of a right relationship with God. We can decide that we do not want a right relationship with God, but we cannot decide that we do not need a right relationship with God. God decided that when He made us. That need can neither be revised nor altered. It is indelibly written by God in the human constitution.

Our *design* determines that we have rational needs. We cannot change that fact. We need a rational worldview. We need an intelligent understanding of life. We are designed for Truth. That is why Jesus said, "And you shall know the truth, and the truth shall make you free" (Jn. 8:32, NKJV).

Our *design* determines that we have moral needs. Those needs are irreversibly written in human nature by God. They are *programmed* into our nature. The fall did not eradicate them. It was people who were fallen, people without the written revelation of God, of whom Paul was speaking when he said:

> For when the Gentiles, who do not have the law, by nature do the things contained in the law, these, although not having the law, are a law unto themselves, who show the work of the law written in their hearts, their conscience also bearing witness, and between themselves their thoughts accusing or else excusing them (Rom. 2:14, 15, NKJV).

The law that is written in the heart of every human being is the same as the moral law that is given in the Ten Commandments. This has been a long recognized fact. Thomas Oden wrote a very helpful paper titled "Without Excuse: Classic Christian Exegesis of General Revelation." He explains concerning his purpose, "The purpose of the paper is to treat general revelation from a theological perspective with special reference to the church fathers and ancient Christian exegetes." In this paper he gives a quotation from Origen in which he comments on the meaning of Romans 2:14, 15. Origen explains:

> When the Apostle says this, he clearly does not mean that the Gentiles keep the Sabbaths or the new moons or the sacrifices which are written down in the Law. For this Law is not what is written on the hearts of the Gentiles. Rather it is that which can be discerned naturally, e. g. that they should not kill, or commit adultery, that they should not steal, nor bear false witness, that they should honor father and mother, etc. It may well be that since God is the one Creator of all, these things are written on the hearts of Gentiles. . . They have the Law written on their hearts by God, not with ink, *but with the Spirit of the living God."*[5]

This basic understanding is innate within each person. When a person puts himself or herself at cross purposes with the morality of the Ten Commandments that person also puts himself or herself at cross purposes with that image of God within and with the Sovereign God of the universe.

Written within the heart and mind of every human being is some appreciation of beauty and excellence and, at least, to some degree an understanding of what is beautiful. That people apologize when things are unkempt or out of order tells us that deep within they have an appreciation of that which is excellent and beautiful. We are designed to function in the likeness of God. The starry skies on a dark night, the beauty of a sunset flanked by clouds, the beauty of fresh fallen snow, the beauty of snow-capped mountains, the beauty of ocean waves as they splatter on the beach, beautiful landscapes, beautiful flowers, the many beautiful birds, and more things than any of us can name tell us that God delights in beauty. The "don't care" attitude and the image of God do not work well together.

Depravity works against the *design* that is woven into the fabric of our nature. But depravity can never destroy that design. By working against the image of God, depravity can make miserable wrecks of people's lives. When a person lets depravity direct his or her life, that person experiences conflict, contradiction, and confusion.

Truly, all human beings are created by God in His image, have fallen into sin, have a depraved nature, and are under the condemnation of eternal death. That is why we, who have accepted Him, have been commissioned by God to win others to Christ.

Analyzing the Challenge Before Us

THE IMPORTANCE OF SIZING-UP THE UNIQUENESS OF THE SITUATION

Everyone who is seeking to reach people for Christ must size-up the situation that he or she is facing. There are some factors that are common to all situations. All human beings have been created by God in His image. That *design* is damaged by the fall, but it is not silent. In each person, a depraved nature is trying to take over the image of God. You might say that the depraved nature is trying to occupy the same space with the image of God. This does not produce two "selves," but a divided self. A self that is in conflict with itself. That puts a person at cross purposes with God and with himself or herself. The one who is made in the image of God is held captive by the depraved nature. This captive is under the sentence of eternal death for his or her sins. Jesus Christ has commissioned us with a message of deliverance from the penalty and the power of sin for these captives. We are God's rescue team.

As we go beyond these points of common ground, we are presented with a variety of ways Satan works through depravity to keep a person captive to sin. With some, he uses the power of addiction to alcohol, addiction to drugs, enslavement to various forms of sexual immorality, and the feeling of despair. There is a loss of hope. I will say more about these problems later. Presently I am concerned about those who are held captive by false worldviews. This captivity could involve various pagan religions or any number of cults. These all have to be considered since pluralism marks our culture.

In working in the United States and Canada, a Christian leader needs to have a working knowledge of, at least, three paradigms: Christianity, modernism, and postmodernism. Even if a person is working to reach people who are influenced by the New Age Movement or the cults, all of this is taking place in a postmodern culture.

My main concern in this chapter is with the influence of the paradigm shift in secular culture from modernism to postmodernism. In communicating the Christian message, it is imperative that we size up the particular situation that we are confronting. It is as if postmodernism is in the very air that we breathe. We have the same Bible and the same gospel that we have always had. But it takes different preparation to rescue those who are being held captive by postmodernism than was the case when modernism was the predominate secular influence.

Modernism was a formidable foe of Christianity. Great losses were suffered, especially in the area of education. There were a few who were rescued from the full grip of modernism. But we did not win very many who were thoroughgoing modernists. However, when it came to the general population, modernism's influence did not permeate the grass roots level of the culture as successfully as the postmodern mood has our present culture. In a general sense, we could say that when modernism was on the throne there was a Christian consensus on the grass roots level of society. Evangelism was much easier and Christianity had such an impact on society that it was frequently said that the United States was a Christian nation. We were not called a secular nation under modernism. We are much further along the road toward being a secular nation under postmodernism than we ever were under modernism. The challenge before us in carrying out the Great Commission in a postmodern culture is much more difficult. But it is not impossible.

A variety of life-threatening situations call for rescue work to be set in motion. The common factor in all of these is that human life is in danger. But there is a wide range of situations that could be considered life-threatening. We would not dare initiate a rescue attempt unless we had some idea of the nature of the danger. Is someone having a heart attack? Has there been a serious automobile wreck? Is a person trapped in a burning building? Is a child lost in a blizzard? Is there a shipwreck at sea? Is someone being held by a group of terrorists? Is some other high-risk circumstance occurring? The nature of the situation determines the qualifications needed by the rescue team, the number of people involved, the type of equipment required, etc. Once we arrive on the scene and assess the situation, we will enlist others who have the necessary qualifications and equipment.

In communicating the Christian message in a postmodern culture, we are in the business of rescuing people from the damning effects of sin in the next life and the detrimental effects of sin in this life. We are in the business of helping people find meaning and purpose in life. We are in the ministry of helping hurting people. If we fail to size-up the challenge of postmodernism, we will at best have only token success.

If we will pay the price that is required to prepare ourselves, I do not believe that any culture is too difficult for us to succeed in reaching people for Christ. Given enough time, I believe churches can be built in these cultures. As I have said earlier, I do not know the time frame of the second coming of Christ. If the coming of Christ is very soon, we may not see any massive movements of revival. However, if Jesus tarries His coming for a long time, I think it is possible for Christianity to become a much stronger factor in our culture here at home and in the rest of the world. I am not advocating a post-millennial eschatology when I say that. I think the question of how soon we will see results depends upon how serious we are about doing God's work. If we go at it with a serious commitment to do God's work God's way, it could be soon. If we do not, God may allow us to go through another "dark ages" before a massive revival will come. Whatever happens, one thing is clear, "Christ will build His church" (Mt. 16:18).

I understand that, apart from God, we cannot reach people. Apart from the work of the Holy Spirit, we will not be able to achieve spiritual results. I also believe that when we are seriously committed to doing God's work God's way, we have the abiding promise of Jesus Christ when He said, "Lo, I am with you always, even to the end of the age" (Mt. 28:20, NKJV). I believe that when we love God, present ourselves as clean vessels to be used of God, and are serious about serving God, He will bless us and we will see the fruit of our labors.

POSTMODERNISM'S REJECTION OF THE CONCEPT OF DESIGN FOR HUMAN BEINGS

In rejecting the notion of definitive Truth, postmodernism rejects the Truth that human beings are created in God's image. I believe the rejection of this Truth by postmodernism explains why we have a more troubled society than we did fifty or sixty years ago. In the days of the Great Depression, people were afraid to die. Now in the midst of plenty, people are afraid to live.

While it is true that modernism also rejected the idea that human beings are created in God's image, the *unbelief* (the denial of the existence of God) of modernism did not permeate the culture as thoroughly as the postmodern mood permeates our present culture. Also, in modernism's approach to morals and ideals its influence was not so much at cross purposes with the image of God as is the case with postmodernism.

Postmodernism denies that human beings are designed by God. In fact, according to postmodernism, human beings have no design. We did not come into existence with a set of needs designed into our being. There is no Truth that preceded our existence that guides our experience. It is as if we were hurled into existence without being accompanied by a factory manual. There is no North Star to guide us. There is no map. There is no compass. There is no universal Truth. There is no collected wisdom. Even animals have instinct to guide them. Human beings have been cast on the sea of life to chart their own course. The trouble is that there is nowhere to go.

Postmodernism promotes the idea of the *social* construction of "truth." It seems to talk about "group thinking" rather than "individual thinking." That would seem to give recognition to the mores and customs of society. However, that is not an apt description of the short history of postmodernism. Instead of manifesting an attitude of acceptance or tolerance, postmodernism in America has been hostile toward the influence of Christianity and modernism (or the Enlightenment) on society.

The promotion of the concept of the social construction of "truth" by postmodernism seems to be self-serving. It seems that the only socially constructed "truth" that it recognizes is that which it constructs, or one that would in no way threaten its own goals. It claims to promote openness, but it is not very open to the traditional values of the Western world. The message of postmodernism is confusing. On the one hand, it seems that postmodernism would recognize a socially constructed consensus on morals. On the other hand, it promotes *privatized morals*. It seems that it will be better if these morals are morally reprehensible to Christians. This especially applies to the area of sex. Postmodernism's failure to make any Truth claims is not to be understood as meaning that they take a neutral position on religious and moral concerns. These apparent contradictions are no problem to postmodernism since it is not bothered by the law of non-contradiction.

LOOKING AT THE POSITIVE SIDE

While we must see the problem side of what we are up against, we must not stop there. If we stop with our negative assessment, we will be very discouraged. We may want to give up in despair. There are some factors that are encouraging. We must look at them.

Theological education is in much better shape now than it was fifty years ago. In the first part of the twentieth century, the situation as it relates to theological seminaries was very bleak. Liberalism had found its way into most theological seminaries. There were only a few seminaries that escaped corruption. It was hard for an evangelical ministerial student to find a seminary to attend. In many cases, if he went to his denominational seminary it would be infested with liberalism. Many lost their faith while in seminary.

Today, there are many solidly conservative seminaries from which a ministerial student may choose. There are many good academic schools. There are many highly qualified professors who are solid in their spiritual commitments. I believe we can also say that there are a number of students who are serious about serving God. The same thing that I have said about seminaries can be said about Bible colleges and Christian liberal arts colleges.

It is amazing what has happened in the area of theological literature in the last fifty years. Those who entered their theological education after 1970 do not know how to appreciate what has been done in the area of theological literature. There was a time when most, then current, academic theological literature was written by liberals. Most academic works written by conservatives were written in the 1800s. That has changed.

It is a strange phenomenon that during the time liberalism was the predominate force in America's theological seminaries the moral and ethical values of the culture in America on the grass roots level were in better shape than they are now. One of the fallacies that conservatives get caught up in is the feeling that the past was always better. Had I not been living fifty years ago, I would probably think that way unless I had researched the matter. In assessing what was happening in theological education fifty years ago, we certainly cannot say that it was better then than it is now. The opposite is true. We may be concerned about the drift of a particular school, but the overall situation is better.

In what I have just said, I do not mean to give credit to theological liberalism. In fairness, I think I should say that liberalism was not destructive to the high ideals of society. During the time that modernism ruled in secular culture, conservative Christianity was a strong force in shaping the culture on the grass roots level. I think that conservative Christianity was very effective in those days because *it said to the human heart what it already knew by general revelation*. The message of general revelation and the message of special revelation concurred on morals and ideals and the matter of guilt and judgment. The difference was that special revelation brought those values and the message of guilt and judgment into clearer focus. The person who came face to face with his or her guilt was a ready candidate for the message of redemption that comes only by special revelation. The Holy Spirit working with general revelation and the Word of God brought many into a saving relationship with Jesus Christ. Another clarification needs to be made. There is no correlation between the permeation of our culture at the grass roots level with the postmodern mood and the fact that conservative evangelical seminaries are stronger now. I think that the presence of many solidly conservative seminaries, Bible colleges, and Christian liberal arts colleges gives us reason for hope.

The Need for Re-examination and Reassessment

From 1960 to 1990 was a very confusing time for Christian schools. The same thing could be said about churches and parachurch groups. But my present concern is with colleges and seminaries. We were confronted with a new kind of questioning from students, parents, and the culture.

Prior to 1960, there were basically two kinds of questioning on college campuses. These kinds of questioning were found among both Christian colleges and universities, and those who made no Christian commitment. One kind had to do with questions that related to very fundamental issues such as: the existence of God, the inspiration of the Bible, the inerrancy of the Bible, the virgin birth of Christ, the deity of Christ, or the bodily resurrection of Christ, etc. Sometimes these questions were from serious personal concerns to the student. At other times they were concerned about how they would answer someone else who might ask these questions.

Another kind of question was related to the true interpretation of matters where Christians were not in full agreement. These questions were about why or whether a particular teaching was true, why a particular conviction was held by some people, why the school had a particular rule, etc. It was always assumed that Truth did exist.

Whether it was the first kind of questions or the second kind of questions, there was always agreement between the student and the teacher, or the student and the administration on one very basic level. There was agreement that Truth existed that made things either right or wrong, true or false, or whether it was an issue where there was room for variation of viewpoint.

In the 1960s, a new kind of questions began to be asked. The "Who's to say?" questions made their entrance. This kind of question had its origin among the radical student movement in the 1960s. We now know that this was the beginning of the entrance of postmodernism on the grass roots level. These questions, when asked on Christian college campuses in those days, did not deal with matters where the Bible plainly says, "Thou shalt," or "Thou shalt not." They dealt with how you apply the principles of the Bible to things not spelled out in the Bible. They dealt with the question of Christian liberty. There are valid questions that can be asked about these areas when they are done with the right attitude. But these questions can also represent the wrong attitude. At least some of what was asked in those days came from the spirit of the age.

Both Christian colleges, private colleges, and state colleges and universities were under pressure to shorten their list of rules. Some of these changes have been for the good, but I believe that we have also suffered some losses.

Now that we have a better perspective on what has taken place on Christian college campuses since 1960, I think we should rethink matters. I think any honest and informed assessment of the changes that have taken place tells us that many of the changes were brought on by pressure from the influence of postmodernism on the culture. From 1960 to 1990 was a period during which postmodernism subdued and dethroned modernism. Postmodernism ascended to the throne as king in secular thought.

This same time period was a time when Christian colleges went through major changes, not in theology, but in the way they handled the matter of student behavior. Many administrators were concerned, but they felt helpless to do any thing about it. The problem applies not only to what to require, but what to promote. It is almost impossible for an administration and faculty to develop a working consensus on what the ideals of Christian behavior are beyond the most literal teachings of the Ten Commandments. I think we should always be open to change when that change is brought about by the highest regard for the Truth. But we need to be sure that proper regard is given to Truth.

Many Christian leaders are frustrated. They are not happy with the way things are, but they do not know what steps to take. There is no consistent, deep concern, nor working consensus in any segment of society today about matters such as politeness, manners, dignity, beauty, and excellence. Most Christian colleges have almost abandoned any attempt to have any influence on their students in these areas.

It is incumbent upon Christian colleges to find some way to make a difference in their students in the areas of morals and beauty, excellence, and ideals. We need to ask, "Did we forfeit too much from the pressure of the influence of postmodernism?" If we did, by God's help, we need to reclaim the territory. We need to be able to develop a working consensus of what is expected of our students and of ourselves as the faculty and administration. A working consensus does not mean that we see eye to eye on every detail. This consensus is not arrived at by someone making authoritative pronouncements. It begins with a commitment of all involved to be like Christ in the totality of our lives. It should be expected that within a working consensus there will be a certain amount of tension. But in a Christian community there should not be hostility and disregard for what is acceptable and what is not acceptable in the community.

THE DEFEAT OF EMPIRICISM AS A WORLDVIEW

While there have been many losses from the influence of postmodernism, there are some things that we can rejoice in. As I have pointed out earlier, Christianity suffered great losses from empiricism. Autonomous reason which rejected all data except the data of observation and experience does not present the challenge to students that it did under modernism. So far as postmodernism is concerned, reason is dead. A student is not encountered nearly so much by the rational arguments against the existence of God, the inspiration of the Bible, and the bodily resurrection of Christ as was the case when modernism was on the throne. Since modernism is not totally dead, these arguments may still be encountered, but they are not the threat they were when modernism was on the throne in secular thought.

While the death of empiricism, as a totalizing worldview, is welcomed by Christianity, its replacement, which is postmodernism, brings a new set of problems. With postmodernism nothing is true in the sense that ideas are either true or false. One approach to life is as good as another if it works for you. What is "true" is whatever meets your needs. The only test of "truth" is internal or subjective validation. There is no tolerance for the exclusive Truth-claims of Christianity.

Prior to the rise of postmodernism, there was a consensus on the idea that Truth existed and that the Truth was what people needed. This helped shape one's approach to evangelism and apologetics. When people had doubts about the truth-claims of Christianity, the prepared Christian would try to see if he could convince the unbeliever that Christianity was indeed true. Evidential apologetics was popular. There was some success in reaching unbelievers who were held captive by modernism.

THE CHANGE OF THOUGHT ON THE NECESSITY OF
OBJECTIVITY IN THE PURSUIT OF KNOWLEDGE

Modernism greatly stressed the objectivity of Truth. Truth existed outside the knower. It was considered an advantage if a person could set aside feelings in the search for Truth. I will make use here of what I said in Chapter 1 under the heading, "Life Oriented." Modifications will be made to make it suitable for use here.

For a long time, there was a tendency in the world of scholarship to make a sharp distinction between the academic, which deals with the content of Truth, and the practical, which deals with the application of Truth. In studying the content of Truth, the ideal was to be objective. It was felt that to combine the study of the content of Truth with the application of Truth was to contaminate objectivity with subjectivity. To be objective was to seek to be detached from the subject under study. A person was to study as if it made no difference what conclusions he reached. It was felt that objectivity was necessary in order to maintain intellectual honesty.

To challenge objectivity as a guiding ideal in the pursuit of Truth should not be considered a challenge to the notion that Truth itself is objective. Truth exists outside of the mind of the knower. At the same time Truth is for life. It is not just a cold, dry collection of abstract and impersonal ideas.

In my early years of teaching in the 1950s, I worked hard to maintain objectivity. I demanded that students write their papers in the third person. I insisted that in an exegetical paper that the students should refrain from introducing anything into their papers besides bare exegesis of the text. I rebuked one student for placing a poem in his paper.

I have come to believe that there are some serious problems in trying to maintain detached objectivity as the guiding ideal in the search for Truth. Objectivity seeks to make a person a neutral investigator of Truth. Why is a person supposed to be more capable of discovering Truth if he is a neutral investigator rather than one who is deeply involved in what he is doing and one who feels strongly about it? Who learns the most about art, a person who is neutral about art, or a person who loves art? Who learns more about baseball, one who studies with a feeling of detachment or one who is deeply involved? We must not wring all the feeling out of Truth if we expect it to speak to life. Thinking and feeling must be found together.

It is an absolute must that we maintain honesty and integrity in our pursuit of Truth. To speak of a dishonest search for Truth is a contradiction of terms. However, to become married to objectivity as a means of trying to guarantee honesty means to divorce the mind from the rest of the personality. Truth is for the total personality. It may take a strong commitment to honesty to be honest when a person is deeply involved in a matter. Yet, this is what must take place. Honesty and deep involvement must be found in the same person in order to reach the highest degree of proficiency in discovering the Truth.

We are not spectators in our search for Truth. We are deeply concerned and involved. We study with a passion. It is particularly important that we study theological Truth as interested and involved persons because theological Truth is for life. It must not be a mere mental exercise. It must be experience oriented.

This problem of over stressing the concept of objectivity was not limited to those in the secular world. It also took its toll in the world of Christian scholarship. Many times authors chose to write in the third person as a means of maintaining a higher degree of objectivity. This caused the author to write as a detached person. To a large extent, this removed his writings from life. There was a missing dimension that kept many outstanding works on theology from speaking to the heart. They were not designed to speak to the heart. That was left for devotional studies.

My change from writing in the third person to writing in the first person was an outgrowth of my own struggles in bringing Truth and life together. I felt strongly enough about this by the time I wrote the first edition of this book ,which was published in 1975, that I wrote it in the first person.

Truth is for the total personality, not just the mind. Truth is objective, but it must be internalized. It must be subjectively experienced. It is only when objective Truth is subjectively experienced that it makes a person free. When Truth does not speak to the total personality, it does not set free. There is a missing dimension when Truth does not speak to the total personality.

I think we can agree with the pioneers of the postmodern movement when they saw that human need was too deep for answers to be found by an objective, detached approach. We are not spectators. We must be deeply involved in the pursuit of Truth. We are in a desperate, life or death struggle. Yet, we must not let our desperate state of mind cause us to fall for something less than the Truth. By all means, we must not let despair cause us to give up. The failure of modernism to produce a rationally consistent and adequate worldview does not mean that such does not exist. There is hope. That hope is found in God, the Bible, and Jesus Christ.

The Positive Contribution of Postmodernism

I think it is obvious to anybody that I am not wanting to give any accolades to postmodernism. However, I do believe that there are some differences that can be attributed to postmodernism that are beneficial. There are three areas in which I believe we have derived benefit from the influence of postmodernism. These have already been dealt with above, but I will give a summary treatment of these and put them in a clearer focus as it relates to the contribution they have made.

THE DEFEAT OF EMPIRICISM

In large measure because of postmodernism, empiricism is no longer a serious threat. The victory of the postmodernists in this instance is not because they refuted the arguments of autonomous reason. They were victorious by pointing out that autonomous reason had failed. Reason through empirical research had done well so far as scientific advancement was concerned. But when it came to the personal needs of mankind, it had failed to fulfill its promises. The time had come to find something else.

Christianity welcomes the defeat of empiricism. However Christianity is not willing to follow postmodernism in announcing the death of reason. Christianity is deeply committed to the law of non-contradiction.

A MOVE IN THE DIRECTION OF A TOTAL PERSONALITY APPROACH TO THE PURSUIT OF TRUTH

I think that postmodernism has played an important part in moving us away from objectivity as the guiding ideal in the pursuit of Truth. This commitment to objectivity tended to divorce Truth from life. For those who were the most deeply involved in this commitment to objectivity, it made Truth look cold and dry. It seemed to wring all of the feeling out of Truth.

In the early 1960s, while I was a seminary student, I did a considerable amount of reading in the works of Emil Brunner. I was never attracted to the neo-orthodoxy of Brunner. But I remember noticing that there was something about Brunner's writings that "grabbed me." Reading Brunner's works was a *total personality* experience. I remember realizing that I did not have the same experience with many of the conservative works that I had read. This was true, even though I agreed with them. I felt like something needed to be done to change this.

Lawrence Crabb has called our attention to this problem. He speaks of "stiff exegesis" that may be technically correct, but does not speak to the deep needs that people have. He explains:

> The Stiff Exegetes . . . unwittingly allow a proper concern for precise interpretation of the Bible to rob the text of its relational and life-changing vitality. . . . The teaching of Stiff Exegetes leaves large and significant areas of human experience untouched—and therefore unchanged. Vital truth that penetrates to the core issues of life has somehow been replaced with technical truth that equips people to pass seminary exams and to preach exegetically correct sermons but not communicate deeply, to relate meaningfully, or to proclaim truth to real human need. An understanding of Scripture that fails to answer the hard questions about how to live is no real understanding at all"[6]

Later in the same book he comments:

> Whenever a Bible-believing church regards its mission as not including ministry to the deep personal struggles hidden in all of us, it is stating in effect that the Bible does not speak to these concerns.[7]

I think some progress has been made in this area. But there is a great need to make more progress in this area.

MORE RECOGNITION OF THE NEED FOR TRUTH TO BE INTERNALLY VALIDATED

Postmodernism has gone too far in insisting that the only validation of Truth is an internal or a subjective validation. However, they are on the right track in rejecting the idea that the only validation for a worldview is an objective validation. There are some things that only require an objective validation. For example, if there is a dispute about how many chairs are in a room, it is possible to settle the dispute by counting them. Feeling is not consulted in deciding how many chairs are in a room. But when it comes to an approach that is to explain the whole of reality, we would expect some kind of internal validation.

We would agree that worldview thinking must have some kind of internal validation. But we would part ways with postmodernism in saying that it is the only validation. We cannot agree with postmodernism's rejection of objective Truth. A worldview must pass tests other than internal validation. I will quote what I said in Chapter 7 on testing worldviews.

I believe that there are four criteria a worldview must meet if it is to be considered true and worthy of serious consideration. These are: (1) Does it answer the *inescapable questions of life?* (2) Is there internal consistency, i.e., is the structure logically related to the foundation? Do all the parts fit consistently together? (3) Is there causal adequacy, i.e., are the causes adequate to produce the effects attributed to them? (4) Does it conform to that which is undeniably true?

The first test would involve an internal validation, but it would involve more than that. No worldview should be accepted if it does not pass the first test. But it must also pass the other three tests. To involve internal validation in this way will not open the flood gates to all kinds of way-out thinking. If some form of rational and objective validation is not employed, error will be unchecked.

While more attention is given to the need of internal validation of Truth, the recognition that Truth needs internal validation is not owed to postmodernism. It has always been true. But it has not always received the emphasis that it needs. Postmodernism can be credited with our increased attention to internal validation. Many Christian thinkers still are uncomfortable with giving place to internal validation.

I will be saying more about this later, but I think general revelation is the basis for the fact that internal validation deserves and requires attention. That we are made in the image of God, which involves God's moral law being written in our hearts, makes an important contribution to the matter of internal validation of Truth. For example, if you tell a person that adultery is wrong, the law of God written in the heart gives internal validation. You are never telling a person something that he or she did not know when you say to them that it is wrong to commit adultery. If he or she denies this, it will be necessary to suppress knowledge that he already has (Rom. 1:18 , 32).

It sometimes bothers us to recognize that unsaved people have made worthwhile observations about worldview thinking and human behavior. This should not surprise us if we keep in mind that every human being is made in the image of God. It is impossible for the image of God to be totally silent in a person.

Charting Our Course

Our responsibility, or should I say, our privilege and opportunity is to serve on God's rescue team. The specific assignment under consideration is the responsibility to rescue those who are held captive by depravity and postmodernism. If we should use the metaphor of fishing, our responsibility is to catch fish from the postmodern sea. I have given considerable time above to sizing up the situation. Considerable attention has been given to the difference between modernism and postmodernism. Attention has been given to what makes it more difficult to reach people since post-modernism has ascended to the throne in secular culture.

Attention has also been given to the identification of the captives whom we, by God's help, are to rescue. These captives have been created by God in His image. They have chosen sin. They are enslaved by depravity. They are under the sentence of eternal death. Jesus Christ has stood in their place under the wrath of God. He paid their penalty in full. He has provided His righteousness to be placed on their account. No matter how much they have sinned, His death and His righteousness will settle their account with God.

Postmodernism has joined with depravity to hold, as captive, the one made in the image of God. Our assignment is not easy. It will take many of us working together in teamwork to effectively perform the rescue. We will each be making a different contribution. With teamwork and with God's help, many can be rescued. When a rescue is made, it is the whole team that made the rescue possible.

One more word about the identification of those who are being held captive by depravity and postmodernism—they may be our sons and daughters. They may be our grandchildren. They may live in our neighborhood. They may be in our Sunday School class. They may be in our youth group. The youth group in a church will probably be the hardest hit of any group in our church. Being a youth minister in a church is serious business. Providing fun experiences and wholesome social opportunities for young people is important. But youth ministry must go much deeper than that. In a church with a sizeable youth group, the youth minister may be more involved with life and death spiritual struggles than anyone else in the church.

THE NEEDS TO BE ADDRESSED

It is not postmodernism that determines the needs of those who are held captive by postmodernism. Their basic needs are determined by God. These basic needs were designed into each person's very being when God created them in His own image. These needs include: being rightly related to God, functioning rationally, thinking and acting morally, relating interpersonally, and relating intrapersonally.

The meeting of these needs is complicated by guilt and depravity. God determines the needs and makes provision for the needs related to guilt and depravity. The guilt of sin places people under the sentence of eternal death (Rom. 6:23; Rev. 20:10; and 21:8). Depravity draws us into sin and seeks to confuse knowledge and suppress Truth (Rom. 1:18; 8:7, 8).

GOD'S PROVISION

Jesus made provision for the only escape from this eternal death by His death and righteousness (Is. 53:6; 1 Pet. 2:24; Gal. 3:13; and 2 Cor. 5:21). The need created by depravity is met by God's provision of regeneration (Jn. 3:3, 5; Tit. 3:5; 2 Cor. 5:17; Eph. 2:1, 2, 10). Those who come to God through Christ receive forgiveness for their sins, are regenerated, and are indwelt by the Holy Spirit (Rom. 8:9). They have God's word to guide and instruct them (2 Tim. 3:16). They have the ministry of their pastor and others who are gifted in the church (Eph. 4:11, 12; Rom. 12:3-8; and

1 Cor. 12:4-31). They also have the fellowship of the saints (1 Jn. 1:3), and the encouragement from others in the church (Heb. 10:25).

THE DIFFICULTY OF OUR ASSIGNMENT

In talking about creation by God in His image, sin, guilt, depravity, judgment, eternal death, atonement, salvation, etc. we are talking about Truth. To use Francis Schaeffer's term, we are talking about "true Truth." We find ourselves at cross purposes with postmodernism. If you do not have "true Truth," you do not have Christianity. We must cling to the words of Jesus when He said, "And you shall know the truth, and the truth shall make you free" (Jn. 8:32, NKJV). As we attempt to rescue those who are lost on the postmodern sea, we must cling to the words of Jesus when He said, "Lo, I am with you always, even to the end of the age" (Mt. 28:20, NKJV).

Most of the people that we will be dealing with are not consciously committed to the tenets of postmodernism. But they are influenced by the postmodern mood. This is particularly true of young people. They are candidates to become full-blown postmodernists if they do not receive the help they need. Those who are brought up in good Christian homes are not exempted from this influence. They are conditioned by relativism and pluralism. They do not feel deeply about sin. Even if they are not convinced by postmodernism's denial of truth, they are numbed by the influence of postmodernism. They are little by little being overwhelmed by the spirit of the age as its influence is manifested in music, clothing styles, and other entertainment genre.

THE REASON FOR HOPE

When we assess the nature and the influence of postmodernism, it is easy to drift into despair. Christianity and postmodernism stand in opposition to each other on the question of Truth, the question of reason, the question of morals, the question of ideals, and the possibility of a rationally consistent worldview.

We need to keep in mind that the one who is held captive by depravity and postmodernism is made in the image of God. The enslaving power of sin is great. But depravity cannot totally silence the image of God.

Postmodernism is attempting to tear the label "sin" off all activity that may appeal to depravity. Postmodernism tells private judgment that it can stamp approval on anything it chooses and call it right. But deep down the inner self knows better. God has unalterably written in every human heart with indelible ink the same moral message that is written in the Ten Commandments. Postmodernism is not able to make either hedonism or nihilism acceptable to the image of God.

Human beings are in desperate need of a worldview. They are in desperate need of a pilot who can navigate the ocean of reality. They are in desperate need of knowledge about their origin. They need to know their true identity. They need help with the present stresses of life. They need to know about life after death. They are in need of a manual from their maker. Postmodernism can neither satisfy these needs nor erase them. The troubled and mixed-up condition of our culture testifies that postmodernism does not make people free.

There is enmity, resistance, and hostility, but the image of God can be appealed to. We have the promise of empowerment by the Holy Spirit (Acts 1:8). Our assignment is difficult, but not impossible. If we will move forward with a heart full of compassion, a mind committed to finding answers, and full commitment to do God's work, we can reach many with the message of hope and freedom. We can make a difference.

Reaching People Before 1960 and Reaching People Since 1990

THE GENERAL POPULATION BEFORE 1960

In the general population prior to 1960, as a rule, it could be assumed that the person that you were talking to was a part of the Christian consensus. We could assume that the person believed in life after death. He or she would believe in Heaven and Hell. He had respect for the Bible. He or she thought that he would get saved before he died. Some would be more concerned about it than others. Some were more resistant than others. But only a few turned a deaf ear to the whole matter of salvation. The soul winner could assume a common ground on belief about God, Jesus Christ, the Bible, and eternity. Approaches like the Romans Road were used and helped many come to faith in Jesus Christ.

THE GENERAL POPULATION SINCE 1990

In the general population in the 1990s, we are faced with an entirely different situation. As I have said many times in this book, "A Paradigm shift has taken place." We can still reach people for Christ. But, when we approach people, it cannot be assumed that the person is in common agreement with us on belief about God, Jesus Christ, the Bible, and eternity. Even if this common agreement exists, we cannot assume that the person has given serious attention to when or whether to make a decision for Christ. It may be that he or she is too satisfied with material prosperity to give attention to eternal matters. However, it is more likely that they are so taken up with the stresses and strains of this life that it draws attention away from giving adequate attention to eternal matters.

Before 1960, people in the general population believed in objective Truth. The objective Truth of Heaven and Hell weighed heavily upon them. You might say that it was a concern for where they would spend eternity that motivated them. When I was saved in 1944, it was 100% because I did not want to go to Hell. I still have respect for that reason, but I have broader reasons for serving God now. Those reasons embrace both the here and now and the hereafter.

Things are drastically different now from what they were before 1960. I hope that what I have said earlier sheds light on why that is true. Postmodernism has either dulled their interest in Christianity or it has turned them away altogether. But it has brought no comfort. The focus is on here and now needs. Even when there is a concern about life after death, they are not as prone to be consumed by it as many were before 1960. They are concerned with how do deal with the stresses and strains of life. They are concerned about emptiness, loneliness, boredom, feeling of rejection, emotional pain, meaning and purpose for life, etc. If it is not their own concern that consumes them, it is someone else's problems. A loved one may be having problems with drugs. A family member may be getting a divorce. The list could go on. Many are candidates for a view that offers help for both the hereafter and the here and now. If Christianity is to get their attention, it must be seen as sympathetic to their here and now needs.

THE ACADEMIC WORLD BEFORE 1960

Students entering colleges and universities, other than Christian schools, prior to 1960 could expect some challenges to be made to their faith. The main area of challenge was in the area of origins—the origin of the universe and man. But there was some important common ground between the modernist and the Christian—both believed in the existence of Truth. Both had great respect for the law of non-contradiction. This gave rise to the popularity of evidential apologetics for evangelistic purposes on college and university campuses.

THE ACADEMIC WORLD SINCE 1990

Under modernism, the emphasis on objective Truth made students look for a standard of Truth outside of themselves. This meant that proving the Christian message to be objectively true was a logical path to follow. Under postmodernism, the emphasis has shifted from objective validation to subjective or internal validation. The shift is away from the objective validation of "true Truth" to "truth for you" and "truth for me."

Postmodernism would not be "post" modernism if it still sought for universal, objective Truth. We would still have modernism. Once a person forsakes the concept of universal, objective Truth, the only thing left is "truth" that is not "true." "Truth" is not "true," for the postmodernist because it passes the test of rational coherence or the test of correspondence to reality, but rather because it "works" for the person. Postmodern "truth" is decidedly pragmatic and utilitarian in nature.

The shift is to the internal or inner person for two reasons. The first reason is that if there is no objective Truth there is no objective validation. The only thing left is internal validation. There is nowhere else to look for validation. The second reason is that the denial of objective Truth leaves people with unmet needs. That is the only way it can be. That is what would lead an artist to produce a painting that conveys the idea that reality is characterized by chaos, confusion, disorder, and has no purpose and meaning and thus giving it the title "Abandoned."[8] Troubled people look inward. That is where their pain is.

Christian evangelism can never surrender the idea that Truth is objective. It must proclaim that it is the Truth that makes people free (Jn. 8:32). But Christianity, to be biblical Christianity, must be interested in the total needs of each person. People have a right to expect their inner needs to be addressed. Christianity is for the total personality. When the Christian message is presented, people should feel like what is happening in their inner-selves is being explained.

Evangelism at the Beginning of the Third Millennium

I will speak of evangelism at the beginning of the Third Millennium, because as we move further into this millennium, circumstances will change. Though cultures change, Truth is unchanging.

In the basic sense, human need is unchanging. The common factors that we must keep in mind at all times and in all places are that human beings are created in God's image, have sinned, and are under the sentence of eternal death. In our rescue work, no matter where we are, we have to take into account that the image of God is being held captive by depravity. Our present concern is with regard to those whom postmodernism has joined with depravity to hold the image of God captive.

Christian theology is timeless. For that reason, the theology of this book is not affected by time or location. However, those comments that are addressed to the shift from modernism to postmodernism are not timeless. They do not fit all locations. The evangelist, pastor, missionary, or soul-winner must analyze the situation that he or she is facing. He must come to an understanding of what is holding the image of God hostage in the location where he is working. He must also come to an understanding of what it is that is hindering the rescue effort in the case or cases where he is involved in a rescue effort.

I believe it is important for missionaries to address the culture where they labor in a similar fashion as I have done in this book with modernism and postmodernism. The situation is not simple anywhere anymore. Even in The US and Canada, in addition to being able to deal with the influence of depravity and postmodernism, a person needs to understand the uniqueness of his own particular situation. He may also need to work on developing a plan of rescue for those who are under the influence of cults, pagan religions, or even Satanism.

Our present purpose is to focus on the culture as it is currently, and will be for sometime, permeated with the influence of postmodernism. Even if there would be some major change soon, the influence of postmodernism would hang on during a transition period.

REACHING THE GENERAL POPULATION

People today are concerned with how to deal with the stresses and strains of life. They are concerned about emptiness, loneliness, boredom, feelings of rejection, emotional pain, meaning and purpose for life, guilt, and anxiety. They are not preoccupied with the question of where they will spend eternity. It is not appealing to them to lay aside their current pain and concerns in order to focus on thoughts about life after death. If Christianity is to get their attention, it must be seen as sympathetic to their needs here and now.

I believe the Christian message is what these people desperately need. Jesus said, "I have come that they might have life, and that they might have it more abundantly" (Jn. 10:10, NKJV). Jesus felt people's pain. He wept at the grave of Lazarus (Jn. 11:35). You can sense the pain that Jesus felt for the Pharisees who were at cross purposes with Him when He said, "O Jerusalem, Jerusalem, the one who kills the prophets and stones those who are sent to her! How often I wanted to gather your children together, as a hen gathers her chicks under her wings, but you were not willing!" (Mt. 23:37, NKJV). Hear the words of Jesus when He said:

> Come to Me, all *you* who labor and are heavy laden, and I will give you rest. Take My yoke upon you and learn from Me, for I am gentle and lowly in heart, and you will find rest for your souls. For My yoke *is* easy and My burden is light (Mt. 11:28-30, NKJV).

We are simply being Christian when we have a compassionate concern for people's hurts and concerns about the problems of this life. But we must not allow our attention to be drawn away from the eternal context in which Christian thought and concerns operate. We must continually remind ourselves and others of the coming Great White Throne judgment. The only way that our guilt could be taken care of was for Jesus Christ, while on the cross, to suffer the full wrath of God for our sins.

Christian thought embraces the whole of reality. It is a worldview. There is no truth that stands outside the Christian worldview. Though it is very comprehensive and the community of believers will never agree on some points, there are a few basic truths that are absolutely essential. If you were to subtract the concepts of sin, guilt, judgment and Hell, you would no longer have Christianity. If you subtract these you have subtracted atonement. That is true because without sin, guilt, judgment, and Hell there is no need of atonement. Without atonement Christianity does not exist.

In a postmodern culture, we must keep alive the doctrines of sin, guilt, judgment, Hell, and a view of atonement that settles the problem of our guilt. It is true that Jesus cares about our hurts in this life. We must give a strong and a continuing emphasis to that fact. But it was not because people were troubled, hurting, and mixed up that Jesus had to go to the cross. He did not undergo punishment for us because we were troubled. He was punished for us because we were guilty. If turning up the volume on the here-and-now needs of people causes us to downplay the truth of guilt, judgment, Hell, and atonement, we will do both Christianity and the people that we are ministering to a serious disservice.

THE NEED TO MINISTER TO PEOPLE'S HERE-AND-NOW HURTS

I bring these words of caution as one who is deeply concerned about helping people with their here and now concerns. I have spent a considerable amount of time talking with people about a very wide range of problems. I was sounding the need of ministering to people's hurts before it received popular attention. I have been doing it for over thirty years.

The first factor that aroused my interest in this area was prompted what I read in the Bible. When we read the Bible, we are confronted over and over again with the truth that God is interested in people's hurts and that He wants us to be interested in people's hurts (Jn. 13:35, Gal. 6:2).

The second factor that influenced me to be interested in ministering to people's hurts grew out of the realization that the oversimplified approach did not work for me. I knew that there had to be answers that would work because I knew that Jesus spoke the truth when He said, "And you shall know the truth, and the truth shall make you free" (Jn. 8:32, NKJV). Slowly, truth began to unfold to me in a way that was meaningful. I shared some of the things that helped me in my classes. I reasoned that if I had a problem, someone else had the same problem. If something had helped me, I reasoned that it would help others too.

The third factor that motivated me to be interested in ministering to people's hurts is that for seventeen out of the more than forty years I have been on the faculty at Free Will Baptist Bible College, I was either dean of men or dean of students. I was not trained in counseling, but I cared about people. I made up my mind that I was, at least, going to try to be of help to those who wanted help. As I worked at doing what I could, and refused to believe that nothing could be done, slowly understanding developed. After things took shape in my mind so that I could organize them into a course, I taught a course titled "Understanding and Helping People."

In several years of counseling, I found meaning in knowing that human beings are designed by God. Understanding the nature of that *design* helped me to understand people, and helped them to understand themselves. That is why in this book I have given such a strong emphasis to the fact that we have a *design* that it is designed into us by God. *Design* determines need.[9]

In ministering to the postmodern culture, the factor that will open more doors to us than anything else will be for us to manifest a genuine interest in people and their needs. We do this because God has planted a love in our hearts that will not be silent. What we do must grow out of a genuine desire to help people—not simply as a means of reaching more people. It will help us reach more people—but if we are going to be Christian, we have no other choice. One of the most important things that we can do in reaching people for Christ is to simply be what a Christian should be. In being Christian, we must manifest a concern for people's needs.

The challenge before us is to determine how we can show genuine concern for people's need in the here and now. When we show concern for people's here and now needs, it will not go unnoticed. In many cases, it will open the door for sharing with them that Christianity exists in the context of eternity. There is a past, present, and future of Christianity. The past of Christianity looks back to eternity past. The future of Christianity takes us into the eternal future.

DEVELOPING THE STORY OF REDEMPTION

God has always existed. There was a time when only God existed. He created the universe and its plant and animal inhabitants. He created Adam and Eve in His image. Adam and Eve sinned. Their sin involved the human race. It introduced sin as guilt and depravity. God set in motion a plan of redemption. In bringing about that plan of redemption, God called the nation of Israel into existence through Abraham. He made a covenant with Abraham that would eventually involve the provision and offer of salvation for everyone who would come to Jesus Christ by faith.

Outside the Book of Job, every book in the Old Testament was written by a descendant of Abraham. It was through Moses, a descendant of Abraham, that God established the Covenant of Law, also referred to as the Mosaic Covenant. This Law gave instructions to the Israelites about how to live and how to worship God. This Law did much to prepare the way for the coming of the Messiah. *Messiah* is from a Hebrew word. *Christ* is from a Greek word. They both refer to the same person. They refer to God's Anointed One.

As time passed on, God made another covenant with David , another descendant of Abraham. He promised David that one of His descendants would be the Messiah. He would be the One who would save His people from their sins. After David there was a period of prophets. In the Old Testament we have several books that were written by these prophets that prepared the way for the coming of Christ.

The time finally arrived when Christ came. He was born of the Virgin Mary. He was given the name of Jesus. He lived a sinless life. In His ministry He gave us the most noble teachings about right and wrong, and good and bad that the world has ever known. He was a person of great compassion. He performed many miracles. These miracles were God's way of stamping His approval on Jesus. It was God's way of saying, "He is who He claims to be. He is My Son. Everything He tells you is true." The Gospels make clear to us that Jesus is fully God and fully man. He is both God and man. He is the God-man.

As it had been planned by God in eternity past, Jesus died on the cross. While He was dying on the cross, He took our sins upon Him and suffered the full wrath of God for our sins. He paid for our sins so we would not have to pay for them by going to Hell. He was buried. But on the third day He came forth victorious over sin, death, Hell, and the grave. When God raised Jesus from the dead, that was the miracle of miracles. That was God's greatest stamp of approval on Jesus. The resurrection from the dead proved beyond all doubt that Jesus was and is the Son of God.

Before He ascended into Heaven, He commanded us to tell people about Him so they could become His disciples. Now He is giving people an opportunity to be saved by believing in Him. He will come again. There are too many things that will happen in connection with the second coming of Christ to list them here. But there will be a time when God will bring things as we know them here and now to a close. Those who are saved will spend eternity with Him. Those who are not saved will spend eternity in Hell.

If you take the context of eternity away, you destroy Christianity. A worldview must deal with eternity past and eternity future. It is only when we think in the context of eternity that we can adequately deal with the present. That was one of the problems with modernism. Without God in the eternal past and the eternal future, they had no adequate basis for ethics, i.e., for human beings living in the here and now. No one has been able to construct an adequate and lasting view of morals and ethics without an eternal frame of reference. I think postmodernism knows this. That is why it settles for relativism.

One of the reasons the cults have posed such a threat to conservative Christians is that almost all of the cults have a developed view of God's plan of the ages. They teach it to ordinary people.

One of the greatest weaknesses of conservative Christianity is that there is very little attempt made, on the local church level, to set forth a developed plan of the drama of redemption. About the only ones who have ever made any wide-scale attempt were the advocates of the view of dispensational premillennialism in its older form. It was popularized by the old Scofield Bible.

While there has been a weakness when it comes to a developed view of the drama of redemption, a knowledge of bare essentials were known widely in the general population until recent years. There was a belief in creation. There was some knowledge that the Bible was divided into the Old and New Testaments. There was a belief in Heaven and Hell. There was some knowledge that Jesus Christ was in some way involved in the individual escaping Hell. That may not be much. But it is vastly more than not having this bare knowledge.

I gave this very brief look at Christianity from eternity to eternity to remind us that that kind of knowledge is very important. It cannot be assumed today. It is necessary for a person to have at least some meager knowledge of how Christ fits into history before he or she can have saving faith.

REACHING THE ACADEMIC WORLD

What I have said above about reaching the general population applies to the academic world. Students are filled with unmet needs. They are hungry. If they are not in a Christian school, they are in the midst of strongholds for the influence of postmodernism. The college years are dangerous years. The influence of drugs, alcohol, and sexual immorality of all kinds is prevalent.

A person who hopes to have success with university evangelism must have some knowledge of the paradigm shift from modernism to postmodernism. He must have knowledge of the subject so he can engage in conversation on the areas of concern. He or she needs to be a good listener in order to pick up on points of interest that can help to turn the discussion to spiritual matters.

One thing to be listening for are indications that the person is struggling with the *inescapable questions of life,* such as: Is there a God? What about right and wrong? What about life after death? Is there meaning and purpose in life? A person should be careful to discern the difference between those who have genuine concerns and those who just want to argue.

A person doing university evangelism should be able to hold his ground on evidence and arguments, but evidential apologetics is not as useful addressing those who are under the influence of the postmodernist paradigm as it was for those under the modernist paradigm. Though the postmodernist does not recognize the validity of the law of non-contradiction, they will try to use it in arguing against Christianity. The Christian should be able to hold his ground well at times like that. But detecting and ministering to the hunger that God has placed within human beings is what will bring the most fruit in the postmodern culture.

We are still in the period of assessment when it comes to university evangelism under postmodernism. It is evident that what was once rather successful is not working so well now. But we must remember that the image of God is not silent on university campuses, and the Holy Spirit still works on university campuses.

The Importance of General Revelation in Ministering in a Postmodern Culture

General revelation has been a much neglected subject. In dealing with the subject of revelation, a small amount of attention is usually given to general revelation to make the treatment of the subject of revelation complete. Sometimes attention is given to general revelation when a person wants to build a case for believing that the heathen are lost. For the most part, the feeling has been that since we have special revelation, general revelation is not of much value to us. It has, in the past, received almost no attention in preaching. In recent years, the subject of general revelation has received more attention among theologians.

GENERAL REVELATION AND GUILT, JUDGMENT, AND HELL

Guilt, judgment, and Hell are based on general revelation, not special revelation. Special revelation sets these truths forth and enlarges upon them. However, it is not necessary for a person to be charged with the disobedience of special revelation in order to stand condemned before God.

In building his case to show that the whole world stands guilty and condemned before God (Rom. 3:19, 20), Paul does not begin by showing that they had violated special revelation. Rather, he begins by showing that people are guilty of violating the message of general revelation.

In Romans 1:18 Paul tells us that, based on general revelation, God's wrath is against: (1) Ungodliness, (2) Unrighteousness, and (3) The suppression of the Truth. These three experiences describe every human being. That means that every human being as he or she stands before God on his own merit is condemned and under His wrath. In building a case to show why all people, *including those who have only general revelation,* are justly under God's condemnation and wrath, Paul makes the following things clear:

1. By general revelation, people know that God exists (Rom. 1:19, 21).

2. By general revelation, people have a knowledge of the eternal power and the attributes of God. This would include the fact that God is holy (Rom. 1:20).

3. This knowledge of the existence and the attributes of God which people have by general revelation renders them without defense before God (Rom. 1:20). This means that no defense can be made that would protect them from the wrath of God.

4. In Romans 1:32, Paul makes it clear that general revelation makes people aware that they are worthy of death.

5. In Romans 2:12-15, Paul makes it clear that the Gentiles who have only general revelation stand condemned before God. They have violated the moral law that is written in their hearts.

6. The verdict in Romans 3:19, 20 is that, as they stand on their own merits, the whole world stands guilty and condemned before God.

7. In Romans 3:23 (NKJV), when Paul says, "For all have sinned and fall short of the glory of God," he was including the Gentile world, as well as the Jews who had sinned against the written Law of God (Rom. 2:12).[10]

Internal Validation of Basic Knowledge about God, Morals, Guilt, Judgment, and Hell

I have called attention to the fact that under postmodernism more attention is being given to inner concerns and internal validation than was the case when modernism was reigning in secular culture. I believe that Paul's teaching on the concepts of God's existence, His basic attributes, human guilt, and divine judgment of human guilt receive internal validation.

GENERAL REVELATION AND THE KNOWLEDGE OF GOD

In Romans 1:19, 20 Paul was saying more than, "It is *possible* for a person to know that God exists and to know something about His attributes." Paul was saying, "Every person has knowledge of God's existence and a basic understanding of His attributes." (Support for these conclusions is more fully developed in my treatment of general revelation in Chapter 3.)

This brings up the question, "What about the person who does not believe in God?" In spite of what the person says, I believe that he or she *does know* that God exists. Having said that, let me make some things clear. I am not saying that the person who says, "I don't believe in God," is lying. I am saying that in his or her deep inner self a knowledge of God *does* exist. The only thing that allows a person to say, "I don't believe in God" and not be lying is that he has *suppressed* that knowledge. Having suppressed that knowledge, a person can say, "I don't believe in God" and not be lying on the conscious level. But if he or she would cease suppressing the truth of God's existence, that truth would come to the surface and God's existence would be acknowledged.

Paul makes it clear in Romans 1:18 that God's wrath is against the suppression of Truth. A person *knows* that which he or she is *suppressing* into the subconscious mind. *Suppressed knowledge is still knowledge.* The Supreme Judge of the universe holds a person responsible for the truth that he or she *suppresses*.

GENERAL REVELATION AND KNOWLEDGE OF MORALS

It is at this point that postmodernism has inflicted the most damage on society. Its damage goes far beyond the damage that was inflicted by modernism in the area of morals. Modernism believed that nature had a "nature" (a character or constitution). In Christian theology, God is the author of this "nature." Nature is morally constituted. The morality of the Ten Commandments is written on every human heart. Though modernism rejects the divine authorship of the moral "nature" in nature, by its reflection on nature it was able to read the basic moral concepts that were written in nature. Though modernism failed to give God the credit, it was able to read with benefit the message of general revelation.

When the person who has been influenced by the conditioning power of postmodernism hears the voice of this moral revelation that is within, he attempts *to deny its validity and to suppress it.* Instead of giving recognition to these concepts, he blames the conditioning power of the influence of the traditional values of Western culture. It is the influence of the imperialistic culture of the Enlightenment, or Christianity seeking to bring him or her under its oppressive power. This approach is taken because he has been influenced by postmodernism to believe that there is no moral "nature" to nature. There is no universal Truth that is written in human nature.

The postmodernist operates on the basis of the hermeneutics of suspicion. He or she believes that the moral teachings of Christianity have as their design to oppress him or her and deny the pleasures of life. The only available freedom then is to have the courage to resist the voice of general revelation. The evidence of freedom is to cast off the restraints imposed by Christianity.

Postmodernism does not recognize that human beings are made in the image of God. But this denial has no power over the fact. A person could deny the law of gravity. But that would not change the reality that if you threw an object into the air it would certainly fall. If a person either denies or tries to ignore the fact of the presence of the image of God within, that will not keep the image of God from springing into action when he or she violates the morality of the Ten Commandments. That fact does not depend on whether the person has ever read or heard of the Ten Commandments. It is based on the premise that the basic morality of the Ten Commandments is written on the heart of every human being. Whenever this moral nature is trampled on, it spells trouble. This is true whether we are talking about an individual or whether we are talking about a society.

As the postmodern influence has infiltrated our culture, it has brought a tide of moral degradation. The disregard of the message of general revelation that is written in the human heart has wreaked havoc on our society. We live in a troubled society, as evidenced by those who seek legal and legitimate help from psychologists, psychiatrists, and pastors. It is also evidenced by those who seek help by illegal drugs and alcohol. Another area that tells us that we live in a troubled culture is the plunge into pornography, sexual immorality, and abortion. Another indicator is the problem of divorce and troubled homes.

For the young and immature, drugs, alcohol, pornography, and sexual immorality seem to offer a life of excitement and fun. I was, by God's grace, spared from these experiences, but I can remember how, as a young person, I thought such people were really enjoying life. Since then, I have come to understand how wrong my assessment was. I have heard too many tales of woe from those who have traveled these roads. I have helped too many people try to deal with the scars that were inflicted by their own experience with these sins and/or the sins of others. I have come to realize that sin is not only *wrong* but *bad*.

We do not understand drug addiction, alcohol addiction, and numberless kinds of addiction until we understand that people who become addicted are looking for answers to deep inner needs. There are basically two reasons that people get involved with drugs. The first reason is that they are looking for fellowship and acceptance rather than an experience with drugs. But the place in which they found acceptance and fellowship was where people were doing drugs. The second reason people get involved in drugs is to kill emotional pain and experience an emotional lift. This reason more likely leads one into addiction. People who are getting along all right do not get involved in drug addiction.

Postmodernism's short history has been negative. Whatever joy it has brought to people has been short-lived. Sin does have pleasure for a season (Heb. 11:25, 26). Trouble and unrest have increased under postmodernism's influence. Postmodernism offers no help. It denies that there is any such thing as a universal and timeless answer to human need.

GENERAL REVELATION AND THE NEEDS OF SOCIETY

General revelation conveys enough truth that, if followed, it could lay the foundation for a reasonably stable society. However, there is always the problem of getting people to follow the truth of general revelation even if they recognize it. But the problem with postmodernism is much greater than that. There is a denial of any universal Truth from any source that instructs human behavior.

What makes our situation under the influence of postmodernism so atypical in human history is that there is an attempt to put together a society that eliminates all religious input.

David Wells reminds us:

> Beneath all other major cultures were religious assumptions, whether these came from Hinduism, Islam, or Christianity itself. There are no such religious assumptions

beneath our culture, however, and this is the first time any major civilization has attempted to build itself this way.[11]

Wells further observes:

> In the nineteenth century in particular, there were numerous attempts to establish a system of morals that did not need to assume the existence of God and his revelation. These experiences were all conducted by a small avant-garde made up of philosophers, novelists, and artists. What has changed is that now the whole society has become avant-garde. It is the whole society that is now engaged in this massive experiment to do what no other major civilization has done—to rebuild itself deliberately and self-consciously without religious foundations. And the bottom line of this endeavor is that truth in any absolute sense is gone. Truth, like life, is fractured. Like experience, it is disjointed. Like our perceptions of ourselves, it is uncertain. It takes on different appearances as we move between the small units of meaning that make up our social experience. Like our manners, it must be adapted to each context and it must remain flexible. It is simply a type of etiquette. It has no authority, no sense of rightness, because it can no longer find any anchorage in anything absolute. If it persuades, it does so because our experience has given it its persuasive power—but tomorrow our experience might be different.[12]

Chuck Colson reminds us:

> There has never been a case in history in which a society has been able to survive for long without a strong moral code. And there has never been a time when a moral code has not been informed by religious truth. Recovering our moral code—our religious truth—is the only way our society can survive. The heaping ash of Auschwitz, the killing fields of Southeast Asia, and the frozen wastes of the gulag remind us that the city of man is not enough; we must also seek the city of God.[13]

The present emphasis on religious pluralism will be short-lived if postmodernism prevails. It must be remembered that postmodernism is secular. Postmodernism is giving lip service to religious pluralism. But the driving force behind postmodernism is not to promote a society where religious pluralism prevails. It is secular to the core. Its aim is to build a society where religion is eliminated. Its aim is to eliminate the influence of both special revelation and general revelation. It should be obvious to all who are old enough to remember what life in America was like prior to 1960 that, as Christians, our liberties are more threatened now than they were prior to 1960.

I am sure there are those who are more or less identified with the postmodern culture who do have a genuine interest in religious pluralism. But all movements that affect masses of people will either die or move toward a logical consistency with their basic premises.

Postmodernism had a secular birth. A secular parent gives birth to a secular child. The failure of modernism brought on the birth of postmodernism. When it became convincingly evident that modernism could not deliver on its promises, postmodernism rose up and dethroned its parent. If postmodernism ceases to be secular, it will cease to be "post" modernism. If a complete disconnection with secularism would occur, whatever resulted from such a move would have to be numbered among the religions of the world. It would either be absorbed into existing religions, or it would become a new religion.

The Rational Needs of Human Beings

THE IMAGE OF GOD AND RATIONAL DESIGN

Colossians 3:10 makes it clear that a basic and very important part of what it means to be in the image of God is that, as human beings, we are in the *rational* likeness of God. The Creator designed rationality into the very essence of our nature. This means that we can reason and think. This not only means that we are *able* to reason and learn—it also means that we have *rational needs*. We *need* to learn. We need to develop a rational understanding of things. We need more than a few fragments of knowledge. We need a comprehensive view of life and thought. We need to develop a rationally consistent worldview or lifeview.

OUR INNER NATURE AND THE LAW OF NON-CONTRADICTION

When our conscious mind becomes aware of what seems to be a contradiction, a caution light comes on. Our deep inner self (the image of God within) does not accept contradictions. The image of God may find it necessary to live with some ideas that it cannot fully reconcile, but that leaves, at least, some level of concern. As human beings, we cannot easily bring ourselves to the point of knowingly accepting contradictions in our thinking. Our whole being cries out against such thinking (non-thinking). Even those who admit contradictions in their thinking do not hesitate to criticize their opponent if they see what appears to be a contradiction in his thinking.

The law of non-contradiction is innate. A child does not have to take a course in logic before he will point out what he or she thinks is a contradiction. In rearing children, it is not uncommon to hear a child say, "You let him do it; why can't I do it?" One of the things that makes me know that people have more intelligence than they use is that everybody can split hairs when it comes to defending his or her own action.

Let us now go back to the question, "If the law of non-contradiction is innate, how do we explain the rise and strength of postmodernism?"

Modernism, as a child of the Enlightenment, thought that unaided reason would be able to solve all the needs of human beings. It sought to make this dream a reality through empiricism. Empiricism proceeded to develop its thinking by reflecting on the data of observation and experience. In leaving out any possibility for the validity of the data of divine revelation, empiricism asserted epistemological atheism. In its epistemology, God was omitted.

The change from modernism to postmodernism was inherent in the epistemology of modernism from the outset. When followed, epistemological atheism would inevitably end in what we now call postmodernism. This is true because without God, there is no foundation for truth, morals, and ideals. Given time, the human mind would inevitably recognize all of this. It did. When this was recognized, the birth pains of postmodernism began.

By the end of World War II, it was becoming evident in the secular community that man's inhumanity to man was making it impossible for the honest observer to hold any longer to the concept of the basic goodness of man. The Korean War gave additional evidence that modernism's utopian dream was not in sight. The evidence was building. Many in the secular community were beginning to judge modernism, as a worldview, to be a failure. By 1960 this thinking began to reach the grass roots level, particularly among college students. We now know that what followed in the 1960s was the beginning of postmodernism.

Postmodernism is not the result of careful research and philosophical thinking. It was not chosen because of its superiority over modernism. Rather, it was a result of the failure of modernism. It was a leap into the realm of the irrational. The only way to remain secular and to reject modernism was to reject the law of non-contradiction. Where else was there to go and still remain secular? If a person was going to reject modernism and still remain secular, he must reject a view that had placed its hope in reason. He had to reject reason, as far as the law of non-contradiction is concerned. When the law of non-contradiction is rejected, reason is gone. Any attempt to hang on to the hope that a solution to man's problems would be solved by reason would be some form of modernism. That was held to be untenable.

Let's go back again to the question, "If the law of non-contradiction is innate, how do we explain the rise and strength of postmodernism?" It is based on a determination, on the part of its adherents to remain secular. They were unwilling to abandon the ship of secularism. They chose to oust modernism and seize control of the ship. There are no other choices for the person who wants to be secular. The choice is either to accept some form of modernism or to reject the law of non-contradiction.

THE NEED TO ADDRESS PEOPLE'S MINDS AND HEARTS

In this book, I have given considerable attention to the *inescapable questions of life*. They are questions such as: Is there a God? If so, what is He like? How do I know what is right and what is wrong? Is there life after death? If there is how do I get ready for it? We do not have to be afraid of saying that all people have these questions. When my wife and I spent four months in Ukraine and Russia in 1996, I was on the lookout to see if there was any evidence that anyone had been able to face life and not face these questions. I found no evidence that anyone had. In a brief sojourn in Japan, I found no evidence that anyone had totally escaped having to deal with such questions. My anecdotal experience is not exhaustive. But neither is it insignificant.

When people go to church, they need to feel like they have been spoken to. They need to feel like what they are hearing explains what is happening inside of them. They need to be developing an understanding of themselves and how to face life. They need to feel like someone in the church would care about their concerns and would be available to answer their questions.

Another person cannot simply act on my confidence that every human being is faced by these or similar questions as growth and development takes place. You have to think about your own experience, you have to start listening for clues as you talk to other people, as you move about in society, as you watch television, etc. You need your own validation that all people are faced with these questions. When you have your own validation, the thinking becomes yours. You can then have freedom in using these ideas. You will have a confidence that will prepare you to speak effectively to other people about what is going on within them. We need to be addressing questions that people are asking at their most basic level of needs.

THE NEED TO KNOW THE ORIGIN OF MAN AND THE UNIVERSE

People want to know about their roots. They want to know their identity. People want to know their family history. If you will find a web-page on the Internet that deals with genealogies, you will find that people are desperately searching for their roots. It is very moving to see how those who were adopted are passionately searching to find their birth parents.

Our interest in family history should tell us something about human beings. It may not take as much in-depth information for some as it will others, but people want to know about the origin of the universe and man. The fact that people have spent millions of hours and billions of dollars trying to build a case for evolution should tell us that human beings are desperately interested in knowing the origin of the human race. We need to give them the only answer that satisfies the deepest needs of the human soul.

THE NEED FOR ANSWERS FOR THE INESCAPABLE QUESTIONS OF LIFE

Those of us who were brought up in church and a Christian home, have blessings that we take for granted. I had no idea how much it meant to believe in God, to believe that God created the universe and man, to believe in the Bible, and to believe that Jesus Christ is the Son of God until the Hippies came on the scene. They did not have answers to the *inescapable questions of life*. They reacted against traditional Western values. They rioted. They sought meaning through drugs. When I saw what it was doing to them not to have the answers to the *inescapable questions of life*, it began to dawn of me how much it meant to me that I did have answers. I was wealthy and did not know it. My Christian life took on new meaning.

THE NEED OF A COMPREHENSIVE GRASP OF CHRISTIAN TRUTH

For a long time, the church world has been plagued with the question of what is the minimum amount of truth and the minimum amount of commitment that it takes to be saved? I believe that this kind of thinking is a serious mistake. It is a mistake for two reasons. First, the New Testament gives no evidence of being obsessed with such an idea. It always moves toward presenting Christianity in its fulness. Second, it is a gross misunderstanding of the needs of human beings as those needs are determined by the image of God within.

We receive conflicting messages from human beings. The reason for this is that within each human being is the presence of a divided self. There is the presence of the image of God, and there is the presence of depravity trying to unseat the image of God. It is depravity, not the image of God, that would like to get by with minimum Christianity and with the least amount of Truth. We have been commissioned to minister to the image of God. We are not to get our signals from depravity. People like it when they see an overall picture develop.

THE NEED OF A DEVELOPED VIEW OF ESCHATOLOGY

People are in great need of a basic understanding of the historical development of the story of redemption from Genesis 3:15 to the cross. They need, at least, an entry level understanding of the Abrahamic Covenant, the Mosaic Covenant, the Davidic Covenant, and the New Covenant. When they get that, they will want to know more. When we talk about people like Abraham, Jacob, Isaac, Moses, and David, we need to go beyond a mere character study. We need to show their importance in the development of the story of redemption.

People need to have a knowledge of Jesus, who He is, His teachings, and how our redemption centers in Him and Him alone. They need to know something about the history of the church. They, at least, need to know the basics of the eschatological future.

In the last several decades, except for a few voices here and there, a developed eschatology has been considered non-essential. The conviction that Jesus will come again and a few of the barest details about final events is considered adequate. Since a person can believe in amillennialism, pre-millennialism, or postmillennialism and still be saved, it is thought that it does not really matter what a person believes. If it does not matter, it will save a lot of time and effort if we ignore the whole subject. Also, if we neglect the subject, we will cut down on tensions. We will have more unity.

Before we write off the subject of eschatology, we should size up the situation. If a person has not studied the subject of eschatology, he may not realize the extent of what eschatology deals with. Amillennialism, premillennialism, and postmillennialism are referred to as views of eschatology. While the word *eschatology* means a study of last things, these views deal with a lot more than the events surrounding the second coming of Christ. These are actually views of the unfolding of the plan of redemption from Genesis 3:15 until we enter the eternal state. We have no right to deny people a knowledge of the unfolding of the plan of redemption. The image of God needs it. If we deny people the knowledge of eschatology, we deny them the knowledge of the unfolding of the plan of redemption.

THE NEED OF A BASIC UNDERSTANDING OF THE SOVEREIGNTY OF GOD, PREDESTINATION, AND THE QUESTION OF FREE WILL

In the church world, the call of the day is for us to tone down differences. This means that there are not many developed treatments of Classical Arminianism, Wesleyan Arminianism, and Calvinism on the local church level. It is either thought that these matters are not very important, or it is thought that they are just for the clergy and theological schools. Even there, these matters are not as high on the level of priorities as books and seminars dealing with "how to get the job done."

It is imperative for us to follow Paul's example when he said, "I kept back nothing that was helpful, but proclaimed it to you," and "For I have not shunned to declare to you the whole counsel of God" (Acts 20:20, 27, NKJV). We must also keep in mind the words of Jesus when, in answer to Satan, He quoted Deuteronomy 8:3, "Man shall not live by bread alone, but every word that proceeds from the mouth of God" (Mt. 4:4, NKJV).

THE DESPERATE NEED OF GIVING PROPER PLACE TO THE RATIONAL NEEDS OF HUMAN BEINGS

While postmodernism undercuts the use of reason, I believe that the need of the day calls for more use of our minds than at any other point in my lifetime, and perhaps anytime in the history of the church. *Since postmodernism rejects reason, we will have to use it more.* It is the design of human beings in the image of God that determines the fact that we need to use reason in ministering to them. We are trying to rescue the image of God. It is rational by design. *We dare not let postmodernism dictate the terms on which we do evangelism.*

Winning arguments is not the way to reach those who are held captive by postmodernism. But we do not set reason aside. We show a deep interest in people's needs and we use reason to help them understand what their needs are and what the answers are. Our ministry must be to the total personality.

The Moral Needs of Human Beings

The moral needs of human beings are very real. They are written by God on the heart of every human being. We do not need to be intimidated by the questions, "Who's to say that lying is wrong?" "Who's to say that stealing is wrong?" "Who's to say that sex outside marriage is wrong?" The answer to those questions is this: "Every human being who will let the image of God within be heard." No external human authority decides these issues. They are settled by God. They are written on the human heart. God has given us an inner moral authority. It comes across loud and clear if we do not suppress it. These are universal morals. Even postmodernism cannot blot these moral truths from the inner self.

If we expect to minister to people's needs, we must turn up the volume on morality. We must sound the note on character and purity. Human beings were not made for sin. We were made for righteousness. Sin and the image of God cannot live together in full harmony. We need to speak convincingly on moral issues in such a way that it speaks to the deep inner self of those who have been influenced by postmodernism. We must speak compassionately, but convincingly, and meaningfully about sin, guilt, judgment, Hell and atonement.

We must maintain a view of Christian liberty that is biblically based. We must not let our thinking on Christian liberty keep us from having a strong voice against sin and for righteousness. If our voice for righteousness and against sin is weakened, we will do a disservice to the image of God within those who are in drastic need of help. We will do a disservice to God and His church. We need to be compassionately interested in the hurts of people. But we must not let them down by failing to point out their guilt and God's provision of atonement.

HUMAN DESIGN AND BEAUTY

God designed us so we could be like Him. We are to reflect His likeness in everything that we do. We cannot study the descriptions of the tabernacle and the temple without being impressed by God's concern for beauty and excellence. The beauty and majesty of God come across very clearly in the Bible.

What God desires of us, in this regard, comes across very clearly in Philippians 4:8 when Paul says:

> Finally, brethren, whatever things are true, whatever things *are* noble, whatever things *are* just, whatever things *are* lovely, whatever things *are* of good report, if *there is* any virtue and if *there is* anything praiseworthy—meditate on these things (NKJV).

The KJV says "Think on these things." Why did Paul say think on these things? It is because thinking changes behavior. Surely, the *noble*, the *lovely*, and the *praiseworthy* translate into a concern for *beauty, excellence,* and *ideals.*

Beauty, excellence, and ideals have been hit hard by the influence of postmodernism. There was a time when, as opportunity presented itself, the underprivileged would move in the direction of the demeanor of those of greater privilege. Postmodernism's influence has been to reverse that trend. The areas that have been hit the hardest on the grass roots level are music and personal appearance. All human beings are made in the image of God. A Christian's body is the temple of the Holy Spirit (1 Cor. 6:19, 20). We must keep in mind who we are.

The problem of music and personal appearance are not going to be solved by issuing decrees. But God has not granted us the privilege of ignoring the problem. Certainly, He has not stamped His approval on the idea of saying that what people do in this area does not matter. If we ignore it, the image of God suffers.

We will not be able to solve the problems in this area by dwelling on *form.* We must deal with *substance. Substance* deals with basic ideas, concepts and principles. It deals with Truth on the foundational level. It deals with universal Truth. *Form* deals with how we manifest the concern expressed by substance. Form can vary, but it must always be appropriate.[14]

As Christians, we constantly find ourselves, on the one hand, having to hold to high standards. On the other hand, we find ourselves needing to deal with these issues without building a wall between us and the people who have these problems. This applies to an endless list of things such as problems related to alcohol, drugs, sex, divorce, etc. We must learn to deal with areas related to beauty, excellence, and ideals the same way. It requires depth and maturity to do this. With some room for variety and tolerance, educational institutions and churches need to develop a working consensus. We must regain the territory that we have lost in these areas. It would be wonderful if we could see some civility restored in the culture. In this endeavor we have depravity against us, but we have the design of the image of God on our side.

In the area of beauty, excellence, and ideals, I feel so inadequate. Sometimes I feel that I should not be playing, even on the B team. But I am concerned, and I must speak out.

HUMAN DESIGN AND THE NEED FOR INTERPERSONAL RELATIONSHIPS

The need for social relationships is *designed* into every human being (Gen. 2:18). God did not leave that up to each individual to decide. We cannot decide whether we need interactive relationships with other people. God decided that and wrote it indelibly and unalterably in the design of every human being. We need to be aware of this fact and we need to keep this before the people in our churches.

This social need applies to all of a person's contacts with people. We need to make people aware of this fact and give them helpful suggestions. We may not be able to have any influence on what happens in other situations. But we must have as our ideal a healthy interaction between the members of the church. We must be sure that visitors are properly greeted. We must make every effort to see that new people are socially integrated into the church.

What I am saying may be supported by promotional research, but that is not why I am saying it. I am saying it because God has designed a need for social relationships within each person. When they are used properly, there is power in the right kind of social relationships. Paul said, "Evil company corrupts good habits" (1 Cor. 15:33, NKJV). It could also be said that good company makes a positive contribution to "good habits."

Deep within every human being there is a need to be a part of . . . have a feeling of belonging . . . a sense of community. A church should furnish this to its membership and make it available for all who acknowledge Christ as Lord who choose to worship with them.

We must see it as a part of our Christian and biblical responsibility to minister to people's interpersonal needs. This extends to family relationships, friendships, employer-employee relations, teacher-student relationships, etc. When we do these things we will be ministering to the needs of the image of God. It will not go unnoticed by those who are made in God's image.

HUMAN DESIGN AND THE NEED FOR INTRAPERSONAL RELATIONSHIPS

Much that is being said about self-esteem and self-image these days needs to be avoided. But we do not need to condemn the whole subject of self-worth. If human beings have any worth at all, there should be a valid way to approach the subject of self-worth. As to the question of whether human beings have value or worth, Jesus settled that when He said, "You are of more value than many sparrows", and when He asked, "Of how much more value is a man than many sheep?" (Mt. 10:31, 12:12, NKJV)

That every human being is made in the image of God gives value to everyone. Christians have been bought by the death and righteousness of Christ. That is the highest price that was ever paid for anything. The purchase price is to be given consideration in giving an estimate on the value of a person. We tend to recoil from the idea of a human being being purchased because it brings to our mind the times when human beings have been sold as slaves. However, this case is different. Jesus paid the price for us so we can be free.

Christian thought makes it possible for a person to have a true sense of self-worth. We have identification value as one who is created by God in His image. A work of art is of more value when it bears the signature of the artist. When God made us, instead of signing His name, He made us to bear His image. That means value beyond estimation. This extends far beyond us being the highest of the animal kingdom! As Christians, we may add Paul's words, "For you are bought with a price" (1 Cor. 6:19, NKJV). No calculator has enough zeros to compute our value. This inestimable value is "given value." It is a value that we have because we are created by God in His image, and because we have been redeemed by Jesus Christ. It has nothing to do with achievement or accomplishment.

A part of what is involved in being made in the image of God is that there is an automatic inner "mechanism" that judges our thoughts and actions as being becoming or not becoming to one who is made in the image of God. When we have a basically consistent record of living in a way that is becoming of one who is made in the image of God, we have a feeling of self-respect and self-satisfaction. There is no gloating in this. If we ride roughshod over the prompting of the image of God within, there are not enough self-esteem classes in the world to free us from the harm we have done to the way we view ourselves. When we achieve worthy goals, there is a valid sense of self-satisfaction. But this feeling of self-satisfaction must always be accompanied with thanksgiving to God and for the human beings that have contributed to the success that we experience.

The Challenge for the Christian Worldview

CHRISTIANITY AND SCIENCE

Modernism failed as a worldview. In many ways we could say that science was viewed as a child of modernism. Science cannot continue to exist without a worldview. I think we must appeal to scientists and invite them back home. I have already pointed out that science had a Christian birth. It came from a Christian womb. Many scientists have been and many scientists are Christians. With the toppling of modernism, you might say that many in the scientific community became orphans.

It is our opportunity and our responsibility to make these scientists welcome. We must let them know that if they will turn to Jesus Christ as Savior and Lord that they will find the answers that modernism could not give. (1) It will meet the deepest needs of their personality. (2) It will give them eternity with Jesus Christ after this life. (3) The Christian worldview forms a solid foundation for scientific research. (4) It will help them develop ethical guidelines to monitor their research.

CHRISTIANITY, MODERNISM, AND POSTMODERNISM

For the masses of the population, we need to let them know that the eventual failure of modernism was always known by Christians. But the secular world would not listen. They had to experience the failure in no uncertain terms. That took about two hundred years.

It should be obvious that postmodernism has no answers. It has no hope for the next life. It really has nothing to offer in this life. It may look like there are some signs of success. But that needs a more careful look. You might say that about the only seeming evidence that postmodernism has is its ability to achieve a goal. In this pursuit, the only thing that matters is to achieve the desired goal and to stay out of jail in the process. Any difficulties that may happen with regard to moral and ethical matters can be handled by the "Spin Doctors."

This success is accompanied by a pathway of devastation. But even if you would grant the seeming success of postmodernism, we need to take a more careful look. Postmodernism, as we have seen, offers no foundation for scientific research. So far as the secular world is concerned, postmodernism left empirical science an orphan.

In its denial of an ordered universe as a foundation for science, postmodernism does not seem to be aware of what it is doing. While it seeks to inflict a death blow to science, it is living off the benefits of the science that it is undermining. Postmodernism could not produce cars, airplanes, televisions, computers, Internet, nor any of the other benefits of empirical science. But it uses them. Where would postmodernism be without modern technology?

Postmodernism is living dangerously. While it has sought to destroy the foundation which gave birth to science and which sustains its continued existence, it is thriving off the borrowed capital of science. The masses of the population have no idea what damage the postmodern termites have done. The image of God is suffering drastically from this attempt to stifle both general revelation and special revelation.

Our responsibility is a serious one. If we do not face up to the seriousness of the situation, and take appropriate steps to do something about it, our children, our grandchildren, the church, the nation, and the world will suffer. To follow the anti-worldview of postmodernism would spell the death of science, the death of any hope for a healthy working consensus on morals, and beauty. If followed long enough, it would mean the death of civilization. Christianity is a message of hope. Paul tells us, "Godliness is profitable for all things, having promise of the life that now is and of that which is to come" (1 Tim. 4:8, NKJV).

A Concluding Challenge

One of the greatest contributing factors to a weakening of Christianity is that we have been operating from an abridged or truncated view of Christianity. Let me explain what I mean. Except for a few isolated instances, a number of Christian doctrines have been written off. At least, this is true so far as the local church is concerned. Eschatology is considered an easy one to write off. Since a person can be saved and be wrong on his eschatology or have no opinion other than Jesus is coming again, it is no big problem to omit it altogether. There are even gains to leaving it off, it is thought, since it tends to be divisive.

The price that is paid for leaving the treatment of eschatology off is that people have no grasp of the development of the drama of redemption from Genesis 3:15 to the eternal state. The main people of the Old Testament are used for character studies without showing the important place that they had in the unfolding of the drama of redemption. Illiteracy prevails when it comes to Israel and the redemptive covenants.

Significant developments of Arminianism or Calvinism are nearly non-existent on the local church level. The emphasis on generic Christianity makes it so a person could go from a church that is denominationally Arminian to one that is denominationally Calvinistic or vice versa and hardly recognize the difference. This may on the surface look like a good thing because it suggests that there is unity.

The problem that comes from leaving off the treatments of Arminianism and Calvinism is that it promotes illiteracy on some of the most important themes in the Bible: the sovereignty of God, predestination, election, depravity, free will, etc. When these doctrines are not dealt with, the result is a deprived Christian experience. It is hard to have any understanding of salvation without the implications of Calvinism and Arminianism working their way into our thinking and our discussions. We must give fully developed views on the areas of thought covered by Arminianism and Calvinism. We must learn to respect one another. We must be able to interact with one another and at the same time maintain a spirit of unity and fellowship. But we must not promote illiteracy in these areas as a way of maintaining unity.

When we see the beauty, excellence, and the majesty of God, and remember that we are to be in the likeness of God, we should be challenged to demonstrate a concern for beauty, excellence, and ideals. This concern translates into a concern for propriety. It is a truncated view of Christianity when there is loss of concern for propriety. The loss of a sense of propriety is traceable to the influence of postmodernism, first in the culture, and then in the churches. Things that do not belong together take place in the same service. Can we live up to Paul's admonition in Philippians 4:8 and show little or no regard for propriety? Is propriety privatized? Are we to abolish all concern for a consensus on propriety?

I think it is important for us to have peace and unity in our churches. But I think resorting to an abridged Christianity is the wrong way to achieve this unity. It is incumbent upon us to develop a complete and comprehensive view of the Christian worldview. All truth is important. Human beings are designed with a need for a comprehensive worldview.

Let us again be admonished by the words of Paul and the words of Jesus. Paul told the Ephesian elders "I kept back nothing that was helpful, but proclaimed it to you," and "For I have not shunned to declare to you the whole counsel of God" (Acts 20:20, 27, NKJV). In answering Satan, Jesus quoted Deuteronomy 8:3, "Man shall not live by bread alone, but *every word* that proceeds from the mouth of God" (Mt. 4:4, NKJV, emphasis mine). Christianity is comprehensive. It touches all the bases. It speaks to the whole of life and thought. We must not settle for *an abridged or truncated view of Christianity.*

I appreciate every sincere effort that anyone has put forth in trying to reach the people whose lives have been influenced by postmodernism. I think when we take a serious look at what we are dealing with, we will see that some of the methods that have been used will either need to be set aside or seriously modified.

Our challenge is great. We must take our responsibility seriously. Every human being is made in the image of God. He or she is made for a positive relationship with God. For that one who is away from God, there is an emptiness that only God can fill. Even in the most hardened person and in the one in the greatest darkness there is a longing for something that they may not be able to identify. But we know what it is. There is something within that longs for a right relationship with God. It is our responsibility under God to learn how, with the help of God, to reach these people and when we do reach them to give them the whole counsel of God.

Now to Him who is able to keep you from stumbling
And to present you faultless
Before the presence of His glory with exceeding joy,
To God our Savior,
Who alone is wise,
Be glory and majesty,
Dominion and power,
Both now and forever.
Amen
—Jude 24, 25, NKJV

APPENDIX 1

Sins of Ignorance and Presumptuous Sins in the Old and New Testaments[1]

In the Old Testament a distinction is made between what the KJV calls "sins of ignorance" and "presumptuous sins." I will wait until we have examined both Old and New Testament teachings on this subject before drawing conclusions on the propriety of these terms to identify these two types of sins.

In dealing with this subject, I will show how the KJV, the NASB, and the NIV translate the Hebrew words that are used to refer to sins of ignorance and presumptuous sins in the Old Testament. I will also show how the LXX translates these terms as well as give the English translation of the LXX given by Brenton.[2] I will simply refer to it as the translation of the LXX.

At the end of the paper, I will append some tables that I have compiled of all of the Hebrew words that deal with sins of ignorance and presumptuous sins. I give a complete list of the occurrences of each word and how it is translated in the versions to which I have just referred. While these words are not always referring to sin, I give all of the references as a means of helping us grasp the meaning of these words. I will also include a list of pertinent Greek words and the places they are used in the New Testament which shed light on the subject that I am dealing with.

An Examination of Old Testament Teachings

THE TWO TYPES OF SIN SET FORTH
The most important passage of Scripture in showing this distinction is Numbers 15:27-30. In the KJV we are told in verse 27 that if a person sinned through ignorance he was to offer a sin-offering. In verse 30 we are told that if a person sinned presumptuously he was to be cut off from his people. There was no sacrifice for presumptuous sins.

The questions before us are: (1) What is the difference in the nature of these two types of sin? (2) Are these distinctions carried over into the New Testament? (3) Does a knowledge of these distinctions have any value for the church today, or is it an investigation of a technical matter to be discussed in a theological meeting and then forgotten?

Presumptuous Sins
When a sin is so serious that there is no sacrifice for it, it is incumbent upon us to try to understand what it is. In Numbers 15:30 the Hebrew that is translated "presumptuously" in the KJV is *bᵉyādh rāmāh*. Both the NASB and the NIV translate "defiantly." The literal translation of the Hebrew is "with a high hand." The LXX has *cheiri huperēphania* and translates "presumptuous hand."

*B*ᵉ*yādh rāmāh* is found in only two other places in the Old Testament: Exodus 14:8 and Numbers 33:3. In both of these references, it refers to the way the Israelites left Egypt. They left with a high hand. In both of these instances, the KJV has "high hand." The reading in the NASB and the NIV for both of these references is "boldly." In both of these places the LXX has *cheiri hupēlēi* and translates "high hand."

In Psalm 19:13 David says, "Keep back thy servant also from presumptuous *sins*" (KJV). The Hebrew (v.14) is *zēdh*. The NASB also translates "presumptuous *sins*." The NIV translates "wilful sins."

The vast majority of translators understand *zēdh* in this verse to refer to presumptuous or wilful sin. However, there are a few that have other views. William S. Plumer reminds us of the wide range of views that have been taken. He comments:

> The Septuagint, Vulgate and Ethiopic for *presumptuous* sins read *strangers*; *Douay*: From my secret sins cleanse me, O Lord; and from those of others spare thy servant; Chaldee: Set thy servant free from the proud; Syriac: From iniquity restrain thy servant; Enema: Withhold thy servant from the proud: Amesius: Withdraw thy servant from the contumacious; Fry: From presumption, etc.; Horsley: From evil spirits, etc.[3]

Mitchell Dahood translates *zēdh* "the presumptuous ones" and gives the following explanation:

> In the present context, the frequent plural adjective *zēdhîm* concretely means "idols or false gods," i.e., those who presume to be God. It derives from *zy/wd*, "to act presumptuously," and enjoys a fine analogue in Ps. xl 5, *r*ᵉ*hābîm*, "arrogant ones, false gods," from *rhb*, "to act arrogantly."[4]

I will develop my reasons later for siding with those who take Psalm 19:13 to refer to presumptuous sins, but let me comment on Dahood's reference to Psalm 40:5 (English trans. 40:4). While Dahood takes *r*ᵉ*hābîm* in this verse to refer to "false gods," it does not appear that many have followed him in this view. The reference is thought to be to proud, arrogant, or defiant persons.

Archdeacon Aglen in *Ellicott's Commentary* takes the position that the reference is to arrogant men. This is based on the fact that in the eight other places where *zēdh* occurs it refers to persons.[5]

Peter C. Craigie translates the verse, "Withhold your servant from presumptuous persons, and let them not rule over me."[6] In his comments he says, "He asks to be protected from presumptuous persons and the control which they could so easily exert over him."[7] Though he gives this translation and interpretation, he gives no reasons for it.

The reason for taking the view that the reference is to persons, as Aglen points out, is that in the eight other places where it is used (see tables) it refers to persons. In all of these references, the KJV translates "the proud" (the article is omitted in Pr. 21:24). The NASB uses "the arrogant," "arrogant men," "the proud," and "proud." The NIV translates "the arrogant," "proud," and "the haughty."

Since all of the other uses of *zëdh* refer to proud or arrogant persons, serious consideration should be given to whether that is its meaning in Psalm 19:13. Though I think it must be considered, I am of the opinion that a careful study of the context decides against that interpretation.

In verse 12 (Hebrew, v. 13) David says, "Who can understand his errors [*s*ᵉgî´oth*]? cleanse thou me from secret [*sāthar*] *faults* (KJV). The NASB and the NIV also translate "errors." Instead of "secret" they have "hidden."

*Ŝ*ᵉgî´oth* is from the same root as *ŝ*ᵉgāgāh* which we will see later refers to sins of ignorance as distinguished from presumptuous sins. Secret or hidden faults would also be in the category of sins of ignorance. Since verse 12 refers to sins of ignorance, the context demands that verse 13 be understood as a reference to presumptuous sins.

Karl Bernhard Moll, in *Lange's Commentary*, explains:

> The plural form of this word [*zidîm*] is in other passages of Scripture always to be regarded properly as of haughty oppressors and is likewise here thus taken by many, finally by Köster and Olsh. But there is no other reference to the oppression of such hostile persecutors (the Sept. and the Vulg. read *zārîm* [strangers]). The context leads to the sphere of moral persuasion, not of protection against external power. The expression **ruler** [A.V., have *dominion*] in the following member of the verse is entirely appropriate and clear only when we regard the plural form as denoting the abstract (Kimchi, Rosem., Delitzsch, Hitzig), which especially recommends itself in an ancient piece of composition. The reference to the evil influence and tempting power of association and intercourse with proud transgressors (DeWette, Hupf., Camph.) forces the abstract into the explanation in order to be endurable, and obscures the contrast that is in the clause Gen. iv. 7, Rom. v. 14, and similar passages which are cited lead directly to an abstract, and *ch$k* = hold back, preserve, is usually connected with an abstract (Gen. xx. 6; 1 Sam. xxv. 39). Still less is it to be supposed that the intentional sins are here *personified* as tyrants (Hengst) which strive to bring the servant of God under their unworthy dominion.[8] (*brackets in original*)

I think the case is conclusive for understanding the reference to be to sins rather than persons, idols, or any other interpretation. I will address the meaning and significance of presumptuous sins later.

Sins of Ignorance

The Hebrew words that are used to refer to sins of ignorance are *ŝāgag* (verb), *ŝāgāh* (verb), *ŝ*ᵉgāgāh* (noun), and *ŝ*ᵉgî´oth* (noun). A study of the tables of these words will reveal that the KJV understood these words to mean "to sin through ignorance," "to err," "to go astray," and to kill "unawares." The NASB understood these words to mean "to sin unintentionally," "to err," "to go astray," and to kill "unintentionally." The NIV understands the words to mean much the same as the NASB. The NIV speaks of killing "accidentally."

I am not sure of the reasons that the KJV, in a number of places, uses the term "sins of igno-rance" or "sinned through ignorance." One of the most probable reasons is that *lo´-yāda'* (lit., did not know), and *biblî dbā `atb* (lit. without knowledge) occur in a few places as qualifying the sins of the type that are referred to as sins of ignorance.

In Leviticus 5:18 the KJV reads, "The priest shall make an atonement for him concerning his ignorance *(šᵉgāgāh)* wherein he erred *(šāgag)* and wist it not *(lo´-yāda')*." "Wist" is the past tense of "wit" which is an archaic word for "know." The NASB translates "sinned unintentionally." The NIV has "committed unintentionally." The LXX translates *lo´-yāda'* by *ouk oida* and translates "knew it not."

Biblî dbā'atb is seen as a qualifying factor of the type of sins under consideration in Deuteronomy 4:42; 19:4; and Joshua 20:3, 5. All of these references refer to the criterion for deter-mining whether a person who had killed someone was qualified to flee to one of the cities of refuge. The KJV translates *biblî dbā'atb* by "unawares," "ignorantly," and "unwittingly." The NASB has "unintentional," and "without premeditation." The NIV translates "unintentionally" in all four places. The LXX translates it twice as *ouk oida* and twice as *akousiōs*. *Ouk oida* is translated "unin-tentionally." In both occurrences of *akousiōs*, it is translated "unintentionally."

Another probable reason the KJV uses the term "sins of ignorance" is the influence of the LXX. In Leviticus 5:18 *šāgag* is translated by *agnoeō* (to know not). *Šāgag* is translated by *agnoeō* in Leviticus 4:13 and 1 Samuel 26:21 (LXX, 1 Kings 26:21). *Šᵉgāgāh is* translated by *agnoia* (igno-rance) in Leviticus 5:18; 22:14; and Ecclesiastes 5:6.

A study of the mention of what the KJV refers to as sins of ignorance makes it clear that, at least, in some cases the person had some awareness of what he was doing. G. F. Oehler's comments are helpful on this point. Concerning *šᵉgāgāh* he says:

> Undoubtedly this expression generally refers to *unintentional* offences (comp. in elu-cidation, Lev. iv.13, v. 2 sq., 17, where *uᵉlo´ yādba`*, "and he knew it not," relates not to ignorance of the command, but to unconsciousness and unpremeditatedness in the offence; see also how the *bišgāgāh* of Num. xxxv.11 is explained in Deut. iv.42 by *biblî-dba`atb*). Still the expression includes more than mere inadvertence, and extends *to errors of infirmity*, of *rashness*, we might say of *levity*. Its opposite is the sin *bᵉyādb rāmāh* "with an uplifted hand," *i.e.* rebelliously, Num. xv. 30, the sin com-mitted defiantly, deliberately, the wilful transgression of the Divine commandments. For the latter there is from the legal viewpoint no sacrifice, but "that soul shall be cut off from his people."[9]

Patrick Fairbairn makes a good case for saying that the type of sins we are dealing with includ-ed some things that the person would have been aware of at the time of the sin. He explains:

> For while we have such things mentioned as touching, even unwittingly, the carcass of an unclean beast, or the person of a man who at the time happened to be in a state of

uncleanness, there is also the case of one who, when solemnly called upon to give evidence regarding a matter of which he had been cognizant, yet, for some selfish reason operating on him at the time, withheld the testimony he should have given (ver.1 [Lev. 5:1]), and the case of one who had pronounced a rash vow or oath, committing himself to do what should either not at all or not in the circumstances have been undertaken (ver. 4 [Lev. 5:4]). These were plainly things which could not have happened without knowledge or consciousness on the part of the transgressor; but they betrayed hastiness of spirit, or the moral weakness which could not resist a present temptation. Viewed in this light, too, they can not be regarded otherwise than specimens of a class; for no one could possibly imagine that moral weakness, displaying itself in the matter of rash swearing, or in a cowardly refusal to give faithful testimony on fitting occasions, was different in kind from such weaknesses when appearing in various other directions. . . . We are certainly warranted to include the sins mentioned in Lev. vi. 1-5 as belonging to the class now under consideration; and among these are lying, deceit, betrayal of trust, false swearing, fraudulent behavior. In further proof of the same thing, we find even adultery mentioned elsewhere [Reference, Lev. xix. 20 given in a footnote], if committed with a bondmaid, as an offence which might be expiated by this class of offerings.[10]

Walter C. Kaiser, Jr. in commenting on Psalm 19:12, 13 expresses concern over the way we categorize the types of sin found in the Old Testament. He explains:

An alarmingly large number of students of the OT divide all sins into two major headings of accidental and deliberate. The Psalmist enumerated three major headings in Psalm 19:12-13: "Who can discern his *errors* [$š^e g\hat{\imath}\,'\hat{o}t$]? Cleanse me from my *hidden faults* [*nistārôt*]. Restrain your servant from wilful sins [*zēdîm*]" (my translation). But if the first two categories of the Psalmist ("errors" and "hidden faults") are merely two subcategories of the "accidental" heading, as Jacob Milgrom concluded, then it is clear that so-called "sins in ignorance" are actually sins of inadvertence." Thus, the designation "unwitting" (KJV, NJV, RSV "ignorance") i.e., "without wit," "without consciousness"—is impossible. The sins of *shegagah* are acts of negligence; the offender knows the law but violates it accidentally and without malice aforethought (e. g., in the case of accidental homicide—Num 35:22ff; Deut 19:4-10; Josh 20:2-6, 9). There is also the sin of inadvertence, where the person acts without knowing all the facts —the ignorance was not about law but about the circumstances—such as the case of Abimelech's taking Sarah, whom he thought was Abraham's sister (Gen 20:9), or when Balaam was unaware that an angel was in the donkey's path (Num. 22:34: "I have sinned. I did not realize you were standing in the road"). Thus, the sinner who commits a sin of inadvertence is conscious of the act, even if he or she is not always aware of its consequences.[11] (*brackets in original*)

I would consider "errors" and "hidden faults" as two subcategories under what the KJV calls sins of ignorance. I would certainly agree that we could not say that all of the sins mentioned in this category were committed by a person who was totally unaware that what he was doing was in violation of the law of God. Both Oehler's and Fairbairn's comments quoted above would support this conclusion.

I think it is important to recognize that "secret" or "hidden" faults are to be considered sin. This is a recognition of the fact that our sins extend beyond our consciousness.

However, I do not think there is justification for creating another category of sins in distinction from the sins of ignorance.

I understand Kaiser's attack when he says, "the designation 'unwitting' (KJV, NJV, RSV 'ignorance') i.e., 'without wit,' 'without consciousness'—is impossible." However, in the light of the Hebrew terms *lo´ yādha'* (lit., did not know), and *biblî-dha`ath* (lit. without knowledge) which qualify some of the sins in this category (especially Lev. 5:18), I would say let's wait until we examine the New Testament teachings on this subject before we decide to throw away the term "sins of ignorance."

A Contrast of the Old Testament Teachings on Sins of Ignorance and Presumptuous Sins

Sins of ignorance and presumptuous sins are best understood when seen in contrast to each other. I want to reserve a more complete discussion of the nature of these two types of sin until we have examined the teachings of the New Testament. But a few statements need to be made to conclude this examination of the Old Testament.

Sins of ignorance would refer to sins of weakness. In some cases the person would have been aware that what he was doing was wrong. In other cases he would not have known at the time. In some cases it would be ignorance of the circumstances rather than ignorance of the law. In other cases what took place could have been an accident.

There might be some question over whether an accidental killing (or some other accidental event) was an actual sin, but for the most part we must conclude that what was classified as a sin of ignorance was, in fact, a sin and required repentance and atonement.

Timothy R. Ashley's comments are insightful when it comes to presumptuous sins. In commenting on Numbers 15:30, 31, he explains:

> The sins hitherto discussed have all been inadvert and are expiable by the appropriate sacrifice. All of these are in sharp contrast to the sins that are said to be *with a high hand (b⁰yā\d rāmâ)*. The same phrase describes the attitude of the Israelites to Pharaoh and the Egyptians at the time of the Exodus (e.g. Exod.14:8; Num. 33:3, usually translated "boldly," or even "defiantly"). The Israelites thought themselves quite beyond the sphere of interference by Pharaoh, and they were confident that he was irrelevant for the future. While the passages in Exod. 14 and Num. 33 provide a posi-

tive evaluation of such an attitude, and the context here clearly calls for a negative evaluation, there are parallels in the attitude: the sinner *with a high hand* considers Yahweh irrelevant for the future; this one sins in an open-eyed and rebellious way, knowing full well what he or she is doing. This kind of rebellion therefore differs from the intentional sin described in Lev. 5:20-26 (Eng. 6:1-7) for which a reparation offering may be made, "when the offender feels guilty" (5:23, 26). The sinner with a high hand feels no guilt; the offense is not sacrificially expiable.[12]

In Numbers 15:30 the person who is guilty of *bᵉyādh rāmāh* (sinning with a high hand) is guilty of *gādhaph* toward God i.e., he blasphemes or reviles God. In verse 31 this person is said to have *bāzāh* (despised) the word of Yahweh. For such a person there was to be no sacrifice for his sins. He was to be cut off from his people. He was to be put to death.

Among those who believe that Psalm 19:13 speaks of presumptuous sins rather than presumptuous persons or idols, there does not seem to be any question about whether it is the same type of sin referred to in Numbers 15:30. Based on the studies that I have made, I would conclude that presumptuous sins do not refer to the nature of the particular sin, but to the attitude toward God that is manifest on the part of the person. Presumptuous sins referred to a conscious, deliberate, defiant, and arrogant attitude of unbelief toward God.

The important question for us now is this: Is the distinction between sins of ignorance and presumptuous sins seen in the New Testament? Let us turn our attention to the New Testament and see.

An Examination of New Testament Teachings

SINS OF IGNORANCE

In the New Testament, comparison of translations is not as helpful as it is in the Old Testament study on this subject. I will limit my use to the NASB except in cases where it is helpful to look at other translations.

While keeping the Old Testament teachings on sins of ignorance in mind, let us examine some references. Consider the words of Jesus when He said, "Father, forgive them for they do not know what they are doing" (Lk. 23:34).[13] Jesus was placing the sin of those who crucified Him into the category of sins of ignorance and therefore it could be forgiven. This is particularly interesting when we observe that "do not know" is a translation of *ouk oida* which in the LXX is used in Leviticus 5:18; Deuteronomy 4:42; and 19:4 with reference to sins of ignorance.

Craig A. Evans points out a connection between the saying attributed to Jesus and sins of ignorance in the Old Testament.[14] I. Howard Marshall refers to these words as "a motif familiar in Luke (Acts 3:17; 13:27; cf. 7:60) and in Jewish and pagan thought."[15] The Jewish thought would, of course, have its roots in the Old Testament sins of ignorance.

The words of Jesus from the cross in His prayer of forgiveness (Lk. 23:34) reminds us of Stephen's prayer which he prayed for those who were stoning him. Stephen said, "Lord, do not hold this sin against them" (Acts 7:60). Though Stephen does not refer to those who stoned him as acting out of ignorance, his prayer indicates that such was the case. We know that was the case of Saul who was in "hearty agreement with putting him to death" (Acts 8:1). Paul makes it clear in 1 Timothy 1:13, to which I will refer later, that the possibility of his being forgiven was based on the fact that he sinned ignorantly.

When Peter was explaining how the lame man had been healed in Acts 3:12-26, he said to the Jews that had disowned Christ and had Him put to death, "And now, brethren, I know that you acted in ignorance, just as your rulers did also" (verse 17). He then proceeded to invite them to repentance so their sins could be wiped away (verse 19). It is obvious that Peter is placing the crucifixion of Christ by the Jews and their rulers in the category of sins of ignorance and for that reason they could be forgiven. The word for "ignorance" here is *agnoia*. In the LXX, *agnoia* is used to refer to sins of ignorance in Leviticus 5:18; 22:14; and Ecclesiastes 5:6.

Both John B. Polhil and David J. Williams suggest a connection is in mind between the ignorance involved in the crucifixion of Christ and the sins of ignorance referred to in the Old Testament. They recognize this to be in distinction from those committed with a "high hand."[16]

Paul in speaking in the synagogue at Pisidian Antioch also spoke of the Jews and their rulers. He said, "The people of Jerusalem and their rulers did not recognize [*agnoeō*] Jesus, yet in condemning him they fulfilled the words of the prophets. . ." (Acts 13:27, NIV).

In 1 Corinthians 2:8 Paul speaks of "*the wisdom* which none of the rulers of this age has understood." He goes on to say, "for if they had understood it, they would not have crucified the Lord of Glory." "Understood" in both occurrences in this verse translates *ginōskō*. In saying that the rulers of this age did not understand what they were doing, Paul is placing their sin in the category of sins of ignorance. The relationship between lack of *ginōskō* (understanding) and *agnoia* and *agnoeō* as used in the LXX is obvious.

With regard to his own situation Paul said, "He [Jesus] considered me faithful, putting me into service; even though I was formerly a blasphemer and a persecutor and a violent aggressor. And yet I was shown mercy, because I acted ignorantly in unbelief" (1 Tim. 1:12, 13). "Acted ignorantly" translates *agnoeō* which in the LXX refers to sins of ignorance in Leviticus 4:13; 5:18; and 1 Samuel 26:21 (LXX, 1 Kings 26:21).

Gordon D. Fee, Thomas D. Lea and Hayne P. Griffin, Jr., and Homer A. Kent, Jr. point to the Old Testament distinction between sins of ignorance and presumptuous sins in explaining what Paul meant when he said that he had "acted ignorantly."[17]

Jesus, Peter, and Paul would have been familiar with the distinction between sins of ignorance and presumptuous sins that was clearly set forth in the Old Testament. It is quite obvious that in the references given above that they were referring to sins of ignorance as distinguished from presumptuous sins.[18]

In Hebrews 9:7, *agnoēma* is translated "ignorance" in the NASB and the NIV. The KJV translates "errors." It is a reference to the sins of ignorance in the Old Testament.

There is another word that we need to give some attention to. In the LXX, *planaō* is used with reference to sins of ignorance in Deuteronomy 27:18; Job 6:24; 19:4; Proverbs 28:10; and it is used twice in Isaiah 28:7. *Planaō* is used several times in the New Testament. I will mention the ones that we might find interesting in the light of our study.

In Matthew 22:29 Jesus said to the Sadducees that they were "mistaken" (*planaō*) about the resurrection because they did not understand (*ouk oida*) the Scriptures (See also Mk. 12:24, 27).

In Hebrews 5:2 an explanation was given of why the High Priest, in the Old Testament, was taken from among men. It was so "he can deal gently with the ignorant (*agnoeō*) and misguided (*planaō*), since he himself is beset with weakness." It is obvious that the writer of Hebrews is recognizing the category of sins of ignorance in this verse.

In James 5:19 James speaks about one who "strays (*planaō*) from the truth." Peter reminds his readers about their past before they came to Christ. He says, "For you were continually straying (*planaō*) like sheep" (1 Pet. 2:25).

In 1 Timothy 6:10 *apoplanaō* is translated "wandered" in "some having longed for [money] have wandered away from the faith."

Some of the occurrences of the noun form (*planē*) are also of interest. In Romans 1:27 Paul refers to homosexuality as error (*planē*). James speaks of one "who turns the sinner from the error (*planē*) of his way" (Jas. 5:20).

Unless the context gives a reason to think otherwise, I would conclude that sins that are described in the New Testament by *agnoia, agnoeō, agnoēma, planaō, planē, apoplanaō* are sins that can be forgiven.

PRESUMPTUOUS SINS

Now the question is: Do we find references to presumptuous sins in the New Testament? In 2 Peter 2:10 with reference to false teachers, Peter says, "Presumptuous are *they*, self-willed, they are not afraid to speak evil of dignities" (KJV). Presumptuous is a translation of *tolmētēs* (only here in N.T.). The NASB translates "daring." These apostate teachers are presumptuous, daring, defiant, and self-willed.

J. A. Motyer, in *The New International Dictionary of New Testament Theology* points out that the verb *tolmaō* occurs in the LXX. It is found in Esther 1:18; 7:5 and in Job 15:12. The noun *tolmētēs* does not occur in the LXX. In the references in Esther he gives the meaning "to have affrontery to" and in Job 5:12 he gives the meaning "what rashness does your heart suggest?" He explains, "The single occurrence of the noun (*tolmētēs*) is clearly in the bad sense. . . , the arrogant man of 2 Pet. 2:10 who brooks no restriction on self-will and recognizes no authority to which he will be answerable."[19] It is obvious that the type sin referred to here is to that which the Old Testament classified as presumptuous sins.

The most significant reference is Hebrews 10:26 where *hekousiōs* is translated "wilfully" in the KJV and the NASB. The NIV translates "deliberately." To illustrate the seriousness of sinning wilfully, the writer explains in verse 28, "Anyone who has set aside [KJV, "despised"] the Law of Moses dies without mercy on *the testimony of* two or three witnesses" (See Deut. 17:2-13). He goes on to say that the punishment would be more severe for one who tramples under foot the Son of God (verse 29).

The only other occurrence of *hekousiōs* in the New Testament is in 1 Peter 5:2 where Peter is telling the elders that they should shepherd the flock "voluntarily." The KJV translates "willingly." The NIV has "willing." In the LXX it is used with reference to the freewill offerings (Lev. 23:38; Num. 15:3; Deut. 12:6; Ezra 1:4, 6; 3:5; and 8:28).

The LXX does not use *hekousiōs* to refer to presumptuous sins. However, *akousios* and *akousiōs* which mean "unwilling" is used several times to refer to sins of ignorance. *Akousios* is used to translate the Hebrew for sins of ignorance in Numbers 15:25, 26; and Ecclesiastes 10:5. *Akousiōs* is used in Leviticus 4:2, 22, 27; 5:15; Numbers 15:24, 27-29; 35:11, 15; and Joshua 20:3, 5, 9. It can hardly be doubted that *hekousiōs* as it is used in Hebrews 10:26 was deliberately chosen as being in contrast with *akousiōs*.

While most commentators do not make mention of a connection with presumptuous sins in commenting on this verse, the only source that I have found that denies that *hekousiōs* harks back to the presumptuous sins of the Old Testament is Ellingworth. He explains:

> Despite **hekousiōs** (v. 26), the author does not develop a distinction between sins which can be forgiven and those which cannot (cf. Mk. 3:28f.; 1 Jn. 5:16f.). Dussant 93 discerns a link between *hekousiōs* = "with a high hand" (e.g., Nu. 15:30) in v. 26 and "falling into the *hands* of the living God" in v. 31; but this is not discernible in the Greek.[20]

I find it difficult when I study Ellingworth's comments on Hebrews 5:2; 9:7; and 10:26 to be sure that I am understanding all that he saying. In commenting on Hebrews 5:2 where *agnoēma* appears, he comments:

> Even in the LXX, however, the category of unwitting sins does not embrace all those which could be dealt with by sacrifice (so Michel): Lv. 6:1-7, for example, provides for an act of wilful disobedience of God's commandments (*paridōn paridēi tas entolas kuriou*) to be dealt with by a combination of restitution, with interest and sacrifice."[21]

It appears to me that Ellingworth is trying to make two kinds of deliberate sins:

(1) Those for which sacrifice could be made (Lev. 6:1-7), and (2) Those for which sacrifice could not be made (Num. 15:30, 31). The first would be deliberate, but would not be with a high hand as would be the case in the second. It seems that he is attempting to put *hekousiōs* in Hebrews 10:26 in the category of deliberate sins for which atonement could be made.

I find myself in agreement with Fairbairn as it relates to the sins mentioned in Leviticus 6:1-7. In commenting on unwitting sins or sins of ignorance he explains, "We are certainly warranted to include the sins mentioned in Lev. vi. 1-5 as belonging to the class now under consideration; and among these are lying, deceit, betrayal of trust, false swearing, fraudulent behavior."[22]

Let us take a closer look at *paridōn paridēi tas entolas kuriou*, which Ellingworth calls to our attention. The LXX translation is "willfully overlooked the commandments of the Lord."

Paridōn is a participle, and *paridëi* is subjunctive. They are two forms of the same word: *paroraō* which means "to overlook." Literally, they would mean "overlooking overlook." In the Hebrew (5:21), we have *mā 'al* followed by *ma'al*. The KJV translates "commit a trespass," the NASB has "sins and acts unfaithfully," the NIV has "sins and is unfaithful."

The important observation to make here is that Leviticus 5:15 has the same Hebrew construction (*mā 'al* followed by *ma'al*) as we find in Leviticus 6:1. The sin of the person in Leviticus 5:15 is classified as *šᵉgāgāh*. That means that sins that are qualified by *mā 'al* followed by *ma'al* can be classified as *šᵉgāgāh*. Whatever other conclusions we arrive at, we must conclude that sins that are qualified by *mā 'al* followed by *ma'al* do not require another category apart from *šᵉgāgāh*. They would still be in the category of sins of ignorance. If by deliberate we mean that a person could have sinned by a conscious choice and still be eligible to offer a sacrifice, I would agree that such was the case, but I would say that such sins would fall in the category of sins of ignorance.

The obvious contrast between *hekousiōs* and *akousiōs* links the sin spoken of in 10:26 with the presumptuous sins of the Old Testament. In commenting on *hekousiōs*, Lidell and Scott explain, "**ta he.**, *voluntary acts*, opp. *ta akousia* which means involuntary."[23] The words "there no longer remains a sacrifice for sins" in 10:26 certainly states that the sin in question could not be forgiven.

It is true that the LXX does not use *hekousiōs* to refer to presumptuous sins. However, before we draw too many conclusions from that, let's make some observations: (1) There are only two places in the Hebrew text that make a clear reference to presumptuous sins: Numbers 15:30 where the Hebrew is *bᵉyādh rāmāh*, and Psalm 19:14 (Eng. v. 13) which is *zëhd*.[24] It will be noted that the Hebrew uses two words for this sin. The LXX (18:13) uses a variant Hebrew reading, "*zārîm*" and translates it as *allotrios* (strangers). This reading eliminates the reference to presumptuous sins from the passage in Psalm 19 so far as the LXX is concerned.

This means that there is only one reference to presumptuous sins in the LXX: Numbers 15:30. The LXX translates *bᵉyādh rāmāh* with *cheiri huperēphania (presumptuous or arrogant hand)*. The Hebrew uses two different ways of referring to presumptuous sins. There is no reason that Greek could not do the same. As I have pointed out above *hekousiōs* is well suited as a contrast with *akousiōs* which referred to sins of ignorance in the Old Testament.

It is of further interest to note, as Ashley pointed out above, that *bᵉyādh rāmāh* is used in both a positive sense when the children of Israel are said to have left Egypt with a high hand and in a negative sense in referring to sinning with a high hand. It should not be thought strange that *hekousiōs* would be used in a positive sense of willing (or voluntary) service on the part of the elder in 1 Peter 5:2, and in a negative sense as presumptuous sin in Hebrews 10:26.

Simon J. Kistemaker in commenting on Hebrews 10:26, observes, "In the Old Testament the distinction is made between sins committed unintentionally and sins committed intentionally. The first can be forgiven; the second cannot." He then gives a list of Old Testament references. He goes on to say:

> The author of Hebrews is rather specific. He writes concerning a person who sins intentionally and who keeps on doing this in open rebellion against God and his Word.

. . . He is not talking about a believer who falls into sin unintentionally and finds for-giveness in grace and mercy. Rather, he points to the same sin that Jesus calls the sin against the Holy Spirit (Matt. 12:32; Mark 3:29) and that John describes as "a sin that leads to death" (I John 5:16). Although he employs different terms, the writer virtual-ly repeats the same thought he expressed in 3:12 and 6:4-6, where he speaks of falling from the living God.[25]

Kaiser also makes a connection between the presumptuous sins of the Old Testament and Hebrews 10:26. In speaking of Numbers 15:30, he comments, "This is similar to what is called the blasphemy of the Holy Spirit in the NT (cf. Heb 10:26-39)."[26]

Others who see a connection between Hebrews 10:26 and the presumptuous sins of the Old Testament are Albert Barnes[27] and Donald Guthrie.[28]

Even if a person would agree that Leviticus 6:1-7 should be classified as a deliberate sin and thus should not be considered as a sin of ignorance, it would seem to me that the evidence is con-clusive for comparing *hekousiōs* in Hebrews 10:26 with *bᵉyādh rāmāh* in Numbers 15:30. What-ever else we might say about the sins referred to in 2 Peter 2:10 and Hebrews 10:26, it is obvious that they fit the description of what was called presumptuous sins in the Old Testament. It is also obvious that the people who are committing them are not to be considered Christians.

Both Old and New Testaments deny the possibility of atonement being made for presumptuous sins. Only a few have suggested a contrary opinion. Arnold C. Schultz, whom I greatly admired, told us in class some years ago that though there was no sacrifice for presumptuous sins before the Day of Atonement that they were covered on the Day of Atonement. He based his opinion on Leviticus 16:16 which reads, "And he shall make atonement . . . in regard to all of their sins." At that time, I did not know enough about the subject to ask a question, so I am not sure how he would have answered an objection to his viewpoint.

Ellingworth points out that Philo "believed that the day of Atonement could deal even with deliberate sins, and appealed to Lv. 16:16 ('all their sins') in support."[29]

Lea and Griffin, after pointing out the distinction between sins of ignorance and presumptuous sins, in commenting on 1 Timothy 1:13 say, "God can bring to salvation wilful sinners as well as 'ignorant' sinners, but both groups need to come to God in faith and repentance. The more wilful the persons, the less likely is their repentance."[30]

I have seen no information in either the Old Testament or the New Testament that would sug-gest that there is forgiveness for presumptuous sins. The statement in Numbers 15:30 that the per-son who was guilty of presumptuous sin was to be cut off from among his people seems to close the case so far as forgiveness was concerned. All of the evidence points to a contrary conclusion.

I am of the opinion that once we grasp what the Old and New Testaments are referring to when they speak of sins of ignorance and wilful sins we will be far more careful how we use the terms. This is particularly true of what we will place in the category of presumptuous sins.

While it is appropriate to refer to these sins as wilful, defiant, and arrogant, I think it is best to use the term presumptuous sins for this type of sins. By using the word "presumptuous" and using

the other words to explain it, we will have a better chance of helping people recognize the seriousness of this kind of sin. It will also offer some help in avoiding confusion. We must be very careful
in making it clear that the sin referred to in Hebrews 10:26 refers to something far more serious
than it would be for a person simply to do something that he or she knows to be wrong.

The Validity of Using the Term "Sins of Ignorance"

When I started my research for this paper, I was inclined to think that "sins of ignorance" was
not a good term for the type of sins that it referred to. I thought that a better term was "sins of weakness." Though I think that sins of weakness is usually an appropriate term for these sins, I am not
ready to discard the term "sins of ignorance" now that I have reached this point in my study. Here
are my reasons:

1. The use of *lo´-yāda'* (not knowing), and *biblî dhā`ath* (without knowledge) which qualify
   some of the sins that fit this category of sins in the Old Testament.
2. The use of *agnoe, agnoia*, and *ouk oida* used in the LXX in translating the Hebrew in referring to this type of sins.
3. The use of *agnoeō, agnoia*, and *ouk oida* in the New Testament in referring to the crucifixion of Christ on the part of the Jews and their rulers, and the persecution of the church
   by Paul. Also, the use of *agnoeō* in Hebrews 5:2 and *agnoēma* in Hebrews 9:7.

While most, when they think of sins of ignorance, think of the Old Testament, there is more evidence in the New Testament for calling these sins sins of ignorance than in the Old Testament. In
fact, after examining the evidence in the New Testament that I cited above, I feel compelled to keep
using the term "sins of ignorance." I do, as a result of this study, still think it is proper to speak of
these sins as sins of weakness, but I dare not discard the term "sins of ignorance."

THE SIGNIFICANCE OF REFERRING TO THESE SINS AS SINS OF IGNORANCE

In the case of accidental killing, the use of *biblî-dha`ath* (without knowledge) meant "with-
out intent," or "without premeditation." The question before us is: What is the meaning of ignorance
when it refers to cases where the person did have a knowledge that what he was doing was in violation of God's law, and therefore, knew that what he was doing was wrong?

Apparently, both Old and New Testaments would have no trouble saying that a person who sins
is ignorant. In some cases, it can be assumed that ignorance does not mean that they were without
knowledge of the essential information. In such cases, without knowledge would mean without
understanding. To sin knowingly represents poor judgment. It indicates an ignorance of what constitutes disvalue and what represents true value. To know something in the full sense of the word
means to have a knowledge of and believe the essential facts, to understand and believe its value,
and to understand and believe its consequences whether good or bad. Anything less than this represents ignorance.

In the light of these observations we gain a deeper understanding of Jesus' words, "And you shall know (*ginōskō*) the truth, and the truth shall make you free" (Jn. 8:32). Peter tells us that knowledge is related to the way we experience grace and grow spiritually. He says:

> Grace and peace be multiplied to you in [or by] the knowledge (*epignōskō*) of God and of Jesus our Lord; seeing that His divine power has granted to us everything pertaining to life and godliness, through the true knowledge (*epignōskō*) of Him who called us by His own glory and excellence (2 Pet. 1:2, 3).

PROBLEMS INVOLVED IN KEEPING THE DISTINCTION BETWEEN SINS OF IGNORANCE AND PRESUMPTUOUS SINS

There are no insurmountable problems in maintaining this distinction. However, there are some problems that I should mention. In Psalm 119:118 (LXX, 118:118), *šāgāh* is translated *apostateō*. The relationship between this word and apostasy is obvious. It may cause us to think that the translators of the LXX understood *šāgāh* to refer to something stronger than sins of ignorance. However, I think it is safe to assume that at this point in time the word *apostateō* had not taken on its more technical meaning of what we would now think of as "commit apostasy." It simply meant to stray, to depart from, or to turn away.

Another problem is found in 2 Peter 2. We find the word *tolmētēs* in verse 10 which I take to be a reference to presumptuous sin. In describing these apostate teachers, Peter says, "But these, like unreasoning animals, born as creatures of instinct to be captured and killed, reviling where they have no knowledge (*agnoeō*), will in the destruction of those creatures also be destroyed" (verse 12).

It catches us off guard when we see *agnoeō* as a part of the description of those who are guilty of presumptuous sins. It is obvious that the kind of ignorance that is described here is what we would call "wilful ignorance." We would expect ignorance to be this kind of ignorance only when the context demands it. In the places where we have seen sins of ignorance discussed, the context has demanded that we distinguish these sins from presumptuous sins.

Conclusions

What does this study of sins of ignorance and presumptuous sins have to say to us as New Testament believers? To get at this we must first be sure that we understand the difference between sins of ignorance and presumptuous sins in the light of a study of both Old and New Testaments.

It is not the name of a sin that determines whether it is a sin of weakness or a presumptuous sin. It is the attitude manifested toward God on the part of the person committing the sin that makes the difference. In the New Testament we have seen that the crucifixion of Jesus by the Jews and the Romans was placed by Jesus, Peter, and Paul in the category of sins of ignorance. Therefore, with repentance it could be forgiven. We also saw that Paul placed his sins of blasphemy and the persecution of the church in the category of sins of ignorance. For that reason he could be forgiven.

Paul's carefulness in pointing this out tells us that if he had been doing the same thing presumptuously forgiveness would not have been available.

It is also clear that to place a sin in the category of sins of ignorance did not mean that it was not a sin. Sins of ignorance place people under the wrath of God. Sins of ignorance carry with them guilt and require repentance and atonement.

When it comes to presumptuous sins (or wilful sins), it is *very important* that we understand that not all sins that involve a conscious choice of the will are presumptuous sins. The vast majority of conscious sins are sins of ignorance, not presumptuous sins. Presumptuous sins are only committed by informed people who do so with a presumptuous, wilful, defiant, arrogant attitude toward God.

I believe that a careful study of the Scripture on this subject reveals that the sins of Christians fit in the category of sins of ignorance. The very fact that we are told that to confess our sins and receive forgiveness (1 Jn. 1:9), and that we have an advocate with the Father if we sin (1 Jn. 2:1) tells us that the sins of a person who is in a state of grace are sins of ignorance.

I have had low moments since I became a Christian. I have not always done the right thing, but I have never seen a time, be I ever so weak, that I did not have a desire to do right and to be right with God. We are not far from the truth if we say, "The only sins that a Christian knowingly commits are the sins that he does not want to commit."

We must not leave the impression that those who are in a state of grace can commit presumptuous sins. Neither Classical Calvinism nor Classical Arminianism should have any trouble with this point.

Implications for the Current Scene

A lack of understanding the positive value of righteousness and the negative value of sin is, according to the Bible, ignorance. At the same time that we are experiencing the greatest advance in scientific knowledge, secular worldview thinking has plunged us into deeper moral and spiritual "ignorance." Gross sin permeates our culture.

Evangelism is far more difficult than it used to be. One of the main reasons for this is that people do not feel deeply about sin. People who are without an adequate knowledge of guilt and the seriousness of sin are not convinced about judgment and Hell. *People who do not believe the bad news about Hell are not ready to receive the good news about salvation through Jesus Christ.* Without deep feelings about sin, we cannot support the biblical teachings about judgment, Hell, and atonement. I believe that, according to Scripture, a failure to grasp the seriousness of sin is ignorance.

Christians do not have the deep feelings that need to characterize a church that will remain strong during the rushing tides of relativism. Theological content at a time when it needs to be stronger tends to be weaker.

It must be remembered that sins of ignorance are still sins and call for repentance and atonement. We must remember that truth makes people free (Jn. 8:32). We need more theological content not less. *The antidote for ignorance is a knowledge of truth.* Moral truth and its recognition of the seriousness of sin must be effectively taught before we can expect people to be interested in the gospel of grace through faith in Jesus Christ.

In order to counter the ignorance that prevails in our day we need Christians who are characterized by a concern for truth as it is revealed to us in Scripture and a depth of experience that Scripture admonishes us to have.

Suggestions for Further Research

My study has organized the biblical material that deals with sins of ignorance and presumptuous sins. This will make it much easier for others to do an in-depth study.

I believe that I have given conclusive evidence for the validity of the term sins of ignorance in referring to those sins that are to be distinguished from presumptuous sins. Also, I believe there are good reasons for using the term presumptuous sins.

I think I have given a strong case for the position that the sin spoken of in Hebrews 10:26 and 2 Peter 2:10 are in the same category as the presumptuous sins spoken of in Numbers 15:30 and Psalm 19:13.

I would like to make the following suggestions in hope that others will look into these areas and help us gain greater insights:

1. Attention needs to be given to how "ignorance" is used when referring to sins of ignorance. This is particularly true when the person has a knowledge that what he or she is doing is wrong. Along with this, attention needs to be given to the importance of Truth.

2. Attention needs to be given to how this study of sins of ignorance and presumptuous sins sheds light on the unpardonable sin mentioned by Jesus in the Gospels, Hebrews 6:4-6; 10:26-29; 2 Peter 2:20-22; and 1 John 5:16, 17.

3. Attention needs to be given to who can commit presumptuous sins. Can an unbeliever? Can a Christian?

4. Attention needs to be given to the history of interpretation: both Jewish and Christian. Also, why has this distinction between sins of ignorance and presumptuous sins received such little attention?

Tables of Hebrew and Greek Words That Are Pertinent to a Study of Sins of Ignorance and Presumptuous Sins

These tables have been prepared with the aid of *The Englishman's Hebrew and Chaldee Concordance of the Old Testament*, *A Concordance of the Septuagint*, and *The Englishman's Greek Concordance of the New Testament*. In dealing with the LXX , the blank cells indicate a different Hebrew reading that the translators were using, the translation that they gave was not pertinent to the subject, or the verse did not appear to be present in the LXX.

A Complete List of the Occurrence of the Words Used
for Presumptuous Sins in the Old Testament

b^eyādh rāmāh	KJV	NASB	NIV	LXX	LXX, Trans
Ex. 14:8	high hand	boldly	boldly	*cheiri hupsēlēi*	high hand
Num. 15:30	presumptuously	defiantly	defiantly	*cheiri huperēphanias*	presumptuous hand
Num. 33:3	high hand	boldly	boldly	*cheiri hupsēlēi*	high hand

zēdh	KJV	NASB	NIV	LXX	LXX, Trans
Ps. 19:13 (Heb., 19:14)	presumptuous	presumptuous	wilful	(18:13) *allotrios,* based on Heb. reading *zārîm*[31]	strangers
Ps. 86:14	the proud	the arrogant	the arrogant	(85:14) *paranomos*	transgressors
Ps. 119:21	the proud	the arrogant	the arrogant	(118:21) *huperēphanos*	the proud
Ps. 119:51	the proud	the arrogant	the arrogant	(118:51) *huperēphanos*	the proud
Ps. 119:69	the proud	the arrogant	the arrogant	(118:69) *huperēphanos*	the proud
Ps. 119:78	the proud	the arrogant	the arrogant	*huperēphanos*	the proud
Ps. 119:85	the proud	the arrogant	the arrogant	(118:85) *paranomos*	transgressors
Ps. 119:122	the proud	the arrogant	the arrogant	(118:22) *huperēphanos*	the proud
Pro. 21:24a	proud	proud	proud	*thrasus*	bold
Is. 13:11	the proud	the proud	the haughty	*anomos*	transgressors
Jer. 43:2	the proud	arrogant men	the arrogant		
Mal. 3:15	the proud	the arrogant	the arrogant	*allotrios*[32]	strangers
Mal. 4:1 (Heb., 3:19)	the proud	the arrogant	the arrogant	*allogenēs*[33]	aliens

zâdhôn	KJV	NASB	NIV	LXX	LXX, Trans
Dt. 17:12	presumptuously	presumptuously	shows contempt	_huperēphania_	haughtiness
Dt. 18:22	presumptuously	presumptuously	presumptuously	_asebeia_	wickedly
1 Sam. 17:28	pride	insolence	conceited		
Pr. 11:2	pride	pride	pride	_hubris_	pride
Pr. 13:10	pride	presumption	pride	_hubris_	insolence
Pr. 21:24b	proud	proud	proud		
Jer. 49:16	pride	arrogance	pride	(29:16) _itamia_	fierceness
Jer. 50:31	most proud	arrogant one	arrogant one	(27:31) _hubristria_	the haughty one
Jer. 50:32	most proud	arrogant one	arrogant one	(27:32) _hubris_	pride
Ezek. 7:10	pride	arrogance	arrogant one	_hubris_	pride
Ob. 3	pride	arrogance	pride	_huperēphania_	pride

zîdh or _zûdh_	KJV	NASB	NIV	LXX	LXX, Trans
Ex. 18:11	dealt proudly	dealt proudly	arrogantly		
Ex. 21:14	presumptuously	presumptuously	deliberately	_epitithēmi_	lie in wait
Dt. 1:43	presumptuously	presumptuously	arrogance	_parabainō_	forced
Dt. 17:13	presumptuously	presumptuously	contemptuous	_asebeō_	commit impiety
Dt. 18:20	shall presume	presumptuously	presumes	_asebeō_	impiously
Neh. 9:10	dealt proudly	acted arrogantly	arrogantly	_huperēphaneō_	behaved insolently
Neh. 9:16	dealt proudly	acted arrogantly	became arrogant	_huperēphaneō_	behaved proudly
Neh. 9:29	dealt proudly	acted arrogantly	became arrogant		
Jer. 50:29	been proud	became arrogant	defied	(27:29) _anthistēmi_	resisted

A Complete List of the Occurrence of the Words Used
for Sins of Ignorance in the Old Testament

šāgag	KJV	NASB	NIV	LXX	LXX, Trans.
Lev. 5:18	erred	sinned unintentionally	committed unintentionally	*agnoeō*	ignorantly trespassed
Num.15:28	sinneth ignorantly	sins unintentionally	sinning unintentionally	*akousiazomai*	committed unwillingly
Job 12:16	the deceived	the misled	deceived		
Ps. 119:67	went astray	went astray	went astray	(118:67) *plēmmeleia*	transgressed

šāgāh	KJV	NASB	NIV	LXX	LXX, Trans.
Lev. 4:13	sin through ignorance	commits error	sins unintentionally	*agnoeō*	trespass
Num. 15:22	erred	unwittingly fail	unintentionally fail	*diamartureō*	transgress
Dt. 27:18	he that maketh to wander	he who misleads	the man who leads astray	*planaō*	make to wander
1 Sam. 26:21	erred	committed error	erred	(1 Kings 26:21) *agnoeō*	erred
Job 6:24	erred	erred	been wrong	*planaō*	erred
Job 19:4	erred	erred	gone astray	*planaō*	erred
Ps. 119:21	err	wander	stray	*ekklinō*	turn aside
Ps. 119:118	err	wander	stray	(118:118) *apostateō*	depart
Pro. 19:27	err	stray	stray		
Pro. 28:10	cause to go astray	leads astray	leads along an evil path	*planaō*	cause to err
Is. 28:7	erred (2) err (1)	reel (3)	stagger (3)	(1) *plēmmeleō* (2) *planaō* (3) *planaō*	1st - trespassed 2nd -erred 3rd - erred
Ezek. 45:20	erreth	goes astray	sins unintentionally		

šᵉgāgāh	KJV	NASB	NIV	LXX	LXX, Trans.
Lev. 4:2	ignorance	unintentionally	unintentionally	*akousiōs*	unwillingly
Lev. 4:22	ignorance	unintentionally	unintentionally	*akousiōs*	unwillingly
Lev. 4:27	ignorance	unintentionally	unintentionally	*akousiōs*	unwillingly
Lev. 5:15	ignorance	unintentionally	unintentionally	*akousiōs*	unwillingly
Lev. 5:18	ignorance	error	wrong	*agnoia*	trespass ignorantly
Lev. 22:14	ignorance	unintentionally	mistake	*agnoia*	ignorantly
Num. 15:24	ignorance	unintentionally	unintentionally	*akousiōs*	unwillingly
Num. 15:25	ignorance	error	not intentional	*akousios* (2)	involuntary (2)
Num. 15:26	ignorance	error	unintentional	*akousios*	involuntary
Num. 15:27	ignorance	unintentionally	unintentionally	*akousiōs*	unwillingly
Num. 15:28	ignorance	unintentionally	unintentionally	*akousiōs*	unwillingly
Num. 15:29	ignorance	unintentionally	unintentionally	*akousiōs*	unwillingly
Num. 35:11	unawares	unintentionally	accidentally	*akousiōs*	unintentionally
Num. 35:15	unawares	unintentionally	accidentally	*akousiōs*	unintentionally
Jos. 20:3	unawares	unintentionally	accidentally	*akousiōs*	unintentionally
Jos. 20:9	unawares	unintentionally	accidentally	(verse 6) *akousiōs*	unintentionally
Ec. 5:6 (Heb., 5:5)	error	mistake	mistake	*agnoia*	error
Ec. 10:5	error	error	error	*akousios*	error

šᵉgîʾoth	KJV	NASB	NIV	LXX	LXX, Trans.
Psalm 19:12 (Heb., 19:13)	errors	errors	errors	*paraptōma*	transgressions

Terms that Sometimes Qualify Sins of Ignorance

lo´-yāda`	KJV	NASB	NIV	LXX	LXX, Trans.
Lev. 5:18	wist it not	`sinned intentionally	committed intentionally	*ouk oida*	knew it not

biblî dhā`ath	KJV	NASB	NIV	LXX	LXX, Trans.
Dt. 4:42	unawares	unintentionally	unintentionally	*ouk oida*	unintentionally
Dt. 19:4	ignorantly	unintentionally	unintentionally	*ouk oida*	ignorantly
Jos. 20:3	unwittingly	without premeditation	unintentionally	*akousiōs*	unintentionally
Jos. 20:5	unwittingly	without premeditation	unintentionally	*akousiōs*	unintentional

A List of Greek Words and New Testament References That Are Pertinent to a Study of Presumptuous Sins and Sins of Ignorance

PRESUMPTUOUS SINS

hekousiōs, Heb. 10:26
tolmētēs, 2 Pet. 2:10

SINS OF IGNORANCE

agneō, Acts 13:27; 17:23; 1 Tim. 1:13; and Heb. 5:2
agnoia, Acts 3:17; 17:30; Eph. 4:18; and 1 Pet. 1:14
agnoēma, Heb. 9:7
ginōskō, 1 Cor. 2:8 (2)
ouk oida, Lk. 23:34
planaō, Mt. 22:29 (with *ou oida*); Mk. 12:24, 27; Heb. 5:2; Jas. 1:16; 5:19; 1 Pet. 2:25; and 2 Pet. 2:15
planē, Rom. 1:27; Jas. 5:20; 2 Pet. 2:18; 3:17; and Jude 11

APPENDIX 2

Legalism in the Book of Galatians¹

Legalism is usually defined as a view that makes law-keeping a condition for salvation: in other words, salvation by works. This is legalism, but it is not the only kind of legalism.

Another kind of legalism tends to make a set of laws the only valid way to set forth ethical responsibility. When this kind of legalism is found among Christians, they tend to take the principles in the New Testament and make laws from them. These "laws" are then added to that which is specifically commanded or forbidden in the New Testament.

The trouble is that each of these two kinds of legalism is usually simply referred to as legalism. This leads to confusion. When someone is called a "legalist," that is usually taken to mean that he believes in salvation by works. But his "legalism" may be the way he expresses ethical obligation; he may not believe in salvation by works at all.

To avoid confusion, I believe we should speak of two kinds of legalism. Salvation by works is *soteriological legalism* (Soteriology refers to the doctrine of salvation). The kind of legalism that seeks to express all ethical obligations in the form of laws is *ethical legalism*. What each form of legalism has in common is a wrong dependence upon law. That is what makes it legalism.

Soteriological legalism incorrectly depends upon law-keeping for salvation. Ethical legalism incorrectly seeks to turn ethical principles into detailed, binding laws. It fails to allow the believer the freedom that goes with Christian liberty. Everyone agrees that Galatians is an attack on legalism.

Even so, if we are going to understand the legalism in Galatians, we must make a distinction between soteriological legalism and ethical legalism. To fail to do so is to misconstrue much of what Paul says.

As I understand it, in the first part of Galatians (through 3:18) Paul is dealing with *soteriological legalism*. Paul makes it unquestionably clear that salvation is conditioned on faith. There is general agreement that Paul refutes salvation by works in this part. The theme of 3:23–4:10 is deliverance from *ethical* legalism. (The concern with ethical legalism is still seen after 4:10, but the basic thrust of Paul's treatment is in 3:23–4:10.) However, since many do not distinguish between soteriological legalism and ethical legalism, there is a tendency on the part of some to think that Paul is also dealing with soteriological legalism in this section. This confuses what Paul is saying.

Let me acknowledge that the word legalism does not appear in Scripture. However, it is a word that is commonly understood to refer to a wrong dependence upon law. If we can show that in addition to refuting salvation by works Paul also spoke against dependence upon law as the basic method of dealing with Christian ethics, we will have established a valid use of the term ethical legalism.

The Periods of Time

The expressions in the passage that deal with periods of time are: "before faith came" (3:23); "after that faith is come" (3:25): "when we were children" (4:3); and "when the fulness of time was come" (4:4).

There is general agreement among commentators on the periods of time involved. "Before faith came," and "when we were children" refer to the time between the giving of the Law at Mount Sinai and the coming of Christ. "When the fulness of time was come" refers to the time after Jesus had come and completed his work.

Opinions are divided over the meaning of faith in "before faith came." In the Greek, the article *the* occurs before the word faith. Greek and English do not use articles alike. For that reason, the English New Testament uses the article at times when it is not in the Greek and at times omits it when an article is in the Greek. In many instances translators disagree concerning when to translate the article and when not to use it. I am of the opinion that the article should be used here, thus reading, "Before the faith came." The question to be decided is: (1) Is "the faith" referred to in 3:23 the act of believing in Christ, which would be subjective faith? or (2) Does "the faith" in 3:23 refer to the body of truth which the believer believes (as in the expression "contend for the faith" in Jude 3)? This would be objective faith. Many are of the opinion that the article, here, refers back to the faith mentioned in 3:22, which is faith in Jesus Christ. They understand the meaning to be "before the time when faith had Jesus Christ as its object" (Alford[2] Burton[3] Eadie[4] Hendriksen[5] and Robertson[6]). This would be subjective faith since it is the exercise of faith in Christ on the part of the believer. The meaning would be, "Before the time when people believed in Jesus Christ."

Others understand faith in 3:23 to be used in the objective sense. Rendall explains, "By the coming of the faith is meant the historic fact of the Christian religion, the spread of the gospel on earth:"[7] John Brown understands "the faith" to mean *the revelation believed*." He goes on to explain: "The phraseology adopted by the apostle, the revelation of faith [the last part of verse 23], makes it evident that faith here refers to doctrine. He speaks of it as "afterwards to be revealed."[8] Lightfoot understands "the faith" to mean "The Gospel, the objective teaching, the system of which 'faith' is the leading feature."[9]

I am of the opinion that "the faith" is a synonym for the New Covenant which was established by Christ. Paul had been talking about the Abrahamic Covenant in 3:15, 16. In 3:17 he reminded the Galatians that the Law, which came 430 years later, could not void the Abrahamic Covenant. Since "the law" refers to the Mosaic Covenant, it is not difficult to believe that "the faith" is a synonym for the New Covenant. The Covenant of Law is spoken of as "the law" because law was its basic principle. The New Covenant is spoken of as "the faith" because faith is its basic principle.

By taking "the faith" to mean the New Covenant, "before the faith came" (3:23) refers to the time before the New Covenant. It was the time when the Covenant of Law was in force. The law served until "the seed [Christ] came" (3:19). "After the faith came" (3:25) refers to the time after the establishment of the New Covenant.

The People Involved

The people prior to the establishment of the New Covenant are referred to as "we" (3:23); "our" and "we" (3:24); and "we" (4:3). The people after the New Covenant has been established are referred to as "we" (3:25); "ye" (3:25); "you" (3:27); "ye" (3:28, 29); "we" 4:5); "ye" (4:6); and "thou" (4:7). Since the time period of 3:23, 24 is the time from the giving of the law to the coming of Christ, "we" and "our" would refer to the Jews who were under the Mosaic Law. The question that remains is: Is Paul referring to believing Jews, or unbelieving Jews, or both? While many commentators do not address this issue, those who do agree that believing Jews were under the law as described in these verses. Lenski takes the position that both believing and unbelieving Jews are referred to, but the main stress is on the believing Jews.[10]

In 4:3 there is a variety of opinions. Some believe "we" refers to Jews only (Lenski[11] and Eadie"[12]). Rendall believes the reference is to Gentiles only.[13] Others believe "we" refers to both Jews and Gentiles (Burton,[14] Duncan,[15] Lightfoot,[16] and McDonald[17]).

The reason some think Gentiles must be included in the "we" of 4:3 is the occurrence of "ye" and "thou" in 4:6-10. These verses obviously apply to Gentiles both in their saved and unsaved experiences.

I believe "we" in 4:3 embraces both Jewish and Gentile Christians. However, when the "we" is traced back into history, it is the history of God's people (Jewish believers in Old Covenant times), not the pre-salvation history of the Gentiles. Brown understands the reference to be to "*The Family of God, the true church, genuine believers.*[18]

I am of the opinion that all of the occurrences of "we" in 3:23–4:3 refer to the people of God. (To call them the "seed of Abraham" would also be appropriate.) The people of God as constituted at the time Paul wrote Galatians were made up of believing Jews and Gentiles. The people of God as they were constituted under the Old Covenant were Jews. I prefer to restrict the name "church" to New Covenant believers, but I share the same basic concept as Brown concerning the continuity of Old and New Covenant believers. There is a conjunctive relationship between Old Testament Israel and the New Testament Church rather than a disjunctive one. This continuity makes it so that both Jewish and Gentile believers can say "we" or "our" in identifying with the spiritual history of the Old Covenant.

The Condition of the People of God Under the Covenant of Law

A proper understanding of what Paul says about the ministry of the law in 3:23, 24 requires that we remember that believers—the people of God—were under the law from Moses to Christ. If the interpretation that I have given to "we" in 3:23–4:3 stands, *we must view Jewish believers before Christ as being under the law*. To put it another way, *saved people were under the law*. It appears that some commentators have failed to keep this in mind in interpreting 3:23, 24. (See commentaries by Bring,[19] Eadie,[20] and Hendriksen[21]).

The key to understanding the condition of the people of God under the law is found in the interpretation of the word translated "schoolmaster" in 3:24, KJV (Greek, *paidagōgos*) and "the elements of the world" in 4:3.

The *paidagōgos* in 3:24 speaks metaphorically of the law. The law was our *paidagōgos*. In ordinary usage, a *paidagōgos* was a trusted slave who was over Greek and Roman boys in wealthy families. He was over the young boy from the ages of about six to sixteen. He went with him wherever he went, protected him, and helped instill the family values in him

When Paul used the word *paidagōgos* to refer to the law that God's Old Testament people were under, he was implying by this that they were immature. The word *paidagōgos* is literally translated child-leader.

In verse 23 Paul said, concerning Old Covenant believers: "We were kept under the law, shut up unto faith which should afterwards be revealed." At first glance, "kept under the law" and "shut up" sound as if it means under the curse and condemnation of the law, and that would not fit believers. But this need not be the case. "Keep" can have the meaning of a protective guarding: "We were guarded (or protected) under the law." The Greek word for "kept" is used enough for protective guarding (Phil. 4:7; 1 Pet. 1:5) to show that there are adequate grounds for giving such a meaning here in 3:23.

A positive meaning must also be given to "shut up." Brown applies these words to the people of God and says, "They were shut up as in a fortress, or confined within certain limits. The general idea is, they were kept in a state of restriction, preserved as a distinct people, and to gain this object, were subjected to many peculiar usages."[22]

Another problem that must be dealt with is the meaning of "that we might be justified by faith" (3:24). Many have read this verse as if the law is used today to lead people to Christ "that we might be justified by faith." Whether that is ever true or not, it is not the meaning here. We have already dealt with the time reference of this verse. It refers to the time from Mount Sinai to Calvary. Also, we have shown that the people were to be considered as Old Covenant Jewish believers.

In the light of these observations, it is necessary to understand the justification by faith in 3:24 to refer to the justification by faith of Old Covenant believers. Lenski supports this conclusion.[23]

It helps if we omit the italicized words *"to bring us."* (Words are italicized in Bible translations to show that there were no words in the Greek from which the italicized words were translated.) It will also help if we understand the Greek preposition *eis* to be temporal (Brown[24] and Picirilli[25]). With this meaning it would be preferable to translate "until" instead of "unto." By translating the verse as follows, the meaning is easier to see: "Wherefore, the law was our child-leader until Christ, that we [Old Covenant believers] might be justified by faith."

Now, let us turn our attention to "the elements of the world" in 4:3. As a result of extensive research, Burton gives the following list of interpretations that have been given to "the elements" (Greek, *ta stoicheia*) in New Testament times:

1. The physical elements of the universe. . . .
2. The heavenly bodies which the Galatians worshiped before their conversion. . . .

3. The spirits that are associated with the stoicheia in the physical sense whether stars or other existences, and so angels and spirits in general. . . .

4. The elements of religious knowledge possessed by men: a description applicable both to the Gentile religions and to Judaism before Christ. Under this term are included ritual observances, but the reference is not to them exclusively nor to them as ritual, but as elementary, adapted to children.[26]

The key to understanding which view given by Burton is the correct view lies in (1) a proper interpretation of "we" in 4:3, and (2) the association of these "elements" with the law.

In the discussion of the people involved, it was my conclusion that Paul referred to both Jews and Gentiles. When "we" is referred back into history, it is the spiritual history of God's people. Once this position is taken, it rules out the application of the "elements" to the Gentiles' pagan history.

In the illustration in 4:1, 2, Paul speaks of the child-heir as being under tutors (Greek, *epitropous*) and governors (Greek, *oikonomous*) until the time appointed of the father. It is obvious that there are some similarities, so far as the metaphorical interpretation is concerned, between the "elements" and the *paidagōgos*. If this is true, Paul is referring metaphorically to the law in 4:3 when he speaks of "the elements of the world." The only interpretation listed by Burton that would be suitable is the one that describes these as the elements of religious knowledge which are elementary in nature and adapted to children. McDonald considers them to be "picture-book lessons of childhood."[27]

The addition of "the world" to "the elements" apparently refers to the ceremonial system's use of the visible and the tangible. It is similar to "the earthly or worldly sanctuary" in Hebrews 9:1.

This ministry of the law as "child-leader" and "elements" is not displaced in Paul's discussion in 3:21–4:10 because it represents *soteriological* legalism. Rather, it was displaced because it represents *ethical* legalism. It was an ethical legalism that was used by God because of the immaturity of His people under the Mosaic covenant. The Covenant of Law made far more use of laws to prescribe responsibility than the New Covenant does. This is evidenced in the Civil and the Ceremonial Laws. However, it is important to keep in mind that the legalism of the Oral Tradition of the Pharisees went far beyond the mild ethical legalism in the Old Testament. Pharisaism was a serious abuse of the ethical legalism of the Old Testament.

The ministry of the law parallels the way we deal with children. In dealing with children, we spell things out in detail. Discipline is inflicted upon children for disobedience. We teach children with an extensive use of the visible to illustrate the invisible. We use extensive repetition with children. All these are characteristics of the Mosaic system: detailed rules, penalties, priestly ritual, repeated sacrifices and the yearly calendar.

Childhood treatment is essential and helpful for children, but both the child and the parent look forward to an approach more in keeping with maturity. The ethical legalism of the law was necessary and helpful during the ministry of the law, but deliverance was desirable later in God's redemptive program.

I use the term ethical legalism to refer to both the moral and the religious life of the people because the religious life was regulated in detail by laws, and obedience to these laws became an ethical responsibility. A limited use of laws does not, within itself, constitute ethical legalism. We find this kind of law in the New Testament. Ethical legalism develops when a preference is given to laws instead of principles in setting forth ethical responsibility.

The bondage (or slavery) to which Paul refers in Galatians 4:3 is not the bondage of condemnation. Rather, it is the bondage of ethical legalism of the Old Covenant in contrast with the liberty of the New Covenant (5:1). Peter called it a "yoke . . . which neither our forefathers nor we were able to bear" (Acts 15:10).

The Condition of God's People Under the New Covenant

In 3:25 the Greek article is before faith: "But after the faith is come we are no longer under a *paidagōgos* [child-leader]." Earlier I pointed out that "the faith" is a synonym for the New Covenant. These observations help us to understand that this verse is telling us that after the establishment of the New Covenant we are no longer under the *paidagōgos*.

In the literal use of the word *paidagōgos*, the Greek or Roman boy was delivered from the *paidagōgos* at 16 or 17. This implies that he had reached a level of maturity; he would no longer be treated like a young child. Paul's implication is that, by delivering us from the *paidagōgos*, God is dealing with us as mature sons.

The view that as New Covenant believers we are dealt with as adult, mature sons receives further support from the use of the word "adoption" in 4:5. In 4:1, 2 Paul explained that a child-heir is under tutors and governors until the time appointed by the father. Release from tutors and governors takes place only after the heir reaches maturity.

In applying this illustration, Paul considers the heirs of God to be dealt with like children prior to the coming of Christ (4:3). "When the fulness of time was come" (4:5) refers back to "the time appointed of the father" in the illustration (4:2). This was the time when the heir reached maturity.

"When the fulness of time was come," something very important took place: "God sent forth his son . . . that we might receive the adoption of sons" (4:5, 6). The "fulness of time" was the time when God viewed his people as being mature enough to be delivered from the *paidagōgos* (the law serving as a child-leader) and from "the elements of the world" (the law as giving elementary moral and spiritual teaching).

In our society, adoption is a legal process by which a person not born in a family is made legally a member of that family. This is not the way Paul is using the word adoption (Greek, *huiothesia*). This word literally means "son-placing." In the context it clearly refers to taking one who is already a child and placing him in the position of a mature or adult son. The only way to interpret the illustration in 4:1, 2 is to understand the time appointed by the father to be the time when the young boy had reached the level of maturity that would allow him to be delivered from the tutors and governors (or *paidagōgos*). It is obvious that 4:5, 6 is drawing a parallel between God's people and the heir of 4:1, 2. It is obvious that the parallel calls for an interpretation that would understand that the time had come for God to consider his people as mature. Thus they would be delivered from the law as child-leader and as elementary teaching.

This interpretation finds good support among those who have carefully studied the use of adoption by Paul (Brown[28], Burton,[29] Hampton,[30] and Tenney[31]). There are others who take the position that adoption (*huiothesia*) refers to the way a person gets into the family of God (Eadie,[32] Hogg and Vine,[33] and Robertson[34]). For reasons already given, I do not think this is the proper interpretation.

That God views New Covenant believers as mature also receives support by the use of the word translated "children" in 3:26. This word (Greek, *huios*) is commonly translated "son." Its use by Paul is to refer to New Covenant believers as adult sons. We, as New Covenant believers, are adult sons (*huioi*) in 3:26, and this is connected with our being delivered from the *paidagōgos* (3:25).

To see the full implications of 3:26 we also need to observe that the article appears in the Greek before faith and would thus be "the faith," synonymous with "the New Covenant" The meaning of the verse is clearer this way: "For ye are all the sons [adult sons] of God through the faith [the New Covenant] in [in union with] Christ Jesus."

The question before us now is: How did God accomplish this change in His people from minority and immaturity to majority and maturity? In 4:4, 5 Paul explains: "But when the fulness of time was come, God sent forth his Son . . . To redeem them that were under the law, that we might receive the adoption of sons."

"To" in the first clause and "that" in the second clause are both translations of the same word (Greek, *hina*, a purpose conjunction). The meaning of verse 5 will be clearer if we translate both of these as "that": "That he might redeem them that were under the law [and] that we might receive the adoption of sons." By looking at the verse this way, we can see that both clauses are dependent upon "God sent forth his Son" (verse 4). This gives two purposes for God's sending His Son: (1) That he might redeem them that were under the law," and (2) "That we might receive the adoption of sons."

The sending of God's Son is what accomplished the change of God's people from the status of children to the status of adults. The way this was accomplished is further amplified by 3:26: "For ye are all the sons of God through the New Covenant in union with Christ Jesus." (For support of the translation "in union with Christ Jesus" see Burton[35] and Lightfoot.[36])

In the New Covenant, the birth, life, death, resurrection and ascension of Jesus represent a much higher level of divine revelation than had existed before. This observation is important because there is a close relationship between knowledge and maturity. The limited knowledge of Old Covenant saints kept them in a state of spiritual immaturity. The revelation of God through the New Covenant opens the way for greater knowledge and a higher level of maturity.

We deal with children and adults in different ways. The way we treat children is good for children, but not for adults. The law method was good for the Old Covenant believers because of their immaturity. A method in keeping with maturity is better for New Covenant believers.

Paul has already told the Galatian Christians that it was a serious mistake to go into *soteriological* legalism. "For as many as are of the works of the law are under a curse" (3:10). He reasoned with them about this error through 3:18. Then, in 3:23–4:10, he explained the folly of the one already saved who would exchange the superior way of New Covenant liberty for the inferior way of Old Covenant legalism. Paul pleads with those who had been converted out of paganism in 4:8: "How turn ye again to the weak and beggarly elements, whereunto ye desire again to be in bondage?" This is what would happen if they were to become involved in the ethical legalism of the Covenant of Law.

Paul warned the Galatian Christians against the folly of going back under the Covenant of law for two reasons: (1) It would exchange salvation by grace, which truly saves, for a soteriological legalism that could never save. (2) It would trade the Christian liberty of the New Covenant for the bondage of the ethical legalism of the Covenant of Law. What adult is there who would go back home to his parents and ask them to treat him like a child!

Some Practical Implications

My purpose has been to show that Galatians 3:23–4:10 treats ethical legalism as the wrong approach to Christian living. Paul presents Christian liberty as the alternative, and as the biblical approach. Although I do not have space to develop detailed practical applications. I do want to offer a few suggestions about what this teaching means in a practical way.

1. Some who tend toward ethical legalism follow what I call "long list legalism." Their approach is to turn biblical principles into a detailed list of rules for conduct. People who do not keep these rules are regarded as questionably Christian. As with the Jewish Pharisees, regulations are devised to cover all uncertain matters, and these regulations take on almost the same authority as the clear biblical prohibitions against adultery and murder. While there may be a degree of comparison of those who tend toward ethical legalism with the Pharisees, the legalism of the Pharisees went far beyond in its multiplication of details anything that we may face today.

2. Others who practice ethical legalism follow what I call "short list legalism." They go to the opposite extreme. They say that unless the Bible specifically calls a certain thing a sin that it is a matter of personal opinion what a person does. They mistakenly believe *they* are the ones promoting "Christian liberty." What they fail to realize is that the *principles* of the New Testament are broader than rules. In condemning one form of legalism they establish another form. The New Testament Christian is responsible to take the principles and apply them to all the situations of life.

3. There is a difference in the way children and adults are governed, and that is the difference between the Mosaic system and the New Testament approach. Children are given more rules, more detail. Adults are given principles. Interestingly enough, the children, with their more detailed rules, are actually less responsible: they are held accountable only for what they have been told. Adults, with broader principles, are actually responsible for more. Their maturer understanding of the implications of the principles means they are accountable to apply those principles in various circumstances whether they have been instructed about all the possible applications or not. The way of Christian liberty is *not* a careless way.

4. In understanding all this, it helps to distinguish *substance* from *form*. A mother may not let a small child leave the yard, for example. Later on, she will say to the teenager, as he drives away,

"Be careful." In both cases, the substance of the concern is safety, but the *form* is very different. Just so, the transition from the Old Covenant to the New brought a change in form, but not in substance. We are never delivered from the substance of God's law, even though the form is very different. This substance, for New Testament adult sons, is in the form of principles that go deeper than mere rules. That is why Jesus could say that lust in the heart is the same as adultery (Mt. 5:27, 28). See also 1 John 3:15.

5. Many of the differences of opinion about Christian standards involve those matters that the New Testament does not specifically mention. There are things that the New Testament specifically condemns, as in Romans 1:29-31; 1 Corinthians 6:9, 10; Galatians 5:19-21; Ephesians 5:3-5—to cite just a few examples. "Christian liberty" has nothing to do with these, nothing delivers us from the obligation to avoid these sins. Christian liberty is concerned only with that which is not clearly identified by the Lord as sin.

How then do we decide about such matters? There are two kinds of situations that arise. First, there are various things we will decide are *wrong*, based on our application of the biblical principles. In such instances, we must refrain. We should also show others just how we understood the principles and reached our decision. We should seek to be persuasive, but we may not be able to demand that they conform to our approach—they *may* "apply" the very same principles in a different way. That does not mean that an organization—a church or institution—cannot require compliance in such matters. It can. Even then, however, we should make clear that these standards are applications of principles rather than expressly given in the New Testament. And we should be careful about our attitudes toward others who *sincerely* apply the principles in a different way, lest we end up in ethical legalism—of the "long list" variety.

Second, there will be things we will decide are *not wrong*, based on our application of biblical principles, and yet we find that other sincere Christians forbid them. Christian liberty, in such cases, is *not* a license to ride roughshod over the welfare of others who differ with us. As Paul said: "Brethren, ye have been called unto liberty; only use not liberty for an occasion to the flesh, but by love serve one another" (Gal. 5:13). Our love for others leads us to avoid doing anything that would result in serious injury to their spiritual lives. This love that limits one's liberty is, you see, one of the *principles* we have been talking about. It is not legalism to refrain from some things we could allow for the sake of love. It is ethical legalism—of the "short list" variety—to ignore others' concerns and insist on doing anything that is not specifically legislated against in the Bible. In such matters as these, Romans 14, 15 and 1 Corinthians 8–10 serve as our guide.

A few years ago, there was some legitimate concern over the prevalence of a trend toward a tendency toward long-list legalism. However, in recent years that trend has greatly diminished. At present, there is far more concern over short-list legalism. The Postmodern Mood has greatly diminished our feelings about sin.

Conclusion

There is no better book than Galatians for refuting soteriological legalism and establishing the doctrine of grace. There is also no better book than Galatians to lay a foundation for Christian liberty as distinguished from ethical legalism.

Furthermore, there is no better book than Galatians to establish the fact that to *reject soteriological and ethical legalism does not have to result in moral timidity and antinomianism*. Paul was the greatest champion of grace and Christian liberty of all time, and still he warned: "For, brethren, ye have been called unto liberty; only use not liberty for an occasion to the flesh, but by love serve one another" (5:13). He also said: "Now the works of the flesh are manifest, which are *these*; Adultery, fornication, uncleanness, lasciviousness, idolatry, witchcraft, hatred, variance, emulations, wrath, strife, seditions, heresies, envyings, murders, drunkenness, revellings, and such like: of the which I tell you before, as I have also told you in time past, that they which do such things shall not inherit the kingdom of God" (5:19-21). And none dare accuse him of legalism, either soteriological or ethical!

Notes

Preface

1. Jacques Barzun and Henry F. Graff, *The Modern Researcher* (New York: Harcourt, Brace, & Co., 1957), 288; cited in *A Manual of Style*, 12th ed. (Chicago: University of Chicago Press, 1969), 236

Chapter 1

1. My wife and I were in Ukraine and Russia from February 1, 1996 until May 26, 1996. We were in Kiev and Odessa in Ukraine. In Russia we were in Seltso (a village near Bryansk), Moscow, Chelyabinsk, Yekaterinburg, St. Petersburg, Novosibirsk, Irkutsk, and Khabarvosk. We were in a number of churches, seminaries, Bible institutes, and conferences. I talked about the *inescapable questions of life* on many occasions. I listened very carefully to see if there was any evidence that anyone had grown up without giving thought to these questions. On many occasions I told the audience that if they knew of anyone who had never experienced these questions to let me know. No one ever mentioned anyone. Our three-week stay in Japan, June 6-28, 1996, did not destroy my confidence that in the process of human development every human being has these *inescapable questions* that will voice themselves from within. There may be some variation in the form of the questions, but there will never be an empty space.

2. In *Biblical Systematics,* published in 1975, I chose to write in the first person. It has become much more common now for works to be written in the first person. I think this is because people are more interested in seeing a relationship between truth and life.

Chapter 2

1. Frances Schaeffer, *Escape from Reason* (Downers Grove, Illinois: InterVarsity Press, c. 1968), 46, 47, 53, 54. (Stephen M. Ashby, Assistant Professor of Philosophy and Religion, Ball State University, Muncie, Indiana, in personal correspondence, points out that "Schaeffer's distinction of *upper story/lower story* knowledge is a more popular, yet, essentially synonymous treatment of what Immanuel Kant calls the noumenal and phenomenal realms." Dr. Ashby has read through the entire manuscript of my book and has made many helpful suggestions.)

2. David Rausch, "Empiricism, Empirical Theology," *Evangelical Dictionary of Theology,* Walter A. Elwell, ed., (Grand Rapids: Baker, 1984), 353.

3. A. J. Ayer and Rudolf were advocates of this view. This approach has fallen into disrepute even among those who once held to a positivist approach. Steve Ashby pointed out that "this took place via the critique of W. V. O. Quine."

4. In general, a paradigm is a model or a way of thinking about something. The word *paradigm*, as it is being used in this book, is a model that a person uses in approaching and interpreting life and thought. We are mainly concerned with the Christian paradigm, the modernist paradigm, and the postmodernist paradigm. Once a paradigm is accepted, it guides and limits the kind of worldview or anti-worldview that can be developed while using that particular paradigm. There is no such thing as a neutral paradigm or non-limiting paradigm. There are at least some presuppositions assumed by any *upper story* paradigm that give rise to a worldview, anti-worldview, or lifeview.

We speak in this chapter of a Christian paradigm, a modern paradigm, and a postmodern paradigm. We could also speak of a Hindu paradigm, a Buddhist paradigm, a Muslim paradigm, etc.

5. John Dillenberger, *Protestant Thought and Natural Science* (Nashville: Abingdon Press, 1960), 23.

6. Ibid., 27-28.

7. Ibid., 28.

8. Ibid.

9. Robert G. Clouse, "Galileo" in *The New International Dictionary of the Christian Church*, J. D. Douglas, ed. (Grand Rapids: Zondervan, 1974), 399.

10. Dillenberger, 86.

11. Ibid., 117, 118.

12. Ibid., 120.

13. Ibid., 219, 220.

14. Ibid., 223, 224.

15. M. H. McDonald, "Deism," *Evangelical Dictionary of Theology*, 304.

16. Joseph Natoli and Linda Hutcheon, eds., "Introduction," *A Postmodern Reader* (Albany: State University of New York Press, 1996), x-xi.

17. Ibid., xi.

18. Thomas C. Oden, "The Death of Modernity and Postmodern Evangelical Spirituality" in *The Challenge of Postmodernism: an Evangelical Engagement*, David S. Dockery, ed. (Wheaton: Victor Books, 1995), 20.

19. Ibid., 23.

20. The law of non-contradiction tells us that the same thing cannot be both A and non-A. If two statements contradict one another, both cannot be true. Both may be false, but both cannot be true. Both modernism and orthodox Christianity agree on this. Postmodernism and much of contemporary Christian theology do not agree on this.

21. Stanley J. Grenz, *A Primer on Postmodernism* (Grand Rapids: Eerdmans, 1996), 49.

22. Morals deal with questions of right and wrong. "Ideals embrace values such as refinement, the lofty, the beautiful, the noble, polish, dignity, poise, honor, good manners, masculinity, ruggedness, strength, femininity, charm, daintiness, and good taste." From my book, *Biblical Ethics* (Nashville: Randall House, 1973), 45.

23. David F. Wells, *No Place for Truth or Whatever Happened to Evangelical Theology?* (Grand Rapids: Eerdmans, 1993), 169.

24. Randolph O. Yeager, *The Renaissance New Testament*, vol. 11 (Gretna, La.: Pelican, 1983), 338.

Chapter 3

1. Allan Bloom, *The Closing of the American Mind* (New York: Simon and Schuster, 1987), 25.

2. Ibid., 27.

3. Ibid., 34.

4. *The Americana Encyclopedia International Edition* (1996), s. v. "Nicolaus Copernicus" by Edward Rosen. For a more complete development of what motivated Copernicus to search the past, see John Dillenberger, *Protestant Thought and Natural Science* (Nashville: Abingdon, 1960), 21-27.

5. Dennis McCallum, "Are We Ready?" in *The Death of Truth*, Dennis McCallum, ed. (Minneapolis: Bethany House Publishers, 1996), 14.

6. Joseph Natoli and Linda Hutcheson, eds., "Introduction," *A Postmodern Reader*, x-xi.

7. Jim Leffel and Dennis McCallum, "Postmodern Impact: Religion," *The Death of Truth*, 201.

8. Chuck Colson, "Can We Be Good Without God?" *Imprimis*, April 1993, vol. 22, no. 4. Reprinted by permission from *Imprimis*, the monthly journal of Hillsdale College, Hillsdale, Michigan.

9. Wells, *No Place for Truth*, 80.

10. Ibid., 86.

11. Michael Bauman, "The Chronicle of Undeception" in *God and Man: Perspectives on Christianity in the Twentieth Century,* Michael Baughman, ed. (Hillsdale, Michigan: Hillsdale College Press, 1995), 11.

12. Ibid., 6.

13. Bernard Ramm, *Special Revelation And The Word of God* (Grand Rapids: William B. Eerdmans Publishing Company, 1961), 17.

14. Louis Berkhof, *Systematic Theology,* 3rd ed. (Grand Rapids: William B. Eerdmans Publishing Company, 1941), 36, 37.

15. See Erickson's treatment of Barth's view of general revelation in Millard J. Erickson, *Christian Theology* (Grand Rapids: Baker Book House, 1985), 163-170.

16. For further study on the meaning of *gnostos,* see my commentary, *Romans, The Randall House Commentary,* Robert E. Picirilli, ed. (Nashville: Randall House Publications, 1987), 26.

17. Franz Delitzsch, *Proverbs, Ecclesiastes, Song of Solomon,* vol. 6 (three vols. in one), James Martin, trans., *Keil and Delitzsch Commentary on the Old Testament in Ten Volumes* (1872, reprint, Grand Rapids: William B. Eerdmans Publishing Co., 1975), 261.

18. For further study on the meaning of *katecho,* see my commentary on Romans, 25.

19. Ibid., 30-32 (for my comments on why I think the knowledge of God in verse 21 is a present knowledge of God).

20. Kenneth S. Kantzer, "The Communication of Revelation" in *The Bible—The Living Word of Revelation,* Merrill C. Tenney, ed. (Grand Rapids: Zondervan Publishing Company, 1957), 262.

21. Carl F. H. Henry, "Divine Revelation and the Bible," in *Inspiration and Interpretation,* John F. Walvoord, ed. (Grand Rapids: William B. Eerdmans Publishing Company, 1957), 262.

22. Aurelius Augustine, *The Confessions of Saint Augustine,* trans. Edward B. Pusey (New York: Washington Square Press, 1960), 1.

23. G. C. Berkouwer, "General and Special Revelation," in *Revelation and the Bible,* Carl F. H. Henry, ed. (Grand Rapids: Baker Book House 1958), 15.

24. Benjamin Brekinridge Warfield, *The Inspiration and Authority of the Bible,* Samuel Craig, ed. (Philadelphia: The Presbyterian and Reformed Publishing Company, 1948), 74-75.

25. If you want your heart warmed and your faith strengthened, read about the preservation and triumph of Christianity in the Former Soviet Union. My wife and I traveled extensively in Ukraine and Russia. We met many who had been imprisoned for their faith under Stalin and Khrushchev. The pain of the slaughter in the Stalin years lives on in Russia. It is fresh in the memory of many whose family members were put to death for their faith.

As I talked with those people about their experiences and read books about the persecution of believers in the Former Soviet Union, the words of Jesus, "I will build my church; and the gates of hell shall not prevail against it" (Mt. 16:18), took on a new depth of meaning. Khrushchev boasted that he would destroy Christianity and march the last Christian across television screens for everyone to see. In spite of the severity of the persecution, the communists were not able to destroy Christianity. Many criminals were converted in prison as a result of the way the Christians stood when they were singled out for special punishment and torture.

26. Carl F. H. Henry, ed., *Baker's Dictionary of Christian Ethics* (1973), s.v. "Natural Law" by Paul B. Henry.

Chapter 4

1. Warfield, *The Inspiration and Authority of the Bible*, 133.

2. Ibid., 165.

3. Ibid., 131.

4. Ibid., 134.

5. Ibid., 113.

6. See Ramm's discussion of "inner forma" and "outer former" Bernard Ramm, *Special Revelation and the Word of God* (Grand Rapids: Eerdmans Publishing Co., 1961), 196-198.

7. R. Laird Harris, *Inspiration and Canonicity of the Bible* (Grand Rapids: Zondervan Publishing House, 1957), 21.

8. H. D. McDonald, *Theories of Revelation* (London: George Allen & Unwin LTD, 1963), 196.

9. Ibid., 218.

10. Ibid., 284-285.

11. Milton S. Terry, *Biblical Hermeneutics* (1883; Grand Rapids: Zondervan Publishing House, n.d.), 203.

12. Ibid.

13. E. R. Cravens, "Footnote," *Revelation* by John Peter Lange in *Lange's Commentary on the Holy Scriptures,* Philip Schaff, trans. and ed. (Grand Rapids: Zondervan Publishing House, n.d.), 98

14. Everett F. Harrison, "The Phenomena of Scripture," *Revelation and the Bible*, Carl F. H. Henry, ed. (Grand Rapids: Baker Book House, 1958), 250.

15. Roger Nicole, "New Testament Use of the Old Testament," *Revelation and the Bible*, 138.

16. The material from this point on to the "Concluding Challenge" is taken from my booklet *Inerrancy* (Nashville: Commission for Theological Integrity of the National Association of Free Will Baptists, ca. 1980). I made modifications to suit the purpose of this chapter.

17. Stephen T. Davis, *The Debate About the Bible* (Philadelphia: The Westminster Press, 1977), 114.

18. Ibid., 83-93.

19. Harold Lindsell, *The Battle About the Bible* (Grand Rapids: Zondervan Publishing House, 1976), 141-160, 185-199.

Chapter 5

1. Fred H. Klooster, "The Attributes of God: The Incommunicable Attributes," *Basic Christian Doctrines,* Carl F. H. Henry, ed. (New York: Holt, Rinehart and Winston, 1962), 24.

2. Stephen Charnock, *The Existence and Attributes of God* (London, 1681, reprint, Grand Rapids: Kregel Publications, 1958), 72.

3. Augustus Hopkins Strong, *Systematic Theology,* three vols. in one, seventeenth printing (Philadelphia: The Judson Press, 1907, 1953), 277.

4. James Oliver Buswell, Jr., *A Christian View of Being and Knowing* (Grand Rapids: Zondervan Publishing House, 1960), 47.

5. Ibid., 41.

6. James Oliver Buswell, Jr., *A Systematic Theology of the Christian Religion,* vol. 1, (Grand Rapids: Zondervan Publishing House, 1962), 47.

7. Ronald H. Nash, *The Concept of God: An Exploration of Contemporary Difficulties with the Attributes of God* (Grand Rapids: Zondervan Publishing House, 1983), 73-83.

8. Henry Clarence Thiessen, *Introductory Lectures in Systematic Theology* (Grand Rapids: William B. Eerdmans Publishing Company, 1949), 128.

9. Ibid., 124.

10. The material under "God is Holy" (p. 72) up to this point was taken from my book, *Biblical Ethics*, 10-12. Changes and additions were made to suit this study.

11. Thiessen, *Introductory Lectures* (1949), 129.

12. Ibid.

13. The material under "God Is Loving" up to this point was taken from *Biblical Ethics*, 12-14, and adapted for use in this study.

14. Thiessen, *Introductory Lectures* (1949), 131.

15. Strong, *Systematic Theology*, 286.

16. Charnock, *The Existence and Attributes of God*, 269.

17. Anthony A. Hoekema, "The Attributes of God: The Communicable Attributes," *Basic Christian Doctrines*, 29.

18. I have learned that since we were there this man has become a believer.

19. "Awesome," *The Oxford Dictionary of New Words: A Popular Guide to Words in the News* (New York: Oxford University Press, 1991), 21.

20. *Evangelical Dictionary of Theology*, 1984, s. v. "Awe."

21. *Evangelical Dictionary of Biblical Theology*, Walter A. Elwell, ed. (Grand Rapids: Baker, 1996), s. v. "Awe, Awesome."

Chapter 6

1. Benjamin Breckinridge Warfield, *Biblical Foundation* (Grand Rapids: William B. Eerdmans Publishing Company, 1958), 79.

2. H. E. Dana and Julius R. Mantey, *A Manual Grammar of the Greek New Testament* (New York: The MacMillan Company, 1955), 140.

3. Ibid., 147.

4. Ibid.

5. Warfield, *Biblical Foundation*, 109.

6. Ibid., 87, 88.

7. Gustav Friedrich Oehler, *Theology of the Old Testament*, a revision of the translation in *Clark's Theological Library* by George E. Day (New York: Funk and Wagnalls, 1883; reprint, Grand Rapids: Zondervan Publishing House, 1950), 88.

8. Buswell, *A Systematic Theology*, vol. 1, 111, 112.

9. Loraine Boettner, *Studies in Theology* (Grand Rapids: William B. Eerdmans Publishing Company, 1947), 121.

10. Warfield, *Biblical Foundation*, 111.

Chapter 7

1. Among those who take approaches that would fit the category of proving Christianity true are Norman Geisler, R. C. Sproul, John Gerstner, and Josh McDowell.

2. I find some kinship with my thinking in the writings of Gordon Clark, Edward John Carnell, Carl F. H. Henry, Francis Schaeffer, and Ronald Nash.

3. I have a special interest in the test of causal adequacy. When I was a small child, my mother assured me that Santa Claus delivered all the toys to all the children in the world on Christmas Eve. The stricter version was that he went down every chimney in the world at midnight. Some neighbor children told me that there was no Santa Claus. They said that my mother and father were Santa Claus. I talked with my mother about it and she assured me that there *was* a Santa Claus. Several things happened that for a while assured me of Santa Claus' existence, but I had inescapable doubts.

I had trouble with the causal adequacy of the Santa Claus theory. Santa Claus was only a man. As a man, he could not deliver toys to all the children in the world in one night. (If I had realized that there were 24 time zones, I might have held on a little longer.) I became philosophically convinced that there was no Santa Claus who delivered toys to all children in the world on Christmas Eve. Since that philosophical victory, I have remained unshaken in my conclusion.

A fictitious story may have value for children if they understand that it is for the pretend world, but fictitious life views for adults need to be discarded.

4. Ibid.

5. Gene Edward Veith, Jr., *Postmodern Times: A Christian Guide to Contemporary Thought and Culture* (Wheaton: Crossway Books, 1994), 57.

6. See the comments on Romans 3:11 in Chapters 2 (p. 23) and 3 (pp. 40, 41).

7. Edward Hopper (1871), "Jesus, Savior, Pilot Me," *Rejoice: The Free Will Baptist Hymn Book* (Nashville: The National Association of Free Will Baptists, 1988), 605.

8. Edward S. Ufford (1851-1929), "Throw Out The Lifeline," *Rejoice*, 354.

9. Buswell, *A Systematic Theology*, vol. 1, 72.

10. Berkhof, *Systematic Theology*, 28.

11. Addison H. Leitch, "The Knowledge of God: General and Special Revelation," *Basic Christian Doctrines*, Carl F. H. Henry, ed. (New York: Holt, Rinehart, and Winston, 1962), 2.

Chapter 8

1. Edwin K. Gedney, "Geology and the Bible," *Modern Science and Christian Faith*, F. Alton Everest, ed. (Wheaton: Van Kampen Press, 1948), 66.

2. Buswell, *A Systematic Theology*, vol. 1, 146.

3. From a personal discussion with Garnett H. Reid, chairman of the Bible Committee, Free Will Baptist Bible College, Nashville, Tennessee.

4. Buswell, 144.

5. Ibid., 145, 146.

6. H. C. Leupold, *Exposition of Genesis*, vol. 1 (Grand Rapids: Baker Book House, 1942), 57.

7. Bernard Ramm, *The Christian View of Science and Scripture* (Grand Rapids: William B. Eerdmans Publishing Company, 1955), 116, 215.

8. Carl F. H. Henry, "Science and Religion," *Contemporary Evangelical Thought*, Carl F. H. Henry, ed. (New York: Harper and Brothers, 1957), 277.

9. Ramm, *The Christian View of Science and Scripture*, 221.

10. Smalley and Fetzer, "A Christian View of Anthropology," *Modern Science and Christian Faith*, 2nd. ed., Alton Everest, ed.(Wheaton: Van Kampen Press, 1950), 161, referred to in Ramm, *The Christian View of Science and Scripture*, 325.

11. Ramm, *The Christian View of Science and Scripture*, 334.

12. Ibid., 335.

13. See Buswell, *A Systematic Theology*, vol. 1, 329-339 for a discussion of gaps in genealogies.

14. Ramm, *The Christian View of Science and Scripture,* 327.

15. John W. Klotz, *Genes, Genesis, and Evolution,* 2nd. ed. (St. Louis: Concordia Publishing House, 1955, 1970), 70.

16. Henry M. Morris, *The Twilight of Evolution* (Grand Rapids: Baker Book House, 1963), 42.

17. Carl F. H. Henry, "Theology and Evolution," in *Evolution and Christian Thought Today,* Russell L. Mixter, ed. (Grand Rapids: William B. Eerdmans Publishing Company, 1955), 217-218.

18. Ibid., 218.

19. Eugenie C. Scott, "Creationism, Ideology, and Science," *The Flight From Science and Reason,* Paul R. Gross, Norman Levitt, and Martin W. Lewis, eds. (Baltimore: John Hopkins Press, 1996 by the New York Academy of Sciences), 518, 519.

20. Robert T. Clark and James D. Bales, *Why Scientists Accept Evolution* (Grand Rapids: Baker Book House, 1966), 6. (For those who want a documented case in addition to the logical case I have presented on this point, I highly recommend this book if it can still be found.)

21. See Endnote 19.

22. Loren Fishman, "Feelings and Beliefs" *The Flight From Science and Reason,* 95.

23. Morris, *The Twilight of Evolution,* 55-56.

24. Ibid., 56.

25. Much of the material used in this chapter was from my booklet, *Issues Among Evangelicals,* published by The Commission on Theological Liberalism [Name later changed to "Commission on Theological Integrity"] of the National Association of Free Will Baptists, Nashville, Tennessee, 1968, 22-57. The material was rearranged and rewritten for this study. A small amount of material was taken from my booklet *Evolution* (Randall House Publications, Nashville, Tennessee, 1973), 3, 4, 8-10.

26. Myra Brooks Welch, "The Touch of the Master's Hand," in *Sourcebook of Poetry,* Al Bryant, ed. (Grand Rapids: Kregel Publications, 1992), 568, 569.

Chapter 9

1. Carl F. H. Henry, "Image of God" in *Evangelical Dictionary of Theology,* 547.

2. Ibid., 341.

3. Berkhof, *Systematic Theology,* 204.

4. Augustine, *The Confessions of Saint Augustine,* 1 (See Chapter 3, note 22).

5. A suggestion by Stephen Ashby (See Chapter 2, note 2).

6. Jean-Paul Sartre, *Existentialism and Human Emotions* (New York: Philosophical Library, 1957), 13-17.

7. Ibid., 49.

8. Veith, *Postmodern Times,* 48.

9. See quotations from Chuck Colson and David Wells in Chapter 3 (pp. 28, 29).

10. Millard J. Erickson, *Christian Theology,* unabridged one vol. ed. (Grand Rapids: Baker, 1985), 502.

11. Ibid., 498.

12. Ibid., 502.

13. Ibid., 503-504.

14. Ibid., 508.

15. Augustus Hopkins Strong, *Systematic Theology,* three vols. in one, (Philadelphia: The Judson Press, 1907), 486.

16. Alan F. Johnson, "Revelation" in *The Expositor's Bible Commentary,* vol. 12, Frank E. Gabaelein, ed. (Grand Rapids: Zondervan Publishing Company, 1981), 475.

17. Berkhof, *Systematic Theology,* 321.

18. Buswell, *A Systematic Theology,* vol. 1, 241.

19. Henry, "Image of God" in *Evangelical Dictionary of Theology,* 547.

20. Gordon H. Clark, "Image of God" in *Baker's Dictionary of Christian Ethics,* Carl F. H. Henry, ed. (Grand Rapids: Baker Book House, 1973), 313.

21. Charles Ryrie, "Depravity Total" in *Evangelical Dictionary of Theology,* 312.

22. From Ashby's suggestions (See Chapter 2, Note 2).

23. J. Matthew Pinson, "Will the Real Arminius Please Stand Up: A Study of the Theology of Jacobus Arminius in Light of His Interpreters," an unpublished paper written for the class History of Christian Theology (450-1650), Professor George Lindbeck, Yale University (May 7, 1993), 18, 19.

Pinson's quotes from Arminius are taken from *The Works of James Arminius,* 2 vols., Trans. James Nichols and William Nichols (Grand Rapids: Baker Book House, 1986). The order of the material in this printing differs from that of the 1956 printing by Baker referred to later in this chapter.

24. Van Til, Cornelius, "Calvinism," in *Baker's Dictionary of Theology,* Everett F. Harrison, ed. (Grand Rapids: Baker Book House, 1960), 340-341.

25. Strong, *Systematic Theology,* 619.

26. Ibid., 601-603.

27. David L. Smith, *With Wilful Intent: A Theology of Sin* (Wheaton: Victor Books, 1994), 363.

28. Pinson, "Will the Real Arminius Please Stand Up?" 15, 16.

29. James Arminius, *The Writings of James Arminius,* vol. 1, trans. James Nichols (Grand Rapids: Baker Book House, 1956), 317-319

Chapter 10

1. Robert Baker Girdlestone, *Synonyms of The Old Testament,* Second ed. (1897; reprint, Grand Rapids: William B. Eerdmans Publishing Company, n. d.), 117- 118.

2. Ibid., 119.

3. H. Dermot McDonald, *The Atonement and the Death of Christ: In Faith, Revelation, and History* (Grand Rapids: Baker Book House, 1985), 167.

4. Alexander M. Renwick, "Gnosticism," *Baker's Dictionary of Theology,* 238.

5. H. Dermot McDonald, *Jesus—Human and Divine* (Grand Rapids: Zondervan Publishing House, 1968. Published by special arrangement with Pickering and Inglis Ltd., London), 20.

6. H. Dermot McDonald, "Nestorius," *New Dictionary of Theology,* Sinclair B. Ferguson and David F. Wright, eds. (Downers Grove: Intervarsity Press, 1988), 457.

7. Strong, *Systematic Theology,* 672.

8. Charles Hodge, *Systematic Theology,* vol. 2 (1871; reprinted at Grand Rapids: William B. Eerdmans Publishing Company, 1986), 403.

9. Thiessen, *Introductory Lectures* (1949), 305.

10. Strong, 695.

11. From a lecture in Systematic Theology by Warren C. Young at Northern Baptist Theological Seminary.

12. Josh McDowell, *The Evidence Demands a Verdict* (San Bernardino: California, 1972), 185-273.

13. See my book, *Romans, The Randall House Commentary,* 13.

14. Buswell, *A Systematic Theology,* vol. 2 (Grand Rapids: Zondervan Publishing House, 1962), 69.

Chapter 11

1. H. Dermot McDonald, *The Atonement and the Death of Christ.*

2. Thiessen, *Introductory Lectures* (1949), 131.

3. Buswell, *A Systematic Theology,* vol. 2, 114.

4. Forlines, *Romans,* 55.

5. I learned the essence of this illustration of a council between the attributes of God from reading the "The Priesthood of Christ" by James Arminius. I read it in the 1951-1952 school year while taking a course on Arminian theology taught by Dr. L. C. Johnson, founding president of Free Will Baptist Bible College. The reading of this message by Arminius greatly helped me develop my understanding and acceptance of the penal satisfaction view of atonement. I was convinced then, and I still am, that Arminius believed in the penal satisfaction view of atonement. [In various editions of *The Writings of James Arminius,* the material is differently. In the set that I have (published by Baker Book House in 1956), "The Priesthood of Christ" is found in volume 1, pp. 2-51. The "Priesthood of the Believer" was "Delivered on the Eleventh day of July, 1603, by Arminius, on the occasion of receiving the Degree of Doctor of Divinity" (p. 2). The illustration of the council between Justice, Mercy, and Wisdom is found on pp. 28-31.]

6. The course on Arminian theology mentioned above was the occasion of my first struggle with exactly what Christ did that made atonement for my sins. It challenged my thinking more than any course that I have ever had. During this time of struggling with the thought of the atonement, I realized that Jesus, to be our redeemer, must satisfy the demands of the Law for perfect obedience and the requirement of the payment of an infinite penalty. It was at that time that I discovered the book by Lorraine Boettner, *Studies in Theology,* 2nd. ed. (Grand Rapids: Eerdmans Publishing Company, 1951), 299-300. This book used the terms *active* and *passive obedience of Christ,* providing the terminology for my developing idea.

7. William G. T. Shedd, *Dogmatic Theology,* vol. 2 (1889; reprint, Grand Rapids: Zondervan Publishing House, Classic Reprint Edition), 436-437.

8. Forlines, *Romans,* 55.

9. See Leon Morris, "Propitiation," *Evangelical Dictionary of Theology,* 888.

10. McDonald, *The Atonement and the Death of Christ,* 345

11. W. J. Conybeare and J. S. Howson, *The Life and the Epistles of St. Paul* (reprint, Grand Rapids: Eerdmans Publishing Company, 1978), 511, note 5. Brackets theirs.

12. Leroy Forlines, "A Study of Paul's Teachings on the Believer's Death to Sin and Its Relationship to a New Life," unpublished M.A. thesis, Winona Lake School of Theology, 1959.

13. Shedd, *A Critical and Doctrinal Commentary on the Epistle of St. Paul to the Romans,* (1879; reprint, Grand Rapids: Zondervan Publishing House, 1967), 148, 149.

14. Shedd, *Dogmatic Theology,* vol. 2, 534.

15. John F. Walvoord, "Identification with Christ," *Evangelical Dictionary of Theology,* 542.

16. Loraine Boettner, *Studies in Theology,* 299.

17. Robert Haldane, *An Exposition of the Epistle of Romans* (1852; reprint, McLean, Virginia: McDonald Publishing Company, 1958), 131, 132.

18. John Miley, *Systematic Theology,* vol. 2 (New York: Hunt and Eaton, 1894), 162.

19. James H. Fairchild, *Elements of Theology* (Oberlin, Ohio: Pearce and Randolf Printers, 1892), 224.

20. Miley, *Systematic Theology,* 163.

21. Charles G. Finney, *Finney's Lectures on Systematic Theology,* rev. ed., James H. Fairchild, ed. (1878; reprint, Grand Rapids: Eerdmans Publishing Company, 1953), 259.

22. Miley, *Systematic Theology,* 163.

23. Fairchild, *Elements of Theology,* 229.

24. Ibid., 227-228.

25. Ibid., 277.

26. Ibid., 278.

27. Finney, *Finney's Lectures on Systematic Theology,* 383-384.

28. For a treatment of the moral influence theory of liberalism, see Albert C. Knudson, *The Doctrine of Redemption* (New York: Abingdon-Cokesbury, 1933). I dealt with Knudson's moral influence theory of atonement in "The Need of Atonement According to Representative Theologians" (unpublished B.D. thesis, Northern Baptist Theological Seminary, 1962).

29. In the thesis mentioned in the note above, I dealt with Emil Brunner's view of atonement. Concerning the question of annihilation, Paul Jewett says: "In His eternal hope, Brunner seems to have given up the doctrine of hell in favor of annihilation of the wicked. A negative decision against Christ in this life will not be changed in the world to come, but it will be terminated." [Paul K. Jewett, Emil Brunner an *Introduction to the Man and His Thought* (Chicago: InterVarsity Press, 1961), 23] Brunner says, "Without detracting from his Holiness, God could make an end of sinful man." [Emil Brunner, *Dogmatics,* vol. 1, "The Christian Doctrine of Man," trans. Olive Wyon (Philadelphia: The Westminster Press, 1950), 274].

30. Berkhof, *Systematic Theology,* 393.

31. Millard J. Erickson, *Christian Theology,* unabridged one vol. ed. (Grand Rapids: Baker, 1985), 825-841. See also Charles Ryrie, *Basic Theology* (Wheaton: Victor Books, 1987), 318-323.

32. "Infant Salvation" in *The New Schaff-Herzog Encyclopedia of Religious Knowledge,* Samuel Macauley Jackson, ed. (1907; reprint, Grand Rapids: Baker Book House, 1950), 491.

33. H. Orton Wiley, *Christian Theology,* vol. 2 (Kansas City, Mo.: Beacon Hill Press, 1952), 132.

34. Forlines, *Romans,* 130.

35. In a quotation given earlier from Shedd, with regard to the union of Christ and the believer, he explains, "Because they are spiritually, vitally, eternally, and mystically one with him, his merit is imputable to them, and their demerit is imputable to him" (Shedd, *Dogmatic Theology,* vol. 2, 534). I believe this same reasoning can be applied to the identification of the Christ with the race in the incarnation.

36. In the quotation from Walvoord given earlier in the chapter, he says, "Christ is identified with the human race in incarnation, but only true believers are identified with Christ" ("Identification with Christ," *Evangelical Dictionary of Theology,* 542.) He makes the observation that the incarnation identified Christ with the race. If that is true, there should be some theological implications derived from this identification. I believe that those implications are pertinent to salvation.

37. See comments on general revelation in Chapter 3, pp. 32, 33.

38. Millard J. Erickson, *Christian Theology,* unabridged one vol. ed. (Grand Rapids: Baker, 1985), 639.

39. Ibid.

40. Ibid., 638.

41. Ibid., 637.

42. Ibid., 638.

43. James Leo Garrett, Jr., *Systematic Theology,* vol. 1 (Grand Rapids: Eerdmans Publishing Company, 1990), 487.

44. Ibid.

45. See page 164.

Chapter 12

1. Charles G. Finney, *Finney's Lectures on Systematic Theology*, rev. ed., J. H. Fairchild, ed. (1878; reprint, Grand Rapids: Eerdmans Publishing Company, 1953), 391, 392.

2. Buswell, *A Systematic Theology*, vol. 2, 146.

3. David Brown, Acts–Romans, in *A Commentary Critical, Experimental and Practical on the Old and New Testaments*, vol. 3, Robert Jamieson, A. R. Fausset, and David Brown (1864–1870; reprint, Grand Rapids: Eerdmans Publishing Company, 1984), 226.

4. Robert Haldane, *An Exposition of the Epistle of Romans* (1852; reprint, McLean, Virginia: McDonald Publishing Company, 1958), 248, 249.

5. William Sanday and Arthur Headlam, *The Epistle to the Romans in the International Critical Commentary*, 5th ed. (1902; reprint, Edinburgh: T. & T. Clark, 1960), 218.

6. Richard Chenevix Trench, *Synonyms of the New Testament*, (1854; reprint, Grand Rapids: Associated Publishers and Authors, Inc., n. d.), 245.

7. Ibid., 243, 244.

8. Ibid., 246, 247.

9. Ibid., 247.

10. Most commentaries agree with the difference noted between "conformed" (Greek *suschēmatizō*) and "transformed" (Greek *metamorphoō*). (For discussions which agree, see Barclay 157, 158; Hendriksen 405, note 338; and Sanday and Headlam 353. For discussions that deny this distinction, see Barrett 232, 233; and Cranfield II:605, 608) [This is noted in my commentary, *Romans*, 321.]

11. Barclay M. Newman and Eugene A. Nida, *A Translator's Handbook on Paul's Letter to the Romans* (New York: United Bible Societies, 1973), 235.

12. Joseph Henry Thayer, *Thayer's Greek-English Lexicon of the New Testament* (1889; reprint, Grand Rapids: Zondervan Publishing House, 1962), 429.

13. For a more complete discussion of the problem of a person's attitude toward himself see my book, *Biblical Ethics* (Nashville: Randall House Publications, 1973), 59-67.

14. For a system of ethics based on the application of the four basic values to the four basic relationships, see my book, *Biblical Ethics*.

15. See Chapter 9, "Designed for a Relationship With the Created Order," pp. 141, 142.

16. Wells, *No Place for Truth*, 169.

17. From "A Mother's Day Address" to the Independence County Chapter of AARP, Batesville, Arkansas. At that time James was the pastor of Allen Chapel Free Will Baptist Church in Batesville, Arkansas. He is now General Director of the Department of Foreign Missions of the National Association of Free Will Baptists, Antioch, Tennessee.

18. Berkhof, *Systematic Theology*, 536.

19. Robert Haldane, *An Exposition of the Epistle of Romans* (1852; reprint, McLean, Virginia: McDonald Publishing Company, 1958), 248, 249.

20. I have discussed earlier in this chapter the problems involved in the use of illustrations under the heading, "The Limitations of Illustrations in Explaining Our Relationship With God." To refer to our subconscious minds as being "programmed" is a metaphor which draws an analogy from computer science. The analogy between the programming of a computer and the programming the subconscious mind is very useful. However, there is a point where the analogy breaks down. Once the program is written, the computer works in terms of *cause* and *effect*. When applied to the subconscious mind, we are not to press the analogy to the point that we eliminate the element of choice.

21. The material under "The Guaranteed Results of Sanctification" up to this point with slight modification is taken from my book, *Biblical Ethics*, 34-36.

22. Most of the material under "Sanctification and Perfection" was taken from my book *Biblical Ethics*, 138-140.

23. This statement is based on the study for my thesis, "Jesus and the Pharisees," an unpublished Th.M. thesis, Chicago Graduate School of Theology, 1970.

24. There was an evidence of concern for basic morality and the virtues that led to refinement on secular college campuses. They had rules to uphold, maintain, and promote these virtues. All this came under attack from the radical student movement in the 1960s.

25. For a more thorough discussion on Christian liberty and legalism, see my book, *Biblical Ethics*, chs. 7 and 8.

Chapter 13

1. Richard Chenevix Trench, *Synonyms of the New Testament* (1854; reprint, Grand Rapids: Associated Publishers and Authors, Inc., n. d), 242.

2. R. C. Sproul, *Willing to Believe: The Controversy Over Free Will* (Grand Rapids: Baker Books, 1997), 73.

3. See page 159.

4. R. C. Sproul, *Chosen by God* (Wheaton: Tyndale House Publishers, Inc., 1986), 118.

5. Robert Haldane, *An Exposition of the Epistle of Romans* (1852; reprint, McLean, Virginia: McDonald Publishing Company, 1958), 248, 249.

6. Berkhof, *Systematic Theology*, 536.

7. Strong, *Systematic Theology*, 536.

8. Berkhof, *Systematic Theology*, 517-520.

9. Ibid., 520.

10. Ibid., 518.

11. Ibid., 518, 519. Translation by Dr. Darrell Holley, professor of Latin at Free Will Baptist Bible College, Nashville, Tennessee.

12. Ibid., 519.

13. John Piper, *The Justification of God* (Grand Rapids: Baker Book House, 1983), 67.

14. Millard J. Erickson, *Christian Theology*, unabridged one vol. ed. (Grand Rapids: Baker, 1985), 932.

15. Ibid., 933.

16. Ibid., 931.

17. Sproul, *Willing to Believe*, 189-202.

18. Edward Mote, "The Solid Rock" in *Rejoice: The Free Will Baptist Hymn Book* (Nashville: National Association of Free Will Baptists, 1988), 419.

19. Forlines, *Romans*, 105.

Chapter 14

1. For a long time those who accepted only the last point of Calvinism called themselves "Calvinists." There is a trend among some to call themselves "Arminian." In fact they are more Arminian than Calvinistic.

2. Lewis Sperry Chafer, *Systematic Theology*, vol. 3 (Dallas: Dallas Seminary Press, 1948), 316.

3. Buswell, *A Systematic Theology*, vol. 2, 145.

4. Millard J. Erickson, *Christian Theology* (Grand Rapids: Baker Book House, 1985), 986, 987.

5. Charles Stanley, *Eternal Security* (Nashville: Thomas Nelson Publishers, 1990), 11, 12.

6. Ibid., 92.

7. M. R. Vincent, *Word Studies in the New Testament,* 2nd ed. (1888; reprint, Wilmington, Delaware: Associated Publishers and Authors, 1972), 1059.

8. Stanley, *Eternal Security,* 35.

9. Forlines, *Romans,* 90-96.

10. Zane C. Hodges, *The Gospel Under Siege: A Study of Faith and Works* (Dallas: Rendención Viva, 1981).

11. William Wilson Stevens, *Doctrines of The Christian Religion* (Grand Rapids: William B. Eerdmans Publishing Company, 1967), 258.

12. Buswell, *A Systematic Theology,* vol. 2, 146.

13. John H. Gerstner, "Perseverance," *Baker's Dictionary of Theology,* 404.

14. Berkhof, *Systematic Theology,* 404.

15. Herman Hoeksema, *Reformed Dogmatics* (Grand Rapids: Reformed Free Publishing Co., 1966), 258.

16. John Henry Thayer, *Thayer's Greek-English Lexicon of the New Testament,* (1889; reprint, Grand Rapids: Zondervan Publishing House, 192), 663.

17. R. C. Sproul brings up an interesting observation about the use of repentance here. He explains: "I think the passage may well be describing true Christians. The most important phrase for me is 'renew again to repentance.' I know there is a false kind of repentance that the author elsewhere calls the repentance of Esau. But here he speaks of renewal. The new repentance, if it is renewed, must be like the old repentance. The renewed repentance of which he speaks is certainly the genuine kind. I assume therefore that the old was likewise genuine" [R. C. Sproul, *Chosen by God* (Wheaton: Tyndale House Publishers, Inc. 1986), 185].

18. J. D. O'Donnell, *Free Will Baptist Doctrines* (Nashville: Randall House Publications, 1974), 78.

19. Robert E. Picirilli, *Perseverance* [a booklet] (Nashville: Randall House Publications, 1973), 20.

20. I. Howard Marshall, *Kept by the Power of God: A Study of Perseverance and Falling Away* (Minneapolis: Bethany House, 1969), 142.

21. Ibid., 146.

22. Ibid., 148.

23. Robert Shank, *Life in the Son: A Study of the Doctrine of Perseverance* (Springfield, MO: Wescott Publishers, 1960), 309.

24. Ibid., 328-329.

25. This paper was presented at the Southeastern Region of the Evangelical Theological Society meeting in Charlotte, North Carolina, March 10, 1995. I have included it in Appendix 1 because it is impossible in this chapter to give adequate attention to this subject.

26. A discussion on the appropriate name for these sins will be found in Appendix 1.

27. J. A. Motyer, "Courage, Boldness," in *The International Dictionary of New Testament Theology,* vol. 1, Colin Brown, ed. (Grand Rapids: Zondervan Publishing House, 1975), 365.

28. Millard J. Erickson, *Christian Theology,* One vol. originally published in three vols. (Grand Rapids: Baker Book House, 1985), 994.

29. Erickson, 993, 994.

30. Shank, *Life in the Son,* 164, 165.

31. John 15:1-8 is frequently referred to as "The Parable of the Vine and the Branches." This passage is more accurately called an allegory. A parable is an extended simile, while an allegory is an extended

metaphor. A simile is a figure of speech introduced by "like" or "as." For example, "red like crimson" or "white as snow" are similes. A parable is an extended simile, e.g., "The kingdom of heaven is like. . . ."

On the other hand, a metaphor omits the *like* or *as*. For example, Jesus said, "I am the bread of life." When we make a distinction between allegories and parables, the Gospel of John is found to have no parables, only allegories. Since an allegory is an extended metaphor, Jesus words, "I am the vine you are the branches" (Jn. 15:5), and His extended explanation of this statement is an allegory. The nature of allegories demands that more attention be given to interpreting their details than for a parable.

32. *The Amplified Bible* (Grand Rapids, Michigan: Zondervan Publishing House, 1987), Heb. 6:7, 8.

33. Some who believe that it is possible for one who is saved to cease to be a Christian and once again be under the wrath of God object to the term "lose salvation." To them it seems that it would say that you could accidentally or without intention lose your salvation. I understand their concern. However, that is not the only meaning that *lose* can have. To "lose something" simply means to no longer be in possession of it.

The term "lose your salvation" is so commonly used that it is almost impossible to say much about the subject without using it. Even if a particular person avoids using the term, it will continue to be used.

34. Picirilli, *Perseverance,* 22.

35. Berkhof, *Systematic Theology,* 547.

36. Ibid., 548.

37. Wayne Gruden, "Perseverance of the Saints: A Case Study from Hebrews 6:4-6 and the Other Warning Passages in Hebrews," in *The Grace of God, the Bondage of the Will,* vol. 1, eds. Thomas R. Schreiner and Bruce A. Ware (Grand Rapids: Baker Books, 1995), 139-150.

38. Berkhof, *Systematic Theology,* 548.

39. Picirilli, *Perseverance,* 25, 26.

40. During the 1960s and 70s, Georgi Vinns was one of the most significant voices in the USSR for religious freedom. This cost him two terms in prison. He had spent eight years in prison when President Carter negotiated his release in 1979. He came to America and set up Russian Gospel Ministries in Elkhart, Indiana. On February 18, 1996, he and his wife visited an Autonomous Baptist Brotherhood Church in Kiev, Ukraine. He had been one of the pastors of this church prior to his imprisonment. This was the first time he had visited this church since his release from prison. Well over a thousand people packed into that church for a three-hour service. Many stood, some of them old people, the entire time, while the much of the crowd filled other rooms in the church. Georgi Vinns died of an inoperable brain tumor January 11, 1998.

41. In the light of the teaching of the Old Testament about presumptuous sins, it seems that 1 John 3:9 should be understood as saying that a Christian cannot choose sin as a lifestyle. It has reference to more than mere repetition of sin. It would be a deliberate choice of sin as a lifestyle. There is a very significant difference between being shamefully defeated by sin and choosing sin for a lifestyle.

Chapter 15

1. A good bit of the material that appears here and there in this chapter was adapted from "Observations About Election" from my commentary, *Romans,* 232-238.

2. Millard J. Erickson, *Christian Theology,* (Grand Rapids: Baker Book House, 1985), 918.

3. Norman L. Geisler, "Freedom, Free Will, and Determinism," *Evangelical Dictionary Of Theology,* 429.

4. J. A. Crabtree, "Does Middle Knowledge Solve the Problem of Divine Sovereignty?" *The Grace of God, the Bondage of the Will,* vol. 2, Thomas R. Schreiner and Bruce A. Ware, eds. (Grand Rapids: Baker Books, 1995), 429.

5. John S. Feinberg, "God, Freedom, and Evil in Calvinistic Thinking" *The Grace of God, the Bondage of the Will*, vol. 2, 463, 464.

6. Gordon H. Clark, *Biblical Predestination* (Philadelphia: Presbyterian and Reformed Publishing Company, 1969), 60.

7. Ibid., 45.

8. Richard A. Muller, "Grace, Election, and Contingent Choice: Arminians Gambit and the Reformed Choice," *The Grace of God, the Bondage of the Will*, vol. 2, 269-270.

9. Ibid., 271.

10. Ibid., 276. Quoted material from William Perkins, *A Treatise of God's Free Grace and Man's Free Will*, in *Workes*, I:704, IA, 709.2C-710.IC.

11. Clark, *Biblical Predestination*, 121.

12. R. K. McGregor Wright, *No Place for Sovereignty: What's Wrong with Freewill Theism* (Downers Grove: Inter Varsity Press, 1996), 41.

13. Buswell, *A Systematic Theology*, vol. 1, 267.

14. Ibid.

15. Loraine Boettner, *The Reformed Doctrine of Predestination* (Philadelphia: The Presbyterian and Reformed Publishing Company, 1969), 78.

16. Ibid., 208.

17. Ibid., 222.

18. Ibid.

19. Feinberg, "God Ordains All Things," *Predestination and Free Will: Four Views of Divine Sovereignty and Human Freedom*, eds. David Basinger and Randall Basinger (Downers Grove: InterVarsity, 1986), 24, 25.

20. Ibid., 37.

21. Boettner, *The Reformed Doctrine of Predestination*, 42.

22. Feinberg, "God Ordains All Things," 32.

23. Crabtree, "Does Middle Knowledge Solve the Problem of Divine Sovereignty?" *The Grace of God, the Bondage of the Will*, vol. 2, 436.

24. Buswell, *A Systematic Theology*, vol. 1, 60.

25. Thiessen, *Introductory Lectures* (1949), 344-349.

26. Henry C. Thiessen, *Introductory Lectures in Systematic Theology*, rev. ed., rev. by Vernon D. Doerksen (Grand Rapids: Wm. B. Eerdmans Publishing Company, 1979), 257-262. The only hint of a change from Thiessen's view of *conditional* election in the first edition to the view of *unconditional* election in the revised edition is found in the "Preface to the Revised Edition." Doerksen explains, "Several of the portions, such as those on inspiration, election, foreknowledge, creation, demons, imputation of sin, and pretribulationism, have been rather extensively revised" (p. ix). [I hardly think anyone unfamiliar the first edition's teaching of *conditional* election would have imagined it after reading the revised edition's treatment supporting *unconditional* election.]

27. J. A. Crabtree, "Does Middle Knowledge Solve the Problem of Divine Sovereignty?" *The Grace of God, the Bondage of the Will*, vol. 2, 449, footnote 18. (Crabtree calls attention to the fact that William Lane Craig alludes to these terms. Then he gives an explanation.)

28. Nash, *The Concept of God*, 54.

29. *Oxford English Dictionary*.

30. Berkhof, *Systematic Theology*, 68.

31. *Merriam Webster's Collegiate Dictionary*, Tenth Edition.

32. Norman Geisler, "God Knows All Things," *Predestination and Free Will: Four Views of Divine Sovereignty and Human Freedom,* eds. David Basinger and Randall Basinger, 76.

33. Ibid., 79.

34. John Miley, *Systematic Theology,* vol. 2 (New York: The Methodist Book Concern, 1894), 273.

35. Ibid.

36. Geisler, "God Knows All Things," *Predestination and Free Will: Four Views of Divine Sovereignty and Human Freedom,* eds. David Basinger and Randall Basinger, 73.

37. Gordon H. Clark, *Biblical Predestination,* 120.

38. Miley, *Systematic Theology,* vol. 1, 166-169.

39. When I finish this book, I want to get back to work on a manuscript that is well over half finished for which I am using the working title, "Understanding Yourself and Others."

40. Clark Pinnock, "From Augustine to Arminius: A Pilgrimage in Theology," *The Grace of God, the Will of Man: A Case for Arminianism,* Clark Pinnock, ed. (Grand Rapids: Zondervan Publishing House, 1989), 25.

41. Ibid., 26.

42. Clark Pinnock, "God Limits His Knowledge," *Predestination and Free Will: Four Views of Divine Sovereignty and Human Freedom,* eds. David Basinger and Randall Basinger (Downers Grove: InterVarsity, 1986), 144.

43. Richard Rice, "Divine Foreknowledge and Free-Will Theism," *The Grace of God, the Will of Man: A Case for Arminianism,* Clark Pinnock, ed. (Grand Rapids: Zondervan Publishing House, 1989), 134.

44. Ibid., 135.

45. Ibid., 136.

46. James Arminius, *The Writings of James Arminius,* vol. 3, trans. James Nichols (Grand Rapids: Baker Book House, 1956), 66.

47. Jack Cottrell, "The Nature of the Divine Sovereignty," *The Grace of God, the Will of Man: A Case for Arminianism,* Clark Pinnock, ed., 111.

48. Cottrell, "Conditional Election," *Grace Unlimited,* Clark H. Pinnock, ed. (Minneapolis: Bethany House, 1975), 59.

49. Ibid., 60.

50. Robert E. Picirilli, an unpublished manuscript, *God's Decrees, Our Faith: Calvinism, Arminianism, and the Theology of Salvation.* (Picirilli is currently, Associate Dean at Free Will Baptist Bible College. For years he was academic dean. He has taught Pauline Writings, Greek, Philosophy, and Calvinism and Arminianism.) The material quoted here can be found in "Chapter 3: The Classical Arminian Doctrine of Predestination," under "Areas of Disagreement," under the sub-point, "The relationship between, certainty, contingency, and necessity."

51. William Lane Craig, *The Only Wise God: The Compatibility of Divine Foreknowledge and Human Freedom* (Grand Rapids: Baker Book House, 1987), 37.

52. Feinberg, "God Ordains All Things," 24, 25.

53. Feinberg, "God, Freedom, and Evil in Calvinistic Thinking," *The Grace of God, The Bondage of the Will,* vol. 2, 463, 464.

54. Ibid., 460.

55. Ibid., 451.

56. Picirilli, *God's Decrees, Our Faith,* "Chapter 3: The Classical Arminian Doctrine of Predestination," under the heading, "Areas of Disagreement," under sub-point, "An emphasis on the nature of man as personal."

57. Richard Muller, "Grace, Election, and Contingent Choice: *Arminius's Gambit and the Reformed Response, The Grace of God, the Bondage of the Will,* vol. 2, 271.

58. Ibid., 277-278.

59. See "God Is Infinite in Relation to Time," pp. 67-70.

60. Geisler, "God Knows All Things," *Predestination and Free Will: Four Views of Divine Sovereignty and Human Freedom,* eds David Basinger and Randall Basinger, 73.

61. Arminius, *The Writings of James Arminius,* vol. 3, 66.

62. William Lane Craig, "Middle Knowledge: A Calvinistic-Arminian Rapprochement," *A Case for Arminianism: The Grace of God, the Will of Man,* Clark Pinnock, ed. (Grand Rapids: Zondervan Publishing House, 1989), 141.

63. Ibid., 141-142.

64. Craig, *The Only Wise God: The Compatibility of Divine Foreknowledge and Human Freedom* (Grand Rapids: Baker Book House, 1987), 131.

65. Ibid., 129.

66. Craig, "Middle Knowledge: A Calvinistic-Arminian Rapprochement," 147.

67. Ibid., 130-131.

68. Craig, *The Only Wise God,* 129.

69. Arminius, *The Writings of James Arminius,* 66.

70. Buswell, *A Systematic Theology,* vol. 1, 60.

71. Berkhof, *Systematic Theology,* 67.

72. Ibid., 60.

73. Picirilli, *God's Decrees, Our Faith,* "Chapter 3: The Classical Arminian Doctrine of Predestination," under the heading, "Areas of Disagreement," under sub-point, "1. The relationship between certainty, contingency, and necessity."

74. Ibid.

75. Ibid., The "b" sub-point under "1. The relationship between certainty, contingency, and necessity."

76. Ibid., The "c" sub-point.

77. Ibid.

78. Ibid.

79. Cottrell, "The Nature of the Divine Sovereignty," *The Grace of God, the Will of Man: A Case for Arminianism,* Clark Pinnock, ed., 111.

80. Berkhof, *Systematic Theology,* 536.

81. Shedd, *Dogmatic Theology,* vol. 1 (1888; reprint, Nashville: Thomas Nelson Publishers, 1980), 406.

82. Thiessen, *Introductory Lectures* (1949), 344

Chapter 16

1. In this treatment of Romans 9, I am drawing heavily from a paper that I wrote by the title, "Election in Romans 9: Conditional or Unconditional?" This paper drew heavily from my Romans commentary. I read this paper at the Southeastern Regional Meeting of the Evangelical Society at Temple University in Chattanooga, Tennessee (ca., 1990). I also read it at the Theological Symposium meeting at Hillsdale Free Will Baptist Bible College (1997). In this paper, I used the NASB. It is more convenient to use the NASB in my treatment of Romans 9 in this chapter.

2. Forlines, *Romans.*

3. Robert Haldane, *An Exposition of the Epistle to the Romans* (London, 1952; reprint, McLean, Virginia: MacDonald Publishing Co., 1958), 467.

4. Everett F. Harrison, *Romans* in *The Expositor's Bible Commentary*, vol. 10 (Grand Rapids: Zondervan Publishing House, 1976), 106.

5. William S. Plumer, *Commentary on Romans* (New York: Anson D. F. Randolph & Co., 1870; reprint, Grand Rapids: Kregel Publications, 1979), 473.

6. Shedd, *A Critical and Doctrinal Commentary on the Epistle of St. Paul to the Romans* (Charles Scribners, 1879; reprint, Grand Rapids: Zondervan Publishing House, 1976), 288.

7. John Piper, *The Justification of God: An Exegetical Study of Romans 9:1-23* (Grand Rapids: Baker Book House, 1983), 100.

8. Adam Clarke, *The New Testament of Our Lord and Savior Jesus Christ, Vol. VI: Romans-Revelation* (T. Mason & G. Lane, 1837, reprinted, Nashville: Abingdon-Cokesbury Press, n.d.), 111-112.

9. F. L. Godet, *Commentary on the Epistle to the Romans*, trans. A. Cusin (Funk and Wagnall, 1883, reprinted, Grand Rapids: Zondervan Publishing House, 1956), 350-51.

10. William Sanday and Arthur C. Headlam, *A Critical and Exegetical Commentary on the Epistle to the Romans*, in *The International Critical Commentary* fifth edition, eds., S. R. Driver, A. Plummer, and C. A. Briggs (1895, reprinted, Edinburgh: T. & T. Clark, 1960), 245.

11. Shedd, *Commentary on Romans*, 285.

12. Hodge, *Commentary on Romans*, 306-307, 312.

13. William Hendriksen, *New Testament Commentary, Exposition of Paul's Epistle to the Romans* (Grand Rapids: Baker Book House, 1982), 323, 24

14. John Murray , *The Epistle to the Romans*, vol. 2. in *The New International Commentary on the New Testament*, F. F. Bruce, gen. ed. (Grand Rapids: William B. Eerdmans Publishing Co.,1982), 15-19.

15. Piper, *Study of Romans 9:1-23*, 48-52.

16. 2 Esdras in *The Apocrypha of the Old Testament*, Revised Standard Version (New York: Thomas Nelson and Sons, 1957), 23.

17. When I was doing research for my commentary on Romans, I visited an Orthodox Jewish Rabbi. I said to him, "When I study about the Jewish view of salvation, I get the idea that they believe that when God called Abraham He unconditionally saved all Jews." He said, "Yes." I then said, "I also get the idea that Jews believed in salvation by works." He said, "Yes." The seeming contradiction did not seem to bother him.

18. E. P. Sanders, *Paul and Palestinian Judaism* (Philadelphia: Fortress Press, 1977), 120.

19. Charles Hodge, *Commentary on the Epistle to the Romans* (First published in 1835, reprinted from the 1886 revised edition, Grand Rapids: William B. Eerdmans, 1983), 70, 71.

20. Douglas J. Moo, *The Epistle to the Romans* in *The New International Commentary on the New Testament*, Gordon D. Fee, ed. (Grand Rapids: William B. Eerdmans Publishing Company, 1996), 573.

21. Ibid., 46, 47.

22. "Resurrection" in *The Jewish Encyclopedia*, vol. 10, Isidore Singer, managing ed. (Funk and Wagnalls, 1907; reprinted by Ktav Publishing House, Inc., 1964).

23. Phillip Birnbaum, *A Book of Jewish Concepts* (New York: Hebrew Publishing Co., 1964), 609, 610.

24. Sanders, *Paul and Palestinian Judaism*, 180.

25. Ibid., 75. See also 236.

26. Ibid., 147.

27. Ibid., 33-59.

28. Forlines, *Romans*, 173, 174.

29. Ibid., 249.

30. Piper, *Study of Romans 9:1-23*, 33.

31. Ibid., 136.

32. Ibid., 44.

33. I think that my treatment of "Justification According to the Penal Satisfaction View of Atonement" in Chapter 11 (pp. 184ff) shows that a person cannot successfully charge me with believing in salvation by works. I believe that I have shown in Chapter 15, under the heading "An Answer to the Third Assumption of Calvinism" (pp. 340, 341), that a person can believe in conditional election without it being based on works.

34. See the treatment of saving faith under the heading "The Question of Synergism," Chapter 13 (p. 260).

35. Piper, *Study of Romans 9:1-23*, 100.

36. M. R. Vincent, *Word Studies in the New Testament* in one volume, second edition (New York, 1888; reprinted at Wilmington, Delaware: Associated Publishers and Authors, 1972), 732.

37. R. C. H. Lenski, *The Interpretation of St. Paul's Epistle to the Romans* (Minneapolis: Augsburg Publishing House, 1961), 606, 607. In the book, the word is *justice* rather than *injustice*, but it is obvious that Lenski meant *injustice*.

38. See H. P. Liddon, *Explanatory Analysis of St. Paul's Epistle to the Romans* (1892; reprinted, Grand Rapids: Zondervan Publishing House, 1961) 162-63. See also Shedd, *Commentary on Romans*, 288.

39. Robert Picirilli, *The Book of Romans* (Nashville: Randall House Publications, 1975), 183.

40. Thomas R. Schreiner, "Does Romans 9 Teach Individual Election unto Salvation?" in *The Grace of God, the Bondage of the Will*, vol. 1, eds. Thomas R. Schreiner and Bruce A. Ware (Grand Rapids: Baker Books, 1995), 99.

41. Piper, *Study of Romans 9:1-23*, 133-34.

42. Ibid., 137.

43. Hendriksen, *Commentary on Romans*, 326.

44. Piper, *Study of Romans 9:1-23*, 159.

45. Ibid., 275.

46. John Brown, *Analytical Exposition of the Epistle of Paul the Apostle to the Romans* (Robert Carter and Brothers, 1857; reprinted, Grand Rapids: Baker Book House, 1981), 338.

47. Forlines, *Romans*, 275-279.

48. Ralph Earle, *Word Meanings in the New Testament*, vol. III, Romans (Kansas City: Beacon Hill Press, 1974), 194.

49. Henry C. Thiessen, *Introductory Lectures in Systematic Theology* (Grand Rapids: William B. Eerdmans Publishing Company, 1949), 129.

50. Shedd, *Romans*, 298.

51. Harrison, *Romans* in *The Expositor's Bible Commentary*, vol.10, 107.

52. Hodge, *Commentary on the Epistle to the Romans*, 321.

53. Murray, *The Epistle to the Romans*, vol. 2., 36.

54. Shedd, *Romans*, 299.

55. Piper, *Study of Romans 9:1-23*, 194.

56. Picirilli, *The Book of Romans*, 187.

57. Lenski, *Romans*, 627.

58. Forlines, *Romans*, 239-241.

59. F. F. Bruce, *The Epistle of Paul to the Romans, Tyndale New Testament Commentaries* (Grand Rapids: William B. Eerdmans Publishing Co. 1963), 177.

60. Hendriksen, *Exposition of Paul's Epistle to the Romans*, 285.

61. August Wilhelm Meyer, *Meyer's Commentary on the New Testament*, vol. 10, *Critical and Exegetical Handbook to the Epistle to the Romans*, Timothy Dwight, ed.; William P. Dickson, trans. and ed. (T & T Clark, 1883; reprinted, Winona Lake, Ind.: Alpha Greek Publications, 1980), 377.

62. Murray, *The Epistle to the Romans*, vol. 1, 320.

63. Godet, *Commentary on the Epistle to the Romans*, 327.

64. Bruce, *The Epistle of Paul to the Romans*, 178.

65. John Wesley, *Explanatory Notes Upon the New Testament*, vol. 2 (reprinted, Grand Rapids: Baker Book House, 1981) pages not numbered.

66. Robert W. Yarbrough, "Divine Election in the Gospel of John," *The Grace of God, the Bondage of the Will*, 49.

67. See my discussion on page 260.

68. Yarbrough, "Divine Election in the Gospel of John," 47.

69. Ibid.

70. Ibid., 47, 48.

71. It appears that some of the Jews thought that it was possible for a person to repudiate his Jewish faith and become an apostate. It seems that some of the Jews were trying to say that Jesus was an apostate. (See Mt. 12:24; 26:65; Mk. 3:22; 14:62-64; Lk. 11:15; and Jn. 8:48.)

72. Yarbrough, "Divine Election in the Gospel of John," 50, footnote 10.

73. Ibid., 52.

74. Ibid., 50.

75. See F. F. Bruce, *Commentary on the Book of Acts* (Grand Rapids: William B. Eerdmans, 1955), 63, 64, for the requirements of being a Jewish proselyte.

76. Ibid., 216.

Chapter 17

1. According to the *Oxford English Dictionary* one of the obsolete meanings of the word *schoolmaster* was "a private tutor." That was one meaning of the word in 1611 when the KJV was translated.

2. See Chapter 15 under "Divine Foreknowledge of Free Human Choices and Acts Not Based on a Spectator Role" (p. 335).

3. Paul Jacobs and Hartmut Krienke, "Foreknowledge, Providence, Predestination," *In the International Dictionary of New Testament Theology*, vol. 1, Colin Brown, ed. trans. from the German, THEOLOGISCHES BEGRIFFSLEXIKON ZUM NEUEN TESTAMENT, 1967-1971 (Grand Rapids: Zondervan Publishing House, 1975), 692-693.

4. *Theological Dictionary of the New Testament*, vol. 1, Gerhard Kittle, German ed., Geoffrey W. Bromiley trans. and ed. from THEOLOGISCHES WÖRTERBUCH ZUM NEUEN TESTAMENT, 1933-1973 (Grand Rapids: William B. Eerdmans Publishing Company, 1964-1974), 716.

5. *The Apocrypha of the Old Testament*, Revised Standard Version (New York: Thomas Nelson, 1957).

6. Forlines, *Romans*, 236.

7. Heinrich August Wilhelm Meyer, *Critical and Exegetical Hand-Book to the Epistle to the Romans*, 5th ed., John C. Moore, B. A. and Edwin Johnson, trans.; William P. Dickson, ed.; Timothy Dwight, American ed.; *Meyers Commentary on the New testament*, vol. 5 (Clark, 1884; reprinted, Winona Lake: Alpha Publications, 1979), 337.

8. Godet, Frédéric Louis, *Commentary on the Epistle to the Romans*, trans. A. Cusin (Funk and Wagnalls, 1883; reprinted at Grand Rapids: Zondervan Publishing House, n. d.) 325.

9. Lenski, *Romans*, 557.

10. Ibid., 562.

11. See Chapter 16 under "The Occurrences of the Word *Eklegomai*" (p. 384).

12. Thomas R. Schreiner, "Does Romans 9 Teach Individual Election unto Salvation?" in *The Grace of God, the Bondage of the Will*, vol. 1, eds. Thomas R. Schreiner and Bruce A. Ware (Grand Rapids: Baker Books, 1995), 99.

13. See Chapter 15 under "The Order of Decrees in Calvinism" (p. 304).

14. James Arminius, *The Writings of James Arminius*, vol. 3, James Nichols and W. R. Bagnall, trans. (Grand Rapids: Baker Book House, 1956), 314.

15. Ibid.

16. See the comments in Chapter 13 under "An Inconsistency in Calvinism" (pp. 260-62) and "The Question of Sovereign Grace" (p. 262-63).

17. Arminius, *The Writings of James Arminius*, vol. 3, 314.

18. Ibid., 315.

19. See the discussion in Chapter 11 under the heading, *"The Ground of Justification"* (pp. 191-92).

20. Forlines, *Romans*, 239

21. Chapter 15, p. 304.

22. Henry C. Thiessen, *Introductory Lectures in Systematic Theology* (Grand Rapids: William B. Eerdmans, 1949), 344.

23. Strong, *Systematic Theology*, 771-773.

24. Millard J. Erickson, *Christian Theology* (Grand Rapids: Baker Book House, 1985), 829-835. For those who would like a more thorough defense of unlimited atonement than I will give, I would recommend Erickson's treatment.

25. Thiessen, *Introductory Lectures in Systematic Theology*, 329-330.

26. See Chapter 5 "Calvinistic Arguments for a Limited Atonement," Chapter 6 "Arguments for a Universal Atonement," and Chapter 7 "New Testament Evidence for Universal Atonement" in Picirilli, *God's Decrees, Our Faith* (unpublished).

27. See Chapter 11 under "Universal Salvation or Limited Atonement a Necessary Result" (pp. 206, 207) and "Double Payment With Regard to Sinners Who Go to Hell" (p. 207).

28. Berkhof, *Systematic Theology*, 393

Chapter 18

1. Robert H. Bork, *Slouching Towards Gomorrah: Modern Liberalism and American Decline* (New York: Harper Collins Publishers, Inc., 1996), 6.

2. See Appendix 2, p. 489.

3. Paul R. Gross, Norman Levitt, and Martin W. Lewis, eds., *The Flight From Science and Reason* (Baltimore: John Hopkins Press, 1996 by the New York Academy of Sciences), 518, 519.

4. William Bennett, *The Death of Outrage, Bill Clinton and the Assault on American Ideals* (New York: The Free Press, 1998).

5. Origen, *Commentarii* quoted in Thomas Oden, "Without Excuse: Classic Christian Exegesis of General Revelation," in *Journal of the Evangelical Theological Society*, vol. 41, no. 1 (March 1998), 55, 67, 68.

6. Lawrence J. Crabb Jr., *Understanding People* (Grand Rapids: Zondervan Publishing House, 1987), 9, 10.

7. Ibid., 52.

8. In the first few paragraphs of this chapter, I mentioned some British paintings of the 1990s that my wife and I saw in a museum in St. Petersburg, Russia. One of these was titled "Abandoned."

9. Prior to deciding to write this book, I had written fifteen chapters about understanding and helping people. I decided to give priority to completing *Quest for Truth,* but my next book project will be on the topic of understanding and helping people.

10. I have dealt with these matters in Chapter 3 under "General Revelation" (pp. 32, 33).

11. Wells, *No Place for Truth,* 80.

12. Ibid., 86.

13. Chuck Colson, "Can We Be Good Without God?" *Imprimis,* April 1993, vol. 22, no. 4. Reprinted by permission from *Imprimis,* the monthly journal of Hillsdale College, Hillsdale, Michigan.

14. Before the devastating effect of postmodernism, the word "appropriate" was a very significant word in our society. People's interest went beyond what is right and what is wrong. There was a concern for *propriety*. I decided to look up the word *propriety* in the thesaurus on my computer. Here is the list of synonyms, "Appropriateness, correctness, seemliness, suitability, breeding, decorum, etiquette, protocol, refinement, proprieties, amenities, civilities, and social graces." All of these are in shambles. We cannot obey the teaching of Philippians 4:8 and sit silently by.

Appendix 1

I have examined many commentaries on Leviticus, Numbers, Psalms, Luke, Acts, 1 Corinthians, 1 Timothy, and Hebrews. About the only ones in the library at Free Will Baptist Bible College that I did not examine were those that were very general in nature. I have called attention to most of the significant comments on this subject. The vast majority of the commentaries on the New Testament are silent. I found no one who has developed the present significance of sins of ignorance and presumptuous sins beyond a few exegetical comments on particular texts.

1. This paper was presented at the meeting of the Southeastern Region of the Evangelical Theological Society when it met at Southern Evangelical Seminary, Charlotte, North Carolina on March 10, 1995. It is included here because of the importance of making the distinction between presumptuous sins and sins of ignorance when studying the doctrine of perseverance. This is particularly true with reference to wilful sin in Hebrews 10:26.

2. Sir Lancelot C. L. Brenton, *The Septuagint Version: Greek and English* (1844, *Apocrypha,* added 1851; reprinted at Grand Rapids: Zondervan Publishing House, 1981).

3. William S. Plumer, *Psalms* in *The Geneva Series of Commentaries* (1867; Edinburgh: The Banner of Truth, 1978), 260.

4. Mitchell Dahood, *Psalms I, 1-50, The Anchor Bible,* vol. 16, William Foxwell Albright and David Noel Freedman, gen. eds. (Garden City: Doubleday and Company, 1966), 124.

5. Archdeacon Aglen, *The Psalms in Ellicott's Commentary on the Whole Bible,* vol. 4, Charles John Ellicott, ed. (1882-1884; reprinted at Grand Rapids: Zondervan Publishing House, n.d.), 115.

6. Peter C. Craigie, *Psalms 1-50,* John D. W. Watts, ed., *Word Biblical Commentary,* vol. 19, David A. Hubbard and Glenn W. Barker, gen. eds. (Waco: Word Books, Publisher, 1983), 178.

7. Ibid., 182.

8. Karl Bernhard Moll, *Psalms in Commentary on the Holy Scriptures*, vol. 9, John Peter Lange, German ed.; Philip Schaff, trans. (New York: Bible House, 1872; reprinted at Grand Rapids: Zondervan Publishing House, n.d.), 154.

9. Oehler, *Theology of the Old Testament*, 300-301.

10. Patrick Fairbairn, *The Typology of Scripture*, new edition, 1900, two vols. in one, vol. 2, (Edinburgh, 1845-47; reprinted at Grand Rapids: Zondervan Publishing House, n.d.), 285-286.

11. Walter C. Kaiser, Jr., *Toward Rediscovering the Old Testament* (Grand Rapids: Zondervan Publishing House, 1987), 131-132.

12. Timothy R. Ashley, *The Book of Numbers, The New International Commentary on the Old Testament*, R. K. Harrison, ed. (Grand Rapids: Eerdmans Publishing Company, 1993), 288.

13. There is a question concerning whether this was a part of the original text. However, those who are aware of the problem usually leave it in and give a word of explanation. Even if a case could be made against the genuineness of these words as belonging to the original text, it does not destroy its significance for our subject. If inserted later, the person who did so would have done so out of an awareness of its connection with the sins of ignorance in the Old Testament. Also, that the crucifixion of Jesus by the Jews and their rulers was considered a sin of ignorance is well established in other places (Acts 3:17; 13:27; and 1 Cor. 2:8).

14. Craig A. Evans, *Luke, New International Biblical Commentary*, W. Ward Gasque, ed. (Peabody, Mass.: Hendrickson Publishers, 1990), 340-341.

15. I. Howard Marshall, *The Gospel of Luke, The New International Greek Testament Commentary*, I. Howard Marshall and W. Ward Gasque, eds. (Grand Rapids: Eerdmans Publishing Company, 1978), 867.

16. John B. Polhil, Acts, *The American Commentary*, vol. 26, David S. Dockery, ed. (Nashville: Broadman, 1992), 133. David John Williams, *Acts, New International Biblical Commentary*, W. Ward Gasque, ed. (Peabody, Mass.: Hendrickson Publishers, 1990), 70.

17. Gordon D. Fee, *1 and 2 Timothy, Titus, New International Biblical Commentary*, W. Ward Gasque, ed. (Peabody, Mass.: Hendrickson Publishers, 1988), 51.

Thomas D. Lea and Hayne P. Griffin, Jr., *1, 2 Timothy, Titus*, vol. 34., David S. Dockery, ed. (Nashville: Broadman Press, 1992), 73-74. Homer A. Kent, *The Pastoral Epistles* (Chicago: Moody Press, 1958), 91.

18. It may be of value to keep these observations in mind when analyzing the significance of *agnoia* in Acts 17:30, Ephesians 4:18; and 1 Peter 1:14.

19. J. A. Motyer, "Courage, Boldness," *The New International Dictionary of New Testament Theology*, vol. 1, Colin Brown, ed. (Grand Rapids: Zondervan Publishing House, 1975), 364-365.

20. Paul Ellingworth, *The Epistle to the Hebrews, New International Greek Commentary* (Grand Rapids: Eerdman's Publishing Company, 1993), 531.

21. Ibid., 276.

22. Fairbairn, *The Typology of Scripture*, vol. 2, 286.

23. Henry George Lidell and Robert Scott, *A Greek-English Lexicon* (1813; Oxford: Claredon Press, 1958), 514.

24. We may think that something we read about in other references in the Old Testament is referring to presumptuous sins, but Numbers 15:30 and Psalm 19:13 are the definitive texts. Whatever we may think about other texts with regard to presumptuous sins would be by application of what we learn from these texts.

25. Simon J. Kistemaker, *Exposition of The Epistle to the Hebrews, New Testament Commentary* (Grand Rapids: Baker Book House, 1984), 293.

26. Kaiser, *Toward Rediscovering the Old Testament*, 132.

27. Albert Barnes, *Hebrews, Notes on the New Testament* (1884-1885; Grand Rapids: Baker, 1983), 237.

28. Donald Guthrie, *The Letter to the Hebrews*, Leon Morris, ed. (Grand Rapids: Eerdmans Publishing Company, 1983), 217.

29. Ellingworth, *The Epistle to the Hebrews*, 532.

30. Lea and Griffin, *2 Timothy, Titus*, 74.

31. See endnote 7 above and the quotation from Moll in the text.

32. Andrew E. Hill explains, "The LXX misread *zēr* for the MT *zēd*, translating *allotrios* 'stranger, foreigner, enemy.' " From Andrew E. Hill, *Malachi, The Anchor Bible* (New York: Doubleday, 1998), 335.

33. It appears that the LXX was reading the Hebrew the same way in Malachi 4:1 (Heb., 3:19) as was pointed out by Hill in note 32. Since *allotrois* and *allogenēs* come from a different Hebrew word, we are not to understand that *zēd* can be understood as "stranger" or "alien."

Appendix 2

1. I read a paper entitled "Legalism in the Book of Galatians" at the Southern Region of the Evangelical Theological Society meeting at Western Kentucky University, Bowling Green, Kentucky around 1980. This paper was shortened and edited for an article for *Dimension*, vol.1, no. 3 (Winter 1984-85), published by Free Will Baptist Bible College, Nashville, Tennessee. I modified this article slightly for inclusion in this appendix.

2. Henry Alford, Galatians, *Alford's Greek Testament*, vol. 3 (1871; reprinted at Grand Rapids: Baker Book House, 1980), 36.

3. Ernest De Will Burton, *A Critical and Exegetical Commentary on the Epistle to the Galatians, The International Critical Commentary* (1921; reprinted at Edinburgh: T. & T. Clark, 1959), 198.

4. John Eadie, *A Commentary on the Greek Text of the Epistle of Paul to the Galatians* (1869, Edinburgh: T. & T. Clark, 1894; reprinted at Grand Rapids: Zondervan Publishing House, n. d.), 279.

5. William Hendriksen, *New Testament Commentary: Exposition of Paul's Epistle to the Galatians* (Grand Rapids: Baker Book House, 1981), 146.

6. Archibald Thomas Robertson, *Word Pictures in the New Testament*, vol. 5 (Nashville: Broadman Press, 1931), 297.

7. Fredric Rendall, *The Epistle to the Galatians, The Expositor's Greek Testament*, vol. 3, W. Robertson Nicoll, ed. (Reprinted, Grand Rapids: William B. Eerdmans Publishing Company, 1983), 173.

8. John Brown, *An Exposition of the Epistle of Paul to the Galatians* (1853; reprinted at Evansville, Indiana: The Sovereign Grace Book Club, 1957), 173.

9. James Barber Lightfoot, *The Epistle of St. Paul to the Galatians* (1865; reprinted at Grand Rapids: Zondervan Publishing House, 1950), 148.

10. R. C. H. Lenski, *The Interpretation of St. Paul's Epistle to the Galatians, to the Ephesians, and to the Philippians* (Columbus: The Wartburg Press, 1946), 194.

11. Ibid.

12. Eadie, *Galatians*, 294.

13. Rendall, *Galatians*, 175-176.

14. Burton, *Galatians*, 216.

15. George S. Duncan, *The Epistle of Paul to the Galatians*, James Moffat, ed. (New York: Harper and Brothers, 1934), 127.

16. Lightfoot, *Galatians*, 167.

17. Hugh Dermot McDonald, *Freedom in Faith, A Commentary on Paul's Epistle to the Galatians* (Old Tappan, New Jersey: Fleming H. Revell Company, 1973), 92.

18. Brown, *Galatians*, 187.

19. Ragnar Bring, *Commentary on Galatians*, Eric Wahlstrom, trans. (Philadelphia: Muhlenburg Press, 1968), 177.

20. Eadie, *Galatians*, 281.

21. Hendriksen, *Galatians*, 146.

22. Brown, *Galatians*, 172.

23. Lenski, *Galatians*, 182.

24. Brown, *Galatians*, 172.

25. Robert E. Picirilli, *The Book of Galatians* (Nashville: Randall House Publications, 1973), 58.

26. Burton, *Galatians*, 515, 516.

27. McDonald, *Galatians*, 92.

28. Brown, *Galatians*, 192.

29. Burton, *Galatians*, 220, 221.

30. Ralph Hampton, "A Biblical and Historical Study of Paul's Doctrine of Adoption" (M. A. thesis, unpublished, Winona Lake School of Theology, 1961), 68, 69.

31. Merrill C. Tenney, *Galatians: The Charter of Christian Liberty* (Grand Rapids: William B. Eerdmans), 150, footnote 128.

32. Eadie, *Galatians*, 300.

33. C. F. Hogg and W. E. Vine, *The Epistle to the Galatians* (Grand Rapids: Kregel Publications, 1921), 188.

34. Robertson, *Word Pictures in the New Testament*, vol. 5, 302.

35. Burton, *Galatians*, 202.

36. Lightfoot, *Galatians*, 149

Author, Subject Index

A

a priori: 9, 56, 57, 61, 67, 343

abortion: 14, 40, 138, 153, 156, 249, 325, 453

Abraham: xv, xix, 121, 185, 265, 346-350, 352, 356-366, 369, 371, 375-377, 380, 381, 383, 385, 387, 448, 458, 471, 491, 516

Abrahamic Covenant: 276, 347, 349-352, 356-358, 362, 377, 385, 404, 458, 490

Adam: xvii, xix, 36, 37, 72, 118, 119, 121, 124, 125, 139, 140, 152, 153, 157, 158, 160-166, 172, 209-214, 274, 300, 301, 306, 328, 332, 336, 337, 339, 340, 397

adoption: 244, 392, 393, 394, 494, 495, 523

affectionate foreknowing: 399

age of accountability: 211

Aglen, Archdeacon: 468, 520

agnostic, agnosticism: 11, 13, 25, 32, 104, 416

Alford, Henry: 266, 490, 522

angels: 37, 65, 69, 84, 142, 150, 158, 169, 204, 208, 275, 315, 406, 471, 493

annihilation: 31, 205, 227, 508

Anselm: 56, 168, 169

anthropomorphic: 65

anti-worldview: 93, 97, 101, 141, 463, 499

antinomianism: 183, 196, 208, 274, 498

Apollinarius, Apollinarians: 171, 175

apologetic, apologetics: xiv, 55, 56, 96, 181, 307, 417, 418, 437, 445, 450

apostasy: x, 269, 280-286, 288, 292, 295-297, 299-301, 349, 353-355, 376, 480

apostate: 281, 283, 284, 288, 289, 352, 475, 480, 518

Aristotelian-Ptolemaic: 9, 10, 412, 427

Aristotle: 9, 32

Arius, Arians: 171, 175

Ark of the Covenant: 189, 190

Arminian, Arminianism: x, xi, xvii, xviii, xx, 39, 158, 165, 166, 208, 235, 258, 259, 260, 261, 263-265, 267, 270, 273, 274, 297, 303, 306, 307, 309-313, 315, 317, 321, 322, 325, 327-331, 333, 334, 336, 341, 343, 362, 363, 365, 369, 384, 385, 387, 394, 405, 409, 458, 464, 481, 507, 510, 513-515

Arminius, Jacobus (James): x, xvii, 158, 159, 165, 166, 265, 322, 323, 325, 329, 332, 333, 401, 403, 506, 507, 514, 515, 519

art: 3, 232, 411, 412, 438, 462

Ascension, the: 182, 194, 495

Ashby, Steven M.: x, xx, 142, 155, 499, 505, 506

Ashley, Timothy R.: 472, 477, 521

assurance: 43, 181, 220, 258, 262, 298, 299, 387

atheism, atheistic: 1, 13, 30, 32, 35, 103, 105, 181, 296, 320, 416, 455

atonement: x, xvii, 22, 73, 75, 165, 166, 168, 169, 179, 181, 183, 184, 185, 187-192, 196-207, 210, 214, 218, 222, 262-266, 269, 270, 272, 291-294, 304, 339-341, 353, 354, 368, 374, 391, 396, 398, 401, 403, 405-407, 427, 443, 447, 460, 470, 472, 476, 478, 481, 506-508, 517, 519

attributes, divine: 65, 67, 70, 72, 73, 75, 77, 79, 87, 96, 106, 174-177, 184, 335, 451, 502, 503, 507

Augustine: 38, 140, 259, 312, 322, 325, 338, 501, 505, 514

authorship, divine: 43, 45, 47, 59, 452

authorship, human: 45, 51, 59, 60

autographs (original manuscripts): 59, 60, 418

autonomy: 10, 26

awesomeness of God: 78

Ayer, A. J.: 499

B

backslider, backsliding: 301

balance: 10, 144, 196, 228, 234, 235, 239, 348

Bales, James D.: 128, 505

baptism: 20, 87, 192

baptize: 192, 208, 215, 277, 298

barbarians: 16, 230, 234

Barnes, Albert: 478, 522

Barrow, J. P.: xx

Barth, Karl: 17, 33, 94, 148, 501

Barzun, Jacques: xii, 499

Bauman, Michael: 31, 501

beauty: xx, 19, 29, 126, 137, 156, 200, 230, 231, 232, 233, 234, 235, 246, 248, 414, 417, 421, 427, 431, 437, 460, 463

Bennett, William: 423, 427, 519

Berkhof, Louis: 32, 107, 139, 151, 154, 155, 206, 236, 260, 261, 274, 291, 292, 294, 317, 333, 338, 339, 408, 501, 504-506, 508-513, 515, 519

Berkouwer, G. C.: 38, 501

Bible, biblical: xiii, xiv, xvi-xix, 6, 7, 11-13, 17, 29, 33, 34, 38, 39, 41, 43-64, 65-67, 73, 75, 77, 78, 91, 93, 95, 97, 99-101, 108-111, 113, 114, 119-121, 125, 129, 130, 131, 137, 138, 141, 150, 153, 154, 164, 178, 180, 185, 187, 198, 208, 211, 217, 218, 224, 227, 229, 232, 239, 241, 246, 248, 249, 253, 255-257, 284, 288-290, 295, 300, 314, 333, 340, 345, 380-382, 388, 391, 398, 400, 403, 413, 418, 426, 429, 432, 436, 437, 439, 440, 444, 447, 449, 457, 460, 464, 481, 496, 497

biblical Christianity: 17, 18, 40, 63, 81, 146, 319, 445

Biblical Ethics: ix, 247, 500, 503, 509, 510

biblical interpretation: 51, 53

Biblical Systematics: ix, xi, xiv, 123, 134, 499

biblical theology: 4, 503

Birnbaum, Phillip: 516

Bloom, Allan: 25, 500

body: xvii, 65, 149, 151-153, 159, 164, 170, 171, 174, 180, 182, 187, 200, 223, 240, 243, 275, 294, 298, 350, 460

Reformation, the: 412

reformed: x, 260, 306-308, 327

regeneration: xii, xviii, 34, 85, 160, 197, 235, 236, 258-264, 269, 270, 274, 280, 338, 339, 340, 342, 362, 381, 442

Reid, Garnett: xx, 115, 504

relativism: 1, 14, 15, 20-23, 27, 28, 30, 146, 205, 230, 239, 245, 249, 387, 419, 424, 443, 449, 481

religion: xx, 12, 32, 97, 123, 124, 125, 254, 350, 422, 425, 432, 446, 454, 455, 490, 493

Rembrandt: 411

remission: 191, 199, 403

remunerative justice: 74

Rendall, Fredric: 490, 491, 522

Renwick, Alexander M.: 171, 506

repent, repentance: 12, 70, 159, 197, 212, 241, 253-256, 276, 277, 279, 280, 283, 284, 293, 296, 299, 347, 354, 373, 378, 404, 409, 472, 474, 478, 480, 481, 511

reprobation: 325, 347, 363, 370, 371, 373, 374

rescue: 66, 98, 99, 104, 167, 432, 441, 442, 443, 446, 459

resistible grace: 315

restoration: 123, 169, 191, 197, 223

Resurrection: xvi, 93, 151, 179, 180, 181, 183, 194, 221, 223, 236, 251, 350, 353, 358, 415, 419, 436, 437, 449, 475, 495

retributive justice: 74, 188, 199, 202

revelation, divine: ix, 5, 8, 12, 13, 17, 18, 21-23, 29-32, 39, 41, 43, 47, 52, 95, 106, 108, 109, 113, 130, 131, 135, 145, 146, 179, 180, 198, 296, 413-415, 420, 455, 495

revelation, general: 32-35, 37, 38, 40, 81, 95, 99, 107, 137, 147, 211, 356, 414, 417, 420, 422, 431, 435, 441, 450-454, 463, 501

revelation, special: 32, 34, 35-37, 39, 40, 43, 81, 95, 167, 211, 356, 414, 420, 435, 450, 454, 463

Rice, John R.: 50

Rice, Richard: 323, 514

righteousness: x, xviii, xix, 38, 55, 73, 137, 139, 140, 156, 158, 163, 164, 165, 185-191, 194, 195, 200, 201, 206, 207, 209-212, 214, 217, 218, 221, 222, 229, 235-237, 241, 250, 260-267, 272, 284, 287, 291-294, 297, 300, 303, 338-341, 346, 347, 350, 361, 363, 364, 366, 368, 369, 375, 377, 378, 401, 423, 442, 459, 461, 481

Robertson, Archibald Thomas: 490, 522, 523

Roosevelt, Franklin D.: 144

Rosen, Edward: 26, 500

Russia: ix-xi, xvii, xix, 1, 77, 156, 275, 284, 297, 305, 411, 456, 499, 501, 520

Ryrie, Charles C.: 155, 506, 508

S

sacrifice: 189, 190, 281, 282, 407, 467, 470, 472, 473, 476, 477, 478

Sadducees: 475

salvation: x, xi, xx, 19, 20, 73, 98, 154, 159, 165, 166, 172, 179, 186, 190, 191, 197, 204-206, 208, 209, 212, 217-219, 221, 224, 230, 241, 243, 253-267, 269, 270, 271, 273-275, 276, 278, 280, 281, 285, 288, 289, 291-293, 295, 297, 298, 299, 301, 303, 304, 306, 311, 313, 320, 327, 339, 340, 341, 343, 346-355, 357, 360, 362-367, 369, 371, 374, 375, 376, 378, 379, 381, 383, 385, 388, 389, 390, 394, 399, 400, 402-404, 407, 408, 418, 419, 423, 443, 444, 448, 464, 478, 481, 489, 491, 496

sanctification: x, xii, xviii, 85, 90, 143, 149, 193, 197, 207, 217-252, 256, 259, 260, 274, 281, 292, 295, 299, 338, 339, 340, 379, 402, 423, 510

Sanday and Headlam: 225, 311, 509, 516

Sanders, E. P.: 348, 354, 355, 516

Santa Claus: 504

Sartre, Jean-Paul: 146, 505

Satan: 63, 84, 85, 101, 122, 169, 179, 339, 433, 460, 466

satisfaction view: xviii, 184, 191, 196, 199, 201, 202, 203, 206, 207, 208,

266, 272, 292, 339, 368, 401, 408, 507, 517

Schaeffer, Francis: xiii, xv, 7, 15, 17, 419, 443, 499, 503

scholarship: 2, 35, 51, 123, 124, 127, 310, 416, 438, 439

Schreiner, Thomas R.: 366, 367, 400, 512, 517, 519

Schultz, Arnold C.: xx, 478

science, scientific: xv, 8-11, 16, 17, 27, 29, 41, 48, 54, 60, 61, 77, 98, 102, 113, 116, 117, 120-122, 125-127, 128-134, 413, 418, 422, 424, 427, 439, 462, 481

Scopes Trial: 416

Scott, Eugenie: 127, 505

Scripture: xvi, 34, 39, 43-51, 54, 57, 59, 61, 68, 70, 73-75, 82, 83, 85, 86, 93, 108, 109, 110, 111, 113, 115, 117, 120, 122, 124, 138, 146, 149, 159, 163-165, 167, 170, 178, 183, 194, 203, 213, 214, 218, 220, 226, 246, 253, 254, 257, 265, 266, 271, 274, 277, 278, 281, 285, 288, 290, 293, 303, 310, 320, 324, 332, 333, 335, 345, 366, 369, 375, 377, 379, 389, 400, 440, 467, 469, 481, 482, 489

secular, secularism: xiii, 9, 13-15, 18, 29, 30, 96, 97, 101, 120, 147, 166, 231, 249, 296, 387, 412, 413, 416, 419, 422, 424, 425, 427, 432, 435-437, 439, 442, 451, 454, 456, 463, 481, 510

self: 103, 138, 150, 151, 156, 187, 193, 227, 228, 239, 255, 432, 443, 452, 458, 459

self-denial: 227

self-determinism, self-determination: 304, 308, 315, 318, 319, 369

self-directed: 158, 315, 319

self-evident: 25, 56, 108, 109, 147, 148

self-worth: 143, 227, 229, 461, 462

Semi-Pelagian: 213

seminary(ies): ix, xi, xvii, xx, 20, 50, 137, 166, 172, 295, 416, 434, 435, 440, 499, 506, 508, 520

sense data: 8, 126

Septuagint: 397, 468, 482

Shank, Robert: 281, 282, 286, 511

Scripture Index

1 Corinthians

2 Corinthians

Galatians

Printed in the United States
4590